Teaching for Diversity and Social Justice

Third Edition

Edited by

Maurianne Adams and Lee Anne Bell
With Diane J. Goodman and Khyati Y. Joshi

Routledge
Taylor & Francis Group

NEW YORK AND LONDON

Third edition published 2016
by Routledge
711 Third Avenue, New York, NY 10017

and by Routledge
2 Park Square, Milton Park, Abingdon, Oxon, OX14 4RN

Routledge is an imprint of the Taylor & Francis Group, an informa business

First edition published by Routledge 1997

Second edition published by Routledge 2007

Library of Congress Cataloging-in-Publication Data
Teaching for diversity and social justice / [edited] by Maurianne Adams and
Lee Anne Bell with Diane J. Goodman and Khyati Y. Joshi. — Third edition.
    pages cm
  Includes bibliographical references and index.
ISBN 978-1-138-02333-8 (hardback) — ISBN 978-1-138-02334-5 (pbk.) —
ISBN 978-1-315-77585-2 (e-book)   1. Critical pedagogy—United States.
2. Social justice–Study and teaching—United States.   3. Multicultural
education—United States.   4. Teachers—Training of—United States.
I. Adams, Maurianne.   II. Bell, Lee Anne, 1949–   III. Griffin, Pat.
  LC196.5.U6T43 2016
  370.11'5—dc23
  2015031677

ISBN: 978-1-138-02333-8 (hbk)
ISBN: 978-1-138-02334-5 (pbk)
ISBN: 978-1-315-77585-2 (ebk)

Typeset in Swiss 721 and Classical Garamond
by Apex CoVantage, LLC

Printed and bound in the United States of America by Sheridan Books, Inc. (a Sheridan Group Company).

Dedication

In Memoriam
John Austin Hunt
October 27, 1930, to July 26, 2015

Contents

Preface

Teaching for Diversity and Social Justice: Third Edition offers a unified framework for helping people understand and critically analyze multiple forms of oppression in the United States. Our approach to social justice education (SJE) includes both an *interdisciplinary conceptual framework* for analyzing multiple forms of oppression and *a set of interactive, experiential pedagogical principles* to help learners understand the meaning of social difference and oppression, both in social systems and in their personal lives. In an increasingly abrasive and polarized U.S. society, we believe that SJE can play a valuable role in helping people develop a more thoughtful understanding of diversity and group interaction, better prepare to critically evaluate inequitable social patterns and institutions, and find ways to work in coalition with diverse others to create more socially just and inclusive relationships, practices, and social structures.

As social justice educators, our goal is to engage people in becoming aware of and analyzing oppressive socio-political processes, and reflecting on their own position(s) and responsibilities in relation to various forms of oppression. We want to help people consider the consequences of socialization into these inequitable systems, and to think proactively about alternative actions given this analysis.

We believe that traditional lecture-and-listen methods will not stimulate the active involvement necessary to reach social justice goals. In our courses and workshops, we draw upon participatory pedagogies for engaging participants with new and challenging information, and we are intentional about sequence, design, and facilitation so that participants reflect on their own experiences in ways that we hope foster new awareness, critique, self-assessment, and conscious choices about the actions they take in the world.

Our approach to social justice is necessarily collaborative. This collaborative approach is reflected in how we have written this book. Some chapters are co-authored and some are single-authored, but all have been read by a number of us and reflect major areas of agreement in our approach to SJE. For these reasons, we use the terms "our" and "we" throughout the book to reflect the broad area of consensus among the community of social justice educators who have produced this volume. We believe that change cannot happen without the ongoing exchange of ideas about direction, goals, and practice by those affected by oppression. As SJE continues to gain currency and visibility, we hope that practitioners, researchers, and activists acknowledge and build upon each other's work in ways that can better prepare all of us to engage the problems we face as a society in committed, sustained, and radically creative ways.

CHANGES IN THIS THIRD EDITION

We have learned a great deal since the publication of earlier editions of *Teaching for Diversity and Social Justice* (TDSJ) in 1997 and 2007, and would like to note here the most significant changes in the third edition. These changes come from suggestions by many users of earlier editions who provided valuable direct and anonymous feedback on what they find most useful about the book and their ideas for improvement.

One of the most significant changes in this edition is that we have moved the detailed curriculum designs (formerly embedded in chapters devoted to a specific form of oppression or "ism"[1]) to the companion website for the book. Instructors and facilitators often need rapid access to downloadable designs, activities, and handouts. New technologies have eased this process, and now much of the instructional material from former editions, plus new material for this edition, will be easily accessible on the website for the book.

Chapters 4–10 are accompanied by website materials that flesh out the design presented in the chapter and support instructors and facilitators in teaching effectively about the particular issue the chapter describes. Part 1 of the website for each chapter, in particular, is designed to help instructors and facilitators carry out the leading ideas and purposes of that chapter. We therefore strongly recommend that educators carefully read the chapter before using the website materials in classes and workshops.

We are uneasy about people using our designs and activities out of context and request that users not share website activities and handouts with people who have not purchased the text to read and understand the theoretical and conceptual frameworks, historical themes, and pedagogical principles that stand behind these materials.

A serendipitous consequence of our decision to move curricular materials to the web was space for more in-depth information in each ism chapter. The information we now offer in these chapters makes it possible for instructors and facilitators to assign them as background reading for students and workshop participants. The new and revised material in each ism chapter includes:

- An explanation of our SJE approach and rationale
- Key terms and definitions
- Central issues and historical legacies for understanding the background of each ism
- Contemporary manifestations of the ism and its intersections with other isms and identities
- Examples of individual and collective action that can challenge the ism and foster greater social justice

In response to the lack of historical knowledge we find among many students and workshop participants, we have been more deliberative in this edition about the historical underpinnings in which contemporary oppression is rooted. History operates as a core construct for discerning how each ism is connected to actions in the past that endure in the present but have come to be taken as given. Understanding these historical legacies is essential for making sense of the maintenance and reproduction of oppression in contemporary life, and provides inspiration and examples of resistance and activism that can encourage students and participants to consider ways to take action in the present.

All of the chapters provide examples where the focus ism intersects with other isms, both in the overall system of oppression and in the complex lives of individuals who hold multiple, intersecting identities. While we continue to find it pedagogically useful to foreground one ism at a time, as in previous editions, here we offer examples of intersections to illustrate the kaleidoscopic and simultaneous nature of multiple forms of oppression as they play out in the lives of individuals and institutions. Each curriculum design acknowledges ways in which different issues overlap and intersect in real-life experiences, policies, and practices. More than ever, seeing the intersections is necessary for understanding how location in systems of oppression affects people in similar and different ways. Understanding the intersections also helps focus interventions that challenge oppression in all of its forms.

We recognize that U.S. manifestations of oppression are embedded in a globalized economy and in its multiple transnational diasporas. It no longer makes sense, if it ever did, to think of U.S.-based issues as separate from their transnational roots or repercussions. The multinational, multiethnic, multicultural, and diasporic dimensions of the topics we teach and their ripple effects on how oppressions play out, and the diversity of the participants in our classes and workshops, make the systematic study of oppression ever more complex. We have tried to show global implications and interconnections through the examples and analyses provided in this new edition.

Following the sections described above, each ism chapter then provides a brief overview of a curriculum design for teaching about that ism that includes learning objectives, key concepts, and activity options. The more detailed design with related activities, materials, and facilitation steps can be downloaded from each ism chapter's website. Each ism chapter concludes with a discussion of the pedagogical and design and facilitation issues specific to teaching about that particular ism. While the preceding chapters on theory (Chapter 1), pedagogy (Chapter 2), design and facilitation (Chapter 3), and core concepts (Chapter 4) provide a comprehensive discussion of SJE content, pedagogy, and design and facilitation strategies, each ism chapter highlights what is especially important for facilitators to know when they teach about the particular ism that chapter addresses.

The first four foundational chapters have been significantly reconceptualized and updated. In Part I: *Theoretical Foundations and Principles of Practice*, Chapters 1–4 lay out the theories, foundations, and frameworks upon which our approach to SJE is based, including the principles of pedagogy and design and facilitation that shape our practice as social justice educators.

Chapter 1 provides an overview of theoretical foundations for understanding the characteristics of oppression in relation to our vision for social justice, based upon lessons for change drawn from social justice movements. Chapter 2 grounds our pedagogy by describing the challenges and opportunities for instructors/facilitators and participants. It summarizes the activist and academic roots of SJE pedagogy and suggests pedagogical principles to guide classroom or workshop teaching and learning. Chapter 3 describes the principles of design and facilitation and the specific facilitation issues that arise in social justice teaching with practical strategies to address them. Chapter 4 then serves as a bridge between the first three foundational chapters and the following ism chapters that apply the theory and principles to specific isms. This bridging chapter focuses upon the core concepts that need to be in all SJE practice, and illustrates ways of "getting started" through a curriculum design for teaching foundational core concepts and processes. This curriculum can be used as a stand-alone introduction to core concepts of SJE or to introduce the SJE approach to one or more specific isms. We strongly encourage users to draw upon Chapter 4 and incorporate these core concepts and principles into their own teaching as they adapt the specific ism designs that follow.

Part II: *Teaching Diversity and Social Justice* describes our approach to teaching five isms or clusters of isms (Chapters 5–11). Chapter 5: *Racism and White Privilege* examines the ways that racism operates differently for different communities of color, including immigrants who are incorporated into the U.S. racial structure when they arrive. This chapter also analyzes the cumulative impact of white advantage and corresponding cumulative disadvantage for people of color that compounds racism over time.

Chapter 6: *Sexism, Heterosexism, and Trans* Oppression* takes an integrative approach that analyzes these three forms of oppression within a single analytic framework. It challenges binary understandings of sex, gender, and sexuality, and looks at these interrelated identity concepts in relationship to sexism, heterosexism, and transgender oppression. To supplement the integrated design, the chapter website offers updated designs and activities for teaching each of these issues separately.

Chapter 7: *Classism* includes a provocative analysis of the historical legacies and contemporary manifestations of class and classism. It focuses on the historical background for classism, the intersections of classism with other forms of oppression, and the reproduction of advantages and disadvantages that accumulate from the intersections of class with race, gender, age, and other forms of oppression.

Chapter 8: *Religious Oppression* uses the lens of Christian hegemony to explore the long history of Christian advantage and the equally long history of disadvantages for different minority religious groups in the U.S. It provides an analysis of historical U.S. and global conflicts in which religion intersects with class and other forms of oppression, and proposes new emphases in the U.S. on religious pluralism as a route to religious justice.

Chapter 9: *Ableism* describes the historical legacies as well as the current manifestations of the construction of a broad continuum of disabilities, including cognitive, physical, and psychological disabilities, chronic illness, and post-traumatic stress disorder. The chapter explores assumptions about what constitutes a "normal" body and mind, how the physical and social environments construct disability, and how ableism is embedded in U.S. language, institutional policies, architecture, and the overall culture.

Chapter 10: *Youth Oppression and Elder Oppression* looks at the way both youth and elders are oppressed in a society that holds very narrow ideas about human capacity defined by age. The SJE approach to the oppression of youth and elders draws upon theories of colonialism as a way of understanding modern formulations of childhood. The challenges posed by this approach to youth and elder oppression are addressed by detailed facilitation notes.

Chapter 11: *Online and Blended Pedagogy in Social Justice Education* is an entirely new chapter that addresses the challenges and possibilities for adapting social justice content and processes, developed in face-to-face formats, to on-line and blended formats. The chapter compares advantages and disadvantages of the two modes, based on experience with both formats, and proposes curricular, materials, and facilitation notes for a blended SJE curriculum design that frankly acknowledges the opportunities and drawbacks of on-line and blended SJE.

Chapter 12: *Critical Self-Knowledge for Social Justice Educators* concludes the book with a discussion of what instructors and facilitators need to know about themselves in order to teach about social justice issues and interact thoughtfully, sensitively, and effectively with students and participants. It explores the importance of self-reflection and self-awareness, and the ongoing process of exploration and growth that are critical to sustaining a commitment to SJE.

TERMINOLOGY AND NAMING

As in previous editions, we highlight the ways in which historical and contemporary hierarchies of advantage and disadvantage not only divide and rank social identity groups, but also name them in ways that convey privileged and subordinated social identities and social positions. We consider these socio-politically potent either/or categorizing processes for entire groups of peoples to be a major hallmark of oppression. At the same time, we recognize that people engage in a continuous struggle to challenge, redefine, and invent anew more meaningful ways to name and describe their lived experiences of the world, and often do so by claiming identities and terminology that stand in opposition to categorizing boxes and dualisms. The either/or boxes of dominant and subordinated categories cannot contain the much richer and messier terrain of lived experience that is always in tension with the constraints of oppression, and the experience of simultaneous privilege and disadvantage in the multiple identities people hold.

This edition takes a more intentionally intersectional approach than earlier editions, and we have not found it easy to find a way to introduce concepts of social identity (one by one, incrementally) while also honoring the intersectional simultaneity by which people experience their identities (Goodman & Jackson, 2012). The relation between the binaries, by which oppression forges unequal social categories and the intersectional simultaneity through which they are experienced, is a paradoxical one (Holvino, 2012). Postmodern analyses of contingency, context, and change challenge, in fundamental ways, the stability of social identities and the very social categories themselves (Holvino, 2012; Renn, 2012). We have tried in this edition to note this tension in the way we represent models and constructs, and to acknowledge that "the map is not the territory."

LANGUAGE

As noted above, resistance to "being" categorized plays out in opposition to the binaries of oppression, and in new ways of naming social identity groups. In the years between editions, we have witnessed the ways that language is in flux, evolving and changing as terms are contested and redefined by communities seeking justice. Thus, keeping up with and respecting the language that groups use to self-name is an important aspect of social justice.

Over the years, names and terms for social identity groups have changed in remarkable ways. One is through the recovery of categories and descriptive terms that previously conveyed negative meanings, such as "queer" (Shlasko, 2005), "trans"(Catalano, 2015), or the noun "Jew" (as distinct from the adjective, Jew*ish*).

And there is shifting consensus of appropriate understanding of aboriginal and indigenous peoples of the Americas—grouped categorically as Native Americans, Native American Indians, American Indians, or identified by specific traditional tribal designations such as Cherokee, Kiowa, and Lakota (Horse, 2012). Since these terms are in fluid usage among different communities within or across social identities, we prefer to leave the choice of appropriate language to specific co-authors in this volume rather than attempt a "one-size-fits-all" policy.

We follow an emerging consensus by capitalizing and not hyphenating specific ethnicities that are derived from geographical areas (African American, American Indian or Native American, Asian American). We capitalize ethnicities that are rooted in proper names, but we do not capitalize racial designations because these are constructed terms with no geographical, ethnic, or national connection. We understand that Latino/a, Native American, and Asian/Pacific Islander are ethnic designations that are often racialized in that they conflate race, ethnicity, and pan-ethnicity, and we acknowledge this as part of the crazy-quilt of an emergent U.S. racialized landscape that absorbs ethnic peoples of color into racially subordinated status. (Irish and Italian ethnic designations, understood to be white, remain invisible and are not seen as explicit racial designations in the same ways.)

When we move to global, diasporic immigration issues, racial/ethnic descriptors become even more problematic. As much as possible, we use terms that are specific to national/geographic origin (people of South Asian descent, for example). We do not use the term Hispanic, recognizing that many people from Spanish-speaking countries resist this categorization as a marker of their Spanish colonizers. We use the preferred term, *Latina/o*. In actuality, people in Latin America do not refer to themselves as either Hispanic or Latino since they define themselves by the country or indigenous population to which they belong (Ecuadorian, Cuban, Brazilian, Quechua, etc.)

We want to encourage the use of inclusive and gender-neutral pronouns (hir, ze; they, their) in our teaching and prefer "they" as a gender-neutral singular pronoun in place of "he" or "she" as one way to be inclusive. Similarly, Latinx is a relatively recent term intended to make Latino/a inclusive of men, women, transgender, genderqueer, and gender-fluid people. While we use Latina/o in this edition as the currently more broadly embraced term, we want to note the ever-changing nature of language to be more inclusive and accurate in describing people. Authors of each curriculum design address other considerations of language usage in their respective chapters.

We recognize that it is problematic to use any single set of terms to convey the complexity of human beings whose identities are derived in part from multiple social identity groups, within the phenomenon of oppression and also within the context of their cultural communities. We no longer use the terms "oppressor" and "oppressed," for example, to refer to specific advantaged or disadvantaged identity groups, because they too often arouse objections as being too broad from participants who cannot reconcile themselves as oppressors when they feel personally quite powerless, or who resist being defined as oppressed as a denial of agency. We also avoid the similarly contested terms "agent" and "target.".

On the other hand, we struggle to find language that doesn't trivialize the power and harm of the oppressive system we want to expose. After wrestling with various terms, we have decided to primarily use the following: Advantaged, Privileged, and Dominant to describe groups with access to social power, and Disadvantaged, Marginalized, and Subordinated for groups who are blocked from access to social power. We think these terms, while far from perfect, focus on the structured roles and outcomes of an oppressive system, and we hope to create an invitational rather than confrontational approach that highlights the function of unequal roles in a system rather than attributes of individual people.

Not all of our contributors agree on uniform terminology, and readers will notice the use of different terms in various chapters. However, all of us do agree on the importance of attending to the systemic features that perpetuate inequality and injustice in our society and of the possibility for individuals to work from wherever they are positioned to challenge and change the system.

Our guiding principle is to adopt language preferred by people from oppressed groups to name themselves: "people of color" rather than "nonwhite"; "gay, lesbian, bisexual" rather than "homosexual"; "people with disabilities" rather than "handicapped." We also note the reclaiming by targeted communities of previously negative terms such as "queer," "crip," "girl," and "trannie" that reframe slurs as positive. We know that naming is a necessarily fluid and sometimes contradictory and confusing process as people/groups insist on defining themselves rather than acquiescing to names imposed by others; we also know that members of marginalized groups may reclaim negative terms amongst themselves, but hear those terms from outsiders as triggers. Social justice educators need to remain sensitive and alert to changes in language, language preferred by specific communities, and outsider/insider terminology. We encourage readers to recognize that such terms will continue to evolve and change, and to appreciate the significance of the power to name oneself as an important aspect of group identity and resistance.

OTHER CONSIDERATIONS

We continue to be disappointed by the citation practices of libraries, reviewers, booksellers, and scholars who fully name the first author only, as in "Adams, et al. (2007)." This practice does not acknowledge and may even discourage collaborative work, since academic rewards and professional visibility tend to accrue to first authors, often presumed senior or primary. We have struggled with the question of how to represent the participation of all members of a collaborative team such that both academic rewards and professional visibility are credited equally to all whose ideas, creativity, and writing contribute to the final product.

Any line of names, however arranged, suggests a ranking order. We regret that we have found no successful alternative to the convention of alphabetical order in listing editors and contributors. However, we place a statement at the beginning of each chapter honoring the nature and value of our collaborative work with a request that people who cite us include the names of all authors. We have, in all cases, acknowledged in full citations all the co-authors of the published work we reference in this book. We consider "et al." an insult to co-authorship.

In the past ten years, we have received feedback from hundreds of people throughout this country and internationally who use and find *TDSJ* a valuable resource. We are gratified to know that our book has been used successfully in many different settings—academic departments (black studies, women's studies, ethnic studies, teacher education, sociology, psychology, seminaries), student affairs, adult formal and non-formal education, workplace diversity and staff development programs, diversity curricula for general education, upper-level high school courses, grassroots organizing, and start-up activist organizations.

Given the challenges to social justice in the world today, and the difficulties overcome by dynamically evolving social justice movements around the world, we expect that the theory, language, and practice of SJE will continue to evolve as it has since earlier editions of *TDSJ*. We hope we have articulated some of these new developments in the current edition, and that our curriculum will inspire new generations of educators and activists in the cause of social justice. We look forward to a continuing dialogue with those who use this book and to the inspiration they give to our ongoing work for social justice.

Note

1 A short-hand term we use to refer to manifestations of oppression that are described in Chapters 5–10 of this volume.

References

Catalano, C. (2015). Beyond virtual equality: Liberatory consciousness as a path to achieve trans* inclusion in higher education. *Equity & Excellence in Education, 48*(3), 419–436.

Goodman, D. J., & Jackson, B. W. (2012). Pedagogical approaches to teaching about racial identity from an intersectional perspective. In C. L. Wijeyesinghe & B. W. Jackson (Eds.), *New perspectives on racial identity development: Integrating emerging frameworks* (2nd ed., pp. 216–240). New York: New York University Press.

Holvino, E. (2012). The "simultaneity" of identities: Models and skills for the twenty-first century. In C. L. Wijeyesinghe & B. W. Jackson (Eds.), *New perspectives on racial identity development: Integrating emerging frameworks* (2nd ed., pp. 161–191). New York: New York University Press.

Horse, P. G. (2012). Twenty-first century Native American consciousness: A thematic model of Indian identity. In C. L. Wijeyesinghe & B. W. Jackson (Eds.), *New perspectives on racial identity development: Integrating emerging frameworks* (2nd ed., pp. 108–120). New York: New York University Press.

Renn, K. A. (2012). Creating and recreating race: The emergence of racial identity as a critical element in psychological, sociological and ecological perspectives on human development. In C. L. Wijeyesinghe & B. W. Jackson (Eds.), *New perspectives on racial identity development: integrating emerging frameworks* (2nd ed., pp. 11–32). New York: New York University Press.

Shlasko, G. D. (2005). Queer (*v.*) pedagogy. *Equity & Excellence in Education, 38*(20), 123–134.

Acknowledgements

This book reflects collaboration among several generations of faculty and graduate students in the Social Justice Education program at the University of Massachusetts Amherst, and the various editions reflect changes in the landscape of diversity and social justice that we have presented in classes, workshops, conferences, activism, and everyday life. The development of the theory and practice described in this volume has truly been a collaborative, multigenerational, and ongoing endeavor.

Many of the new features in this third edition were suggested by anonymous users of earlier editions who took the time to fill out detailed questionnaires about how they use the book in their classes and their suggestions for changes. Their input has helped make this a better edition. Each of the new editions of this book rests on the shoulders of those who went before.

This volume benefits from the thoughtful designs offered in earlier editions that provided a foundation for new directions developed by new teams of authors in the current edition. In particular, we want to thank Bailey Jackson and Rita Hardiman for their vision of SJE expressed in earlier editions. Their work continues to inspire and prepare social justice educators.

For chapters in earlier editions, we thank Barbara Love, Rosemarie Roberts, and Charmaine L. Wijeyesinghe on Racism; Steven Botkin, Diane Goodman, JoAnn Jones, Tanya Kachwaha, and Steve Shapiro on Sexism; Katja Hahn, Bobbi Harro, Linda McCarthy, Davey Shlasko, and Tom Schiff for chapters on Heterosexism and Transgender Oppression; Katja Hahn, Donna Mellon, and Gerald Weinstein for Antisemitism chapters; Pat Griffin, Mary McClintock, Laura Rauscher, and Robin Smith for Ableism chapters; Sharon Washington, Barbara Love, and Gerald Weinstein on Knowing Ourselves; Beverly Daniel Tatum and JoAnn Jones on Knowing Our Students; and Linda Marchesani on the Multiple Issues Course Overview that has been integrated into the revised and updated Design chapter and the Chapter 4 website.

We continue to learn and be inspired by graduate students in the Social Justice Education program at the University of Massachusetts Amherst School of Education, who teach the courses and workshops described here, and SJE graduates who are co-authors in this edition. Their creativity, resourcefulness, and passion for teaching contributed greatly to this book and sustained us in our ongoing learning about forms of oppression and approaches to SJE. Many of our colleagues and students took time, under tight deadlines, to provide thoughtful feedback to early drafts of these chapters. Some of them provided new material for chapter websites, and we name them in those specific acknowledgements. We owe a special debt to Davey Shlasko for superb editorial help on several chapters, and to Eun Lee and Jess McDonald for creative solutions to multiple formatting, design, and citation challenges.

We want to thank our authors in this new edition for rising to the challenge of incorporating substantial new material into the chapters and preparing detailed activities, handouts, and resources for the website. In most cases, we have read, reviewed, and helped revise each other's work. It takes a village—a generous community of activists, educators, and scholars.

We are fortunate to work with an amazing editor in Catherine Bernard, who has supported us in re-envisioning this new edition and creating a companion website. Her generosity and firmness, her unflagging belief in this project and in us, her flexibility to help us meet the challenges in our personal lives, the care with which she has read each of our chapters, and her determination that "yes, we will finish this book on time," make her a uniquely supportive editor. The evolution of this edition could not have happened without her clarity and commitment. We also thank Marlena Sullivan, who read and cross-checked chapter designs with website activities and handouts, with an eagle-eye and thoughtful analysis that prevented many errors and omissions. Autumn Spalding has shown grace under pressure, generosity, patience and clarity in leading us through the copyediting challenges during final edits for the book and the website activities. It is a rare and great gift to have such thorough, supportive, and attentive editors.

Finally, the experience of collaborating as an editorial and writing team with two new people has been a stimulating and rewarding experience. Our energizing conversations about the work before us have challenged and stretched our understanding of SJE as we worked on this edition. We have also been excited to work with new authors, some of whom were once our students and are now our colleagues. It is a joy and a fulfillment to see the work of social justice educators grow, stretch, and influence.

Each of us has critical people in our lives and at our home institutions without whose support (personal, professional, financial) the time and commitment we put into this book would not have been possible. It would overwhelm our readers to try to list them here. They know who they are, and they have our heartfelt appreciations.

PART I

THEORETICAL FOUNDATIONS AND PRINCIPLES OF PRACTICE

Theoretical Foundations for Social Justice Education

Lee Anne Bell

WHAT IS SOCIAL JUSTICE?

Social justice is both a goal and a process. The *goal* of social justice is full and equitable participation of people from all social identity groups in a society that is mutually shaped to meet their needs. The *process* for attaining the goal of social justice should also be democratic and participatory, respectful of human diversity and group differences, and inclusive and affirming of human agency and capacity for working collaboratively with others to create change. Domination cannot be ended through coercive tactics that recreate domination in new forms. Thus, a "power with" vs. "power over" (Kreisberg, 1992) paradigm is necessary for enacting social justice goals. Forming coalitions and working collaboratively with diverse others is an essential part of social justice.

Our *vision* for social justice is a world in which the distribution of resources is equitable and ecologically sustainable, and all members are physically and psychologically safe and secure, recognized, and treated with respect. We envision a world in which individuals are both self-determining (able to develop their full capacities) and interdependent (capable of interacting democratically with others). Social justice involves social actors who have a sense of their own agency as well as a sense of social responsibility toward and with others, their society, the environment, and the broader world in which we live. These are conditions we not only wish for ourselves but for all people in our interdependent global community.

WHAT IS JUSTICE?

Philosophers and others have long debated the question, "What constitutes justice?" Our definition of social justice draws on theories that describe justice as a fair and equitable *distribution of resources* (Rawls, 1999, 2003) with the imperative to address those who are least advantaged (Rawls, 2001). We also draw on theories that affirm the importance of fair and equitable *social processes* (Young, 2011), including recognition and respect for marginalized or subjugated cultures and groups (Young, 1990). We see these two aspects as intertwining, acknowledging that social justice must address *both* resources and recognition. Resources include fair distribution of social, political, and symbolic, as well as economic, assets. Recognition and respect for all individuals and groups requires full inclusion and participation in decision-making and the power to shape the institutions, policies, and processes that affect their lives.

Diversity and social justice are distinct though interconnected terms. *Diversity* refers to differences among social groups such as ethnic heritage, class, age, gender, sexuality, ability, religion, and nationality. These differences are reflected in historical experiences, language, cultural practices, and traditions that ought to be affirmed and respected. Concrete and genuine knowledge of different groups, their histories, experiences, ways of making meaning, and values is important to the social justice goal of recognition and respect.

Social justice refers to reconstructing society in accordance with principles of equity, recognition, and inclusion. It involves eliminating the *injustice* created when differences are sorted and ranked in a hierarchy that unequally confers power, social, and economic advantages, and institutional and cultural validity to social groups based on their location in that hierarchy (Adams, 2014; Johnson, 2005). Social justice requires confronting the ideological frameworks, historical legacies, and institutional patterns and practices that structure social relations unequally so that some groups are advantaged at the expense of other groups that are marginalized. In our view, diversity and social justice are inextricably bound together. Without truly valuing diversity, we cannot effectively address issues of injustice. Without addressing issues of injustice, we cannot truly value diversity.

WHAT IS SOCIAL JUSTICE EDUCATION?

The definition of social justice education presented in this book includes both an *interdisciplinary conceptual framework* for analyzing multiple forms of oppression and their intersections, as well as *a set of interactive, experiential pedagogical principles and methods/practices*. In this book, we use the term "oppression" rather than discrimination, bias, prejudice, or bigotry to emphasize the pervasive nature of social inequality that is woven throughout social institutions as well as embedded within individual consciousness. The conceptual framework and pedagogical approach of social justice education provide tools for examining how oppression operates both in the social system and in the personal lives of individuals from diverse communities.

The goal of social justice education is to enable individuals to develop the critical analytical tools necessary to understand the structural features of oppression and their own socialization within oppressive systems. Social justice education aims to help participants develop awareness, knowledge, and processes to examine issues of justice/injustice in their personal lives, communities, institutions, and the broader society. It also aims to connect analysis to action; to help participants develop a sense of agency and commitment, as well as skills and tools, for working with others to interrupt and change oppressive patterns and behaviors in themselves and in the institutions and communities of which they are a part.

Working for social justice in a society and world steeped in oppression is no simple feat. For this reason, we need clear ways to define and analyze forms of oppression in order to discern how they operate at individual, cultural, institutional, and structural levels, historically and in the present. We hope the theoretical framework presented here—the pedagogical processes presented in Chapter 2, the facilitation and design information in Chapter 3, and the core concepts and introductory design presented in Chapter 4—will help readers make sense of, and hopefully act, more effectively against oppressive circumstances as these arise in different contexts.

WHY THEORY?

Articulating the theoretical sources of our approach to social justice education serves several important purposes. First, theory enables social justice educators to think clearly about our intentions and the means we use to actualize them in educational contexts/settings. It provides a framework for making choices about what we do and how, and for distinguishing among different approaches. Second, at its best, theory also provides a framework for questioning and challenging our practices so that we remain open to new approaches as we encounter inevitable problems of cooptation, resistance, insufficient knowledge, and changing social conditions. Ideally, we will keep coming back to and refining our theory as we read emerging scholarship on oppression, participate in and learn from social justice movements, and continually reflect upon the myriad ways oppression can alternately seduce our minds and hearts, or inspire us to further learning and activism. Finally, theory has the potential to help us stay conscious of our position as historically and geographically situated subjects, able to learn from the past as we try to meet current conditions in the specific contexts in which we live, in more effective and imaginative ways.

UNDERSTANDING OPPRESSION

Oppression is the term we use to embody the interlocking forces that create and sustain injustice. In this book, we focus on how oppression is manifested through racism, classism, sexism, heterosexism, transgender oppression, religious oppression, ableism, and youth and elder oppression. In order to work toward a vision of justice, it is essential to understand how oppression operates institutionally and personally in everyday life. The features of oppression that social justice educational strategies are intended to expose, analyze, and challenge can be seen as interwoven strands in a social fabric that renders oppression durable, flexible, and resilient, as shown in Fig. 1.1. In order to work against oppression effectively, we need to understand the component strands and how they weave together to reinforce and strengthen each other in maintaining an oppressive system.

1A: Features of Oppression

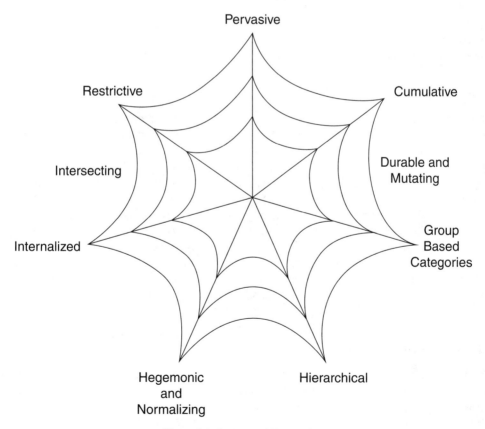

Figure 1.1 Features of Oppression

The dictionary definition of oppression includes such terms as domination, coercion, cruelty, tyranny, subjugation, persecution, harassment, and repression. These terms describe important overt features of oppression but do not capture the more subtle and covert aspects of how oppression is normalized in everyday life. Below we define and discuss both overt and subtle features that characterize oppression as restrictive, pervasive, and cumulative; socially constructed, categorizing, and group-based; hierarchical, normalized, and hegemonic; intersectional and internalized; and durable and mutable. These features are illustrated with examples that show how they interlock with one another to sustain the overall system. While presented as separate terms, these features in fact interweave and mutually reinforce each other in ways that are not as simple to tease apart as a list of discrete terms might suggest. Rather, they should be understood as interlocking constituent parts of a dynamic process.

RESTRICTIVE

On the most general level, oppression denotes structural and material constraints that significantly shape life opportunities and sense of possibility. Oppression restricts both self-development and self-determination, delimiting the person one can imagine becoming as well as the power to act in support of one's rights and aspirations. It encapsulates the fusion of institutional/systemic discrimination with personal bias, bigotry, and social prejudice through a complex web of relationships and structures that saturate everyday life. For example, the national mythology of the American Dream claims that anyone who works hard enough can get ahead, yet evidence shows that people who grow up poor today have the same odds of staying poor as their grandparents did, regardless of how hard they work or what their aspirations are. Further, intergenerational mobility in the U.S. is significantly lower than other countries (Chetty, Hendren, Kline, Saez, & Turner, 2014).

PERVASIVE

Oppression is institutionalized through pervasive practices grounded in history, law, economic policy, social custom, and education that rationalize and maintain hierarchies among individuals and groups. Individuals are socialized into this system and internalize the dynamics that sustain it. Woven together through time and reinforced in the present, these individual, interpersonal, and institutional practices interact to create and mutually reinforce an all-encompassing, pervasive system. The more institutionalized, sophisticated, and embedded these practices become, the more difficult it is to see how they have been constructed in the first place and how they have come to be taken for granted as inevitable and unchangeable. For example, the pervasiveness of racism is spread across multiple institutions in our society that mutually reinforce one another. Racial profiling by police, employment discrimination, negative images in the media, the inability to get bank loans at the same rates as whites, under-resourced schools, and inadequate health care all interact to support a pervasive system of racism (see Chapter 5).

CUMULATIVE

Oppression accumulates through institutional and social patterns, grounded in history, whose effects aggregate over time. Historical context and detail can reveal the relationships between particular actions, practices, and policies from the past and their structural and cumulative outcomes in the present. For example, the racial wealth gap that exists today is rooted in slavery and genocide that set white and non-Native people on the road to wealth at the expense of enslaved Africans, dispossessed Native Americans, and exploited Asian and Latino workers. In order to address the racial wealth gap that exists today, it is important to understand the pervasive and cumulative factors that created and continue to sustain it.

For example, the current situation of extreme poverty and isolation of Native American peoples is a result of a long legacy of historical, legal, economic, and educational policies that stripped them of land, rights, cultures, religious practices, and languages through forced relocation, conversion, mass extermination, boarding schools aimed at "removing the Indian" from the child, and paternalistic government oversight. Stereotypes and misinformation perpetuated through movies, textbooks, and popular culture sanitize and rationalize this history.

The corresponding benefits for non-Native people, who profit from appropriated Indian land and wealth that has grown exponentially over centuries, are rendered invisible. Today, the relative success of the non-Native, white majority is attributed to their work ethic and character, while the lack of success of Native peoples is ascribed to problems in their communities rather than the historical, political processes that create and sustain differential outcomes. Mainstream television, media, children's books, cartoons, and popular culture socialize non-Indians to view Native people as quaint artifacts of the past who have vanished or as mascots for sports teams and wealthy casino owners. Most non-Indian people in the U.S. know very little about the present circumstances of Native peoples, their living cultures, or how government policies constructed and perpetuate the dire circumstances they face. Likewise, most non-Native people are unaware of their share in the cumulative benefits reaped from this process of dispossession. All of these conditions combine to describe the pervasive impact of the oppression Native Americans face as a result of racism, colonialism, religious oppression, and economic imperialism.

The cumulative properties of oppression are also evident in the concept of microaggressions. These are the daily, constant, often subtle, and seemingly innocuous, covert and overt negative messages and actions directed toward people from marginalized groups (Sue, 2010). Because they are incessant and difficult to respond to, they take a cumulative toll on the psyche of individuals who are oppressed. Microaggressions "are in fact, a form of everyday suffering that have been socially and systemically normalized and in effect minimized" (Huber & Solorzano, 2015, p. 304). They show the tangible, cumulative ways oppression manifests in the daily lives of people who experience them.

SOCIALLY CONSTRUCTED CATEGORIES

Social construction is the process by which society categorizes groups of people. In the U.S., constructed social categories are based on race, class, gender, sexuality, age, religion, and other social markers. The ways in which a society categorizes social identity groups are embedded in its history, geography, patterns of immigration, and social-political context. The group categories upon which oppression is based, such as gender roles or racial designations, are not "real," but through implicit beliefs and social practices that operate as if real, they become so in practice. Social constructions are used to rationalize differential treatment or allocation of resources and to explain social reality in ways that make inequitable outcomes seem inevitable.

For example, the construction of distinct racial groups was produced to justify particular social, economic, and political practices that justified the enslavement, extermination, segregation, and exploitation of other "races." The meaning-making system of race gained force and power through its reproduction in the material practices of the society across historical eras. Anti-miscegenation laws and segregation in housing, employment, schooling, and other areas of social life reproduced and reinforced race as a social category. Thus, using, and continuing to use, race to allocate resources and opportunities made race real in practice. Today, the idea of race is so taken for granted that it is difficult to see the apparatus that created it in the first place (Leonardo, 2013).

The social construction of gender provides another example. Gender divides humans into categories of male and female with dichotomous masculine or feminine identities, traits, and social roles. A socialization process that treats presumed gender differences as innate reinforces these constructs and makes them appear "natural" (i.e., that there are only two genders—male and female; or that boys are naturally active and rambunctious, while girls are passive and sweet). Such assumptions are supported and reinforced through social norms, roles, and interpersonal and organizational practices that regard and treat males and females accordingly. The assumption that females are innately more emotional and empathic than males is reflected in an organization of labor that slots females in the majority of caretaking roles and positions, where they typically earn lower wages than men, face limits on advancement, and remain the primary caretakers of both children and elders. Despite the many advances women have made in the past few decades, this division continues to show up in social science research on employment, the division of labor at work and at home, and prevalent stereotypes about male and female roles (World Economic Forum, 2014).

Social constructions presented as natural and inevitable are difficult to question and challenge. Once their provenance comes into question, however, imagining alternative scenarios becomes possible. Part of the work of social justice education and social justice movements is to expose and take apart oppressive constructs, understand how they have been created and maintained, and then reconstruct more just ways to organize social life. The construct of gender has been valuably problematized by queer theory (Turner, 2000). "A central endeavor of feminist, queer, and trans activists has been to dismantle the cultural ideologies, social practices, and legal norms that say that certain body parts determine gender identity and gendered social characteristics and roles" (Spade, 2011, p. 61). Once this construction is challenged, the way is open to imagining a system of "gender self-determination for all people and to eliminating coercive systems that punish gender variance" (Spade, 2011, p. 59).

History, geography, patterns of immigration, and socio-political context are important to how identities are categorized and constructed. For example, the group labeled "Hispanic" in the United States is extremely diverse, comprised of people from many different countries of origin who speak various languages; they are from divergent racial, ethnic, and socio-economic groups and arrive in the United States under widely different conditions of immigration, colonization, or slavery, and over different time periods (Anzaldúa, 1987; Oboler, 1995). The category may include a Spanish-speaking, upper-class white man from Cuba as well as a dark-skinned, Mayan speaking, Indian woman from Guatemala. The dominant society lumps them together in a group labeled "Hispanic" to which certain attributions, assumptions, and stereotypes are applied. Yet their experiences are so divergent as to have little in common at all but for the common group experience of cultural, ethnic, and linguistic oppression based on their categorization and location in a U.S. hierarchy. Indeed, this lumping is often the basis for political organizing among different groups labeled Latino/as who organize as a pan-Latino/a group. The same is true for pan-Asian organizing that cuts across national origins, language, conditions of immigration, and other factors.

Individuals, of course, push back against limiting labels, often through reclaiming and redefining these terms. Social group identities can be consciously embraced and affirmed as a fundamental aspect of self-definition in opposition to oppression. The emergence of black consciousness, gay pride, feminist solidarity, disability rights, the gray panthers, red power, la raza, and other self-chosen labels demonstrates the significance of self-ascribed group status for resisting devaluation by the dominant society (Young, 1990). In fact, individuals may embrace multiple self-ascriptions and align with others in complex coalitions that defy easy categorization ("crips" of color, black lesbian feminists, QTPOC (queer &/ or trans people of color). Social justice is concerned with recognizing and respecting the differences and distinctions valued by diverse individuals and groups, not with forcing conformity to a unitary norm, while at the same time challenging hierarchies that divide and discriminate among groups.

In actual practice, neither individual identities nor social groups are homogeneous or stable. Identity categories interact with and co-constitute one another in different geographic and historical contexts to create unique social locations (Hankivsky, 2014). Essentialist notions of group identity as fixed ignore the fluid and changing ways that people experience themselves, both as individuals and as members of different social groups, over the course of a lifetime (Anzaldúa, 1987; Hurtado, 2003; Mohanty, Russo, & Torres, 1991). We need to "recognize the ways in which positions of dominance and subordination work in complex and intersecting ways to constitute a subject's experiences of personhood" (Nash, 2008). Queer theory pushes further to challenge and deconstruct categories of identity that have been normalized and to question assumptions of uniformity within groups that mask important differences among individuals inside any particular category (Marcus, 2005; Warner, 1999). "Despite our desperate, eternal attempt to separate, contain, and mend, categories always leak" (Trinh, 1989, p. 94).

POWER HIERARCHIES

Social groups are sorted into a hierarchy that confers advantages, status, resources, access, and privilege that are denied or rationed to those lower in the hierarchy. Social groups are not simply different, but ranked in a hierarchy. Thus, individuals are positioned as *dominant* or *advantaged* in relation to other groups that are *subordinated* or *disadvantaged*. Power hierarchies create and maintain a system of advantage and disadvantage based on social group membership.

Dominant groups hold the power and authority to control, in their own interests, the important institutions in society, determine how resources are allocated, and define what is natural, good, and true. They are seen as superior, more capable, and more credible—as normal—compared to those who are differently situated. People in dominant groups are socialized to accept their group's socially advantaged status as normal and deserved, rather than recognizing how it has been conferred through systems of inequality. Thus, one of the privileges of dominant group status is the luxury to see oneself as simply an individual. Group status is typically invisible and unmarked, as is evident in how jarring it is when someone comments on maleness or whiteness or straightness in most settings. A white man, for example, is rarely defined by "whiteness" or "maleness." If he does well at his job, he is acknowledged as a highly qualified individual. If he does poorly, the blame is attributed to him alone.

Subordinated or marginalized groups are represented as less than, inferior, and/or deviant. People who are oppressed are not seen as individuals but as representatives or members of social groups (Cudd, 2006; Young, 1990). For people in subordinated groups, social group membership trumps individuality. They can never fully escape being defined by their social group memberships and the ascriptions the dominant society applies to their group. A Puerto Rican woman, for example, may wish to be viewed as an individual and acknowledged for her personal talents and abilities. Yet she can never fully escape the dominant society's assumptions about her racial/ethnic group, language, and gender. If she excels in her work, she may be seen as atypical or exceptional. If she does poorly, she may be seen as representative of the limitations of her group. In either case, she rises or falls not solely on the basis of individual qualities, but always partly as a member of the social group(s) with which she is identified.

Thus, those in subordinated groups are caught in a contradiction created by an oppressive system that claims they are free individuals but treats them according to group status. Whether or not individuals in the same social group define themselves in the same way, they must deal with the stereotypes and assumptions attributed to their group and used to rationalize hierarchical relationships. A person's self-defined group identity may be central, as religious identity is to a traditionally observant Jew or Muslim. Or it may be mainly background, only becoming salient in certain interactional contexts, as Jewish identity may become for an assimilated Jew when confronted with antisemitism, or as Muslim identity may become for an Arab or Indian targeted by anti-Muslim prejudice (Malik, 2010). Regardless, they must struggle for individual self-definition within the burden of oppressive attributions, assumptions, and practices toward their group(s).

Young (1990) developed the concept of five faces of oppression to distinguish families of concepts or conditions that constitute oppression differently in the lives of different groups. The five faces are: exploitation, marginalization, powerlessness, cultural imperialism, and violence. In our teaching, we often use these five terms as a heuristic device to illustrate the shared and different ways oppression plays out and is experienced among different groups of people. In some of the ism chapters in this book, the five faces are used as a tool to examine how oppression operates for that oppression (see Chapter 8, Religious Oppression, and Chapter 9, Ableism, for examples).

HEGEMONIC AND NORMALIZED

The concept of hegemony was developed by Gramsci to explain how domination and control are maintained not only through coercion but also through the voluntary consent of both those who are dominated and those who gain advantage because of the oppression of others (Simon, 2002). Through hegemony, the reproduction of advantage and disadvantage come to be assumed as natural, normal, "business as usual," even by those who are disempowered.

Woven so effectively into the social fabric, the processes and effects of oppression become normalized, thus making it difficult to step outside of the system to discern how it operates—like fish trying to understand the water in which they swim. For example, the exclusion of people with disabilities from many jobs does not require overt discrimination against them. Business as usual is sufficient to prevent change. Physical barriers to access go unnoticed by those who can walk up the stairs, reach elevator buttons and telephones, use furniture and tools that fit their bodies and functional needs, and generally move in a world that is designed to facilitate their passage, and thus support and maintain policies that seem perfectly natural and fair from the privileged vantage point of those not affected.

In hegemonic systems, power is relational and dynamic, something that circulates within a web of relationships in which we all participate, rather than something imposed from top down (Foucault, 1980). Power operates not simply through persons or groups unilaterally imposing their will on others, but through ongoing systems that are mediated by well-intentioned people acting, usually unconsciously, as agents of oppression by merely going about their daily lives. Hegemony and structural injustice are thus produced and reproduced by "thousands or millions of persons usually acting within institutional rules and according to practices that most people regard as morally acceptable" (Young, 2011,

p. 4). In such a system, responsibility for oppression often cannot be isolated to individual or institutional agents but is rather more indirect, collective, and cumulative.

Hegemony is also maintained through "discourse," which includes ideas, texts, theories, language, and ideology. These are embedded in networks of social and political control that Foucault (1980) called "regimes of truth." Regimes of truth operate to legitimize what can be said, who has the authority to speak, and what is sanctioned as true (Kreisberg, 1992). For example, until women began speaking out about spousal abuse, a husband's authority to physically control his wife often went unchallenged, rendered invisible through the language of family privacy and presumptions of sexual consent in marriage. Received wisdom that young people are irresponsible and immature, or that old people are no longer capable of contributing to society in meaningful ways, are other examples of hegemonic discourse.

Through hegemony, the roles and rules, institutional norms, historical accounts, and social practices of dominant groups come to be accepted as the natural order. The advantages of dominant groups and the disadvantages of marginalized groups are normalized through language, ideology, and cultural/material practices. For example, despite rhetoric that the United States is a secular nation, Christian symbols, holidays, and rituals are routinely integrated into public affairs and institutions. Other religious and spiritual traditions held by large numbers of Americans, including Jews, Muslims, Hindus, Sikhs, and Native Americans, are invisible or marginalized, so much so that when members of these groups protest, they are often viewed as challenging the American (i.e., Christian) way of life (Kruse, 2015) (see Chapter 8).

In a similar vein, the material and other advantages of whites as a group are normalized and justified as fair and deserved. As a group, whites earn more money and accumulate more assets than African Americans, Native Americans, and Latina/os; hold the majority of positions of power and influence; and command the controlling institutions in society (Demos, 2015; Lipsitz, 2006; Oliver & Shapiro, 2006). White-dominated institutions restrict the life expectancy, infant mortality, income, housing, employment, and educational opportunities of people in these groups, while enhancing opportunities for white people (Smelser, Wilson, & Mitchell, 2001). When we look beneath the normalizing assumptions that support the status quo, we can see that advantages are not the inevitable result of hard work in a fair system, but rather the created effects of a system rigged in favor of whites in countless and cumulative ways (see Chapter 5).

INTERNALIZED

Through the process of socialization, members of a society appropriate and internalize social norms and beliefs to make meaning of their experiences (Vygotsky, 1978) and to fit in, conform, and survive. As part of this process, people learn and incorporate oppressive stereotypes and beliefs reflected in the broader society. Such stereotypes and beliefs circulate through everyday language and cultural scripts (L. A. Bell, 2003; Bonilla-Silva, Lewis, & Embrick, 2004) that frame their assumptions and interactions with others. In this way, oppression is internalized so that it operates not only through external social institutions and norms, but also through discourse and practice (Fanon, 1968; Freire, 1970; Memmi, 1965; Miller, 1976).

The processes of socialization and internalization illustrate how an unjust status quo comes to be accepted and replicated by those who benefit as well as by those who suffer from oppressive norms. Attribution and internalization are thus reciprocal and mutually reinforcing processes. People may adopt oppressive beliefs and stereotypes attributed to their group, regardless of their particular social locations. To varying degrees, poor people and affluent people alike internalize the attribution that people who are poor deserve and are responsible for poverty, and that the success of wealthy people is merited and deserved. Attributions that youth are irresponsible and incapable of serious commitments, or that elders are slow and less vital than middle-aged people in their "prime," are taken as true by people of all ages.

Conditions of oppression in everyday life are reinforced when we accept systems of domination without question or challenge. As eloquently put by Audre Lorde, "the true focus of revolutionary change is to see the piece of the oppressor inside us" (1984, p. 123). Both those who are advantaged and those who are penalized play a role in maintaining oppression. When members of penalized groups accept and incorporate negative attributions of their group fostered by the dominant society, they collude in supporting the system of oppression (Fanon, 1968; Freire, 1970; Memmi, 1965; Miller, 1976). They may go along because they internalize the false belief that the system is legitimate and/or as a means of survival. Women, for example, may actively accept the belief that men are more capable in politics and business and women more naturally suited to housework and childcare, and unquestioningly adopt assumptions about female limitations and negative stereotypes of women as weak, overemotional, and irrational. Or women may consciously reject such stereotypes, but go along with male dominance as a means of survival, because to challenge may mean risking jobs, relationships, and physical security. Internalized subordination exacts a psychic toll, generating feelings of powerlessness, inferiority, and even self-hatred. It may prompt hiding oneself from others, resignation, isolation, and hopelessness in those who go along with it (Pheterson, 1990).

Those in advantaged positions also adopt and internalize oppression and perpetuate norms, policies, and practices that support the status quo. Through internalized domination, individuals in the advantaged group learn to look at themselves, others, and the broader society through a distorted lens in which the structural privileges they enjoy and the cultural practices of their group are taken to be universal, superior, and deserved (Jost, Banaji, & Nosek, 2004; Piff, 2014). Internalized domination has psychic consequences, too, including false feelings of superiority, self-consciousness, guilt, fear, projection, and denial (Frankenberg, 1993; Pharr, 1988).

Internalized domination and internalized subordination can cause members of both dominant and subordinated groups to devalue or turn on members of their own group who challenge the status quo (Bivens, 2005). Such "horizontal hostility" (Freire, 1970; White & Langer, 1999) blocks solidarity and prevents organizing for change. For example, GLBTQ people who stay in the closet in order to survive may resent activists who insist on publicly working to challenge discrimination against their group. This division within the community helps to maintain the system of heterosexism and transgender oppression, and prevents solidarity and working together for change. People in dominant groups also engage in horizontal hostility toward members of their group who challenge the status quo. For example, white people label other white people who challenge racist practices as "troublemakers," "extremists," or "bleeding hearts." Pressure against rocking the boat or "making trouble" can keep people in dominant positions from challenging inequality and discrimination. By simply doing nothing and going along with business as usual, people perpetuate an unequal status quo.

Internalization and collusion are further complicated by the fact that most people, through the intersecting identities they hold, may experience privilege and penalty simultaneously. Thus, a middle-aged white woman may focus on the penalties she experiences based on a subordinated gender status but ignore the privileges she obtains through her dominant race and age status. A middle- or upper-class man with a disability may focus on his subordinated status as a disabled person and remain unaware of the privileges he receives through dominant class and male status.

However, internalized subordination and domination can be unlearned through consciousness-raising, examining and challenging oppressive attitudes and assumptions that have been internalized, and imagining and enacting new ways of being. Harro (2008) traces the way individuals learn and internalize their roles through interaction with family and other institutions in society. She also uses the same model to illustrate how individuals can come to consciousness about their roles in the system and take action at various points to challenge and change oppressive relationships and actions (Harro, 2008). Love (2013) calls this developing a liberatory consciousness (described further in the final section of this chapter).

INTERSECTIONAL

Each form of oppression has distinctive qualities and historical/social legacies that distinguish it from other forms of oppression, and we believe that learning about the specific legacies and historical trajectories of different groups is critical for understanding the specific ways different forms of oppression operate. At the same time, we recognize that different forms of oppression interact with and co-constitute one another as interlocking systems that overlap and reinforce each other, at both the systemic/institutional level and at the individual/interpersonal level (Collins, 1990; Crenshaw, 2003).

Telescoping in on a single form of oppression can provide valuable information for understanding the particular historical contexts and contemporary manifestations of that oppression. Panning out to focus on the broader pattern of interlocking systems yields important knowledge about general features of oppression that cut across specific forms and about how different forms mutually reinforce each other. Focusing on the intersections where different forms of oppression meet in the lives of particular individuals can reveal the differential impacts of varying locations within the overall system of oppression.

Racism and sexism, for example, can be examined as mutually reinforcing systems that operate according to similar principles of social construction, categorization and hierarchy, normalization, hegemony, etc. However, race and gender also operate in particular and distinctive ways depending on historical context and normative social practices. Understanding the distinctive ways in which racism and sexism function can be helpful for determining how best to challenge each one at a particular point in time (Luft, 2009). For example, Luft argues that given the essentialism with which gender is currently viewed by large numbers of people and renewed debates about "innate" gender differences at this particular moment in our history, a decision to focus on deconstructing gender roles and tracing the interests behind them may be most effective. Whereas, in an era where color blindness is constantly invoked to deny or minimize the existence of racism, a focus on deconstructing race may inadvertently support claims that the U.S. is "post-racial" and "beyond racism." In this case, a decision to demonstrate the reality of "race" in terms of social outcomes (poverty, incarceration, disenfranchisement, etc.) may be more effective for challenging racism (Luft, 2009).

Valuable learning about how oppression operates can also be drawn from pinpointing what happens to individuals and groups who are differently situated at the intersections of multiple oppressions. For example, the experiences of transgender people who are also poor and of color sheds light on how class and race can interact with gender expression to render some individuals and groups more invisible and expendable than others who may also be oppressed. Focusing on poor women of color, or homeless lesbians and trans women, provides another example where attention to the unique impacts of violence toward particularly situated women can provide a more nuanced understanding of the problem of gender violence. Such an intersectional approach to gender violence can reveal how strategies predicated on the experiences of white, middle class, heterosexual, and cisgender women may not address the particular problems and obstacles faced by poor women, women of color, lesbian, bisexual, or transgender women because of their different locations within intersecting forms of oppression (Cho, 2013).

For each form of oppression, we can be purposeful in looking at how it intersects with other forms:

> We challenge individuals to see interconnections by "Asking the other question." When I see something that looks racist, I ask, "Where is the patriarchy in this?" When I see something that looks sexist, I ask, "Where is the heterosexism in this?" When I see something that looks homophobic, I ask, "Where are the class interests in this?"
>
> (Matsuda, 1987, p. 1189)

Intersectionality operates at the level of identity, as well as the level of institutions and the overall system, in ways that are multiplicative (Wing, 2003), and simultaneous (Holvino, 2012). Individuals experience their lives based on their location along all dimensions of identity and thus may occupy positions of dominance and subordination at the same time (Collins, 1990; Crenshaw, 2003). For example, an upper-class professional man who is African American (still a very small percentage of African Americans overall) may enjoy economic success and professional status conferred through being male, and class privilege and perhaps dominant language and citizenship privilege as an English-speaking native-born citizen, yet face limitations not endured by co-workers who are white. Despite economic and professional status and success, he may be threatened by police, unable to hail a taxi, and endure hateful epithets as he walks down the street (Ogletree, 2012). The constellation of identities that shape his consciousness and experience as an African American man, and his varying access to privilege, may fluctuate if he is light or dark skinned; Ivy League educated or a high school dropout; heterosexual, gay, or transgender; incarcerated or unemployed; or a tourist in South Africa, Brazil, or Europe, where his racial status will be differently defined.

From our perspective, no single form of oppression is the base for all others; all are connected and mutually constituted in a system that makes them possible. We find it useful to identify where and how different isms coalesce or diverge in particular historical, geographical, and institutional periods (Weber, 2010) in order to understand the "technologies of categorization and control" (Wacquant, 1997, p. 343) that operate to discipline human beings to accept injustice. While Chapters 5–10 each zero in on one form of oppression, they also point to the interconnections with other forms throughout their discussion and design.

In our approach, we argue for the explanatory and political value of identifying the particular histories, geographies, and characteristics of specific forms of oppression as well as the intersections across isms that mutually reinforce them at both the systemic and individual levels. Focusing on one facet of a prism does not remove it from its broader context, but provides a way to highlight and focus in order to ground learning at a particular point in time.

DURABLE AND MUTABLE

A final feature of oppression is its resilience and ability to shape-shift into new forms to prevail against challenges to it. The civil rights movement was successful in eliminating de jure segregation, but the system of racism evolved to create new ways to segregate and discriminate while calling itself "post racial." Obviously, overt discrimination still exists, but racism has also become more subtle and insidious. For example, Haney-Lopez (2014) examines how overt racist appeals from politicians that were more prevalent in the past have morphed into coded language and images ("dog whistle politics"). Veiled statements that link public goods such as health care and welfare, to race have been successful in getting white voters to support policies that favor the wealthiest few, even though it harms their own self-interest in gaining access to these services.

CONSEQUENCES FOR ALL

Oppression has consequences for everyone. People in both marginalized and advantaged groups are dehumanized by oppression (Freire, 1970). Thus, a goal of social justice education is to engage all people in recognizing the terrible costs of maintaining systems of oppression. For example, when millions of Americans are homeless and hungry, those who are comfortable pay a social and moral price. The cost of enjoying plenty while others starve is the inability to view our society as just and see ourselves as decent people. Just as important, it also prevents a clear view of underlying structural problems in the economic system that ultimately make all people vulnerable in a changing international economy that disregards national boundaries or allegiances. The productive and creative contributions of people who are shut out of the system are lost to everyone. Rising violence and urban decay make it increasingly difficult for anyone to feel safe. Reduced social supports, limited affordable housing, and scarcities of food and potable water loom as a possible future for all who are not independently wealthy, particularly as people reach old age.

The impetus for change more often comes from those on the margins, since they tend to see more clearly the contradictions between myths and reality and usually have the most incentive to change (Collins, 1990; Freire, 1970; Hartsock, 1983; Harding, 1991).The "subjugated knowledge" of oppressed groups defines the world and possibilities for human existence differently and offers valuable alternative analyses and visions of what is possible (Collins, 1990; Wing, 2003). Cho argues that "looking to the bottom" is an inclusionary way to understand oppression because "restructuring the world according to those who are multiply disadvantaged will likely and logically mean that those who are singularly disadvantaged will also be unburdened" (Matsuda, 1987, p. 2012). Listening to and learning from the analyses and experiences of members of multiply marginalized groups can lead to a clearer understanding of how oppression operates, and can suggest more imaginative alternatives for socially just relationships and institutional policies.

For example, in a world controlled by and built to accommodate supposedly able-bodied people, those who want to challenge ableism must discern the institutional, legal, social, and educational patterns and practices, as well as individual biases and assumptions, that restrict full access and participation of all people. Those who have direct experience with ableism are likely to be more aware of the barriers and to have ideas about how to make institutions and physical environments more inclusive.

Those advantaged by the system also have an important role to play in joining with others to challenge oppression. They can expose the way advantage works from the inside and articulate the social, moral, and personal costs of maintaining privilege. Those in dominant groups can learn to see that they have an investment in changing the system by which they benefit, by recognizing they also pay a price (Goodman, 2011). Some argue this commitment comes through friendship (Spelman, 1988), others that it comes only through mutual struggle for common political ends (Mohanty, Russo, & Torres, 1991). Throughout human history, there have always been people from advantaged groups who used their power and position to actively fight against systems of oppression (Aptheker, 1993; Wigginton, 1992; Zinn, 2003). White abolitionists, middle- and upper-class anti-poverty crusaders, and men who supported women's rights are examples. Those who are advantaged are able to unmask the role dominants play in maintaining the system and articulate the high moral and societal cost of privileged status in an unequal society (Thompson, Schaefer, & Brod, 2003).

WORKING FOR SOCIAL JUSTICE

Given that systems of domination saturate both the external world and our individual psyches, how do we challenge and change them? In a context where we are all implicated, where we cannot escape our social location, how do we find standpoints from which to act (Lewis, 1993)? A commitment to social justice requires a moral and ethical attitude toward equality and possibility, and a belief in the capacity of people to transform their world (Freire, 1970; Weiler, 1991). Oppression is never complete; it is always open to challenge, as is evident if we understand history and learn lessons from past movements for justice. The next section discusses concepts that have been developed and successfully used in the struggle for social justice in the past. These legacies, together with the creativity and ingenuity of current struggles, provide a set of practices that we can build on to guide social justice work in the present.

DEVELOP A CRITICAL CONSCIOUSNESS

Freire created the notion of critical consciousness in his work to help Brazilian peasants become aware of the political and social patterns that enforced their oppression, rather than accept these conditions as fated or inevitable (1970). Critical consciousness meant working in solidarity with others to question, analyze, and challenge oppressive conditions in their lives rather than blame each other or fate. The goal of critical consciousness is to develop awareness or mindfulness of the social and political factors that create oppression, to analyze the patterns that sustain oppression and the interests it serves, and to take action to work democratically with others to reimagine and remake the world in the interest of all.

Critical consciousness connects the personal with the socio-political to understand both external systems of oppression and the ways they are internalized by individuals. Feminist consciousness-raising groups in the early 1970s sought to help women make these connections through examining patriarchal structures in the family and other institutions while exploring how women internalized patriarchal ideas and values as appropriate and/or inevitable. Through consciousness-raising groups, women collectively uncovered and deconstructed the ways that the system of patriarchy is reproduced inside women's consciousness as well as in external social institutions. In so doing, they challenged conventional assumptions about human nature, sexuality, family life, and gender roles and relations (Combahee River Collective, 1986; Evans, 1979; Firestone, 1970). Feminist practice also sought to create and enact new, more liberating ways of thinking and behaving as equals in society. Consciousness-raising processes are a powerful way to examine and critique normative assumptions and our own, often unconscious, investments in supporting them. Consciousness-raising processes have been fruitful for many oppressed groups seeking to raise awareness about their situation.

DECONSTRUCT THE BINARIES

Gay and lesbian rights activists in the 1980s and 1990s exposed normative assumptions about family, love, relationships, and gender roles to analyze straight supremacy and heteronormativity (Gilreath, 2011). Queer and transgender scholars and activists question binary categories and assumptions of uniformity within any constructed category. The inadequacy of defining the experience of individuals and groups in simplistic binary terms is reflected in the work of bisexual and transgender people within feminist and gay/lesbian movements who refuse the categories as well as their content (Butler, 2004) and experiment with multiple ways of expressing and enacting identities. Since oppression works through setting up dualistic frames that privilege some groups and exclude others, deconstructing the binaries and recognizing the individual and social complexities and variety they hide can be an important tool for change. Activists and educators in a range of social movements have analyzed how binary categories work to perpetuate oppression, while at the same time deconstructing and exploding categories that sort and rank people into either/or boxes (black/white, straight/gay, male/female, young/old, disabled/non-disabled). This experimentation with categories to push back against the binary categorizations through which oppression operates is evident in a range of social movements.

DRAW ON COUNTER-NARRATIVES

Critical Race Theory (CRT) analyzes and challenges mainstream narratives in law, history, and popular culture that uphold the status quo (D. Bell, 1992; Delgado & Stefancic, 2013; Matsuda, 1996). Through counter-storytelling, CRT seeks to destabilize "stock stories" that valorize the legitimacy of dominant groups. Critical historical methods draw on counter-narratives to "demarginalize" (Davis & Wing, 2000) and center the roles that Native American people, working class people, African Americans, immigrants from various ethnic backgrounds, Latina/os, Asian Americans, people with disabilities, and women of all groups have played in challenging oppression (Fleischer & Zames, 2001; Lerner, 1986; Zinn, 2003, 2004). Such counter-narratives unearth suppressed and hidden stories of marginalized groups, including stories of their resistance to the status quo, and provide evidence as well as hope that oppressive circumstances can change through the efforts of human actors (L. A. Bell, 2010). Historical counter-narratives show, for example, how diverse coalitions organized to abolish slavery, extend suffrage to women, create unions and improve working conditions for laborers, challenge anti-immigrant policies, fight for Native sovereignty, and advocate for gay/lesbian and transgender rights.

A critical historical approach requires an understanding of history as not linear but rather multiple and simultaneous:

> The events and people we write about did not occur in isolation but in dialogue with a myriad of other people and events. In fact, at any given moment millions of people are all talking at once. As historians we try to isolate one conversation and to explore it, but the trick is then how to put that conversation in a context which makes evident its dialogue with so many others—how to make this one lyric stand alone and at the same time be in connection with all the other lyrics being sung.
>
> (Barkley-Brown, 1991, p. 2)

The counter-stories to the status quo developed within different social movements and inspire emerging social movements today. The civil rights movement continues to excite the imagination of people here and around the world who apply its lessons to an understanding of their particular situations and adapt its analyses and tactics to their own struggles for equality. Just as Native American, Asian American, Chicano, and Puerto Rican youth in the 1960s and 1970s styled themselves after African-American youth in the Student Nonviolent Coordinating Committee (SNCC) and the Black Panther Party (Marabel, 1984;

Oboler, 1995; Okihiro,1994), young people today draw from and expand upon these images to inspire their own activism.

We can also learn from new counter-stories that emerge to build on, challenge, and reinvent older counter-stories. For example, building resistance through discovering and claiming a shared identity was a critical part of social movements following colonialism (Memmi, 1965). Emerging movements today draw from these stories, but they understand that identity politics has limitations that can prevent people from seeing dynamics across issues and communities and prevent effective cross-group understanding and coalition building (Guinier & Torres, 2002). As they work across multiple identities and projects, they fashion new counter-stories about how oppression works and how diverse coalitions can strategize to challenge the status quo.

As formerly marginalized or hidden historical stories are reclaimed, people in the present weave anew an understanding of the interconnections among struggles for justice. The more we know about the historical experiences and perspectives of diverse peoples, the more we are able to understand the interlocking systems that produce inequality. As importantly, we gain ideas and strategies for working with diverse others across coalitions in more effective, inclusive, and egalitarian ways (Bly & Wooten, 2012; Roberts & Jesudason, 2013).

ANALYZE POWER

Another lesson from earlier social movements is the need to examine the dynamics of power and the interests it serves. Such analyses remind us to continually ask the questions, "In whose interest do systems operate?" and "Who benefits and who pays?" regarding prevailing practices. These questions help to expose hierarchical relationships and hidden advantages and penalties embedded in purportedly fair and neutral systems. They reveal how power operates through normalizing relations of domination by presenting certain ideas and practices as rational and self-evident, as part of the natural order. Once people begin to question what has previously been taken for granted, the way is open to imagine new possibilities and practices.

New Left movements of the 1960s drew on Marxist theory to shift the focus to the structural rather than individual factors that maintain oppressive economic and social relations. They critique as anti-democratic normative assumptions that conflated democracy with capitalism and stigmatize alternative ways to arrange economic and social life. Grounded initially in anti-racist civil rights movements, the New Left critiqued the hypocrisy of espousing ideals of democracy and personal liberty while repressing democratic ideas. Their goal was to organize to hold accountable those in power by exposing hypocrisy and evasion in policies presented as fair and democratic but that obscured cynical self-interests (Bowles & Gintis, 1987).

These lessons were brought to life again in the Occupy Wall Street movement that galvanized thousands of people across the country and the world to challenge the dominance of Wall Street in government decision-making and government bailouts following the market crash of 2008. The Occupy movement illustrated the importance of connecting the dots across institutions to understand how power operates to maintain dominance under the guise of neutrality. It also provoked creative ideas about alternative possibilities to this system in both process and structure (Gitlin, 2012; van Gelder, 2011). More recently, a group called the "Hedge Clippers" is using public venues to expose and teach about how hedge funds use the money they gain from favored tax policies to buy political influence and shape public policy on education and other areas, in unaccountable and undemocratic ways that disguise as altruistic their self-serving interests.

LOOK FOR INTEREST CONVERGENCE

The notion of "interest convergence" (D. Bell, 1992) is another useful tool for analyzing how systems of oppression modulate, sometimes appearing to respond to charges of injustice when it serves their interest, but ultimately continuing to maintain dominance. For example, critical race theorists argue that racial integration of the armed forces during World War II was an instance of interest convergence (D. A. Bell, 1980). When anti-lynching and anti-Jim Crow agitation in the U.S. coincided with establishment fears that the Germans would use American racism to attack U.S. claims about democracy, these disparate interests converged to support desegregating the armed forces. The U.S. government could neutralize communist critiques while meeting the interests of anti-racism advocates for change. At the same time, racism restabilized through policies that reinforced segregation in housing and prevented black soldiers from using the G.I. Bill to purchase housing in newly built suburbs, where property values would grow and lay the basis for the future prosperity that whites were able to enjoy.

The concept of interest convergence can be useful for strategizing ways to take advantage of potential alignments of interest with groups we might otherwise oppose in order to move a particular change forward (Milner, 2008). At the same time, understanding interest convergence can help groups be realistic about the limits of such coalitions and prepare to change tactics when different strategies are needed.

MAKE GLOBAL CONNECTIONS

Transnational activists and scholars help us understand the ways that oppression is shaped by geographic and historical contexts and interactions across national borders. They offer an analysis of transnational capital and its impact on labor, migration, gender, and ethnic relations, and national development in different parts of the world (Dirlik, 1997; Mohanty, 2003; Sandoval, 2000). Global feminism (Mohanty, 2003), global critical race feminism (Davis & Wing, 2000), and transnational feminisms (Fernandes, 2013) highlight the leadership of women at the margins and focus on how to understand the shared and distinctive problems women face under post-colonial systems and U.S. imperialism as they identify local strategies and solutions to address their particular contexts (Dirlik, 1997).

A comparison of two immigrants to the U.S. from Uganda illustrates the insights that a transnational perspective can offer for understanding local conditions in different parts of the world. Purkayastha (2012) describes the situation as follows. The ancestors of both a black and an Indian immigrant may have lived in Uganda for generations and been expelled by the Amin dictatorship. Both immigrants may have suffered under gendered/racialized migration policies in the U.S. that impacted their arrival. However, the black Ugandan's experience of racism is likely to be similar to that faced by African Americans, while the Indian Ugandan is more likely to experience the racism faced by Muslims and "Muslim-looking" people. If they return to Uganda, they will encounter a different set of privileges and penalties in a black-majority country that privileges the black migrant. If they move to India, the reverse may occur, with the Indian Ugandan experiencing the privileges of the Indian majority, privileges that would not be extended to the black Ugandan. When the Indian Ugandan is Muslim or lower-caste Hindu, a different set of hierarchies would apply. Taking a global perspective enables us to be more thoughtful about how we design policies and organize coalitions to meet the diverse needs of individuals in different locations and contexts.

BUILD COALITIONS AND SOLIDARITY

Because of the complexities and interconnections among different forms of inequality, we believe that eradicating oppression ultimately requires struggle against all its forms, and that coalitions among diverse people who can offer perspectives from their particular social locations provide the most promising potential for creating change. Working in collaboration with diverse groups is essential for building collective strength and developing strategies that draw on the energies, insights, and access to power of people who are differently positioned. Working at the intersections across groups and identities is an important coalitional strategy, because it links processes of subordination/domination and prevents compartmentalizing issues (Cho, 2012). When one group fails to acknowledge the ideas and needs of other groups in a coalition, it only serves to strengthen the power relations that each is attempting to challenge. Thus, thinking and working across intersections can prevent working at cross-purposes:

> For example, when feminists fail to acknowledge the role that race played in the public response to the rape of the Central Park jogger, feminism contributes to the forces that produce disproportionate punishment for black men who rape white women, and when antiracists represent the case solely in terms of racial domination, they belittle the fact that women particularly, and all people generally, should be outraged by the gender violence the case represented.
>
> (Crenshaw, 1991, p. 1282)

The Black Lives Matter movement against police brutality and the destruction of black lives illustrates the potential of a coalition of people from diverse groups working together as allies. African Americans, and other people of color, including queer people of color who have taken the lead in this movement, have forced U.S. society as a whole to confront the ugly truth of racism. White allies, such as the group Showing Up for Racial Justice (SURJ, www.showingupforracialjustice.org), work to mobilize support and commitment in white communities to pressure for change and participate in actions where laying white lives on the line is more likely to garner police protection and media attention.

As individuals and groups, our visions can only be partial. Coalitions bring together multiple ways of understanding the world and analyzing the oppressive structures within it. Specific skills of perspective taking, empathic listening, and self-reflection are critical. Furthermore, since all forms of oppression are interactional and co-constitutive with each other, alliances among people from diverse social locations and perspectives may perhaps be the only way to develop interventions muscular enough to challenge systemic oppression (Crenshaw, 2003; Roberts & Jesudason, 2013).

We take the position that everyone has a role to play in dismantling oppression and generating a vision for a more socially just future. Those who are marginalized take the lead in articulating an analysis of power from the vantage point of their particular geographic and social locations and contexts, but all of us need to develop the capacity for reflecting on our locations and recognizing the perspectives of others who are differently positioned.

> Reflexivity acknowledges the importance of power at the micro level of the self and our relationships with others, as well as the macro levels of society . . . to recognize multiple truths and a diversity of perspectives, while giving extra space to voices typically excluded.
>
> (Hankivsky, 2014, p. 10)

Holvino (2012) argues for "simultaneity": making an effort to hold onto our multiple identities so that we can flexibly speak from our complex experiences and resist pressures to oversimplify identity. She urges us to build coalitions and alliances that go beyond goals of individual empowerment to focus on building a social justice movement.

Accountability and solidarity, while aspirational and philosophical ideals, also ask us to be concrete in our goals for working in coalition with others so we can be clear about where our commitments overlap and where they do not. Most coalition work is organized around concrete goals that members of different groups in a coalition agree upon, even as other issues and goals may conflict (McGrath, 2007). Being clear helps coalitions make pragmatic alliances and work together for a common end, even when members do not agree on other goals.

FOLLOW THE LEADERSHIP OF OPPRESSED PEOPLE

Listening to the voices of those at the margins and following their lead is another important practice for social justice. The disability rights movement slogan, "Nothing about us without us" (Charleton, 1998), affirms the principle that no decisions should be made without the full participation of those affected by the decision. Unless people from the subordinated group are central to defining, framing, developing, and leading responses to inequities and social problems, the same power dynamics that we are trying to change will be reproduced, and the solutions are likely to fail. For example, youth need to be involved with issues that affect their lives in schools and the community. Likewise, poor people need to name the issues and help set the agenda for addressing poverty-related concerns. The right to self-determination and autonomy has been a goal of all social justice movements from the start.

The benefits of following the lead of those who have been marginalized can be seen in the movement for gay rights. Until GLBTQ people organized to challenge heterosexism, assumptions of heterosexual privilege went mostly unchallenged and invisible in our society. Gay rights advocates began to expose social norms, rituals, language, and institutional rules and rewards that presume the existence of exclusively heterosexual feelings and relationships. They critiqued language and symbols of love, attraction, family, and sexual and emotional self-development that largely ignored the existence of gay, bisexual, transgender, and other possibilities of human potential. Now trans and queer-identified people question the questioners, raising new critiques of sexuality and gender that were not as visible in earlier movements. Their work showed how the regime of heterosexism operates not only to oppress gay, lesbian, bisexual, and transgender people, but also to constrain and limit heterosexuals to narrowly gender-defined rules of behavior and options for self-expression as well.

BE AN ACCOUNTABLE AND RESPONSIBLE ALLY

Frequently, those from dominant groups, outside the communities they intend to help, come in with, and try to impose, pre-conceived ideas about what a community "needs." Such a stance reflects and reinforces unequal power relationships and a "savior" mentality. People in dominant groups must respectfully listen to how oppressed people define their own needs, work with them to support getting those needs met, and operate in solidarity with their organizations, efforts, and social movements (Kivel, 2006). It means ongoing action that demonstrates a sustained passion for and willingness to engage in social justice work over the long haul (Edwards, 2006). The decision about who to name as an ally is most credibly done by members of the oppressed group(s) within which one is in coalition

(Edwards, 2006). Thus, allyship also requires humility, a willingness to listen and learn, and a commitment to do the work without expectation of reward or recognition (Goodman, 2011).

Social justice organizing is stronger when both those who benefit and those who are disadvantaged by a particular ism, or cluster of isms, are able to work together in a sustained way to create change. The term "ally" is often used to convey the position of those in the dominant group who work in coalition with oppressed others, as in white people being allies to people of color (Broido & Reason, 2005), but we believe people from all social groups and positions can be allies to each other. A person's motivation to act in support of social justice can range along a continuum from individual self-interest focused on "me," to relational self-interest that is mutual or shared "you and me," to interdependent self-interest focused on a broader "us" (Goodman, 2011). Allyship can be problematic when it stays at the level of individual self-interest and fails to move to a broader self-interest. As blogger Mia McKenzie of Black Girl Dangerous puts it:

> Allyship is not supposed to look like this, folks. It's not supposed to be about you. It's not supposed to be about your feelings. It's not supposed to be a way of glorifying yourself at the expense of the folks you claim to be an ally to. It's not supposed to be a *performance*. It's supposed to be a way of living your life that *doesn't* reinforce the same oppressive behaviors you're claiming to be against.
>
> (No More "Allies," Sept. 30, 2013, www.blackgirldangerous.org/
> 2013/09/30/no-more-allies/#.Uk3lbYbDYqI.email)

We can recognize that individuals may be at different stages in awareness and thus be better or lesser prepared to be effective and reliable allies (Edwards, 2006).

This critique leads us to emphasize the importance for all people, particularly those in dominant groups, of being accountable and responsible to the others with whom they work in coalition. Accountability and responsibility connote mutuality in defining goals and actions, and answerability to those with whom we are collaborating. Another word for this is solidarity.

CONCLUSION

As historical circumstances change and emerging social movements take up issues of oppression in the United States and throughout the world, new definitions and understandings will continue to evolve. Through highlighting the historical and contextual nature of this process, we hope to avoid the danger of reifying systems of oppression as static, or treating individuals as one-dimensional and unchanging. History illustrates both how tenacious and variable systems of oppression are, and how dynamic and creative we must continue to be to rise to the challenges they pose. The concepts and processes we present in this text are continuously evolving. We hope the work presented in this third edition will contribute to an ongoing dialogue about social justice education theory and practice in ways that can have positive impacts on our world.

References

Adams, M. (2014). Social justice and education. In M. Reisch (Ed.), *Routledge international handbook of social justice* (pp. 249–268). London: Routledge.

Anzaldúa, G. (1987). *Borderlands/la frontera: The new mestiza*. San Francisco: Aunt Lute Books.

Aptheker, H. (1993). *Anti-racism in U.S. history: The first 200 years*. Westport, CT: Praeger.

Barkley-Brown, E. (1991). Polyrhythms and improvization: Lessons for women's history. *History Workshop, 31* (Spring 1991), 85–90. Retrieved from http://www.jstor.org/stable/4289053

Bell, D. (1992). *Faces at the bottom of the well: The permanence of racism*. New York: Basic Books.

Bell, D. A. (1980). Brown v. Board of Education and the interest convergence dilemma. *Harvard Law Review, 93*(3), 518–533.

Bell, L.A. (2003). Telling tales: What stories can teach us about racism. *Race, ethnicity and education, 6*(1), 3–28.

Bell, L. A. (2010). *Storytelling for social justice: Connecting narrative and the arts in anti-racist teaching*. New York: Routledge.

Bivens, D. (2005). What is internalized racism? In M. Potapchuk, S. Liederman, D. Bivens, & B. Major (Eds.), *Flipping the script: White privilege and community building* (pp. 43–51). Silver Spring, MD: MP Associates, Inc. and Conshohocken, PA: Center for Assessment and Policy Development (CAPD). Retrieved from http://www.capd.org/pubfiles/pub-2005–01–01.pdf

Bly, L., & Wooten, K. (2012). *Make your own history: Documenting feminist and queer activism in the 21st century*. Los Angeles: Litwin Books.

Bonilla-Silva, E., Lewis, A., & Embrick, D. G. (2004). "I did not get that job because of a black man . . .": The story lines and testimonies of color-blind racism. *Sociological Forum, 19*(4), 555–581.

Bowles, S., & Gintis, H. (1987). *Democracy and capitalism: Property, community, and the contradictions of modern social thought*. New York: Basic Books.

Broido, E. M., & Reason, R. D. (2005). The development of social justice attitudes and actions: An overview of current understandings. In R. D. Reason, E. M. Broido, T. L. Davis, & N. J. Evans (Eds.), *Developing social justice allies. New directions for student services, no. 110* (pp. 69–81). San Francisco: Jossey-Bass.

Butler, J. (2004). *Undoing gender*. London: Taylor & Francis.

Charleton, J. I. (1998). *Nothing about us without us: Disability oppression and empowerment*. Berkeley: University of California Press.

Chetty, R., Hendren, N., Kline, P., Saez, E., & Turner, M. (2014). Is the United States still a land of opportunity? Recent trends in intergenerational mobility. *American Economic Review: Papers and Proceedings, 104*(5), 141–147.

Cho, S. (2013). Post-intersectionality. The curious reception of intersectionality in legal scholarship. *Du Bois Review, 10*(2), 385–404.

Collins, P. H. (1990). *Black feminist thought: Knowledge, consciousness and the politics of empowerment*. New York: Routledge.

Combahee River Collective. (1986). *The Combahee River Collective statement: Black feminist organizing in the seventies and eighties*. Latham, NY: Kitchen Table, Women of Color Press.

Crenshaw, K. (1991). Mapping the margins: Intersectionality, identity politics, and violence against women of color. *Stanford Law Review, 43*(6), 1241–1299.

Crenshaw, K. W. (2003). Traffic at the crossroads: Multiple oppressions. In R. Morgan (Ed.), *Sisterhood is forever: The women's anthology for a new millennium* (pp. 43–57). New York: Washington Square Press.

Cudd, A. (2006). *Analyzing oppression*. New York: Oxford University Press.

Davis, A., & Wing, A. K. (2000). *Global critical race feminism*. New York: New York University Press.

Delgado, R., & Stefancic, J. (2013). *Critical race theory: The cutting edge* (3rd ed.). Philadelphia: Temple University Press.

Demos (2015). *The racial wealth gap: Why policy matters*. Retrieved from http://www.demos.org/publication/racial-wealth-gap-why-policy-matters

Dirlik, A. (1997). *The post-colonial aura: Third world criticism in the age of global capitalism*. Boulder, CO: Westview Press.

Echols, A. (1989). *Daring to be bad: Radical feminism in America*. Minneapolis: University of Minnesota Press.

Edwards, K. E. (2006). Aspiring social justice ally development: A conceptual model. *NASPA Journal, 43*(4), 39–60.

Evans, S. (1979). *Personal politics: The roots of women's liberation in the civil rights movement and the new left*. New York: Knopf/Random House.

Fanon, F. (1968). *The wretched of the earth*. New York: Grove Press.

Feinberg, L. (1996). *Transgender warriors: Making history from Joan of Arc to Ru Paul*. New York: Farrar, Strauss and Giroux.

Fernandes, L. (2013). *Transnational feminisms in the U.S.: Knowledge, ethics and power*. New York: New York University Press.

Firestone, S. (1970). *The dialectic of sex: The case for feminist revolution*. New York: Morrow.

Fleischer, D., & Zames, F. (2001). *The disability rights movement: From charity to confrontation*. Philadelphia: Temple University.

Foucault, M. (1980). *The history of sexuality*. New York: Vintage Books.

Frankenberg, R. (1993). *The social construction of Whiteness: White women, race matters*. Minneapolis: University of Minnesota Press.

Freire, P. (1970). *Pedagogy of the oppressed*. New York: Seabury.

Frye, M. (1983). *The politics of reality: Essays in feminist theory*. Freedom, CA: The Crossing Press.

Gilreath, S. (2011). *The end of straight supremacy: Realizing gay liberation*. New York: Cambridge University Press.

Gitlin, T. (2012). *Occupy nation: The roots, the spirit and the promise of Occupy Wall Street*. New York: Harper Collins.

Goodman, D. (2011). *Promoting diversity and social justice: Educating people from privileged groups*. New York: Routledge.

Guinier, L., & Torres, G. (2002). *The miner's canary: Enlisting race, resisting power, transforming democracy*. Cambridge, MA: Harvard University Press.

Haney-Lopez, I. (2014). *Dog whistle politics: How coded racial appeals have reinvented racism and wrecked the middle class*. New York: Oxford University Press.

Hankivsky, O. (2014). *Intersectionality 101*. Vancouver, BC, Canada: The Institute for Intersectionality Research and Policy, Simon Fraser University. Retrieved from http://www.sfu.ca/iirp/documents/resources/101_Final.pdf

Harding, S. (1991). *Whose science, whose knowledge?* Ithaca, NY: Cornell University Press.

Harro, B. (2008). Updated version of the cycle of liberation. In M. Adams, W. J. Blumenfeld, R. Castenada, H. W. Hackman, M. L. Peters, & X. Zuniga (Eds.), *Readings for diversity and social justice* (pp. 463-469). New York: Routledge.

Hartsock, N. (1983). *Money, sex and power: Toward a feminist historical materialism*. New York: Longman.

Hertz, T. (2006). *Understanding mobility in America*. Washington, DC: Center for American Progress.

Holvino, A. (2012). The "simultaneity" of identities: Models and skills for the twenty-first century. In C. L. Wijeyesinghe & B. W. Jackson (Eds.), *New perspectives on racial identity development: Integrating emerging frameworks* (pp. 161–191). New York: New York University Press.

Huber, L. P. & Solorzano, D. G. (2015). Racial microaggressions as a tool for critical race research. *Race, Ethnicity and Education, 18*(3), 297–320.

Hurtado, A. (2003). *Voicing Chicana feminisms*. New York: New York University Press.

Johnson, A. (2005). *Privilege, power and difference*. New York: McGraw-Hill.

Jost, J. T., Banaji, M. R., & Nosek, B. A. (2004). A decade of system justification theory: Accumulated evidence of conscious and unconscious bolstering of the status quo. *Political Psychology, 25*, 881–919.

Kivel, P. (2006). *Uprooting racism: How white people can work for racial justice* (3rd ed.). New York: New Society Publishers.

Kreisberg, S. (1992). *Transforming power: Domination, empowerment, and education*. Albany, NY: State University of New York Press.

Kruse, K. M. (2015). *One nation under God: How corporate America invented Christian America*. New York: Basic Books.

Leonardo, Z. (2013). *Race frameworks: A multidimensional theory of racism and education*. New York: Teachers College Press.

Lerner, G. (1986). *Women and history*. New York: Oxford University Press.

Lewis, M. (1993). *Without a word: Teaching beyond women's silence*. New York: Routledge.

Lipsitz, G. (2006). *The possessive investment in whiteness: How white people profit from identity politics*. Philadelphia: Temple University Press.

Lorde, A. (1984). *Sister outsider*. Trumansburg, NY: Crossing Press.

Love, B. J. (2013). Developing a liberatory consciousness. In M. Adams, W. J. Blumenfeld, R. Castaneda, W. Hackman, M. L. Peters, & X. Zuniga (Eds.), *Readings for diversity and social justice* (3rd ed., 601–606). New York: Routledge.

Luft, R. E. (2009). Intersectionality and the risk of flattening difference: Gender and race logics, and the strategic use of antiracist singularity. In T. Berger & K. Guidroz (Eds.), *The intersectional approach: Transforming the academy through race, class and gender*. Chapel Hill, NC: University of North Carolina Press.

Malik, M. (2010). *Anti-Muslim prejudice: Past and present*. New York: Routledge.

Marabel, M. (1984). *Race, reform, and rebellion: The second reconstruction in Black America, 1945–1982*. Jackson: University of Mississippi Press.

Marcus, E. (1992). *Making history: The struggle for gay and lesbian equal rights*. New York: Harper Perennial.

Marcus, S. (2005). Queer theory for everyone: A review essay. *Signs, 31*(1), 191–218.

Matsuda, M. (1987). Looking to the bottom: Critical legal studies and reparations. *Harvard Civil Rights-Civil Liberties Law Review, 22*, 323–399.

Matsuda, M. (1996). *Where is your body? And other essays on race, gender and law*. Boston: Beacon Press.

McGrath, C. (2007). Coalition building. In G. L. Anderson & K. G. Herr (Eds.), *Encyclopedia of activism and social justice* (pp. 359–361). Thousand Oaks, CA: Sage.

Memmi, A. (1965). *The colonizer and the colonized*. Boston: Beacon Press.

Miller, J. B. (1976). *Toward a new psychology of women*. Boston: Beacon Press.

Milner, H. R. (2008). Critical race theory and interest convergence as analytic tools in teacher education policies and practices. *Journal of Teacher Education, 59*(4), 332–346.

Mohanty, C. T. (2003). Feminism without borders: Decolonizing theory, practicing solidarity. Durham, NC: Duke University Press.

Mohanty, C. T., Russo, A., & Torres, L. (1991). *Third world women and the politics of feminism*. Bloomington: Indiana University Press.

Morris, J. (1991). *Pride against prejudice: Transforming attitudes to disability*. Philadelphia: New Society Publishers.

Nash, J. C. (2008). Rethinking intersectionality. *Feminist Review, 89*, 1–15.

Oboler, S. (1995). *Ethnic labels, Latino lives*. Minneapolis: University of Minnesota Press.

Ogletree, C. (2012). *The presumption of guilt: The arrest of Henry Louis Gates, Jr. and race, class and crime in America*. New York: Palgrave McMillan.

Okihiro, G. Y. (1994). *Margins and mainstreams: Asian American history and culture*. Seattle: University of Washington Press.

Oliver, M. L., & Shapiro, T. M. (2006). *Black wealth, white wealth* (2nd ed.). New York: Routledge.

Pharr, S. (1988). *Homophobia: A weapon of sexism*. Inverness, CA: Chardon Press.

Pheterson, G. (1990). Alliances between women: Overcoming internalized oppression and internalized domination. In L. Albrecht and R. Brewer (Eds.), *Bridges of power: Women's multicultural alliances* (pp. 34–48). Philadelphia: New Society Publishers.

Piff, P. K. (2014). Wealth and the inflated self: Class, entitlement, and narcissism. *Personality and Social Psychology Bulletin, 40*(1), 34–43.

Piven, F. F., & Cloward, R. (1982). *The new class war: Reagan's attack on the welfare state and its consequences*. New York: Pantheon.

Purkayastha, B. (2012). Intersectionality in a transnational world. *Gender & Society, 26*, 55–66.

Rawls, J. (1999). *A theory of justice*. Cambridge, MA: Harvard University Press.

Rawls, J. (2001). *Justice as fairness: A restatement*. Cambridge, MA: Harvard University Press.

Reagon, B. J. (1983). Coalition politics: Turning the century. In B. Smith (Ed.), *Home girls: A black feminist anthology*. New York: Kitchen Table Press.

Roberts, D., & Jesudason, S. (2013). Movement intersectionality: The case of race, gender, disability, and genetic technologies. *Du Bois Review, 10*(2), 313–328.

Said, E. W. (1993). *Culture and imperialism*. New York: Knopf.

Sandoval, C. (2000). Methodology of the oppressed. Minneapolis: University of Minnesota Press.

Simon, R. (2002). *Gramsci's political thought*. London: Lawrence & Wishart.

Smelser, N. J., Wilson, W. J., & Mitchell, F. (Eds., National Research Council). (2001). *America becoming: Racial trends and their consequences* (Vol. 1). Washington, DC: National Academies Press.

Spade, D. (2011). Some very basic tips for making higher education more accessible to trans students and rethinking how we talk about gendered bodies. *The Radical Teacher, 92*, 57–62.

Spelman, E. (1988). *Inessential woman: Problems of exclusion in feminist thought*. Boston: Beacon Press.

Sue, D. W. (2010). *Racial microaggressions in everyday life. Race, gender, and sexual orientation*. Hoboken, NJ: John Wiley and Sons.

Thompson, C., Schaefer, E., & Brod, H. (2003). *White men challenging racism*. Durham, NC: Duke University Press.

Trinh, T.M.H. (1989). *Woman, Native, other*. Bloomington: Indiana University Press.

Turner, W. (2000). *A genealogy of queer theory*. Philadelphia: Temple University Press.

Van Gelder, S. (2011).This changes everything: Occupy Wall Street and the 99% movement. San Francisco: Berrett-Koehler Publishers.

Vygotsky, L. (1978). *Mind in society*. Cambridge, MA: Harvard University Press.

Wacquant, L. (1997). Three pernicious premises in the study of the American ghetto. *International Journal of Urban and Regional Research*, 21(2), 341–353.

Warner, M. (1999). *The trouble with normal: Sex, politics and the ethics of queer life*. New York: The Free Press.

Weber, L. (2010). *Understanding race, class, gender and sexuality: A conceptual framework* (2nd ed.). New York: Oxford University Press.

Weiler, K. (1991). Freire and a feminist pedagogy of difference. *Harvard Educational Review*, 61(4), 449–474.

White, J. B., & Langer, E. J. (1999). Horizontal hostility: Relations between similar minority groups. *Journal of Social Issues*, 25(3), 537–559.

Wigginton, E. (Ed.). (1992). *Refuse to stand silently by: An oral history of grass roots social activism in America, 1921–1964*. New York: Doubleday.

Wing, A. K. (2003). *Critical race feminism: A reader*. New York: New York University Press.

World Economic Forum. (2014). *Global gender gap report: 2014*. Retrieved from http://reports. weforum.org/global-gender-gap-report-2014/

Young, I. M. (1990). *Justice and the politics of difference*. Princeton, NJ: Princeton University Press.

Young, I. M. (2011). *Responsibility for justice*. New York: Oxford University Press.

Zinn, H. (2003). *A people's history of the United States: 1492–present*. New York: Harper-Collins.

Zinn, H. (2004). *Voices of a people's history of the United States*. New York: Seven Stories Press.

2

Pedagogical Foundations for Social Justice Education

Maurianne Adams

In this chapter, we describe our approach to social justice teaching, the theories we draw upon, and the pedagogical principles that guide our practice. Here, the focus is on *how we teach* (classroom processes, group dynamics, participant interactions) as distinct from *what we teach* (subject matter, course content, core concepts described in Chapters 1 and 4–11), even though we know that these are inseparable in practice. The chapter works together with Chapters 1 and 3 to connect content and process for social justice education (SJE).

This chapter explains the theoretical and activist roots of our pedagogy as well as our reasons for preferring certain pedagogical activities and processes over others. First, we provide our definition and goals for SJE pedagogy. Next, we explain why experiential pedagogy is so important to our approach. Third, we review the theoretical and activist foundations that inform our approach to pedagogy; and finally, we elucidate the pedagogical principles that derive from these foundations with examples to illustrate them.

WHAT IS SJE PEDAGOGY?

Social justice education pedagogy is based upon a set of principles and practices for teaching about oppression and social justice. SJE pedagogy aims to generate active engagement with social justice content through learning processes that are consistent with the goals of social justice. The priority of social justice educators is to affirm, model, and sustain socially just learning environments for all participants, and by so modeling, to offer hope that equitable relations and social structures can be achieved in the broader society. Thus, the pedagogical choices we make as social justice educators are as important as the content we teach, so that *what* participants are learning and *how* they are learning are congruent. In this chapter, we foreground pedagogy, while never losing sight of the inextricable connection to content we temporarily move to the background.

Pedagogy of the Oppressed (Freire, 1970) is a book whose integration of vision, theory, analysis, and practice has had incalculable influence on generations of social justice educators and activists. In the spirit of Freire, we use the term *praxis* to describe the integration of learning goals with pedagogical processes that together encourage reflection and action to create change. This approach is in keeping with the tradition of critical pedagogy where the term *pedagogy* similarly conveys a holistic sense of the entire educational enterprise that is in need of critique and change, including schooling, curriculum, and pedagogy (Apple, Au, & Gandin, 2009; Darder, Baltodano, & Torres, 2008; Sandoval, 2000; Shor, 1987).

For Freire, pedagogy was an instrument to awaken oppressed peoples from their subordinated status into a consciousness of their oppression, with the expectation that once awakened, they would themselves take actions to effect change. Freire's pedagogical materials ("codes") and questions ("dialogue") were drawn from the everyday lives of his participants, and were thus immediately recognizable and meaningful to them. In Freirean pedagogy, instructors and facilitators identify and organize resources and initiate dialogue so that, through dialogue, the participants move to the center of their own learning and develop critical consciousness (Freire's term is *conscientização*).

By contrast, most U.S. formal schooling supports the status quo through both the "explicit" curriculum (what gets valued and taught) and the "hidden" curriculum (the policies, procedures, and pedagogies through which teaching takes place) (Beyer & Apple, 1998; Margolis, 2001; Nieto & Bode, 2008). In our traditional educational system, at all levels, the explicit as well as the hidden curricula reflect and reproduce larger societal dynamics of power and inequality. Assumptions that the content of learning is neutral ignore the privileging of some academic subjects over others, the focus on dominant social groups at the core of the curriculum, and the approaches to teaching and learning that advantage socially dominant groups and marginalize and exclude others based on race, gender, and class-based stereotypes of smartness, academic preparation, or the cultural values embodied by traditional academic practices. Social justice education challenges traditional education through applying principles of social justice to both the explicit and hidden curriculum to expose unequal power relations that privilege some while disadvantaging others at individual, institutional, and societal levels.

Freire's term "banking education" critiques a pedagogy dominated by experts with authority who pour knowledge into the empty heads of novices expected to listen passively and receive pre-digested information. As a metaphor, "banking education" connotes the inequitable economic sorting produced by education aimed at "how well people fit the world the oppressors have created, and how little they question it" (Freire, 1970, p. 57). A social justice pedagogy must necessarily differ from pedagogies of "banking education" to challenge the visible as well as hidden influences of curriculum, and facilitate the skills and knowledge that can challenge injustice and create change. In an anti-banking approach to learning, "the students—no longer docile listeners—are now critical co-investigators in dialogue with the teacher" (Freire, 1970, p. 62). Social justice educators think of our pedagogy as *praxis* informed by the interaction of theory, reflection, and action.

WHY EXPERIENTIAL PEDAGOGY IS CENTRAL TO SJE

Participants in SJE courses and workshops are encouraged to engage actively with learning and with each other to explore challenging ideas and feelings that inevitably emerge in the process of learning about oppression. Often, they hear perspectives and learn information that contradict what they had previously believed or might still consider to be true. Such learning can pull the rug out from under the status quo on which their lives have been built. The questions that participants tangle with, and the insights and commitments they arrive at in response to these challenges, have enormous personal and policy consequences. *Thus, SJE needs a pedagogy that acknowledges the challenges and opportunities participants face when confronted with new knowledge and perspectives, and that supports them in a learning process that is personally and intellectually challenging.*

Participants experience strong (often unexpected) emotions when their previous beliefs are contradicted by new information and perspectives that challenge what they have taken to be true. The different perspectives presented in SJE classes ask for a level of complexity that can be challenging for those accustomed to thinking in dichotomous and dualistic ways about issues they had considered clear-cut. When perspectives have been shaped by family, school, or religious authorities, participants may question or resist the authority of instructors and information that challenge their entrenched worldview. They may not be prepared to use analytic frameworks when enmeshed in their own personal experiences. They may need structure as well as role models to support them in reaching for new awareness and working with more complex, self-reflective, and nuanced thinking skills. Thus, *SJE needs a pedagogy that acknowledges the emotional as well as cognitive aspects of learning, and that encourages and models processes for dialogue, critical inquiry, and complex thinking.*

Social justice education courses or workshops incorporate the everyday experiences of participants who come from different social and cultural backgrounds, who bring different points of view, whose life experiences differ, and who seem at times to inhabit entirely different social and intellectual universes. The differences as well as the commonalities among participants from different social identities and social positions offer powerful opportunities for interactive and collaborative learning where the learning community acknowledges everyone's capacity to contribute and values everyone's desire to learn. The learning community is a place where the concrete and the personal (the experiential learning) are connected and coordinated with the abstract and the theoretical (readings, lectures, presentations about social systems and historical legacies). This coordination of concrete with abstract, individual with systemic, experiential with theoretical, requires "meta" level thinking skills.

Social justice education embodies an analysis of oppression that is both outside and inside the classroom or workshop at one and the same moment. Oppression is "outside" in that the information about historical and contemporary manifestations of oppression, as well as resistance and actions taken for social justice, exist "out there" in the world. At the same time, the system of oppression is "in here"—in the learning community— providing opportunities for instructors and peers to note how oppression is reproduced in the group. There are also opportunities to acknowledge the possibilities for social justice "in here," in moments where participants become more self-aware and develop new ways of interacting and collaborating through mutual respect, equality, and inclusion.

The coordination of personal, individual experience with larger structural and societal reference points shows the continuity of the past into the present. Just as manifestations of oppression in the outer world get reproduced inside the classroom or workshop, so too do historical legacies of injustice and oppression. Our histories are not only "out there" in the world but also "in here" in the thoughts and assumptions carried from participants' families and home communities into the shared learning community. Thus, the "outside world" comes into the learning community through the histories and experiences brought there by participants, as well as the "in the moment" interactions that illustrate broader patterns of oppression. *Thus, SJE needs a pedagogy that creates learning communities where members share and learn from each other's experiences, reflect on their own and other's experiences to make sense of larger structural systems of advantage and disadvantage, and create new meanings for themselves.*

Although some of the challenges and opportunities described above may not be unique to SJE, the constellation of subjective knowledge, challenging information, charged emotions, multiple perspectives, differing social identities, and the coordination of concrete experiences with abstract frameworks requires a specific pedagogy. This pedagogy draws upon and is nourished by cognitive and social psychology theory, and experiential, activist communities of practice. It is a pedagogy that is experiential, participant-centered, inclusive, collaborative, and democratic. It draws attention to social identity and social position, explores contradictions from the social world, engages emotions as well as thought, and acknowledges the reproduction of systemic inequalities of advantage and disadvantage in group processes.

THE THEORETICAL AND ACTIVIST FOUNDATIONS THAT INFORM SJE PEDAGOGY

Social justice educators draw from an extensive body of literature as well as activist antecedents to inform and nourish our work. As social justice educators, knowing the roots of our practice can provide us with confidence and guidance for making intentional and informed decisions about what we are doing and why we are doing it. Knowing and being able to articulate the theoretical and empirical foundations of our pedagogy also makes our work convincing and credible to others who approach learning from different traditions.

This root system draws upon scholarly as well as social movement traditions as far-reaching as (for example) adult literacy and grassroots education; Freire and the Highlander Folk School; black studies, ethnic studies, and women's and gender studies; critical pedagogy; cognitive and social identity development; experiential education; and group dynamics, intergroup dialogue, and laboratory and T-(training) group education. An inclusive list of the academics and activists whose shoulders we stand on would be far longer than this, and they have been amply acknowledged elsewhere (Adams, 2007, 2010, 2014).

We have drawn from educators and psychologists who study the affective, personal, social, cognitive, and experiential dimensions of teaching and learning in academic and activist contexts. The cross-fertilization between grassroots activism and academic study has established a flexible repertoire of processes and practices that no longer require justification, and can be used and researched on their own merits. Yet, it remains important to acknowledge the traditions that undergird our pedagogical approach and the tools we use, to ground our work philosophically and pragmatically, and to keep us connected to the activism that is at the heart of SJE.

By way of identifying common elements and interconnections, these traditions are grouped into these three "extended families" or communities of scholarship and practice:

1. Consciousness-raising processes within social liberation movements. These include Freire's work on literacy emerging at the same time as, although independent of, U.S. social movements and global anticolonial movements, all of which developed and used similar consciousness-raising practices.
2. Social learning processes (active and experiential) articulated within a social-psychological framework and directed to educational reform and anti-discrimination education by Allport (1954/1979), Dewey (1909/1975), and Lewin (1948).
3. Cognitive, life span, and social identity development theories and models that enable instructors/facilitators to anticipate and facilitate shifts in meaning-making as participants become aware of self and others within the context of oppression. These theories explain participant efforts to achieve more complex and adequate ways of making meaning in a multilayered social world, and suggest pedagogies that provide "scaffolding" that starts where the learners are to provide footholds and supports for more complex modes of learning and thinking.

After reviewing these three families of scholarly and activist roots, we discuss specific SJE pedagogical principles that grow out of these fields. Understanding these principles, and the sources from which they derive, can enable social justice educators to become more knowledgeable, intentional, and effective in their practice.

ACTIVIST CONSCIOUSNESS-RAISING SOCIAL MOVEMENTS OF THE 1960S AND THE WORK OF PAULO FREIRE

Community activists worked in tandem with social psychologists during the half-century following the 1954 *Brown v. Board of Education* decision to generate public awareness of the damages wrought by racially segregated schools, public facilities, and residential neighborhoods. At the same time, black consciousness movements in the U.S. and in Africa generated civil rights and anti-colonial movements (Sherif & Sherif, 1970) and influenced the "consciousness-raising" that was key to the women's movement in the U.S. (Evans, 1980). Through consciousness-raising, subordinated peoples became aware of daily inequities and were led by these insights towards analyses that theorized and directed action against their oppression (Sarachild, 1975; Sherif & Sherif, 1970). Consciousness-raising was one of the tools by which the personal became the political.

Personal testimonies demonstrate the power of consciousness-raising within the civil rights and women's movements (Howe, 1964/1984; Rachal, 1998). For example, Florence Howe's initial exposure to what became feminist pedagogy occurred during the Mississippi Voter Registration Summer of 1964 (Howe, 1964/1984); and black women activists in the civil rights movement discovered their feminism once they became conscious of the patriarchy practiced by their black male colleagues in the struggle (Evans, 1980).

During this formative period, Freire (1970) was offering in Brazil and Guinea-Bissau a dialogic- and inquiry-based model parallel to the consciousness-raising of U.S. social movements. His approach elicited "generative themes" from participants that reflected specific experiences of oppression as well as possibilities for concrete action (Au, 2009; Shor, 1987). Freire's approach reinforced not only the experiential focus of U.S. social movements, it also opposed the prevailing mode of "banking" education in U.S. schooling (students as consumers, knowledge as deposits). It is impossible to overestimate Freire's impact on the formal and informal multicultural and critical education reform movements during the closing decades of the 20th century. As well, Freirean theory and pedagogy was influential in indigenous, literacy-based, popular, participatory, labor organizing, and/or grassroots and anticolonial movements throughout the Americas and globally (Brookfield & Holst, 2011; Zajda, Majhanovich, Rust, & Sabina, 2006).

In a later generation, the educator-activist Jean Anyon similarly noted that "the experience of participation *itself*" provides the impetus for people to take action against local instances of injustice (2009, p. 389). This is an important dimension of Freirean and critical pedagogy, namely that participants engaging together with critical information, awareness, and understanding of social inequities can take corrective action. Anyon's phrase—"experience of participation *itself*"— reinforces the *praxis* of Freire's literacy circles, and of the voter registration drives that accompanied the experimental schooling of the Mississippi Summer (Rachal, 1998). This consciousness raising through active participation is also illustrated by the changes in domestic work, spousal relationships and gendered work-places that followed in the wake of consciousness-raising within the women's movement.

SOCIAL LEARNING, SOCIAL PSYCHOLOGY, AND EDUCATIONAL REFORM: DEWEY, ALLPORT, AND LEWIN

John Dewey's contribution to SJE pedagogy comes from his emphasis on experiential education as a means of engaging students with real-world social issues. Dewey wrote that "Apart from participation in social life, the school has no moral end nor aim" (1909/1975, p. 11). This commitment to social experience posed powerful ideological as well as pedagogical challenges to traditional "lecture and listen" or "read my mind" pedagogies that characterized formal schooling. In this way, Dewey paved the way for the cross-cultural and intergroup pedagogies developed in response to *Brown v. Board of Education* in schools and community settings involved in school desegregation.

There is a direct through-line from the work of Dewey to Allport's classic *The Nature of Prejudice* (1954/1979), in which Allport delineated the norms, in-group and out-group social categories, and manifestations of prejudice that poisoned the possibilities for the pluralistic, democratic education envisioned by Dewey. Allport's still-illuminating analysis has shaped subsequent anti-racism and intergroup thinking and practice (Dovidio, Glick, & Rudman, 2005). His insights about racism, stereotypes, discrimination, and the conditions needed for positive intergroup relations have been elaborated and used by generations of anti-racist educators in developing guidelines for effective anti-racist learning communities.

Intergroup relations within school, community, and residential settings draw upon these guidelines to promote intergroup contact based on the following: Equal status within the contact situation despite unequal social status; common goals; intergroup cooperation; and support from authorities (instructors, facilitators, school systems) (Pettigrew, 1998; Pettigrew & Tropp, 2006). With the work of Allport and those who came after, social psychology established templates for the affective, cognitive, and social processes necessary for intergroup contact to be a reliable educational intervention against racism and other forms of prejudice. The evolution of Allport's conditions for intergroup contact have shaped SJE's understanding of preconditions needed for socially just learning communities. Despite the variety of curricular topics in SJE that range from the broadly cultural and structural to the deeply personal and experiential, SJE depends on small-group pedagogical processes to bring people together into a cohesive and inclusive learning community.

Other useful sources in the social psychology and the social learning literature include: Kurt Lewin's (1948) studies of group dynamics; Bronfenbrenner's (1979) ecological developmental psychology; social identity theory (Abrams & Hogg, 1990; Sherif & Sherif, 1970); experiential, social-learning reforms identified with John Dewey (1909/1975); and the application of psychological research to challenging the "separate but equal" doctrine in *Brown v. Board of Education* (Pettigrew, 1998; Pettigrew & Tropp, 2006). Social justice educators draw on these theories to understand how participants work through the contradictions to previous ways of thinking that they encounter in intergroup settings and to design pedagogical tools that will engage contradictions productively. Social justice educators have drawn on developmental as well as social psychology for our understanding of processes of personal meaning-making and personal change, and of how to help participants develop a broader and more inclusive world view (Adams, Perry-Jenkins, & Tropp, 2014; Cole, 1996; Kegan, 1982; Rogoff, 2003).

Lewin's research on group dynamics and the role of feedback demonstrated the impact that individual participants have on group process and organizational culture, and how easily the latter reproduce and reinforce the former (Benne, 1964; Bradford, Gibb, & Benne, 1964). His team developed simulations and role-plays in a set of procedures called "laboratory training" that provided opportunities for members of interracial groups to "get into the shoes of the other" (Lippitt, 1949). Structured, facilitated group feedback enabled participants to achieve "in the moment" insight into themselves and each other in groups of diverse individuals. Much of what we now know about socially mixed group dynamics and the role of group norms and guidelines in establishing a positive learning community for SJE derives from these sources.

The group dynamics literature provides many useful ideas about staging or designing experiential activities for learning in the "here and now," facilitated through process observation and feedback (Bradford, Gibb, & Benne, 1964; Pfeiffer & Jones, 1972–80). Theories such as Tuckman's (1965) stages of group development—Forming, Norming, Storming and Performing—offer perspectives on how groups evolve that alert facilitators to the opportunities as well as pitfalls at various stages in a group's evolution. In Lewin's spirit, social justice educators have learned how to use films, discussions, simulations, and structured interactions as specific, socially situated prompts for personalizing challenging abstractions about racism, classism, and other oppressions. These experiences are then interpreted and analyzed (processed) from multiple perspectives, with feedback on group process from participants and facilitators.

More recently, the pedagogical tools associated with Lewin and Allport have been tested in structured intergroup dialogues and classes to assess the conditions that govern effective intergroup contact and cross-group interpersonal communication (Pettigrew & Tropp, 2006). These tools are now widely used in educational and community settings to build cross-group relationships and to practice cross-group communication skills (Dovidio, Glick, & Rudman, 2005; Engberg, 2004; Stephan & Vogt, 2004). The intergroup pedagogies have benefited from research that links specific outcomes in awareness and critical thinking about injustice to a range of social justice pedagogical tools (Gurin, Nagda, & Zúñiga, 2013; Zúñiga, Lopez, & Ford 2012).

COGNITIVE, LIFE SPAN, AND SOCIAL IDENTITY DEVELOPMENT THEORIES AND MODELS

Social justice education poses cognitive challenges for participants, not only through the content on social injustice, but also because of the questions it raises about participants' unexamined beliefs, biases, misinformation, stereotypes, and entrenched modes of thinking. Social justice education pedagogical strategies have been developed to pose contradictions and support participants' reflection on their intellectual and emotional attachments to attitudes and beliefs learned in trusted home, school, and religious communities. Critical reflection about one's social positions and identities, and critical thinking about structural inequities, are SJE objectives that challenge and stretch participants, both cognitively and emotionally. Thus, cognitive development and social identity development theories provide valuable information for addressing these challenges.

Cognitive development provides useful frameworks for understanding and facilitating the challenges participants negotiate in an SJE course or workshop. Developmentalist Robert Kegan describes the tension between polarities of assimilation and accommodation in how individuals respond when our current world view is contradicted by new experiences or information (1982). This process of adaptation, which Kegan calls "equilibration," occurs when individuals are confronted with new knowledge. They can either "assimilate" the experience into an already established epistemology or world view that remains unshaken by the new experience, or they can "accommodate" and shift the current world view to incorporate new experiences (Kegan, 1982, p. 44). When individuals accommodate new experiences or information, their mode of meaning-making becomes increasingly more complex and inclusive as they develop new (metacognitive) capacities for reflecting on their own thinking.

Assumptions from cognitive development theory that support SJE goals include: 1) the importance of personally relevant meaning-making and not merely the acquisition of abstract knowledge as central to learning; 2) cognitive dissonance as both the fuel and the combustion spark that can generate dissatisfaction with established ways of thinking; and 3) the effect of the dissatisfaction generated by cognitive dissonance that can lead either to "assimilation" of the dissonant material into the established meaning-making system or "accommodation" of this material into more complex and critical meaning-making processes (i.e., a shift in meaning-making.) Although "models" of development present different pathways and use different terminology, all speak to these three key principles. See, for example, college student and adult development (Brookfield, 1987, 2013; Perry, 1970, 1981); student intellectual development (Baxter-Magolda, 1992); reflective judgment (King & Kitchener, 1994); and women's ways of knowing (Belenky, Clinchy, Goldberger, & Tarule, 1986).

In all such models, thinking evolves from a mode of dualistic either/or options to a mode of more complex and relativistic thinking, then to the use of metacognitive skills that enable a person to hold various options in mind while weighing or evaluating evidence. This evolution is not necessarily unidirectional and can recycle in response to new topics or experiences. For example, someone who is a complex, nuanced thinker on familiar topics may be drawn to simple, either/or terms when encountering information or experiences that are entirely new. The evolution of cognition can also appear gendered, contrasting "separate" thinking generally attributed to men (standing outside, making judgments, objective) with "connected" thinking generally attributed to women (getting inside, joining with, subjective) (Belenky, Clinchy, Goldberger, & Tarule, 1986). Both modes or styles are needed in SJE problem-posing and both styles should be cultivated to generate cognitive complexity.

Theories of cognitive development offer explanations for how momentous shifts in meaning-making take place and can be encouraged, modeled, and supported through the decisions facilitators make about pedagogy and sequence. Social justice education can be seen as a "pressure cooker" for cognitive dissonance which, presented in ways that are not overwhelming, opens opportunities for more abstract, complex, and critical thinking. Such new approaches to meaning-making involve cognitive skills that can be practiced and developed by listening to the perspective of others, reflecting upon one's own beliefs and values, and taking a critical and inquiring stance toward experts and authority. Through such engagement, reliance on clear-cut certitudes may give way to acceptance of a world characterized by doubt and uncertainty, and in need of independent, critical inquiry.

The specific "stage" models of some of the theorists mentioned above, while valuable and illuminating, have been challenged as unnecessarily fixed or unilinear descriptions of more complex and multilayered mental and emotional phenomena. The language of "modes of knowing" offers a less linear way of describing a process whose evolution reaches forward in complexity and nuance while also cyclical and reflexive in its unfolding. For example, Baxter-Magolda (1992) differentiates "modes of knowing" that she characterizes as *absolute* (acquiring knowledge from authorities), *transitional* (understanding rather than acquiring knowledge and valuing peers as sources of knowledge), *independent* (thinking for oneself, internal agency for making meaning), and *contextual* (integrating one's own and others' ideas). This model displays changes in modes of thinking about one's own role as a learner, the roles of peers and teachers, the role of assessment, and the framing of the nature of knowledge. Thus, it is more easily and directly applicable to the social justice classroom and can be used to shape an instructor's decisions about appropriate pedagogies based on "where the students are" in their meaning-making, their view of the instructor as resource or "expert," and of their peers as sources of knowledge (Adams, 2002; Adams & Zhou-McGovern, 1994).

Another developmental resource for social justice educators comes from the Russian "cultural-historical" developmentalist Vygotsky. He situates cognitive development within the social and cultural context where socialization takes place—a context that includes education as well as family and community life (Cole, 1990, 1995, 1996; Moll, 1990; Rogoff, 2003; Vygotsky, 1978). This cultural-historical approach highlights the role of "mediation" as people engage with each other within specific informal and formal systems of interaction. Vygotsky called these "zones of proximal development" to convey the zone between a person's current developmental range, and socially provided opportunities that challenge and stretch development beyond the range.

The zone of proximal development becomes a space of mediation and interdependence between the individual and other members of the social organization whose collaborative activities prompt further development in the "less competent" member. As a person develops agency, skills, and knowledge through interaction with others, these become internalized (Moll, 1990). In SJE, peers with different perspectives, skills, and cultural assets will be more or less competent in making new meanings from the variety of learning opportunities that emerge in SJE classes and workshops.

This approach to cognitive development is explicitly *constructivist* and *historical*. It emphasizes historical and social construction of meanings and language, the role of socialization, psychological processes of internalization, and development that is mediated, all of which speak directly to the pedagogies of SJE. It is an elastic rather than a static approach to development in cultural context, because that which has been historically constructed can be changed, and that which has been internalized can also, through the development of internal agency, be questioned, challenged, replaced, and transformed.

Examples of the relevance of this cultural-historical approach can be found in recent research on intergroup dialogue where specific skills can be modeled and internalized, enabling participants to practice and become more proficient (Hopkins & Domingue, 2015; Zúñiga, Lopez, & Ford, 2012). Intergroup dialogue promotes complex, multilayered thinking, uses participant experiences as the subject for reflection, and coordinates various sources of knowledge. New skills are modeled, scaffolded, and practiced to become part of the internal cognitive repertoire.

Because oppression takes place on multiple levels, an important goal of SJE pedagogy is that participants understand the interactions among individual misinformation or prejudice, institutional discrimination or marginalization, and cultural and social structures that advantages some groups while disadvantaging others. Because people live in and are socialized at all three levels of society, it is important that participants have the opportunity to practice thinking across levels so that they become skillful at recognizing such multilayered examples in everyday life. Without a theory of oppression or an understanding of cultural, structural, and institutional reproductions of oppression, individual experiences and stories do not "add up" to something more that leads to greater understanding. In SJE, much of the new meaning-making for participants takes place in the coordination of the experiential and the structural, and such coordination may feel like a stretch for participants of any age or educational background (Bidell, Lee, Bouchie, Ward, & Brass, 1994; King & Shuford, 1996). Pedagogies that support this coordination between personal and abstract include intergroup dialogue, peer panels focused on concrete experiences of privilege or disadvantage, film clips, and small discussion groups, in all cases "mediated" by discussion prompts, processing of insights, or short reflection papers.

Developmental theory offers explicit ways for facilitators to recognize the "cognitive dissonance" that participants experience, model new ways of thinking that can incorporate the dissonant material, and provide the mediation and scaffolding that supports the process (see Tatum, 1992 for an illustration). These theoretical and pedagogical traditions offer SJE instructors a wealth of perspectives and tools for helping students develop and embrace new understandings about social justice issues.

SOCIAL IDENTITY FORMATION AND DEVELOPMENT

Social identity as a concept gained currency with *Identity, Youth and Crisis* (Erikson, 1968), which popularized the notion of an adolescent "identity crisis" as part of the identity-formation process that characterized young adulthood. The possibilities for growth are suggested by the tension between crisis and commitment within each stage of psychosocial development (Marcia, 1966) similar to the "equilibration" between assimilation and accommodation described above (Kegan, 1982).

The idea of an explicitly *racial* identity development was stimulated by the civil rights and black consciousness movements (Sherif & Sherif, 1970). The black racial identity development models of Cross (1971, 1991, 2001) and Jackson (1976, 2001) show their cognitive and psychosocial roots through terms such as "identity conversion," "encounter," and "transition" to convey the mechanisms and the intensity through which challenges to a current stage of racial identity might spur the transition to new understandings of racial identity:

> [A]person might experience enough cognitive or emotional dissonance to stimulate the beginning of a stage transition . . . The transition from one stage to another usually occurs when an individual recognizes that his or her current worldview is either illogical or contradicted by new experiences and/or information . . . [or] detrimental to a healthy self-concept.
>
> (Jackson, 2001, p. 16)

The foundational models of racial identity development started out as "stage" models with specific developmental goals that enabled people to understand their racial privilege or subordination at each stage. As the models evolved, they became more nuanced descriptions of meanings that people make of their social identities and relative advantage or disadvantage, in relation to culture, intergenerational family socialization, and multiple other socialization factors (Cross & Phagen-Smith, 2001; Jackson, 2001, 2012). Developmental models designed to examine other social identities followed this pattern. These models include "coming out" models of gay liberation (Cass, 1996; Cox & Gallois, 1996), feminist identity models (Bargad & Hyde, 1991; Downing & Roush, 1985), disability identity (Gill, 1997), white identity development (Helms, 1995), and ethnic and racial identity development models that reflect the ethnic/racial complexities of identity for immigrant communities of color (Duany, 1998; Hurtado, Gurin, & Peng, 1994; Kim, 2001).

Most of the social identity development models identify a similar sequence: 1) accepting and internalizing the dominant ideology and values that assume the superiority of the dominant group and the inferiority of the subordinated group; 2) questioning, rejecting, and resisting the dominant ideology and oppressive systems and thus the way their social group is characterized; 3) exploring, redefining, and developing a new sense of social identity that is not rooted in the norms and values of superiority and inferiority; and 4) integrating and internalizing the new identity along with a commitment to social justice. Significant demographic, social and cultural, and theoretical issues have led social identity models to veer away from the unidirectionality implied by "identity development" and toward a more interactional notion of "identity formation" (Hurtado, Gurin, & Peng, 1994; Wijeyesinghe, 2001). Notions of identity formation acknowledge the fluidity of identity, changes in salience of identity in different contexts, and the social and cultural communities within which identity is formed, challenged, and reworked.

There have been numerous challenges and changes to theories of social identity development. In retrospect, we see that it was an oversimplification to tie social identities to rigidly social categories of advantage or disadvantage (based on race, gender, sexuality, class, religion, disability, and age). Instead, we now see how advantage and disadvantage shift depending on context and location within systems of oppression (Cross, 2001; Hurtado, Gurin, & Peng, 1994; Jackson, 2012). For example, transnational migration has focused attention on the dilemmas posed for peoples of color who enter a U.S. racial system that is different from the systems of racial classification and hierarchy in their home countries (Gallegos & Ferdman, 2012; Holvino, 2012; Hurtado, Gurin, & Peng, 1994). Identity models must account for the intersection of identities and contexts. Binary models of social categorization are contested and do not adequately describe an individual's understanding of their identity (Holvino, 2012; Wijeyesinghe, 2012). In addition, there is often a tension between one's self-attribution of identity and the attributions made about oneself by others.

Despite these caveats, the social identity development literature provides a valuable lens to help social justice educators understand the perspectives of diverse individuals and to consider what might be useful to support their growth. A participant's social identities may shape their response to particular social justice content and to group dynamics. An understanding of social identity development enables facilitators to anticipate and understand interactions among members of the same identity group who express different understandings of their identities and the isms to which they are connected, as well as the interactions and differing understandings among people from different identity groups. For example, if a man says something a woman finds sexist, members of the group may have a range of responses. Some women may agree that the statement was offensive, while other women may come to the defense of the man. Some men may feel that people are overreacting while other men might recognize the sexism and want to be an ally to the women who are offended. These various reactions may, in part, be shaped by one's identity development and consciousness about sexism. Seeing these dynamics, in turn, provides the facilitator with some indication of where participants may be in their identity development process and thus can offer opportunities to challenge participants to think more critically about these different perspectives.

Social identity development theories also offer participants a framework for examining current ways of thinking and feeling, and to see the possibility of moving to a position that feels more authentic and liberating. Students can be exposed to particular theories of social identity development (around a particular social identity) and asked to look for how this model resonates or not with their own journey. Often people find that they can relate to aspects of the theory and that this normalizes their feelings and experiences. For people who may be struggling at the earlier phases, the latter phases offer positive images of what continued growth can look like. This can be especially important for participants who feel mired in difficult emotions such as guilt, shame, and rage.

It is crucial that instructors/facilitators understand that a stage or level serves as a metaphor or indicator for meaning-making in relation to oppression and not a fixed category for placing people in boxes. Terms such as *lens, world view, perspective,* and *consciousness level* are equally appropriate as metaphors or indicators. Beverly Tatum uses the metaphor of a spiral staircase to describe the internal sense of how "what one sees" changes over time and with new experiences:

> As a person ascends a spiral staircase, she may stop and look down at a spot below. When she reaches the next level, she may look down and see the same spot, but the vantage point has changed.
>
> (Tatum, 1992, p. 12)

What "develops" is a person's increasingly informed, differentiated, and inclusive understanding of within-group and between-group commonalities and differences, and a personalized awareness of how these understandings bear on one's sense of identity and everyday behaviors.

THE PEDAGOGICAL PRINCIPLES THAT INFORM SJE PRACTICE

Whether we are novice or seasoned social justice educators, each classroom or workshop experience feels "new" because of the mix of participants and the unknown dynamics and issues that may arise. Time and again, as educators, we go back to the drawing board as we consider the challenges and opportunities of SJE. We continue to enlarge our repertoire of pedagogical resources and facilitation skills, hoping to become more effective "instruments of others' learning" (a phrase I learned from a mentor, Norma Jean Anderson). Our pedagogy is strengthened through apprenticeship and mentorship, collaboration and experimentation, as well as through ongoing reading and reflection on scholarship and activism. While the authors cited above have been invaluable, learning "how to do" is a matter of ongoing experimentation and practice. Nonetheless, a set of pedagogical principles affords a helpful guide, and we ask that the following principles be considered in that spirit.

Although the six pedagogical principles appear as a list, they should be understood as *concurrent, not sequential, approaches and processes*. It is only the linear format of writing principles one at a time that makes them *seem* sequential. In reality, these processes are likely to be happening simultaneously, although some approaches may be introduced earlier or later in the life of a learning community. The pedagogical principles are as follows:

Principle 1: Create and maintain a welcoming and inclusive social justice learning environment based on clear norms and guidelines agreed to by the entire learning community.

Principle 2: Help participants acknowledge their own multiple positions within systems of inequality in order to understand how oppression operates on multiple levels.

Principle 3: Anticipate, acknowledge, and balance the emotional with the cognitive components of SJE learning.

Principle 4: Draw upon the knowledge and experiences of participants and the intergroup dynamics in the room to illustrate and discuss social justice content.

Principle 5: Encourage active engagement with the issues and collaboration among participants.

Principle 6: Foster and evaluate personal awareness, acquisition of knowledge and skills, and action-planning processes to create change.

Each principle is discussed in more detail below with examples of how the principle applies in SJE teaching.

Principle 1: Create and maintain a welcoming and inclusive social justice learning environment based on clear norms and guidelines agreed to by the entire learning community.

How the class or workshop begins and the tone that is established at the outset sets the stage for the rest of the learning experience. Thus, SJE pays special attention to how an inclusive environment is established and how participants are welcomed into the environment and engaged actively in shaping the norms and guidelines for the learning community.

Entry Points and Getting Started

The "first thing in the door" for participants will shape their initial impressions of each other and their comfort level with SJE. So how to get started is important and can involve such entrance activities as ice-breakers, introductions, and establishing the norms and guidelines for a learning community. This principle is illustrated in the following chapters, all of which focus initially on how to "get started" and establish the learning community. Participants need to feel from the very beginning that the learning community will be inclusive, personalized, and experiential. They need to know that they will be challenged, but they will be safe as they engage with difficult issues on which many of them will have different perspectives. As facilitators, we think about their experience as soon as they come in the door and plan activities to acknowledge and to relieve the anxieties they inevitably bring to such a project.

We try to avoid the passivity or anxiety participants may feel as they enter the room and then sit silently waiting for something to happen. This inaction and discomfort can be avoided by providing active "entry" activities that participants can join immediately, so that the class or workshop gets started before it seems officially to start. (One of my earliest mentors in experiential teaching, Norma Jean Anderson, called this "a raggedy beginning.") These ice-breakers can begin immediately as participants enter or after the course or workshop has officially begun. For example, activities where participants are provided a list of prompts for mingling and asking questions to "collect" information from each other break the ice by getting people actively involved from the outset. They also provide a way for participants who do not know each other to connect in informal and fun ways and "break the ice" typical of new encounters. Similarly, a structured approach to introductions provides opportunities to share personal experiences and associations related to the topic to be explored so that participants begin to see similarities and differences with other members of the group. The facilitator always tries to set the tone and model the process by going first.

Setting Up an Inclusive Learning Community

Greeting participants through experiential activities illustrates what they can expect from an inclusive learning environment that is characterized by mutual respect, careful listening and learning from each other, and acknowledgment that everyone's participation is important. The review of logistics—time frame, breaks, bathroom options, taking care of personal needs, putting aside distractions such as cell phones and text messaging devices—can also be tied to the social justice rationale for doing so. Facilitators can communicate *why* we pay attention to bathroom locations (gender-neutral, gender-identified), time frames (different health or fatigue thresholds), and cell phone or text message policies (focus on the learning community rather than unshared communications). Similarly, the overview of an agenda for the day or the curriculum for the semester can explain *why* the learning design has been set up a certain way, why some topics were chosen and others not, where there is flexibility to change the agenda or curriculum, and when opportunities will be available for asking questions and making comments.

Early among the tone-setting activities, participants need to know what to expect of an "SJE approach." Instructors/facilitators should present some succinct, engaging, personalized remarks about what SJE is, the characteristics of the SJE approach they are using, the assumptions they make, what they hope the participants will achieve, and why they believe that a learning community needs to be inclusive, active, and respectful. These remarks set a tone of transparency as facilitators explicitly describe their approach and assumptions about SJE.

Taking the time to talk about the challenges and discomfort they may experience lets participants anticipate and take responsibility for noticing and monitoring their own reactions. The experiences and subjects they feel comfortable and knowledgeable about (their "comfort zone") will be challenged as they are encouraged to engage with new information and experiences and consider new insights (their "learning edge"). The "comfort zone" can be visualized as a circle with the learning edge on its periphery, conveying two seemingly contradictory expectations simultaneously: First, the "learning edge" is located on, not beyond, the periphery of comfort, yet not so far outside as to seem unreachable; and second, the notion of a comfort zone whose periphery is a learning edge helps to distinguish between "comfort" (which we do not aim for, since we are looking for challenge and growth) and "safety" (which we require to avoid emotional or physical danger). In many ways, this approach models the idea of scaffolding and working with the zone of proximal development.

Finally, it is also helpful to discuss "triggers"—words, behaviors, experiences, or content that stimulate emotional responses because of their painful, negative, or demeaning associations. We need to discuss "triggers" in advance so that participants are prepared to handle them effectively when they arise. These concepts enable participants to take ownership for monitoring and learning from their feelings and reactions rather than avoiding or fleeing at the first sign of discomfort.

Clear and Explicit Norms, Guidelines, and Shared Expectations for the Learning Community

The preliminary activities described above are intended to relax participants, immediately engage them with each other and with the subject matter, and provide a preliminary overview of SJE. We then collaboratively establish norms and guidelines to help sustain and monitor the learning community.

The time invested in an inclusive, transparent, and explicit process by which norms and guidelines are generated and discussed is time well spent. The process of developing norms and guidelines is one in which participants express their hopes, worries, and goals for the workshop or class, and it enables them to agree to a set of norms and guidelines that will help them reach their goals and negotiate potential pitfalls. The norms and guidelines should be posted and referred to throughout a class or workshop. They provide reminders in difficult moments, when participants are feeling misunderstood or when air time is being taken up by too few people or by people with entitlement, that the participants have committed to an inclusive and respectful learning community. Additional guidelines can always be added as needed, but the important thing is to ensure that they are followed. No one gets a "free pass" from observing the norms and guidelines of the learning community.

Principle 2: Help participants acknowledge their own multiple positions within systems of inequality in order to understand how oppression operates on multiple levels.

In SJE classrooms and workshops, participants learn to reflect upon their own (multiple, simultaneous) social identities and statuses, and to examine how these connect with larger systems of oppression. They also explore how institutional and cultural dynamics impact them as members of particular social groups.

A key component of SJE pedagogy is having participants explore their social identities and socialization experiences. Their identities and experiences as members of particular social groups are lenses through which they make meaning of their lives and the world. Participants may have deeply considered some aspects of their identity but not others. It is important that participants explore how their social identities and cultural backgrounds inform their world views and lived realities. Sharing their own stories and hearing those of others are powerful ways to help participants reflect on their own experiences and note commonalities and differences with others who have similar and different social identities.

Most people are even less likely to have thought about the dominant and subordinated statuses social positions they occupy in relation to different forms of oppression, or their intergenerational legacies of advantage or disadvantage. This is especially true for individuals' privileged identities. How do individuals' dominant or subordinated status affect their access to resources, social power, and opportunities? These explorations are key to making connections between the personal and systemic levels at which oppression operates. Having participants acknowledge the various dominant and subordinated statuses they hold helps them begin this exploration.

The exploration of social identities and positionality is further complicated by an intersectional perspective. Participants need opportunities and support to examine the interaction among their multiple social identities and positions of advantage and disadvantage. An understanding of oppression is gained when participants consider the contexts or settings in which certain social identities become more salient. One way to encourage this exploration is to have participants form small groups that focus on a single social identity—such as race, gender, sexuality, class, religion, or ability. Within each small group, they identify their status (privileged or marginalized) in relation to that identity and share concrete experiences to illustrate. For example, participants of color in a group formed around race can discuss their similar and different experiences with racism. As a second stage, within the same groups, they can talk about the ways in which other social identities are experienced simultaneously in the specific settings or situations under discussion and consider how these identities impact their experiences of advantage and disadvantage. In the example above, participants of color next discuss their experiences of relative advantage and disadvantage based on class or age, gender, religion, or ability. They can then move to considering different settings or issues and discuss how these intersecting identities would be experienced differently or other identities would be more salient. Continuing the example, participants could discuss how their experiences of race and its intersections with other identities differ when they are in predominantly white schools or workplaces, or at "home" in racially homogeneous churches or community settings. Within these examples, they can reflect on how gender, class, and other identity markers shape their experiences in different settings, and compare and contrast their own experiences with those of others in the group.

The kaleidoscope of social identities can come into clearer focus as specific social identities, and their privileged or disadvantaged positions, shift in relation to one or another or the issues under examination (Adams & Marchesani, 1997). The intersections of identities will, if named and explored within the pedagogy, be felt to be "simultaneous," not "additive" (Goodman, 2014; Holvino, 2012). Like other complex content that benefits from scaffolding and sequencing, Goodman and Jackson (2012) suggest a progression for helping individuals understand racial identity and racism from an intersectional perspective that could be useful with other forms of identity and oppression. Explorations of social identities and statuses place participants within systems of oppression that categorize and rank people based on their social group memberships. Having participants look at their own and others' experiences through that lens helps them see how they are situated within these systems of inequality and how they are affected by them.

Another way participants can personally relate to different forms of oppression is to make connections between their own experiences and institutional and cultural manifestations of oppression. They can see how these dynamics or concepts are not some abstraction but part of their own realities. For example, many ism designs in this book use Young's "Five Faces of Oppression"—exploitation, marginalization, cultural domination, powerlessness, and violence (1990). Participants not only hear historical and current examples to illustrate the points, but they can look at how these "faces" are present in their own experiences and communities. Similarly, in additional to simply defining or describing privilege, participants can list the ways they experience privilege in their own lives. When exploring different isms in the media, participants can critically reflect on media to which they have been and are exposed. They can examine how the institutional policies and practices in their organization or school advantage or disadvantage people based on their different social identities, and develop action strategies to address them. Sometimes it is useful to first present concepts or theories and then have participants make the connection to their own lives; other times, participants can explore their personal realities and then connect them to larger systemic dynamics and analysis.

Learning is most powerful when it is relevant. Situating students' lives within the social justice content not only makes the learning relevant, it helps illuminate the reality of oppression in their lives. It provides lenses to understand what they see and experience. Theories of oppression and social justice issues become not just abstract ideas but ways to understand oneself, others, and the world in order to create change.

As the developmental literature illustrates and Freire reminds us, facilitators need to start from "where" participants are—in their social identities and awareness of issues, in their ways of knowing, in their openness and interest in SJE issues:

> The educator needs to know that . . . [y]ou never get *there* by starting from *there*, you get *there* by starting from some *here* . . . This means, ultimately, that the educator must not be ignorant of, underestimate, or reject the "knowledge of living experience" with which [participants] come to school.
>
> (Freire, 1994, p. 58)

A journey where the facilitator starts from the participants' "here" to achieve some mutually agreed upon "there" recurs in Freire's pedagogical dialogue with Myles Horton, *We Make the Road by Walking* (1990). The "we" is as important as any other word in that aphorism.

Principle 3: Anticipate, acknowledge, and balance the emotional with the cognitive components of SJE learning.

Social justice learning is emotionally and cognitively challenging because it asks participants to not only explore new ideas and content that may clash with their assumptions about the world, but it also asks them to examine their own socialization and participation in perpetuating injustice. These are not "neutral" topics. Facilitators need to expect and plan for the range of intellectual and affective responses that commonly arise.

Working With Cognitive Challenges in SJE

Given the cognitive complexity of social justice content and expectations that participants will be making connections between concrete and abstract examples of oppression, and between the personal and systemic levels on which it operates, some participants are inevitably going to feel cognitively challenged. Cognitive challenges arise when participants are asked to think complexly and with nuance about mutlilayered SJE issues; reflect on their own social experience using social justice concepts (metacognition); take another's perspective (social perspective taking); or utilize underdeveloped skills such as self-reflection, analysis, critical thinking, communication, listening, and planning action (Kuhn, 1990). All of these cognitive skills can be identified, developed, and practiced, as documented in recent intergroup dialogue research (Gurin, Nagda, & Zúñiga, 2013; Hopkins & Domingue, 2015).

The models discussed earlier of cognitive development and social identity development enable instructors to anticipate the challenges posed for participants by complex, multifaceted, real-life issues. Facilitators can intentionally structure activities that will help participants grapple with new content and practice the cognitive skills named above. For example, instructors can plan activities that ask participants to hold several ideas or experiences in their minds (or posted in the room) for exploration. During a group "brainstorm" to generate different ideas, facilitators might ask participants to analyze the content in particular ways: To physically draw links or connect concrete examples with overarching structural patterns. Students can work in small groups and make "mind maps" for ideas that they think are connected. These "mind maps" can be posted for "gallery walks" during which participants with post-its can add their own thinking. This model of "inclusive" thinking considers all of the ideas in the room through listing them, making connections, and critically evaluating them. In "scaffolding" greater complexity and mutlilayeredness in thinking, facilitators will want to ask participants to talk about how it feels to forge new connections, and have them consider how they can use the processes being modeled in the classroom or workshop in other contexts.

The scaffolding of participant thinking is an important cognitive developmental tool. The facilitator is not doing the thinking for participants, but noting what comes up during group discussion and encouraging participants to make connections and map relationships among similar ideas. This process shifts the authority and modeling from facilitator to participants, endorses the value of multiple perspectives, demonstrates how complex thinking becomes "internalized" through considering various perspectives or information sources on an issue, and forges relationships among participants that can lead to subsequent group projects or activist coalitions.

For participants whose habitual mode is to think in binaries of either/or, right or wrong, and true or false, this approach can feel initially quite challenging. It can be useful to encourage such participants to first consider new ideas before evaluating them, and to not rule out perspectives until they have tried to understand them from the inside-out (Belenky, Clinchy, Goldberger, & Tarule, 1986). It is often the case that dualistic thinkers have been taught to accept authorities (parental, religious, political, other teachers) without critique, and are unsettled when the views they have absorbed are contradicted in the SJE classroom or workshop. These contradictions need to be handled respectfully and thoughtfully by facilitators, in order to leave participants in the driver's seat as they negotiate contradictions for themselves and feel their own way forward. Encouraging metacognition and perspective-taking as valuable life-long cognitive tools can help them step out of their comfort zone and try on new ways of thinking as they engage with the issues at hand.

This approach can also prod transitional or "relativistic" (Perry, 1970, 1981) thinkers to ask themselves, "How do I evaluate ideas? How do I make decisions or commitments?" Considering "from the inside" (connected knowing) and making evaluations and judgments "from the outside" (separate knowing) is a further practice in expanding cognitive flexibility that draws upon the feminist approach to cognitive development (Baxter-Magolda, 1992; Belenky, Clinchy, Goldberger, & Tarule, 1986).

Small-group discussions, peer panels, caucus groups, concentric circles, and fish bowls are pedagogies that provide opportunities in which participants who have been more accustomed to lecturer as authority figure and an either/or world view get to hear from peers as "experts" on their own experiences, or discover "expertise" is not necessarily the property of people with particular credentials but is something that is broadly shared.

It is unusual, even within higher education, to ask participants to think about their thinking, and at the same moment to acknowledge their feelings. Both require a level of self-reflection and "meta" cognition that is rarely encouraged. But without such parallel attention to thoughts and feelings, participants cannot learn to identify or manage the toll that their emotions might be taking on the clarity of their thinking—or its influence on the conclusions they reach about serious social justice issues in their everyday world.

Social justice education can be thought of as a "pressure cooker" toward complexity, metacognition, and self-reflection upon one's own experiences and emotions. It is helpful for social justice educators to have the cognitive development literature as a "go to" for recommendations about options to address these challenges. One recommendation is to acknowledge that social justice is a complicated area, and that authorities disagree on how best to move forward on the many injustices we will be noticing in a course or workshop. As disagreements among authorities (including participants claiming the authority of their experience) emerge during discussions, the instructor can point out such contradictions. For dualistic thinkers, the fact that experts disagree can be both challenging and liberating. For relativistic thinkers, the evaluation of options (data, logic, evidence) poses a challenge that is also an opening for internal agency. In keeping with the cognitive developmental view that contradictions (cognitive dissonance) fuel new ways of thinking, facilitators can use probing questions to encourage deeper thinking: "What are the different factors that might lead people to different conclusions on the same topic? What are the factors that led you to your conclusions? If these factors seem incomplete for arriving at a convincing decision, where might you go to get needed additional perspectives or new information?"

Worksheets for films or peer panels providing different viewpoints can encourage participants to identify with speakers who offer more than two options, perspectives, or proposed solutions to problems. This "personalizing" is important, and it may be useful to have "real people" (invited speakers and panelists) rather than "talking heads" in films. It is helpful to frame these as "experience-based points of view" rather than "debates," since debates rarely call for more than two opposing viewpoints, whereas "experience-based points of view" can disclose three or more. Participants can be encouraged to conduct interviews (as an outside-of-class assignment) to identify different perspectives derived from different experiences as a way of challenging a single dualistic viewpoint.

Upon listening to the personal experiences and perspectives of others—through small-group discussions, organized speakers' panels, films, videos, or other media—participants may feel more comfortable imagining how they might themselves experiment with and incorporate other ways of thinking or feeling. Based on the personal testimonies of others (peers are often the most powerful "evidence" for participants), facilitators can help participants clarify a "third way" to think about a given issue.

Working With Emotions in SJE

Although emotion is closely intertwined with and at times indistinguishable from cognition, we focus on emotion as well as cognition because each offers a different entry point to social justice learning, and each poses a distinctive set of challenges. In SJE, emotions are particularly important, because they can interfere with openness to new awareness (anxiety, uncertainty, shame) and because the display of emotion disrupts traditional assumptions about calm, neutral, objective classroom discourse.

Participants may feel a range of apparently contradictory feelings. Some may feel anxious that they will say or do something stupid or wrong, or that they will unintentionally insult or antagonize other participants. Others may feel excited about being able to share their perspectives and learn from their mistakes. Some may worry about exposing aspects of their own marginalized identities that they do not want to reveal to strangers—and/or they may feel relief at being able to discuss these issues in a supportive setting. Participants may be unsettled by the disconnect between what they learned at home or from peer groups about peoples from marginalized groups, and what they are now being exposed to in a social justice workshop or course—and they may feel relief and appreciation to find their questions and feelings reinforced and valued in SJE. Participants may feel fear of being overwhelmed by complex and challenging conceptual frameworks that are entirely new to them, and concepts that challenge their current world view—and they may eagerly welcome the opportunity to think deeply and explore new ideas. Participants may feel anger and outrage about historical and current instances of inequality and injustice—and invigorated by opportunities to take action.

The establishment of norms and guidelines as an early phase of the learning community offers an important way to acknowledge and manage the "fears" and anxiety as well as the "hopes" and excitement that participants bring to SJE. Clear guidelines help to surface, acknowledge, and alleviate anxiety about what the course will entail and how people will be treated, and provide an opportunity to develop new skills in a supportive setting. For example, facilitators may say, in so many words, that participants are likely to feel anxious, judgmental, curious, defensive, excited, and/or hopeful, and they should not be surprised when these different feelings surface. Facilitators may disclose feelings such as uncertainty, anxiety, or joy that we ourselves have experienced—and continue to experience—in our own journeys as social justice learners, noting that SJE involves a lifelong journey with surprises, twists, and turns. Facilitators can mention some of the activities planned to acknowledge participants' hopes and concerns, and find similarities and differences with others. Facilitators can explain that we pay attention to emotions because they can either inhibit or facilitate learning, and that no one in the room is alone or will be unsupported in having strong feelings about oppression and social change. Instructors can encourage participants to think in advance about how they might handle these feelings so they can stay engaged when feelings arise.

Attention to the emotional ingredients of participant learning is not a one-time endeavor, attended to once and then put aside. Interventions in the moment, especially when participants and/or facilitators are triggered, need to be thoughtful, measured, and respectful. Remarks that may seem offensive or insulting should be taken (at least the first time they are expressed) as honest statements that need to be explored respectfully, perhaps by asking what evidence the remarks are based on, or whether there are other ways to frame them. Instructors can remind participants that none of us are responsible for what we have learned or the ways we have been socialized, but once we become conscious of privilege and disadvantage, and the misinformation or stereotypes we hold about each other, we are responsible for maintaining and acting on our new levels of awareness. These commitments place us on perpetual "learning edges" and we become accountable for not falling back into old habits.

Instructor/facilitator or participant interventions in the moment may heighten emotion for everyone in the room, as participants watch whether prior agreements about norms and guidelines, honest mistakes, learning edges, and respectful dialogue are honored for all. Facilitators might ask participants to help in calling attention to violations of norms and guidelines. The concept of comfort zones/learning edges serves as a helpful reminder that there are challenges for all participants in a social justice learning community, including the instructor/facilitator. All can be encouraged to use those terms to communicate instances where they feel challenged or stuck.

Principle 4: Draw upon the knowledge and experiences of participants and the intergroup dynamics in the room to illustrate and discuss social justice content.

The content in SJE does not only come from "out there" through readings, media, and guest speakers, but also arise within the group itself. Activities are created and intentionally structured so that participants not only reflect on their own experiences, but also hear about and learn from the experiences of others. Participants are able to broaden their frames of reference and increase their knowledge from hearing the thoughts, opinions, and lived realities of others in the group.

For some people, this is one of the few opportunities they have for open discussion with other individuals who are different from themselves. There is also power in hearing information firsthand and in person, especially from people with whom you have a connection. Learning from each other does not replace the additional resources instructors introduce, especially if the group is relatively homogeneous, but contributes to and enhances the learning experience. Even in a group that appears similar, instructors can help participants consider how other identities intersect to encourage a more nuanced and complex understanding of a shared social identity.

Bringing one's experiences "into the room" is one form of experiential education. Activities that invite participants to share stories, experiences with advantage and disadvantage, and examples from their lives outside of the classroom make their experiences and examples part of the curriculum. A second, equally important, mode of experiential education is the interpersonal communications and interactions that occur in the "here and now" among participants. The group dynamics in the room thus provide fertile educational material. As both the instructor and students notice and comment on the interactions in the class, people can learn about how interpersonal and group dynamics operate in everyday encounters outside the learning community. The workshop or classroom becomes a "laboratory" to explore different cultural styles of communication and conflict, and the dynamics of advantage and disadvantage, so that these can be recognized and addressed outside in community or workplace interactions.

Through reflecting on group dynamics, we help participants analyze social relations of power and privilege by noting things such as who speaks and for how long, who gets interrupted, whose views are listened to or dismissed, how people's body language and emotional expressiveness gets interpreted, and with whom individuals sit and who is included in small groups. When conflict or other dynamics occur, we can use those as teachable moments to explore how they connect to larger social issues and patterns of behavior. Attending to and working through interactions in class, students develop and practice tools for analysis and skills for interacting in other settings. Engaging in conversations and small- and large-group activities with people who are both similar and different provides participants with opportunities to develop comfort and competencies they can use in other parts of their lives.

Principle 5: Encourage active engagement with the issues and collaboration among participants.

In the past several decades, educators have acknowledged that learning is something more than a spectator sport, and that learning requires active participation, a sense of personal relevance, engaged discussion and dialogue, and the opportunity to try out new skills—in other words, learning requires "doing" (Bonwell & Eison, 1991; Johnson, Johnson, & Smith, 1991; Silberman, 1998). The growing influence of Vygotsky in education has also brought "activity" into focus as the space in which adults and peers, or peers with other peers, engage in "doing" and solving problems or developing skills that are social in nature, that are needed in a real world of social interaction and not a "school" world of passive learning (Gallimore, 1992; Sannino, Daniels, & Gutierrez, 2009).

The pedagogy of SJE is a pedagogy of activity, embedded in multiple social contexts (the content, the learning community, the self in relation to others). There is an immense active-learning pedagogical literature on how to form groups, structure tasks, facilitate collaboration, use small- or large-group discussion techniques, and structure dialogue or debate, role playing or simulations, cooperative or collaborative projects, and scaffold learning tasks (Barkley, Cross, & Major, 2005; Boal, 1979; Bonwell & Eison, 1991; Daniels, 2001; Johnson, Johnson, & Smith, 1991; Lakey, 2010; Schutzman & Cohen-Cruz, 1994; Silberman, 1998; Slavin, 1995). The literature on intergroup dialogue is also grounded in active learning (Gurin, Nagda, & Zúñiga, 2013; Zúñiga, Lopez, & Ford, 2012), and the entirety of this volume is based upon active learning.

Social justice education pedagogies presume active engagement by the entire learning group, and activities designed to involve everyone. For example, students engaged in a fish bowl activity need either to be fully engaged in addressing the issues at hand (the "fish" in the bowl) or fully engaged in active listening as participants who form the perimeter of the bowl (the outer circle of observers). Not only do participants take turns as the "fish" or the "bowl," but "active listening" skills need to be taught and used. No one gets "time out" to passively sit back and observe, except during agreed-upon breaks.

Active learning includes physically moving around, through circle activities such as "Common Ground" or "Concentric Circles," or moving to different discussion spaces to generate examples for "Five Faces" or intervention options for different oppression scenarios. "Gallery Walks" get small groups moving around to look at each other's newsprint gallery before returning to their seats (or continuing to stand) for whole-group discussions.

In SJE, not only is active learning important in its own right, it provides the basis for new awareness, insight, knowledge, and action. Kolb's learning style model (1981, 1984) is useful in that it balances reflection with action—and thus action with reflection (Anderson & Adams, 1992). It is worth noting that Kolb's model supports an experiential pedagogy that also includes fairness and inclusivity through learning options that reflect a range of learning styles.

Principle 6: Foster and evaluate personal awareness, acquisition of knowledge and skills, and action-planning processes to create change.

Learning objectives and evaluation need to be aligned in any educational process, however informal or formal the workshop or classroom setting. Whether evaluation is expressed through encouragement or through grades, or some combination of the two, it conveys a clear message about what is valued and recognized. If we are to "walk the talk" about learning goals, we need also to recognize progress in participant awareness, readiness, and skills to create change.

In SJE courses in academic settings, students are accountable for learning core concepts (as they would in any other academic class), for writing papers, and for completing and reflecting upon the readings and other assignments (research, interviews, group projects) typical of academic courses. If instructors have been consistent in articulating the purposes of SJE, we will have established clarity about why awareness is important, why correct information needs to replace misinformation, how core concepts serve as organizers for this body of knowledge, and why participants need to explore (whether or not they take action) instances of inequality, prejudice, and discrimination, and consider what would be needed within their spheres of influence to move toward greater inclusion, fairness, and justice.

Instructors should take care not only in deciding what SJE learning outcomes to evaluate, but how such evaluation is conducted. For example, instructors in academic courses can create rubrics for grading, in which completeness and thoughtfulness of answers, or documentation of perspectives in response to the instructor's carefully sequenced questions, are the basis for the grade (Stevens & Levi, 2005). It is especially important in an SJE class or workshop, where participants may not yet understand that there are no "right/wrong" answers to complex questions, that participants not feel compelled to guess the "correct" answer on issues where instructors and participants might reasonably disagree. However, in cases on which we do want students to master a body of material—such as an understanding of core concepts or "Five Faces" or the different levels of oppression—we need to be clear about the material for which they are accountable and may even hold a review session to model the kinds of responses that are appropriate.

Final grades can be based on points for work completed and turned in using a scale that is presented at the beginning of a semester. Thus, responses to assigned readings or short papers can be designated specific points on a scale of timeliness, thoughtfulness, and completeness. An SJE approach to grading requires planning and effort on the part of instructors to develop clear rubrics, point systems, and guidelines for all assignments. Participants need to understand the nature of the task and why it is part of the overall SJE project. This approach to grading is quite different from the subjectivity involved in evaluating student writing in many classes, where the criteria for what is "competent" or "excellent" is often not accessible to students, especially students from marginalized cultures where there is not the cultural capital that derives from intergenerational higher education experiences and degrees.

When action-planning projects are part of the design or curriculum, as they are in Chapters 4–11, it is important to convey that the purpose of such assignments are for participants to understand the planning necessary for any kind of action. In SJE, we encourage planning collaborative change projects that will model inclusiveness, fairness, and justice in relationships, in communities, and in work or professional organizations. We encourage but do not require that such plans be implemented, since that could be considered personally intrusive and beyond the scope of a course—although not beyond the scope of professional classes or workshops whose major purpose is the creation of change , or the motivation that participants often feel to work toward social justice. Chapters 4–11 offer many activities through which participants can identify situations that cry out for remedy, coalitions they can establish or participate in for mutual support and planning for change, intentional considerations of resources needed and challenges anticipated in change efforts, skill sets and assets they bring to change efforts and their potential risk levels, and the help and resources needed from others.

We do not assess or grade the actual change effort, except in situations where SJE workshops have been set up to lead to change (such as in workshops with domestic labor organizers, environmental activists, anti-racist advocates, class action coalitions, or interfaith dialogue groups). In those settings, connecting awareness, skills, and action will be front and center in the learning outcomes and goals of the workshop.

As students in K–12 and higher education settings explore the legacies and current manifestations of oppression and injustice, they want to do something that can make a difference for the better, and learning to plan for change is an important skill that SJE courses can help them to develop (Tatum, 1994). It is our responsibility to help those participants who are motivated to create change to identify the skills they need for effective action; the resources and assets already available within their own spheres of influence and those they need to access by tapping into other coalitions; and the knowledge, partners, and allies they can work with to effect and sustain the desired change. In the context of SJE as conceptualized in this volume, we at least open the door and provide frameworks and rubrics to begin the coalition-building and planning process.

Participant self-assessment about what they have learned is an equally important part of the overall assessment process, whether formal or informal. Even in an academic, credited, and graded classroom, there is tremendous value in having students write self-assessment self-reflection papers that have been structured by questions that probe and ask for connections between the concrete and abstract, as well as describing "aha" moments of insight. As a final written product, these self-reflection papers provide closure for participants and a source of insight for instructors. Final papers such as these have contributed greatly to our sense of what is possible, and which pedagogies are most effective in different contexts and with different groups. Such self-assessments are different in quality, kind, and value than typical exams, research papers, and assignments. Through both formal and informal assessment processes, both instructors and students can reflect on and gauge the impact of the learning process. Participants can leave further equipped to implement change around issues and in contexts that are personally relevant.

CONCLUSION

As social justice educators, our goal is to create the kind of socially just relationships, communities, institutions, and society that we ourselves want to live in. Thus, our pedagogies need to model the equity, fairness, inclusiveness, reciprocity, and justice for which we are striving. Because we are educators as well as social justice activists, we think of formal and informal education settings as key sites to embody and model the goals of social justice and to enact processes toward those goals. We hope to provide learning communities where we can, together, develop and practice cross-group understanding, empathy, and collaboration; conduct a critical analysis of our interpersonal interactions, social institutions, culture, and society; embrace the opportunity to practice skills and build coalitions that enable taking action to challenge injustice; and together imagine the better world to which we aspire.

References

Abrams, D., & Hogg, M. A. (Eds.). (1990). *Social identity theory: Constructive and critical advances.* New York: Springer-Verlag.

Adams, M. (2002). Charting cognitive and moral development in diversity classes. *Diversity Digest,* 6(1/2), 21–23.

Adams, M. (2007). Pedagogical frameworks for social justice education. In M. Adams, L. A. Bell, & P. Griffin (Eds.), *Teaching for diversity and social justice* (2nd ed., pp. 15–34). New York: Routledge.

Adams, M. (2010). Roots of social justice pedagogies in social movements. In T. K. Chapman & N. Hobbel (Eds.), *Social justice pedagogy across the curriculum: The practice of freedom* (pp. 59–86). New York: Routledge.

Adams, M. (2014). Social justice and education. In M. Reisch (Ed.), *The Routledge international handbook of social justice* (pp. 249–268). New York: Routledge.

Adams, M., & Marchesani, L. (1997). Multiple issues course overview. In M. Adams, L. A. Bell, & P. Griffin (Eds.), *Teaching for diversity and social justice: A sourcebook* (pp. 261–275). New York: Routledge.

Adams, M., Perry-Jenkins, M., & Tropp, L. (2014). Pedagogical tools for social justice and psychology. In C. V. Johnson, H. Friedman, J. Diaz, Z. Franco, & B. Nastasi (Eds.), *The Praeger handbook on social justice and psychology* (Vol. 2, pp. 227–248). Santa Barbara, CA: Praeger.

Adams, M., & Zhou-McGovern, Y. (1994). The sociomoral development of undergraduates in a "social diversity" course: Developmental theory, research and instructional applications. Paper presented at an annual meeting of the American Educational Research Association (AERA). New Orleans, LA: ERIC. ERIC Document Reproduction Service No. ED380345.

Allport, G. W. (1954/1979). *The nature of prejudice* (unabridged, 25th anniversary ed.). Reading, PA: Addison-Wesley.

Anderson, J. A., & Adams, M. (1992). Acknowledging the learning styles of diverse student populations: Implications for instructional design. In L.A.B. Border & N.V.N. Chism (Eds.), *Teaching for diversity: New directions for teaching and learning* (#49, pp. 19–34). San Francisco: Jossey-Bass.

Anyon, J. (2009). Critical pedagogy is not enough: Social justice education, political participation, and the politicization of students. In M. W. Apple, W. Au, & I. A. Grandin (Eds.), *The Routledge international handbook of critical education* (pp. 389–393). New York: Routledge.

Apple, M. W., Au, W., & Gandin, L. A. (2009). *The Routledge international handbook of critical education*. New York: Routledge.

Au, W. (2009). Fighting with the text: Contextualizing and reconceptualizing Freire's critical pedagogy. In M. W. Apple, W. Au, & I. A. Grandin (Eds.), *The Routledge international handbook of critical education* (pp. 221–231). New York: Routledge.

Bargad, A., & Hyde, J. S. (1991). Women's studies: A study of feminist identity development in women. *Psychology of Women Quarterly*, *15*, 181–210.

Barkley, E. F., Cross, K. P., & Major, C. H. (2005). *Collaborative learning techniques: A handbook for college faculty*. San Francisco: Jossey-Bass.

Bartolomé, L. (1994). Beyond the methods fetish: Toward a humanizing pedagogy. *Harvard Educational Review*, *64*(2), 173–194.

Baxter-Magolda, M. B. (1992). *Knowing and reasoning in college: Gender-related patterns in students' intellectual development*. San Francisco: Jossey-Bass.

Belenky, M. F., Clinchy, M. B., Goldberger, N. R., & Tarule, J. M. (1986). *Women's ways of knowing: The development of self, voice, and mind*. New York: Basic Books.

Benne, K. D. (1964). History of the T-group in the laboratory setting. In L. P. Bradford, J. R. Gibb, & K. D. Benne (Eds.), *T-group theory and laboratory method: Innovation in re-education* (pp. 80–136). New York: John Wiley.

Beyer, L. E., & Apple, M. W. (Eds.). (1998). *The curriculum: Problems, politics, and possibilities* (2nd ed.). Albany, NY: State University of New York Press.

Bidell, T. R., Lee, E. M., Bouchie, N., Ward, C., & Brass, D. (1994). Developing conceptions of racism among young white adults in the context of cultural diversity coursework. *Journal of Adult Development*, *1*(3), 185–200.

Boal, A. (1979). *Theatre of the oppressed*. London: Pluto Press.

Bonwell, C. C., & Eison, J. A. (1991). *Active learning: Creating excitement in the classroom*. Association for the Study of Higher Education (ASHE)-ERIC Higher Education Report No. 1. Washington, DC: George Washington University, School of Education and Human Development.

Bradford, L. P., Gibb, J. R., & Benne, K. D. (Eds.). (1964). *T-group theory and laboratory method: Innovation in re-education*. New York: John Wiley.

Bronfenbrenner, U. (1979). *The ecology of human development*. Cambridge, MA: Harvard University Press.

Brookfield, S. D. (1987). *Developing critical thinkers: Challenging adults to explore alternative ways of thinking and acting*. San Francisco: Jossey-Bass.

Brookfield, S. D. (2005). *The power of critical theory: Liberating adult learning and teaching*. San Francisco: Jossey-Bass.

Brookfield, S. D. (2012). *Teaching for critical thinking: Tools and techniques to help students question their assumptions*. San Francisco: Jossey-Bass.

Brookfield, S. D. (2013). *Powerful techniques for teaching adults*. San Francisco: Jossey-Bass.

Brookfield, S. D., & Holst, J. D. (2011). *Radicalizing learning: Adult education for a just world*. San Francisco: Jossey-Bass.

Cass, V. C. (1996). Sexual orientation identity formation: A western phenomenon. In R. P. Cabai & T. S. Stein (Eds.), *Textbook of homosexuality and mental health*. Washington, DC: American Psychiatric Press.

Catalano, C. J. (2014). *Welcome to Guyland: Experiences of trans* men in college* (Doctoral dissertation). Retrieved from WorldCat. Amherst, MA: University of Massachusetts, Amherst.

Cole, M. (1990). Cognitive development and formal schooling: The evidence from cross-cultural research. In L. C. Moll (Ed.), *Vygotsky and education: Instructional implications and applications of sociohistorical psychology* (pp. 89–110). New York: Cambridge University Press.

Cole, M. (1995). Culture and cognitive development: From cross-cultural research to creating systems of cultural mediation. *Culture and Psychology*, *1*(1), 25–54.

Cole, M. (1996). *Cultural psychology: A once and future discipline*. Cambridge, MA: Harvard University Press.

Cox, S., & Gallois, C. (1996). Gay and lesbian identity development: A social identity perspective. *Journal of Homosexuality*, *30*(4), 1–30.

Cross, W. E. (1971). The Negro-to-black conversion experience: Toward a psychology of black liberation. *Black World*, *20*(9), 13–27.

Cross, W. E. (1991). *Shades of black: Diversity in African American identity*. Philadelphia: Temple University Press.

Cross, W. E. (2001). Patterns of African American identity development: A life-span perspective. In C. L. Wijeyesinghe & B. W. Jackson (Eds.), *New perspectives on racial identity development: A theoretical and practical anthology* (pp. 243–270). New York: New York University Press.

Cross, W. E. (2012). The enactments of race and other social identities during everyday transactions. In C. L. Wijeyesinghe & B. W. Jackson (Eds.), *New perspectives on racial identity development: Integrating emerging frameworks* (2nd ed., pp. 192–215). New York: New York University Press.

Cross, W. E., & Phagen-Smith, P. (2001). Patterns of African American identity development: A life-span perspective. In C. L. Wijeyesinghe & B. W. Jackson (Eds.), *New perspectives on racial identity development: A theoretical and practical anthology* (pp. 243–270). New York: New York University Press.

Daniels, H. (2001). Vygotsky and pedagogy. New York: Routledge.

Darder, A., Baltodano, M. P., & Torres, R. D. (Eds.). (2008). *The critical pedagogy reader* (2nd ed.). New York: Routledge.

Dewey, J. (1909/1975). *Moral principle in education.* Carbondale, IL: Southern Illinois Press.

Dovidio, J. F., Glick, P., & Rudman, L. A. (Eds.). (2005). *On the nature of prejudice: Fifty years after Allport.* Malden, MA: Blackwell.

Downing, N. E., & Roush, K. L. (1985). From passive acceptance to active commitment: A model of feminist identity development for women. *The Counseling Psychologist, 13*(4), 695–709.

Duany, J. (1998). Reconstructing racial identity: Ethnicity, color, and class among Dominicans in the United States and Puerto Rico. *Latin American Perspectives, 25*(3), 147–172.

Engberg, M. E. (2004). Improving intergroup relations in higher education: A critical examination of the influence of educational interventions on racial bias. *Review of Educational Research, 74*(4), 473–524.

Erikson, E. H. (1968). *Identity, youth and crisis.* New York: Norton.

Evans, S. (1980). *Personal politics: The roots of women's liberation in the civil rights movement and the new left.* New York: Random House.

Freire, P. (1970). *Pedagogy of the oppressed.* New York: Herder & Herder.

Freire, P. (1994). *Pedagogy of hope: Reliving pedagogy of the oppressed.* New York: Continuum.

Gallegos, P. V. & Ferdman, B. M. (2012). Latina and Latina ethnoracial identity orientations: A dynamic and developmental perspective. In C. L. Wijeyesinghe & B. W. Jackson (Eds.), *New perspectives on racial identity development: Integrating emerging frameworks* (2nd ed., pp. 51–80). New York: New York University Press.

Gallimore, R. (1992). Developmental perspectives. In F. K. Oser, A. Dick, & J-L Patry (Eds.), *Effective and responsible teaching: The new synthesis* (pp. 155–222). San Francisco: Jossey-Bass.

Gill, C. (1997). Four types of integration in disability identity development. *Journal of Vocational Rehabilitation, 9,* 39–46.

Goodman, D. (2014). The tapestry model: Exploring social identities, privilege, and oppression from an intersectional perspective. In D. Mitchell, Jr., C. Simmons, & L. Greyerbiehl (Eds.). *Intersectionality in higher education: Theory, research, and praxis.* New York: Peter Lang Publishing.

Goodman, D. J., & Jackson, B. W. (2012). Pedagogical approaches to teaching about racial identity from an intersectional perspective. In C. L. Wijeyesinghe & B. W. Jackson (Eds.), *New perspectives on racial identity development: Integrating emerging frameworks* (2nd ed., pp. 216–242). New York: New York University Press.

Gurin, P., Nagda, B. R. A., & Zúñiga, X. (2013). *Dialogue across difference: Practice, theory, and research on intergroup dialogue.* New York: Russell Sage Foundation.

Hamako, E. (2014). *Improving anti-racist education for multiracial students* (Doctoral dissertation). Retrieved from WorldCat. Amherst, MA: University of Massachusetts, Amherst.

Helms, J. E. (1995). An update of Helms's white and people of color racial identity models. In J. G. Ponterotto, J. M. Casas, L. A. Suzuki, & C. M. Alexander (Eds.), *Handbook of multicultural counseling* (pp. 181–198). Thousand Oaks, CA: Sage.

Holvino, E. (2012). The "simultaneity" of identities: Models and skills for the twenty-first century. In C. L. Wijeyesinghe & B. W. Jackson (Eds.), *New perspectives on racial identity development: Integrating emerging frameworks* (2nd ed., pp. 161–191). New York: New York University Press.

Hopkins, L. E. (2014). *Beyond the pearly gates: White, low-income student experiences at elite colleges* (Doctoral dissertation). Retrieved from WorldCat. Amherst, MA: University of Massachusetts, Amherst.

Hopkins, L. E., & Domingue, A. D. (2015, in press). From awareness to action: College students' skill development in intergroup dialogue. *Equity & Excellence in Education, 48*(3).

Horton, M., & Freire, P. (1990). *We make the road by walking: Conversations on education and social change.* Philadelphia: Temple University Press.

Howe, F. (1964/1984). Mississippi's Freedom Schools: The politics of education. In F. Howe (Ed.), *Myths of coeducation: Selected essays, 1964–1983* (pp. 1–17). Bloomington, IN: Indiana University Press.

Hurtado, A., Gurin, P., & Peng, T. (1994). Social identities—A framework for studying the adaptations of immigrants and ethnics: The adaptations of Mexicans to the United States. *Social Problems, 41*(1), 129–151.

Jackson, B. W. (Ed.) (1976). *Black identity development*. Dubuque, IA: Kendall Hunt.

Jackson, B. W. (2001). Black identity development: Further analysis and elaboration. In C. L. Wijeyesinghe & B. W. Jackson (Eds.), *New perspectives on racial identity development: A theoretical and practical* anthology (pp. 8–31). New York: New York University Press.

Jackson, B. W. (2012). Black identity development: Influences of culture and social oppression. In C. L. Wijeyesinghe & B. W. Jackson (Eds.), *New perspectives on racial identity development: Integrating emerging frameworks* (2nd ed., pp. 33–50). New York: New York University Press.

Johnson, D. W., Johnson, R. G., & Smith, K. A. (1991). *Active learning: Cooperation in the college classroom*. Edina, MN: Interaction Book Company.

Kegan, R. (1982). *The evolving self*. Cambridge, MA: Harvard University Press.

Kim, J. (2001). Asian American identity development. In C. L. Wijeyesinghe & B. W. Jackson (Eds.), *New perspectives on racial identity development: A theoretical and practical anthology* (pp. 67–90). New York: New York University Press.

King, P. M., & Kitchener, K. S. (1994). *Developing reflective judgment: Understanding and promoting intellectual growth and critical thinking in adolescents and adults*. San Francisco: Jossey-Bass.

King, P. M., & Shuford, B. C. (1996). A multicultural view is a more cognitively complex view: Cognitive development and multicultural education. *American Behavioral Scientist, 40*(2), 153–164.

Kolb, D. A. (1981). Learning styles and disciplinary differences. In A. W. Chickering (Ed.), *The modern American college: Responding to the new realities of diverse students and a changing society*. San Francisco: Jossey-Bass.

Kolb, D. A. (1984). *Experiential learning: Experience as the source of learning and development*. Englewood Cliffs, NJ: Prentice Hall.

Kuhn, D. (Ed.) (1990). *Developmental perspectives on teaching and learning thinking skills*. Basel, Switzerland: Karger.

Lakey, G. (2010). *Facilitating group learning: Strategies for success with diverse adult learners*. San Francisco: Jossey-Bass.

Lewin, K. (1948). *Resolving social conflicts: Selected papers on group dynamics*. New York: Harper & Row.

Lippitt, R. (1949). *Training in community relations*. New York: Harper & Row.

Marchesani, L., & Adams, M. (1992). Dynamics of diversity in the teaching-learning process: A faculty development model for analysis and action. In M. Adams (Ed.), *Promoting diversity in college classrooms: Innovative responses for the curriculum, faculty and institutions* (New Directions for Teaching and Learning, no. 52, pp. 9–21). San Francisco: Jossey-Bass.

Marcia, J. E. (1966). Development and validation of ego-identity statuses. *Journal of Personality & Social Psychology, 3*, 551–558.

Margolis, E. (Ed.) (2001). *The hidden curriculum in higher education*. New York: Routledge.

Matos, J. (2015). La familia: The important ingredient for Latina/o college student engagement and persistence. *Equity & Excellence in Education, 48*(1), 437–454.

Moll, L. C. (Ed.) (1990). *Vygotsky and education: Instructional implications and applications of sociohistorical psychology*. New York: Cambridge University Press.

Nieto, S., & Bode, P. (2008). *Affirming diversity: The sociopolitical context of multicultural education* (5th ed.). Boston: Pearson.

Perry, W. G. (1970). *Forms of intellectual and ethical development in the college years*. New York: Holt, Winston & Rinehart.

Perry, W. G. (1981). Cognitive and ethical growth: The making of meaning. In A. Chickering (Ed.), *The modern American college* (pp. 76–116). San Francisco: Jossey-Bass.

Pettigrew, T. F. (1998). *The intergroup contact hypothesis reconsidered*. New York: Basil Blackwell.

Pettigrew, T. F., & Tropp, L. R. (2006). A meta-analytic test of intergroup contact theory. *Journal of Personality & Social Psychology, 90*(5), 752–783.

Pfeiffer, J. W., & Jones, J. E. (Eds.). (1972–1980). *A handbook of structured experiences for human relations training* (Vols. I–VII). San Diego, CA: University Associates.

Rachal, J. (1998). We'll never turn back: Adult education and the struggle for citizenship in Mississippi's Freedom Summer. *American Education Research Journal, 35*(2), 167–198.

Renn, K. A. (2012). Creating and re-creating race: The emergence of racial identity as a critical element in psychological, sociological, and ecological perspectives on human development. In C. L. Wijeyesinghe & B. W. Jackson (Eds.), *New perspectives on racial identity development: Integrating emerging frameworks* (2nd ed., pp. 11–32). New York: New York University Press.

Rogoff, B. (2003). *The cultural nature of human development*. New York: Oxford University Press.

Sandoval, C. (2000). *Methodology of the oppressed*. Minneapolis: University of Minnesota Press.

Sannino, A., Daniels, H., & Gutierrez, K. D. (Eds.). (2009). *Learning and expanding with activity theory*. New York: Cambridge University Press.

Sarachild, K. (1975). Consciousness-raising: A radical weapon. In Redstockings (Ed.), *Feminist revolution* (pp. 144–150). New York: Random House.

Schutzman, M., & Cohen-Cruz, J. (Eds.). (1994). *Playing Boal: Theatre, therapy, activism*. New York: Routledge.

Selman, R. L. (1980). *The growth of interpersonal understanding: Developmental and clinical analyses*. New York: Academic Press.

Sherif, M., & Sherif, C. (1970). Black unrest as a social movement toward an emerging self-identity. *Journal of Social & Behavioral Sciences, 15*(3), 41–52.

Shor, I. (Ed.) (1987). *Freire for the classroom: A sourcebook for liberatory teaching*. Portsmouth, NH: Heinemann.

Silberman, M. (1998). *Active training: A handbook of techniques, designs, case examples and tips*. San Francisco: Jossey-Bass.

Slavin, R. E. (1995). *Cooperative learning* (2nd ed.). Boston: Allyn & Bacon.

Stephan, W. G., & Vogt, W. P. (Eds.). (2004). *Education programs for improving intergroup relations: Theory, research, and practice*. New York: Teachers College Press.

Stevens, D. D., & Levi, A. J. (2005). *Introduction to rubrics: An assessment tool to save grading time, convey effective feedback, and promote student learning*. Sterling, VA: Stylus.

Tatum, B. D. (1992). Talking about race, learning about racism: The application of racial identity development theory in the classroom. *Harvard Educational Review, 62*(1), 1–24.

Tatum, B. D. (1994). Teaching white students about racism: The search for white allies and the restoration of hope. *Teacher's College Record, 95*(4), 462–476.

Tuckman, B. (1965). Developmental sequence in small groups. *Psychological Bulletin, 63*(6), 384–399.

Vygotsky, L. S. (1978). *Mind in society: The development of higher psychological processes*. Cambridge, MA: Harvard University Press.

Wijeyesinghe, C. L. (2001). Racial identity in multiracial people: An alternative paradigm. In C. L. Wijeyesinghe & B. W. Jackson (Eds.), *New perspectives on racial identity development: A theoretical and practical* anthology (pp. 129–152). New York: New York University Press.

Wijeyesinghe, C. L. (2012). The intersectional model of multiracial identity: Integrating multiracial identity theories and intersectional perspectives on social identity. In C. L. Wijeyesinghe & B. W. Jackson (Eds.), *New perspectives on racial identity development: Integrating emerging frameworks* (2nd ed., pp. 81–107). New York: New York University Press.

Wijeyesinghe, C. L. & Jackson, B. W. (Eds.). (2001). *New perspectives on racial identity development: A theoretical and practical anthology*. New York: New York University Press.

Wijeyesinghe, C. L. & Jackson, B. W. (Eds.). (2012). *New perspectives on racial identity development: Integrating emerging frameworks* (2nd ed.). New York: New York University Press.

Young, I. M. (1990). *Justice and the politics of difference*. Princeton, NJ: Princeton University Press.

Zajda, J., Majhanovich, S., Rust, V., & Sabina, E. M. (Eds.). (2006). *Education and social justice*. New York: Springer.

Zúñiga, X., Lopez, G. E., & Ford, K. A. (Eds.). (2012). Intergroup dialogue: Engaging differences, social identities, and social justice. *Equity & Excellence in Education, 45*(1), 1–236.

3

Design and Facilitation

Lee Anne Bell, Diane J. Goodman, and Mathew L. Ouellett*

INTRODUCTION

Social justice education (SJE) courses do not simply convey content; they also engage participants in examining social identities, power, privilege, and structural inequalities in our society and in their own lives. Thus, social justice courses are cognitively challenging, emotionally charged, and personally unsettling. They can also be transformative, as participants develop greater personal awareness, expand knowledge that counters dominant narratives, and commit to making changes in themselves and their environments. Given this complexity, social justice educators should be intentional about their curriculum choices and pedagogical approaches if they are to successfully accomplish social justice educational goals. Therefore, thoughtful consideration of the interrelated issues of design and facilitation are essential.

Design includes all the planning, assessment, and evaluation activities that facilitators/instructors engage in prior to, during, and after meeting with participants. Design includes setting an agenda for the course or workshop, selecting reading and other course materials, planning activities, and organizing small- and large-group procedures for engaging participants actively. In traditional academic courses, design also includes constructing syllabi, exams, and other assessments. *Facilitation* refers to the leadership strategies and skills that instructors use to actively engage participants in learning, mediate interactions within the group, and guide interpersonal and group dynamics as part of the learning process. Both aspects are key to social justice teaching and are complementary and interconnected.

Attention to design and facilitation creates a classroom or workshop community or holding environment within which active and engaged learning can take place. As *designers*, we want to clearly think through and organize materials, activities, and sequencing at every stage in the process. As *facilitators*, we want to intentionally model effective communication skills and respect for differences. We also want to encourage ways of interacting that are inclusive, respectful, honest, and courageous, and support people to challenge injustice in our relationships and the institutional systems of which we are a part.

While our approach in this book is to foreground one ism at a time, we always want to keep in mind that isms intersect on both structural and personal levels, and they mutually inform and reinforce each other in various contexts. Participants are personally situated within matrices of oppression that will differentially affect their connections to, and experiences with, the topic under discussion, and this should inform our planning and facilitation. We also want to be mindful that our own social identities and positionality as instructors will impact our responses to students and course material, and plan for this as well. (We discuss this further in Chapter 12.)

In this chapter, we map out the design and facilitation frameworks and strategies we have developed to guide our social justice teaching. While in practice, design and facilitation are integrally related, for the sake of clarity we focus first on overarching principles of design and then on facilitation strategies. In the facilitation section, we also delve into design considerations at different phases of a class or workshop. We hope readers will see the interconnections between the two sections as they use these design and facilitation guidelines to develop their own social justice practice.

DESIGN PRINCIPLES

Well-designed curriculum sets the stage for easier and more effective facilitation. Marchesani and Adams (1992) identify four dimensions to consider for addressing diversity and equity in a classroom or workshop: 1) *instructor*, 2) *students*, 3) *curriculum*, and 4) *pedagogy*. Briefly, the four dimensions address these questions: "Who are we as instructors?" "Who are our students?" "What do we teach?" and "How do we teach it?" To these four dimensions, we add one more: 5) *classroom climate and group dynamics*, which affects and is affected by all four other dimensions: "How do the climate and interactions in the classroom affect learning?"

Among other contributions, the model shown in Fig. 3.1 reminds instructors of the multilayered and interacting facets in the design and teaching of social justice courses. Each dimension offers a point of entry for considering how a course may be shaped and improved.

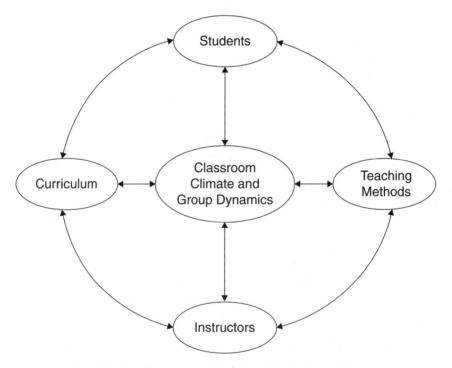

Figure 3.1 Five Dimensions of Diversity and Equity in the Classroom
Adapted from Marchesani & Adams (1992)

DIMENSION 1: SELF/INSTRUCTOR: WHO WE ARE

The first dimension addresses who we are as instructors/facilitators. We bring ourselves into the classroom, including our social identities, cultural styles, preferred teaching approaches, personalities, knowledge bases, triggers, and biases (see Chapter 12). It is especially important in social justice education that educators explore how we are shaped by our intersectional social identities and consequent positionality, and how these affect our teaching (Palmer, 1997). Consciously attending to personal growth and development is essential, ongoing work for social justice educators. We can benefit by considering such questions as these:

- *What social justice related topics am I most and least comfortable teaching?*
- *With which students am I most and least comfortable?*
- *Which students am I most/least effective educating?*
- *How do my social identities and positionality affect my teaching?*
- *What behaviors or issues trigger me in the classroom?*
- *How do I handle conflict? How well do I manage my reactions to conflict?*
- *How do I ensure that I am continuing my own process of development as a social justice educator?*
- *How am I staying current on the topics I teach?*

By examining our competencies and areas for further growth, we can design classes and workshops that match our skills and styles and be conscious of the areas where we will need to grow as instructors. (Chapter 12, *Critical Self-Knowledge for Social Justice Educators*, provides a thorough discussion of these issues.)

DIMENSION 2: STUDENTS—WHO WE TEACH

The second dimension addresses getting to know the participants in our classes and workshops. Important factors to consider are the multiple social identities, interests, expectations, needs, prior experiences, lived realities, and learning preferences that participants bring to the course. Knowing about our students helps us develop appropriate learning goals and activities, and anticipate and plan for participant reactions and interactions in the course.

Multiple Social Identities and Positionality

Participants' various social identities and positionality within matrices of domination and subordination are important for numerous reasons. Social identities shape participants' lived experiences and relationship to the issue being explored. Those who have multiple subordinated identities often bring a different world view and different needs to the course than participants with a single or no subordinated identity. In a sexism course that is multiracial with a mix of sexual identities, for example, we can anticipate and provide ways to explore how participants encounter sexism differently through their diverse experiences with heterosexism and racism (among other forms of oppression). Instructors also can be attuned to possible feelings of isolation or hyper-visibility, depending on the makeup of the group or the organization in which the class is being offered—for example, being one of the few Latino/a students or staff in a predominantly white course or institution.

While we should not assume *how* participants' social identities shape their knowledge, experiences, and perspective, we can recognize that identities do inform the way they relate to the issues. Facilitators can anticipate dynamics between and among people from privileged and marginalized groups and design accordingly. Some design strategies that facilitators can tailor to the specific needs of individuals and groups include explicit class agreements that address power dynamics and different styles of communication, caucus groups, where participants from the same identity group can share experiences with each other, experiential activities that actively engage participants, process questions that include various degrees of complexity, and choices of readings and assignments tailored to the particular group.

Social Identity Development

We can expect that participants will be at different places in their social identity development related to different forms of oppression. (Chapter 2 provides a more thorough discussion of social identity development theory.) Social identity development helps us understand how students enter our classes with different levels of awareness of their own social identities in relation to larger social structures of privilege and oppression. Participants in earlier phases of identity development may have done little critical thinking about their social identities and are likely to be operating from the ideology and values of the dominant culture. Participants in other phases of growth may be more conscious of their social identities and may be more focused on resisting the dominant paradigm and changing systems they see as oppressive.

Reflecting on where participants are in their individual social identity development allows us to understand how participants from the same social identity group may have very different reactions to the same content. For example, an incident where a young black man is seriously injured by a white police officer may be viewed differently by two students who are both African American, depending on their positionality and prior knowledge. A black male student who grew up in a predominantly white, affluent neighborhood, and who has had no personal interactions with police, may view this situation as an isolated incident and the behavior of one bad cop; while another black male student who is an African American Studies major, and/or who has had similar dealings with police, may see this as a continuation of a history in which police victimize and subordinate black people. While social identity development theory is not a diagnostic tool, it can help us anticipate dynamics among participants at similar and different points in their process, consider how to meet their diverse learning needs, and facilitate class dynamics more skillfully.

Interests and Motivations

Each participant brings to the course or workshop a unique combination of work and life experiences. Insight into participants' personal and professional interests and motivations can help us shape learning activities, supplemental materials, and group experiences to be as relevant as possible to participants' lives and future goals. For example, are participants graduate or undergraduate students? Traditional or nontraditional age, or a mix? Experienced with or new to social justice content? Is the course/workshop required or voluntary? Such information can help guide pedagogical choices, too. If the course includes a variety of participants, the use of caucuses or work groups based on majors, career orientations, or job roles may be helpful to promote a sense of applicability and connection to participants' interests.

Previous Experiences and Comfort

Participants generally will have had varying opportunities to develop personal awareness and to think critically about social justice issues. For some participants, this is their first time exploring these topics and learning in a diverse group. Others may have grown up in families that talked comfortably about this subject matter and may have lots of experience discussing controversial topics. Some people may have had very positive (even transformative) experiences in social justice courses or workshops, while others may have had very negative ones. Some participants are used to being in an academic setting and debating views, while others are less familiar with formal educational environments.

In some settings, participants may not expect to be engaged actively or experientially. Consequently, an activity may feel risky and emotionally challenging to some participants but not to others. Particular pedagogical strategies can allow for different levels of comfort, such as ensuring that there is time for personal reflection or sharing in pairs before asking people to contribute to a whole-group discussion. Recognizing differences in readiness and experience can help us design learning experiences that foster participation by everyone and provide levels of challenge that promote learning for all.

Relationships Among Participants

Another aspect to consider in designing classes/workshops are the organizational levels and type of relationships among participants. Past, present, and future relationships of participants can directly affect current group dynamics. Differences in power, placement in the organizational hierarchy, or educational attainment can lead participants to have varying degrees of confidence that it is safe enough to be open about their experiences, engage in large-group discussions, or participate in personally revealing learning activities. For example, participants from the same department or work setting who hold different statuses may have concerns about whether what they say and do will be used against them by supervisors or higher-ranking colleagues. Feelings of vulnerability may make it seem too risky to be direct and honest about feelings, experiences, and perceptions in front of other participants. Individuals in high-level positions as well may not want to appear ignorant or vulnerable in front of those they supervise.

It is important to understand the relationships that participants bring into the room with them. Are the participants strangers or an ongoing work group? Do some participants directly supervise others? Have the participants had prior experiences with each other that may have already built trust or called it into question? Knowing something about the participants' prior experiences with each other helps us to plan accordingly. There may be a greater need to include writing exercises, such as brief response exercises or journaling, or more paired discussions in which participants select their own partner. Caucus groups—homogeneous groups organized around particular identities, such as white and people of color/multiracial caucus groups to discuss racism—offer an excellent opportunity to aggregate insights and perspectives that individuals may feel too vulnerable to offer personally in a mixed group. Caucus groups typically report back in an anonymous way key points to the larger group so the group as a whole can learn from these insights.

Accommodations / Modifications

By knowing about participants, we can better anticipate and design learning experiences that will accommodate individual learning needs. The presence of international participants for whom English is not a first language, or participants with learning disabilities, may require that we make modifications to ensure an equitable learning experience for all. For example, this may mean modifying the formats of readings, videos, and class activities. Universal Design (discussed in detail in Chapter 9) is a useful model to ensure that all students can fully benefit and participate.

Pre-assessment Options

One way to obtain relevant information is to use classroom assessment techniques as described by Angelo and Cross (1993), such as a prior learning survey or brief "minute paper" exercises. For example, it may be helpful in a variety of instructional settings to ask participants to fill out an inventory or profile in which they identify their social group memberships and prior experiences in social justice education courses or trainings. Informal pre-assessment activities can be completed beforehand; for example, facilitators can interview participants individually before the session or convene a focus group with representative class members. If that proves impractical, facilitators can send out a brief individual survey in which participants describe their prior experiences, hopes, and fears, and learning goals for the upcoming class or workshop. In a similar way, having participants complete a brief quiz on prior knowledge can provide a sense of the range of understanding that participants are likely to bring to the topic of the class or workshop. Facilitators can also talk with individuals who are knowledgeable about social justice issues and familiar with participants or the community from which they come (Angelo & Cross, 1993).

There are many structured activities that can be used in the initial session to help students learn each other's names, get to know a bit about each other, and give the facilitator a chance to get a better sense of participants' prior experiences, expectations, and views. For example, Chapter 5, *Racism and White Privilege*, uses an activity called the "Prevalence of Race Continuum." This activity asks participants to respond to a series of statements ("You speak a language other than English at home"; "You have studied people who look like you in history class"; "You have ever felt racial tension in a situation and were afraid to say anything about it") by moving to signs in the room that say "True for Me," "Not True For Me," and "Neutral/Don't Know." This activity is a relatively low-risk way to get into the topic of race and lets the facilitator get a sense of who is in the group and their experiences with the topic of race. Curriculum adjustments can then be made based on the information about student identities, experiences, and interests gleaned from these activities.

DIMENSION 3: CURRICULUM—WHAT WE TEACH

The third dimension addresses choices instructors/facilitators make about what content, perspectives, and voices to include in the course. Three broad goals for social justice education courses are to increase personal awareness, expand knowledge, and encourage action. The relative emphasis we place on each of these goals will vary with the specific learning goals for a particular workshop or course. For example, with novice groups, it may be useful to focus on developing personal awareness and knowledge of social justice content, and select curriculum materials that provide information and help participants reflect on their own experiences in relation to that content; whereas with an experienced group, it may be more useful to focus on how to apply and take action on what the participants have learned, and select curriculum materials and content that serve that goal.

Establish Learning Outcomes

It is important that social justice educators have clear and realistic learning outcomes for the whole course or workshop, for each module/session, and for the individual activities we use. While it can be tempting to build curriculum around particular activities that we find exciting, instruction should be driven by our goals for learning, not activities. Establishing learning outcomes offers benefits for both participants and instructors. Facilitators will be better organized and prepared to communicate to participants what is most important to learn and why. We are also better able to communicate our expectations for how participants will demonstrate successful progress toward these learning goals.

Fink (2013) suggests three questions for developing learning outcome goals. The first question, *What do you want learners to know?* addresses cognitive learning goals and communicates what is most important for participants to know by the end of the course or workshop. The second question, *What do you want learners to be able to do?* addresses kinesthetic learning goals and communicates the skills in which participants are expected to demonstrate proficiency by the end of the course. The third question, *What critical perspectives do we want learners to understand and practice using?* addresses the particular dispositions (sometimes referred to as habits of mind) of social justice education. For example, instructors may want participants to develop and demonstrate dispositions of critical self-reflection and the ability to use a social justice/equity lens to analyze situations thoughtfully.

Clear, realistic, and flexible learning outcome goals help facilitators make decisions more effectively in the moment and as the course unfolds to assess whether or not the group is on track. Sometimes facilitators need to adapt learning goals based on what they learn in the process of working with participants. Having clarified beforehand the priorities related to content, skills, and values, instructors can more easily distinguish what comments, questions, and activities are most central to student learning and which are not. This helps to assess if a question or activity, albeit interesting or fun, may be at best optional, or at worst a digression or distraction, from what is most important and central to the course or workshop focus.

Choosing Activities and Materials

Based on the learning outcomes, facilitators can identify instructional materials and activities that best match the needs of the group. As instructors decide on materials, it is useful to consider such questions as: *Who is included? What is included? How is it included? From whose perspective?* and *Using what sources?* For example, in a course that addresses LGBTQ issues, are a range of people's experiences included? From whose perspective are these issues being examined? Are readings or films written or produced by LGBTQ people? Are LGBTQ people seen only as victims, or are examples of strength, resilience, resistance, and change included? Instructors should always avoid content that presents people from disadvantaged groups in tokenized, stereotypical ways, and seek materials that reflect the diversity of experiences within a social identity group. In making these choices, we benefit as instructors from being mindful of how our own social identities, knowledge base, and values influence our decisions about what to include or not.

Context

Program, department, institutional, community, and/or discipline-specific expectations may also shape learning outcome goals. Curricular goals in many pre-professional programs (nursing, social work, engineering, and teacher education) may reflect both institutional and national professional accreditation guidelines. For example, courses in social work or education may be expected to address specific learning outcomes established by their national accrediting bodies. Grassroots and community organizations may have a different set of expectations and goals than university settings. It is important to understand the context for which the course or workshop is being designed in order to design curriculum appropriately.

DIMENSION 4: PEDAGOGY—HOW WE TEACH

The fourth dimension addresses how facilitators engage with participants, with the content and with each other to promote learning. The degree to which this is done successfully determines whether an inclusive teaching and learning environment will be created and sustained. Social justice and diversity courses/workshops can be transformative experiences. However, such growth comes only after confronting and critically analyzing previously held concepts, theories, and beliefs. The process of addressing what may well have been limited or missing information, unconscious or unintentional bias, and the feelings attached to such positions is both an affective and cognitive process. How instructors model self-reflection, critical analysis, and openness to feelings and ideas is as much a part of the growth experience for students as the theoretical content.

Utilize a Range of Appropriate Pedagogical Strategies and Approaches

Facilitators, as do all people, have learning style preferences, and unless we make conscious choices, we may fall into teaching in ways that reflect our learning style preferences rather than meeting the needs of the group. Effective educators learn to utilize a range of pedagogical strategies to meet the needs of a range of learners as well as to help them stretch and expand their repertoire. The work of Bloom and Krathwohl (1956) on learning taxonomies and Kolb (1984) on learning style preferences offer useful frameworks for designing and facilitating social justice educational experiences.

Bloom and Krathwohl (1956) developed a model to show how learning progresses systematically and identified three domains of learning: cognitive (intellectual), affective (social–emotional), and kinesthetic (skills and behaviors). Further research on this model has shown that sustained learning happens most when learners are appropriately engaged across all three domains simultaneously (Anderson & Krathwohl, 2000; Bloom & Krathwohl, 1956). An example of socio-emotional learning might be to ask participants to purposefully connect with someone whose experiences and perspectives differ from their own. Cognitive learning may be exemplified by listening to a lecture, reading assignments, or learning new theories and definitions. Kinesthetic learning can be seen in experiential activities that enact and explore the dynamics of oppression, such as using role-playing to explore different perspectives, and using music and art to express learning. Kinesthetic activities can be invaluable in helping learners synthesize and integrate skills, practice new behaviors, and process emotions:

- Simulations and speak-outs, for example, engage participants in a direct and concrete manner (*concrete experience*).
- The processing questions that follow an activity, film, or lecture utilize *reflective observation*.
- Conceptual models such as the Five Faces of Oppression or Cycle of Socialization employ *abstract conceptualization*.
- Action projects that ask participants to apply learning to their particular contexts exemplify *active experimentation*.

Physical Environment and Logistics

How we teach particular content and the specific activities we choose also depend on the physical environment and the timing of the class or workshop. It is helpful for facilitators to consider the following questions:

- *What is the space like? Is it stadium seating with unmovable chairs or open space with flexible seating?*

- *How well does the space lend itself to different kinds of groupings, experiential activities, and use of educational technology?*
- *What kind of technology is available for us and for students?*
- *Will the design of the physical structure present any challenges to access, sightlines, and mobility for students?*
- *What time of day is the session? Early morning, late afternoon, or evening when energy may be low?*
- *What activities or events immediately precede or follow that may affect participants' engagement? For example, is the class right before lunch or following another long class?*

STRUCTURING ACTIVITIES

As mentioned above, we believe that it is important for social justice educators to have clear learning objectives for the activities we use and explicit criteria for determining how students will measure progress toward these goals. In general, the internal structure of activities follows a basic progression such as the one shown in Fig. 3.2.

1. Identify Key Concepts and Establish Learning Objectives and Evaluation Criteria
2. Establish How Learners Will Demonstrate Progress
3. Select or Design Learning Activities and Allot Time for Each Activity
4. Organize Directions and Procedures for Each Activity and Gather Equipment and Materials Needed
5. Develop Processing Format and Questions for Each Activity
6. Sequence Learning Activities

Figure 3.2 Steps in Structuring Activities

1. Identify key concepts and establish learning objectives and evaluation criteria.

Given the vast amount of material on any social justice issue, instructors need to identify the main ideas they want to address. Key concepts introduce new information or conceptual frames for participants to use in examining course content, issues raised in discussion, and their own experiences. In an Ableism class, for example, participants may be introduced to the concept of stereotyping by exploring stereotypes of people with disabilities and examining the roots of these stereotypes historically and in their own socialization.

It is important that social justice educators have clear learning objectives for each of the activities used in order to establish criteria for determining whether or not we have been successful in meeting our goals. Instructors should also be intentional about the purpose of a particular activity so they can facilitate it effectively.

2. Establish how learners will demonstrate progress.

It is essential to identify how students will demonstrate successful progress toward the key learning goals by the end of the course or workshop. Participants will value a clear explanation of what is expected of them and how their progress will be assessed. If you are teaching a course for credit, the students can benefit from knowing the required assignments, seeing models of exemplary work, and having a rubric that describes levels of success. In other settings, participants can develop action plans to demonstrate what they have learned and report on their progress.

3. Select or design learning activities and allot time for each activity.

Each learning activity is a structured interaction with one or more key concepts. As discussed earlier, knowing our students is an essential first step in choosing relevant and developmentally appropriate learning activities. Examples of activities include: role-plays, case studies, simulations, brainstorming, interactive lecture, video, small- or large-group discussions, worksheets, or writing prompts. Activities are generally designed to engage participants with the issues experientially, cognitively, and/or emotionally, and provide ways for them to interact with the content, each other, and with us as instructors at different points in the course. Some questions that can help guide the selection of activities include:

- *What is the composition of this particular group of participants?*
- *What range of prior knowledge and experiences might they bring to this activity?*
- *How does this activity align with and advance progress toward one or more key learning goals?*
- *How does this activity fit with what participants have just been doing and with what they will be asked to do next?* (Later in the chapter, we will discuss sequencing learning activities.)

It is important to anticipate and allocate sufficient time for the full activity, including processing the activity and addressing questions or concerns that may emerge from the group. It can be easy to underestimate how long it will take to complete and then debrief an activity sufficiently, especially for facilitators who are new to experiential learning or to the specific activity. If too little time is allocated for processing and synthesizing the learning outcomes that the activity is designed to promote, participants will be left to make sense of activities on their own without the benefit of facilitator guidance and the perspectives of other participants.

While there are no explicit rules about timing, we suggest that facilitators initially plan to debrief or process an activity for about three times the amount of time the actual exercise or activity takes to do. The more experience with a specific activity, the better able a facilitator will be to judge what students will likely need. It is helpful to provide participants with estimated time frames for each activity, while noting that these can be modified if needed. Leading thoughtful and probing discussions after an activity is at the heart of facilitation in social justice education courses and can often make the difference between high-quality and superficial learning.

4. Organize directions and procedures for each activity and gather equipment and materials as needed.

To facilitate a successful activity, facilitators need to become familiar with the procedures of the activity and to develop directions that will guide participants through a clearly defined and logical sequence of learning. When introducing an activity, it is important to communicate what the learning objectives are, how these fit into the overall curriculum, why this activity is relevant to their learning, and what is expected of them as participants.

It is also important to assemble ahead of time and in the right quantities what participants may need (e.g., directions, handouts, newsprint, videos, scissors, masking tape, index cards, post-its, supplemental resources) in order to complete activities. Additionally, make sure to set up and test technology beforehand.

5. Develop processing format and questions for each activity.

Processing refers to the systematic and guided reflection that follows an activity. The steps involved in processing often include time for individual reflection and analysis (often done in small- and large-group discussions). The goal of processing is to help participants build on prior knowledge, reflect on their learning, construct personal meaning, identify questions and contradictions, and consolidate new learning. Processing also helps facilitators assess how well participants are making sense of an activity and key learnings.

Before asking students to participate in discussions, a brief writing prompt can be used to give participants the opportunity to first reflect individually on how they felt about the activity and what they learned. This strategy can be particularly valuable for students who are shy or prefer time for reflection before engaging with others. Discussions are important opportunities for participants to deepen analysis of the activity and the meanings they draw from it. Discussions can take place in pairs, small groups, or caucuses, depending on the activity. Through discussion, participants can clear up points of confusion, share observations, and receive feedback from us and other participants. In discussions, it is important to normalize respect for the expression of divergent perspectives while also encouraging students to challenge their own and others' thinking.

After a period of personal reflection and group discussion—which match the learning style modes of *concrete experience* and *reflective observation*—it is time to shift the dialogue toward *abstract analysis* of the oppression issues raised in the activity by inviting participants to discuss how the activity illustrates particular dynamics of oppression. We invite them to identify questions, contradictions, or insights raised by the activity, and to discuss connections to other concepts. For example, following a role-play about sexual harassment, we might ask participants, "How did the actions of men and women in this role-play reflect gender socialization?" "In what ways are the power dynamics in this situation similar to other forms of oppression?" "How might the experiences of women from different racial groups compare in this situation?" Participants can also be asked how they might apply the learnings from this and other activities to their lives.

6. Sequence learning activities.

We consider several factors in selecting and sequencing activities so that the overall flow of the course makes sense to participants. Careful sequencing also enables us to introduce concepts and activities in an incremental way that builds upon student prior awareness and learning at different phases of the course (Brooks-Harris & Stock-Ward, 1999; Weinstein, 1988).

Lower to higher risk. Learners need to feel safe enough to express and examine deeply held feelings, confusions, and assumptions about oppression issues. Lower-risk activities in the beginning of a social justice education course are designed to help participants get acquainted, develop a sense of group cohesion, practice interaction guidelines that support honest engagement and learning, and acquire some basic concepts and information before moving to activities that require more risky disclosure of feelings and perspectives. Moving from individual reflection to discussions in pairs or small groups before engaging in whole-group discussions is also a way to progressively increase the level of risk and to build in support as discussions proceed.

Concrete to abstract (or abstract to concrete). This sequencing principle reflects our belief that participants learn best when their understanding of oppression is firmly rooted in concrete experiences and examples that provide a foundation for analysis of abstract concepts, theory, and the multiple levels on which oppression operates. Participants can then examine material in the context of concrete examples that illustrate the theoretical ideas being discussed. For instance, in exploring the portrayal of a marginalized group in the media, participants could be asked to watch TV shows and note the ways members of that group are portrayed (concrete). Then they could read an analysis of how that group has historically been and is currently reflected in the media, and consider the sociological significance (abstract) of the way the group has been reflected in the media. It may make sense to start with the abstract and then connect it to concrete examples when there is limited time or participants are particularly interested in theory or expert opinion.

Personal to institutional/cultural (or institutional/cultural to personal). In most of our courses, we begin with personal content, then introduce an institutional and cultural focus. We start with a personal focus because this level is more accessible to participants for initial exploration of the topic. After examining their own experiences and socialization, they can consider new information (e.g., readings, lectures, and discussions) that asks them to reflect critically on assumptions and experiences using new information and conceptual frameworks that explore how oppression operates on institutional and cultural levels. In some cases, it might be more appropriate for a group to start with the institutional/cultural and then move to the personal if a broader perspective would be useful first.

Difference to dominance (or diversity to social justice). This sequencing principle first focuses on helping participants describe and understand their own experiences as members of different social groups and listen to others in the course share their experiences and perspectives. The focus is on respecting, understanding, and acknowledging difference. After this exchange, the concepts of dominance, social power, and privilege are introduced to help participants understand that difference is not neutral, and that social groups are valued differently and have greater or lesser access to social and personal resources and power.

What? So what? Now what? These questions are a handy shorthand for how to sequence and organize processes as well as content. The first question, *"What?"* asks what knowledge and awareness we want participants to gain. The second question, *"So what?"* helps students understand *why* this information or awareness is important or relevant. And the third question, *"Now what?"* addresses the implications of what participants have learned and the next steps to be taken given this new knowledge and awareness.

Other considerations related to sequencing ensure that activities are varied. Instructors need to balance activities that allow participants to move about (active), such as experiential exercises and role-plays, with ones that require more sitting and listening (passive), such as lectures and movies. How students are grouped, such as individual reflection, paired sharing, and small-group and large-group activities also need to be rotated.

DIMENSION 5: CLIMATE AND CLASSROOM DYNAMICS

The previous four dimensions (i.e., "Who we are as instructors," "Who are our students," "What we teach," and "How we teach") each affect how participants experience the learning environment of the course or workshop. We suggest climate and classroom dynamics be considered a fifth dimension since both are so central in social justice education and are shaped by the other four dimensions. Some questions that can help identify important factors of climate and classroom dynamics include the following:

- *Do all participants feel heard and respected?*
- *Do participants see us as trustworthy and knowledgeable?*
- *Are participants able to engage with each other in ways that support learning?*
- *Do the content and the pedagogy feel relevant and culturally inclusive?*

The better the facilitator is at creating and sustaining an inclusive climate—by designing and implementing structures and activities that enable participants to engage honestly and thoughtfully with course material and each other—the more likely participants will be open to express and explore unexamined beliefs and values, and learn.

Making adjustments as the class unfolds. More times than not, the design that instructors have prepared prior to the start of the course requires adjustment once the course begins. The flexibility to make needed design adjustments based on what is happening in the moment is an essential skill. Many factors can necessitate redesigning a course. Pre-assessment information about participants may be incomplete or inaccurate. Incidents in a class may require a change in design to capitalize on a spontaneous learning opportunity or "teachable moment" that presents itself during the class. Student expectations for the course may not match the design. Activities may take longer than the time allotted for them in the original design and instructors need to change plans as a result. Informal student evaluations in the midst of the course may signal the need to alter the design. In all of these cases, it is necessary to reevaluate the design and decide how to make adjustments that will maintain the flow of the course while addressing the essential key concepts and learning goals.

Designing for accessibility. Universal instructional design (UID) is a useful planning model for making social justice education courses accessible to a broad spectrum of participants with and without disabilities (Burgstahler & Cory, 2008). Universal instructional design is an adaptation of the universal design model used to enhance architectural accessibility in the physical environment. Just as ramps and automatic doors for building entrances, books on tape, and auditory signals at traffic lights are useful to everyone, UID is intended as a guide for curriculum planning to serve the needs of all participants. Rather than focus on accommodating "special needs," UID principles are integrated into the planning process for all courses. For example, instructors using UID principles routinely ensure the following in their course planning: Wheelchair-accessible spaces, accessible and gender-neutral toilet facilities, instructional materials in a variety of formats (e.g., large print, audio, closed-captioned), adaptable activities (e.g., stand up or raise hand), and flexibility in time for students to complete tests and assignments. Making sure that all aspects of the learning environment are accessible to all participants is essential (Burgstahler & Cory, 2008).

The range of potential disabilities may make it impossible to pre-plan for all of them, but UID principles call on instructors to plan for as many disabilities as are reasonable. As a routine aspect of pre-assessment, instructors should ask participants in each class about their specific learning needs, either before the course begins or at the first class meeting. By incorporating these principles in course planning, instructors are far better prepared to provide appropriate accommodations when needed. Additionally, such efforts send a proactive message about the instructor's commitment to providing an inclusive classroom where every student is welcome and supported to excel.

ASSESSMENT

An important part of design is developing ways to assess participant learning and course/facilitator effectiveness. Assessment and feedback strategies allow instructors to better understand and meet individual participants' needs as well as the needs of the group. Planning evaluation procedures as part of course or workshop design enables instructors to be intentional about selecting methods of assessment that match learning activities and align with the specific learning goals. Assessments can include formative and summative evaluations, and formal and informal mechanisms for feedback and evaluation, of the participants, the course or workshop, and the instructors/facilitators.

Student/Participant Assessment

Student/participant assessment can be accomplished through formative and/or summative evaluations.

Formative participant assessment. Formative assessment methods are designed to provide students the opportunity to receive regular, informal feedback on work in progress. Formative assessment strategies can be used to identify which learning activities successfully prepare students to demonstrate the knowledge and skills needed to meet the course/workshop goals. For example, at the end of a session, facilitators can ask students to write down one or two things they learned from the session and any questions or confusions they still have. Collecting such information at the end of a class or session will help the instructor prepare to address these issues in the next class or session.

Summative participant assessment. Summative assessment measures are designed to grade and/or evaluate performance for uses such as assigning final grades or evaluating participation in community or workplace learning experiences. Traditional examples of summative assessment measures include quizzes, mid- or final-term exams, and term papers. In other settings, they might also include case studies, videos, interview exercises, community service learning projects or other small-group assignments, journals, and reflective essays or action plans. Grades and evaluation should always be based upon assigned work and clear performance criteria. In college environments, this may include questions about assigned texts and other readings, preparation of homework assignments, and completion of in-class activities; written papers that follow a sequence of reflective questions or structured guidelines; and a final essay exam, based on broad conceptual questions prepared in advance that test participants' ability to effectively utilize new concepts and knowledge (Suskie, 2004).

We may disagree, even dislike and disavow, some of the views expressed by participants in these assignments, and we will always ask questions and/or give constructive feedback (Walvoord & Anderson, 2009). Course grades derive from evaluation and assessment activities that are clearly aligned with key outcome goals and learning activities. Students may be concerned about giving "politically correct" answers. A neutral grading scheme, based on work completed and knowledge demonstrated, rather than views or opinions, can be reassuring to students and a fairer basis for assessment.

Grade points and grade percentages can be set in advance for each assignment. Students may find it helpful to see models and examples of successful assignments. Our goal is that participants will demonstrate their ability to think critically, examine prior beliefs and assumptions, increase knowledge, grapple with theoretical and conceptual interconnections, recognize course concepts in real-world examples, and identify potential plans of action (Walvoord & Anderson, 2009).

Course/Workshop Assessment

In the same way participants benefit from feedback, it is important for instructors to gather feedback about the course or workshop as well. Such information can help us determine what works and what can be changed or improved for the future. It can also be a source of information about our strengths and challenges as facilitators. Like student assessments, course assessment can be undertaken using both formative and summative strategies.

Formative course/workshop assessment. Classroom/workshop assessment techniques provide participants the opportunity to give instructors feedback on what they do or do not understand and for instructors to get a clearer, real-time sense of the progress participants are making. Formative evaluation can be informal: asking open-ended questions such as, *"What learning activities have been most effective in helping you to learn more about ableism?" "What made these activities effective?"* and *"How comfortable do you feel participating in class at this point?"* We can draw upon anonymous feedback periodically throughout the course and do informal check-ins with students, especially when we notice issues such as reduced participation, hostility, confusion, or boredom.

Formative evaluation can also be formal: Instructors develop specific questions about learning activities, sequencing, reading assignments, and grading criteria, and ask participants to rate them on a Likert scale. Formative evaluation of student work has the advantage of enabling instructors to make mid-course changes in the content or learning activities based on how well students are making progress toward their goals.

Summative course/workshop assessment. Summative evaluation can make use of institutionally designed forms or those created by the instructor to evaluate the course/workshop as a whole. End-of-semester course-based assessment strategies provide a useful longitudinal perspective on what curricula, learning activities, and assessment practices work well for different students. Looking at student feedback on a course over several semesters can help instructors anticipate which particular topics or exercises will challenge students, refine assignments, and pilot innovative learning activities. Such reflection can also stimulate deeper insights into how a particular module, workshop, seminar, or course links to other courses, programs, and department and institutional learning goals (e.g., general education, disciplinary majors or minors, certificate programs, etc.).

Instructor/Facilitator Assessment and Professional Development

Instructor engagement in an ongoing self-assessment process can be extremely valuable. Instructors grow and develop the same way students do. We benefit from formative and summative feedback and a long-term perspective on our development. A number of resources can foster teacher critical reflection and growth. Two of the most popular and least-intrusive techniques are to keep a daily journal and to foster opportunities for informal debriefings and discussion with trusted colleagues. Whether teaching alone, co-facilitating, or team-teaching, you can develop an ongoing relationship with a trusted peer to provide valuable opportunities for reflection, review, and improvement (see Ouellett & Fraser, 2005, for a team interview guide).

An all-too-human tendency can be to skim over participant evaluations and zero in on any negative comments to the exclusion of everything else. However, it is important to reflect on and integrate the full scope of feedback. One strategy for doing this is to find time after the end of the course to sit down with the other instructor and the course evaluations and take note of the general themes of what the evaluators say went well and suggestions they made for changes or improvements in the course content and teaching.

Identifying what is going well so that you can continue those practices is as important as focusing on what needs improvement.

For instructors of social justice and diversity related courses/workshops, however, Student Evaluations of Teaching (SETs) and other forms of evaluation can be limiting in at least two ways. Research shows that women and people of color often receive lower course ratings in general (Amos, 2014; Hamermesh & Parker, 2005; Huston, 2006), and in social justice courses, this can be especially true. Participants bring their biases and projections that influence how they perceive and evaluate facilitators. The complexity of facilitating social justice courses, as well as the time it may take for students to grow and develop, may not be easily captured in the time frame in which students are asked to complete course evaluations. Courses that are required versus those that are elective may also receive lower evaluations. Give these realities, it is particularly important to be able to discuss and reflect on this feedback with trusted colleagues to help assess what is useful.

Together, summative and formative assessment measures of students, the course, and the instructor create a communication flow between the facilitator and participants, both during and after the course. Ongoing assessment allows for mid-course corrections on the part of instructors (e.g., the need to give more explicit directions or clarify expectations, provide more examples, clear up questions related to reading) and on the part of students (e.g., reflect on their pattern of contributions to discussions or small group projects, sharpen their theoretical understanding, or revise and resubmit written work). Such embedded assessment practices benefit participants and the overall course/workshop design process as well as instructor development.

SUMMARY OF DESIGN PRINCIPLES

We have offered the design tools in this section of the chapter as a guide to help instructors have confidence that what they have planned will enable participants to explore difficult social justice issues in the most constructive and supportive learning environment possible. We provided activity-sequencing guidelines to help participants understand the dynamics of oppression in their own lives and in the larger society. We hope the design principles described above will also be useful and adaptable for developing new designs for social justice education classes that meet the particular needs of the groups you teach. With practice, these principles can become a routine part of planning and a basis from which to create and explore new activities and approaches to social justice education.

FACILITATION PRINCIPLES

In this section, we hope to highlight facilitation as well as show how design and facilitation are interconnected. Planning and designing ahead of time provide the essential scaffolding and tools for learning. Once the course begins, facilitation issues come to the fore. Facilitation involves managing the group dynamics and guiding participants through activities and the learning process. There are many aspects to good facilitation that include both task and process roles. At different times, instructors may need to guide the discussion by asking questions, be a role model by demonstrating respectful communication or sharing personal stories, present information, manage interpersonal conflict, begin and end an activity, observe and name classroom dynamics, or offer conceptual analysis. One of the skills of good facilitation is being able to utilize the appropriate role and task when needed (see Griffin & Ouellett, 2007, pp. 97–106).

GENERAL FACILITATION STRATEGIES

Before we discuss specific facilitation strategies that may be useful to address particular situations, we share some approaches that can be helpful throughout a class or workshop. While responses are best when they are situational and contextual, these are some general strategies that are useful to keep in mind.

Seek Understanding Before Responding

In general, we want to make sure that individuals feel heard as well as ensure that we understand them correctly before responding. This approach allows us to develop more thoughtful and effective responses. Immediately challenging what someone says can heighten defensiveness and close people off to further discussion. Instead, facilitators can follow three steps: *Reflect, Question, and then Add.* To first paraphrase or repeat back in your own words what you heard someone say can be powerful. It allows individuals to know that they are heard, ensures that the facilitator accurately understands what participants are saying, and provides an opportunity for participants to clarify statements that may not convey their intention.

For example, the instructor might say, *"It sounds like you think that . . ."* or *"Let me be clear, you believe that . . ."* Next, ask questions to further clarify their perspective, such as: *"What led you to believe that . . .?" "Can you tell me more why you think that?" "Can you explain what you mean by that?"* Then, once individuals feel heard and the instructor has greater understanding of their perspective, the facilitator can decide on the most appropriate response. Some options might be to add information or correct misinformation, open it up to the class for other thoughts, build on the comment to move onto new topics, or simply thank them for sharing their view. The point is not to do this process in every situation in a rote manner, but to be mindful of being respectful and gaining clarity before replying.

Get Distance and Gain Perspective

Often when we are in the middle of a situation, we can get caught up in the immediate dynamics and do not see the bigger picture. Especially in complex or challenging moments, it can be useful to try to get some distance, intellectually and emotionally, and gain perspective. Warren refers to this as "getting off the dance floor and getting up on the balcony" (2005, p. 620). "From the balcony" we can better see patterns and dynamics. She encourages instructors to "listen to the song beneath the words." Distance can often help facilitators discern the underlying issues, what is really being communicated. Instructors can also gain perspective by taking a break to reflect on the classroom dynamics, closely attend to the communication and participation patterns and non-verbal behaviors to look for the deeper issues, take a few moments to breathe and refocus their attention, and talk with a co-facilitator or other colleague to process feelings and observations in the moment before reengaging.

Share Observations Non-Judgmentally

Simply stating what you notice in a neutral and non-judgmental way can bring issues to the fore and allow for their discussion in a more thoughtful way. Observations about group dynamics can help surface underlying feelings and assumptions that can promote greater learning. Participants can also be taught and encouraged to share their own observations in constructive ways. Some examples of observations might be, *"When Susan shared her powerful story, no one responded. I'm wondering how people are feeling?"* Or *"I've noticed that when I ask people to share an example of how they've experienced privilege, several people shared stories of how they've been marginalized. I'm wondering if it seems harder to think about one's privilege?"*

Consider Timing, Tone, and Word Choice

Whether reflecting back what a student says, offering a different perspective, or sharing an observation, the timing, tone, and word choice we use matter. These qualities can make the difference between sounding respectful and insightful or judgmental and disparaging. The timing of a comment can have very different impacts depending on where the group is in its group development. The following examples illustrate how facilitators can consider timing and tone in their interventions. In reference to sharing observations, initially instructors may share observations that are less threatening but help them assess the group, such as *"I notice people are very quiet. I'm wondering if people are reluctant to share their views or if people simply need a break."* At a later point, facilitators might make an observation that could have a deeper impact, for example, *"I notice that the spokespeople for the small group report–outs have all been men, even though men make up only a quarter of the class. I'm wondering what people make of that."*

Similarly, timing may affect how an instructor responds to a comment such as, *"I don't see color. I think we should just be color-blind and treat everyone the same."* At the beginning of the class, the instructor might say *"Thank you for sharing your perspective. That is a sentiment many people have. Throughout the class we'll be discussing why people believe that and the impact that approach may have on creating equity."* At this point, the instructor may not want to directly challenge the statement, but rather focus on encouraging people to share their views while indicating that this view will not go unexplored. Also, asking for other students to comment rather than the instructor can often expand the discussion. Later in the course, the instructor might respond to that statement by drawing on the class material and discussions and greater class cohesiveness to examine the problems with claiming a color-blind stance.

DESIGN AND FACILITATION AT DIFFERENT PHASES OF A CLASS/WORKSHOP: CONFIRMATION, CONTRADICTION, AND CONTINUITY

With these general facilitation strategies and design principles in mind, we next explore Kegan's (2009) framework of *confirmation, contradiction*, and *continuity* to highlight common design features and related facilitation issues and strategies that occur in different phases of a course. Kegan, a developmental psychologist, describes the changing ways people make meaning of themselves, others, and the world, and the environments needed to support this developmental process. We use Kegan's framework as a helpful heuristic for attending to the changes that occur over time in a social justice education course so as to anticipate the needs of participants at each stage in the process. The first stage, *confirmation*, highlights the need for creating a holding environment where participants can take risks and be vulnerable so as to be able to look at their own socialization and be open to learning about oppressive issues in which we are all implicated. Once a safe-enough holding environment is created, we move to the *contradiction* stage, where prior beliefs and understandings will be challenged and held up for examination. During this stage, we want to unsettle assumptions and encourage exploration, questioning, and risk-taking. The *continuity* stage addresses the need for closure and continuity beyond the course or workshop.

In this stage, we want to help participants pull together and summarize what they have learned, and plan for how they will act on what they have learned and continue learning once they leave the course. While we consistently see this progression from confirmation to contradiction to continuity in the course/workshop overall, we also see these stages occur and reoccur throughout the course/workshop as well, and we respond accordingly. For example, throughout the course or workshop, we can help participants make connections to how they might apply this information (continuity), or at particularly challenging moments in the course, we may include more ways to sustain a confirming environment (e.g., group building activities).

Table 3.1 shows design issues and facilitation strategies for each facilitating environment.

Phase One: Confirmation

From a social-psychological perspective, consciously or unconsciously, people develop and internalize a set of beliefs about social justice issues simply through living in this society. Each of us could be said to be *embedded* in a particular way of making sense of the world. Left unchallenged, this embeddedness leads us to take for granted our world view as given, natural, and true, as simply "the way things are." In the social justice education classroom, these beliefs will be exposed to critical examination and questioning, unsettling the "taken for granted" worldview. This challenge inevitably disturbs a person's equilibrium, can be experienced as threatening, and will often raise a person's defenses.

Corresponding facilitating environment

The way participants experience the environment of the classroom has a powerful effect on whether or not they are willing to grapple with conflicting information, cognitive dissonance, and internal disequilibrium. If the environment is perceived as too threatening, a person's defenses may become fairly rigid. They will tend to ignore challenges to their world view and rationalize conflicting information to fit their present belief system. In

Table 3.1 Facilitation and Design Issues at Different Stages

Facilitating Environment	Design Issues	Facilitation Strategies
Confirmation	• Introductions • Learning outcomes, agenda/syllabus, and expectations • Group norms for respectful interactions • Activities to develop a supportive and inclusive learning environment	• Set and model tone • Model self-disclosure • Acknowledge the significance of feelings • Ally fears and concerns
Contradiction	• Content that deepens or challenges current learning about oppression • Sharing of personal stories • Opportunities for full discussion and reflection	• Ensure equitable participation and constructive class behavior/dynamics • Surface different perspectives • Challenge inaccurate information and views • Manage conflict and different perspectives • Acknowledge and manage feelings • Utilize and address silence • Address avoidance • Reduce and manage resistance • Manage facilitator reactions
Continuity	• Identify actions for social justice • Identify support • Provide closure • Evaluate class/workshop	• Discuss appropriate action • Address need for support and potential changes in relationships • Deal with immobilizing feelings

other words, they may cling to their "comfort zone" and be unwilling to consider any new material or openly engage in activities.

However, if the environment is perceived as supportive, a person's defenses can be more permeable. In this case, despite the experience of internal conflict, the person may be attracted to new information and become willing to grapple with the contradictions and discrepancies they perceive. Facilitators are always balancing the need for both challenge and support in order to maximize participant learning.

It is common in social justice education for participants to want to feel "safe" or to create a "safe" environment. However, we know that people will rarely feel completely "safe," especially those from marginalized groups. The meaning of "safety" is often different for students depending on their social location(s), and instructors need to consider the differences in needs and experiences of students from dominant and subordinated groups (Sensoy & DiAngelo, 2014; Garran & Rassmussen, 2014). Some facilitators refer to creating a "safe enough" environment (Bell, 2010). Holley and Steiner describe a safe space as a "climate or environment where students are able to take risks, honestly and openly express their views, and engage in growth promoting learning without fear of psychological or emotional harm" (2005, p. 50).

We believe facilitators must maintain an environment that is respectful and inclusive, whether or not facilitators choose to use some version of the word "safe." Participants need to be able to express their thoughts, feelings, questions, and perspectives without being personally attacked or silenced. Facilitators also should create an environment where they can challenge language and behavior that is offensive or hurtful. We must help students understand the impact of their words or behavior, even if their intent is not to be harmful. Such a climate enables participants to be more open to critically examine their world views and take learning risks. Creating a supportive space for learning and growth is an ongoing process, not a discrete goal.

While we want all participants to feel that the class is a respectful and supportive environment in which they can actively engage, this does not mean they will never be challenged or uncomfortable. We believe that feeling uncomfortable at times is a valuable and expected part of an effective social justice education class. Such feelings of discomfort can be experienced intellectually (e.g., encountering a challenging new perspective, new information, or experience), emotionally (getting feedback from other participants about how one's behavior or attitudes affect others in the class), or physically (experiencing shortness of breath, accelerated heartbeat, or perspiring) and are important learning opportunities for all participants in the class regardless of their social identities. This discomfort can be the basis for intellectual breakthroughs, increased personal insight, and changes in behaviors, awareness, and actions. We can remind participants that discomfort is part of an ultimately growthful and liberating process.

We refer to these moments of discomfort as "learning edges" and invite participants to notice and explore when they are on a learning edge rather than retreat to their comfort zone of familiar beliefs and experiences. Differentiating "safety" and "comfort," and reframing discomfort as an essential aspect of learning in social justice education, helps participants to better understand their feelings and to reframe discomfort as an opportunity to learn. Learning to notice the signs of being on a learning edge is a useful mechanism for realizing when we care deeply about something or experience challenges to taken-for-granted assumptions. In social justice education courses, such self-awareness is an explicit learning outcome goal. At the beginning of the course, facilitators can explicitly ask students to consider how they typically deal with this type of discomfort and name strategies for how they can stay engaged when this occurs.

In a social justice education course, it is desirable that the facilitator get to know participants, help them get to know each other, and enable them to develop a secure enough sense of themselves as a group that they can relax into the learning opportunity. If we can establish a positive group atmosphere and develop trust at the beginning and reinforce it throughout, we can avoid some pitfalls and more easily manage issues that arise. Creating a constructive space entails developing trust among participants as well as with the facilitator. Establishing a confirming environment can greatly reduce resistance and other difficult dynamics, both at the onset and later on in the class.

For these reasons, the initial phase of a social justice education course is very important. Our goals in this phase are to create an environment in which participants feel *confirmed* and validated *as persons* even as they experience challenges to their belief system. We want to construct a community of learners that is supportive and trustworthy and that fosters positive interdependence, the sense that individuals are responsible for their own and other's learning. Our hope is that in such an environment, uncomfortable and challenging issues can be raised and explored, and participants can express discomfort, sadness, confusion, anger, and fear, and know they will be treated with dignity and respect.

Design Features of the Confirmation Phase

To create a *confirming* environment, we want to help people break the ice and become more familiar with each other. We also want to establish and model guidelines of listening respectfully and speaking truthfully from our own experience. We often identify stereotypes and assumptions that the culture fosters about different groups, and acknowledge the misinformation we all receive in order to make it possible to openly examine taboo topics. Once participants experience support and realize they are not expected to have all the answers, they can be confused or uninformed, and they are allowed to make mistakes despite their best intentions, they may be able to relax their defenses enough to engage with classroom activities and information that question their assumptions about social reality. Some specific design components of the confirmation phase include: 1) introductions, 2) learning outcomes, agenda/syllabus, and expectations, 3) group norms for respectful interactions, and 4) activities to develop a supportive and inclusive learning environment.

1. Introductions: Introductions of the instructors and participants recognizes the unique identity of each person and lets people know they will not be treated as anonymous, but are indeed central to the course. By learning each other's names and getting to know one another, the participants start to develop a sense of community and group cohesiveness. Participants begin to understand that they will be asked to learn about and listen to each other.

2. Learning outcomes, agenda/syllabus, and expectations: This component provides an explicit structure that participants can rely upon and can allay some fears as to what the course will entail. Participants can be informed of expected attendance, class participation, and assignments. The agenda, outcomes, and expectations can also be developed with or adjusted to meet the needs of a particular group. These components help participants anticipate what the focus of the course will be, have some sense of what will occur, and share responsibility for following and achieving these objectives. Participants can also begin to identify and develop their own goals for learning.

3. Group norms for respectful interactions: Participants come to social justice workshops and courses with widely varying prior experiences and degrees of knowledge. We assume that all participants have internalized oppressive messages from the dominant culture and lack accurate information about many social issues. Most have had few opportunities to think critically about their social identities and systemic inequalities, or to engage with people whose lived realities and perspectives may be very different from their own.

It is useful for both instructors and participants to anticipate and plan for the affective and cognitive dynamics that can arise when people express divergent perspectives on topics about which they have strong feelings and deeply held beliefs. We can suggest that participants engage with "critical humility" and openness and recognition that we all are in the process of learning. Students can be encouraged to be curious and ask questions to deepen their understanding of different perspectives and experiences instead of just countering with their own viewpoint. Creating a list of mutual expectations and guidelines for interaction, and asking the class to agree to observe them, is one convention that sets the stage for constructive interactions (see DiAngelo & Sensoy, 2014, and Garran & Rassmussen, 2014, for further discussion of guidelines).

In the process of developing these agreements, we can clarify with the group what is meant by different terms (e.g., respect), discuss differences in conflict and communication styles, and coach participants in strategies for successful intergroup dialogue. We can explicitly name the ways that power and privilege often play out in interactions among people from dominant and subordinated social groups, and ask participants to develop agreements that can mitigate or interrupt such interactions in the class. For example, one guideline might be "consider how your own social positionality (such as your race, class, gender, sexuality, ability status) informs your perspectives and reactions." As instructors, we can use group agreements to ensure that dynamics of power and dominance are not unintentionally recreated in our classroom discussions. We can hold students accountable for contributing to a climate in which everyone's participation is valued.

4. Activities to develop a supportive and inclusive learning environment: In addition to introductions, activities early in the course are designed to establish a norm of interaction and self-disclosure. These activities help create group cohesiveness and a sense that everyone has something to learn and contribute. Initial interactions should be lower risk so that participants can comfortably practice what for many might be a novel experience of sharing feelings and personal experiences in the context of a classroom or workshop. Pairs and small-group activities are good vehicles for this type of relationship-building. For examples, in several ism chapters, the activity "Common Ground" is used. This activity uses a list of prompts to identify commonalities and differences among group members.

Facilitation Issues and Strategies for the Confirmation Phase

Participants observe both what facilitators do as well as what we say. Some of the central facilitation issues in the confirmation phase include: 1) setting and modeling the tone of the class, 2) modeling self-disclosure, 3) acknowledging the significance of feelings, and 4) allaying fears.

1. Set and model tone: As previously discussed, it is critical in this initial phase to establish a constructive tone and practice using group agreements or guidelines. As facilitators, we attempt to model and support the norms we hope to establish. Co-facilitators are also role models in their interactions with each other, and should demonstrate respectful dialogue and an effective collaborative relationship. Some components of setting the tone include supporting risk-taking, modeling respect, and integrating humor and fun with serious issues.

Support risk-taking: As participants share their views, personal experiences, feelings, and questions in the initial class activities, facilitators can affirm and validate their willingness to take risks. We can reinforce the notion that there are no "stupid" questions. Simply stating, *"Thank you for sharing that"* or *"I appreciate your willingness to raise that issue"* conveys that we do, in fact, value their openness.

Model respect: Not only can we respond in positive ways when people take initial risks, but we can consistently model respectful interactions. This may include paying thoughtful attention to students as they speak, not talking over them, using their correct or preferred name and gender pronouns, and interrupting comments or behaviors from others that are dismissive or insulting. Additional strategies include building on students' comments, paying attention to equitable access to airtime, inviting quiet students or those who have not spoken yet to participate, and keeping activities generally on time.

Integrate humor and fun. Creating an atmosphere that is both serious and light helps to set a friendly and supportive tone. We want to treat social justice content as the serious issue it is, while incorporating activities that include humor and playfulness that can keep students engaged, release feelings, build community, and challenge the assumption that learning about oppression is simply depressing; working for justice can be joyful, too.

2. Model self-disclosure: When instructors model appropriate levels of self-disclosure and the kind of responses sought in a particular activity, it demonstrates for participants how to share about oneself and make personal connections with the content. It also builds rapport with participants and illustrates that it is safe for them to share about themselves. Appropriate self-disclosure on the part of the facilitator serves the learning needs of the students, not the personal development of the instructor.

3. Acknowledge significance of feelings in the learning process: As previously discussed, social justice education is both a cognitive and affective process. During a social justice education course, many different feelings arise as participants grapple with perspectives and information that challenge their previous understanding. It is important to acknowledge that these feelings are a natural and appropriate part of the learning process. Providing participants with some guidance for how to recognize, listen to, and learn from feelings encourages their expression in ways that help rather than hinder learning. The introduction of concepts such as "learning edge," "comfort zone," and "triggers," for example, provides participants with a language and a process to use in examining and making sense of feelings that arise. This can be an opportunity to clarify the difference between "safety" and "comfort." Being uncomfortable is a typical and productive reaction when confronting contradictions and challenges to what we have learned in the past and is an essential part of confronting social injustice. Discomfort is not necessarily a sign that we are unsafe or in danger.

4. Allay fears and concerns: Some fears or worries may be addressed when the learning outcomes, agenda, and expectations are presented and discussed. Instructors also can speak specifically to some of the concerns people may have, such as worrying about being blamed or shamed for their ignorance or for being part of the privileged group, or being unsupported when offensive stereotypes about one's group are made by other participants. We can communicate our assumptions that highlight our approach of not blaming people for how they were socialized or for not having accurate information, encouraging responsibility once we become conscious, recognizing that we all have work to do to overcome the ways we internalize and perpetuate oppression, and that we all have a role to play in its eradication. We can also reiterate (and model) to participants that we will enforce the agreed-to guidelines that interrupt disrespectful, inequitable, and oppressive group dynamics. Participants can also be reminded that they can have the option to pass or participate at a level that feels appropriate for them.

Phase Two: Contradiction

If we have succeeded in creating a supportive environment, participants may now feel secure enough to open up to contradictions to their old belief system and begin a process of exploration, to find their "learning edge" and live with the inevitable discomfort. They become willing to examine and differentiate ideas and feelings and try on different ways of making sense of the world. This process can be confusing, disorienting, and, at times, frightening. Participants might feel out of control, without known boundaries or familiar ground, and may experience a sense of loss or *surrender* as they literally "excavate the ground they stand on" (Barker, 1993, p. 48).

As they learn new information, they may also experience strong emotions such as anger, resentment, and a sense of betrayal by those who were supposed to tell them the truth about the social world. At the same time, they may feel a sense of freedom as they consider, discard, and eventually construct new ways of making sense of the world or of conceptualizing and naming their experiences.

Corresponding facilitating environment

The supportive environment for the contradiction phase is one that allows participants to immerse themselves fully in whatever contradictions and conflicts arise as a consequence of engaging previously unknown ideas and exploring their own and others' feelings and experiences. The course content and process deliberately pose and explore contradictions, and encourage participants to make sense of the new material they encounter. This process is akin to Freire's notion of education for critical consciousness (1970, 1973).

At this point, the environment shifts. It does not overprotect or enable participants to avoid feelings of discomfort, confusion, fear, and anger. Such feelings are an inevitable and ultimately helpful part of the learning process. Through engaging with challenging information and participating in experiential activities, participants are encouraged to let go of the comfortable and familiar and explore new territory.

This phase is not only challenging for students—intellectually and emotionally—but often the most challenging for instructors as well, since we are creating dissonance and raising emotions through the information and experiences we provide. This phase requires skillful facilitation to process effectively. As students engage with material that is more personally challenging, and possibly encounter more conflict in the classroom or workshop, facilitators can revisit some of the activities and facilitation strategies utilized in the confirmation phase to help participants stay connected to each other, the instructor, and the material as they feel increasingly uncomfortable.

Design Features of the Contradiction Phase

Activities in the contradiction phase encourage participants to face the challenges posed by new information and different perspectives. Learning activities in the contradiction phase can focus on any of the several key concepts identified in Chapter 4 and exemplified in the course designs in this volume, such as socialization, historical legacies, and manifestations at the individual, institutional, and societal/cultural levels; power and privilege; and allies and advocacy. Some key design components of the contradiction phase include: 1) content that deepens or challenges current understanding, 2) sharing of personal stories, and 3) opportunities for full discussion and reflection.

1. Content that deepens or challenges current understanding: There are numerous ways instructors can offer students opportunities to deepen or challenge their current understandings. Readings, different types of media, experiential activities, presentations, panel discussions, guest speakers, field trips, and various discussion formats are some of the resources and approaches facilitators use.

2. Share personal stories/experiences: Asking participants to share their personal experiences with the content allows them to reflect on their own experiences and to listen to and reflect on the experiences of others. Hearing personal stories can be very powerful in supporting learning and changing attitudes and beliefs. Personal stories make abstract concepts concrete and can promote empathy (Bell, 2010; Eisner, 2002; Greene, 2007; Soohoo, 2006). For instance, hearing first-hand a gay student's experiences of harassment is often more evocative than solely hearing facts and statistics about bias incidents. Hearing a white person talk about coming to terms with white privilege and struggling to find responsible ways to be an ally will likely be more powerful than a list of directives.

3. Provide opportunities for full discussion and reflection: Facilitators can create a variety of structures that allow participants to deeply grapple with the content. We use a range of discussion formats, including whole-class, small groups, triads, and pairs to ensure that all participants have the opportunity to speak. Caucus groups create the space for people with a similar social identity to discuss their ideas, questions, and experiences with each other without relying on or worrying about the reactions from people with a different social identity. Instructors can ask students, both during and after class, to keep a journal or respond to prompts to further their personal reflection.

Because the activities in a social justice education course are designed to raise contradictions and challenge participants to rethink their understanding of social power relationships, discussions can be intense as participants engage with conflicting perspectives and challenging new content. We can scaffold activities and content by providing ample opportunity to process or collectively reflect on and discuss reactions to the activities. Processing is an intentional and systematic way to guide discussion of a class activity so as to encourage the expression of divergent perspectives, explore contradictions, and encourage participants to derive cognitive as well as affective understanding from the activity. After each class activity, we lead participants through a processing progression that typically begins with their own individual reactions to the activity, then guides them through more abstract analysis of the oppression issues raised in the activity, and finally focuses on how they can apply this new information.

Facilitation Issues and Strategies for the Contradiction Phase

As previously noted, the contradiction phase can pose some of the greatest challenges to facilitators. Instructors need a range of skills to handle the numerous dynamics that can occur and help ensure that the class remains a respectful and supportive environment where participants can take intellectual and emotional risks and engage deeply. Some key facilitation issues typical of the contradiction phase include: 1) ensure equitable participation and constructive class behavior, 2) surface different perspectives, 3) challenge inaccurate information and views, 4) manage conflict and different perspectives, 5) acknowledge and manage feelings, 6) utilize and address silence, 7) address avoidance, 8) reduce and manage resistance, and 9) manage facilitator reactions. Strategies for responding to participant reactions are also discussed in Chapters 5–12 in the context of specific single-issue courses/workshops.

1. Ensure equitable participation and constructive group behavior: As the course content and experiences get more challenging and the emotional reactions become stronger, facilitators need to ensure that the class remains a constructive learning environment. Facilitators need to carefully monitor and manage the group and power dynamics so that all participants continue to be heard. We can limit and ensure equitable amounts of airtime for participants. For example, when one person or a small group dominates discussions, or when some participants are always silent, the facilitator can make space for others to participate in a number of ways. Consider these examples:

- One participant has taken an active role in class discussions, contributing to every conversation. The facilitator says, *"Before we hear from you again, Steve, I'd like to see if some of the people who have not spoken up would like to say something."*

- The facilitator notices that a quiet participant has been trying to say something, but she keeps getting cut off by other, more active participants. The facilitator says, *"Maria, it looks like you've been trying to get into this discussion. What would you like to say?"*
- The facilitator notices that five participants have not said anything during large-group discussions. He says, *"Let's do a quick pass around the circle. Each person share a short sentence that describes your reaction to this activity. Choose to pass if you wish."*

The instructor may also use dyads for a brief amount of time to simultaneously get everyone in the group talking, or ask participants to respond to a brief writing prompt as a way to help them organize their thoughts and prepare to offer comments aloud.

In this phase, it is particularly important for instructors to pay attention to the power dynamics in the class. These patterns can be expressed in a variety of ways, such as students from dominant groups dismissing the personal experiences or views of people from marginalized groups or expecting them to speak for their whole group, or individuals from dominant groups feeling intimidated and afraid to say something wrong lest they be verbally attacked by individuals from the subordinated group or other members of their dominant group. While we want to encourage participation, we do not want to allow any student(s) to control, dominate, or subvert the class to their own particular agenda (Sensoy & DiAngelo, 2014). Participants can be reminded to use critical humility and encouraged to ask questions to better understand someone's perspective as opposed to just asserting their viewpoint. It can be useful for participants to practice just listening, especially to those from marginalized groups, before allowing dialogue. Facilitators need to enforce the agreed-upon guidelines if students act in ways that violate the norms and erode the learning community, or group members are likely to view the guidelines as fraudulent (see Bell, 2010, pp. 100–104). Instructors need to be especially sensitive to comments or behaviors that silence other students. Facilitators will often write up the agreed-upon norms and guidelines to post in the room. Then, when a challenge emerges, it is useful to go back to the posted agreements, talk about the specific guideline that may be relevant, and perhaps elaborate or add to it. The guidelines thus become a "living document" during the life of the learning community. Consider these examples:

- A participant rolls her eyes and looks away when a man tries to challenge her belief in the fairness of affirmative action programs. The facilitator says to her, *"We may not all agree, but we need to be able to disagree respectfully. We need to express our disagreement in ways that are consistent with our discussion guidelines."*
- A white student interrupts a black student who is describing an incident of racial bias by saying, "You're just playing the race card!" The instructor stops the white student and asks him to allow the other student to finish his story. During the subsequent discussion, the instructor asks the white student, *"Instead of challenging his story and analysis, is there a question you could ask that might help you understand why he experienced the situation as racially biased?"*
- A student reacts to another student by saying, "You're so homophobic if you believe that!" The facilitator responds, *"We agreed there will be no name calling. How else could you express your ideas without making it a personal attack?"*
- An upper-middle-class student, in response to a panel presentation by working-class activists, immediately starts to discount their experiences by saying, "My parents worked hard for what they have." The instructor intervenes and asks, *"Instead of negating what they said, let's first look at what was new information for you."*

Instructors can highlight and affirm behaviors that positively contribute to the class as a way to reinforce constructive group dynamics. In the contradiction phase, it is important to continue to validate personal risk-taking as the class goes more deeply into the subject. Instructors can support and encourage participants to take risks in exploring perspectives, feelings, and awareness that contradict or stretch their prior understanding. They can validate participants who express confusion or ask questions that reflect their personal struggle with issues discussed in the course. And they can acknowledge and appreciate comments and behaviors when students disagree in a constructive manner, support the learning of another student, or ask thoughtful and challenging questions that advance the conversation. Consider these examples:

- *"I know it was difficult to share that, but I appreciate your honesty."*
- *"When you asked that question, it really opened up the discussion in interesting ways. Thank you for raising that."*
- *"I know it's uncomfortable to look at our biases. I respect people's willingness to do this hard work."*

2. Surface different perspectives: Instructors need to not only ensure equitable and constructive participation, but to actively elicit a variety of perspectives so that different viewpoints can be openly aired and explored. When there is limited participation, the group misses out on learning from other's experiences and perspectives. Instructors should allow contradictions and tensions to emerge, and resist the tendency to smooth over tensions, resolve contradictions, or relieve uncomfortable moments in class.

These experiences are an essential part of the learning process in a social justice education course. As long as participants adhere to the agreements, the experience of discomfort with new perspectives and tension among different perspectives can help them work through their own learning. In addition, facilitators need to balance allowing the conversation to evolve and flow depending on the group while staying mindful of the objectives of the particular discussion or activity. Flexibility is important, as is ensuring that we are consciously leading the class in a direction that meets the learning goals and not simply getting distracted by tangents.

Invite and provide various viewpoints. Facilitators can actively solicit divergent perspectives by summarizing what has already been said and asking for other viewpoints or providing other perspectives and asking for students' reactions (whether as part of a discussion or in writing). Exposure to divergent perspectives enables participants to work with contradictions and have their own thinking challenged, clarified, and extended. Instructors can ask, *"What do other people think?"* or *"Some people believe that . . . what do you think about that?"*

Share facilitators' experiences. In addition to the students, facilitators can also share their experiences and perspectives in ways that can advance learning. Through talking about their own stories or views, facilitators can provide additional information, offer a missing perspective, and make it safer for others to share their thoughts and experiences. However, facilitators need to choose carefully when to disclose their personal reactions or stories, and be clear about the purpose of this disclosure. It is never appropriate for facilitators to work out their own issues during a class or workshop. This important work is better attended to at some other time. If facilitators tell too many personal stories or talk about their experiences too much, participants might begin to discount the course as the facilitator's "personal agenda," and it can subvert the focus from a participant-centered to a facilitator-centered environment. All personal disclosure by facilitators should be for the purpose of helping participants achieve a better understanding of the topic.

It would be disingenuous to pretend that a social justice education course is neutral or objective any more than are any other courses. Participants are correct in perceiving that there is a particular perspective represented in a social justice education course. It is essential, however, that there is room for all perspectives to be heard and challenged respectfully. When facilitators or participants squelch the expression of views or experiences that are counter to the underlying beliefs guiding the course, social justice education courses are vulnerable to charges of political correctness. We assure participants that we all have prejudices, assumptions, and limited perspectives, and we encourage them to see the course as an opportunity to consciously examine them. They can then choose views based on new information and understanding, rather than allowing our unexamined attitudes and beliefs to guide our thinking.

3. *Address inaccurate information and views*: As students share their views, inevitably they will express some erroneous or distorted information. It is important that these inaccuracies get addressed. We want to keep people engaged yet not allow incorrect or insensitive statements to go unchallenged. How a facilitator responds to inaccurate, or in some cases offensive, statements depends on numerous factors, including the effect of the statement on individuals in the group, the timing in the overall course and specific class, the facilitator's relationship with the individual, and the group dynamics. Sometimes instructors need to directly correct misinformation or curtail offensive remarks. Often, the approach described earlier of reflecting, questioning, and adding can be helpful to respond to inaccurate beliefs.

Reflecting: As we discussed earlier, reflecting can be a useful general strategy. In the contradiction phase, one of the most effective ways to encourage participants to think more deeply and critically is to reflect back what they say. Hearing their own words reflected back to them can enable participants to understand the impact of their statements and to identify underlying assumptions. Consider this example:

- The facilitator repeats a participant's statement, *"So, what you are saying is that poor and homeless people have the same opportunity for advancement as people who have more financial resources, they just need to try harder?"*

In some situations, when participants listen to their statement reflected back to them, they can hear their faulty logic and clarify their perspective. In many cases, reflection alone is not sufficient. Participants may say things that are factually incorrect and that reflect commonly held misconceptions. Inaccurate statements need to be addressed and corrected, not simply reflected. There are a variety of ways a facilitator can respond to erroneous beliefs, including asking questions, depersonalizing the comment and then addressing it, and directly correcting the statement.

Asking questions: Posing questions is often an effective way to challenge assumptions, solicit factual information, and redirect discussion. Rather than directly challenging participant perspectives through statements, questions can encourage participants to examine their own assumptions and values in a respectful way, and to differentiate between anecdotal and individual experience, and the sociologically and historically grounded experiences that are generally true of a group. Questions can also help participants understand when they are repeating an unexamined belief or perspective. One question we use is, *"Can you say how you came to this perspective?"* Examples of other questions include:

- *"What kinds of portrayals of Latino/a people do you see in the movies and on television? How do these portrayals affect your perception of what Latino/a people are like?"*

- *"What might be some other reasons that parents of low-income students don't come to school events besides that they are uninterested in their children's education?"*

Depersonalizing the statement: A facilitator can respond to an inaccurate or stereotypical comment directly and sensitively by first depersonalizing the statement and then focusing on the correct answer. The instructor can address the issue as a commonly held belief or connect it to class concepts. Consider these examples:

- *"John says he believes, as do many people, that people of color commit more crimes than do whites. However, as statistics from the Department of Justice show us . . ."*
- *"When we talked about structural racism, we talked about the disproportionate involvement of people of color in the criminal justice system. How does institutional racism contribute to the perception that people of color are more likely to be criminals?"*

Correcting: Sometimes it is useful, even essential, to directly intervene and provide accurate information. This is particularly important if the statement may be harmful or inflammatory to other participants. Consider these examples:

- A participant states his belief that gay men want to be women. The facilitator says, *"People who identify as another gender are called transgender. Transgender people can be gay, lesbian, heterosexual, bisexual, or may identify their sexuality in an entirely different way. Most gay men are as comfortable as heterosexual men with identifying themselves as men."*
- A student claims that women who are drinking at parties and get raped are just as responsible as the man for what happened. The instructor responds, *"It's never a person's fault for being sexually assaulted. Our laws and policies are clear that the alleged perpetrator is responsible for ensuring there is consent."*

Facilitators need to decide which strategies and combinations of strategies are most appropriate considering the particulars of a given situation. There is no simple formula. In some cases, we may feel stuck in the moment and unsure of how to respond to a comment that clearly needs a response. Even if we are uncertain about what to do, we cannot ignore statements that are toxic to the group and learning process. Some options can be to acknowledge the statement and its impact, and then create space to develop a response, either in the present or later on (below we discuss how to deal with facilitator reactions). Facilitators could state, *"Many people had a strong reaction to that statement"* followed by giving participants an opportunity to do a "one-minute paper"—writing their thoughts on what just happened and the effect it had, or doing a brief sharing in pairs. If the comment occurs at the end of a class, the instructor can follow-up on email or an online discussion format, or note that this will be discussed at the next meeting. The instructor can also bring in additional information at a following session and revisit the issue.

4. Manage conflict and different views: Conflict and disagreement can be healthy and play an important role in social justice education. Instructors often cite lack of preparation or skills for knowing how to effectively address conflict, and a concomitant fear of losing control of discussions, as primary obstacles to initiating a social justice education (see Chapter 12). Inviting conflict and emotional dissonance, other than in the most traditional forms of argumentation and debate, seems counterintuitive to maintaining "proper" classroom or workshop decorum. The initial response of many instructors to potential conflict in the classroom is to shut down any disagreement, ignore the emotional and affective tone in a class, and keep a tight focus on intellectual and informational content. In the social justice education classroom, conflict and dissonance are a valued, even necessary, part of the process that enable values, beliefs, and ideas to emerge so that different perspectives can be explored. Our goal is to work through immediate conflicts and emotions so as to understand the individual, institutional, and cultural implications of the topic at hand. We do so by encouraging participants to consider and analyze multiple perspectives on any given topic. Important learning opportunities are missed if participants do not have the opportunity to honestly express feelings, concerns, questions, and disagreements.

There are a number of things the facilitator can do to help ensure that conflict is constructive. First is to enforce the agreed-upon guidelines for interaction, particularly no personal attacks. In addition, the facilitator can slow down the interaction, making sure each person is heard before another person speaks. Often conflict will escalate and become unproductive if people do not feel adequately understood. Facilitators can paraphrase what someone says before another person speaks, or ask the next speaker to do so before adding to the conversation. They can ensure that people are not interrupted and have the opportunity to complete their thoughts. Using a "talking stick" or an object to hold if someone is the recognized speaker can also be helpful. If the conflict gets centered between just a couple of people, facilitators can invite other views or perspectives.

Facilitators can also take a break to give everyone a chance to reflect on the interactions, share their thoughts and feelings with a partner, or free write for a few minutes. We can then ask people to share their reflections. Facilitators can also note common ground and areas of agreement. We can also put the issues being discussed into broader context and relate it to the class concepts, moving it away from personal disagreements, such as, *"While you are raising different ways of addressing the gaps in educational achievement, you both agree that this is an issue that needs attention. You both recognize the role parents play in this process. Let's look at what we know about educational opportunity from the reading we have done."*

It is important that facilitators help participants achieve some degree of closure, not to enforce agreement or to answer all questions, but to help participants pull thoughts together so that they are ready to make a transition to the next activity or to end the class session. In summarizing a discussion, facilitators and participants identify themes that emerged, unresolved questions, insights gained, divergent perspectives, and other important points raised. Time to reflect enables participants to step back, summarize their learning, and develop cognitive as well as experiential understanding of the issues raised in the activity. For example, during a classism course, the facilitators might say, *"From this discussion it appears that we have several different understandings of how to define social class in this group. Can we name those differences?"* or *"I notice a conflict in this discussion between what many of us have believed about equal opportunity in the past and what we are beginning to see about the effects of class differences on economic opportunity."* We do not expect participants to end a discussion feeling that they have completely resolved their discomfort with different ideas and perspectives. Some disorientation is a sign that participants are grappling with new awareness and knowledge. We encourage them to notice discomfort, stay on their learning edge, and consider new ideas and questions rather than retreat to the comfort of more familiar perspectives.

5. Acknowledge and manage feelings: For some facilitators and participants, the expression of feelings in a classroom is an unusual experience. This is because traditionally, education environments have discouraged the public expression of emotions as inappropriate. Some participants (e.g., women and some ethnic and racial groups) have been penalized for showing emotions in the classroom and criticized as less rigorous thinkers, less analytical, or unable to frame an impartial argument (Rendon, 2009). In social justice education classes, many feelings arise as people deeply explore systemic inequality, such as anger, guilt, sadness, and frustration. While no one should feel that intense emotion is required for effective learning, all should be prepared for the expression of honest feelings that may arise at different times in the course, and remember that important learning can come from openness and listening closely to the experiences and feelings of others. Facilitators can help participants recognize feelings and manage them or work them through. They can remind students that feelings are a common and normal part of this process. Hearing from other people with similar feelings can be validating and make it easier for participants to accept their own reactions. Consider these examples:

- A participant begins to cry as she recalls how a younger brother with a developmental disability was teased by classmates at school. The facilitator says, *"It seems like that is still a painful memory for you. Thanks for telling us about this experience. It is a powerful reminder of how deeply name-calling can affect us. Do other people have similar memories?"*
- A facilitator asks participants to go around the circle and give a one-word description of what they are feeling in reaction to an intense video about the Holocaust.
- After a panel presentation by a group of people with disabilities in an ableism course, the instructor asks participants to think about or write down their feelings as they heard different panelists talk about how they deal with obstacles they face because of ableism, such as *"What feelings did you have as you listened to the panelists' stories?"* *"What did the panelists say about their experiences as people with disabilities attending this school that you had never thought about before?"*

Some students may become immobilized by feelings of guilt, or the fear of saying the wrong thing or revealing their prejudices. Facilitators can remind students that we are not at fault for having misinformation, and shift the focus to understanding our cultural conditioning. Personal sharing from the facilitators about their own learning process and errors they have made can help students work through these feelings. The introduction of a conceptual model can also provide participants with a way to understand emotions in a broader theoretical context, or it can focus the discussion to proceed more productively. For example, facilitators can refer to the oppression model, the cycle of socialization, identity development theory, or learning edge/comfort zone models discussed in the introductory module to help participants understand and normalize their experience (see Chapters 2 and 4). For example:

- A white participant is ashamed because she could not identify any African American historical figures on a short quiz. The facilitator responds, *"How does the cycle of socialization we talked about earlier help us to understand how we have been kept from knowing about cultures different from our own?"*
- An Asian American student who has struggled with perfectionism and thought it was her personal problem is relieved to learn about the model minority stereotype as a way to understand her experience in a broader context.

Participants may need support managing their feelings of anger or frustration. We can discuss how to appropriately express their anger at realizing the extent of the oppression they or others face by providing opportunities to share their feelings through class activities and finding other constructive outlets, such as speak outs, social change organizations, or support groups. We can assist students from privileged groups to deal with their guilt and help them transform guilt into taking accountable action. Instructors can encourage students to simply sit with their feelings for awhile, providing support and assurance that this is a normal part of the process. Models of social identity development (see Chapter 2) or other descriptions of personal growth regarding social oppression can offer students a vision of how feelings and views can be transformed in a liberatory way (Goodman, 2011; Warren, 2005).

6. *Use silence*: Facilitators and participants alike are often uncomfortable with silence in a classroom or workshop. It can be more helpful to students when facilitators wait after asking a question, rather than either answering their own question or posing questions in quick succession to fill a silence. In the social justice education classroom, silence can have many different meanings. Participants often need silence to think about new information or to articulate perspectives on an issue. A brief period of silence is useful to provide participants time to think through their perspectives, experiences, feelings, and ideas before launching into group discussions. This is especially important for participants whose first language is not English or who need time to reflect before responding.

Differentiating productive silence from bored or fearful silence is an important facilitator skill. Signs of a fearful or uncomfortable silence include lack of eye contact among participants, yawning, physical shifting and movement in seats, or tense expressions on faces. However, facilitators should not assume that a period of silence necessarily reflects fear, discomfort, or unwillingness to continue pursuing a topic under discussion. Silence can often be a learning opportunity and deepen the discussion. One strategy that is helpful for bridging these moments is a brief writing assignment—asking participants to write down their feelings at that moment or turning to a neighbor to share their thoughts—to provide a way to acknowledge and clarify reactions before moving on. Another strategy is to do a quick "whip" around the circle, in which each participant in turn says one word that describes their feelings at that moment. Sometimes simply commenting on silence opens the discussion, enabling it to restart and potentially deepen individual understanding. Consider these examples:

- In response to a processing question, the group is silent and no one is making eye contact. The facilitator says, *"I'm not sure what this silence means. Can anyone say what you are thinking or feeling right now?"* or *"Let's just sit with this silence and give all of us time to sort out our feelings. When someone feels ready to answer one of the processing questions, please do."*
- An emotional exchange between a Jew and a Gentile about the prevalence of antisemitism on campus leads to a long period of silence. The facilitator says, *"Why don't we each take a few minutes to jot down what we are feeling right now. Then we can talk with a partner before we come back to the whole group."* Or the facilitator could say, *"This topic clearly generates strong feelings,"* thus normalizing an emotional, as well as intellectual, response to the topic.

7. *Address avoidance*: It is not uncommon for participants to shift away from a topic that makes them uncomfortable or if they feel another issue is more pressing. Sometimes facilitators can acknowledge the importance of the new topic but remind participants of the focus of the discussion, class, or workshop. Other times, instructors can find ways to connect the issue raised to the class or workshop focus. Facilitators can also name when they notice a pattern of certain topics being avoided and discuss it openly with the participants.

In social justice education, it is common for participants to prefer to talk about their subordinated identity(ies) rather than consider their privileged identity(ies). In some cases, participants may want to consider only a particular subordinated identity but not another of their subordinated identities. From an intersectional perspective, it is important to recognize the interconnections among different forms of oppression and how they mutually constitute each other. However, we do not want students to avoid the in-depth exploration of a particular aspect of social inequality.

Instead of simply dismissing a shift in focus, there are numerous ways facilitators can ask students to consider how their other identities affect and are affected by the form of oppression that is being centered. For example, in a racism workshop, white women who try to shift the focus to their identity as women, but not on their whiteness, could be asked to think about how their whiteness affects their experience of being a woman and how this differs for women of color; or they could be asked how being a woman shapes their experience of being white and having white privilege relative to white men. We can also ask about how their experience and understanding of sexism might help them understand and/or block understanding of racism. What are some of the similarities and differences? Often, once people have had the opportunity to acknowledge the issue that is most central to them, they are more able to explore other issues. Facilitators should support an intersectional focus while foregrounding a particular form of oppression or social identity for the sake of learning about a specific form of oppression.

8. Reduce and address resistance: The contradiction phase is when instructors are most likely to face resistance from participants based on an inability or unwillingness to consider new perspectives or engage in critical self-reflection. This resistance is different than participants expressing prejudiced or inaccurate views. The inability to constructively engage in the learning process is often a sign that defenses are high, and that the dissonance is too threatening.

Resistance can be expressed in many ways by members of both advantaged and disadvantaged groups. Instructors from marginalized groups are likely to encounter more resistance, especially from participants from privileged groups (see Chapter 12). Some behaviors that can indicate resistance might be: refuting every fact that is shared, attacking the facilitator as biased, dismissing other student's experiences, or simply disengaging. Having one's world view challenged—especially one's belief in meritocracy, being asked to acknowledge unasked-for privilege, or to understand how one is discriminated against, are painful and uncomfortable experiences. If the confirmation phase was done well, there is usually less resistance and it is more easily managed, since some basic trust and degree of safety has been established.

There are numerous strategies that can help shift resistance (Beeman, 2015; Goodman, 2011, 2015; Ouyang, 2014). First, the facilitator should try to *assess* what is creating the resistance, i.e., what may be provoking this level of fear or anxiety. This assessment may allow us to make more effective responses. People often feel that they are being told they are bad or wrong and do not feel heard. Their core beliefs or understanding of themselves and the world are being questioned. They may fear what social change would look like and mean for them. If so, consider *revisiting some of the activities in the confirmation phase*. We can affirm who people are and recognize their strengths and qualities that align with social justice (e.g., their strong work ethic, their caring for other people, or their concern for fairness); and we can continue to foster trust and rapport among students and with the facilitator, and ask participants to refer back to the discussion of comfort zone and learning edge to recall how they planned to deal with defensive feelings if they arose. The facilitator can remind students that this exploration is not about personal blame but about understanding how we are part of larger systems that impact our lived realities and those of others.

We can *build on students' current knowledge*, recognizing the nuggets of truth in their perspectives, rather than suggesting that everything they believe is false. If participants tend to refute what they hear from the facilitator or other students, *encourage them to research or explore information for themselves.* It is almost never effective to continually try to convince a student who is being resistant to accept a particular piece of information or viewpoint. For example, participants who no longer believe that sexism is a problem can be asked to research the representation of women as heads of Fortune 500 companies, on corporate boards, or in other major positions of power. Students can be asked to make observations that reveal power inequities or discrimination, such as how people are represented in the media or treated in stores. Materials and activities that allow participants to *examine issues from a distance* can be less threatening and raise less resistance. Case studies, vignettes, and analogies can be used to help students develop a social justice perspective, and identify and analyze power dynamics without feeling personally implicated or attacked. Instead of focusing at an intellectual level, the facilitator can shift to a more personal level. Sometimes hearing personal stories, whether in person or through media, can help students make a more *personal or empathic connection.* Some students can make the link between their own experiences of feeling marginalized, discriminated against, or treated unfairly to relate to the oppression experienced by another group.

Certain participants may experience feelings of "too much, too soon." It may be necessary *to "back up" and allow students to go at a slower pace.* For example, if a heterosexual participant is completely unwilling to explore issues of homophobia and heterosexism, it may first be necessary for that participant to spend time learning more about the impact of gender role stereotypes on personal development and interpersonal relationships.

Students may feel less threatened by changes in the status quo by discussing the ways they and all people are harmed by oppression, and what alternatives might look like that could be beneficial to all. Instructors can look for ways to *heighten students' investment* in particular social justice topics or equity more generally. How might understanding oppression help them in their work or interpersonal relationships or in helping the U.S. live up to its stated values of equal opportunity for all?

Our goal as facilitators is to help participants build resilience and internal resources that enable them to think critically, and to tolerate ambiguity and complexity, so that they can choose behaviors and attitudes that are congruent with their commitments to social justice.

9. Manage facilitator reactions: Emotional reactions in the course of social justice education are a natural and human response for facilitators as well as participants. Facilitators can be triggered by statements participants make, just as participants can trigger emotional reactions in each other (see Chapter 12 for further discussion about facilitator reactions). A facilitator who feels emotionally triggered needs to stay in the facilitator role and attend to group needs, but the facilitator can also respond honestly. Instructors may need to make conscious efforts not to react inappropriately to a student's remark or behavior. It is important for facilitators to recognize their own feelings and reactions, and to have strategies to deal with such situations. Some options include self-talk (telling oneself to calm down, not to take it personally, to just stay in the moment), reframing the situation, taking some deep breaths, letting students know that you had a strong reaction to that comment, and taking a break to collect oneself and think about what to do. A co-facilitator, especially one who holds different social identities, can be helpful in these situations, because rarely are both facilitators triggered at the same time. The one who is not triggered can think more clearly about what leadership role to take in the moment.

Phase Three: Continuity

Once participants have left familiar ground and explored new territory, both affectively and intellectually, they are in a position to integrate what they have learned and establish a new foundation. This balance is gradually achieved as a new set of beliefs becomes "home base" for interpreting experience and creating meaning. The past is not wholly rejected, but reinterpreted and reconstructed into a new frame of reference.

Corresponding Facilitating Environment

The environment once again shifts to encourage the development of stability and *continuity* based on new insights and knowledge. Activities are designed to help participants articulate and confirm what they have learned, and to think about what this might mean for their actions beyond the course or workshop. Opportunities are provided to imagine taking new actions, the likely consequences of such actions, and the types of support that could be called upon to sustain these changes.

Design Issues for Continuity

During the continuity phase of the course, participants turn their attention to thinking about how to integrate new awareness and knowledge into their lives and to bring their experience in the course to a close. We focus on helping participants identify actions they want to take as they further their learning and concretize their new perspectives in actions. Our intention is to help participants feel optimistic about social change rather than feel overwhelmed by the enormity of social oppression. We want all students to feel a sense of agency—that they can play a role challenging inequities and fostering justice. It is important to allow students to choose and develop their own action plan suited to their particular learning and comfort level. Participants need to think about how to nurture and sustain their developing understanding of, and commitment to, acting against social injustice. The following guidelines help in planning this phase of the course.

1. Identify actions for social justice: Instructors can encourage participants to identify actions that match their personal level of comfort and skill. This means acknowledging and valuing actions at all levels of risk. Actions could include reading more about issues, committing to attending lectures or arts events on social justice themes, participating in social justice discussions and actions online, objecting to biased jokes or comments in their classes or at the family dinner table, or joining a social change or ally group on campus or in the community. For example, instructors can provide students with opportunities to map out action plans with concrete steps to successfully accomplish their goals. Several of the ism chapters provide action planning activities.

2. Identify support: Developing support for new awareness of and commitment to address social justice issues that extends beyond the course/workshop boundaries is an essential part of helping participants bridge the gap between the class and their school, work, and personal lives. Helping participants develop support groups from the class or learn about existing community or campus groups to join provides a way for participants to nurture relationships with others who share their developing commitments.

3. Provide closure to the class/workshop: Instructors can help participants achieve a sense of closure by providing a way for them to summarize what they learned, appreciate classmates, and identify next steps in continuing their learning. Closing activities can take a range of formats. Several of the ism workshops ask students to share an action they plan to take or one thing they want to remember from the workshop.

4. Solicit feedback: Whether or not it is formally required, it is usually helpful to get feedback about the class or workshop. Since doing social justice education is always a work in progress, it is useful to hear what participants found helpful and solicit suggestions for improvements, both in terms of our facilitation and the class content.

Facilitation Issues in Continuity Phase

Instructors need to help participants transition out of the class. Many participants report missing the stimulation and support provided in social justice classes or workshops. Sometimes participants are concerned about how they will continue their social justice process without the structure of the class, while others are eager to go out and change the world. Participants need assistance thinking through how they can move forward in constructive ways.

1. Deal with immobilizing feelings: It is not uncommon for students to be overwhelmed by the enormity of social inequality and feel powerless to make any significant change. We hope that in our classes and workshops, students will have learned about ways people have resisted oppression and supported movements for justice. Reminding students of these efforts can help reinforce that social change is sometimes a slow process, but societal changes can and do occur through the myriad actions, big and small, that people make together. We can point to actions in their communities that have led to greater equity. Participants can think about their spheres of influence and how they specifically can make an impact. Being part of groups and collective actions can help mitigate feelings of disempowerment and foster a sense of being part of a larger struggle for justice.

Students from marginalized groups may feel overwhelmed, helpless, confused, despairing, hopeless, and/or angry at the enormity of oppression that members of their group face. We can acknowledge such feelings while also encouraging participants from marginalized groups to identify sources of power within their group to make change and resources that can support their efforts. Providing examples of role models from their group who have worked for justice can provide inspiration and encouragement as well as practical tools and strategies. Helping students recognize the value of group support and affirmation from peers who share their social identities is important for developing strength and courage for facing the broader world.

Students from privileged groups may feel guilty or ashamed of their social identity or unearned advantages, feelings that may impede their work for justice. We can remind them that immobilizing guilt only serves to maintain the unjust status quo. In fact, it is a privilege to claim that one feels too guilty to act. Instead, individuals can be encouraged to consider how to use their privileges to foster social change. How can they use their resources, personal connections, education, time, and credibility to support social justice efforts and work in solidarity with people from other groups? They can study and learn from role models in the past and present who are examples of how people from advantaged groups can accept their social identity and become powerful change agents. Students can connect with others from their privileged group to deal with their feelings and explore how to effectively work in solidarity with people from other social groups.

2. Discuss appropriate action: Participants may leave a course with much enthusiasm and desire for creating social change. Assessing their competencies and areas for growth can help individuals determine what kind of activities are most appropriate for them at this time. It is our responsibility to help students think through their actions so their impact matches their intentions.

Some individuals take on a missionary role, trying to convert everyone they know to adopt their social justice perspective. Instructors should remind students that other people have not shared their class experience and talk with them about how to communicate their new knowledge and excitement in respectful and effective ways. Students can share their learnings with others without imposing or insisting that others adopt these same views. Students may develop a judgmental attitude, looking down on others from their social group who have not developed the same degree of social consciousness. Instructors need to work with students to develop the respect and compassion for those from their own social identity group who have not critically examined issues of oppression. They can remind students of their own ongoing journey and of the things that were helpful to them in their learning and development that might inform how they can interact with others.

Participants from privileged groups may try to "help" or "save" people from marginalized communities. However well intentioned, this can be experienced as patronizing and disrespectful of others' cultures and competencies. Instructors should discuss how students can work in collaboration and solidarity with subordinated groups, listening to their needs, valuing their experiences, and supporting their goals. As people from dominant groups work for social change, there needs to be a sense of accountability to people from the marginalized group to ensure that they are acting in ways that in fact are serving the larger social justice vision.

When people leave the class/workshop with a heightened awareness of social justice issues, they may find it hard to relate in the same ways to their friends and family. Students may notice and be more offended by biased comments, jokes, and beliefs. They may find they have less in common with people currently in their social network. We can discuss with them how to find support for their new views while renegotiating current relationships, and help them explore ways to stay engaged with family members while they continue on their social justice journey. We can share ideas for how to deal with changing friendships. We can help prepare students to manage and make decisions about the relationships in their life and find what they need to continue their growth.

BUILDING SKILLS FOR WORKING TOGETHER

People from all social groups can work together as allies and build coalitions to plan and engage in action for change. In our courses and workshops, participants begin this process by learning to listen across differences to understand and value the perspectives of others who are different from themselves. By engaging in small- and large-group activities in the classroom, they are learning skills to work together and manage group dynamics. Planning action within a supportive group of others can challenge and help clarify misguided attempts to be lone heroes or to decide what other groups may need or want. We hope that all of these actions will help prepare participants to take what they have learned in the class or workshop out into the world and their daily lives.

CONCLUSION

As the chapter reflects, both design and facilitation are critical and interconnected elements of successful social justice education. A well-designed class or workshop takes into account the various dimensions of social justice education (instructor, students, curriculum, pedagogy, and classroom climate and dynamics) and provides a thoughtful and solid foundation for the course. Effective facilitation creates a supportive and respectful environment in which participants are invited to discuss and raise questions about new information and perspectives, and to choose new beliefs and actions based on a critical examination of their own values, skills, and knowledge base. The design and facilitation issues and strategies discussed in this chapter can assist facilitators in planning and conducting classes in which all participants, from both advantaged and disadvantaged groups, are engaged in a positive and productive learning experience for all.

Note

* We ask that those who cite this work always acknowledge by name all of the authors listed rather than either only citing the first author or using "et al." to indicate coauthors. All collaborated on the conceptualization, development, and writing of this chapter.

References

Amos, Y. T. (2014). To lose is to win: The effects of student evaluations in a multicultural education class on a Japanese faculty with a non-native English Accent. *Understanding and Dismantling Privilege*, 4(2), 116–133. Retrieved from http://www.wpcjournal.com/article/view/12220

Anderson, L. W., and Krathwohl, D. R. (Eds.) (2000). *A taxonomy for learning, teaching, and assessing: A Revision of Bloom's taxonomy of educational objectives*. Saddle River, NJ: Pearson.

Angelo, T., & Cross, P. K. (1993). *Classroom assessment techniques: A handbook for college teachers*. San Francisco: Jossey-Bass.

Barker, P. (1993). *Regeneration*. New York: Penguin.

Beeman, A. (2015). Teaching to convince, teaching to empower: Reflections on student resistance and self-defeat at predominantly white vs. racially diverse campuses. *Understanding and Dismantling Privilege*, 5(1), 13–30. Retrieved from http://www.wpcjournal.com/article/view/12211/PDF%28Beeman%29

Bell, L. A. (2010). Storytelling for social justice: Connecting narrative and the arts in antiracist teaching. New York: Routledge.

Bloom, B. S., & Krathwohl, D. R. (1956). *Taxonomy of educational objectives: The classification of educational goals, by a committee of college and university examiners. Handbook 1: Cognitive domain*. New York: Longmans.

Brooks-Harris, J. E., & Stock-Ward, S. R. (1999). *Workshops: Designing and facilitating experiential learning*. Thousand Oaks, CA: Sage Publications.

Burgstahler, S., & Cory, R. (2008). Universal design in higher education: From principles to practice. Cambridge, MA: Harvard Education Press.

DiAngelo, R., & Sensoy, O. (2014). Leaning in: A student's guide to engaging constructively in social justice content. *Radical Pedagogy*, 11(1), 2.

Eisner, E. (2002). *The arts and the creation of mind*. New Haven, CT: Yale University Press.

Fink, D. (2013). *Creating significant learning experiences: An integrated approach to designing college courses*. San Francisco: Jossey-Bass.

Garran, A. M., & Rassmussen, B. (2014). Safety in the classroom: Reconsidered. *Journal of Teaching in Social Work*, 34(4), 401–412. doi: 10.1080/08841233.2014.937517

Goodman, D. (2011). *Promoting diversity and social justice: Educating people from privileged groups* (2nd ed.). New York: Routledge.

Goodman, D. (2015). Can you love them enough to help them learn? Reflections of a social justice educator on addressing resistance from white students to anti-racism education. *Understanding and Dismantling Privilege*, 5(1), 62–73. Retrieved from http://www.wpcjournal.com/article/view/12208

Greene, M. (2007). Imagination, oppression and culture: Creating authentic openings. In a collection of works by Maxine Greene curated by the Maxine Greene Foundation. Available at https://maxinegreene.org/uploads/library/imagination_oc.pdf

Griffin, P., & Ouellett, M. (2007). Facilitating social justice education courses. In M. A. Adams, L. A. Bell, & P. Griffin (Eds.), *Teaching for diversity and social justice: A sourcebook* (pp. 89–113).

Gutiérrez y Muhs, G., Niemann, Y. F., González, C. G., & Harris, A. P. (2012). *Presumed incompetent: The intersections of race and class for women in academia*. Logan, UT: Utah State University Press.

Hamermesh, D. S., & Parker, A. M. (2005). Beauty in the classroom: Instructors' pulchritude and putative pedagogical productivity. *Economics of Education Review*, 24, 369–376.

Holley, L. C., & Steiner, S. (2005). Safe space: Student perspectives on classroom environment. *Journal of Social Work Education*, 41, 49–64.

Huston, T. A. (2006). Race and gender bias in higher education: Could faculty course evaluations impede further progress toward parity? *Seattle Journal for Social Justice*, 4(2), Article 34.

Kegan, R. (2009). *The evolving self: Problem and process in human development*. Cambridge, MA: Harvard University Press.

Kolb, D. A. (1984). *Experiential learning: experience as the source of learning and development*. Englewood Cliffs, NJ: Prentice Hall.

Marchesani, L., & Adams, M. (1992). Dynamics of diversity in the teaching-learning process: A faculty development model for analysis and action. In M. Adams (Ed.), *Promoting diversity in college classrooms: Innovative responses for the curriculum, faculty, and institutions* (pp. 9–19). New Directions for Teaching and Learning, No. 52. San Francisco: Jossey-Bass.

Obear, K. (2013). Navigating triggering events: Critical competencies for social justice educators. In L. M. Landreman (Ed.), *The art of effective facilitation: Reflections from social justice educators*. Sterling, VA: Stylus.

Ouellett, M., & Fraser, E. (2005). Teaching together: Interracial teams. In M. Ouellett (Ed.), *Teaching inclusively: Resources for course, department and institutional change in higher education*. Stillwater, OK: New Forums Press.

Ouyang, H. (2014). Transforming resistance: Strategies for teaching race in the ethnic American literature classroom. *Understanding and Dismantling Privilege, 4*(2), 204–219. Retrieved from http://www.wpcjournal.com/article/view/12280/pdf_11

Palmer, P. (1997). *The courage to teach*. San Francisco: Jossey-Bass.

Rendon, L. (2009). *Sentipensante (sensing/thinking) pedagogy: Educating for wholeness, social justice and liberation*. Sterling, VA: Stylus Press.

Sensoy, Ö., & DiAngelo, R. (2014). Respect differences? Challenging the common guidelines in social justice education. *Democracy & Education, 22*(2), Article 1.

Soohoo, S. (2006). *Talking leaves: Narratives of otherness*. New York: Hampton Press, Inc.

Suskie, L. (2004). *Assessing student learning: A common sense guide*. Bolton, MA: Anker Publishing.

Vargas, L. (1999). When the other is the teacher: Implications of teacher diversity in higher education. *The Urban Review, 31*, 359–383. Retrieved from http://dx.doi.org/10.1023/A:1023290300660

Walvoord, B., & Anderson, V. J. (2009). *Effective grading: A tool for learning and assessment in college* (2nd ed.). San Francisco: Jossey-Bass.

Warren, L. (2005). Strategic action in hot moments. In M. L. Ouellett (Ed.), *Teaching inclusively* (pp. 620–630). Stillwater, OK: New Forum Press.

Weinstein, G. (1988). Design elements for intergroup awareness training. *Journal for Specialists in Group Work, 13*(2), 96.

4

Getting Started

Core Concepts for Social Justice Education

Maurianne Adams and Ximena Zúñiga*

This chapter is a bridge that connects the frameworks in the first three chapters with the specific ism chapters that follow. In it, we present core concepts that instructors and facilitators can use in taking a social justice education (SJE) approach. We urge instructors to review the core concepts and design presented in this chapter as a "prequel" to the chapters that follow. This chapter provides generic material for setting up and introducing a course or workshop and notes for processing activities.

We do not claim that these core concepts are the only way to approach SJE. Even the authors in this volume think about and use these core concepts differently. We encourage readers to consider other frameworks or perspectives that support their understanding of social justice as they develop their own SJE practice.

The core concepts, design, and activities are intended to be used by instructors and facilitators in two different ways. First, the material in this chapter can introduce participants to core concepts that will shape their SJE approach to one or more specific social justice isms. Second, the chapter components can be used as a stand-alone introductory approach to SJE without application to any specific ism. If used as an introduction to one or more isms, these core concepts should be introduced up front and then elaborated in connection to each ism addressed in the course or workshop series. Used this way, the concepts have a cumulative impact for participants as they apply the core concepts to each new social justice issue, and grasp the analytic value of these concepts and their application to multiple SJE topics.

Part 1 of this chapter presents seven core concepts that we consider key to the SJE approach described in Chapter 1. Part 2 introduces a sample for teaching the core concepts as an introduction to one or more isms or as a stand-alone class or workshop, along with an explanation of the pedagogical rationale for the design. Part 3 examines facilitation issues likely to emerge when addressing the core concepts during a class or workshop, with recommendations about ways to anticipate and address them.

PART I: CORE CONCEPTS OF OUR APPROACH TO SJE

All of the seven core concepts presented below are equally important. The sequence in which they are listed reflects our preferences for how and when they appear in overview SJE courses (and in the sample design that follows). The concepts we consider "core" for an introduction to SJE or for a stand-alone SJE course or workshop are:

* The differences between an SJE approach and a diversity approach;
* The pervasiveness of systems of oppression at all levels of social organization;
* The social construction and historical legacies of oppression;
* The socialization process by which oppression is learned and reproduced;

- Individual and group identities in the context of socially constructed categories and positionalities of privilege and disadvantage;
- Intersectionality among social identities, social group memberships and institutional forms of oppression;
- The importance of critical awareness, knowledge, and skills to challenge, resist, and take effective action for change.

We find these core concepts to be effective for introducing social justice issues to a variety of participant groups. We are also aware that different social justice approaches use different core concepts and terminology. In some contexts, instructors and facilitators may want to also help participants explore different terminology and their implications. For example, some instructors, facilitators, and/or participants may be more familiar with terms and frameworks such as patriarchy, misogyny, false consciousness, post-colonialism, post-structuralism, neo-liberalism, Marxism, or criticality. Different sets of terminology offer different entry points and frameworks, and emphasize different perspectives and modes of analysis. Such concepts can be incorporated or set alongside the SJE approach described here and will generate fruitful discussions.

DIFFERENCES BETWEEN DIVERSITY AND SOCIAL JUSTICE APPROACHES

A *diversity* approach generally emphasizes the social, cultural, and other differences and commonalities among social identity groups based on the ethnic, racial, religious, gender, class, or other "social categories" generally recognized within the U.S. (These will differ transnationally as well as historically.) The goals of a diversity approach include appreciation of differences among and within groups in a pluralistic society.

A diversity approach does not necessarily include issues of inequality as fundamental to the ways in which diversity is experienced in the U.S. It is also unlikely to address the ways in which social group differences have been used historically and in the present day to rationalize and justify the damage done by inequality and injustice within the larger society, or the ways in which privileges and disadvantages are situated within a larger context of systemic inequality and oppression.

For example, a diversity approach might focus on understanding the cultural values, religious affiliations, educational experiences, families, national and language origins for specific ethnic groups, like Puerto Rican or Mexican Latinos/as, or U.S.-born African Americans, or Afro-Caribbeans (Cubans, Dominicans, Haitians). Yet this approach often remains silent on the biases and daily microaggressions people from these groups encounter, the pervasive discrimination in employment and educational tracking, and the systemic disadvantages these groups face within the system of U.S. racism.

Similarly, discussions on religion framed by a diversity approach may focus on the beliefs and modes of worship of different faith traditions. They usually do not consider how U.S. Christian hegemony creates disadvantage for religious or nonreligious groups in the U.S. who are not identified as Christian. Members of these groups may experience daily microaggressions if their faith requires that they cover their heads (Jewish men wearing a kippa, Muslim women wearing hijab, Sikhs wearing turbans), they may have difficulty getting time off to observe holidays, and they may be pressured to participate in Christian holidays and rituals.

In contrast, *social justice education* focuses attention on the ways in which social group differences of race and ethnicity, national origins, language, religion, gender, sexuality, class, disability, and age interact with systems of domination and subordination to privilege or disadvantage different social group members relative to each other. We use the term *social justice education* as distinct from diversity education to capture an emphasis upon unequal social structures, supremacist ideologies, and oppressive politics and practices by which members of dominant social groups, whether knowingly or unconsciously, perpetuate their own social and cultural privilege to the disadvantage of marginalized or subordinated social groups.

An SJE approach is based on a vision of society organized upon principles of social justice, and draws on a theory of oppression to analyze the ways in which societies fall short of such a vision (see Chapter 1; Adams, 2014; Rawls, 2003; Sen, 2009; Young, 1990). The goals of an SJE approach include awareness and understanding of oppression, acknowledgement of one's role in that system (as a privileged or disadvantaged social group member), and a commitment to develop the skills, resources, and coalitions needed to create lasting change.

STRUCTURAL INEQUALITY OCCURS AT EVERY LEVEL OF SOCIETY: INDIVIDUAL, INSTITUTIONAL, AND SOCIETAL/CULTURAL

Structural inequality plays out and can be analyzed at every level of social organization, from the most individual and personal, to the most abstract and societal. The terms that we use in this book—individual, institutional, and societal/cultural—refer to the levels of social organization at which inequality is maintained and reproduced.

The individual level refers to persons in themselves and in relationship with others; it includes "internalized" understandings of privilege or inequality within a person's individual consciousness as well as attitudes and behaviors that play out interpersonally.

The institutional level refers to social institutions such as schooling, banking and finance, and criminal justice institutions that enforce the law and political institutions that create the law. The institutional level can also refer to smaller units within larger institutions or organizations, such as a particular school district, a particular classroom within a school system, or a police department or prison within the larger legal system.

The cultural and societal levels refer to the broad abstract understandings that pervade a social system. At the cultural level, we examine prevailing norms and values that govern communication style, gender roles, family structure, expectations of physical and mental capacities, relationship to time and place, aesthetic standards, and more. The term *norm* means that certain ways of being are viewed as correct and *normal* while differences are defined as wrong, unhealthy, or *abnormal*. Culture is not one thing, but an aggregate of many norms, expectations, attitudes, and behaviors that are expressed by individuals and institutions. Likewise, society is an aggregate of institutions that reproduce attitudes and values from the dominant culture, and in their cumulative interactions convey the feeling that one is living within a cohesive system that can be described as *society*.

We find the three levels—individual, institutional, and societal/cultural—useful for drawing general distinctions among levels of social organization, and for describing interactions among them. For some groups of participants, these terms may not seem sufficiently nuanced. They may want additional terms to differentiate between the intrapersonal (within the self) and interpersonal (between several individuals), or to describe the dynamics within groups of people (such as a working group, a club, or a family) that are too small or informal to be "institutional" and yet often are the groupings within which the policies and practices of an institution get understood, carried out, and rewarded. Similarly, it may seem difficult to grasp the meaning of "the culture" or "the society" except through the interplay of specific institutional players such as the media, the rhetoric deployed by politicians running for public office, or the policies and practices that provide or prevent access to health care or school systems or safe neighborhoods.

Social psychologists, sociologists, and social workers describe both the individual and small-group interrelations as *micro* and differentiate these from *meso* (schools, organizations, or communities) and *macro* (the overarching economic, cultural, social, and legal dimensions of social structure). These terms can help to elucidate more subtle distinctions, but they are generally not interchangeable on a one-to-one basis with the terms individual, institutional, and cultural/societal as we use them here (Kirk & Okazawa-Rey, 2013). We call attention to these different terminologies because instructor/facilitators may find one or the other more useful depending upon context. For the purpose of describing social organization, we rely on the terms individual, institutional, and societal/cultural, while acknowledging that any single set of terms chosen to describe something as complex as social organization will remain incomplete.

The dynamics of an overarching cultural and societal system of inequality that is maintained and reproduced institutionally and by individuals can be envisioned as a three-dimensional "cube" (Hardiman, Jackson, & Griffin, 2007) as shown in Fig. 4.1.

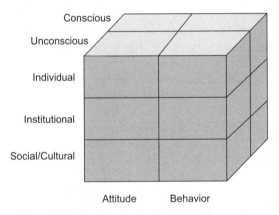

Figure 4.1 Three-Dimensional Matrix of Oppression
Source: Hardiman, R., Jackson, B. W., & Griffin, P. (2013).

The "cube" captures the three horizontally drawn levels (cultural, institutional, individual) described above, and complicates those levels with two additional factors: The difference between attitudes and behaviors, and the distinction between conscious and unconscious. It is obvious that individuals can have conscious and unconscious beliefs and behaviors; likewise, institutions have attitudes (policies) and behaviors (practices) that may be conscious or unconscious (i.e., official or unofficial) and which create advantage or disadvantage for members of different social identity groups. The distinctions between attitudes and behaviors, conscious and unconscious, also play out at the abstract levels of culture and society. This visual representation is a useful pedagogical tool to help participants see how these levels intersect (Hardiman, Jackson, & Griffin, 2007, p. 39).

The Individual Level

At the individual level, the focus is on understanding the individual attitudes and behaviors that maintain one or more forms of oppression, intentionally or unintentionally. Because these attitudes and behaviors are learned through processes of socialization, the cycle of socialization, which we address later in this chapter, is a useful conceptual organizer.

Terminology at the individual level: Conscious and unconscious, attitude and behavior, stereotype, implicit bias, microaggression, prejudice.

At the individual level, we use terms like *bias* and *prejudice* to refer to negative attitudes toward marginalized or excluded groups. These attitudes are often based on unexamined *stereotypes*, or overly generalized assumptions and beliefs about groups of people that are embedded in the dominant culture and that many people reproduce through their attitudes and behaviors. These stereotypes may be negative (women are too emotional and not good at math) or they may seem positive (Asians are unemotional and good at math), but in both cases, they "essentialize" everyone in the social identity group based on partial information, misinformation, or missing information.

Although often based on a kernel of truth, stereotypes are inaccurate and damaging in several ways. First, the kernel of truth on which a stereotype is based is often taken out of historical context and exaggerated. For example, the stereotype that Jews are "clannish"— i.e., prefer to socialize with other Jews—does not consider the history of forced isolation of European Jews in walled ghettos for many centuries. Without this context, the characterization makes light of a long history of violent relocation by implying that its cultural ripple effects are mere matters of preference.

Second, stereotypes often target one group based on a characteristic that is shared by many other groups who aren't targeted thus. Continuing the example above, in cities (where new immigrants moved to be close to acquaintances from the "old country"), there are still neighborhoods that are primarily inhabited by people of Irish, Italian, or Polish descent, and many in these groups prefer "in-marriage" rather than "intermarriage" for their children, but they are not called "clannish." The stereotype applies a value judgement to Jews in particular for an ethnic-centered communalism typical of many other communities.

Third, stereotypes overgeneralize and ignore diversity within a group. Contrary to the stereotype, most Jews socialize widely with non-Jews and many intermarry with non-Jews. But the stereotype is leveraged against all Jews (even those who are not European and have no particular relationship to this stereotype's historical reference), whether or not its characterization describes them. Thus, the stereotype erases historical legacies of oppression, assigns judgement to one group for behavior that is considered unproblematic for other groups, and is grossly inaccurate in attributing to all what might be the understandable behavior of some.

Stereotypes are reinforced by selective attention to behaviors that match stereotypes and ignore or rationalize behaviors that contradict them. For example, when a man of color mugs someone, his behavior may be interpreted as typical of his group and magnified by media attention. When a white person commits a similar crime, their behavior is usually interpreted as an individual fault or outlier, not part of a broader pattern and not worthy of much media attention. Similarly, when a Muslim person plans or commits an attack, they are labeled "terrorist" and their behavior is interpreted as stemming from their religious tradition. Meanwhile, white Christian men (who commit the majority of mass shootings in the U.S.) are seen as individual actors, and their behavior is attributed to mental illness or a response to personal feelings of alienation, rather than ascribed to their race and/or religion. The media is quick to label them "lone wolves."

Examples of individual-level attitudes and behaviors, based on stereotypes, that contribute to oppression include:

- The belief that women are available for sexual attention and/or sex in the workplace and other public and private spaces, including the belief that women "ask for it" by their dress or demeanor, along with behaviors that violate women's boundaries based on these assumptions;

- An implicit bias against black or Latino men that includes the belief they are dangerous and criminal, reflected in women holding their purses close to their bodies and drivers shutting car windows and locking the doors as they drive through a poor, racially marked neighborhood;
- The assumption that people with physical disabilities have impaired thinking, or that all elders are hard of hearing, and the behavior of speaking differently to them than one would to a presumed-able younger adult;
- The belief that all gay men are promiscuous, and related behaviors such as invalidating gay men's partnerships or doubting their ability to interact appropriately with children.

We differentiate at all levels between attitudes and behaviors, but it is not always clear where the line between conscious or unconscious might fall. Someone may be conscious of their behavior but not realize that it is based on an unconscious attitude, or they may be conscious of a particular attitude without recognizing its connection to an unconscious stereotype. The research on *implicit bias* offers a useful analytic tool to understand the *impact* of biases, whether conscious or unconscious. Individuals (as well as institutions) often deny their *intention* to discriminate, but research demonstrates that implicit biases inform attitudes and shape behaviors (Banaji & Greenwald, 2013; Kirwan Institute, 2013). Sometimes an implicit bias or unconscious stereotype rises into conscious thought at the moment we catch ourselves acting upon it.

Microaggressions are a particular kind of individual-level behavior. These are commonplace, everyday interactions that intentionally or unintentionally reinforce a person's subordinated status within a system of oppression (Sue, 2010). Members of marginalized groups experience a cumulative impact from the barrage of behaviors that express stereotyped assumptions and biases from members of privileged groups (Sue 2010; Huber & Solórzano, 2014). For example:

- At a predominantly white college, a black student in a single day might overhear racial slurs, have someone question whether they got unauthorized help on a well-written paper, be left out of an invitation to a team meeting, or ignored at a social gathering.
- A low-income student may overhear disparaging remarks about poor people, encounter friends' assumptions that everyone in the group has middle-class privilege, get invited to participate in a valuable extracurricular learning experience for which they can't afford the fee, or be told that the way they speak in informal settings makes them sound unintelligent.
- A transgender person may be called the wrong pronouns, asked what their "real" name is, stared at, asked inappropriately personal questions about their anatomy, or told that they're in the "wrong" restroom.

These experiences, amplified by repetition and reinforcement in the institutions and the culture at large, result in cumulative experiences of racism, classism, or trans* oppression that are far more powerful than each seemingly insignificant interaction would suggest.

Internalized Subordination and Domination

An important dimension of domination and subordination is the "intrapsychic" or intrapersonal ways they operate within an individual, usually unconsciously. *Internalized subordination* refers to ways in which members of marginalized and disadvantaged groups, through their socialization, internalize the dominant group's negative ideology about their group, and come to accept a definition of themselves that is hurtful and limiting, causing them to think, feel, and act in ways that accept the devaluation of their group. For example, a woman on a hiring committee may doubt the credentials or abilities of women applicants while accepting the qualifications of men without question. Internalized subordination also operates when target group members curry favor with dominant group members and distance themselves from their own group. For example, some people with disabilities that are not readily apparent may distance themselves from people with more apparent disabilities in an attempt to escape stigma (see Chapter 9, Ableism).

Internalized domination describes the behaviors, thoughts, and feelings of privileged or advantaged group members who, through their socialization, have learned to think and act in ways that express entitlement and privilege. Because the advantages of privileged groups have been normalized culturally, members of privileged groups see the resources and opportunities they get as the natural order of things, rather than as a result of a social system that provides them with advantages denied to other social groups (McIntosh, 1989).

Examples of internalized domination include:

- Men unthinkingly talk over and interrupt women in conversation, while simultaneously labeling women as chatty.
- White people who are native speakers of English expect that they will be treated well and accommodated in public spaces, but without a thought cut in front of people of color waiting in line, or demand to be waited on first when a new speaker of English takes time at the cash register.

Internalized domination is supported by all the mechanisms of socialization, and particularly by an educational system that renders disadvantaged group members invisible or devalued by failing to acknowledge their contributions or importance (Loewen, 1995).

One further dimension of oppression that occurs primarily at the individual level can be described as *horizontal oppression*. This term comes from the terms "horizontal violence" and "horizontal hostility," used by Pharr (1997) to describe the situations in which members of marginalized or subordinated groups misdirect their rage at other members of their own group rather than at the more dangerous and powerful members of advantaged groups. For example, a woman may make sexist remarks about another woman's attire, or a working-poor parent may discourage a child from pursuing higher education and instead tell them to accept their future role as an underpaid provisional worker.

Horizontal oppression also works within and among advantaged groups. For example, white people may cast aspersions on white organizations or individuals that are working for racial justice, Christians may discourage other Christians from educating themselves about non-Christian religious communities, or children who do not have disabilities may tease other children for making friends with a child who does have a disability.

Horizontal and vertical manifestations of oppression can be mutually reinforcing. For example, in the early years of the U.S. labor movement, stereotypes and hostility about subordinated racial groups and newly arrived immigrants were used to break up unionizing efforts among mill and factory workers. Vertical hostility across race was used to foment horizontal violence and exclusion within the working class.

The Institutional Level

At the institutional level, oppression is produced, reproduced, and maintained by the policies and practices of institutions such as government agencies, business and industry, banking and finance, K–12 and post-secondary education, religious organizations, and the legal system (including divorce and custody law, mechanisms of inheritance such as wills and trusts, police and criminal courts, civil fines, and prisons). The *institutional level* refers both to broad fields such as health care and the media, and to specific organizations such as a sports team or a congregation. Institutions maintain and reproduce advantage and disadvantage by whom they employ, how they recognize and reward success, and whose transgressions they punish. The policies and practices of privilege or exclusion reflect such institutional norms.

The relationship between individual bias and institutional discrimination is complex. On one hand, institutions reinforce the socialization of individuals into systems of oppression through discriminatory policies and practices. On the other hand, individual attitudes or behaviors are often the vehicles by which a discriminatory institutional policy is carried out. For example, a career counselor in a high school where students are tracked into separate Advanced Placement and vocational tracks may evaluate the potential for college bound vs. vocational students based on their own implicit biases or prejudices about students' family background, neighborhood, or use of accented or vernacular English. In such a case, the counselor's implicit biases based on race and class (individual level) play out through the school's tracking system (institutional level) to produce long-term, material, and discriminatory consequences for student access to higher education and employment. Counselors who become aware of their implicit biases can choose to avoid individual-level discrimination, but in order to address the institutional level, they must work to change policies and practices as well as their own behavior.

Examples of discriminatory institutional practices and policies include:

- Dress codes for front office or sales positions that advantage people who meet dominant beauty norms and disadvantage those who do not (including people with disabilities, people perceived as gay or queer, and people who wear ethnically or religiously marked attire such as head coverings);
- Workplace schedules that institute mandatory days off for major Christian holidays, while non-Christians who want time off for their religious holidays must file a request and use vacation time or unpaid leave;
- Health insurance policies that specifically exclude transition-related health care for trans* people even when the same medications and procedures are covered for cisgender people;
- Youth curfews restricting people under an age threshold from being in public spaces during certain times of the day.

Often, oppression plays out in institutions at both institutional and individual levels. A discriminatory policy exists at the institutional level, but an individual must carry it out. Or, an individual acts based on an implicit bias, and the impact of their behavior is magnified by their institutional role as a manager or policy maker. The lack of safeguards to prevent decision makers' individual bias from governing institutional policies and practices is itself an example of institutional-level oppression.

Oppressive policies and practices are often difficult to notice, because they seem built-in, inevitable features of monolithic structures. For example, many application and intake forms require people to indicate gender and provide only two options. This practice, along with the broader norm of assuming that sex and gender are binary, is so pervasive that most people do not notice it. But for people who are trans* and/or intersex, it means they may be required to misrepresent themselves or be excluded entirely.

Institutional-level oppression can go unnoticed because many oppressive policies seem neutral at first glance. Often they do not state an explicit discriminatory intent, yet their impact reinforces inequality. For example, college admissions policies reward applicants for extracurricular experiences, such as volunteer activities or travel abroad, that are only available to people with significant class privilege. Such policies do not explicitly say that the college wishes to prioritize wealthy applicants, and the policies may be rationalized by seemingly reasonable explanations. Still, the impact is to disadvantage applicants from poor and working-class backgrounds whose need to work prevents volunteer activity or travel, while advantaging those from professional and owning-class backgrounds.

Unofficial institutional practices, such as norms of dress, appearance, communication, group interaction, and self-presentation are generally not apparent to people in privileged groups because they have always "fit in" with the organizational culture. For members of marginalized groups, however, the daily experiences of trying to figure out or being reminded that they don't match accepted norms contributes to the cumulative impact of oppression.

The Societal and Cultural Level

Social systems and cultural norms convey messages about what is correct and expected by the larger society. In an oppressive society, the superior position of the privileged and advantaged groups is maintained and reproduced both through the networks of institutions that make up the society, and through unquestioned belief systems and norms that support and give meaning to those systems.

For excluded and marginalized peoples, the cultural norms and structural obstacles they experience at local banks, hospitals, police forces, realtors, and schools convey a seamless web of oppression that presses on them everywhere they turn. This web, although made up of specific institutions and interactions, becomes an overwhelming cultural and societal force. The reproduction of cultural norms and structural patterns "add up" to a system of advantage and disadvantage that is much larger than the sum of its parts.

Dominant norms and practices take place at a societal and cultural level, although their specific manifestations are most clear at the institutional level. It can be difficult for participants in social justice courses and workshops to make meaningful distinctions between these two levels. The point is not to categorize each example as one level or the other, but rather to strive to hold an understanding that examples at the individual and institutional levels interact and reinforce each other and are upheld by broader cultural/societal patterns and structures.

Examples of cultural norms and societal practices include:

- Policies that prevent gay or lesbian couples from adopting children because of the cultural norm that heterosexual couples are the only "good" parents;
- The often-repeated belief that female survivors of rape provoked their rapists through their dress or behavior;
- The ubiquitous practice of building new homes that are not accessible to people with mobility impairments;
- The culturally reinforced reluctance to vote for non-Christian politicians (including atheists) because of an assumption that only religious people can be trusted to act morally.

OPPRESSION IS SOCIALLY CONSTRUCTED BY HISTORICAL LEGACIES EMBEDDED IN INSTITUTIONS AND BELIEF SYSTEMS

Today's oppression grows out of the legacy of yesterday's accumulated and persistent inequality. Many contemporary manifestations of oppression gain strength from the assumption that something "has always been done this way." When we examine historical legacies, we better understand how different manifestations of oppression evolved as they did, and why they have persisted. We can also begin to imagine how things might have turned out differently. Novelist William Faulkner's famous statement, "The past is never dead. It's not even past" conveys this sense of the continuity of history and why we must dig deep into the past if we are to build a better future.

The term *social construction* refers to the idea that norms, ideas, and institutions that may now seem natural or inevitable actually grew out of specific historical and social processes. When, as children, we learn norms around respectful communication between children and adults, acceptable behavior in public and private spaces, and expectations of men and women, these norms seem absolute. But in fact they vary across cultures and shift over time within cultures. Abstract ideas like democracy, peace, and romantic love are socially constructed, as are the very concepts on which social identity categories are based—race, ethnicity, sex, gender, sexual orientation, disability, childhood, and adulthood.

The social construction of institutions is perhaps easier to trace, because we can often point to a discrete beginning. Institutions emerge in specific contexts, driven by the goals and interests of individuals and groups with the power to implement their decisions at those times. From the perspective of the present, institutions like K–12 schooling, health care based in hospitals and clinics, or the apparatus of representative democracy seem to be settled matters of fact. But U.S. public schools were created in the early 19th century (Fraser, 1999). Hospitals are a recent invention, only replacing doctors' house calls in the mid-20th century after the practice and technology of health care had become so specialized that it required bringing patients to designated buildings. Our system of representative democracy was outlined at the founding of the country but has undergone significant evolution as groups fought to be included, and as the electoral campaign process was transformed by technologies of mass media and a shifting economy.

Institutions tend to perpetuate themselves and often outlive their original intentions. For example, long-term incarceration of criminals began in the late 18th century as a well-intentioned alternative to the public humiliation of whipping and hanging, and was the first penal system in the Western world intended to rehabilitate as well as punish. Within less than 100 years, strong evidence showed that incarceration, especially solitary confinement, was in fact more damaging than rehabilitative. But by that time, other institutions had grown up around incarceration that had their own interests to protect (McLennan, 2008), and all of these institutions are more entrenched today. Private prisons contract with states to fill prison beds for profit, unions for prison guards protect their members' job security, outside companies hire prisoners at extremely low wages, and politicians cite incarceration as proof that they are "tough on crime." Questions about whether incarceration diminishes crime, or is appropriate for a particular crime, or is cruel and unusual, or is racially biased, bump up against established institutions and accepted ideas that perpetuate the status quo. Thus, consideration of the historical legacies of social institutions—in connection with why they were established and who now benefits—enables participants to understand how historical and cultural forces shape the manifestations of oppression we see today.

It is often challenging for participants to think about how social identity categories are also social constructions with tangled historical roots. For example, "race" is a complicated social construction that was created and used to subordinate peoples with darker skin color for the purposes of enslavement, economic exploitation, and/or colonization and conquest (see Chapter 5). The fluidity and instrumental nature of racial categories is captured by the term "racialization"—*"the extension of racial meaning to a previously racially unclassified relationship, social practice, or group"* (Omi & Winant, 2015, p. 111, italics in the original). The process of racialization helps explain how the U.S. has racialized geographically and historically diverse migrants through a shifting color line that sorts people into a racially stratified workforce (see also Chapters 7 and 8). Rather than a biological or even purely cultural fact, race is a social fact constructed through legal, economic, cultural, and other forces in the service of creating and maintaining inequality.

In social justice classes and workshops, exploring social construction and historical legacies enables participants to understand that oppression inherited from the past is not immutable or inevitable. With this insight, change becomes not only possible, but also plausible. Freire described the maintenance of oppression "not as a closed world from which there is no exit, but as a limiting situation which [we] can transform . . . [H]umans live in a world which [we] are constantly re-creating and transforming" (Freire, 1970, pp. 31, 79–80).

While oppressive norms, ideas, and institutions are defended on the assumption that they couldn't be any other way, movements of resistance and change are often undermined by the accusation that their ideas are too new and unprecedented. Activists participating in the Occupy movement were acting in the spirit of populist and direct democratic practices that carried forward the U.S. historical tradition of 18th century populist rent revolts (Zinn, 2003) that bear striking resemblance to today's foreclosure resistance projects. Trans* activists are told that trans* issues are difficult to understand because they are so "new," although in fact trans* people have been organizing and advocating for their rights in the U.S. since the mid-20th century, and people who did not fit into their society's primary gender categories have existed throughout time and across cultures.

Exploring historical legacies of social justice movements can help participants see current social justice work as legitimate and feasible, and inspire them to build upon past efforts to create new openings for social justice. It also creates opportunities for participants to learn from the strategies of past movements, including what worked well and what was problematic. Participants can learn about the importance of coalitions across differences and of intersectional analysis and action, not as buzzwords but as practical and ethical concerns that activists have grappled with over time.

Historical legacies are transnational as well as U.S.-centered, and it is important to understand the interconnections among global and U.S. instances of oppression and resistance. For example, the 20th century Black Consciousness and anti-apartheid movements in South Africa were linked to the civil rights and racial consciousness movements in the U.S. Likewise, 19th and 20th century anti-colonial nationalist movements in Africa, Arabia, and the Americas were inspired in part by anti-colonial aspects of the American Revolution and the anti-monarchy ideas from the French Revolution.

Although the historical legacies described in this volume refer primarily to U.S. manifestations of oppression, they provide a foundation for asking broader questions: How does racism in the U.S. differ from racism elsewhere, and what historical forces led to those differences? How does violence against less-powerful religious group differ from one geographic context to another in the past and present? Especially in classes or workshops with participants who themselves or whose families migrated from outside the U.S., instructors and facilitators will be wise to make room for discussion of how categories like gender, sexuality, race, and religion are constructed differently in other places.

THE ROLE OF SOCIALIZATION AND HEGEMONY IN MAINTAINING SYSTEMS OF OPPRESSION

Socialization refers to the lifelong process by which we inherit and replicate the dominant norms and frameworks of our society, and learn to accept them as "common sense." In particular, we learn to think of social identity categories as essential and natural, and of social hierarchies as inevitable. Our socialization processes rarely point out that our norms perpetuate a world view based upon the maintenance of advantage for some, relative to disadvantage for others.

"The internalization of socially rooted and historically developed activities is the distinguishing feature of human psychology," in that external events and interpersonal processes are transformed into intrapersonal ones (Vygotsky, 1978, pp. 56–57). This general principle of socialization is the ongoing process by which external activities and processes become reconstituted as part of an interior self applies to the internalization of oppressive activities and processes.

Oppression depends on the internalization and acceptance of advantaged and disadvantaged social group relationships within the social hierarchy of the larger society. Disadvantaged social groups can live within a system of oppression that injures them or deprives them of certain rights without having the language or consciousness (Freire used the term "conscientizção") to name the oppression or to understand their situation as an effect of oppression, rather than the natural order of things. Memmi (1957, 1991) described this as "psychological colonization," whereby disadvantaged groups internalize their oppressed condition and collude with the oppressive ideology and social system, a process Freire referred to as "playing host to the oppressor" (1970, p. 30).

In this volume, we use a framework called "the Cycle of Socialization" (Harro, 2013a), shown in Fig. 4.2, as a shorthand for the role of institutions in socializing us into oppressive systems from childhood throughout the lifespan.

The cycle signifies the way socializing interactions within our families, schools, peers, and religious institutions, and through the media, are not one-time events, but continue throughout our lives. Our "first socialization" takes place through interactions with members of immediate and extended family, teachers, and other trusted adults. The messages we receive are usually mutually reinforcing, although sometimes contradictory (e.g., between messages received at home and at school). Such contradictions offer space to question received norms.

Socialization continues through interactions with institutions and through cultural messages that are reinforced in adulthood. Through cumulative encounters with social institutions like medical systems, police, courts, banks, and workplaces, we learn the roles we are expected to play in order to navigate institutions successfully as a person with our social identities. Whether consciously or not, we are reminded again and again of how we are privileged and/or disadvantaged relative to others. When we are conscious of being disadvantaged, we may feel that it's not fair, or if we have advantages, we may accept them as normal and deserved. To the extent that the process is not interrupted, we transmit these norms and assumptions to the next generation, thus perpetuating the cycle.

There are many opportunities for challenging and interrupting socialization into an oppressive system. An encouraging heuristic to explore side-by-side with the Cycle of Socialization (Harro, 2013a) is the Cycle of Liberation (Harro, 2013b). These two models, taken together, indicate how individuals can become conscious of their roles in the system, build skills and knowledge to resist the norms they have learned, and disrupt the cycle on an individual level. At a broader level, social movements can organize resistance to oppressive norms and structures in the larger society. For example, people with disabilities work as individuals and in community to claim a sense of their own value and beauty as people. They also form organizations to advocate for structural and cultural changes that increase opportunities for self-determination and interdependence. Poor and working-class people support each other to resist internalizing messages that they are undeserving, organize to share resources to meet each other's needs, and advocate for policy changes to increase economic equality. People in privileged roles can break out of the Cycle of Socialization

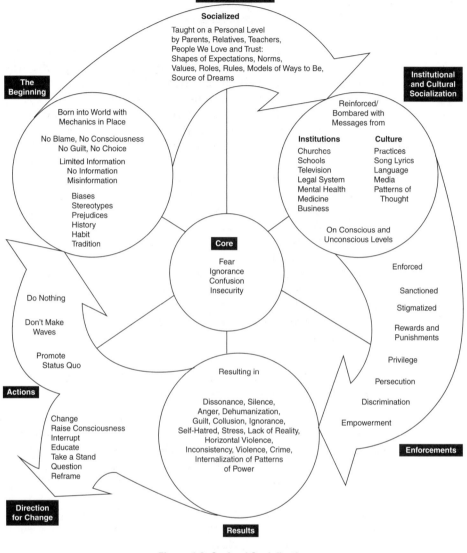

Figure 4.2 Cycle of Socialization

Source: Harro, B. (2013a).

and choose to become allies and change agents in collaboration with disadvantaged groups (Broido, 2000).

The dominant norms we are socialized to accept can be described as *hegemonic*. Hegemonic norms wield power, because most people behave in accordance with social norms without being told or forced to do so and judge harshly those who behave otherwise. For those who benefit from the norms by virtue of their membership in privileged social groups, going along with business as usual provides unquestioned access to social advantages. One of the subtlest advantages is the ability to see oneself and be seen as "normal," in contrast with those considered different, strange, alien, or "other." People are marginalized as "different" relative to the often unnamed, dominant group, and are excluded and disadvantaged on the basis of that difference (Brookfield, 2005; Johnson, 2006; see also Chapter 1).

Hegemonic norms are reinforced and sustained at all levels of society, and come to feel compulsory, as if there is no safe way to behave other than the expected norm. This feeling is accompanied by tangible material rewards for conforming and punishments for diverging from the norm.

For example, heterosexuality is an enforced norm. People who are heterosexual don't need to "come out" because it is the assumed default. Individuals and couples who are heterosexual (or perceived as heterosexual) can experience themselves as normal and unremarkable, and encounter institutions designed to meet their needs (at least on the dimension of sexual orientation). If they want to have children through pregnancy or adoption, their fitness as parents is unlikely to be questioned. If it is necessary to make decisions for each other during medical emergencies, they can be confident that hospitals will recognize their right to do so. Meanwhile, people who are lesbian, gay, bisexual, and queer are continually reminded that they do not fit the norm, starting with the need for a "coming out" process of realizing and disclosing their sexual orientation. If they want to have children, many people will doubt their fitness as parents, and adoption agencies may legally reject them. When they file for a birth certificate, they may have to amend a form that only has spaces for one mother and one father. Legal documents like health care proxies and wills may be ignored by hospitals and courts that choose not to recognize their relationship.

The pervasive cultural, institutional, and individual reinforcement of heterosexuality as the norm means that most people across identity categories go through life with a more or less conscious understanding that heterosexuals fit the norm while queer, bisexual, lesbian, and gay people do not. Norms form part of a pervasive hegemonic system that can seem enormously difficult to change.

INDIVIDUALS EXPERIENCE PRIVILEGE AND DISADVANTAGE RELATIVE TO HOW THEY HAVE BEEN CATEGORIZED INTO SOCIAL IDENTITY GROUPS

Each of us has multiple *social group identities* that are based on our *social group memberships*. Both are based on *categories* that are socially constructed and have long roots in established historical legacies, as described above. These categories represent ways of sorting people and establishing privileges or exclusions based solely on their social group memberships. There is almost always a history of injustice behind the establishment of these social categories.

Participants who are not familiar with the idea of *social categories, social group memberships*, and *social identities* may confuse these with specific *social roles* (such as parent-child, teacher-student, doctor-patient). Although social roles are also constructed and often are attached to power differences, they are not essentialized to the same extent as social group memberships.

Social group memberships are also not the same as *voluntary club* or *team memberships* (Republican-Democrat, hockey player-Little League member, volunteer for Big Brothers Big Sisters). One key difference is that we are free to join and leave such groups without feeling or being perceived as a "different person" as a result of the change (unlike when someone undergoes religious conversion or gender transition, for example). There may be overlaps and interactions among one's social group memberships and identity (e.g., as a Latina), social roles (e.g., as a mother, a wife, and a college teacher) and voluntary memberships (e.g., on a Board of Directors for an Upward Bound program). Nevertheless, the distinction is important because of the strength of socially constructed hegemonic meanings attached to social group memberships and identities.

Social categories, social group memberships and social identities. The core concepts of social category and social identity are closely related but not the same. Social categories are socially constructed, with historical legacies, enforced hegemonic meanings, and widespread unquestioned acceptance. Although socially constructed and therefore potentially changeable, social categories and the meaning attached to them tend to remain relatively stable. Thus, we tend to experience our social group memberships as fixed, natural, and inevitable, and accordingly our social identities—how we "identify with" our social group memberships—feel like inherent traits.

Some social group memberships are inherited from our families (such as race and ethnicity) or from the group we are assigned to at birth (such as class and sex). Some are relatively fixed, while others may emerge or change over time. Our social class or terms for ethnic self-identification may change with economic circumstances, migration, political organizing, and other life events that impact our access to resources (Hurtado & Gurin, 2004). People born with no disabilities may acquire a disability through accident, illness, or aging; and all of us start off as children, move as we age into the category of adult, and if we're lucky eventually become elders. Although we often talk about one social identity at a time, in actuality we experience them simultaneously. One is not separately a white person, an elder, and male; one is an old white man. Each unique combination of social identities carries its own social meanings and its own combinations of advantages and disadvantages.

As individuals, we do not choose the hegemonic meanings that are attached to our social group memberships. Yet we do have some degree of agency in how we make meaning of our social identities. For example, members of disadvantaged social groups often contest derogatory terms applied to their group by reclaiming these terms and giving them positive meaning. Hence, the embracing of "queer" by people who see themselves as outside social norms of heterosexuality and/or binary gender, as an affirmative spin on a term that has been used as a negative slur (and is still negative to some people). Similarly, "Black" and "Afro-Latino" have been embraced as positive umbrella terms for communities of color who affirm their African heritage, despite specific ethnic identities they might also claim (African American or Dominican), and in contradiction to the pejorative associations attached to Blackness in the dominant culture.

In addition to reclaiming terms, sometimes communities and movements seek to replace terms whose meanings are offensive, outdated, and/or inaccurate. Shifts in the words groups use to describe themselves, and that may eventually be adopted by government and other institutions, reflect new layers in the construction of social categories. In social justice workshops and courses, we ask that participants become aware of changes in terminology and meanings associated with social group memberships over time. For example, terms like "retarded," "idiot," and "feebleminded" originated as medical diagnoses. The terms were used to stigmatize and disenfranchise people within the medical system, in legal proceedings, and in communities. Because of this oppressive history, disability advocates have pushed for a shift to language that is more descriptive, less value-laden, and uses "people first" phrasing to recognize that someone's disability is not the only salient fact about them, such as "people with intellectual disabilities." In 2010, these efforts gained legal recognition in Rosa's Law, which changed the references to "mental retardation" in many federal statutes to refer instead to "intellectual disability."

Border identities. Social group categories are often constructed as binary, but the reality of how identities play out, especially across different contexts and settings, is far more complex. Sometimes identities do not fall clearly on one side of an advantaged/disadvantaged binary. We acknowledge this nuance with the idea of *border identities*, identities that border but do not fully fit either category. Examples of border identities include people of mixed racial backgrounds, children adopted and raised by parents of a different race than their own, and young adults who are over the age of legal majority but still treated as young or immature.

The concept of "border identity" is open to contestation. For example, bisexual individuals might in some ways be considered to occupy a border location between heterosexuality and gay/lesbian identity. However, many bisexual people see themselves as a specific identity category whose subordinated status is experienced differently from the subordination of gays or lesbians. Similarly, the social identity of multiraciality or mixed-race has emerged as a separate social category, not "in between" dominant and subordinated groups, but rather occupying a unique location with its own specific experiences of domination and subordination. In this redefinition, the concept of border identity makes room for individuals to identify with both their multiple-family heritages and their own lived experiences in an identity category that differs from their parents' identity category.

Advantage and disadvantage attached to social group membership. In this volume, we present six forms of oppression, each of them based on social categories of advantage and disadvantage—racism; classism; religious oppression; ableism; youth/age oppression; and sexism, heterosexism and transgender oppression (considered together). These isms are rooted in U.S. and global categories of domination and subordination. A central task for instructors and students in justice education courses is to understand, explore, and compare how people are privileged and/or marginalized on the basis of both particular social group memberships and intersecting group memberships.

Almost everyone has some identities that confer advantage (privilege) and others that confer disadvantage. People are often less aware of their advantaged identities and more aware of their disadvantaged identities. The salience of particular identities may also vary depending on context and other factors, but they all matter. For example, Barack Obama is widely referred to as the first black president of the U.S. In addition to being black, he is also male, heterosexual, and Christian; benefits from considerable financial and educational privilege as a lawyer and college professor; and is the biracial son of a white mother. His blackness is salient in public discourse because his success as a leader contradicts many of the dominant associations with blackness, while his privileged identities may seem unremarkable because they are shared with most other political leaders. Yet those privileged identities probably played an important role in securing voters' confidence in him, even though the privileges they confer are less secure than they would be for a politician who is white. Thus, it is rarely useful to categorize someone simply as advantaged or disadvantaged; instead, we encourage consideration of *how* someone is advantaged and/or disadvantaged by particular social group memberships and combinations of social group memberships.

Privilege. People are often unaware of privileges accorded to them based on dominant social group memberships, because those privileges have been *normalized* to be expected. By contrast, people who are denied the same privileges are often painfully aware of them. Advantaged groups sometimes oppose social justice change efforts because they fear losing privileges that they assume to be their "rights" even though those so-called rights are not enjoyed by everyone. *Privileges* are benefits based on social group membership that are available to some people and not others, and sometimes at the expense of others. Some privileges are material—such as access to adequate health care—while others are nonmaterial—such as the ability to experience oneself as normal and central in society. The concept of *privilege* reminds us that such benefits are not earned, but rather result from social advantage relative to others' disadvantage (Case, 2013; Johnson, 2006; Kimmel & Ferber, 2009; Wildman, 1996; see also Chapter 1).

Some examples of privileges include:

- White men can count on being perceived as professional and their expertise as legitimate.
- Heterosexual couples, especially those who conform to norms of gender expression, can count on their relationships being seen as natural.
- Owning-class and professional middle-class young people can make decisions about which career paths to pursue without worrying about supporting themselves or their family members financially.

Many further examples of privilege can be found in each ism chapter.

SOCIAL GROUP MEMBERSHIPS, IDENTITIES, AND FORMS OF OPPRESSION ARE INTERSECTIONAL AT ALL LEVELS

Intersectionality suggests that our various advantaged and disadvantaged social group memberships do not act independent of one another, or in a simply additive way. Rather, they interrelate to create specific experiences of oppression that are not reducible to one or another identity (Crenshaw, 2003; Hankivsky, 2014). For example, people of color who experience racial microaggressions are complicated by gender (for women and for men alike, as well as those whose gender expression is outside the norm), by religion (given the ways that religions associated with the Arab or Asian diaspora are racialized or the Black Church historically kept outside of white Christianity), by class (given the ways in which economic advantage or disadvantage are linked to racial classification), and so on (Cross, 2012; Wijeyesinghe & Jackson, 2012).

Patricia Hill Collins proposes

> placing Black women's experiences at the center of analysis . . . through a both/and conceptual lens of the simultaneity of race, class, and gender oppression and of the need for a humanist vision of community [that] creates new possibilities for an empowering Afrocentric feminist knowledge. Many Black feminist intellectuals have long thought about the world in this way because this is the way we experience the world.
>
> (Collins, 2000, pp. 221–222)

She points out that "a system of interlocking race, class, and gender oppression" for any historical or contemporary context will offer a more accurate and inclusive framework that focuses attention on both the core and the intersecting systems of oppression. "Assuming that each system needs the others in order to function creates a distinct theoretical stance that stimulates [our] rethinking" (Collins, 2000, p. 222). Collins further proposes a "paradigmatic shift" that asks that we think inclusively about other structures of oppression (age, sexual orientation, religion, ethnicity) and conceptualize all such oppression, and resistance, at all three levels "of personal biography; the group or community level of the cultural context created by race, class, and gender; and the systemic level of social institutions" (Collins, 2000, p. 227).

This paradigmatic shift replaces additive or binary models of oppression through models of intersecting axes of race, gender, social class, and other social categories that operate at all three levels of social organization (the individual, cultural, and institutional)—each representing sites of domination as well as potential sites for resistance. But there is a limit to the generalizability of this approach (as in Fig. 4.3), which is "centered" at the core of intersecting axes. Although this "center" conveys the centrality of any one system of oppression, it generates further inquiry, whether the "center" implies some core identity, a "fixity

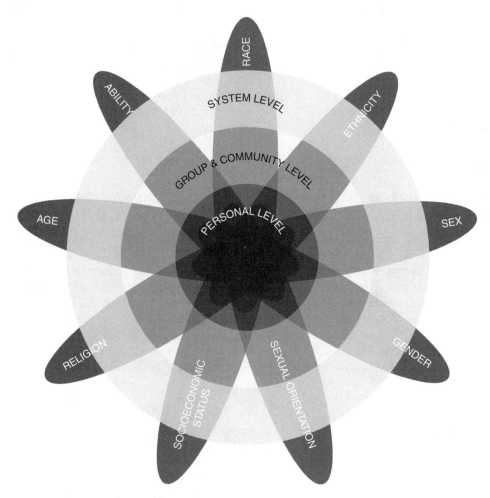

Figure 4.3 Matrix of Interlocking Systems and Levels of Oppression and Resistance
Adapted by Zúñiga, X. & Lee, E. Y. (2015).

or status" that "does not adequately represent the fluidity of identities" for a "self" that is always in process (Holvino, 2012, p. 171). Instead, Holvino further pushes the envelope to reconceptualize identity as "simultaneity," which means "the *simultaneous processes of identity, institutional and social practices*, which operate concurrently and together to construct people's identities and shape their experiences, opportunities, and constraints"; and by "*processes of identity practice*," Holvino means, "the ways in which differences like race, ethnicity, gender, class, and sexuality produce and reproduce particular identities that define how individuals come to see themselves and how others see them" (2012, p. 172, author's italics). Wijeyesinghe visualizes a de-centered universe of social identities as simultaneously and mutually affecting field forces through gravitational pull (Wijeyesinghe, 2012, pp. 98–99).

Thus, it becomes clear that intersections occur at the same moment not only within personal experience, but also at institutional, systemic, and cultural levels that have impacts in the moment and also across time, affecting individuals and social groups. For example:

- Policies like "stop and frisk," "three strikes," and unequal enforcement of drug laws, which disproportionately impact black and brown men and women who are economically disadvantaged;

- Hiring practices that prioritize academic credentials over life experience, and salary negotiations based on previous salary that tend to benefit people who are white, male, and have relative class privilege;
- Media "handlers" for top-level political candidates who strive to identify their candidates with the middle class, emphasize Christian family values, assume heterosexuality (especially if there is no visible spouse or partner), and downplay the extremes of youth or age.

Each ism chapter in this book foregrounds a single issue for purposes of depth and clarity, without losing sight of intersections. Participants are asked to focus on a single social identity for in-depth exploration. This focus also prevents dynamics where participants may divert attention from a topic they find challenging (white women facing the advantages of racism) to one that is less challenging (trying to shift focus to sexism). At the same time, we recognize that participants experience themselves intersectionally. Even as we focus on one ism at a time, we hold the understanding that our identities and experiences are not actually separable, and make room to explore intersections in each design.

THE IMPORTANCE OF CRITICAL AWARENESS, KNOWLEDGE, AND SKILLS TO CHALLENGE, RESIST, AND TAKE EFFECTIVE ACTION FOR CHANGE

Important goals of SJE include helping participants recognize oppressive situations when they encounter them, and developing the knowledge and skills to take action when possible (Pasque & Harris, 2013). These goals are built into some of the core concepts addressed earlier in this chapter, such as making the transition from a "Cycle of Socialization" into a "Cycle of Liberation" using the questions in the cycle of socialization as openings for change (Harro, 2013b). Instead of feeling hopeless and overwhelmed by the pervasive and damaging impacts of oppression on entire groups of people, we want to help participants turn attention to places where they can take action to create change, both as individuals and through coalitions and networks with others (Duncan-Andrade, 2009; Tatum, 1992; West, 2004, Zúñiga, 2013). Thus, we build into our SJE curricula activities to build awareness, knowledge, skill, and practice for change.

Barbara Love has framed individual preparation as "developing a liberatory consciousness" (in homage to Freire), and she identifies awareness, analysis, action, and accountability/allyship as key ingredients for individual action (2013). Awareness and analysis involve identifying places where the normalization of systems of privilege and disadvantage should be questioned, resisted, and changed at all levels—social, cultural, institutional, and personal. As noted earlier, these often overlap.

Learning to question oneself and others, and to resist and transform hegemonic norms and oppressive practices, can take many forms. Historical accounts of past and recent people's struggles for human and civil rights, and for equity and justice, provide powerful illustrations of how members of different social groups have struggled—for basic human rights to food, safety, shelter, minimal wage—as well as for civil rights, educational equity, immigration reform, redistribution of wealth, and against different forms of violence, including hate crimes, violence against women, and police brutality against men and women of color. One important lesson from reading and studying people's struggles is that we must not despair. As Zinn puts it, through the study of history, "we can find not only war but resistance to war, not only injustice but rebellion against injustice, not only selfishness but self-sacrifice, not only silence in the face of tyranny but defiance, not only callousness but compassion" (2002, p. 4). Things do change as result of such struggles. The study of history can motivate and inspire people to create and sustain change.

Individuals also can learn to recognize and interrupt their own complicity in the reproduction of systems of privilege and oppression (Case, 2013; Leondar-Wright, 2005; Pittelman, 2005; Wildman, 1996; Young, 2011). As Collins (2000) observes, we often fail to see how our own values, ideas, and behaviors contribute to perpetuate someone else's mistreatment or disadvantaged location. Thus, increased knowledge and awareness of how we have been socialized to participate in the reproduction of systems of privilege and oppression is a critical first step toward envisioning and working toward social justice.

However, recognizing our role in the perpetuation of injustice versus acting on that injustice take two very different mind-sets, and moving from one to the other involves intentional steps. Love's (2013) "liberatory consciousness" outlines a path for navigating the transition from awareness to analysis, taking action and being accountable.

Participants need to develop their communication and collaborative skills and practice different ways of intervening in difficult situations. These can be practiced in classrooms and workshops through role-plays, especially if they are based on scenarios developed by participants of real-life situations in which they wish they could act.

It is often the case, however, that unjust policies and practices require more than a single individual to create and sustain change. Institutions are complex entities, and change calls for assets from multiple members of coalitions within and outside the institution or community, as well as across advantaged and disadvantaged identity groups (Anyon, 2005). The process of "action planning" proposed in all the chapter designs stresses intentional planning that includes critical analysis, collaboration, seeking multiple perspectives and information sources, and building dialogue and networks across divides. Effective change plans take into account step-by-step timelines, resources, considerations of obstacles, spheres of influence, and risk levels for participants.

Intentional planning and critical analysis include understanding how various forms of privilege and oppression are connected at the psychological, interpersonal, intergroup, structural/institutional, and global levels. This calls for self-awareness of identities and positionality among members of networks and coalitions; it values reciprocity as distinct from "do-good-ism"; it requires intergroup communication skills in order to work across differences; and it needs leadership as well as followership skills to share responsibility collaboratively. It takes a vision of the end goal, so one will know whether or not the desired change has been achieved. These challenging processes are addressed by a growing literature on intergroup dialogue and cross-identity coalitions (Gurin, Nagda & Zúñiga, 2013; Lakey, 2010; Leondar-Wright, 2014; Rose, 2000).

Activists use a range of terms to talk about change at the individual or institutional levels. *Allies* are people who work in alliance with others toward a shared goal of change. *Allies* might be members of privileged groups who are ready to leverage their privilege toward change. They might be people who have transformed disadvantage into empowerment to work on their own behalf and those of others. Other terms include *activists*, *advocates*, and *change agents*, all of whom are likely to be individuals working within *coalitions* or *networks* within communities or organizations. Change at the cultural and societal level calls for broad-based social movements (Leondar-Wright, 2014).

There are countless opportunities in our personal lives to question oppressive beliefs and discriminatory practices and policies, and to work in alliance with others to change them. For example:

- People can interrupt offensive jokes and educate friends about the impact of microaggressions.
- A teacher can incorporate social justice issues into courses not ordinarily focused on social justice.

- A community organizer can create networks of school administrators and service providers to create continuity of support for the children of migrant workers or homeless youth.
- Men can choose to do their fair share of childcare and housework even though sexism would let them get away with not doing it, and make themselves accountable to women in their lives.
- A person with financial resources can make micro-loans to people in need, and donate money to organizations led by poor people.
- People of all ages can make commitments to practice awareness, analysis, action, and accountability in their relationships and interactions.

While the tools for creating change at the personal and interpersonal level may include our own growing awareness, knowledge, commitments, passions, and skills for interrupting oppression and the increased capacity to leverage support for social justice actions in our own sphere of influence, these tools may not be sufficient to challenge hegemonic forces at the institutional and cultural level. We can certainly take active roles in organizations and institutions to change policies and practices impacting people's lives, but we are likely to be more effective to promote change beyond personal and interpersonal contexts by engaging in collective action. Forging pathways for collective action may require understanding the role of social movements in contributing to the most durable instances of change (Pharr, 1997; Tilly, 1978). Social movement methods such as protests, strikes, sit-ins, boycotts, and informing the public of specific discriminatory policies have been historically effective in advancing social justice goals. Along with historical examples, instructors and participants should be aware of current-day alliances, coalitions, and networks that are taking effective action toward legal, structural, and economic changes (Zúñiga, 2013).

Not everyone who participates in a social justice course will choose to take action. Still, it is important that participants be equipped with the tools and skills to translate their visions and ideas into action plans, as well as to identify what may propel and sustain their motivation to act on their principles (Goodman, 2011; Zúñiga, Nagda, Chesler, & Cytron-Walker, 2007).

For example, participants can be supported to:

- Practice intergroup communication skills, including learning to listen well, express emotions, ask clarifying questions, and address conflicts across social identities;
- Recognize examples of oppression in everyday life;
- Learn to navigate oppressive dynamics with awareness, and think creatively about options for responding;
- Develop the capacity for empathy for the experiences of individuals and groups different from us;
- Analyze current and historical examples of social action, particularly of other students or young people who are so engaged;
- Develop action plans with the support of peer mentors who have had experience doing similar efforts.

The examples listed above represent essential methods and skills for translating core concepts into action, advancing social justice goals in one's spheres of influence, and engaging in the complex communication and decision-making needed to create transformative change at personal, institutional, and cultural levels. Supporting participants to find confidence and competence, inspiration, and courage for the long haul is an important goal for social justice educators.

PART 2: SAMPLE DESIGN FOR TEACHING CORE SOCIAL JUSTICE CONCEPTS

The design that follows embodies the core concepts using principles of design and facilitation from the two preceding chapters. The focus on how to teach core concepts offers a bridge from Chapter 1 to the designs in the ism chapters that follow.

The design also draws upon the pedagogical principles offered in Chapter 2. These principles are implicit in the design, and include creating an inclusive social justice learning community; attending to participant emotions as they engage with SJE concepts; emphasizing active, engaged, and collaborative learning; using activities that enable participants to connect personal experiences of their various social identities to abstract SJE concepts; and encouraging personal growth and collaborative efforts toward change. Although SJE pedagogy, design, and facilitation (like social justice theory) have already been examined in the preceding three chapters, here we provide an example of the implementation of these frameworks to help instructors and facilitators get started.

Instructors/facilitators should be aware that the core concepts are not only key content but also central to the learning process of an SJE course. The dynamics of oppression that are "out there" in the larger social world are also "in here" in learning communities. Social justice education is not a matter of abstract knowledge alone; it involves the lived experience of facilitators and participants in the class. Participants bring a range of prior experiences to social justice courses, including different levels of knowledge of and comfort with social justice content, as well as different levels of skill for self-reflection and complex thinking. The interplay of these elements within the social justice learning community requires special attention to the sequence and scaffolding of learning activities and the flexibility of design, pedagogy, and facilitation. While a repertoire of pedagogy, sequence, and facilitation strategies is used to plan ahead and anticipate potential challenges, social justice instructors and facilitators also need to remain alert and flexible to revise the anticipated sequence of activities and adapt the pedagogy as situations evolve.

This part of the chapter offers a sample four-quadrant design. It can serve as a stand-alone course or workshop that introduces the core concepts of SJE, or it can serve as the introductory segment of a single- or multiple-ism course or workshop. Whichever way this design is used, its effectiveness resides in foregrounding the core concepts. Taken together, the core concepts help us analyze various manifestations of oppression in the past and present. The ism-oriented chapters that follow this chapter, although they also present core concepts, do so in a way that is embedded in the exploration of one ism. Here, we focus attention on the core concepts as content in and of themselves. We call attention to the pedagogical and design decisions we have made so that instructors and facilitators who might want to make other choices can do so without losing sight of the core concepts that are the crux of our approach.

The general progression of the design is the following. Quadrant 1 begins by establishing a learning community with various active-learning pedagogies that enable participants to get to know each other individually. It then briefly introduces the core concepts of our SJE approach. The personal learning focus of Quadrant 2 builds on these core concepts, even though some, such as the interrelationship of "levels" (individual, institutional, cultural and societal) are not explored in depth until later. By introducing the concepts early, we help participants contextualize the personal work they will do in Quadrant 2 in developing awareness of socialization processes, social categories, social group memberships, and social identities. Quadrant 3 takes participants to the bigger picture (institutional and cultural/societal levels). The focus is on historical legacies, social construction, and analysis of current examples of oppression. Quadrant 4 focuses on "what next" by presenting frameworks and rubrics that participants can use to identify opportunities for change and develop action plans.

As discussed in Chapter 3, this design strives for a balance among different learning styles, between formal and informal learning modes, and between self-focused reflection and engagement with others. Opportunities for creating such balance will differ depending on the specific needs and contexts of each set of participants and facilitators. We offer this design for illustrative purposes only, and explain (in Part 3) *how* and *why* we chose the options presented in this design, rather than suggest (incorrectly) that one size fits all. We encourage instructors and facilitators to use this design as an example of how to apply concepts of pedagogy, design and facilitation from Chapters 2 and 3, and consider how best to embody those concepts in their own work.

Detailed activity descriptions, along with handouts and other materials needed to implement the design, are available on the Chapter 4 website. Where the design calls for a lecture presentation, we have not provided a script; rather, we assume that instructors and facilitators will use content already presented in this chapter, other chapters, and/or additional sources to prepare their lecture.

Design for Teaching Core Concepts of SJE

Quadrant 1: Introductions, Learning Community, and SJE Approach
1. Welcome Activity
2. Introductions
3. Creating Learning Community
4. Comfort Zones, Learning Edges & Triggers
5. SJE Approach
6. Closing Activity

Quadrant 2: Cycle of Socialization, and Social Identity and Positionality
1. Check-In and Opportunity to Revisit Guidelines
2. Cycle of Socialization
3. Personal Identity and Social Identity
4. Social Group Membership, Positionality, and Intersectionality
5. Experiences of Advocacy or Empowerment
6. Closing Activity

Quadrant 3: Institutional Manifestations and Historical Legacies
1. Historical Overview
2. Current Examples of Oppression
3. Web of Oppression
4. Unweaving the Web
5. Closing Activity

Quadrant 4: Action and Change
1. Envisioning Change
2. Taking Action Terminology
3. Frameworks for Creating Change
4. Action Continuum and Spheres of Influence
5. Action Planning
6. Affirmations

QUADRANT 1: INTRODUCTIONS, LEARNING COMMUNITY, AND SJE APPROACH

Learning Objectives [content and process outcomes]:
1. Develop a collaborative and respectful learning community, based on personal and group norms and guidelines
2. Distinguish SJE approach from other approaches (such as diversity education)
3. Identify key elements of SJE approach to oppression and its manifestations at various levels and types

Key Concepts:
- Social justice, diversity, SJE
- Oppression as a structural and societal phenomenon
- Various manifestations of oppression: Levels and types
- Comfort zones, learning edges, triggers

Activities and Options:

1. Welcome: We offer two options, both icebreakers in which participants get to know each other. Option A allows participants to mingle freely, while in Option B, interactions are more structured.

2. Introductions:

   Option A: In dyads, participants introduce each other using suggested prompts.

   Option B: Participants introduce themselves to the whole group by sharing something about the meaning of their names. This provides an early opportunity to begin thinking about salient social identities on a personal level.

   Option C: Common Ground is a more structured opportunity for sharing, and highlights commonalities and differences within the group.

3. Learning community: Both options establish group norms and guidelines; Option A is an abbreviated version and Option B contains more in-depth discussion based on participants' hopes and concerns.

4. Comfort zone, learning edge, and triggers: Presentation and discussion of these concepts and their definitions, particularly as they concern the use of group guidelines.

5. SJE approach: Presentation of SJE approach to oppression and its manifestations at personal, institutional, societal, and cultural levels. The different options focus on some or all core concepts using different conceptual organizers.

6. Closing activity: Opportunity to bring some closure to this segment before transitioning to a different topic, taking a break, or ending a session.

QUADRANT 2: CYCLE OF SOCIALIZATION, AND SOCIAL IDENTITY AND POSITIONALITY

Learning Objectives:

1. Understand processes of socialization within institutional structures, including internalization and reproduction of received messages (both conceptually and personally)

2. Understand the concept of social identities and their relationship to statuses of advantage and disadvantage

3. Become aware of intersections of multiple identities and statuses

Key Concepts:

- Socialization, reproduction, and internalization
- Social categories, social group memberships, and social group identity
- Social status and position: Advantage, inclusion, social power, and privilege; disadvantage, exclusion, powerlessness, and marginalization
- Intersectionality: Intersections of multiple (different) social group identities and location
- Advocacy and empowerment

Activities and Options:

1. Check-in and opportunity to revisit learning community guidelines.

2. Cycle of Socialization: Both options review the cycle of socialization model. Option A uses a lecture presentation including visual representations of the cycle, and Option B involves participants in an activity based on the cycle.

3. Personal identity and social identity:

   Option A: Instructors and facilitators can prepare their own lecture presentation on personal and social identity by drawing upon the text in Chapter 4 (and the PowerPoint slides provided for Quadrant 1 on Part 1 of the Ch. 4 Website).

   Option B: An interactive activity generates examples of these two concepts with participant input.

4. Social group memberships, positionality, and intersectionality:
Option A: An interactive lecture presentation on these core concepts.
Option B: Participants take an individual inventory, followed by small group discussion, of situations in which they have felt advantaged or disadvantaged based on their social group memberships.
5. Experiences of advocacy or empowerment: This activity encourages participants to draw on their own experiences to share personal examples of advocacy or empowerment.
6. Closing activity: Opportunity to bring some closure to this segment before transitioning to a different topic, taking a break, or ending a session.

QUADRANT 3: INSTITUTIONAL MANIFESTATIONS AND HISTORICAL LEGACIES

Learning Objectives:
1. Awareness of the multiple manifestations of oppression at different levels: Individual, institutional, and cultural, and how they intersect and reinforce each other to create a hegemonic "web" of oppression
2. Awareness of how hegemony and the "web" of oppression impacts individuals
3. Understanding of social construction and hegemony as links between historical legacies and contemporary manifestations
4. Exploration of current impacts of selected historical legacies as well as historical resistance movements
5. Understanding of current institutional examples as well as efforts toward change

Key Concepts:
- Institutional manifestations of oppression
- Concepts of social construction and hegemony
- Role of historical legacies behind current institutional manifestations
- Historical and current intersections
- Historical examples and current opportunities for resistance and change

Activities and Options:
1. Historical overview: Option A is a lecture presentation noting key episodes for each of three different isms and addressing social construction and hegemony. Option B is a group in which participants discuss key historical events related to different isms and generate examples of current-day manifestations.
2. Current examples of oppression: Both options ask participants to generate a variety of examples of contemporary manifestations of oppression. Option A uses the "levels and types" framework and Option B uses the "Five Faces of Oppression" framework.
3. Web of oppression: An interactive, kinesthetic activity demonstrating how interconnections among institutional manifestations of oppression create a ubiquitous "web."
4. Unweaving the web: A continuation of the web of oppression focusing on its impermanence and highlighting opportunities for change.
5. Closing activity: Opportunity to bring some closure to this segment before transitioning to a different topic, taking a break, or ending a session.

QUADRANT 4: ACTION AND CHANGE

Learning Objectives:
1. Explore some of the different pathways individuals and groups can take to envision change, plan, initiate, and create change

2. Develop skills for planning for change in one's personal life, community, or workplace
3. Understand key considerations for initiating a change plan such as: Individual and collective action, action continuum, and spheres of influence
4. Consider specific frameworks for creating individual and collective change
5. Plan a realistic and feasible action plan to effect change toward social justice

Key Concepts:
- Models for creating change: Liberatory consciousness, Cycle of Liberation, action continuum, and spheres of influence
- Action planning skills (identifying goals, clarifying roles, assessing risks/challenges, social support, and resources)
- Empowerment, allyship, and advocacy

Activities and Options:
1. Envisioning change: An opportunity to visualize ways of creating change in small groups and the large group.
2. Taking action terminology: Supports the development of a shared language for taking action and creating change.
3. Frameworks for creating change:
   Option A: Uses Love's Four Elements of Liberatory Consciousness to encourage participants to think about their own agency in systems and possibilities for liberation.
   Option B: Uses Harro's stages of the Cycle of Liberation to structure an activity focusing on self-empowerment, building community, and transforming institutions and organizations.
4. Action continuum and spheres of influence: Encourages discussion about possible action steps participants can take to begin to create changes in their personal lives and the lives of their communities.
5. Action planning: Individual and small-group activity that supports participants to generate realistic action plans.
6. Affirmations: An opportunity to affirm the learning and to bring closure to the four quadrants before transitioning to a different topic or ending the course/workshop.

PART 3: FACILITATION ISSUES FOR CORE SJE CONCEPTS

An intentional SJE learning community is grounded in the principles described in the preceding chapters on theory, pedagogy, facilitation, and design. Those chapters offer different entry points as well as judgment calls in the preparation of social justice courses and workshops. This stand-alone or introductory session on core SJE concepts involves decisions about the following questions concerning sequence and facilitation:

1. Where and how to start?
2. How to build an inclusive learning community?
3. How to bring participant social identities and social positions into focus?
4. How to work with expression of emotions and challenges posed by complex ideas?
5. How to balance focusing on specific identities with acknowledging and exploring intersections?

6. How to provide the knowledge and skills needed to move toward taking action for change?

7. How to provide closure at the conclusion of the course/workshop? or How to transition from this opening segment of a longer course/workshop?

WHERE AND HOW TO START?

In considering where best to begin a workshop or course focusing on core concepts, we draw on the principle of scaffolding (see Chapters 2 and 3) and the framework of "confirmation, contradiction, and continuity" (Kegan, 1982). An important decision for instructors and facilitators is whether to begin with "big picture" knowledge and awareness of social systems, or to start with self-knowledge and personal awareness. Factors to consider include the characteristics of the ism, the readiness of participants, and the time available. If we choose to begin with the "big picture," we start by explaining what we mean by a social justice approach. The approach taken in this design is to start with the personal, by building community and engaging participants.

Therefore, we devote Quadrant 1 to welcoming, active sharing, and community-building activities that immediately get participants engaged with each other and with the topic. This establishes that the class will be interactive and that what participants bring to the class will be part of the content for discussion. We interactively establish norms and guidelines for the learning community and introduce the concepts of comfort zones, learning edges, and triggers. Even before we introduce the SJE approach and core concepts, participants have already begun to make personal connections to the content. Once this active learning environment has been established, we can make the transition to some of the "big picture" concepts of historical legacies, social categories, social group membership, and reproduction of oppression at different levels of social organization—concepts that will be explored in greater depth in Quadrants 2 and 3.

HOW TO BUILD AN INCLUSIVE LEARNING COMMUNITY?

The development and maintenance of an SJE learning community is an ongoing process that needs explicit and careful attention early and throughout the course or workshop. This is a generic process that can be adapted for any SJE course or workshops. We begin with an opening (or upon-arrival) activity that serves as a meet-and-greet or icebreaker, before the session starts officially. We go over the agenda, do logistical announcements, and introduce our frameworks and assumptions, all of which contribute to setting the tone as much as the attention paid to introductions and establishing norms and guidelines. The agenda can be a simplified form of the instructors' session plan, such as the four-quadrant design illustrated in this chapter and the chapters that follow. Reviewing the agenda provides an opportunity for participants to see what lies ahead and to express questions or concerns, which instructors can note, and either respond to immediately or address later in an emended design. Logistical announcements should include information about the building and surroundings (where to find restrooms, food to purchase, accessibility information, etc.), approximate times when breaks will happen, and so on. This is also a good time to remind participants of the opportunity to tell instructors about any accessibility needs that have not yet been communicated.

Norms and guidelines, generated by the participants as a way of acknowledging and addressing their hopes and concerns, is one key element that should happen near the beginning. The norms and guidelines for the learning community should be based on the desire of participants to learn and their agreement to respect each other, as well as their willingness to engage with the subject matter and take responsibility for their own learning. It should include procedures that allow participants to reflect on how the learning community is doing as the class or workshop continues (e.g., mid-way feedback forms, group process checks).

As participants propose guidelines, facilitators may need to post clarifying questions with regard to guidelines that are overly general. Often the answers to such clarifying questions reveal assumptions based in cultural, linguistic, generational, or gendered differences. For example, the indicators of listening vary across cultures. It is important to note these differences in how our various identities and experiences impact our expectations and desires for a learning environment. Facilitators should be careful not to have too many guidelines that limit or restrict communication, honesty, and difference of expression, especially differences that are likely to be connected with social identities.

In generating guidelines, participants often mention a concern about whether the course/workshop will be a "safe" place to take risks. Similarly, many participants come into SJE with worries that they will "make a mistake" and "push the buttons" of ("trigger") someone else. Often these participants are afraid that they will be "called out" or personally attacked for saying something or repeating a stereotype they've heard in the popular culture (Helmreich, 1982) that is offensive and that triggers other participants.

These are learning opportunities, when everyone is outside the comfort zone and on a learning edge. Facilitators may want to repeat the distinction between safety and comfort. Participants often find it reassuring to know that although there will be times when everyone is uncomfortable, the facilitator and the participants are in agreement that no one will be personally attacked. The concepts of comfort zones, learning edges, and triggers can help to introduce the idea that discomfort is sometimes productive for learning. They can also serve as guides to help participants understand and explore their reactions to course content, activities, and other participants' perspectives.

These discussions establish the expectation of a challenging environment in which discomfort is expected and can be a sign of growth and learning, and in which efforts to stretch oneself are supported. Facilitators can assure participants that in order to learn and grow, they need a learning environment in which mistakes can be made, difficult questions can be asked, contradictory information and experiences can be explored, and where people can find ways to support each other and draw on each other's different experiences to expand their own knowledge, awareness, and skills (Goodman, 2011; Wasserman & Doran, 1999).

Next, we present information to participants about comfort zone, learning edge, and triggers (see Activity 4 on the website). After explaining the concepts of comfort zones, learning edges, and triggers, facilitators can invite participants to identify a process for naming triggers and being conscious of learning edges in ways that encourage open and respectful dialogue. This could be as simple as inviting participants who feel triggered or pushed beyond their learning edge to say so. Such practices can generate significant learning opportunities later on in the course.

A more practical aspect of group norms and guidelines has to do with the use of personal electronics during the course/workshop. On one hand, participants should be allowed to use devices that act as accommodations for them (e.g., in the case of participants with learning disabilities who use laptops to take notes). On the other hand, the trust of the learning community can be challenged or damaged if participants are checking their email or social networks while peers are sharing personal stories or examples of experiences with oppression. Technology should be used when it supports, rather than interrupts, participants' ability to listen respectfully and respond meaningfully. For example, this often means that participants will use laptops during lectures, but put them away during group discussions. Participants who must read or respond to texts during a session (for example, if they have a childcare emergency) should step outside to do so, just as they would to take a phone call. In general, we find that framing this guideline as a matter of mutual respect motivates participants to minimize distracting uses of technology, because they recognize that they want to feel respected and heard when they are sharing.

Once established, the guidelines can be used as a reference point for processing group interaction throughout the course or workshop. For example, the facilitator might periodically ask the group to consider how successful they have been in adhering to the guidelines, or ask if there are guidelines participants need to add, delete, modify, or clarify.

In addition to the specific activities that serve to build a learning community in Quadrant 1 (especially establishing guidelines), facilitators' informal behavior is important. Participants will often be alert to any inconsistencies on the part of the facilitator, so it is worth making an extra effort to plan how participants will enter the room and how they will be greeted, even before the session begins. Throughout the course, community-building needs to be sustained through active facilitation of individual and group learning, sometimes including the informal interaction among participants. Community-building should be introduced intentionally, and then honored and maintained with care and attention through ongoing debriefs and closures for course or workshop segments.

HOW TO BRING PARTICIPANT SOCIAL IDENTITIES AND SOCIAL POSITIONS INTO FOCUS?

Our core concepts highlight the complex relationships between individuals' social identities and systemic patterns of oppression. The design provides many opportunities to notice and highlight these interconnections as they emerge in conversation. For example, we can help participants link someone's personal anecdote to larger institutional or cultural/societal patterns that the group has read or discussed, or we can ask the group for personal examples that illustrate institutional or cultural/societal patterns. The back-and-forth between personal and system examples enables participants to recognize these linkages in situations outside the classroom or workshop.

Many participants are unaware of the multiple ways in which they are implicated in the issues we are discussing. Some will strongly identify with one social group identity that feels vulnerable or subordinated, while others will deny or feel shame about their privileged social group identity. Many participants are unaware of the ways in which their own behaviors, communication patterns, and attitudes may reflect and reproduce some of the larger patterns of advantage and disadvantage that are discussed as course topics. People from privileged groups especially may not be aware of how they come across to others.

Facilitators can use the introductory activities in Quadrant 1 to assess participants' readiness and anticipate potential gaps in understanding and tensions in communication. Facilitators' observations about which concepts participants struggle with or get defensive about can inform decisions about how best to approach these concepts later when they are addressed in greater depth. For example, when participants are struggling with the concept of privilege, the facilitator might turn to activities listed among additional resources in Part 2 of the chapter website.

The value of the experiential learning approach that we use in SJE comes from the discussion ("processing") of activities in which social identities become visible, and in which participants learn by doing. It is important to remember that the learning emerges not from the activity itself so much as the discussion in which participants process what they noticed, how they felt, and new insights they derived about themselves, the group, and the material under examination. This is why activities that encourage speaking and listening are so important early on as crucial pathways for learning for reflective learning (Stassen, Zúñiga, Keehn, Mildred, DeJong, & Varghese, 2013).

WORKING WITH EXPRESSION OF EMOTIONS AND CHALLENGES POSED BY COMPLEX IDEAS

In a stand-alone SJE course or workshop that focuses on core concepts, particular participant concerns are likely to emerge. Sometimes participants may have strong emotional reactions to the content or to interactions that occur in the course/workshop.

One such challenge can occur when participants express the view that some isms are more important than others and should get priority attention. Facilitators can address this by noting that all forms of oppression are damaging, that different forms of oppression have greater or lesser salience at different points in time or different contexts, and that it is divisive and serves no purpose to debate the priority of one over the other. Facilitators can also comment that no one form is the root cause for the others. Thus, SJE does not prioritize class conflict or patriarchy or another system, but rather approaches all forms of oppression as having similar dynamics needing to be addressed in the interests of social justice for everyone.

Another participant view that can come across as resistance is that people who belong to disadvantaged groups have an "agenda" and that people in privileged groups are to blame. Facilitators can address the notion that oppressed people may have an "agenda" by appreciating the energy and forcefulness with which oppressed people have brought social injustice to the forefront of everyone's consciousness. Changing a society in the direction of social justice takes everyone's effort, and people with privilege can use access to resources to advocate and work for change.

Defensiveness on the part of people with social advantage—or anger on the part of people who experience disadvantage—can be addressed it two ways. First, facilitators can acknowledge and validate emotions and provide opportunities to reflect on emotional reactions through free writing or pair shares. Second, facilitators can connect anger or shame about instances of oppression in the present moment to the historical legacies that shaped current realities and that none of us created. The focus on historical legacies allows participants to put aside defensiveness, resentment, or fear that they are personally being blamed in order to see how current inequities and injustices have long roots in the past. Rather than blaming past actors, we can understand the past and learn from it to create a better future. Anger and outrage are essential "fuel" to generate change. Discussion can focus on how to use one's feelings as motivation to work with others who share one's outrage about injustice and oppression.

Whether or not an explicit guideline has been established about responding to triggers, facilitators can remind participants that everyone is there to learn. Participants who feel triggered can be invited to describe their feelings so that their feelings can be validated and others can learn from the experience. The facilitator can also provide context for why certain statements might be triggering. Those whose statements triggered others can be asked to listen rather than defend their comments, to sit on their "learning edge" and pay attention to a different perspective. Remind participants that we are more interested in the impacts of comments than on a speaker's intention, although it is also useful to explore the (mis)information or experience that a triggering experience is based on. Encourage participants to view these discussions as "food for thought" rather than attempts to change an individual participant's views on the spot. No one can focus effective attention on personal learning when they feel defensive or chastised.

There are many choices for facilitators to intervene when members experience triggers, such as stereotypes about their group, expressed by others who may be oblivious about the impact. These moments provide learning opportunities about the difference between intention and impact, the consequences of microaggressions experienced by subordinated peoples on a regular basis, and the defensiveness of privileged people when accused of wrongdoings they don't understand.

We use these difficult moments with generosity, not blame, and talk about the "learning edge" that all of us experience in such moments. We may discuss and model for participants how to give feedback in thoughtful ways. We may ask participants to tell us what kind of feedback would be most useful, or to help the group understand why the words or the situation was triggering.

Facilitators learn to share the opportunities to intervene in challenging interactions. It is not the role of the facilitator to rescue someone from other participants' responses to something they have said or done, unless there is a clear concern about safety. As a learning community matures and gains experience in honoring its own norms and guidelines, facilitators might turn to the group to ask whether there are other approaches to an idea or opinion that has been voiced. That becomes an opportunity to explore, openly, the (mis) information behind stereotypes or the socialization that led to assumptions that are now being challenged in SJE contexts.

The emotional responses that emerge during discussions of social justice are often linked to participants' prior experiences and roles in families and social systems. Participants are often not aware of beliefs or misinformation until they are challenged, and they may be surprised by the strength of emotions associated with these beliefs. Participants may get unexpectedly "triggered" or activated during the course of a discussion. Participants may react to each other in ways that are not helpful in maintaining a (safe) learning community. These are some of the reasons we emphasize the importance of clear norms and guidelines from the very beginning of a class or workshop, so that we can refer back to them as they (inevitably) become challenged or violated.

Instructors and facilitators should anticipate how they themselves feel about the public expression of feelings and emotions in classes or workshops, and to prepare for them in advance (see Chapter 12). Experienced instructors tell participants (as part of the norms and guidelines) that they will have a range of emotional (as well as cognitive) responses to this material, and ask that they offer guidelines that will help everyone through these moments. Also, the advance presentation of concepts about comfort zones, learning edges, and triggers provides maps or guideposts to help participants understand and explore their emotional reactions to class activities and other participants' perspectives (Obear, 2013).

It helps if facilitators acknowledge, upfront and early in a course or workshop, that some of the new ways of thinking are likely to challenge old ways of thinking, and that information may emerge that challenges accepted stereotypes. By alerting participants in advance, they can be better prepared for the times that will happen. Facilitators might also want to explain that SJE courses and workshops will present experiences and perspectives that contradict older ways of thinking, and that by working through these contradictions (problem-solving), participants will develop new thinking skills that will help them solve problems in other parts of their lives. These facilitative "alerts" become preemptive strikes, enabling participants to be ready and armed for challenges to outmoded or previously held world views.

FINDING A BALANCE BETWEEN SINGLE ISM/IDENTITY FOCUS AND THE INTERSECTIONS WITH OTHER ISMS/IDENTITIES

It can be difficult to hold onto more than one ism at a time and to look at the intersection among isms, yet explorations that ignore intersectionality are incomplete. In our approach, we try to find a balance by foregrounding one ism while holding others in the background as a first step.

Facilitators can model making connections between SJE isms—keeping the focus on a specific subject while showing the connections to other subjects, and looping back to the main subject. It is often helpful to demonstrate these examples visually by drawing inter-connections on the board. Facilitators can in-the-moment devise, on chalkboard or news-print, lists of personal examples in one column and lists of institutional, cultural, societal, or historical examples on the other, and draw dotted lines to connect them. Or facilitators can ask for a free-wheeling brainstorm that they record on chalkboard or newsprint, and then ask for help in connecting various "levels" from the brainstorm. Writing is an espe-cially useful tool to hold one thought in place while figuring out another, and offers a more grounded approach for participants who are struggling with intersectionality.

Facilitators can remind participants of their goal that participants will come away from these classes and workshops understanding the ism by having focused on it in some depth, while also appreciating that social identities and social justice issues are always complicated by their intersections at all levels and in all contexts.

INCORPORATING POSSIBILITIES FOR ACTION AND CHANGE

Our constructivist emphasis on the historical legacies behind current manifestations of oppression—as well as the historical legacies of resistance and change—creates numerous opportunities throughout a course or workshop to imagine change in the present that will reshape the future (Pasque & Harris, 2013). Opportunities for action and change are explored throughout our design, not only through a segment devoted to action planning toward the end (although the focused action planning activities are in Quadrant 4). Cur-rent and historical examples of social action and activism are used to inspire participants and to help imagine new possibilities as well as conceptual frameworks such as Harro's Cycle of Liberation and Love's Developing a Liberatory Consciousness. In some cases, facilitators may wish to start a course by imagining a different world without oppression, or they may want to integrate action planning throughout the sequence. The sequencing of action and change is an important element of course or workshop design, as is an approach to facilitation/instruction that is hopeful and explores openings for change.

In some organizational contexts, encouraging students/participants to take action may be discouraged or risky. In some individual cases, participants may not intend to take action against the forms of oppression addressed in the course/workshop. In these situa-tions, facilitators can frame the action-focused segments as opportunities to build skills in planning and collaboration that can be useful in many different family, community, and work situations. Participants' work in action planning will therefore be hypothetical—that is, what might you do, how might you do it, whom might you work with, what steps might you take. In other contexts, where encouraging real action is fair game, participants may actually implement their action ideas. Action projects can be woven into the design of a course and scaffolded to build the capacity for informed action and collaboration (Zúñiga, Nagda, Chesler, & Cytron-Walker, 2007).

On the continuum from action "against inclusion and social justice" to actions "for diversity and social justice," action for positive change can take many forms—from an understanding and analysis of one's own role (usually unrecognized and unacknowledged) in the hegemonic structures that create inequality (Young, 2011) to a willingness to engage with new social movements (Anyon, 2005). Domingue and Neely (2013) encourage instructors/facilitators to frame social action as an ongoing journey, not as one or more isolated events; to act, not to react; and to challenge themselves to re-imagine what change can be. Their key suggestions include:

- Emphasize social action at the beginning of courses or workshops, and maintain the focus throughout;
- Provide current historical examples of activism, especially by students and youth (see King, Rizga, & Palermo, 2008);
- Promote opportunities for student or community leadership and hold participants accountable;
- Provide frequent, consistent support through frequent check-ins, coaching, and celebrations of victories (Domingue & Neely, 2013).

CLOSURE OR TRANSITION

Since participants' learning experiences about key concepts are often emotional, it is important to acknowledge the closure of this course or workshop. Even if this design is used as a segment of a longer course or workshop, the completion of the segment should be marked. Facilitators should communicate appreciation of the individual and collaborative efforts of the learning community, and express hope that participants will build on what they have learned, develop new skills, continue to take risks, and maintain the bonds they have forged.

In those cases in which this is the beginning of a longer class or additional workshops, facilitators can use the transition as an opportunity to gather feedback about what participants feel worked well for them, and what they would like to see changed as they continue in this learning community. Facilitators can also provide some continuity by previewing what is to come in the next phase of a course or series of workshops.

Note

* We ask that those who cite this work always acknowledge by name all of the authors listed rather than either only citing the first author or using "et al." to indicate coauthors. All collaborated on the conceptualization, development, and writing of this chapter.

References

Adams, M. (2014). Social justice and education. In M. Reisch (Ed.), *Routledge international handbook of social justice* (pp. 249–268). London: Routledge.

Anyon, J. (2005). *Radical possibilities: Public policy, urban education, and a new social movement.* New York: Routledge.

Banaji, M. R., & Greenwald, A. G. (2013). *Blindspot: Hidden biases of good people.* New York: Delacorte Press.

Broido, E. M. (2000). The development of social justice allies during college: A phenomenological investigation. *Journal of College Student Development, 41*(1), 3–18.

Brookfield, S. (2005). *The power of critical theory: Liberating adult learning and teaching.* San Francisco: John Wiley & Sons.

Case, K. (Ed.). (2013). *Deconstructing privilege: Teaching and learning as allies in the classroom.* New York: Routledge.

Collins, P. H. (2000). *Black feminist thought: Knowledge, consciousness and the politics of empowerment* (2nd ed.). New York: Routledge.

Crenshaw, K. W. (2003). Traffic at the crossroads: Multiple oppressions. In R. Morgan (Ed.), *Sisterhood is forever: The women's anthology for a new millennium* (pp. 43–57). New York: Washington Square Press.

Cross, W. E. (2012). The enactment of race and other social identities during everyday transactions. In C. L. Wijeyesinghe & B. W. Jackson (Eds.), *New perspectives on racial identity development: Integrating emerging frameworks* (2nd ed., pp. 192–201). New York: New York University Press.

Domingue, A. D., & Neely, D. S. (2013). Why is it so hard to take action: A reflective dialogue about facilitating for social action engagement. In L. M. Landerman (Ed.), *The art of effective facilitation: Reflections from social justice educators* (pp. 231–252). Sterling, VA: Stylus Publishing.

Duncan-Andrade, J.M.R. (2009). Note to educators: Hope required when growing roses in concrete. *Harvard Educational Review, 79*(2), 181–194.

Fraser, J. (1999). *Between church and state: Religion and public education in a multicultural America.* New York: St. Martin's Press.

Freire, P. (1970). *Pedagogy of the oppressed.* New York: Herder & Herder.

Goodman, D. (2011). *Promoting diversity and social justice: Educating people from privileged groups* (2nd ed.). New York: Routledge.

Gurin, P., Nagda, B. A., & Zúñiga, X. (2013). *Dialogue across difference: Practice, theory, and research on intergroup dialogue.* New York: Russell Sage.

Hankivsky, O. (2014). *Intersectionality 101.* Vancouver, BC, Canada: The Institute for Intersectionality Research & Policy, Simon Fraser University. Retrieved from http://www.sfu.ca/iirp/documents/resources/101_Final.pdf

Hardiman, R., Jackson, B. W., & Griffin, P. (2013). Conceptual foundations. In M. Adams, W. J. Blumenfeld, C. Castañeda, H. W. Hackman, M. L. Peters, & X. Zúñiga (Eds.), *Readings for diversity and social justice* (3rd ed., pp. 26–35). New York, NY: Routledge.

Hardiman, R., Jackson, B. W., & Griffin, P. (2007). Conceptual foundations for social justice education. In M. Adams, L. A. Bell, & P. Griffin (Eds.), *Teaching for diversity and social justice* (2nd ed., pp. 35–66). New York: Routledge.

Harro, B. (2013a). The cycle of socialization. In M. Adams, W. J. Blumenfeld, C. Castañeda, H. W. Hacksman, M. L. Peters, & X. Zúñiga (Eds.), *Readings for diversity and social justice* (3rd ed., pp. 45–51). New York: Routledge.

Harro, B. (2013b). The cycle of liberation. In M. Adams, W. J. Blumenfeld, C. Castañeda, H. W. Hacksman, M. L. Peters, & X. Zúñiga (Eds.), *Readings for diversity and social justice* (3rd ed., pp. 618–624). New York: Routledge.

Helmreich, W. B. (1982). *The things they say beyond your back: Stereotypes and the myths behind them.* New Brunswick, NJ: Transaction.

Holvino, E. (2012). The "simultaneity" of identities: Models and skills for the twenty-first century. In C. L. Wijeyesinghe and B. W. Jackson (Eds.), *New perspectives on racial identity development: Integrating emerging frameworks* (2nd ed., pp. 161–191). New York: New York University Press.

Huber, L. P., & Solórzano, D. G. (2014). Racial microaggressions as a tool for critical race research. *Race Ethnicity and Education, 18*(3), 297–320.

Hurtado, A., & Gurin, P. (2004). *Chicana/o in a changing U.S. society: The Mexican American experience.* Tucson, AZ: University of Arizona Press.

Johnson, A. G. (2006). *Privilege, power, and difference* (2nd ed.). New York: McGraw-Hill.

Kegan, R. (1982). *The evolving self: Problems and process in human development.* Cambridge, MA: Harvard University Press.

Kimmel, M. S., & Ferber, A. L. (Eds.). (2009). *Privilege: A reader* (2nd ed.). Boulder, CO: Westview Press.

King, J., Rizga, K., & Palermo, T. (2007, Dec. 27). Top youth activism victories of 2007. *The Nation.* Retrieved from http://www.thenation.com/article/top-youth-activism-victories-2008/

Kirk, G., & Okazawa-Rey, M. (2013). Identities and social locations: Who am I? Who are my people? In M. Adams, W. J. Blumenfeld, C. Castañeda, H. W. Hackman, M. L. Peters, & X. Zúñiga (Eds.), *Readings for diversity and social justice* (3rd ed., pp. 9–15). New York: Routledge.

Kirwan Institute. (2013). *State of the science: Implicit bias review.* Columbus, OH: Ohio State Kirwan Institute for the Study of Race and Ethnicity.

Lakey, G. (2010). *Facilitating group learning: Strategies for success with diverse adult learners.* San Francisco: Jossey-Bass.

Leondar-Wright, B. (2005). *Class matters: Cross-class alliance building for middle-class activists.* Gabriola Island, BC, Canada: New Society Publishers.

Leondar-Wright, B. (2014). *Missing class: Strengthening social movement groups by seeing class cultures*. Ithaca, NY: Cornell University Press.

Loewen, J. W. (1995). *Lies my teacher told me: Everything your American history textbook got wrong*. New York: Simon & Schuster.

Love, B. J. (2013). Developing a liberatory consciousness. In M. Adams, W. J. Blumenfeld, R. Castañeda, H. W. Hackman, M. L. Peters, & X. Zúñiga (Eds.), *Readings for diversity and social justice* (3rd ed., pp. 601–605). New York: Routledge.

McIntosh, P. (1989). *White privilege: Unpacking the invisibility knapsack*. Wellesley, MA: The National SEED Project on Inclusive Curriculum, Seeking Educational Equity & Diversity (SEED). Retrieved from http://nationalseedproject.org/white-privilege-unpacking-the-invisible-knapsack

McLennan, R. M. (2008). *The crisis of imprisonment: Protest, politics, and the making of the American penal state, 1776–1941*. New York: Cambridge University Press.

Memmi, A. (1957, 1991). *The colonizer and the colonized* (expanded ed.). Boston: Beacon Press.

National Catholic Educational Association (NCEA, n.d.). *U.S. Census Bureau race and ethnicity reporting for NCEA data collection*. Arlington, VA: NCEA. Retrieved from http://ncea.org/

Obear, K. (2013). Navigating triggering events: Critical competencies for social justice educators. In L. M. Landerman (Ed.), *The art of effective facilitation: Reflections from social justice educators* (pp. 151–172). Sterling, VA: Stylus Publishing.

Omi, M., & Winant, H. (2015). *Racial formation in the United States* (3rd ed.). New York: Routledge.

Pasque, P. A., & Harris, B. L. (2013). Moving from social justice to social agency: Keeping it messy. In K. Kline (Ed.), *Reflection in action: A guidebook for faculty and student affairs professionals* (pp. 133–151). Sterling, VA: Stylus.

Pharr, S. (1997). *Homophobia: A weapon of sexism* (expanded ed.). Berkeley, CA: Chardon.

Pittelman, K. (2005). *Classified: How to stop hiding your privilege and use it for social change*. Brooklyn, NY: Soft Skull Press.

Population Reference Bureau (PRB, 2009). *The 2010 census questionnaire: Seven questions for everyone*. Washington, DC: PRB. Retrieved from http://www.prb.org/Publications/Articles/2009/questionnaire.aspx

Rawls, J. (2003). *Justice as fairness: A restatement*. Cambridge, MA: Harvard University Press.

Rose, F. (2000). *Coalitions across the class divide: Lessons from the labor, peace and environmental movements*. Ithaca, NY: Cornell University Press.

Sen, A. (2009). *The idea of justice*. Cambridge, MA: Harvard University Press.

Stassen, M., Zúñiga, X., Keehn, M., Mildred, J., DeJong, K., & Varghese, R. (2013). Engagement in intergroup dialogue: Listening, speaking and active thinking. In P. Gurin, B. A. Nagda, & X. Zúñiga (Eds.), *Dialogues across differences: Practice, theory and research on intergroup dialogue* (pp. 211–242). New York: Russell Sage Foundation.

Sue, D. W. (2010). *Microaggressions in everyday life: Race, gender, and sexual orientation*. Hoboken, NJ: John Wiley & Sons.

Tatum, B. D. (1992). Talking about race, learning about racism: The application of racial identity development theory in the classroom. *Harvard Educational Review, 62*(1), 1–24.

Tilly, C. (1978). *From mobilization to revolution*. Boston: Addison-Wesley.

U.S. Bureau of the Census (U.S. Census Bureau, n.d.). *Race*. Washington, DC: U.S. Census Bureau. Retrieved from http://www.census.gov/quickfacts/

Vygotsky, L. S. (1978). *Mind in society: The development of higher psychological processes* (M. Cole, V. John-Steiner, S. Scribner, & E. Souberman, Trans.). Cambridge, MA: Harvard University Press.

Wasserman, I. C., & Doran, R. F. (1999). Creating inclusive learning communities. In A. L. Cooke, M. Brazzel, A. S. Craig, & B. Greig (Eds.), *NTL reading book for human relations training* (8th ed., pp. 307–310). Alexandria, VA: NTL Institute for Applied Behavioral Sciences.

West, C. (2004). *Democracy matters: Winning the fight against imperialism*. New York: Penguin.

Wijeyesinghe, C. (2012). The intersectional model of multiracial identity: Integrating multiracial identity theories and intersectional perspectives on social identity. In C. L. Wijeyesinghe & B. W. Jackson (Eds.), *New perspectives on racial identity development: Integrating emerging frameworks* (2nd ed., pp. 81–108). New York: New York University Press.

Wijeyesinghe, C., & Jackson, B. W. (2012). *New perspectives on racial identity development: Integrating emerging frameworks* (2nd ed.). New York: New York University Press.

Wildman, S. M. (1996). *Privilege revealed: How invisible preference undermines America*. New York: New York University Press.

Young, I. M. (1990). *Justice and the politics of difference*. Princeton, NJ: Princeton University Press.

Young, I. M. (2011). *Responsibility for justice*. Cambridge, MA: Oxford University Press.

Zinn, H. (2003). *A people's history of the United States: 1492–present*. New York: Harper-Collins.

Zinn, H. (2002). *You can't be neutral on a moving train*. Boston: Beacon Press.

Adapted by Zúñiga, X. & Lee, E. Y. (2015), Social Justice Education, University of Massachusetts, Amherst. In Collins, P. H. (1990), *Black feminist thought: Knowledge, consciousness, and the politics of empowerment*. New York, NY: Routledge.

Zúñiga, X. (2013). Chapter introduction; Selections for working for social justice: Visions and strategies for social change. In M. Adams, W. J. Blumenfeld, R. Castañeda, H. Hackman, M. L. Peters, & X. Zúñiga (Eds.), *Readings for diversity and social justice* (3rd ed., pp. 589–647). New York: Routledge.

Zúñiga, X., Nagda, B. A., Chesler, M., & Cytron-Walker, A. (2007). Intergroup dialogues in higher education: Meaningful learning about social justice. *ASHE-ERIC Higher Education Report Series*, 32(4). San Francisco: Jossey-Bass.

PART II

TEACHING DIVERSITY AND SOCIAL JUSTICE

5

Racism and White Privilege

*Lee Anne Bell, Michael S. Funk, Khyati Y. Joshi, and Marjorie Valdivia**

INTRODUCTION

Assertions that we are now a "post-racial" society are belied by the 2015 spate of police shootings and killings of unarmed African American men and women, and the murders of nine African Americans in a prayer group in South Carolina by a white man professing white supremacist ideology. These shocking events dramatically illustrate that racism is alive and well in 21st century United States. Attempts to overturn the Voting Rights Act and gerrymander districts to advantage white candidates, as well as deep and ongoing racial and economic segregation, are through lines from an earlier era when de jure segregation was the law of the land. This chapter is intended to help readers understand the patterns and practices that evolved historically to become the system of racism that continues in the U.S. today, a system that impacts everyone—including new immigrants who are incorporated into the racial structure when they arrive.

OUR APPROACH

We start from the premise that race is a *social construction* that has material and psychological consequences in the lives of people from different racialized groups. Social construction signifies that "race" is a concept invented by humans, not a biological reality, and that we are one species called homo sapiens. Although there are physical differences within the human population, these do not represent distinct and separate biological categories. The construction of race as a way to categorize people has a long history that illustrates how race has been used to interpret human differences and justify socio-economic arrangements that benefit the white racial group (Frederickson, 2003; Montagu, 1997; Smedley & Smedley, 2011). Thus, race is a powerful idea that impacts people's lives, psychologically and materially, in consequential and enduring ways.

A second premise in our approach is that it is important to understand both the distinctive and shared ways that racism operates on different communities of color, both historically and in the present, as well as through intersections with other forms of oppression. The foundational frames for racism in this country are based on colonization and genocide of the indigenous people and the enslavement of Africans. We add additional lenses to discern how racism manifests in both similar and different ways for people from other racialized groups (Asian American, Latina/o, Arab American, biracial/multiracial). Further, we look at how race intersects with class, gender, sexual orientation, religion, age, and other axes of identity to provide a more nuanced understanding of how racism functions in different contexts and communities.

We contextualize racism within an understanding of U.S. connections to the broader world. From the outset, the U.S. has been involved in colonial adventures justified by racist ideas about manifest destiny and white superiority. Wherever the U.S. expropriated natural resources and labor from other nations to support economic and/or foreign policy objectives, the negative effects on the home economic and political systems of affected countries impelled streams of migration to the U.S. (Gonzalez, 2011; Takaki, 2008). The contemporary slogan among immigration activists, "We are here because you were there," illustrates this circular connection (Rumbaut, 1996). For example, large numbers have emigrated to the United States as a result of U.S. interventions that made life in their countries of origin unsafe (Nicaragua, El Salvador) or not economically feasible (Mexico, Haiti).

Later in the chapter, we examine how racism manifests at institutional/systemic levels (housing, schooling, employment, the criminal justice system, health care, etc.) as well as at individual/interpersonal levels. We also identify promising policies and practices to address racism in institutional and civic life.

DEFINITION OF KEY TERMS

RACISM

We define *racism* as a pervasive system of advantage and disadvantage based on the socially constructed category of race. Racism is enacted on multiple levels simultaneously: Institutional, cultural, interpersonal, and individual. Institutional structures, policies, and practices interlock with cultural assumptions about what is right and proper to justify racism. Individuals internalize and enact these assumptions through individual behavior and institutional participation. Woven together, these interactions create and sustain systemic benefits for whites as a group, and structure discrimination, oppression, dispossession, and exclusion for people from targeted racial groups.

ETHNICITY

Ethnicity is often confused with, but is distinct from, race. While "race" relates to physical features (skin tone, hair texture, eye color, bone structure), ethnicity relates to nationality, region, ancestry, shared culture, and language. It is also socially constructed. Racial designations tend to eclipse or render invisible specific ethnic and national origins. Ethnicity is an attribution that signifies group affiliation with others who share values and ways of being. As social categories, ethnicity and race function differently.

Racial categories are imposed from outside for the purpose of ranking and hierarchy. Historically, racial categories ensured that European adventurers, colonists, and settlers could seize land for cultivation and enslave people for profit. This theft was justified by a belief system that asserted Europeans/whites were superior to others deemed inferior (indigenous peoples, Africans, Arabs, Asians). Ethnic categories are generated from within, to maintain a people's sense of community and connection, especially if they are peoples in diaspora, living among others whose ethnicity (and perhaps race) differs. Communities sometimes prefer to describe themselves using ethnic rather than racial designations.

INDIVIDUAL/INTERPERSONAL RACISM

Racism at the personal/interpersonal level is an individual phenomenon that reflects prejudice or bias. Individuals may intentionally express or act on racist ideas and assumptions. For example, a white person who proclaims that Asian people are devious or untrustworthy, or who spouts racial epithets against black and Latina/o people, is expressing overt, conscious racism.

More common are covert, unconscious, or unintentional actions of individuals who may honestly believe they are not racist. This implicit bias (Holroyd, 2015) or aversive racism (Dovidio & Gaertner, 2000), because it is typically not explicit or conscious, is frequently more difficult to identify and address. For example, a white person who unconsciously clutches personal belongings in the presence of black or Latino men, or who is amazed that an immigrant from Latin America or Asia speaks "good" English, is exhibiting implicit bias and unconscious, aversive, or covert racism.

INSTITUTIONAL RACISM

Racism at the institutional level is reflected in the policies, laws, rules, norms, and customs enacted by organizations and social institutions that advantage whites as a group and disadvantage groups of color. Such institutions include religion, government, education, law, the media, the health care system, and businesses/employment. For example, a criminal justice system that justifies racially disproportionate stop-and-frisk policies on U.S. streets and highways (Ogletree, 2012) and higher incarceration rates of black and brown people (Alexander, 2012) is an institutionalized expression of racism. Institutional racism is exemplified in the structured inequality of a school funding system based on property taxes that unfairly benefit wealthier (whiter) communities at the expense of poorer (brown and black) communities. Laws that prevent undocumented workers or immigrants from accessing health care or public services are another example of institutional racism.

SOCIETAL/CULTURAL RACISM

Social norms, roles, rituals, language, music, and art that reinforce the belief that white (European) culture is superior to other cultures reflect cultural racism. Normative assumptions about philosophies of life; definitions of good, evil, beauty, and ugliness; normality and deviance; and perspectives on time provide the justification for social oppression (Hardiman & Jackson, 2007, cited in Adams, Bell, & Griffin, 2007). Asserting English as the official language of the United States and viewing people who speak with a Spanish or Chinese accent as less educated and cultured than people who speak with a French or British accent are examples of cultural racism.

Cultural racism can also be expressed through the appropriation rather than appreciation of the cultural creations of people from marginalized groups. For example, white youth who adopt hip-hop dress, styles, and language while remaining ignorant of the culture that produced these forms are exhibiting cultural racism. Non-native people who claim Native American heritage but know nothing about the specific history and culture of diverse Native communities, nor have any present-day interaction with them, is another example.

OVERT RACISM

Overt racism refers to conscious attitudes and behaviors (public or private) that intentionally harm people of color (as individuals or groups) or define them as inferior to whites and less entitled to society's benefits. Overt racism is illustrated in the violence and discrimination typical of the Jim Crow era—from lynching to legally sanctioned segregation in housing, schooling, and transportation. Today, overt racism can be seen in skinhead attacks on people of color, the violence perpetrated by racist police, renewed arguments about cultural deficits (Valencia, 2010), and attempts to diminish or suppress the voting rights of people of color.

COVERT RACISM

In contrast to overt discrimination, covert racism is hidden and unacknowledged. Examples of covert racism include cultural and religious marginalization, color-blind racism, and tokenism. Covert racism is often not recognized as discriminatory by members of the dominant white group. It is disguised with language that downplays the clearly racial aspects of the discrimination by invoking "non-racial" explanations that are more acceptable in the broader society (Bonilla-Silva, 2013; Coates, 2008). Racial code words such as "inner city," "law and order," and "welfare" are successfully used by right-wing politicians to covertly associate government programs with people of color so that white voters will reject such programs, even against their own self-interests (Haney-López, 2014). The existence of covert discrimination is more difficult to prove than acts of overt racism, and is now more commonplace.

RACIAL MICROAGGRESSIONS

Microaggressions are acts of disregard or subtle insults stemming from, often unconscious, attitudes of white superiority. Microaggressions include the commonplace experiences of people of color being ignored by a sales clerk or followed in a store by security guards, hearing white people argue against affirmative action by saying "the most qualified person should get the job" (as if affirmative action ignores or undermines qualified applicants), or being complimented for speaking "good English." Microaggressions reflect denigrating hidden messages: "You are not important enough to be noticed"; or "You are automatically suspect"; or "People of color are less qualified"; or "You are a foreigner, not a true American" (Sue, Lin, Torino, Capodiluco, & Rivera 2009).

While microaggressions appear innocent and harmless to members of the white dominant group, the constant burden they place on people of color has a cumulative, harmful psychological, physiological, and academic toll (Solórzano, Ceja, & Yosso, 2000; Kohli & Solórzano, 2012). Whites often assume that microaggressions are personal disputes rather than acts of racism, and they minimize their impact; for example, they may say, "I'm sure that wasn't what they meant" or "You are reading too much into this."

These seemingly innocuous but constant events are mediated by institutional racism and "allow us to 'see' the tangible ways that racism emerges in everyday interactions" (Huber & Solórzano, 2015, p. 302). The connection between microaggressions and institutionalized racism is important. Assumptions that someone is less intelligent or more dangerous have material consequences (discriminatory actions in hiring, or higher incidences of arrest, incarceration, and death or injury at the hands of police).

INTERNALIZED RACISM

As part of the socialization process, people from all racialized groups internalize messages, about their own group as well as about other social groups, that reinforce racism. Internalized racism plays out differently for whites as the dominant group than for people of color, who are marginalized and targeted by racism. We all breathe in racist ideology, but with psychic effects that differentially impact white people and people of color.

Internalized racism among people of color occurs when they believe and/or act on negative stereotypes about themselves and their group as less capable, not as entitled, or more violent than whites. Internalized racism may be conscious or unconscious. A person of color who is repeatedly passed over for promotion may blame themselves for not working harder, rather than recognizing the possibility that this may be a manifestation of racist attitudes or an insider white network from which they are excluded. It may also take the form of denying one's ethnic or cultural background—not speaking one's native language or not eating ethnic food—in an effort to conform to white norms. Internalizing such negative messages can be psychically debilitating (Joseph & Williams, 2008; Williams, 2011).

STEREOTYPE THREAT

Stereotype threat describes the fear of confirming negative stereotypes about one's racial, ethnic, gender, or cultural group. The term was coined by Steele and Aronson (1995), whose research showed that black college students performed worse than white peers on standardized tests when told, before taking the tests, that their racial group tends to do poorly on such exams. When race was not emphasized, however, black students performed similarly to white peers. This concept is often misinterpreted to explain racial test score gaps as *solely* due to stereotype threat, ignoring group differences in access and opportunities to acquire test-related knowledge (Steele & Aronson, 2004). Like microaggressions, stereotype threat exists because of racism in the broader society.

INTERNALIZED DOMINANCE

Internalized dominance occurs among white people when they believe and/or act on assumptions that white people are superior to, more capable, intelligent, or entitled than people of color. It occurs when members of the dominant white group take their group's socially advantaged status as normal and deserved, rather than recognizing how it has been conferred through racialized systems of inequality. Internalized dominance may be unconscious or unconscious. A white person who insists that anyone who works hard can get ahead, without acknowledging the barriers of racism, is consciously or unconsciously expressing internalized dominance. Whites who assume that European music and art are superior to other forms are enacting internalized dominance.

UNEARNED RACIAL ADVANTAGE/PRIVILEGE

These are unearned benefits or advantages white people receive that are denied to or at the expense of people of color. In the U.S., we are not accustomed to discussing racial *advantage* or focusing on those who benefit from racism. Instead, discussions about race typically focus on those at the receiving end of discriminatory policies and practices. We cannot talk meaningfully about racism, however, without identifying and focusing on the white group positioned at the top of the social hierarchy that reaps the advantages of racism. For whites, "race is a valuable social, political and economic resource that gives them access to power and resources, and protects them from negative pre-judgments based on physical features, language, and other cultural factors" (Lawrence, Sutton, Kubisch, Susi, & Fulbright-Anderson, 2004, p. 17).

Racial advantage and disadvantage are two sides of the same coin of racism. For example, many Americans, particularly white Americans, believe the playing field has leveled and our society operates as a meritocracy in which, despite race or station, anyone willing to work hard can get ahead (Hochschild, 1995; Samuel, 2012). Yet research repeatedly shows that segregated schools and neighborhoods, job discrimination and pay inequity, a racialized school-to-prison pipeline, and enduring legacies of past discrimination mean that working hard is not enough to overcome institutionalized privilege and disadvantage (Oliver & Shapiro, 2006; Rugh & Massey, 2010; Shapiro, Meschede & Osoro, 2013). White privilege enables white people to benefit psychologically and materially from accumulated advantage, whether they seek it or not.

THE RACIAL IDEOLOGY OF WHITE SUPREMACY

The racial ideology of white supremacy describes the belief system that rationalizes and reproduces white advantage in the political, social, and cultural institutions of society. This belief system holds that white people, white culture, and things associated with whiteness are superior to those of other racial groups. It assumes as normal and rational that the interests and perceptions of white individuals are central in society (Gillborn, 2006, p. 318). Unlike overt white supremacist groups, this racial ideology may be unexamined or unconscious. Relations of white dominance and subordination of others are reenacted daily throughout institutions and social settings in a society where whites overwhelmingly control material resources, and ideas about entitlement are widespread (Ansley, 1997).

COLLUSION

Collusion describes when people from any racial group support the system of racism by consciously or unconsciously going along. Conscious collusion occurs when people of color knowingly (though not always voluntarily) accede to their own mistreatment or the mistreatment of other people of color in order to survive or maintain status, livelihood, or some other benefit, as when a person of color silently endures racist jokes told by a supervisor or coworkers, or participates in putting down people of color from their own or other subordinated racial groups. Collusion also occurs when white people go along with racist jokes or putdowns in order to fit in or out of fear of being ostracized if they disagree and go against white norms (Hardiman, Jackson, & Griffin, 2013).

COLOR-BLINDNESS

We recognize the problematic ableist language of this term, but we reference it as used by scholars to describe an important social phenomenon. Color-blind ideology (or color-evasiveness—purporting to not notice race in an effort to not appear be racist), asserts that ending discrimination merely requires treating individuals as equally as possible, without regard to race, culture, or ethnicity. Color-blindness, by overlooking the cumulative and enduring ways in which race unequally shapes life chances and opportunities for people from different groups (Massey, 2007), actually reinforces and sustains an unequal status quo. By leaving structural inequalities in place, color-blindness has become the "new racism" (Bonilla-Silva & Forman, 2000). It also ignores cultural attributes that people value and deserve to have recognized and affirmed (Bell, 2016).

RACE-CONSCIOUSNESS

Race-consciousness signifies being mindful of the impact of policies and practices on different racialized groups in our society. Race-consciousness can motivate a desire to become informed about how injustice occurs and to be intentional about seeking redress (Bell, 2016). Race-consciousness contradicts color-blindness through actively seeking to perceive, understand, and challenge racism. It also paves the way for imagining a more just and inclusive society that affirms diversity rather than reducing it to a white normative ideal.

INTERSECTIONALITY

Race and racism intersect with other social identities and forms of oppression, and position individuals and groups differently in the system of racism by virtue of gender, class, sexuality, ability, and other social markers (Collins, 2012; Crenshaw, 1995). Intersectionality operates on both individual and institutional/systemic levels. For example, a woman of color who is poor and disabled experiences racism differently than an upper-class, able-bodied, heterosexual man of color. At the systemic level, racism and classism are deeply intertwined and interlocking systems that sustain inequalities in such institutions as schooling, housing, and the criminal justice system (see Chapter 7, *Classism*). In this chapter, we focus on race as central, while always acknowledging the ways that race intersects with other social group memberships and isms to shape the particular experiences of differently positioned people of color.

HISTORICAL LEGACIES AND KEY CONCEPTS

In this section, we discuss two key concepts that we believe are essential to convey in a course or workshop on racism. One is understanding the different ways that racism operates on diverse communities of color. The other is understanding the cumulative and systemic nature of white advantage. Then we discuss central themes in U.S. history that undergird the racism that continues to operate today. Given the current emphasis on color-blindness and post-racialism, it is necessary to understand these historical underpinnings and their continuing impacts in the present.

RATIONALIZATIONS FOR WHITE SUPREMACY

One key concept a course on racism needs to convey is the archetypal nature of oppression and dispossession that built white wealth at the outset through the exploited labor of enslaved Africans and the stolen land of Native Americans, and justified this process through an ideology of racial superiority (Feagin, 2002). This structure of exploitation and rationalization was then extended to other groups of color, including Latino/as and Asians, who were viewed as inferior and/or foreign.

Smith (2010) proposes three different "logics" or ways of rationalizing white supremacy: Genocide, Slavery, and Orientalism. The logic of Genocide centers on an "indigenous/settler binary" that rationalizes the right of settlers to take over land (as well as appropriate cultural and religious practices) from indigenous people who are claimed to have "disappeared." The process of disappearing indigenous people continues through controlling and minimizing those who can claim Indian status to suit white interests (Glenn, 2015). This logic encourages non-Native groups to accept as unproblematic the appropriation of Native lands, and the demeaning use of Native images as mascots and in popular media.

The logic of Slavery operates through the control of black bodies for the economic gain of whites. This logic is evidenced in slavery, and the sharecropping and convict-leasing systems following slavery, that created ongoing financial rewards to white individuals and corporations, who profited from conditions of neo-slavery in which blacks could neither leave nor be fully compensated for their labor (Blackmon, 2008). This logic operates currently in the increasingly privatized prison industrial complex that incarcerates black and brown people, while creating commercial rewards for white entrepreneurs and political and economic benefits for the predominantly white communities where prisons are located (Alexander, 2012; Hallett, 2006; Shichor, 1995).

The third logic, Orientalism, describes how peoples, cultures, religions, and nations of Arabia and Asia are seen as inferior to the West and as a perpetual danger to the Western (U.S.) world order (Said, 1994). This logic manifests in anti-immigrant rhetoric and policies that target immigrants of color as foreign threats, regardless of how long they have lived here, as well as in the racial profiling of Arab Americans, and others presumed to be Muslim, as necessary to fight terrorism (Hagopian, 2004).

Latino/as can be seen to fit variously into two different logics. Their labor has been exploited to create white wealth from the very beginning (logic of Slavery) and they have been defined as inferior and a danger to the U.S. way of life (logic of Orientalism) (Feagin & Elias, 2012). The colonization of Mexican land, U.S. employment practices such as the Braceros program that recruited and exploited Mexican workers and then expelled them when they were no longer needed, as well as military projects in Latin America that created instability and the desire to flee to safer land, are the backdrop to immigration issues today. We will not find ways to remedy these injustices without an understanding of this history and its ongoing consequences.

While these logics intertwine and reinforce each other, recognizing the distinctive ways they work can provide a nuanced understanding of how racism(s) function in different communities, contexts, and historical circumstances. Recognizing different rationales for racism also calls attention to the distinctive histories of different groups and avoids conflating their experiences of racism as the same. For example, when Asian Americans are held up as a "model minority," it is often to reinforce attributions of black inferiority. Similarly, when Asian Americans are portrayed as outsiders who cannot be assimilated, it reinforces stereotypes held by non-Asians, including African Americans, of Asians as perpetually foreign (Kim, 1999; Tuan, 2001).

Understanding the contradictory ways racism works on diverse communities of color helps us see how groups can be pitted against each other and become complicit in perpetuating each other's victimization (Kim, 1999; Martinez, 1996; Perea, 1997). Working against racism most effectively would require coalitions that address economic racism, genocide, and settler colonialism simultaneously (Grande, 2015; Smith, 2010).

CUMULATIVE AND COMPOUNDING WHITE ADVANTAGE

A second key issue for teaching about racism is to convey the history of cumulative advantages for whites and corollary disadvantages for other racialized groups resulting from unjust policies and practices that endure into the present. The advantaged position of whites (presented as natural, deserved, the result of merit and hard work) obfuscates the systematic ways in which whites have reaped the benefits of a privileged status from before the start of the Republic (Feagin, 2002; Gonzalez, 2011; Takaki, 2008). Whites as individuals and as a group are "stakeholders in a centuries-old oppressive hierarchical structure of opportunities, wealth and privileges . . . It is part of the historical and structural reality of being positioned as 'white' to be part of the oppressor, privileged class" (Feagin & Elias, 2012, p. 942).

The enduring effects of compounding white advantage, and corollary disadvantage for blacks and people from other racially marginalized groups, are effaced when uninformed whites complain about affirmative action programs intended to address this history. For example, housing policies that underwrote the ability of white families to create wealth through home ownership—wealth that they could use to send their children to college or start a business—were explicitly denied to blacks and other people of color. This wealth gap grows under current policies and practices that fail to address this history (Demos, 2015; Shapiro, Meschede, & Osoro, 2013).

RACIAL CATEGORIZATION AND HIERARCHY

One of the most persistent ideas in U.S. history has been belief in the existence of distinct racial categories that mark groups of people as physically and intellectually different. In the early years of the nation, racial categorization and hierarchy evolved hand in hand to define some groups as inherently superior (those who were white/light skinned) and other groups as inferior (those with darker skin). This idea meshed well with a colonial and revolutionary system that espoused principles of equality and rights but had to rationalize the enslavement of human beings (Smedley, 1993). At first, identity was a more fluid concept, where religious and class distinctions were more salient than race. As wealthy planters embraced a system of chattel slavery, however, they wrote laws that turned Africans into a permanent racial caste. Also, for the first time the word "White," rather than "Christian" or "Englishman," began appearing in colonial statutes (Jacobson, 1998; Roediger, 1999; Zinn, 2003).

The illogic of race as a construct was personified in the "one-drop rule" that defined as black anyone known to have even "one drop" of African ancestry. According to the "one-drop" rule, a person of mixed heritage was black, fixed to the racial group with the least social status. Thus, a one-eighth portion of African ancestry could determine one's status as African American, regardless of a seven-eighths white ancestry. Illustrating the illogic of this system, states developed different rules of classification (from one drop in one state to one quarter in another) so that a person could literally change races by crossing state lines.

Over the course of the 19th century, laws began to codify race and rigidly enforce racial segregation. The Supreme Court in Plessy v. Ferguson (1896) cemented segregation as the law of the land for nearly 60 years. Not until 1967, in the *Loving v. Virginia* Supreme Court ruling, did the ban on interracial marriage become unconstitutional at the national level. While Plessy is best known for the "separate but equal" decision, it also reveals a great deal about whiteness. In his brief, Plessy argued that being forced to sit in the "colored" car, even though he was seven-eighths white, deprived him of valuable property—whiteness and the privileges it conveys. Subsequent court cases recognized "whiteness as property" (C. I. Harris, 1993) by allowing defamation actions for people who were mis-identified as not white (Leong, 2013).

Understanding that race has always been a dynamic concept helps us understand that race is not fixed, but fabricated through legal and social structures to the benefit of those in power. The invention of racial categories and their placement in a hierarchy reveal how advantage and disadvantage, now embedded in our legal and social systems, perpetuate racism in the 21st century.

RACE AND THE REGULATION OF IMMIGRATION

While U.S. mythology lauds our "nation of immigrants," today immigration is often seen as a threat to the "American way of life" that puts immigrant communities under suspicion, as in the "illegalization" of Mexicans and others from Central and South America (Chacon & Davis, 2006), and the mistreatment of people of Middle Eastern and South Asian descent since September 11, 2001 (Jamal & Naber, 2008; Mishra, 2013; Peek, 2011; Singh, 2013). Immigration and immigration control are hot topics that result in discussions and debates about who should enter, who fits in, and who is a threat to the American way of life. Efforts by local legislators, politicians, and anti-immigrant groups to regulate the benefits, privileges, and rights available to undocumented persons have grown. States have passed laws like Alabama HB 56 and Arizona SB 1070, called "show me your papers law"

(Archibold, 2010), that encourage racial profiling of immigrants, restrict immigrant rights, and perpetuate xenophobia (Campbell, 2011).

Immigration restrictions, then and now, are part of the legal and social fabric of the nation. When Europeans were entering the U.S. via Ellis Island in the 1840s, there were no such restrictions (Ngai, 2004). Not until Asian immigration (with Filipinos arriving in New Orleans via the Caribbean, followed by Chinese, Indian, Korean, and Japanese via Angel Island) were limits and restrictions to immigration imposed (Lee & Yung, 2010).

With the arrival of large numbers of immigrants from Asia, the White Anglo Protestant population became concerned about the character of the nation. Organizations such as the Immigration Restriction League and the Know Nothing Party, influenced by prevalent beliefs in "scientific racism," lobbied government officials to restrict immigration. The nativist lobbying efforts were successful in getting Congress to pass legislation that dramatically affected the demographic make-up of the country. First, Congress passed the 1882 Chinese Exclusion Act, which restricted the immigration of Chinese laborers—the first time in U.S. history that a group of people were prohibited entry because of national origin (Lee & Yung, 2010).

Nativist lobbying also led to passage of other restrictive immigration laws that further shaped the makeup of the nation the U.S. would become. The Immigration Act of 1917 barred immigration from most of Asia, excluding Japan. Koreans, Indians, Chinese, Malays, and others were prohibited from entering the U.S., thus closing U.S. doors to Asian immigrants.

Nativist organizations on the East Coast, agitated by the increase in southern and eastern European migration, succeeded in getting the Immigration Act of 1924 passed, virtually closing the door on these groups. Immigration from Europe was pegged to 2% of the total of any nation's residents already here, as reported in the 1890 census. Those most impacted were from southern and eastern Europe and predominantly non-Protestant, specifically Jewish, Catholic, and Eastern Orthodox. The Immigration Act of 1924 established for the first time limits on immigration based on preserving America's "racial" composition. President Coolidge, as he signed the bill into law, said "America must be kept American" (Ngai, 2004).

Ethnic groups considered white today were not always socially accepted as such. Throughout our history, there have been shades of white, where skin color and European origin intersected with social disadvantage, as they did with the Irish, Italian, and eastern European immigrants who arrived in large numbers in the 19th century (Brodkin, 1998; Jacobson, 1998). These populations were seen as less "white" than northern European Protestants, and the advantages of whiteness were selectively and grudgingly extended to them. While granted citizenship, they were subjected to social discrimination ("no Irish need apply"), and spoken of as a threat to the American social order. One of the factors impacting the shading process was religion: The "less white" populations were Catholic, Jewish, or Orthodox Christian, unlike their Protestant European predecessors, who came from British, German, or Scandinavian stock. Another factor was class background (Brodkin, 1998; Jacobson, 1998).

Thus, entrance into a racially coded U.S. society has meant that the economic and social experiences of immigrants considered white have been different from those considered non-white. While European immigrants, such as the Irish, Italians, Greeks, Poles, and Jews, faced considerable hostility and discrimination upon arrival, and were initially considered inferior by the Anglo-Saxons who preceded them (Foner, 2005; Jacobson, 1998), by the second and third generation they had gained social and economic mobility and gradually "became" white. This change in racial status came at the price of giving up their native languages, cultural traditions, and ethnic identities (Brodkin, 1998), while the cutoff of

European immigration created the conditions for the second generation to more readily assimilate into U.S. society (Ngai, 2004).

Not until the Immigration Act of 1965 was the door to immigration reopened, and today most migrants are from Mexico, China, India, Philippines, Cuba, Vietnam, El Salvador, Korea, and the Dominican Republic. At the same time, and despite the claim of being a "nation of immigrants," immigration is still selectively open to people based on criteria of desirability and need. For example, the Immigration Act of 1965 prioritized engineers and health care professionals. Subsequent immigration laws, such as the 1986 Immigration Reform and Control Act (IRCA), gave priority to family reunification and to children, parents, and siblings of U.S. citizens. In the late 1990s, executive orders prioritized workers in the technology industry, predominantly from India and China. Having an understanding of how and when the immigration doors have opened and closed, and for which groups, explains our racial demographics today. It is not coincidental that the white ethnic population is the largest segment of society; it is a direct product of U.S. immigration policy.

CITIZENSHIP AND EXCLUSION

Today, individuals who immigrate to the U.S. are for the most part able to become citizens once they have fulfilled criteria such as the residency requirement and passing a citizenship test. This process is known as naturalization. Citizenship not only confers formal legal status but also belonging and recognition of who is American (Glenn, 2011). However, not all who arrived on our shores have been able to become citizens. Exclusion from citizenship is a key theme for understanding the legacies of institutionalized racism. One of the lasting legacies of exclusion from citizenship is that Asians, once considered "aliens ineligible for citizenship," are still seen as foreigners, even those who are third- or fourth-generation Americans.

Racial restrictions on citizenship started almost from the birth of the United States. In 1790, Congress limited naturalization to immigrants who were "free white persons of good character" (Haney-López, 2006). Not all white men had been free, as is often assumed, or there would have been no need to add "free" to "white" (Painter, 2010). In the notorious *Dred Scott* decision of 1857, the Supreme Court declared that people of African descent, whether slave or free, could not be American citizens. While African Americans and Native Americans were ultimately allowed to become citizens, with the 14th Amendment and Indian Citizenship Act of 1924, respectively, they continued to be kept from full participation in democratic society through Jim Crow segregation, and actions such as the poll tax that tried to keep them from voting and participating in public life. Mexican Americans who were in the Southwest at the time of the Mexican American War attained citizenship automatically through the Treaty of Guadalupe Hidalgo in 1848, which annexed to the U.S. the land on which they were living. Mexican Americans, however, also experienced Jim Crow segregation and restrictions on their ability to exercise citizenship rights.

The same groups that opposed immigration were also successful in lobbying for alien land laws to restrict land ownership to citizens. These laws targeted Asians, particularly Japanese, and barred them from owning land. In a reciprocal way, citizenship was often directly tied to land ownership, and indirectly tied to race, and excluded Asian and others from the right to vote (Keyysar, 2009).

Between 1878 and 1952, 52 racial prerequisite cases were initiated, including two heard by the U.S. Supreme Court. Racial prerequisite cases were brought by immigrants whose applications for citizenship were rejected because they were deemed not white. In these cases, Syrian, Filipino, Hawaiian, Indian, Mexican, Chinese, and Japanese individuals attempted to prove that they were white in order to become U.S. citizens. Such cases set racial parameters for citizenship (Haney-Lopez, 2006).

The two cases heard by the Supreme Court were *Takao Ozawa v. U.S.* (1922) and *U.S. v Bhagat Singh Thind* (1923). Ozawa was born in Japan, moved to Hawaii and then California, and had lived in the United States for 20 years when he applied in 1914 for naturalization. The U.S. government rejected his application on the grounds that he was not "white." Ozawa sued, but the Supreme Court ruled that he was not eligible to become a citizen using the pseudo-scientific argument that, as someone who was part of the "Mongoloid" race, he was not white (Haney-López, 2006).

The Supreme Court in *U.S. v Bhagat Singh Thind* used the opposite reasoning from Ozawa. Even though the Court recognized that Indians were "scientifically" classified as Caucasians, it concluded that they were in fact "nonwhite" in popular U.S. understanding. The lawyers for the United States attacked Thind's "meltability" by defining Hinduism as an alien and barbaric system not fit for membership in the "civilization of white men." The Ozawa and Thind decisions were later extended to rule ineligible for citizenship Koreans, Thais, Vietnamese, Indonesians, and other peoples of Asian countries. These cases show the fluid nature of race and the legal codification of whiteness in defining citizenship and who would be included and excluded.

While racial restrictions on citizenship that had been put in place with the Naturalization Act of 1790 were eliminated in 1952, they have an enduring legacy on race relations today. Many of the aforementioned groups continue to be marked as alien, different, even unpatriotic. While these groups today can gain legal citizenship, they continue to be seen as unassimilable and forever foreign.

RACIAL CLASSIFICATIONS AND CHANGING CENSUS CATEGORIES

One of the legacies of the racial prerequisite cases is a census classification system based on the social construction of race and the privileges and disadvantages it allocates. Census classifications illustrate the construction of race along a color line dividing white from "nonwhite" Americans and the attempt to categorize people into single or "pure" races over the course of our history. These classifications have led to "taxonomic nightmares" (Lee, 1993) where racial, ethnic, religious, and linguistic categories are confused and conflated.

The evolution of the census offers a fascinating exploration of the construction of race and the political and economic interests that shaped the changing ways people have been classified since the first census in 1790. Humes and Hogan (2009) trace these changes in classification in decennial censuses from 1790 to 2010 and show the preoccupation with race and ancestry since the beginning. Scientific racism and concerns about racial purity, as well as the impact of waves of immigration from different parts of the world at different periods of U.S. history, are evident in attempts to define and redefine "racial" categories that continually leaked.

The racial categories in the census have also been contested from the very beginning by peoples for whom the classifications did not fit their self-definitions, and who understood how such categorization regulated access to the benefits of citizenship. For example, in the early years, census categories reflected and bolstered restrictive immigration policies as well as Jim Crow practices. In more recent times, the census has been used to allocate resources to remedy past discrimination. All of these factors contribute to the ongoing contestation and changing language of the census up to the present day.

Pan-ethnic group labels developed by the census, such as Asian American, Arab American, and Hispanic/Latino, illustrate some of these tensions. For example, based on racial prerequisite cases brought by Syrians, people in the pan-ethnic group "Arab American" are classified racially as white. Yet, according to Kayyali (2013), the racial designation does not always conform with self-ascriptions that are national (Syrian, Lebanese, Palestinian), religious (Christian, Muslim), regional (Middle East, Africa) or linguistic (Arabic, Turkish). Organizations that represent the interests of Arab Americans have proposed various ways to change the census to reflect this diversity. They do this for two reasons. First, to honor the self-ascriptions of the diverse peoples under this umbrella. Second, to differentiate those not treated as "white" so that their needs will not be overlooked by social services and federal agencies (Kayyali, 2013). At the same time that pan-ethnic labels obscure differences that matter to people from diverse regions, religions, and languages, they also have opened up spaces for cross-group organizing and support.

BIRACIAL AND MULTIRACIAL PEOPLE

More recently, the census has been preoccupied with how to count the growing population that identifies as "biracial" or "multiracial" (Humes & Hogan, 2009). Of course, this population has existed from the beginning, but it has been concealed by racial categorization systems constructed to maintain white dominance. For example, the one-drop rule, created and used to police the color line, defined as black anyone who might now call themselves biracial or multiracial.

Prior to the Supreme Court decision *Loving v. Virginia in* 1967, interracial marriage was illegal in many states. In 1960, less than 1% of U.S. marriages were interracial. By 2010, there were 5.4 million interracial or interethnic married-couple households, or 9.5% of all married-couple households (Pew, 2015). Between 2000 and 2010, the number of white and black biracial Americans more than doubled, while the white and Asian biracial group increased by 87% (Pew, 2015). With the option to mark one or more races introduced in the 2000 census, the multiracial population become much more visible:

> In 2000, 2.4% of Americans identified multiracially, and in 2010, the figure increased to 2.9 percent. Among Americans under the age of 18, the multiracial population increased by 46% since 2000, making multiracial children the fastest growing youth group in the country. Demographers project that the multiracial population will continue to grow so that by 2050, 1 in 5 Americans could claim a multiracial background.
> (Pew, 2015, p. 11)

The experiences and attitudes of multiracial people differ depending on the races that make up their background, how they see themselves, and how the world sees them (Wijeyesinghe, 2012). In the Pew (2015) report, the majority of multiracial adults with a black background reported that most people view them as black or African American, and their experiences and social interactions lead them to align closely with the black community. Multiracial Asian adults, and biracial white and Asian adults, say they feel more closely connected to whites than to Asians. Among biracial adults who are white and American Indian (the largest group of multiracials), only 22% say they have a lot in common with American Indians, whereas 61% say they have a lot in common with whites (Pew, 2015). The different racialized experiences and orientations of people who define themselves or are defined by others as multiracial are reflected in tensions within the multiracial movement over how to deal with racism (see Hamako, 2009).

COLORISM AND COLOR HIERARCHY

Colorism refers to bias that favors light skin over dark skin linked to racial hierarchy. People of color who consciously or unconsciously accept the color prejudices of the broader society, and any people who uses skin tone and ideals of European beauty to evaluate others, are employing colorism. Research has linked colorism to darker-skinned people receiving inferior education, lower salaries and marriage rates, and longer prison terms (Knight, 2013).

Colorism can be traced to slavery, where it was common for white slave owners to engage in sexual intercourse with enslaved black women. The lighter-skinned offspring of these unions, though remaining as slaves and not acknowledged by their fathers, received "privileges" that darker-skinned slaves did not have (less physically demanding jobs and domestic chores inside the house). After slavery, African Americans employed colorism through the "brown paper bag test": If a person's skin was darker than a paper bag, they would not be admitted to social clubs, churches, and black fraternities and sororities (Knight, 2013).

The media promotes colorism by perpetuating white ideals of beauty through the disproportionate use of light-skinned models in magazines and television, while darker-skinned African American men are presented disproportionately as violent and dangerous. Portrayals in the media that equate dark skin with crime, violence, lack of intelligence, and poverty perpetuate colorism. Colorism is a global phenomenon in every racial/ethnic group where there is skin tone variation, and occurs in Latin America, Asia, Africa, and the Arab world (Glenn, 2009).The booming business in skin-bleaching products signifies the enduring legacy of colorism.

THE SHIFTING COLOR LINE

Increasing racial diversity has resulted in movement from a predominantly black/white binary conversation on race, to one that acknowledges the complexities posed by Asians, Latina/os, Native Americans, people from the Middle East and North Africa, and biracial/multiracial peoples who do not fit this binary. The shift to a "new" racial frame has been variously characterized as white-nonwhite (Warren &Twine, 1997), black-nonblack (Lee & Bean, 2004), or evolving into a more complex triracial hierarchy or "pigmentocracy" that includes the categories white, honorary white, and collective black (Bonilla-Silva, 2004). According to Bonilla-Silva, a triracial system would look more like the racial order in Latin America or the Caribbean, where race conflict is buffered by an intermediate group based on class and color gradations. In a triracial system, intermarriage with whites and economic mobility for some groups of Asians and Latino/as would move them to an honorary white category. However, the "collective black" category would still keep African Americans and dark-skinned Latino/as at the bottom. Overall, this system would still enforce a racial hierarchy.

Warren and Twine (1997) argue that "the back door to whiteness" is open to Asian Americans. Because they are not black and are relatively economically successful, and they have an image as the model minority, Warren and Twine suggest that some Asian Americans are poised to "become white." Their schema connects racial superiority (whiteness) and economic success—a connection that does not hold true in all situations where race and relative economic success are mediated by religion, gender and sexuality, age, and disability.

Regardless, the color line and the determination of position and mobility remain under the control of the dominant white group:

> Members of subordinated groups may adopt mainstream habits and values, change their names, drop their native language or religious affiliation in order to be accepted into the dominant group, but it is always the dominant group that determines who will be allowed access.
>
> (Lawrence, Sutton, Kubisch, Susi, & Fulbright-Anderson, 2004, n.p.)

LINGUICISM AND LINGUISTIC PROFILING

The term *linguicism* (Skutnabb-Kangas, 1988) or *language domination* (Dardar & Uriarte, 2008) describes prejudice and discrimination based on language. Linguicism, like racism, can be overt or covert, conscious or unconscious, and reflects dominant attitudes and beliefs about the value and relative ranking of languages, accents, and ways of speaking. Linguistic discrimination is also linked to color and class. Thus, French and Castilian Spanish are seen as high-status languages, while Spanish spoken by Mexicans, Dominicans, and Puerto Ricans, or French Creole spoken by Haitians, are demeaned, thus reinforcing a hierarchy that valorizes European (white) language, culture, and values. English-only policies based on the normalization of English as "standard" support the stigmatization of other languages and the people who speak them. English-only movements relate to nativism and anti-immigrant sentiments against immigrants of color from Asia, Latin America, and Africa.

Linguistic profiling is the auditory equivalent of visual racial profiling and can have equally negative consequences for those perceived to speak with an undesirable accent or dialect (Baugh, 2003). Linguistic profiling is evidenced in housing and employment discrimination cases where applicants who "sound black" or who speak with a Spanish or Asian accent are denied housing or employment (Subtirelu, 2015). The fact that linguistic profiling takes place over the phone or written correspondence makes it difficult to prosecute. "It is subtle, not in your face, not slamming down the phone. But not following up by calling back or mailing material, is just as malicious as saying, 'I won't give you insurance because you're Black or Mexican'" (quoted in Baugh, 2003, p. 160).

CURRENT MANIFESTATIONS OF RACISM AND POSSIBLE RESPONSES

The themes mentioned above provide a framework for understanding how racism is produced and reproduced in each generation as people are socialized into the systems that sustain racism. These themes are important for understanding the racial system we have inherited. The following section illustrates the connections between these themes, how they manifest in major institutions in society, and what is needed to challenge their impact and create change.

MANIFESTATIONS OF RACISM AT THE INSTITUTIONAL/SOCIETAL LEVEL

While racism impacts all institutions, we focus on the particular racial dynamics in seven mutually reinforcing arenas: Housing, education, the labor market, the criminal justice system, the media, politics, and health care (see Fig. 5.1). Racial differences in opportunities and outcomes in these institutions are particularly critical to a person's (and group's) social, economic, and political standing in society. Despite civil rights advances and purportedly more liberal attitudes, race serves as a reliable predictor of racially unequal levels of access, participation, and success in these institutions. Taken together, these mutually reinforcing institutional manifestations of racism create a pervasive system that can make it feel impossible to escape.

Housing

The impact of where one lives is profound and plays a critical role in access to quality education, decent jobs, adequate public transportation, health, and economic well-being.

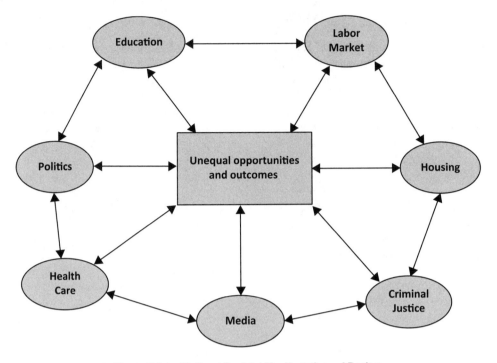

Figure 5.1 Institutional/Societal Manifestations of Racism

Home ownership is the major way that middle-class families can accumulate wealth and pass it on to the next generation (Oliver & Shapiro, 2006). In 2013, the median wealth of white households was thirteen times that of black households, and more than ten times that of Latina/o households (Pew Research Center, 2014).

This legacy of wealth disparity stems largely from generations of housing discrimination engendered by policies of local, state, and federal governments as well as the actions of individuals. Racial prejudice and discrimination on the part of individual white politicians, officials, loan officers, developers, and individuals who seek to live in homogeneous white communities clearly play an important part. Also essential is the way segregation and discrimination have been underwritten by deliberate public policy decisions that supported, justified, and enforced segregation and created the racial landscape in which we live today (Lipsitz, 2011; Rothstein, 2014).

Racially segregated housing was produced and enforced by Federal Housing Administration (FHA) policies and real estate and mortgage lending practices based on race that determined who could live where and in what type of housing (Katznelson, 2005; Lipsitz, 2006). These practices included red-lining and racial zoning, which determined who would be eligible for FHA loans to buy housing, and restrictive covenants that prevented white homeowners from selling to black families. Blockbusting and racial steering by realtors deliberately incited white fear of reduced property values if black families moved into their neighborhoods so that whites would sell low; then realtors could profit by selling high to black families who were desperate for access to decent housing (Rothstein, 2014). New Deal housing policies also subsidized white-only suburban development alongside the parallel destruction of black neighborhoods through failure to maintain municipal services, and the use of eminent domain to confiscate black-owned properties for business purposes and urban renewal projects that benefited white developers. Such practices over the past 60 years excluded people of color at all socio-economic levels from significant home ownership while advantaging white people by comparison (Katznelson, 2005; Lipsitz, 2011). Disparities in home ownership rates, typical home equity, and neighborhood values contribute substantially to the wealth gap between whites on the one hand, and Latinos and blacks on the other (Demos, 2015).

Many such practices continue today. For example, studies show that banks are less likely to offer a mortgage to a black applicant than to a white applicant who has the same earnings, the same educational level, and a comparable job (Savage, 2012). Research also reveals that people of color pay more in interest rates than white people pay for similar mortgages (Gramlich, 2007). The most recent housing crisis led many potential homeowners of color to borrow from predatory lenders in the form of sub-prime loans. The consequences have been disproportionate displacement, eviction, and foreclosure for people of color in the recent economic downturn (Miller & Garran, 2008; Rugh & Massey, 2010). The median loss from the housing crash for white families was 16% of their wealth, while black families' median loss was 53% and Latino families 66% (Demos, 2015). There is evidence that women of color have been impacted most (Hill, 2012). Gentrification in newly desirable urban centers is now reproducing segregation patterns as poor and low-income people of color are forced out of cities into inner-ring suburbs in the face of escalating rents and housing prices (Kruse, 2005).

In a weblike manner, discrimination in housing markets and residential segregation are associated with "concentrated disadvantage," the compounding of racial disadvantage with socio-economic class that can isolate a community from resources, limit the usefulness of local networks, and expose neighborhood residents to negative social conditions (Massey & Denton, 1993). Such discrimination shows up in poor health outcomes (Centers for Disease Control, 2013) and limited educational and employment opportunities (Pager & Shepherd, 2008). These racist practices over generations compound and perpetuate the historical cumulative advantage for whites and cumulative disadvantage for people of color.

Practical programs and regulatory reforms exist that begin to address the problems enumerated above, but more needs to be done. Individuals and organizations could advocate for policies that encourage mixed-income, integrated neighborhoods. Landlords could be prohibited from turning away tenants whose rent is subsidized (Rothstein, 2014). Outer-ring suburbs could be required to repeal zoning ordinances that prohibit construction of affordable housing and to accommodate a "fair share" of low-income populations, as New Jersey has attempted to do (Rothstein, 2014). Stricter enforcement of anti-discrimination laws in housing would increase the ability of people of color to buy homes in higher-value neighborhoods, where they can get the same return on their investment as white homeowners (Demos, 2015). In a major victory for housing justice, the Supreme Court in June 2015, in a 5–4 decision, ruled that policies that segregate minorities in poor neighborhoods, even if they do so unintentionally, violate the Fair Housing Act.

Authorizing Fannie Mae and Freddie Mac (lending institutions that are backed by the government) to make loan modifications for struggling homeowners would help to protect the home equity wealth of black and Latina/o homeowners (Demos, 2015). Recent ally campaigns, such as the "No One Leaves Project" launched by students at Harvard Law School and similar projects in Florida, work with community members facing displacement from bank foreclosure. Such projects strive toward economic justice through training that ensures community residents understand their rights, and foster political agency, leadership, and empowerment to fight back (http://www.springfieldnooneleaves.org/). One recent report estimates that if disparities in home ownership rates were eliminated so that blacks and Latina/os were as likely to own their own homes at the same percentage as whites, the wealth gap would decrease by 28% for Latinos and 31% for blacks (Demos,

2015). If public policy equalized the return on homeownership so that blacks and Latinos saw the same gains as whites, the wealth gap would be reduced by 16% for blacks and 41% for Latinos (Demos, 2015).

Education

Housing segregation preserves a system of educational apartheid that filters educational resources and opportunities to white areas with higher property taxes to pay for good schools, while further marginalizing low-income and poor neighborhood residents where property taxes and financial resources for schools are lower. Segregation in housing, schools, friendship, work, and other areas in turn contributes to white ignorance about people of color and stereotyping and discrimination at individual and cultural levels (Bonilla-Silva, 2013; Cashin, 2004; Frankenberg, 2013). School segregation is largely based on and follows housing segregation.

K–12 Education

Court cases to end racial segregation (*Brown v. Board of Education*), along with cases on the provision of bilingual education (*Lau v. Nichols*) and inclusion of students with disabilities (Individuals with Disabilities Education Act, or IDEA), had brief periods of successful implementation during the 1970s and early 1980s, when public policies, government, and the courts used their power to support change. Since that period, a backlash to busing, bilingual schooling, and integration have rolled back much of the progress that was made. According to Orfield & Lee (2005, p. 18), more than 60% of black and Latino students attend high-poverty schools, compared with 30% of Asians and 18% of whites. Market-driven "reforms" and the growth of charter schools in many cases have exacerbated and increased segregation and inequality, especially in poor neighborhoods (Orfield & Frankenberg, 2013). Studies show, for example, that charter schools are more segregated than public schools attended by black children and that the focus on charters has deflected from integration efforts and exacerbated racial segregation (Frankenberg & Siegel-Hawley, 2009). Students in racially segregated schools of any kind face the negative consequences of overcrowded and inadequate facilities, a less rigorous curriculum, less access to highly qualified teachers, fewer opportunities to take Advanced Placement courses where they could get points toward college admission, and inadequate information about financial aid, college opportunities, and other avenues to well-paying careers (Carter & Welner, 2013).

Although the U.S. student population is increasingly racially and linguistically diverse, the teaching force remains overwhelmingly white and monolingual (Landsman & Lewis, 2011). Teachers who are less knowledgeable about students' families and communities are typically less aware of the challenges of racism their students face (Bell, 2003a; Delpit, 2013; Ladson-Billings, 2009). These social and cultural disconnects often manifest in disciplinary actions and "zero tolerance" policies that treat black and Latino students more harshly than suburban counterparts, and contribute to a school-to-prison pipeline from an early age. Increasingly, African American and Native American females also suffer from disproportionate disciplinary action. For example, black girls in elementary and secondary public schools between 2011–2012 were suspended at a rate of 12% compared to their white counterparts at 2%; and Native American girls were suspended at a rate of 7% higher than their white male peers (Vega, 2014).

It is well documented that working-class Latinos, Native Americans, and African Americans are overrepresented in special education programs (Losen, Orfield, & Jeffords, 2003).

While it is important not to discount the significance of students receiving appropriate support to meet their educational needs, the students in these populations are too often mislabeled. The combination of over-disciplining and the overrepresentation of students of color in special education programs raises even more concerns considering the links between special education and decreased college enrollment and high school graduation (Oesterreich & Knight, 2010).

The dire educational circumstances facing domestically born low-income children of color are also faced by large numbers of children of immigrants of color, who settle in highly segregated neighborhoods where poverty, violence, and substandard schools are the norm. Immigrant children in high-poverty, segregated neighborhoods face declining returns to education (for each succeeding generation, progress based on educational attainment declines), in effect replicating the ways that decades of racism have dampened educational and economic success among African Americans, Native Americans, Puerto Ricans, and Mexican Chicano/as (Foner, 2005; Spring, 2003).

Many children of immigrants (the 1.5 and second generation) lead transnational lives and call multiple places home (Foner, 2011; Joshi, 2006; Levitt & Waters, 2002; Soehl & Waldinger; 2012). Many are bilingual or at least exposed to another language, and they often live in homes where another language is spoken. Juggling multiple realities can reinforce a strong sense of self and identity for those who are able to view the world and their experiences from a dual frame of reference (Coll & Magnuson, 2014; Sánchez & Machado-Casas, 2009). For others, however, the effects of prejudice and discrimination can have cumulative and long-lasting negative effects on their sense of identity, group identification, and academic achievement (Suárez-Orozco, Pimentel, & Martin, 2009). The interaction of linguicism and racism generate "backlash practices" (Tejeda & Gutierrez, 2006) that target immigrants of color and impoverish learning through "English-only" legislation and banning bilingual education from schools (Alamillo et al., 2005; Valenzuela, 1999). In several states, secondary school programs that focus on cultural and ethnic empowerment, which have a proven track record of creating access to college, face elimination. For example, in Tucson, Arizona, a highly successful Ethnic Studies Program that taught inclusive narratives of United States history and pride in language and heritage was banned, thus penalizing English language learners for using their cultural assets in the service of learning.

Black, Latina/o, and Native American youth can internalize negative stereotypes and low expectations for academic achievement held by others in ways that heighten stereotype threat and dampen their performance (Steele, 2010). Asian-American and Asian students, on the other hand, are often marginalized through double-edged, so-called "positive" stereotypes of a "model minority" whose diligence, frugality, and willingness to sacrifice are presumed to propel upward mobility for all Asians (Tuan, 2001). While academic achievement is to be celebrated, generalizations don't account for the academic struggles of students who don't fit the stereotype. Expectations of success can create debilitating anxiety when individuals are expected to produce results because of "positive" stereotypes about their group, such as "the model minority" (Cheryan & Bodenhausen, 2000). Educators must understand how stereotype threats operates through both "positive" and negative attributions, and become knowledgeable about the experiences of the diverse ethnic groups they teach.

The model minority label further obscures serious problems in the Asian community and has been used to justify omitting Asian Americans from federal funding, university admissions, and some special minority programs. Lumping together Asians from many different national origins, languages, and economic situations into one group obscures the stratification among various Asian groups who enter the racialized U.S. system under different immigration rules. For example, well-educated South Asian (Indian and Pakistani) and East Asian (Chinese and Korean) immigrants, who have been preferred by immigration rules, experience mobility and social integration very differently than less well-educated compatriots from those countries or refugees from Vietnam and Cambodia.

This sorting of racial groups, valorizing some over others, minimizes racism as a determining factor in achieving success in the U.S. while policing standards for how members of other racialized groups should behave. When individual members of one social group embrace "positive" stereotypes of their group in order to avoid negative stereotypes applied to other groups, they may play into racial hierarchy. Such hierarchy and division is then used by the dominant white group to discredit claims of injustice by African Americans and others who demand social equality (Kim, 1999).

Higher Education

Racial disparities are also evident in higher education (Orfield, Marin, & Horn, 2005). Currently, eight states have successfully legislated anti-affirmative action policies in favor of "race-neutral policies" despite evidence that African Americans, Latina/os and Native Americans are grossly underrepresented within institutions of higher of education (DeSilver, 2014). While data support the increasing educational gains for blacks over the past two decades, this is largely due to the increased participation of black women. As a result, the gender gap is most extreme among black students, with black females earning 68.3% of associate degrees awarded to black students compared to black males, who earned 31.7% of these degrees (Knapp, Kelly-Reid, & Ginder, 2011). In four-year institutions, this gap is almost a 2:1 ratio (Kim, 2011).

Blacks and Latinos are overrepresented in community colleges (Carnevale & Strohl, 2013). While community colleges can serve as a viable option for these students, black and Latino students also face poor odds of successfully transferring and completing a degree at a four-year institution. This combination of factors contributes to racially disparate college graduation rates, with a larger percentage of white students graduating in five years than black and Latina/o students from predominantly white institutions, even in instances where blacks and Latinos have comparable levels of college readiness and test scores (Carnevale & Strohl, 2013). In fact, barriers to degree completion have actually widened in the past ten years (Demos, 2015).

It is not uncommon for students of color to report being overwhelmed by feelings of isolation, experiences of hostility from peers, and the racial microaggressions they encounter in daily interactions (Solórzano, Ceja, & Yosso, 2000; Sue, 2010; Watkins, 2012). Many incidents on campuses in the past few years, such as "affirmative action bake sales," white fraternity parties with "ethnic themes," and overt racist songs are rooted in racial stereotyping and hostility toward race-conscious campus policies. The "I Am Harvard Too" campaign, organized by a coalition of student organizations and replicated at colleges across the country, highlighted these all too common experiences with racism and microaggressions.

While the current campus context replicates racism in the larger society, it also provides spaces where students can develop knowledge and skills to understand and challenge racism. As places that have historically inspired agitation for social change, colleges can provide the opportunity to form cross-racial coalitions to work for common goals of equality and inclusion. Academic courses, in a variety of disciplines that address and analyze the historical and current social, economic, and legal inequities that exist, can offer a much-needed framework for helping students understand present realities and their historical context, and identify ways to address such issues on campus and in the larger society.

Education about racism provides a vehicle for civic engagement and social responsibility, and the opportunity to translate awareness into action that enables students to take their learning beyond the campus and into their daily lives.

Labor Market

The labor market is another area where racism manifests in interlocking ways with other manifestations. Discriminatory hiring practices segregate workers of color into job categories with lower wages and fewer opportunities for advancement. Employment and wage discrimination makes it difficult enough to afford housing, even without housing segregation. In combination, housing and workplace segregation compound each other. Workers of color, particularly working-class workers of color, often have to live in segregated communities farther away from job sites and rely on substandard public transportation that makes their commute longer and more costly. Native Americans isolated on reservations or in segregated urban communities and Latino/as have faced similar patterns of exclusion. Such entrenched patterns contribute to cumulative disadvantage for people of color and a corollary cumulative advantage for whites.

Labor market participation rates illustrate the significant role race plays in determining access to and type of employment. For example, the highest-paying occupational categories in management, professional, and related occupations are dominated by whites (39%) and Asians (50%), compared with blacks (29%) and Hispanics (20%) (U.S. Bureau of Labor Statistics, 2014). At the lower end of the occupational ladder, we see the reverse: Latinos are overrepresented in lower-paying fields of agriculture (50%), grounds maintenance (45%), and maids and housekeeping (44%), while blacks are slotted into jobs as aides in nursing, psychiatric, and home health care (36%); bus drivers (27%); and security guards and gaming surveillance officers (27%). Asians make up a majority of manicurists, pedicurists, skin care specialists, barbers, and cosmetologists (57%), as well as 29% of software developers, and 22% of physicians and surgeons. Whites are at the top of the occupational pyramid, accounting for 96% of farmers, ranchers, and agricultural managers; 93% of construction managers; and 91% of chief executives (U.S. Bureau of Labor Statistics, 2014).

Black and Latina/o workers are not only paid less, but they are also likely to be employed in jobs that do not provide benefits such as health coverage, paid leave, and retirement plans (Demos, 2015). Having to pay more out of pocket for such benefits means they have less money to invest in the future and build wealth. Studies have shown that networks and personal connections maintain this skewed occupational picture (Mullainathan, 2015; Smith, 2005). Since people in the U.S. lead such segregated lives, whites benefit disproportionately from social networking advantages.

According to the latest census report, there are more people living below the poverty line than at any time in the last half century. In 2013, the overall unemployment rate was highest for blacks (13.1%), American Indians and Alaska Natives (12.8%), and Latina/os (9.1%); and lowest for Asians (5.2%) and whites (6.5%) (U.S. Bureau of Labor Statistics, 2014.) Among teenagers, blacks had the highest unemployment rate—38.8%, followed by Latina/o teenagers 27.5%; whites, 20.3%; and Asians, 19.7%. As a result, blacks, Latinos, and Native Americans have been hit hardest during the most recent recession, where their already-high poverty rates increased (Tavernise, 2011). While 25 to 33% of the gap between the earnings of whites and African Americans, Native Americans, and Latinos can be explained by educational differences, these groups are less likely to receive a quality education that leads to college graduation. Black youth who are not enrolled in college, for example, have a 29.2% unemployment rate compared to white peers not enrolled in college, who have a 14.1% unemployment rate (U.S. Bureau of Labor Statistics, 2014). One study shows that being black affected job opportunities more than or as much as a criminal history. In fact, whites with a criminal history were shown to have equal or better chances of gaining employment than non-criminal offender blacks (Pager, 2007).

Biased hiring and layoff practices add to these disparities. Studies show that employers were 50% less likely to call for an interview applicants with common black names on their resumes than applicants with common white names, even though all applicants in the study had exactly the same resume (Bertrand & Mullainathan, 2004). During the recession of the early 2000s, black workers lost jobs at twice the rate of white and Latino workers. Low-wage service jobs that have replaced manufacturing jobs continue to discriminate against black workers and other workers of color (Pager, Western & Bonikowski, 2009).

Access to decent jobs determines to a large degree whether or not one can buy a home, accumulate assets, and use these assets to improve the life chances for one's offspring.

> Just 50 years after Martin Luther King offered his dream to our nation at the foot of the Lincoln memorial, Blacks earned 62 cents for every dollar of White earned income, however only secured 10 cents of net wealth while Latinos earned 68 cents for every dollar of White earned income, but only 16 cents of net wealth.
>
> (United for a Fair Economy, 2012, p. 5)

Enforcement of anti-discrimination laws in hiring that are already on the books would make an important difference. Agitating for a federal job creation program, such as the Works Progress Administration (WPA) employment programs during the New Deal, would put people back to work and benefit the general public through providing goods and services, such as improved infrastructure, child and elder care, and cultural enrichment (Demos, 2015). Raising the minimum wage, as happened in Seattle, would boost incomes of lower-paid black and Latino workers. Making it easier for workers to form unions would also help, since "Blacks and Latinos see greater wage premiums as a result of union membership than white workers, and union membership does more to increase access to key employment benefits such as health coverage and retirement plans" (Demos, 2015, p. 31). For Latino workers, immigration policy changes that protect their rights are also critical. Individuals can support such efforts by learning about and supporting campaigns to increase the minimum wage and reduce employment discrimination.

Media

In its many forms (newspapers, magazines, social media, books, radio, television, movies), the media provides the backdrop for how society views and responds to people from different racial groups. Media can inflame and propagate racism, as well as provide information to counteract it. Media themes shape public opinion and public policy, the responses of bureaucracies and individual public officials, as well as the attitudes and behavior of the public at large.

Negative representations in the media about particular social groups increase the likelihood that viewers will develop stereotypes about that group (Cortes, 2000). For example, when media highlights black and Latino men as criminal, it perpetuates racial stereotypes; normalizes racially defined, negative characteristics attached to these groups; and ultimately legitimizes racial hierarchy (Bunche Center, 2014). A study that analyzed the 345 most-viewed U.S. television shows from 1987–2009 showed severe underrepresentation of Latinos, Asian Americans, and Native Americans, and a tendency to depict ethnic minorities stereotypically (Entman & Rojecki, 2001; Leavitt, Covarrubias, Perez, & Fryberg, 2015; Tukachinsky, 2015).

The social power to control images of people of color is overwhelmingly in white hands, and thus tends to reflect the preferences, stereotypes, and misinformation of the dominant group. In 2013, for example, white men had controlling interest in 87.34% of full-power television stations in the United States (Federal Communications Commission, 2014). In contrast, people of color own only 5.83% of full-power television stations in total (Federal Communications Commission, 2014). In Hollywood and television, the vast majority of producers, writers, and actors are white men.

> When marginalized groups in society are absent from the stories a nation tells about itself, or when media images are rooted primarily in stereotype, inequality is normalized and is more likely to be reinforced over time through our prejudices and practices.
> (Bunche Center, 2014, p. 5)

Social media, as a virtual public sphere, also serves as a platform for racism. *Cyber-racism* (Daniels, 2009) includes racial bias on the Internet through racist websites, images, blogs, online comments, as well as racist comments, images, or language in text messages, online correspondence, and social media sites (http://www.racismnoway.com.au/about-racism/cyber-racism/index.html). For example, in 2013, General Mills shut down a Cheerios commercial depicting an interracial couple because of the racist commentary in response to the video (Martin, McCann, Morales, & William, 2013).

Social media has also been utilized to bring awareness to longstanding issues about racism. In the example above, the racist commentary resulted in more attention to the ad, with many viewers weighing in to support the interracial family in the ad to counterbalance the negative comments. In this case, social media was also used as a way to fight racism. Several Native American nations have been fighting against the use of Native Americans as team mascots for years, such as protests against the National Football League's Washington Redskins team's use of a racist team mascot. In 2013, the Oneida Indian Nation, in collaboration with the National Congress of American Indians, the United South and Eastern Tribes, the National Indian Education Association, and various supporters across an array of institutions, created a "Change the Mascot" initiative that is gaining ground around the country (http://www.changethemascot.org/).

Political Participation and Representation

The 114th Congress, seated in January 2015, was heralded as the most diverse in our history, but according to the *Washington Post*, it is 80% white, 80% male, and 92% Christian (Bump, 2015). While more diverse than the previous Congress, still, four out of five members are white and male. Such skewed representation is kept in place by several factors: Big money in politics that favors incumbents, an old boy network that grooms and promotes people like themselves for political office, gerrymandered districts that often control who can win (with specifically racial outcomes), and suppression of voting among youth and people of color, to name a few.

This situation is not new in American history. Despite our heralded claims of democracy, the right to vote has been contested throughout U.S. history with white, male property-holders resisting the inclusion of "nonwhites," women, and working-class people (as well as prisoners, aliens, and those deemed morally and mentally unfit to vote) (Keyssar, 2009). This exclusionary cycle is operating again as conservatives propose legislation to restrict voting rights through new barriers to voter registration, shortening early voting periods, adding new requirements for registered voters, and rigging the Electoral College in some states (Keyes, Millhiser, Van Ostern, & White, 2012). The Supreme Court in 2013 (in a 5/4 split) eliminated Section 4 of the Voting Rights Act, which required states with a history of minority voter suppression to clear changes to their voting laws with the federal government, thus paving the way for further exclusion based on race.

These exclusionary attempts are driven by fears of the potential impact of the growing pool of young voters and voters of color at a time when the proportional white population is declining. Between 1988–2008, the number of minority voters increased from 15% to 26% (Keyes, Millhiser, Van Ostern, & White, 2012). Combined with a more liberal youth vote, the collective impact of these groups presents a growing threat to entrenched political power.

The right to vote is more important than ever, especially at state and local levels, where political representation can have the most impact. Many coalitions and organizations are working to educate people about the importance of defending voting rights, including the Voting Rights Coalition, Fair Vote, and the NAACP Legal Defense Fund. Others, such as Project Vote, work for the restoration of voting rights to former felons and encourage young people to get involved in electoral politics. Rock the Vote, Campus Compact, and the National Coalition on Black Civic Participation are other organizations that teach about and foster civic engagement among youth.

The Criminal Justice System

Racial discrimination and prejudice deeply affect the criminal justice system in areas such as profiling, sentencing, access to adequate legal representation, incarceration, and parole (The Sentencing Project, 2014). Prominent author, Michelle Alexander, contends black Americans are living in an era that represents the New Jim Crow (Alexander, 2012). Whereas in the past the U.S. racial caste came in the form of chattel slavery and segregation, the contemporary system is created through the targeted surveillance and disproportionate imprisonment of blacks and Latinos. Federal, state, and city policies, such as the war on drugs, three strikes, and stop-and-frisk have led to the over-incarceration of people in poor and working-class black and Latino/a communities (Alexander, 2012). For example, African Americans comprise roughly 13% of the U.S. population, yet they represent almost 50% of the prison population (Miller & Garran, 2008).

A growing body of scholarship suggests that a significant portion of such disparity may be attributed to implicit racial bias held by Americans of all races who implicitly associate black Americans with adjectives such as "dangerous," "aggressive," "violent," and "criminal." This implicit bias affects how law enforcement officers do their job (The Sentencing Project, 2014). Disparities have been well documented in traffic stops and drug law enforcement. Whether California's three-strikes law, Arizona's SB 1070 and Safe Neighborhoods Act, or New York City's stop-and-frisk, these policies foster a culture that encourages racial profiling and the hyper-surveillance of poor and working-class communities of color without fear of repercussion.

Once racial minorities enter the criminal justice system, they continue to face bias at every stage of litigation, from the counsel that defendants receive (especially those who are poor) to the prosecutorial decisions about which cases to pursue, who to prosecute, what charges to bring, and what sentences to seek (including capital punishment) (The Sentencing Project, 2014). Evidence shows that implicit racial bias affects the ability of judges and juries to evaluate guilt and innocence objectively, and skews their judgment of cases with black defendants toward guilty regardless of the evidence presented (The Sentencing Project, 2014; Stevenson, 2014). Supreme Court decisions expanding the discretion of law enforcement personnel in searches has also had a detrimental effect, and the Court has thus far been unwilling to look at racially disparate impacts of their decisions (The Sentencing Project, 2014).

The various consequences of imprisonment may include losing the right to vote, an inability to receive financial aid, and a perpetual stigma that carries over into the search for employment. Incarceration rates for men are higher than for women, yet the rate at which women are incarcerated, disproportionately women of color, has grown faster than the rate for men in recent years, particularly since welfare reform and harsher penalties for drug crimes have been implemented. The number of women in prison increased by 646% between 1980 and 2010 (The Sentencing Project, 2012).

Juvenile detention rates reveal similarly deep racial disparities. African American children and adolescents are nearly five times more likely to be involved in the justice system than white peers; and Latino and American Indian children and adolescents are between two and three times as likely to be confined (Y. R. Harris, 2014). As noted in the research literature, for African American men, there is a school-to-prison pipeline (Curtis, 2014; Morris, 2012). In New York City, African American and Latino youth comprise 95% of those entering juvenile detention centers, even though they represent only two-thirds of all youth in New York City. Significantly, half of youth who enter detention come from only a quarter of New York City neighborhoods with the highest levels of poverty, poor housing, and under-performing schools (Prisco, 2011). Similarly disproportionate rates can be found in other urban communities across the country.

In addition to arrest and false convictions, police brutality continues to plague the black community. Racial bias within the police force and lack of attention to police relations with the community reflect implicit bias as well as explicit racist attitudes (U.S. Department of Justice, 2015). The number of black men who have been stopped by police with no probable cause and then killed when they talked back or tried to flee has become a national disgrace (U.S. Department of Justice, 2015).

Important reforms include establishing a national commission to examine racial disparities and make recommendations for systemic reform at all levels of the criminal justice system; scaling back the war on drugs, especially for low-level offenders; eliminating mandatory minimum sentencing; and abolishing capital punishment. Further recommendations include the adoption of racial impact statements for proposed sentencing policies, procedures to assess disparate racial impact, and training for all professionals in the justice system about implicit bias (The Sentencing Project, 2014).

The Immigration Industrial Complex

Racial profiling is rising both at the Mexican border and in interactions with those perceived to be terrorists based on anti-Muslim stereotypes. The focus on expelling undocumented immigrants from the nation has intersected with the prison industrial complex to create what has been dubbed the *immigration industrial complex,* referring to "public and private sector interests in the criminalization of undocumented migration, immigration law enforcement and the promotion of anti-illegal rhetoric" (Golash-Boza, 2009, p. 295). The immigration industrial complex is demonstrative of how fear and prejudice are utilized to construct a system that polices and monitors individuals based on citizenship status and geographic, racial, and religious identity. Since 9/11, anti-immigrant and nativist sentiment have fueled a deportation plan to expel undocumented immigrants from the nation.

Undocumented, not "illegal," immigrants are a large revenue source for private prisons. In 2012, Corrections Corporation of America (CCA), the largest operator for private prisons in the world, earned $1.7 billion in revenue— a quarter of it generated through contracts with Immigration Customs Enforcement (ICE) (Fang, 2013). In 2013, CCA spent $1 million lobbying for government contracts for prisons for undocumented immigrants (Justice Policy Institute, 2011). Lobbying for private prisons impacts immigration policy, in particular when the group consists of government officials. For example, the Arizona state legislator responsible for the SB 1070 legislation, which invites racial profiling of anyone suspected of being undocumented, happens to be a board member of the lobbying group American Legislative Exchange Council (ALEC). In fact, 30 of the 36 co-sponsors of the SB 1070 bill received campaign contributions from three major private prison companies: CCA; The Geo Group, Inc.; and Management and Training Corporation (MTC) (Freed Wessler, 2010).

Immigration policy represents a conundrum for politicians when anti-immigrant sentiments are in conflict with U.S. corporate and military interests. Many employers rely upon undocumented and low-skilled immigrant workers who they can pay less, prevent from unionizing, and let go during economic downturns. The military, when lacking volunteer citizens, rely heavily on immigrants who enlist in the armed services in exchange for the opportunity to become documented.

Immigration reform advocates work to change laws that block paths to citizenship. However, those such as the Fair Immigration Reform Movement (FIRM) see changing the law as only one part of their mission. They also seek to help local immigrant rights organizations better represent the needs of their communities, and help their members achieve legal status and democratic participation as citizens and voters. They also work to build alliances among immigrant communities and native-born, low-income, and people of color groups (www.fairimmigration.org).

Health Care

Numerous studies reveal health disparities among whites and communities of color, even when socio-economic status and education levels are controlled (Gomez & Lopez, 2013; Horner-Johnson, Fujiura & Tawara, 2014). For instance, African American women who are college graduates have a higher infant mortality rate than white women who dropped out of high school (http://www.unnaturalcauses.org/). African Americans have the highest cancer rates and deaths from cancer, are twice as likely as their white counterparts to suffer from diabetes, and represent 49% of individuals who are HIV-infected in the United States (Washington, 2007). Blacks and Latinos represent 86% of children infected with HIV.

Only a fraction of African American deaths are related to hereditary causes. Instead, a history of egregious medical experiments, distorted diagnoses from medical professionals, and an overall failure to humanize the experience of ailing African Americans by the medical field greatly contribute to sustaining health disparities (Washington, 2007). The phrase *Iatrophia* describes African Americans' fear of medical professionals and institutions (Washington, 2007). Instead of ascribing African American anxieties to paranoia, it is important to examine the historical context that shapes blacks' contemporary relationship to the field of mental health and medicine. In 1850, American psychiatrists pathologized enslaved Africans who ran away from slave owners, diagnosing them with an illness called drapetomania (Metzel, 2010). Since the civil rights movement, there has been a tendency to over-diagnose black men with schizophrenia—so much so that currently, they are three times more likely to be diagnosed as such, contributing to the impact of stress due to racism.

Mistrust of and mistreatment by the field of health is not unique to the black community. Recent Latino immigrants are among the healthiest ethnic groups in the United States; however, within five years of immigrating, Latino immigrants' health falls to the bottom. This phenomenon is referred to as the *Latino Paradox* (http://www.unnatural causes.org/video). Multiple factors, including environmental racism, contribute to this decline. Predominantly Latino and black neighborhoods have been labeled "food deserts" where healthy food is hard to come by, but there is an overabundance of fast food chains and liquor stores. Research has found residents of food deserts are more likely to die at an earlier age due to heart disease and high blood pressure (Dutko, Ver Ploeg, & Farrigan, 2012). Additionally, black and Latino neighborhoods are less likely to have green space, clean air, and recreational facilities where it is safe for children to play, and more than twice as likely to have toxic facilities such as sewage plants, dump and disposal sites, or transportation depots (unnatural causes.org).

In addition to physical health, racism generates mental health consequences. The term "racial battle fatigue" describes the psychological toll of living with the stresses of racism and daily microaggressions (Smith, Allen, & Danley, 2007). Immigrant communities of color are impacted by hate crimes committed on the basis of race/ethnicity, national origin, and religion that have steadily increased since the mid-1980s, and spiked after the attacks of September 11, 2001 (Ingraham, 2015; Muslim Public Affairs Council, 2015). In the year following the bombing of the World Trade Center, hate crimes against Arab American and South Asian (Alsultany, 2008) Sikhs (who were presumed to be Muslim based on their appearance) were 17 times higher than in the previous year (Orfalea, 2006). Immigration issues post 9/11 are increasingly linked to national security concerns, creating new and complex issues for many immigrants of color. Proposed legislation would require a national social identification card for air travel, opening a bank account, collecting social security, and accessing most government services.

These daily stresses have a deleterious impact on the health and well-being of recent immigrant populations. In 2011, Asian American elderly women and those between the ages 18–22 had the highest rate of attempted suicide at 13.5%. Unrealistic expectations to fit into the "model minority" myth add pressure to assimilate to U.S. norms. Moreover, youth often internalize expectations to perform as "super minorities" and fail to seek help or support when needed (Teranishi, 2002). In 2014, teen-aged Latinas unfortunately surpassed the aforementioned numbers with a 15.6% attempted suicide rate (CDC, 2015). These troubling rates are exacerbated for undocumented Latinas, who are less likely to seek medical assistance or mental health resources as a result of fear of deportation. This population is also at great risk for sexual assault and abuse given their vulnerability (CDC, 2015).

Polls show that most physicians and the public at large erroneously think that there are no longer racial disparities in health care (Kaiser Family Foundation, 2008). Thus, raising the awareness of the general public and of health care providers about documented racial/ethnic disparities in care is an important first step. Improving the capacity and number of providers in underserved communities who understand health disparities and their causes can ensure better responses and earlier interventions to reduce disparities. Equally important is the expansion of health insurance coverage to provide equal access to adequate health care (http://kff.org/disparities-policy/issue-brief/eliminating-racialethnic-disparities-in-health-care-what/). Finally, addressing environmental racism and its impacts is an important step toward addressing many negative health outcomes for communities of color. Of course, eliminating racism in public life would ameliorate the physical and mental toll on people of color exacted through living with racism.

MANIFESTATIONS OF RACISM AT THE INDIVIDUAL LEVEL

The previous section focused on manifestations of racism at the institutional and societal level. This section examines racism at the individual level. While people may recognize overt forms of racial harassment as individual racist behavior, they may be less likely to recognize more subtle forms of racism. Racism tends to be conceptualized as conscious attitudes and behaviors that are intended to harm individuals or groups of color, or to define them as inferior to whites and therefore less entitled to society's benefits. Many immigrants who experience racism often do not recognize or categorize it as such since they assume it is only something that happens to African Americans. Some examples of overt racism at the individual level are when people of color are called racial epithets or when immigrants (or those perceived to be immigrants) are told, "Go back to where you came from." Emails with explicit racist jokes or images, or nooses hung on doors, are other examples of intentional, overt individual racism.

Covert or unintentional racism is more commonplace. Racial microaggressions are examples of unconscious racial bias. There are many types of racial microaggressions. One type is marginalization or exclusion. To experience marginalization or exclusion is to be relegated to the sidelines, or to be rendered racially or culturally invisible. Marginalization and exclusion occur, for example, when people of color are not invited to social events or into work groups, or are not accepted into white fraternities and sororities, or white people avoid sitting next to people of color. People from the Caribbean, Africa, and South Asia are sometimes ridiculed or ostracized for eating foods with spices unfamiliar to those in the dominant group (Joshi, 2006; Waters, 2009). Biracial and multiracial people are marginalized when their life experiences are not acknowledged in discussions around race and racism, or they are forced to choose one identity.

Questioning a person of color's identity, cultural authenticity, or "Americanness" are other forms of racial microaggression. For example, Asian Americans face the "forever foreign syndrome," the assumption that an Asian is automatically from somewhere else and not a real American (Tuan, 2001). They confront questions like the ubiquitous, "Where are you from? No, where are you *really* from?" As a result, Asian Americans are perceived as less patriotic (Xu & Lee, 2013). Latinos face similar questions about whether or not they are "legal," and they are called the derogatory term "illegal aliens." Native Americans often need to justify their identity and authenticity to people who ask how much "Indian" blood is in their lineage. Conversely, individuals who are not Native American can be hurtful or offensive to indigenous people by romanticizing the lived experience of Native Americans and engaging in the commodification of Native American cultural items and practices.

Claiming color-blindness can also be a manifestation of unconscious individual racism. When white people say, "I don't see color" or "I treat everyone the same, we are all just the human race" they are often trying to avoid being seen as racially biased. Despite what may be good intentions, by not acknowledging race, they fail to respond to a person of color's distinctive identity, needs, and experiences, and the impact of racism in their lives. Color-blind racism avoids direct racial discourse and thereby effectively safeguards existing structures of racial privilege.

It can be difficult to separate individual and institutional racism. When a person engages in racist behavior, they may be enacting their own racial bias and/or reflecting the culture and practices of the institution of which they are part. When white fraternities host "Ghetto Thug" or "Border Patrol" themed parties, they operate on stereotypes and create unwelcome environments for students of color. When they are allowed to do so without consequence, the institution is enabling that behavior. Asian Americans may encounter individual racism from individuals who make fun of their accents or physical features, or stereotype them as "math nerds." When counselors and teachers channel them into math and science fields regardless of personal interest or aptitude, individual and institutional racism intersect and mutually enforce each other. When African Americans and Hispanics are met with stereotyped assumptions by classmates that their admission to college or getting a job was based on affirmative-action, or that they are "natural" athletes but not intellectual, they face individual racism. A teacher who more harshly disciplines a black student than a white student, or a police officer who treats a black person more aggressively than a white person, may be evidencing both individual racism and the norms of their institutions. In either situation, it is important to recognize and address the bias and discrimination and see how individual racism and institutional racism are interconnected. Individual attitudes, beliefs, and behaviors affect institutional policies and practices, and institutional culture and norms affect individual behavior.

MOVING TOWARD JUSTICE

Learning about the long history of racism in the U.S., and its contemporary manifestations and consequences, can leave people feeling helpless to dismantle entrenched patterns. Love (2000) argues for the development of a "liberatory consciousness" that "enables individuals to live their lives in oppressive systems and institutions with awareness and intentionality, rather than on the basis of the socialization to which they have been subjected" (p. 599). Cultivating awareness and intentionality are antidotes to despair and become the basis for hope and taking accountable action against racism.

The "web of resistance" is an intervention intended to unite people around the possibility for change by developing greater consciousness about racism and working with others to take action against it (Werkmeister Rozas & Miller, 2009). Drawing on Freire's notion of critical consciousness, Love (2000) argues for developing awareness and analysis as a basis for taking accountable action in alliance with others. Similarly, Werkmeister Rozas & Miller (2009) focus on developing a combination of internal strategies to resist racism and external strategies to develop action with others to challenge racism.

The web of resistance illustrates points of connection where internal and external strategies link up to build internal capacities and coalitions with others (Werkmeister Rozas & Miller, 2009). These two aspects are mutually reinforcing and essential aspects of anti-racism work. In alliances and coalitions, "individuals both support and constructively challenge each other to go further in their own process while making strides to stand up against institutional forces that harbor and perpetuate racism" (Werkmeister Rozas & Miller, 2009, p. 36). Developing a liberatory consciousness is part of envisioning and creating the society we want. We need to dream and enact together an anti-racist agenda that can "complete our democracy" through living these principles in our daily lives (Guinier & Torres, 2002). In the Racism Workshop Design that follows, we include a module addressed to ongoing education, involvement, and anti-racist action that builds on the ideas outlined above.

We also believe that hope is generated through learning about the actions of individuals and groups, historically and in the present, on whose work and ideas we can build. Here, we share a few contemporary examples of such work to challenge racism in the institutions described in the previous section. One example, The People's Institute for Survival and Beyond (www.pisab.org), supports education, community organizing, and activism (including youth activism) to challenge racism in communities and organizations. Race Forward (www.raceforward.org) works to advance racial justice through research, advocacy, and activism. Groups like Teachers for Justice (www.teacherforjustice.org), Teaching for Change (www.teachingforchange.org), and the New York Collective of Radical Educators (www.nycore.org) work with students and parents to challenge practices that harm young people of color and to advocate for their right to well-resourced, culturally responsive, and anti-racist schooling. The UCLA Civil Rights Project (www.civilrightspro ject.ucla.edu) illustrates ways to promote school and neighborhood integration that would improve schooling outcomes for all (Tefera, Frankenberg, Siegel-Hawley, & Chirchigno, 2011).

Immigrant youth activism, under the United We Dream network (www.unitedwedream. org), has garnered widespread attention through narratives that show young people wanting to learn and serve their country by, for example, wearing graduation caps and gowns at DREAM protests, donating blood, praying with religious leaders, and at one point, holding a "study-in" in a Senate cafeteria. Dreamers have built coalitions with other groups, working with African Americans to resist black vs. brown rhetoric and supporting LGBT rights to build mutually supportive agendas (www.dissentmagazine.org/online_articles/ the-dreamers-movement-comes-of-age).

People across the country, from all racial groups, have mobilized to bring national attention to these issues and to demonstrate solidarity. The campaign BlackLivesMatter#, which began with the killing of Trayvon Martin in Florida, has expanded to affirm the

> . . . lives of Black queer and trans folks, disabled folks, black-undocumented folks, folks with records, women and all Black lives along the gender spectrum. It centers those that have been marginalized within Black liberation movements. It is a tactic to (re)build the Black liberation movement.
> (Black Lives Matter, http://blacklivesmatter.com/about/)

Grassroots organizations for health justice can be found in many states. Such organizations advocate for universal health care, particularly for those in poverty. Some organizations focus on the link between food deserts in inner city and isolated rural locations and how these contribute to obesity. Michelle Obama's "Let's Move" campaign makes these links and advocates for urban gardens, healthy school lunch programs, and engaging children in physical activities. Still other groups focus on monitoring air quality in urban areas and addressing health problems, such as asthma, that are disproportionate in poor communities. Other examples of organizations to address racism and its different manifestations have been noted throughout this chapter.

The above sections works ambitiously to provide a framework and contemporary context for understanding how various racial and ethnic groups are affected by the ubiquitous web of institutional structures that preserve a white dominant society, and the individual and interpersonal forms of racism that contribute to it. The examples above also illustrate how racism intersects with classism, sexism, ageism, and other forms of oppression. We hope this overview will help people understand the roots and effects of racism and the very real threat racism poses to democratic principles and values. Ultimately, change will come when common people demand that our government live up to the promise of democracy codified in our Constitution and Bill of Rights. This promise has inspired, and continues to draw, people from all over the world; people whose belief in these principles strengthens our commitment to them.

RACISM WORKSHOP DESIGN

The design presented below aims to provide participants with an introductory overview and understanding of racism. A number of the activities included in this design assume that facilitators are familiar with social justice education (SJE) core concepts and the conceptual frameworks described in Chapters 1 and 4. The design focuses on helping participants develop an historical and conceptual understanding of racism and white advantage at the individual, institutional, and cultural levels. It also focuses on helping participants take action to challenge racism in their personal and institutional lives.

This design, like others in this volume, uses four quadrants as a way to sequence learning goals, key concepts, and activities. The quadrants generally follow the sequence, "What? So what? Now what?" Quadrant 1 focuses on developing a shared language to talk about racism, defining key terms, and building a learning community in which participants from diverse racialized groups can honestly examine their own socialization about racism in personal terms. Quadrant 2 moves to a historical and conceptual understanding of the construction of race and its historical legacies and contemporary manifestations on multiple levels. Quadrant 3 examines the construction and perpetuation of white privilege and advantage in maintaining an unjust status quo. Finally, Quadrant 4 turns to taking accountable action against racism and developing action plans for change. We use the four-quadrant design to keep the learning sequence in focus, and it can be easily adapted to short workshops or semester-long courses.

The quadrant design is immediately followed by learning objectives and core concepts specific to each of the four quadrants, as well as brief descriptors of the activities (with at least one option) needed to carry out the design. Actual instructions, facilitation notes, and handouts for each of the activities can be found on the Racism website that accompanies this volume.

Following the four-quadrant design with its learning outcomes, core concepts, and activities, the chapter closes with a general discussion of pedagogical, design, and facilitation issues central to teaching about racism. Specific considerations of pedagogy, design, and facilitation for each of the activities are explained more fully on the website.

Racism Design: Overview of the Quadrants

Quadrant 1: Connecting to Self and Developing Shared Language	Quadrant 2: Historical and Conceptual Understanding of Racism
1. Welcome, Introductions, Community Norms (40 min)	1. Opening Warmup (30 min)
2. Social Identities (30–90 min)	2. Social Construction of Race (60–80 min)
3. Assumptions and Stereotypes (30–45 min)	3. Contemporary Systemic Racism and Racial Microaggressions (70–90 min)
4. Definitions (15–90 min)	4. Closing (10–15 min)
5. Socialization Processes (35–60 min)	5. Homework Assignment (5 min)
6. Closing (10–15 min)	
Quadrant 3: Unearned Advantage and White Privilege	**Quadrant 4: Possibilities for Change and Taking Action**
1. Check-in and Opening Activity (45 min)	1. Opening Activity (30 min)
2. Construction of White Advantage (90 min)	2. Creating Accountability and Solidarity (60 min)
3. White Privilege in Everyday Life (30–45 min)	3. Taking Action (40–60 min)
4. Journal Reflection and Closing (20 min)	4. Closing and Wrap-Up (15–20 min)

For each quadrant, we provide the associated learning outcomes and a choice of activities for each of the topics listed in the quadrant. We have provided a choice of activities as a way of accommodating small vs. large groups, workshops vs. college courses, etc.

QUADRANT 1: CONNECTING TO SELF AND DEVELOPING SHARED LANGUAGE

Learning Objectives for Quadrant 1:
- Create a positive learning environment through developing community agreements/ guidelines for support and risk taking

- Explore personal learning/experiences about race and racism to begin to develop understanding of the ways that racism is communicated and reinforced at systemic, institutional, and cultural levels
- Develop a shared understanding of key terms and ideas, including racial formation, race, racism, socialization, and social construction
- Explore institutional and cultural forms of racism

Key Concepts: stereotypes, personal bias, cycle of socialization, assumptions, social location (fill in as needed)

Activities

1. Welcome, Introductions, and Overview of Developing Community Norms (40 min):
   A. Community Agreements-Guidelines: Invites participants to collectively develop a set of agreements/guidelines for a positive and effective learning experience that encourages people to take appropriate risks and step out of their comfort zone in order to learn. The activity also acknowledges that participants enter from different social locations and asks them to consider how to create a safe enough space for all.
   B. Hopes and Concerns: This activity elicits the hopes and concerns of participants in order to make them explicit to all and lays the groundwork for creating community agreements.
   C. Liberation Buddies: Gives participants the opportunity to create self-selected smaller groups, to have a space to connect and check in with each other regarding their learning.
2. Social Identity Activities:
   A. Cultural Chest (60 min): This social identity activity invites participants to share a symbol or artifact that is meaningful for them as a member of various social groups, provides an opportunity to celebrate our multiple identities, and examines the intersections of our different identities.
   B. Mapping Identity (60 min): This social identity activity asks participants to map aspects of their identity of which they are proud and others that they have felt embarrassed or sad about. They compare these aspects with how others may view them and identify stereotypes they have experienced as a result.
3. Assumptions and Stereotypes Activities (30–45 min):
   A. Assumptions Activity (30–45 min): This activity gives participants the opportunity to explore personal assumptions and inquire about the utility of leaning on stereotypes.
   B. Naming Stereotypes Activity (30–40 min): This activity gives participants the opportunity to explore stereotypes about different racial groups that they have stated or have heard at some point.
4. Definitions:
   A. Definition Matching Activity (30 min): Provides the group with a set of terms that helps develop a language to be able to engage in a discussion about racism, as well as creating a foundation for a more in-depth understanding of racism.
   B. Racism in the U.S. Quiz (60–90 min): Addresses the needs of content learners and is not administered to be graded or examined by the facilitator. Provides a snapshot of race and racism in the U.S., both historically and contemporarily.
   C. Levels and Types of Racism Mini Lecturette (15 min): Intended to provide the group with an understanding of the different levels that racism is manifested.

5. Socializations Processes Activities:
    A. Cycle of Socialization (35–40 min): Intended to give participants the opportu-
        nity to explore their socialization process through individual, cultural, and insti-
        tutional interactions and norms, and how these teach us to accept the system of
        racism and white privilege/advantage.
    B. Earliest Memories Personal Time Line (60 min) (critical incident activity with
        guided imagery): Provides participants with the opportunity to examine early
        memories related to race in order to explore learned (consciously and uncon-
        sciously) messages about race, their own racial group, and other racial groups.
        Participants are able to begin to analyze how they are socialized about race and the
        multiple levels on which racism has affected their lives.
6. Closing Activities: These closing activities help to wrap up the session and give the
    facilitator and group a sense of what has been learned and how people are responding
    to the session. This can also help facilitators plan for the next session.
    A. Closing Whip (10–15 min):
        •   One thing you learned today that you want to remember?
        •   One question that you are still grappling with in regards to the material cov-
            ered today? Allow individuals to pass if they wish to do so.
    B. Three Adjectives (10 min): Each person select one adjective to describe how you
        felt when you first arrived today, how you felt at the middle of the session, and
        how you are feeling now. Go around and each person say your three words (you
        may pass if you wish). Facilitator also responds.

QUADRANT 2: HISTORICAL AND CONCEPTUAL UNDERSTANDING OF RACISM

Learning Objectives for Quadrant 2:
•   Understand how racism operates in U.S. history and contemporary life
•   Understand covert and overt racism and microaggressions
•   Identify and analyze the material consequences of racial construction for people
    of color

Key Concepts: social construction, institutional racism, white normativity,
white privilege, microaggressions, intent v. impact, logics of racism

1. Opening Activities:
    A. Journeys to the U.S. (20 min): Participants learn about and reflect on their own
        heritage, as well as learn about each other's heritage. They will see that not every-
        one came to America for the same reasons.
    B. Prevalence of Race Continuum (20 min): In this activity, participants begin to
        explore their own racialized experiences as well as how their experiences relate to
        those of their peers.
2. Social Construction of Race Activities:
    A. The Stories We Tell About Race (*Race: The Power of an Illusion*, Episode 2) (80
        min): This episode traces the social construction of race and its consequences for
        people of color in the U.S.
    B. The "Logics" of Racism (30 min): This activity engages participants in identify-
        ing the distinctive ways racism operates for different groups of people depending
        upon the particular historical experiences of each group. Participants learn the
        three logics and apply them to examples of contemporary racism.

3. Contemporary and Systemic Racism Activities:
   A. The Web of Institutional Racism (60–70 min): This activity helps participants make connections about the ways racism operates across different social institutions.
   B. The Impact of Microaggressions (20 min): This activity provides participants with an understanding of the concept of microaggressions, a critical aspect of contemporary racism.
   C. Racial Bullying and Micro-Aggressions (60–90 min): This activity uses a film to help participants identify examples of racial bullying and microaggressions and to consider the role of bystanders in perpetuating these forms of racism.
4. Closing Activity:
   A. Sculpting Power Dynamics (10–15 min): This activity engages participants in representing the power dynamics discussed above in a creative and physical way and reinforces what has been learned in the session.
5. Homework:
   A. Homework: Looking at Institutions (5 min): Name an institution you want to know more about; bring 1–2 examples of how racism operates in this institution to the next class.
   B. Homework: Tracking Everyday White Privilege: Participants will be given a handout that helps them track the number of times in a day they observe or benefit from white privilege.

QUADRANT 3: UNEARNED ADVANTAGE AND WHITE PRIVILEGE

Learning Objectives for Quadrant 3:
- Understand the cultural and institutional privileges/advantages attached to "whiteness" in the U.S.
- Recognize examples of white privilege in everyday interpersonal interactions and institutional, social, and cultural life

Key Concepts: white privilege, white normativity, unearned advantage, institutionalized whiteness

1. Exploring the Impact of Racism Interpersonally (45 min): Deal with homework from previous session, where appropriate.
   A. Race and Privilege Common Ground Activity/Step in, Step out (30 min): This activity allows participants to experience the impact of white privileges/advantages and to see how these separate people from one another.
   B. White Privilege Inventory Checklist (30 min): Participants complete an inventory and add up the number of privileges they have in society in comparison to others in the group as a basis for discussion of different social locations.
2. Construction of White Privilege (90 min) (select one from the following two options):
   A. Construction of White Privilege: *Race: The Power of an Illusion*: Episode 3 (45 min): This segment demonstrates how law and public policy create advantages for whites at the expense of other groups in ways that normalize (or make invisible) white advantage.
   B. History of Racism Timeline: Participants are provided with a timeline to identify examples of events that perpetuate white norms and white normativity.
3. White Privilege Dialogue and Discussion Activities (60–90 min):
   A. Beads Activity (30–45 min): This symbolic activity highlights the impact of racial segregation and encourages participants to examine their own spheres of influence.

B. Tracking Everyday White Privilege (30 min): Handout and instructions given as homework—see Quadrant 2. Discuss participants' findings when tracking to see how many times in a day they benefit from white privilege or see white privilege.

4. Journal Reflection, Pair Share, and Closing Activity (30 min):
   A. Journal Reflection and Sharing (10 min): Suggested prompts: How does understanding white privilege help you better understand racism and the way that it is maintained and reinforced? How might having an understanding of white privilege help you challenge racism?
   Pairs Share (10 min): Encourage active listening and purposeful sending.
   B. Closing Circle (10 min): Go around the circle and invite each participant to share one lingering question from the session. Or share a feeling, emotion, thought (one word) based on material engaged with today.

QUADRANT 4: POSSIBILITIES FOR CHANGE AND TAKING ACTION

Learning Objectives for Quadrant 4:
- Plan concrete ways of taking action
- Construct visions of liberatory alternatives and develop actions plans to reach them
- Build coalition and work with others

Key Concepts: accountability, solidarity, acting as allies, spheres of influence

1. Opening Activities (20–30 min):
   A. Liberation Envisioning Concentric Circle (15 min): This exercise encourages participants to imagine the "ideal world" they would like to live in and to openly reflect upon what they as individuals, as well as others, will need to do for this world to be realized.
   B. Check-In and Emotional Timeline (30 min): Each participant graphs with days or dates of course sessions along the horizontal axis and numbers from 1–5 their least and most emotional moments in the course. In small groups, participants share as a way to review course and highlight key moments of learning.
2. Advocate Ally Accountability and Solidarity (60 min):
   A. Spheres of Influence (15 min): This activity is intended to 1) give participants the opportunity to gain an understanding that the action an individual can take against oppression can occur in different parts of their life, given that we all are part of different spheres in which we have influence, and 2) identify where in their own spheres of influence they can take action.
   B. Cycle of Liberation (30 to 45 min): This activity is intended to give participants the opportunity to become familiar with the cycle of liberation and to identify their location in the cycle of liberation at the moment.
3. Taking Action Activities:
   A. Scenarios for Taking Action (40–60 min): Scenarios provide participants with the opportunity to offer an analysis of how racism occurs individually and institutionally in everyday occurrences. The activity seeks to develop the appropriate skills to disrupt racist attitudes and behaviors, and to foster the confidence to act.
   B. Design a Non-Racist Institution (40 min): This activity asks participants to pull together what they have learned and to imagine alternatives to racism in institutional patterns and practices. Participants look at different institutions (education/schools, criminal justice, housing, etc.) and ask, "What would a non-racist

or anti-racist housing policy look like?" (for instance). This forms the basis for making personal commitments regarding next steps.

    C. Intersections and Collaborations Activity (45 min): This activity is intended to provide participants with the opportunity to understand how building a coalition across difference is critical for addressing oppression by challenging participants to see "our" issues as broader, to reframe "our" issues and see the inclusion and exclusion in the framework we use, and to understand how we can build community around diverse identities and agendas.

4. Closing and Wrap-Up:

    A. One Sentence Declaration or Commitment (15–20 min): This activity enables participants to publically announce a specific commitment toward eradicating racism.

    B. Liberation Pairs or Accountability Buddies (15–20 min): This activity is designed to add a support system for participants outside of the specified learning community. It encourages participants to be accountable to one another as each works to transform the various levels and types of racism.

PEDAGOGICAL, DESIGN, AND FACILITATION ISSUES IN TEACHING ABOUT RACISM

Teaching about racism in the United States is an intellectually, emotionally, and politically challenging project, complicated by the lack of supportive spaces to think and talk about racism in diverse groups and learn about differences in racial experiences. Limited knowledge regarding the nation's racial history, the illusion that our nation is in a "post-racial state," and the pervasiveness of "color-blind" ideology contribute to this challenge. Like other isms, racism not only operates at different levels (individual, institutional, cultural and societal), it also interconnects with other forms of oppression, adding further complexity to teaching about racism. Also, individuals have a wide range of feelings and experiences, misinformation, confusion, and bias about the topic of racism, all of which impact openness to the learning experience and engagement with the topic. Below we discuss some of the typical challenges that arise in teaching about racism and ways that facilitators can respond effectively to these challenges.

DEALING WITH EMOTIONAL CONTENT

Issues of trust and safety are often present for participants in a course on racism. Thus, it is important to collectively develop community agreements/guidelines to foster a positive learning experience. Working together to develop and *practice* the guidelines is crucial (see Chapter 3). Facilitators should be active role models from the start, willing to acknowledge their own thoughts and feelings, and expose the socialized attitudes and assumptions about other racial groups they have uncovered, examined, and changed in their own process of coming to consciousness and learning about racism. The concepts of comfort zone and learning edge provide useful tools to help participants monitor their internal reactions and consciously work at staying open to learning, even when feeling challenged emotionally and intellectually.

Participants, particularly white participants, may feel embarrassed to share ignorance and misunderstandings of racism, or to expose their own racist assumptions and socialization. White participants may be cautious because they are afraid of offending people of color; people of color may be cautious because they don't feel safe enough to trust white facilitators and/or participants. White participants may wait for people of color to teach them about racism, assuming that they themselves know little about racism and need to hear about it from the "people who have had it done to them." Some people of color may assume that they know everything there is to know about racism from their own experiences, and they may be skeptical that they will learn anything new. Others may assume the role of "expert" to teach white participants about racism. Facilitators must be attentive to such issues, so that participants of color are not asked to be educators or spokespeople for their racial group, and to ensure that they, too, can expand their learning about racism.

Activities that examine early experiences have an emotional weight that facilitators should acknowledge and be prepared to address. For some people of color, recounting early experiences with racism can revive situations where they or members of their family were targets of prejudice, discrimination, or violence, bringing up the emotions felt at an earlier time. For some white people, realizing that parents and others they love and trust have taught them stereotypes about other racial groups, and/or engaged in racist behavior, may cause discomfort, anger, or sadness. It is helpful to note that one of the costs of racism is the emotional pain and dehumanization it causes all people living in a racist system.

Facilitators should create a safe-enough space that people can express some of those painful emotions while maintaining a productive learning environment (Bell, 2010). It can be useful to remind participants that feelings are neither right nor wrong, but simply feelings. Acknowledging feelings is an important step in distinguishing feelings from thoughts and in determining actions based on conscious choice rather than unconscious socialization. While it is important to acknowledge the feelings and emotions of participants, facilitators must make sure that the focus does not end up centering the emotions of white participants at the expense of participants of color. For example, white women are often overwhelmed by emotion when they begin to learn about racism and their own unconscious participation. The challenge for facilitators is to acknowledge the pain of racism while keeping the focus on developing consciousness and action to address racism. People of color have experienced racism and the emotions of its injustice, and they are more likely to need acknowledgement of their experiences of racism, to gain knowledge about how it functions, and to learn about actions that can be taken to challenge racism.

Caucus groups are one way to address the differing needs of participants from diverse racial groups at different points in the course. White caucus groups provide a space for white participants to express emotions, confusion, and lack of awareness or knowledge, and get support from white peers. Participants of color caucus groups likewise provide a space for expressing anger, pain, sadness, and confusion, and get support from racial peers. After caucus groups, it is important to bring groups back together to share learning and move forward as a cohesive learning community. In forming caucus groups, facilitators should take into account the makeup of the class. For example, providing options for biracial and multiracial participants to meet as a separate caucus group, or for African Americans and Latina/os to decide whether to meet as one group or separately, are issues to be considered. Sometimes white participants may want to focus on other identities (religious, gender) to avoid dealing with whiteness, and facilitators must help them keep the focus on race and racism.

DEALING WITH COMPLEX HISTORICAL INFORMATION

Creating opportunities for participants to talk about and reflect upon their life experiences in the context of accurate historical information can help them understand how their experiences are shaped by systemic patterns of institutional and cultural racism and white privilege/advantage. Learning about our own implication in conditions that constrain, oppress, and even imprison other people is often quite painful, but it can also generate better understanding of how power functions in society to perpetuate racism (Preskill &

Brookfield, 2009). Such knowledge can help participants understand the racial problems we still face today, making it possible to imagine solutions and take steps to address them. It also helps participants move from a perspective of individual blame to one of recognizing the significance of systemic forces. Given the fact that racism is a complex, multifaceted phenomenon, it can be overwhelming, so it is important to encourage inquiry and going beyond surface analysis without expecting immediate closure or simple answers.

Since many people do not know this history, they are likely to assume that the United States has made steady progress in eliminating racism and that racism is now a problem of (now rarely expressed) individual bigotry or discrimination. Facilitators must be able to discuss knowledgeably the historical development of racism in the United States, and the myriad ways racism manifests in contemporary times. For example, participants with white immigrant ancestors may be honestly confused about the different trajectories of African Americans, white immigrants, and immigrants of color ("If my parents could make it in America, why can't they?"). Without knowledge of the historical barriers to progress and of how white advantage has been constructed and perpetuated through government and other institutional policies and practices, participants who hold this view may not be able to understand the very different experiences of other groups. It is important to acknowledge that while their family members did work hard, they did not face the same barriers African Americans and immigrants of color faced. The use of historical information can help them understand the construction of whiteness as a vehicle to maintain privilege, as well as the costs for white immigrants who gave up language and culture in exchange for the advantages of whiteness (Haney-López, 2006). Such information provides a context for seeing that African Americans and immigrants of color are not offered the "choice" to become white or enjoy the privileges that whiteness affords. In general, content knowledge puts personal experience in social and historical context.

The racism history timeline is an effective way to introduce this material, as it lays out how racism has manifested over time in different periods of U.S. history. Using the timeline, participants can trace laws and practices that created disadvantage for groups of color and the corollary development of white advantage at different points in our history. This history shows the connection between whiteness and property (Harris, 1993), citizenship rights (Keyssar, 2009), and the accumulation of wealth to pass on to future generations (Oliver & Shapiro, 2006). *Readings for Diversity and Social Justice* (Adams, Blumenfeld, Castaneda, Hackman, Peters, & Zuniga, 2013) provides articles that critically examine the advantages and disadvantages people receive based on racial social group membership.

UNPACKING "COLOR-BLIND" TALK

Many people espouse color-blindness by invoking Martin Luther King's dream to assert that they are not racist, as in the phrase "I don't see color, I just see people." In fact, people are socialized to pretend to not notice difference (see Fig. 4.2, the Cycle of Socialization) and many incorporate the injunction that to notice or comment on difference is wrong (Bell, 2003b). Color-blind ideology positions race as a taboo topic that cannot be openly discussed and thus makes it more difficult to address the racial problems that persist in our society (Haney-Lopez, 2014).

Participants need information that can help them understand how color-blind ideology actually reproduces racism (Bonilla-Silva, 2015). This requires naming and acknowledging the ways institutional racism shapes life chances and opportunities. It also means acknowledging and appreciating difference as a positive value and understanding positive race-consciousness as a critical step toward imagining and creating racial justice (Bell, 2016).

It is important for facilitators to provide language and tools for thoughtful and open dialogue about race. Our goal is to help participants examine how they have been socialized to ignore race and to look at their own racial identities within the broader context of racism. This can be particularly difficult for white participants who are unable or unwilling to tolerate the disequilibrium and stress of facing the realities of racism and white involvement in maintaining the status quo (DiAngelo, 2011). We want to enable students to wrestle with what they have internalized about race and racism, reflect on their social location in relation to other racial groups, and consider their own complicity when following business as usual (Choi, 2008). The Cycle of Socialization helps participants examine their own socialization process and consider points of intervention to go against this socialization.

As a racial ideology, "color-blindness" argues that ending discrimination requires treating everyone the same, without acknowledging racial, cultural, or ethnic identities, or the very unequal positions from which some start because of past discrimination. Historical information, clear definitions, and examples of how racism operates on different levels provide language and tools for discussing cumulative advantage and disadvantage that reveal how "equal" treatment can be inequitable. For example, people of color who attend underfunded schools in poor neighborhoods face educational, health, and economic barriers to attending college that other groups do not. Treating everyone the same will not ameliorate those barriers. Making up for inequities in material resources, knowledge, and cultural capital may require different actions to address the unique needs and experiences of different groups. Such targeted actions represent equitable, not equal, treatment.

ACKNOWLEDGING CONFERRED WHITE PRIVILEGE

White privilege defines the unearned advantages granted to white people on the basis of racial group membership. White privilege is normalized in such a way that the majority of whites are unaware of and take for granted the privileges or advantages they receive (McIntosh, 2001). At first, acknowledging the existence of white privilege can be difficult for white individuals who may be resistant to seeing how they have personally benefited from white privilege. Without an understanding of cumulative white privilege throughout history, some may discount examples of cultural or institutional racism as atypical. Others may believe that there is reverse racism in education and employment as a result of affirmative action and other non-discrimination policies. Some may feel that the slight increase in the number of people of color in positions in government, the media, and other professions is an indication of the end of racism. Some resistance to the concept of white privilege might be the result of the salience of other marginalized social identities. For example, a white working-class person might have difficulty accepting the ways in which they benefit from white privilege given their experience with class inequality.

When encountering these challenges, it is important to encourage participants to say more about what they understand the issue to be, so that they go beyond a surface analysis to look at the assumptions underlying their position. People often base their positions on taken-for-granted societal norms and beliefs that require deeper reflection. Becoming comfortable with challenges to "common sense" understandings of racial injustice can be difficult for individuals who have never considered such issues before. Helping individuals analyze their own statements rather than arguing with them is more likely to encourage openness to considering alternative information and analysis.

Introducing levels and types of racism provides a useful framework for helping participants examine taken-for-granted understandings. Also important are social science data and analyses about actual representations and outcomes in such areas as education, employment, wealth accumulation, and health for different groups in our society. Understanding the difference between individual prejudice and social power to oppress is also important. It may be a good idea to refer to Lorde's writing about oppression not having a hierarchy (Flynn, 2010).

An intersectional perspective can also be useful here—keeping the focus on racism while acknowledging the impact of other form of oppressions. Individuals experience manifestations of racism in distinct ways due to the intersection of their social identities. Furthermore, a focus on the complexity of identity helps participants see the diversity that exists within social groups so they don't essentialize all members of a group as the same (Jones & Wijeyesinghe, 2011).

Not all white people benefit in the same way, given other social identities. Yet, instead of this shifting the focus off of cumulative white advantage, participants can consider how their other social identities affect their experience of white privilege and how their white privilege affects their experience of their other social identities and advantage and disadvantage. How does my whiteness affect my experience of class? How does my class affect my experience of whiteness and white privilege? Individuals' different social identities must be honored through the content of the curriculum as well as through the process, while keeping race at the forefront of our focus (Grant & Zwier, 2011).

DEALING WITH RESISTANCE

Given the complexity of the topic, facilitators may encounter resistance when teaching about racism. Tatum (1992) suggests four strategies that can help address student resistance to learning about racism. These include: 1) creating a safe classroom space through the use of community guidelines, 2) creating opportunities for students to generate their own knowledge by assigning hands-on assignments to be completed outside of the class, 3) providing students with a developmental model they can utilize to help understand their own process of emerging awareness about racism, and 4) exploring strategies that empower students as change agents, such as giving students an opportunity to create their own action plans for addressing racism.

Facilitators should assure participants that difficult conversations are part of the learning process about racism, and that difficulties that arise can be aired and openly examined together (Miller, Donner, & Fraser, 2004). One useful strategy can be dividing participants into caucus groups based on social identities for small-group conversations before reconvening to share points from their separate discussions. See Goodman (2011) and Chapter 12 for further suggestions for facilitators.

HELPING PARTICIPANTS UNDERSTAND RACISM AND IMMIGRATION

Some participants, including U.S. born people of color, may have a hard time seeing how immigrants of color are impacted by racism and may view racism as only a black/white issue. Misconceptions and misinformation about immigrants can support negative stereotypes about them. For example, some might say that immigrants today are "illegal" and be unaware that there was no such category during earlier waves of "white" immigration. Others may complain that undocumented people don't pay taxes and are "leeches on the system," since they do not know that undocumented people actually pay a lot into a system whose benefits they are unable to access.

It is useful to keep track of the assumptions and misconceptions raised in discussion as well as language used by participants when referring to immigrants so that these terms and assumptions can be analyzed in historical context. It is important to note how patterns of migration have been impacted by larger economic, social, and political factors, and the ways that immigration policy controls who is included or excluded on the basis of race (and also class, gender, national origin, political affiliation, sexual orientation, and disability). Help participants see that migration has been both forced and voluntary, often corresponding to the demand for cheap labor and U.S. political and military intervention that displaced people. They can learn about and trace the patterns of xenophobia and nativism that have occurred throughout history to blame immigrants for problems such as unemployment, crime, overburdened social services, and other issues. It is also helpful for participants to see that social justice movements have successfully organized to fight against racism and anti-immigration xenophobia throughout U.S. history.

Note

* We ask that those who cite this work always acknowledge by name all of the authors listed rather than either only citing the first author or using "et al." to indicate coauthors. All collaborated on the conceptualization, development, and writing of this chapter.

References

Adams, M., Blumenfeld, W., Castaneda, R., Hackman, H., Peters, M., & Zuniga, X. (2013). *Readings for diversity and social justice* (3rd ed.). New York: Routledge.

Adelman, L., & Smith, L. M. (Executive Producers) (2008). *Unnatural causes: Is inequality making us sick?* [Documentary Film Series]. United States: California Newsreel.

Alamillo, L., Palmer, D., Viramontes, C., & Garcia, E. (2005). California's English-only policies: an analysis of initial effects. In A. Valenzuela (Ed.), *Leaving children behind: How Texas-style accountability fails Latino youth* (pp. 201–224). Albany: State University of New York Press.

Alexander, M. (2012). *The new Jim Crow: Mass incarceration in the age of colorblindness*. New York: The New Press.

Alsultany, E. (2008). The prime time plight of the Arab Muslim American after 9/11. In A. Jamal & N. Naber (Eds.), *Race and Arab Americans before and after 9/11: From invisible citizens to visible subjects* (pp. 204–228). Syracuse, NY: Syracuse University Press.

American Civil Liberties Union (2015). Arizona's SB 1070 Law. Retrieved from https://www.aclu.org/feature/arizonas-sb-1070?redirect=arizonas-sb-1070

Ansley, F. L. (1997). White supremacy (and what we should do about it). In R. Delgado & J. Stefancic (Eds.), *Critical white studies: Looking behind the mirror*. Philadelphia: Temple University Press.

Archibold, R. C. (2010). Arizona enacts stringent law on immigration. *New York Times*, April 24. Retrieved at: http://www.nytimes.com/2010/04/24/us/politics/24immig.html?_r=0

Baugh, J. (2003). Linguistic profiling. In S. Makoni, G. Smitherman, A. F. Ball, & A. K. Spears (Eds.), *Black linguistics: Language, society and politics in Africa and the Americas* (pp. 155–168). New York: Routledge.

Bell, L. A. (2003a). Telling tales: What stories can teach us about racism. *Race, Ethnicity and Education*, 6(1), 3–28.

Bell, L. A. (2003b). Sincere fictions: The pedagogical challenges of preparing white teachers for multicultural classrooms. *Equity and Excellence in Education*, 35(3), 236–245.

Bell, L. A. (2010). *Storytelling for social justice: Connecting narrative and the arts in antiracist teaching*. New York: Routledge.

Bell, L. A. (2016). Telling on racism: Developing a race-conscious agenda. In H. A. Neville, M. E. Gallardo, & D. W. Sue (Eds.), *The myth of racial color blindness: Manifestations, dynamics, and impact* (pp. 105–122). Washington, DC: American Psychological Association.

Bertrand, M., & Mullainathan, S. (2004, Sept.). Are Emily and Greg more employable than Lakisha and Jamal? A field experiment on labor market discrimination. *The American Economic Review*, 94(4), 991–1013.

Bivens, D. (2005). What is internalized racism? In M. Potapchuk, S. Leiderman, D. Bivens, & B. Major (Eds.), *Flipping the script: White privilege and community building* (pp. 43–51). Silver Spring, MD: MP Associates, Inc. Retrieved from http://www.mpassociates.us/pdf/FlippingtheScriptmostupdated.pdf

Blackmon, D. A. (2008). *Slavery by another name: The re-enslavement of Black Americans from the Civil War to World War II*. New York: Doubleday.

Bonilla-Silva, E. (2004). From bi-racial to tri-racial: Towards a new system of racial stratification in the USA. *Ethnic and Racial Studies*, 27(6), 931–950.

Bonilla-Silva, E. (2013). *Racism without racists* (4th ed.). Lanham, MD: Rowman and Littlefield.

Bonilla-Silva, E. (2015). More than prejudice: Restatement, reflections, and new directions in critical race theory. *Sociology of Race and Ethnicity*, 1(1), 73–87.

Bonilla-Silva, E., & Dietrich, D. (2011). The sweet enchantment of color-blind racism in Obamerica. *The Annals of the American Academy of Political and Social Science*, 634(1), 190–206.

Bonilla-Silva, E., & Forman, T. A. (2000). "I am not a racist but . . .": Mapping white college students' racial ideology in the USA. *Discourse and Society*, 11(1), 50–85.

Brodkin, K. (1998). *How Jews became white folks and what that says about race in America*. New Brunswick, NJ: Rutgers University Press.

Bump, P. (2015, Jan. 5). The new Congress is 80 percent white, 80 percent male and 92 percent Christian. *The Washington Post*. Retrieved from http://www.washingtonpost.com/news/the-fix/wp/2015/01/05/the-new-congress-is-80-percent-white-80-percent-male-and-92-percent-christian/

Bunche Center (2014). *2014 Hollywood diversity report: Making sense of the disconnect*. Los Angeles: Ralph J. Bunche Center for African American Studies at UCLA. Retrieved from http://www.bunchecenter.ucla.edu/wp-content/uploads/2014/02/2014-Hollywood-Diversity-Report-2-12-14.pdf

Calefati, J. (2010, May 12). Arizona bans ethnic studies. *Mother Jones*. Retrieved from http://www.motherjones.com/mojo/2010/05/ethnic-studies-banned-arizona

Campbell, K. M. (2011, Spring). The road to SB 1070: How Arizona became ground zero for the immigrants' rights movement and the continuing struggle for Latino civil rights in America. *Harvard Latino Law Review*, 14, 1–21.

Carnevale, A. P., & Strohl, J. (2013). *Separate & unequal: How higher education reinforces intergenerational reproduction of white privilege*. Washington, DC: Georgetown Public Policy Institute, Center on Education and the Workforce.

Carter, P. L., & Welner, K. G. (2013). *Closing the opportunity gap: What America must do to give every child an even chance*. New York: Oxford University Press.

Cashin, S. (2004). *The failures of integration: How race and class are undermining the American dream*. New York: Public Affairs.

Centers for Disease Control and Prevention (2013). *CDC Health disparities and inequalities report United States – 2013. Vol 62, No 3*. Washington, DC: Author.

The Century Foundation. (2013). *Bridging the higher education divide: Strengthening community colleges and restoring the American dream*. Retrieved from http://www.tcf.org/assets/downloads/20130523-Bridging_the_Higher_Education_DivideREPORT-ONLY.pdf

Chacon, J. A., & Davis, M. (2006). *No one is illegal: Fighting racism and state violence on the US-Mexico border*. Chicago: Haymarket Books.

Cheryan, S., & Bodenhausen, G. V. (2000). When positive stereotypes threaten intellectual performance: The psychological hazards of model minority status. *American Psychological Society*, 11(5), 399–402.

Choi, J. A. (2008). Unlearning colorblind ideologies in education class. *Educational Foundations*, 22, 53–71.

Coates, R. (2008). Covert racism in the USA and globally. *Sociology Compass*, 2(1), 208–231.

Coll, C. G., & Magnuson, K. (2014). The psychological experience of immigration: A developmental perspective. In M. M. Suárez-Orozco, C. Suárez-Orozco, & D. Qin-Hilliard, *The New Immigrant and the American Family: Interdisciplinary Perspectives on the New Immigration* (pp. 69–110). London: Routledge.

Collins, P. H. (2012). Looking back, moving ahead: Scholarship in service to social Justice. *Gender & Society*, 26(1), 14–22.

Cortes, C. E. (2000). *The children are watching: How the media teach about diversity*. New York: Teachers College Press.

Crenshaw, K. W. (1995). Mapping the margins: Intersectionality, identity politics, and violence against women of color. In K. Thomas (Ed.), *Critical race theory: The key writings that formed a movement* (pp. 357–383). New York: The New Press.

Curtis, A. J. (2014). Tracing the school-to-prison pipeline from zero-tolerance policies to juvenile justice dispositions. *Georgetown Law Journal*, 102(4), 1251–1277.

Daniels, J. (2009). *Cyber racism: White supremacy online and the new attack on civil rights*. Lanham, MD: Rowman & Littlefield.

Dardar, A., & Uriarte, M. (2013). The politics of restrictive language policies: A postcolonial analysis of language and schooling. *Postcolonial Directions in Education*, 2(1), 6–67.

Delpit, L. (2013). *"Multiplication is for white people": Raising expectations for other people's children*. New York: The New Press.

Demos (2015). *The racial wealth gap: Why policy matters*. New York: Demos. Retrieved from http://www.demos.org/publication/racial-wealth-gap-why-policy-matters

DeSilver, D. (2014, Apr. 22). *Supreme Court says states can ban affirmative action; 8 already have*. Washington, DC: Pew Research Center Fact Tank. Retrieved from http://www.pewresearch.org/fact-tank/2014/04/22/supreme-court-says-states-can-ban-affirmative-action-8-already-have/

DiAngelo, R. (2011). White fragility. *International Journal of Critical Pedagogy*, 3(3), 54–70.

DiTomaso, N. (2013, May 5). How social networks drive black unemployment. *The New York Times*. Retrieved from http://opinionator.blogs.nytimes.com

Dovidio, J.F., & Gaertner, S.L. (2000). Aversive racism and selection decisions: 1989 and 1999. *Psychological Science*, 11(4), 315–319.

Dutko, P., Ver Ploeg, M., & Farrigan, T. (2012, Aug.). *Characteristics and influential factors of food deserts* (Economic Research Report No. 140). Washington, DC: U.S. Dept. of Agriculture, Economic Research Service. Retrieved from http://www.ers.usda.gov/publications/err-economic-research-report/err140.aspx

Entman, R. M., & Rojecki, A. (2001). *The black image in the white mind: Media and race in America*. Chicago: University of Chicago Press.

Fang, L. (2013). How private prisons game the immigration system. *The Nation*. Retrieved from http://www.thenation.com/article/173120

Feagin, J. (2002). White supremacy and Mexican Americans: Rethinking the black-white paradigm. *Rutgers Law Review*, 54(4), 959–987.

Feagin, J., & Elias, S. (2012). Rethinking racial formation theory: A systemic racism critique. *Ethnic and Racial Studies*, 36(6), 931–960.

Federal Communications Commission (2014). *Report on ownership of commercial broadcast stations*. Retrieved from https://apps.fcc.gov/edocs_public/attachmatch/DA-14-924A1.pdf

Flynn, J. E. (2010). Creating the dialogic space: Critical pedagogy with the oppressed and the oppressor. *Wisconsin English Journal*, 52(1), 1–12.

Foner, N. (2005). *In a new land: A comparative view of immigration*. New York: New York University Press.

Foner, N. (2011). *The next generation: Immigrant youth in a comparative perspective*. New York: New York University Press.

Frankenberg, E. (2013). The role of residential segregation in contemporary school segregation. *Education and Urban Society*, 45(5), 548–570.

Frankenberg, E., & Siegel-Hawley, G. (2009). *Equity overlooked: Charter schools and civil rights policy*. Los Angeles: The Civil Rights Project, UCLA. Retrieved from https://escholarship.org/uc/item/0kq1t80f

Frederickson, G. (2003). *Racism: A short history*. Princeton, NJ: Princeton University Press.

Freed Wessler, S. (2010, Oct. 8). NPR investigation: Private prison companies helped write SB 1070. *Colorlines*. Retrieved from http://www.colorlines.com/articles/npr-investigation-private-prison-companies-helped-write-sb-1070

Gillborn, D. (2006). Critical race theory and education: Racism and anti-racism in educational theory and praxis. *Discourse: Studies in the cultural politics of education*, 27(1): 11–32.

Glenn, E. (2011). Constructing citizenship: Exclusion, subordination, and resistance. *American Sociological Review* 76, 1–24.

Glenn, E. N. (Ed.). (2009). *Shades of difference: Why skin color matters*. Palo Alto, CA: Stanford University Press.

Glenn, E.N. (2015). Settler colonialism as structure: A framework for comparative studies of U.S. race and gender formation. *Sociology of Race and Ethnicity*, 1(1), 54–74.

Golash-Boza, T. (2009). The immigration industrial complex: Why we enforce immigration policies destined to fail. *Sociology Compass*, 3(2), 295–309.

Gomez, L. E., & Lopez, N. (Eds.). (2013). *Mapping race: Critical approaches to health disparities research*. New Brunswick, NJ: Rutgers University Press.

Gonzalez, J. (2011). *Harvest of empire: A history of Latinos in America* (revised ed.). New York: Viking.

Goodman, D. (2011). *Promoting diversity and social justice: Educating people from privileged groups* (2nd ed.). New York: Routledge.

Gramlich, E. M. (2007). *Subprime mortgages: America's latest boom and bust*. Washington, DC: Urban Institute Press. Accessed June 17, 2015, from the ProQuest ebrary.

Grande, S. (in press). *Red pedagogy: Native American social and political thought* (10th anniversary revised ed.). Lanham, MD: Rowman & Littlefield.

Grant, C.A., & Zwier, E. (2011). Intersectionality and student outcomes: Sharpening the struggle against racism, sexism, classism, ableism, heterosexism, nationalism, and linguistic, religious, and geographical discrimination in teaching and learning. *Multicultural Perspectives, 13*(4), 181–188.

Grant-Thomas, A., & Orfield, G. (Eds.). (2008). Twenty-first century colorlines: Multiracial change in contemporary America. Philadelphia: Temple University Press.

Gualtieri, S. (2009). *Between Arab and white: Race and ethnicity in the early Syrian American diaspora*. Oakland, CA: University of California Press.

Guinier, L., & Torres, G. (2002). *The miner's canary: Enlisting race, resisting power, transforming democracy*. Cambridge, MA: Harvard University Press.

Hagopian, E. (Ed.). (2004). *Civil rights in peril: The targeting of Arabs and Muslims*. Chicago: Haymarket Books.

Hallett, M.A. (2006). *Private prisons in America: A critical race perspective*. Thousand Oaks, CA: Sage Publications.

Hamako, E. (2009). *The multiracial movement: Conflicts & learning goals. Comprehensive exam*. University of Massachusetts, Amherst.

Haney-López, I. (2006). *White by law: The legal construction of race*. New York: New York University Press.

Haney-López, I.F. (2014). *Dog whistle politics: How coded racial appeals have reinvented racism and wrecked the middle class*. New York: Oxford University Press.

Hardiman, R., Jackson, B., & Griffin, P. (2007). Conceptual foundations for social justice education. In M. Adams, L.A. Bell, & P. Griffin (Eds.), *Teaching for diversity and social justice* (2nd ed.) (pp. 3566). New York, NY: Routledge.

Hardiman, R., Jackson, B., & Griffin, P. (2013). Conceptual foundations. In M. Adams, W. Blumenfeld, R. Castaneda, H. Hackman, M. Peters, & X. Zuniga (Eds.), *Readings for diversity and social justice* (3rd ed., pp. 26–35). New York: Routledge.

Harris, C.I. (1993). Whiteness as property. *Harvard Law Review, 106*(8), 1707–1791.

Harris, Y.R. (2014). Juvenile detention in the US. *Oxford Bibliographies* (Childhood Studies, subject). doi: 10.1093/obo/9780199791231–0153

Hill, A. (2012). *Reimagining equality: Stories of gender, race and finding home*. Boston: Beacon.

Hochschild, J.L. (1995). *Facing up to the American dream: Race, class and the soul of the nation*. Princeton, NJ: Princeton University Press.

Holroyd, J. (2015). Implicit bias, awareness and imperfect cognitions. *Consciousness and Cognition, 33*, 511–523.

Horner-Johnson, W., Fujiura, G.T., & Tawara, D.G. (2014, Oct.). Health disparities research at the intersection of disability, race, and ethnicity. *Medical Care, 52*(10), Suppl. 3, pp. S1–2. Retrieved from www.lww-medicalcare.com

Hoxby, C.M., & Murarka, S. (2009). *Charter schools in New York City: Who enrolls and how they affect their students' achievement* (Working Paper No. 14852). Cambridge, MA: National Bureau of Economic Research. Retrieved from http://www.nber.org/papers/w14852.pdf?new_window=1

Huber, L.P., & Solórzano, D.G. (2015). Racial microaggressions as a tool for critical race research. *Race, Ethnicity and Education, 18*(3), 297–320.

Humes, K., & Hogan, H. (2009). Measurement of race and ethnicity in a changing, multicultural America. *Race Social Problem, 1*, 111–131.

Ingraham, C. (2015, Feb. 11). Anti-Muslim hate crimes are still five times more common today than before 9/11. *The Washington Post*. Retrieved from http://www.washingtonpost.com/news/wonkblog/wp/2015/02/11/anti-muslim-hate-crimes-are-still-five-times-more-common-today-than-before-911/

Jacobson, M.F. (1998). *Whiteness of a different color: European immigrants and the alchemy of race*. Cambridge, MA: Harvard University Press.

Jamal, A., & Naber, N.C. (2008). *Race and Arab Americans before and after 9/11: From invisible citizens to visible subjects*. Syracuse, NY: Syracuse University Press.

Jones, S.R., & Wijeyesinghe, C.L. (2011). The promises and challenges of teaching from an intersectional perspective: Core components and applied strategies. *New Directions for Teaching and Learning, 125*, 11–20.

Joseph, V., & Williams, T.O. (2008). "Good niggers": The struggle to find courage, strength, and confidence to fight internalized racism and internalized dominance. *Democracy and Education, 17*(2), 67–73.

Joshi, K. (2006). *New roots in America's sacred ground: Religion, race, and ethnicity in Indian America*. New Brunswick, NJ: Rutgers University Press.

Justice Policy Institute (2011, June). *Gaming the system: How the political strategies of private prison companies promote ineffective incarceration policies*. Retrieved from http://www.justicepolicy. org/uploads/justicepolicy/documents/gaming_the_system.pdf

Kaiser Family Foundation (2008, Oct.). *Eliminating racial/ethnic disparities in health care: What are the options?* Retrieved from http://kff.org/disparities-policy

Katznelson, I. (2005). *When affirmative action was white: An untold history of racial inequality in the twentieth century*. New York: W. W. Norton.

Kayyali, R. (2013). US census classifications and Arab Americans: Contestations and definitions of identity markers. *Journal of Ethnic and Migration Studies*, *39*(8), 1299–1318.

Keyes, S., Millhiser, I., Van Ostern, T., & White, A. (2012). Voter suppression disenfranchises millions, race, poverty & the environment. *Public Property Popular Power: New Majority Rising*, *19*(1), 11–12.

Keyssar, A. (2009). *The right to vote: The contested history of democracy in the United States*. New York: Basic Books.

Kim, C.J. (1999). The racial triangulation of Asian Americans. *Politics and Society*, *27*(1), 105–138.

Kim, Y.M. (2011). *Minorities in higher education* (2011 supplement). Washington, DC: American Council on Education.

Knapp, L. G., Kelly-Reid, J. E., & Ginder, S. A. (2011). *Postsecondary institutions and price of attendance in the United States: 2010–11; Degrees and other awards conferred: 2009–10, and 12-month enrollment: 2009–10* (NCES 2011–250). Washington, DC: National Center for Education Statistics. Retrieved from http://nces.ed.gov/pubsearch

Knight, W. (2013). Colorism. In C. Cortés (Ed.), *Multicultural America: A multimedia encyclopedia*. (pp. 547–550). Thousand Oaks, CA: SAGE Publications, Inc.

Kohli, R. (2014). Unpacking internalized racism: Teachers of color striving for racially just classrooms. *Race, Ethnicity and Education*, *17*(3), 367–387.

Kohli, R., & Solórzano, D.G. (2012). "Teachers: Please learn our names!" Racial microaggressions and the K-12 classroom. *Race, Ethnicity and Education*, *15*(4), 1–22.

Kruse, K.M. (2005). *White flight: Atlanta and the making of modern conservatism*. Princeton, NJ: Princeton University Press.

Kucsera, J., & Orfield, G. (2014). *New York State's extreme school segregation: Inequality, inaction and a damaged future*. Los Angeles: The Civil Rights Project/Proyecto Derechos Civiles, University of California at Los Angeles.

Ladson-Billings, G. (2009). *The dreamkeepers* (2nd ed.). San Francisco: Jossey-Bass.

Landsman, J.G., & Lewis, C.W. (Eds.). (2011). *White teachers/diverse classrooms: Creating inclusive schools, building on students' diversity, and providing true educational equity*. Sterling, VA: Stylus.

Lawrence, K., Sutton, S., Kubisch, A., Susi, G., & Fulbright-Anderson, K. (2004). *Structural racism and community building*. Washington, DC: The Aspen Institute Roundtable on Community Change.

Leavitt, P.A., Covarrubias, R., Perez, Y., & Fryberg, S.A. (2015). "Frozen in time": The impact of Native American media representations on identity and self-understanding. *Journal of Social Issues*, *71*(1), 39–53. doi: 10.1111/josi.12095

Lee, E., & Yung, J. (2010). *Angel Island: Immigrant gateway to America*. Oxford, NY: Oxford University Press.

Lee, J., & Bean, F. D. (2004). America's changing color lines: Immigration, race/ethnicity, and multiracial identification. *Annual Review of Sociology*, *30*(1), 221–242.

Lee, S.M. (1993). Racial classifications in the U.S. census: 1890–1990. *Ethnic and Racial Studies*, *16*(1), 76–94.

Leong, N. (2013). Racial capitalism. *Harvard Law Review*, *126*(8), 2151–2226.

Levitt, P., & Waters, M. C. (2002). *The changing face of home: The transnational lives of the second generation*. New York: Russell Sage Foundation.

Li, P. (2014). Recent developments hitting the ceiling: An examination of barriers to success for Asian American women. *Berkeley Journal of Gender, Law & Justice*, *29*(1), 140–167.

Lipsitz, G. (2006). *The possessive investment in whiteness: How white people profit from identity politics*. Philadelphia: Temple University Press.

Lipsitz, G. (2011). *How racism takes place*. Philadelphia: Temple University Press.

Losen, D.J., Orfield, G., & Jeffords, J.M. (Eds.). (2003). *Racial inequality in special education*. Cambridge, MA: Harvard Educational Publishing Group.

Love, B. J. (2000). Developing a liberatory consciousness. In M. Adams, W.J. Blumenfeld, R. Castenada, H. W. Hackman, M. L. Peters, & X. Zuniga (Eds.), *Readings for diversity and social justice* (pp. 599–603). New York: Routledge.

Martin, R., McCann, H., Morales, M. E., & Williams, S. M. (2013). White screen/white noise: Racism and the Internet. University of Kentucky Libraries, Library faculty and staff publications, Paper 244. Retrieved from http://uknowledge.uky.edu/cgi/viewcontent.cgi?article=1245&context=libraries_facpub

Martinez, E. (1993). Beyond black/white: The racisms of our time. *Social Justice, 20*(1–2), 22–34.

Martinez, E. (1996). Beyond black/white: The racisms of our time. In M. Rogers & G. Ritzer (Eds.), *Multicultural experiences, multicultural theories* (pp. 236–246). New York: McGraw-Hill.

Massey, D. S. (2007). *Categorically unequal: The American stratification system.* New York: Russell Sage Foundation.

Massey, D. S., & Denton, N. A. (1993). *American apartheid: Segregation and the making of the underclass.* Cambridge, MA: Harvard University Press.

McIntosh, P. (2001). White privilege: Unpacking the invisible knapsack. In P. Rothenberg (Ed.), *Race, class and gender in the United States: An anthology* (pp. 188–103). New York: St. Martin's Press.

Metzel, J. (2010). *The protest psychosis: How schizophrenia became a black disease.* Boston, MA: Beacon Press.

Miller, J., Donner, S., & Fraser, E. (2004). Talking when talking is tough: Taking on conversations about race. *Smith College Studies in Social Work, 74*(2), 377–392.

Miller, J., & Garran, A. (2008). *Racism in the United States: Implications for the helping professions.* Belmont, CA: Thomson Brooks/Cole.

Mishra, S. (2013). Race, religion, and political mobilization: South Asians in the post-9/11 United States. *Studies in Ethnicity and Nationalism, 13*(2), 115–137.

Montagu, A. (1997). *Man's most dangerous myth: The fallacy of race* (6th ed., abridged student ed.). Walnut Creek, CA: Sage Press.

Morris, M. W. (2012). *Race, gender and the school to prison pipeline: Expanding our discussion to include black girls.* New York: African American Policy Forum.

Mullainathan, S. (2015). *Racial bias even when we have good intentions.* Retrieved from http://www.nytimes.com/2015/01/04/upshot/the-measuring-sticks-of-raciam-bias-html

Muslim Public Affairs Council (MPAC) (2015). *Statistics: What you need to know.* Retrieved from http://www.mpac.org/programs/hate-crime-prevention/statistics.php

Ngai, M. M. (2004). *Impossible subjects: Illegal aliens and the making of modern America.* Princeton, NJ: Princeton University Press.

Oesterreich, H. A., & Knight, M. G. (2010). Facilitating transitions to college for students with disabilities from culturally and linguistically diverse backgrounds. In M. Adams, W. Blumenfeld, R. Castañeda, H. W. Hackman, M. L. Peters, & X. Zuniga (Eds.), *Readings for diversity and social justice* (2nd ed., pp. 513–518). London: Routledge.

Ogletree, C. J. (2012). *The presumption of guilt.* New York: Palgrave-McMillan.

Oliver, M. L., & Shapiro, T. M. (2006). *Black wealth/white wealth: A new perspective on racial inequality* (2nd ed.). New York: Routledge.

Omi, M. (1986). *Racial formation in the United States: From the 1960s to the 1990s.* New York: Routledge.

Orfalea, G. (2006). *The Arab Americans: A history.* Northampton, MA: Olive Branch Press.

Orfield, G., & Frankenberg, E. (2013). *Educational delusions: Why choice can deepen inequality and how to make schools fair.* Berkeley, CA: University of California Press.

Orfield, G., & Lee, C. (2005). *Why segregation matters: Poverty and educational inequality.* Cambridge, MA: Civil Rights Project, Harvard University.

Orfield, G., Marin, P., & Horn, C. L. (Eds.). (2005). *Higher education and the color line: College access, racial equity, and social change.* Cambridge, MA: Harvard Education Press.

Pager, D. (2007). Marked: Race, crime, and finding work in an era of mass incarceration. Chicago: University of Chicago Press.

Pager, D., & Shepherd, H. (2008). The sociology of discrimination: Racial discrimination in employment, housing, credit, and consumer markets. *Annual Review Sociology, 1*(34), 181–209.

Pager, D., Western, B., & Bonikowski, B. (2009). Discrimination in a low-wage labor market: A field experiment. *American Sociological Review, 74*(5), 777–799.

Painter, N. I. (2010). *The history of white people.* New York: W. W. Norton & Company.

Peek, L. A. (2011). *Behind the backlash: Muslim Americans after 9/11.* Philadelphia: Temple University Press.

Perea, J. F. (1997). The black/white binary paradigm of race: The normal science of American racial thought. *California Law Review, 85*(5), 127–172.

Pew Research Center (2014). *Wealth inequality has widened along racial, ethnic lines since end of Great Recession.* Retrieved from http://www.pewresearch.org/fact-tank/2014/12/12/racial-wealth-gaps-great-recession/

Pew Research Center (2015). *Demographic and economic data by race.* Retrieved from www.pewso
cialtrends.org/2013/08/22/chapter-3-demographic-economic-data-by-race/

Preskill, S., & Brookfield, S. (2009). Learning to analyze experience. In Preskill, S., & Brookfield, S. (Eds.), *Learning as a way of leading: Lessons from the struggle for social justice* (pp. 105–125). San Francisco: Jossey-Bass.

Prisco, G. (2011). *When the cure makes you ill: Seven core principles to change the course of youth justice.* New York: Correctional Association of New York.

Roediger, D.R. (1999). *The wages of Whiteness: Race and the making of the American working class* (rev. ed.) London: Verso.

Roediger, D. (2007). *The wages of whiteness: Racism and the making of the American working class* (2nd ed.). London: Verso.

Rothstein, R. (2014). *The making of Ferguson: Public policy and the root of its troubles.* Washington, DC: The Economic Policy Institute.

Rugh, J.S., & Massey, D.S. (2010). Racial segregation and the American foreclosure crisis. *American sociological review, 75*(5), 629–651.

Rumbaut, R.G. (1996). Origins and destinies: Immigration, race, and ethnicity in contemporary America. In S. Pedraza & R. G. Rumbaut (Eds.), *Origins and destinies: Immigration, race, and ethnicity in America* (pp. 21–42). Belmont, CA: Wadsworth Publishing Company.

Said, E. (1994). *Orientalism.* New York: Vintage.

Samuel, L.R. (2012). *The American dream: A cultural history.* Syracuse, NY: Syracuse University Press.

Sánchez, P., & Machado-Casas, M. (2009). At the intersection of transnationalism, Latina/o immigrants, and education. *The High School Journal, 92*(4), 3–15.

Savage, C. (2012, July 12). Wells Fargo will settle mortgage bias charges. *The New York Times.* Retrieved from http://www.nytimes.com/2012/07/13/business/wells-fargo-to-settle-mortgage-discrimination-charges.html?_r=0

The Sentencing Project. (2012). *Incarcerated women.* Retrieved from http://www.sentencingproject.org/doc/publications/cc_incarcerated_women_factsheet_sep24sp.pdf

The Sentencing Project. (2014). *The state of sentencing 2014: Developments in policy and practice.* Retrieved from http://sentencingproject.org/doc/publications/sen_State_of_Sentencing_2014.pdf

Shapiro, T. (2004). *The hidden cost of being African-American.* New York: Oxford University Press.

Shapiro, T., Meschede, T., & Osoro, S. (2013, Feb.). *The roots of the widening racial wealth gap: Explaining the black-white economic divide* (Research and Policy Brief). Waltham, MA: Institute on Assets & Social Policy, Brandeis University. Retrieved Feb. 5, 2014, from http://iasp.brandeis.edu/pdfs/Author/shapiro-thomas-m/racialwealthgapbrief.pdf

Shichor, D. (1995). *Punishment for profit: Private prisons/public concerns.* Thousand Oaks, CA: Sage Publications.

Singh, J. (2013). A new American apartheid: Racialized, religious minorities in the post-9/11 era. *Sikh Formations* (ahead-of-print), pp. 1–30.

Smedley, A. (1993). *Race in North America: Origin and evolution of a worldview.* Boulder, CO: Westview Press.

Smedley, A., & Smedley, B. (2011). *Race in North America: The origin and evolution of a worldview* (4th ed.). New York: Westview Press.

Smith, A. (2006). Heteropatriarchy and the three pillars of white supremacy. In *Incite! Women of color against violence* (anthology, pp. 66–73). Cambridge, MA: South End Press.

Smith, A. (2010). Indigeneity, settler colonialism, white supremacy. *Global Dialogue, 12*(2), 1–13.

Smith, S. (2005). "'Don't put my name on it": (Dis)trust and job-finding assistance among the black urban poor. *American Journal of Sociology, 111*(1), 1.

Smith, W. A., Allen, W. R., & Danley, L.L. (2007). "Assume the position . . . you fit the description": Psychological experiences and racial battle fatigue among African American male college students. *American Behavioral Scientist, 51,* 558–578.

Soehl, T., & Waldinger, R. (2012). Inheriting the homeland? Intergenerational transmission of cross-border ties in migrant families. *American Journal of Sociology, 118*(3), 778–813.

Solórzano, D., Ceja, M., & Yosso, T. (2000). Critical race theory, racial microaggressions, and campus racial climate: The experiences of African American college students. *The Journal of Negro Education, 69,* 60–73.

Spring, J. (2003). *Deculturalization and the struggle for equality: A brief history of the education of dominated cultures in the U.S.* New York: McGraw-Hill.

Steele, C. (2010). Whistling Vivaldi: And other clues to how stereotypes affect us. New York: W.W. Norton & Company.

Steele, C. M., & Aronson, J. (1995). Stereotype threat and the intellectual test performance of African Americans. *Journal of Personality and Social Psychology, 69*, 797–811.

Steele, C. M., & Aronson, J. (2004). Stereotype threat does not live by Steele and Aronson (1995) alone. *American Psychologist, 59*(1), 47–55.

Stevenson, B. (2014). *Just mercy: A story of justice and redemption.* New York: Spiegel & Grau.

Suárez-Orozco, C., Pimentel, A., & Martin, M. (2009). The significance of relationships: Academic engagement and achievement among newcomer immigrant youth. *The Teachers College Record, 111*(3), 712–749.

Subtirelu, N. C. (2015). "She does have an accent but . . .": Race and language ideology in students' evaluations of mathematics instructors on RateMyProfessors.com. *Language in Society, 44*(1), 35–62.

Sue, D. W. (2010). *Racial microaggressions in everyday life: Race, gender, and sexual orientation.* Hoboken, NJ: John Wiley and Sons.

Sue, D. W., Capodilupo, C. M., Torino, G. C., Bucceri, J. M., Holder, A. M. B., Nadal, K. L., & Esquilin, M. (2007). Racial microaggressions in everyday life: Implications for clinical practice. *American Psychologist, 62*, 271–286.

Sue, D. W., Lin, A. I., Torino, G. C., Capodiluco, C. M., & Rivera, D. P. (2009). Racial microaggressions and difficult dialogues on race in the classroom. *Cultural Diversity and Ethnic Minority Psychology, 15*(2), 183–190.

Sullivan, L., Meschede, T., Dietrich, L., & Shapiro, T. (2015). *The racial wealth gap: Why policy matters.* New York: Demos.

Takaki, R. (2008). *A different mirror: A history of multicultural America, revised.* Boston: Little, Brown & Co.

Tatum, B. D. (1992). Talking about race, learning about racism: The application of racial identity development theory in the classroom. *Harvard Educational Review, 62*(1), 1–25.

Tavernise, S. (2011, Sept. 13). Soaring poverty casts spotlight on "lost decade." *The New York Times.* Retrieved from http://www.nytimes.com/2011/09/14/us/14census.html

Tefera, A., Frankenberg, E., Siegel-Hawley, G., & Chirchigno, G. (2011). *Integrating suburban schools: How to benefit from growing diversity and avoid segregation.* Los Angeles, CA: Civil Rights Project/Proyecto Direcho Civiles.

Tejeda, C., & Gutierrez, K. D. (2006). Fighting the backlash: Decolonizing Perspectives and pedagogies in neocolonial times. In P. Pedraza & M. Rivera (Eds.), *Latino Education: An agenda for community education research* (pp. 261–294). New York: Routledge.

Teranishi, R. (2002). The myth of the superminority: Misconceptions about Asian Americans. *The College Board Review, 195*, 16–21.

Tuan, M. (2001). *Forever foreigners or honorary whites? The Asian ethnic experience today.* New Brunswick, NJ: Rutgers University Press.

Tukachinsky, R. (2015). Where we have been and where we can go from here: Looking to the future in research on media, race, and ethnicity. *Journal of Social Issues, 71*(1), 186–199.

United for a Fair Economy (2012). *State of the dream 2012: The emerging majority.* Retrieved from http://faireconomy.org/sites/default/files/State_of_the_Dream_2012.pdf

U.S. Bureau of Labor Statistics (2014). *Labor force characteristics by race and ethnicity, 2013. Report 1050.* Washington, DC. Retrieved from http://www.bls.gov

United States Department of Education (2012). *New data from U.S. Department of Education highlights educational inequities around teacher experience, discipline and high school rigor.* Retrieved from http://www.ed.gov/news/press-releases/new-data-usdepartment-education-highlights-educational-inequities-around-teache

United States Department of Justice, Civil Rights Division (2015, Mar. 4). *Investigation of the Ferguson police department.* Retrieved from http://www.justice.gov/sites/default/files/opa/press-releases/attachments/2015/03/04/ferguson_police_department_report.pdf

Valencia, D. (2010). *Dismantling contemporary deficit thinking: Educational thought and practice.* New York: Routledge.

Valenzuela, A. (1999). *Subtractive schooling.* New York: SUNY Press.

Vega, T. (2014, Dec. 10). Schools' discipline for girls differs by race and hue. *The New York Times.* Retrieved from http://www.nytimes.com/2014/12/11/us/school-discipline-to-girls-differs-between-and-within-races.html

Ver Ploeg, M., & Farrigan, T. (2009, Sept. 3). *Access to affordable and nutritious food: Measuring and understanding food deserts and their consequences* (Report to Congress). Washington, DC: U.S. Dept. of Agriculture, Economic Research Service. Retrieved from http://www.ers.usda.govhttp://www.ers.usda.gov/http://www.ers.usda.gov/

Warren, J. W., & Twine, F. W. (1997). White Americans, the new minority? Non-blacks and the ever-expanding boundaries of whiteness. *Journal of Black Studies, 28*(2), 200–218.

Washington, H. A. (2007). *Medical apartheid: The dark history of medical experimentation on black Americans from colonial times to the present*. New York: Doubleday Press.

Waters, M. C. (2009). *Black identities*. Cambridge, MA: Harvard University Press.

Watkins, N. L. (2012). *Disarming microaggressions: How black college students self-regulate racial stressors within predominately white institutions* (Dissertation). New York: Columbia University Libraries. Accessed via ProQuest, UMI Dissertations Publishing, 2012. 3519081.

Werkmeister Rozas, L. W., & Miller, J. (2009). Discourses for social justice education: The web of racism and the web of resistance. *Journal of Ethnic & Cultural Diversity in Social Work*, *18*(1–2), 24–39.

Wijeyesinghe, C. L. (2012). The intersectional model of multiracial identity: Integrating multiracial identity theories and intersectional perspectives on social identity. In C. L. Wijeyesinghe & B. W. Jackson (Eds.), *New perspectives on racial identity development* (pp. 81–107). New York: New York University.

Wildman, S. M. (2006). The persistence of white privilege. *Journal of Law and Policy*, *18*(6), 245–265.

Williams, T. O. (2011, Jan.). *A process of becoming: U.S. born African American and black women in a process of liberation from internalized racism* (Doctoral dissertation). Available from Proquest, Paper AAI3465244.

Winant, H. (2004). *The new politics of race: Globalization, difference and justice*. Minneapolis: University of Minnesota Press.

Xu, J., & Lee, J. C. (2013). The marginalized "model" minority: An empirical examination of the triangulation of Asian Americans. *Social Forces*, *91*(4), 1363–1397.

Zinn, H. (2003). *A people's history of the United States: 1492–present*. New York: Harper-Collins.

6

Sexism, Heterosexism, and Trans* Oppression

An Integrated Perspective

*D. Chase J. Catalano and Pat Griffin**

An increasing focus on same-sex marriage and abortion legislation, the growing visibility of transgender identities—including transgender characters in popular culture and television—and debates about who belongs in an historically women's college have raised debates and questions about sex, gender, and sexuality. As the attention heightens the fervor of these discussions, what becomes clearer are how questions about one of these social identities, and the forms of oppression that impact them, have implications for the others. We have reached a point where it is crucial to rethink common assumptions about these categories and reconceptualize how we understand others and ourselves.

This chapter describes an integrated approach to teaching about sexism, heterosexism, and trans* oppression in which all three of these manifestations of oppression are examined simultaneously. An integrated approach is based on the assumption that all three of these manifestations of oppression are best understood in relationship to each other. Heterosexism, sexism, and trans* oppression are systems of privilege afforded to heterosexuals (heterosexism), cisgender men (sexism), and people whose gender identity and/or gender expression conform to cultural and social expectations for women/girls and men/boys (trans* oppression). Groups disadvantaged by these systems of oppression are lesbian, gay, bisexual, queer people (heterosexism), cisgender women, trans* women and intersex women (sexism), and people whose gender identity or gender expression do not conform to binary cultural norms and expectations (trans* oppression).

The emergence of a trans* rights movement separate from the lesbian, gay, and bisexual rights movements highlights the limitations of binary understandings of sex, gender, and sexuality, and challenges social justice educators to sharpen our awareness and understanding of these interrelated identity concepts in relationship to sexism, heterosexism, and trans* oppression. This more complex understanding requires that education about sexism, heterosexism, and trans* oppression pay more attention to the relationships among all three. The workshop design described in this chapter addresses the intersection and relationships between sexism, heterosexism, and trans* oppression to help prepare those who will facilitate either a single-issue workshop or an integrated design. Single-issue workshops/course modules on sexism, heterosexism, and trans* oppression are available on the website associated with this chapter.

This chapter includes a discussion of: a) key terms essential to teaching about sexism, heterosexism, and trans* oppression; b) the assumptions and rationale for an integrated approach to teaching about sexism, heterosexism, and trans* oppression; c) historical themes among sexism, heterosexism, and trans* oppression; d) current manifestations of sexism, heterosexism, and trans* oppression; and e) an integrated design for teaching about sexism, heterosexism, and trans* oppression; and f) a discussion of pedagogical and facilitation issues for teaching an integrated design.

KEY TERMS ESSENTIAL TO TEACHING ABOUT SEXISM, HETEROSEXISM, AND TRANS* OPPRESSION

Before going further into a discussion of an integrated approach to teaching about sexism, heterosexism, and trans* oppression, several terms that are a key part of this conversation need to be defined. All facilitators, whether they are using an integrated approach or not, need to know these definitions to assist participants in understanding the interconnections and complexities among these three forms of oppression. Because of this interrelationship, identity concepts associated with sex, gender, and sexual orientation are often confused or conflated. This lack of understanding is accentuated because the language associated with sexism, heterosexism, and trans* oppression is continually evolving as our understanding of these manifestations of oppression becomes more sophisticated, differentiated, and nuanced.

Among the key concepts that need clarification are: a) biological/assigned sex, b) gender assignment, c) gender identity, d) gender expression, e) gender role, f) sexual orientation, g) trans*, h) cisgender, and i) intersex. Each of these terms is discussed below.

a) *Biological/assigned sex*: Biological/assigned sex is the physical, hormonal, and genetic characteristics with which we are born that are the basis for assigning female or male sex. The two categories of biological sex assume "that every human being is either male or female" (Kessler & McKenna, 1978, p. 1). However, not all infants are born with a clearly differentiated biological makeup. Intersex (formerly hermaphrodite) refers to babies born with some combination of male and female biological sex characteristics (Kessler, 1998; Preves, 2003). Some medical experts estimate that one in 4,000 babies born each year is intersex (Fausto-Sterling, 2000). Though these babies are typically healthy, binary cultural assumptions and expectations often lead physicians and parents to immediately assign these children to either male or female through surgery and subsequent hormone therapy and social reinforcement of the assigned sex (Chase, 2012; Kessler, 1998).

b) *Gender assignment*: Gender assignment is the assignment of gender that typically occurs simultaneously with the assignment of sex at birth, and based on the doctor's interpretation of the visual appearance of a baby's external genitalia, with males assigned the gender of boy and females as girls (Messerschmidt, 2009). Although sex and gender are commonly used interchangeably, it is important to make distinctions between the terms. We use biological/assigned sex to refer to the physical sex designation that appears on birth certificates and other legal documents, and gender to refer to socially constructed roles, behaviors, activities, and attributes that a given society considers appropriate for men and women. Sex is generally understood as a designation attributed to physiological and biological factors that foster individual classification as one of the two expected sex categories, male and female. Gender assignment, since it is usually conflated with the gender binary, uses the categories man or boy and woman or girl.

c) *Gender identity*: Gender identity is how we identify our own gender, typically using terms boy/man and girl/woman, which may or may not align with the sex assigned to one's body at birth. Most people's gender identity matches the gender and sex they were assigned at birth (cisgender). However, for some people, their gender identity is incongruent with the gender and sex they were assigned at birth. Some people assigned a male gender at birth identify as girls/women, and some people assigned female at birth identify as boys/men. Moreover, the spectrum of gender identities is much broader than the simple Western-based woman/man binary (Browne, 2004; Fausto-Sterling, 2000; Hird, 2000; Lorber, 1996). Once the expected woman/man binary is challenged, as it is in non-Western cultures (Nanda, 2014) and some Native American cultures (Blackwood, 1997), other gender identities emerge. In U.S. culture, genderqueer is a gender identity that is often used to signify being outside of and resistant to containment in a man/woman gender binary (Harrison, Grant, & Herman, 2012; Nestle, Howell, & Wilchins, 2002).

d) *Gender expression*: Gender expression is the behavioral, aesthetic, and psychological characteristics by which a person communicates their gender identity. One's gender expression may or may not conform to cultural expectations and may challenge the gender role binary. Gender expression complicates and challenges the assumed naturalness of binary gender roles as the "correct" expression of gender identity of men as masculine and women as feminine, as defined by the dominant culture.

e) *Gender role*: Gender role is the socially constructed, historically and culturally grounded behavioral and psychological characteristics expected of women (femininity) and men (masculinity). Gender roles are assumed to be a "natural" expression of gender identity. Over the last forty years, terms like androgynous, and more recently genderqueer, gender non-conforming, and gender fluid, have emerged as challenges to the masculine/feminine binary and to the "naturalness" of assuming gender expression is a product of biological sex (Nicholson, 1995).

f) *Sexual orientation*: Sexual orientation is a person's predominant sexual and emotional attractions toward someone of the same sex (lesbian or gay), "opposite" sex (heterosexual), both sexes (bisexual), or any sex (queer/pansexual). Of course, these distinctions require the expectation that attraction or physical intimacy is based on a person's biological/assigned sex or body morphology, and as earlier described, gender and sex may not be as clearly distinguished. For example, Marine (2011b) defines queer people as those who "are distinguishable by the ways in which their identities defy socially prescribed norms of gender identity and sexual orientation" (p. 5). Historically, sexual orientation has been described variously as an innate and unchangeable characteristic, a fluid behavioral choice, and an identity that must be viewed in historical and cultural context (Katz, 1995).

g) *Trans**: Trans* is an identity category describing a person whose gender identity does not conform to the sex or gender they were assigned at birth or who transgresses the boundaries of gender norms ascribed to their assigned sex and gender categories at birth (Feinberg, 1996; Stryker, 2008). In this chapter, we use trans* as an umbrella description that includes a broad spectrum of identities, such as trans* woman, trans* man, gender non-conforming, gender fluid, transgender, transsexual, and genderqueer. Historically, transsexual was defined as people who choose to and could access biomedical transition processes to change their bodies through surgeries and/or hormone treatments to better match their gender identity (Meyer, Bockting, Cohen-Kettenis, Coleman, DiCeglie, Devor, Gooren, Hage, Kirk, Kuiper, Laub, Lawrence, Menard, Monstrey, Patton, Schaefer, Webb, & Wheeler, 2001). The use of trans* (with an asterisk) instead of transgender as a broad identity term allows for the inclusion of a variation of body modifications, hormonal uses, and/or gender expression choices (Johnson, 2013; Killerman, 2012; Nicolazzo, 2014; Tompkins, 2014).

h) *Cisgender*: Cisgender is an adjective describing a person whose gender identity is congruent with their gender assigned at birth. The use of cisgender provides an affirmative way of describing non-trans* gender identities (Aultman, 2014; Enke, 2012; Serano, 2009; Stryker, 2008). Cisgender individuals are not necessarily gender-conforming in terms of their gender expression. For example, a cisgender woman may prefer to wear clothes typically thought of as masculine or style her hair in a way that is typically associated with men. Similarly, trans* individuals can be gender-conforming in their gender expression by choosing a gender expression that is congruent with traditional gendered expectations for women or men—for example, trans* men who prefer to wear suits and ties or trans* women who wear dresses and makeup.

i) *Intersex*: Intersex refers to a group of medical conditions (formerly called hermaphroditism) describing people who are born with what are deemed to be genital, chromosomal, and/or reproductive capacity anomalies, or whose genitals at birth are not easily classified as male or female, or whose bodies develop hormonally after birth in such a way that their bodies are not easily classified as male or female (Chase, 2012).

Confusion about and conflation of these identity concepts are often based on two assumptions. One assumption is that there is a "normalized" and consistent relationship among gender assigned at birth, gender identity, gender expression, and sexual orientation that is based on biological sex. According to this normalized perspective, once biological sex is identified based on the appearance of external genitals, a gender is assigned that matches the biological sex. Each person's gender identity, gender expression, and sexual orientation are expected to conform to cultural expectations and are assumed to remain consistent over a lifetime. For example, a biological male assigned a male sex at birth is expected to identify as a boy/man (gender identity), appear and act in masculine ways (gender expression), and have a heterosexual sexual orientation. A biological female who is identified as a girl at birth is expected to identify as a girl/woman, appear and act in feminine ways, and have a heterosexual sexual orientation.

Biological/assigned sex, assigned gender, gender identity, gender expression, and sexual orientation are assumed to be binary concepts; that is, a person is either male or female, man or woman, masculine or feminine, gay/lesbian, or heterosexual. From a dominant cultural perspective, the diversity of biological sex, gender identity, gender expression, and sexual orientation outside these expected binaries, and discontinuities among these identity categories, is perceived as abnormal, inferior, or disruptive to social and cultural norms. When babies are identified as intersex at birth, they are often immediately assigned either male or female sex based on the cultural expectations for external sex anatomy. This decision is usually made by physicians in consultation with the parent(s), as is now required by law. This assignment is sometimes accompanied by surgical intervention on healthy infants to create genitals that are consistent with the gender assignment decision and to meet binary cultural expectations.

Failure to conform to sex, gender, and sexual orientation binaries leads to the potential for stereotyping, discrimination, and oppression. Many of the stereotypes associated with one or more of these different social identity groups are based on assumptions of congruence among them. Examples of identity stereotypes include: That gay men (sexual orientation) are effeminate (gender expression), or that trans* people (gender identity) are lesbian or gay (sexual orientation), or that cisgender females (sex) are more emotional and relational than cisgender men, or that bisexual people are really gay. These examples illustrate assumed congruence with the binary.

Understanding and differentiating the relationships among these identity concepts will help to dispel stereotypes and increase appreciation for the range of sex, gender, and sexual orientation diversity concealed by assumptions about what is normal. Assumptions about what is and is not normal are the basis for the perception of hierarchical relationships among different sexes, sexual orientations, and gender identities that result in oppression based on sex, gender identity, and sexual orientation.

RATIONALE FOR AN INTEGRATED APPROACH TO TEACHING ABOUT SEXISM, HETEROSEXISM, AND TRANS* OPPRESSION

Part of the rationale for using an integrated approach to teach about heterosexism, sexism, and trans* oppression rests on an understanding of relationships among patriarchy, misogyny, biological determinism, and genderism, and how these belief systems support and reinforce oppression based on sex, gender, and sexual orientation. These shared foundations suggest that effective education about sexism, heterosexism, and trans* oppression must attend to all three forms of oppression to best understand the complexities of each one as well as the interconnections among all three.

Patriarchy is a social system in which cisgender and many trans* men are positioned as the primary authority figures who occupy roles of political leadership, moral authority, and control of property. Patriarchal belief systems serve as a rationale for male privilege and female subordination. Under patriarchy, male-identified behaviors and attributes are highly valued, and female-identified behaviors and attributes are devalued, or valued only for their position of subordination in relationship to men, the needs of men, and under the control and protection of men (Johnson, 1997).

Misogyny, a complement to patriarchy, is the hatred or dislike of women and values or concepts associated with females (Gilmore, 2007). Misogyny has historical roots in most world cultures, religions, and philosophies, and has persisted in contemporary societies as a foundation for resistance to feminism or any assertions of women's equality (Clack, 1999). Misogyny can be manifested in numerous ways, including the denigration and degradation of women, preference for male children, violence against women, and sexual objectification of women. Misogyny is also an underlying factor in masculinist values that require boys and men to avoid exhibiting any behaviors or attitudes that are associated with femininity or women-identified values. At its most insidious, misogyny is internalized by women who reinforce women's subordination and their own inferiority.

Biological determinism is the belief that biological factors, such as an individual's genes or physiological make-up (as opposed to social or environmental factors), determine how a person behaves, and that these biological factors place limits on the ability to change. Biological determinism supports the belief that masculinity and femininity are natural expressions of a person's biological sex, that heterosexuality is the only normal sexual orientation (heterosexism), and that gender assigned at birth based on the appearance of external genitals is always correct. Cisgender people who deny the self-affirmed gender of a trans* man or woman reflect the biological-determinist belief that a trans*man is "really" a woman or that a trans* woman is "really" a man based on the sex they were assigned at birth. Biological determinism also refutes the existence of genderqueer or gender-nonconforming gender identities as possible or authentic. Critics assert that the principles underlying biological determinism serve mainly as a pseudo-scientific justification for maintaining a status quo in which inequities based on such characteristics as race, sex, class, and sexuality benefit historically privileged social groups (Lewontin, Rose, & Kamin, 1984).

Scientists have attempted to determine whether sexual orientation is an innate characteristic with a basis in biology (Weill, 2009). These studies have failed to demonstrate conclusively that such a biologically determined relationship exists, but they do suggest that there may be some biological components related to one's sexual orientation (DeCecco & Parker, 1995; Mustanski, Chivers, & Bailey, 2002). In contrast, Roughgarden (2009) offers how diversity of sexual orientations and gender identities has always existed, but argues that it is our interpretations that have been limited. Some lesbian, gay, bisexual, trans*, and queer (LGBTQ) people describe their experience of their sexual orientation or gender identity as consistent across their lifetime, which leads them to believe they are, in fact, "born that way." Nevertheless, the personal experiences of individual people and how they identify their sexual orientation or gender identity exist in the context of social, historical, and cultural factors that shape how they think about themselves. It is important to respect the integrity of these personal experiences, and at the same time acknowledge that the dynamics of oppression are rooted in systems of thought—biological determinism, for example—that support hierarchies of privilege and subordination. What we do know is that sexual orientation and gender identity are far more complicated and fluid than the either/or binaries that form the foundation for heterosexism, sexism and trans* oppression would allow, and that the social meanings attached to one's identity must be viewed within these larger systems of oppression.

In an interesting paradox, biological determinism is sometimes used by LGBTQ activists to claim that LGBTQ people are "born" and that their sexual orientation identity is rooted in their biology. This claim is used to argue that discrimination against LGBTQ people on the basis of an innate identity is unreasonable and akin to discrimination on the basis of sex or race. Anti-LGBTQ activists, on the other hand, believe that homosexuality is an abnormal/sinful behavior that can be changed and therefore is not biologically determined.

Genderism, as an extension of biological determinism, is the classification of male and female or masculine and feminine into two distinct and opposite sex and gender binary categories. These binaries encompass biological sex, gender assigned at birth, gender identity, and gender roles/expression, and assume a consistent, natural, and congruent relationship among these components of gender (Bilodeau, 2009). Conformity with this binary confers privilege and the assumption of normality, while non-conformity is associated with inferiority, abnormality, and subordination (Hill & Willoughby, 2005). Any deviation from conformity to the expected consistency among gender assigned at birth, gender identity, gender expression, and a heterosexual sexual orientation dilutes the experience of privilege. For example, a cisgender heterosexual man whose gender expression does not conform to expected masculine expectations is afforded less social status than a cisgender heterosexual man who does conform to expected masculine gender expression.

These four belief systems form a common foundation for viewing as normal a status quo based on sexism, heterosexism, and trans* oppression. An integrated approach to teaching about heterosexism, sexism, and trans* oppression challenges a status quo in which privilege and power accrue to cisgender gender-conforming heterosexual males over all others. The extent of their privilege, however, is mediated by the intersections of other social identities, such as race and class. A poor or working-class white man, or a Latino man with a disability, will still experience privilege based on their male identity, but it will be mediated by these other intersecting disadvantaged identities.

Similarly, cisgender women; trans* men and women; lesbian, gay, bisexual, and queer people; and intersex people are subjected to varying levels of subordination and privilege according to their individual identity profiles. For example, though cisgender women of any sexual orientation have relatively more access to privilege than trans* women do, they are subjected to sexism (and heterosexism in the case of lesbians and bisexual women). Cisgender gay men may enjoy male privilege in relationship to all women, but heterosexism limits their access to privilege relative to cisgender heterosexual men.

Patriarchy and misogyny combine to justify sexism directed at cisgender gender-conforming women of any sexual orientation, trans* women, and intersex women. Through the lenses of patriarchy and misogyny, gay men, bisexual men, and trans* women have abdicated their birthright to male privilege, and in doing so, deserve a subordinate status in relationship to cisgender gender-conforming heterosexual males. Trans* men, lesbians, and bisexual women, from a patriarchal perspective, aspire to a pseudo-male status, abdicating their "natural" and subordinate roles as women. Fueled by misogyny, violence toward trans* men, lesbians, bisexual women, and cisgender women is often ignored, condoned, or blamed on the victims for their failure to conform to normalized gender and sexual expectations. This misogynistic violence also serves as a warning about the consequences of failing to conform to sex, gender, and sexual orientation norms.

These perspectives are reinforced by genderism and biological determinism in that anyone who defines their identity outside of the biological and gender binary-based definitions of man or woman, gay or straight, is regarded as inferior or unnatural and thus deserving of subordination, violence, pity, or ridicule. Identities such as bisexual, intersex, trans*, or other identities that occupy identity spaces between the opposite poles of gender/sex binaries challenge the either/or imperative of genderism and the notion of a binary by defining their identities outside of its either/or parameters.

SOCIAL CONSTRUCTIVISM AS FOUNDATIONAL FOR TEACHING ABOUT SEXISM, HETEROSEXISM, AND TRANS* OPPRESSION

Social constructivism provides a useful pedagogical foundation for teaching about sexism, heterosexism, and trans* oppression. In contrast to biological determinism and genderism, social constructionism is a theoretical construct grounded in sociology that asserts that social meaning is created (Berger & Luckman, 1966). According to a social constructivist view, humans attribute meaning to concepts according to our cultural, historical, and personal socialization. As a socially constructed concept, the meaning of gender changes according to shifts in cultural, historical, and personal perspectives, rather than having fixed or essential qualities that transcend historical or cultural contexts. For example, though same-sex sexuality has been acknowledged throughout history as a behavior, the concept of a "homosexual" identity or naming oneself as gay or lesbian originated in the late 19th century (Katz, 1995). (We use "homosexual" in its historical context as the term used in the 19th and early 20th centuries to refer to individuals with same-sex attractions.)

A social constructivist perspective on sex, gender, and sexual orientation challenges genderism and biological determinism as two important foundations of sexism, heterosexism, and trans* oppression, and interrupts the assumption of consistency among biological sex, gender assigned at birth, gender identity, and sexual orientation.

A social constructivist perspective also challenges the inevitability of "natural" power hierarchies and the essential nature of these aspects of identity (Johnson, 2006). By disrupting dominant understandings of gender, sexuality, and sex, a social constructionist perspective destabilizes hierarchies and assumptions of superiority and inferiority upon which sexism, heterosexism, and trans* oppression are justified. If sex, gender, and sexuality are understood as socially constructed concepts, then the interlocking systems of oppression based on these identities are called into question.

BENEFITS AND CHALLENGES OF AN INTEGRATED APPROACH TO TEACHING ABOUT SEXISM, HETEROSEXISM, AND TRANS* OPPRESSION

Historically, many social justice educators have used "single issue" designs in which sexism, heterosexism, and trans* oppression are addressed as separate, but related, topics. Novice facilitators, or students who are enrolled in their first social justice education (SJE) course, might find that a single-issue design provides a useful introduction to not only the form of oppression under study, but also the overall dynamics of oppression in general. One of the benefits of a single-issue design is the ability to explore in-depth each form of oppression and the dynamics of how that manifestation of oppression is operationalized on an individual, institutional, and cultural level. Single-issue approaches enable facilitators to include more content about a particular form of oppression, as well as allow more time for focused self-reflection, awareness, and action related to the particular form of oppression under examination. Such a design allows for significant exploration of one form of oppression raising awareness of how, for example, sexism is a part of all facets of life and socialization, but experienced differently depending on a person's intersection with other social identities. The inclusion of activities that prompt students to explore how various intersecting identities—such as race, class, and (dis)ability—affect the manifestation of oppression under study in a single-issue design is an important benefit of effective single-issue design.

Even if facilitators do not adopt an integrated approach, the overlap among sexism, heterosexism, and trans* oppression should inform how we address each one in a single-issue design. For example, a single-issue sexism class focuses on ways that males are advantaged and females are disadvantaged individually, institutionally, and culturally. Male privilege and female subordination are mediated by sexual orientation, gender expression, and trans* identity as well as other intersecting identities, such as race or class, and these complications should be acknowledged. In addition, participants in sexism classes do not experience the world solely according to their affirmed gender, and addressing these other intersections is necessary to help them make sense of their own lived experiences.

In similar ways, heterosexism operates according to stereotypes and assumptions about gender expression associated with gay men and lesbians, and nontraditional gender expression is often the basis for assuming that someone is lesbian or gay. Trans* people, whose gender identities and expression challenge binary assumptions about gender, call into question traditional binary sexuality labels such as heterosexual, lesbian, gay, or bisexual. It is important to address these issues in a single-issue heterosexism workshop.

Trans* oppression needs to be examined within the contexts of both sexism and heterosexism. Because trans* identities challenge the gender binaries that support both sexism and heterosexism, sexism and heterosexism curricula must be attentive to assumptions about sexual orientation and gender that perpetuate binary thinking. For example, forming groups by gender or sexual orientation should avoid forcing participants to choose based on binary assumptions about gender identity and sexual orientation that will exclude people whose identities challenge these binaries.

Similarly, heterosexism must be addressed in studying sexism and trans* oppression, and sexism must be addressed in studying trans* oppression and heterosexism. For example, in a sexism course, assuming that all participants have intimate relationships with someone of another gender or sex when discussing relationship violence ignores that trans* and intersex people are also targeted by sexist violence. Often the way we examine and talk about relationship and sexual violence is based on heterosexist assumptions, such as using gender boxes as a starting point to understand gender-based violence; however, this process often makes trans* and queer identities and relationships invisible (Mogul, Ritchie, & Whitlock, 2011). Likewise, in a trans* oppression course, facilitators should be alert to the interactions of sexism and heterosexism that affect the experiences of trans* women and men in ways that differ from cisgender participants, who have more accepted gender identities and expression. These examples demonstrate how sexism, heterosexism, and trans* oppression, though based on power imbalances among different identities, are also overlapping systems that are best understood in relation to each other.

While there are benefits to a single-issue design, there are also challenges in addressing sexism, heterosexism, or trans* oppression separately. One challenge is the potential reinforcement of binaries through lack of attention to multiple genders and sexual orientations. Another is ignoring the ways that sexism, heterosexism, and trans* oppression are interlocking systems. Further, a focus on one specific identity or one form of oppression creates a false sense of singularity that does not reflect how any person experiences the world. For example, using men and women as universalized categories to discuss sexism may be useful for a basic understanding of the dynamics of sexist oppression, but not attending to all genders perpetuates the gender binary that undergirds sexism. Further, all women do not experience sexism the same way based on the intersections of other social identities (the experiences of trans* women, lesbians, bisexual, and heterosexual women are not the same in relation to sexism). All heterosexual men do not benefit from heterosexism the same way. The experience of heterosexual privilege by heterosexual trans* men or by heterosexual men who are gender non-conforming is different from that of heterosexual gender-conforming cisgender men.

In a single-issue design, participants may feel compelled to focus on some gender or sexual identities without having the space to understand how those identities interact with each other to influence incidents of privilege or disadvantage. Cisgender lesbians or bisexual women have different relationships with men in their lives, and a focus on "(heterosexual) dating violence" in a sexism class can render their experiences invisible. These potential omissions in a single-issue design can unintentionally evoke a sense of a "hierarchy of oppressions" (Lorde, 1984), which does not ultimately benefit efforts for liberation and change.

In contrast to the single-issue approach, in this chapter we describe an integrated approach to teaching about sexism, heterosexism, and trans* oppression. In an integrated design, sexism, heterosexism, and trans* oppression are simultaneously addressed. Participants are invited to examine privilege and disadvantage based on membership in multiple sex, gender, and sexual orientation identities.

The challenges in adopting an integrated approach to addressing sexism, heterosexism, and trans* oppression are important for facilitators to consider. An integrated approach can make facilitation and design more complex, and create confusion among participants about privilege and disadvantage as they address these topics in the context of the added complications of intersections of sex, gender, and sexuality at the same time. Understanding sexism, heterosexism, and trans* oppression as interlocking systems of oppression calls for caution in the use of language typically used to describe differential power relationships among social identity groups. Being "privileged" or "disadvantaged" is dependent on the ability to group people into binaries of power and powerlessness. These binaries do not adequately describe the complexities of privilege and disadvantage that emerge when oppressions are examined as interlocking systems.

Cisgender, gender-conforming, heterosexual men have the greatest access to power and privilege in relationship to sexism, heterosexism, and trans* oppression. In varying degrees, depending on memberships in different subordinated social groups, all other sex, gender, and sexual orientation identities are disadvantaged in a sexist, heterosexist, and trans* oppressive society. For example, attempting to compare the experiences of privilege or disadvantage enjoyed by a black cisgender gay man and a white trans* heterosexual woman is a complicated and nuanced process of acknowledging the integrated effects of their multiple identities.

An integrated approach requires that facilitators are knowledgeable about sexism, heterosexism, and trans* oppression, and the interconnections among them. It is not always a given that a facilitator who is knowledgeable about one or even two of these forms of oppression will be prepared to lead an education program integrating all three. Heterosexism, sexism, and trans* oppression each have distinctive manifestations of the overall characteristics of oppression common to all. For example, heterosexism imposes legal barriers to marriage, adoption, and custody of children, and access to spousal benefits for gay, lesbian, bisexual, and queer people not imposed on heterosexual people. Sexism creates a power system in which women are paid less than men (which is even more apparent within different marginalized racial groups), in which barriers to leadership positions in business and government limit women, and in which sexual violence poses a persistent threat. Trans* oppression results in a lack of access to biomedical transition options (hormones and/or surgeries), barriers from insurance companies that exclude such treatments, and refusals to accept or acknowledge trans* identity, as well as lack of legal protections for employment and housing. Facilitators using an integrated approach must be aware of the differing types of manifestations, and give time and attention to these distinctions.

As an example, homophobia (a pathological fear or hatred of lesbian, gay, or bisexual people), transphobia (a pathological fear or hatred of trans* people or anyone whose gender identity or gender expression defies cultural expectations), and misogyny are gender-based forms of violence that target all women and LGBTQ people. This violence is often a response to women and LGBTQ people who refuse to accept their subordinate status or whose visibility disrupts the status quo. Homophobia or transphobia are often the underlying motives for violence toward people of all sexual orientations or gender identities who violate gender norms and expectations (men who are perceived as effeminate, women who are perceived as masculine, and people who are perceived as gender confusing). Misogyny is often the underlying motivation behind violence toward women who are perceived as too strong, too smart, or too independent, or men who are perceived as not manly enough.

Looking at marginalized genders and sexualities together allows for a deeper analysis of those forms of violence, and the shared features of all three forms of oppression. For example, disgust with same-sex attraction that turns to violence shares a theme of dehumanization and a sense of superiority present in the sexual assault of women and violence in response to women's rejection of sexual advances by men. Issues of sexual assault cross all boundaries of sexual identities, because rape is not about sex, it is about power. Similarly, relationship violence is not specific to cisgender heterosexuals, but it can be present in relationships regardless of the sexual orientation or gender identity of the people involved. Survivors of gender- and sexual-based violence experience similar fears, such as secondary trauma from reporting violence to untrained or skeptical authorities resulting from disbelief and victim blaming. An integrated approach enables participants to understand that the dynamics of sexism, heterosexism, and trans* oppression share common roots in misogyny and patriarchy. This approach allows participants to better understand the interconnections of power structures that privilege the view that violence directed toward cisgender heterosexual women, lesbians, gay men, and bisexual and trans* people is "normal" or "expected." While an integrated approach allows for a more complex understanding of these issues, thinking outside of binaries and about the complicated interrelationships among sex, gender, and sexual orientation, and related oppressions, is cognitively and emotionally challenging.

The benefits of an integrated approach to sexism, heterosexism, and trans* oppression may outweigh the challenges if facilitators are prepared to guide participants through these complexities. Sexism, heterosexism, and trans* oppression are interconnected yet distinct from each other; therefore, an integrated design requires that students have opportunities to understand these distinctions, and at the same time learn about their common roots and manifestations. Our lived experiences of sexism, heterosexism, and trans* oppression are mediated by our simultaneous membership in different gender and sexual orientation identities as well as the intersections of other social identities, such as race or class. Examining how sexism, heterosexism, and trans* oppression affect our lives can help participants better understand how they can be both privileged and disadvantaged in any given situation.

The shift toward focusing on marginalized genders and sexualities together gives space for more intentional conversations, examples, and discussions about the salience of these identities and interactions with other social identities.

MOVING TOWARD JUSTICE: FEMINIST; LESBIAN, GAY, BISEXUAL, AND TRANS* RIGHTS MOVEMENTS

The histories of people with marginalized genders (women and trans* people) and sexualities (gay, lesbian, bisexual, queer people) and their liberation movements are distinctive, yet they share common themes. Each of these liberation movements have struggled with inclusion and exclusion, and with adequately addressing intersecting identities such as racial, religious, class, and ability diversity, either within the movement or as part of their larger advocacy efforts. Historically, feminist movements have excluded queer women, trans* people, poor and working-class women, and women of color while focusing on the needs of white, heterosexual, middle-class, cisgender women (Hooks, 2000; Spellman, 1988). Gay and lesbian liberation movements have excluded bisexual and trans* people, and racism is an ongoing issue in the predominately white LGBT rights movement. Lesbians often feel marginalized by white gay men within the LGBTQ movement. Trans* movements have excluded genderqueer people and those disinterested in biomedical transition options. Though many trans* men and women do not undergo surgery or hormone treatment as part of their gender transitions, they have been made to feel invisible and marginalized within trans* advocacy circles that prioritize the identities of trans* people who do take hormones and have gender-affirmation surgeries (Ekins & King, 2006).

All three movements challenge major cultural and institutional barriers that perpetuate oppression based on sex, gender, and sexual orientation. The right to control reproductive decisions, the right to marry the person of one's choice, the right to live as one's affirmed gender, the right to be treated with dignity and equality at work and in the public sphere, are all ongoing struggles that have roots in the histories of the feminist and LGBTQ liberation movements.

The histories of the social justice movements in the United States that challenge sexism, heterosexism, and trans* oppression reveal the ways in which these separate liberation movements are interwoven, and how they developed and built on other earlier social justice movements. It is important for facilitators contemplating an integrated and intersectional approach to sexism, heterosexism, and trans* oppression to be aware of these historical and contemporary complexities.

Feinberg (1996) asserts that the roots of these three forms of oppression can be found in historical shifts from agrarian and communal cultures to more feudal societies, in which men who owned property and the institutions that they created increasingly stigmatized and persecuted trans* people, LGBTQ people, and cisgender heterosexual women in order to consolidate and protect their interests. An important part of this process was invalidating and subordinating women and all people whose identities challenged the gender binary and superiority of cisgender, gender-conforming heterosexual men. Once these property-owning men ascended to power, religion, psychology, medicine, government, and other social institutions enforced social norms and laws that protected and reinforced their privileged status (Feinberg, 1996).

The United States feminist movement has its roots in the first Women's Rights Convention in Seneca Falls, New York, in 1848. In 1897, Dr. Magnus Hirschfield, a German homosexual (the language used at the time) founded the Scientific Humanitarian Committee, the first known homosexual rights organization. The first U.S. gay rights group, the Chicago Society for Human Rights, was founded by Henry Gerber in Chicago in 1924. Though trans* people's existence is documented throughout history in multiple cultures around the world, the 1990s are commonly recognized as the decade in which a visible and vibrant trans* rights movement emerged and separated from the earlier conceptions of trans* identity as a pathological condition under the control of medical experts (Feinberg, 1996).

Prior to these initial stirrings of liberation, women were essentially the property of their fathers and then husbands, with no legal rights separate from men they were associated with. It was legally and socially acceptable for men to beat their wives and to demand that they engage in marital sex. Rape in a marital relationship was not legally recognized. Lesbian, gay, bisexual, and trans* people were stigmatized alternatively as sinful spawns of Satan, depraved psychopaths, sex-crazed freaks, criminals, and threats to family and community. Women who defied the restrictions placed on them, and all lesbians, gay men, and trans* people, were subjected to medical experiments, medication, physical abuse, incarceration, and hospitalization—all with the goal of forcing them to conform to dominant sex, gender, and sexual expectations.

FEMINIST MOVEMENTS

Feminism, described as a movement to end sexism and sexist exploitation and to empower women, provided the conceptual lens for the 19th century women's rights advocates and early 20th century suffragists, the second-wave feminists as well as third-wave feminists fighting for women's rights, and against all forms of gender-based violence and exploitation in all spheres of life around the world. Historically, first-wave feminism is associated with 19th and early 20th century movements. The second wave of feminism began in the early 1960s, and the third wave of feminism is associated with contemporary movements to challenge patriarchy and sexism.

Wyoming was the first state to legalize women's right to vote in 1890, but it took twenty years of lobbying, led by political organizations like the National American Women's Suffrage Association, before women in the United States won the right to vote in 1920, with the passage of the 19th amendment to the U.S. Constitution. Though decidedly middle-class and white, the feminist movement's early leaders encouraged women to demand equality in the home and at work.

In the United States, Betty Freidan's book, *The Feminine Mystique* (1963), awakened the consciousness of white middle-class women all across the United States and spurred the organization of informal consciousness-raising groups, where (mostly white, presumed heterosexual) women met to challenge their subordinate relationship to men and to support each other in challenging the sexist status quo (Morgan, 1970). The National Organization for Women (NOW) was founded in 1966, and the U.S. Supreme Court struck down the final state law prohibiting abortion in 1967. Feminists saw the legalization of abortion as a key step in liberating women to control their bodies and their destinies in both public and private spheres. Building on these successes, women's rights organizations spearheaded efforts to pass the Equal Rights Amendment (ERA) in the U.S. House and Senate in 1971 and 1972. Unfortunately, in 1982, the amendment fell three states short of the 38 needed for passage.

Since the 1980s, the feminist movement has continued to focus on a broad range of issues. The latest wave of feminism began to grapple with issues of racism, classism and heterosexism in the movement's membership and goals. Feminist scholars, including many women of color and lesbians, challenged the concept of "universal womanhood" as social constructionism and postmodernism influenced and disrupted the white, heterosexual, middle-class paradigm that dominated the feminist movement of the second wave (Hooks, 2000; Smith, 2000; Spellman, 1988). In addition, feminists from all parts of the world began to work together to make connections among sexism, poverty, religion, and race to expand the complexity and reach of feminist aspirations for women's empowerment. As young feminists join the movement and make it their own, the destabilization of concepts such as "gender" and "feminine" challenges modern feminist thinking. The inclusion and acceptance of trans* women and their issues in feminist and lesbian organizations also constitutes a challenge to historical thinking about such basic ideas as who we include in our definitions of "woman." Just as some LGBTQ people have reclaimed epithets like "queer," some young feminist "grrls" reclaim terms like "slut" and "bitch" as ways to subvert commonly accepted sexist words and to strip them of their power to hurt or limit (Klein, 2011).

LESBIAN, GAY, AND BISEXUAL RIGHTS MOVEMENTS

Though the Chicago Society for Human Rights was the first gay rights organization in the United States, the homophile movement of the late 1940s and 1950s represented the most organized early efforts to change public consensus on homosexuals as sick and perverted. The homophile movement focused on political reform to decriminalize homosexuality by providing educational programs for medical experts. The goal was to increase tolerance of homosexuality and win the support of physicians and psychiatrists, who could be allies in efforts to stop the widespread persecution of homosexuals in the 1950s (Jagose, 1996). During the 1950s, homosexual men and women were stigmatized as communists and sexual predators, who threatened the foundations of Western civilization and American freedom. During the House Un-American Activity Committee hearings led by Senator Joseph McCarthy, government workers and others suspected of being communists or homosexuals were publicly discredited and their careers ruined as they were subjected to widespread discrimination. Deeply closeted men and women were arrested in police raids of gay bars and private homes, and their names were routinely published in local newspapers, which often resulted in loss of jobs and homes, estrangement from friends and family, as well as public ridicule.

Secret organizations like the Mattachine Society and Daughters of Bilitis played key roles in educational and political campaigns, as well as providing support for a largely closeted membership. Though open to women, the Mattachine Society was primarily a male organization and focused on issues of concern to homosexual men. The Daughters of Bilitis developed out of a need for an organization that focused on the needs of lesbians (D'Emilio, 1983). Though the Mattachine Society's original goals were much more in tune with later liberationist elements of the gay and lesbian rights movement, by the late 1950s they became much more conservative, focusing on increasing tolerance for homosexuals by transforming public attitudes (Jagose, 1996). Homophile organizations of this era often are characterized as "assimilationist" because of their efforts to encourage lesbians and gay men to adopt dress and mannerisms that conformed to traditional gender expectations of the time. These organizations rejected anyone who transgressed these gender norms, such as drag queens, butch lesbians, or other trans* identified people, who were often associated with the primarily working-class bar culture (Jagose, 1996)—in much the same way that feminist organizations of the 1960s and 1970s shunned lesbians out of fear that their visibility would distract from their mission of addressing concerns such as access to birth control, abortion rights, and equal pay.

Neither the Mattachine Society nor the Daughters of Bilitis achieved widespread public recognition or appeal to lesbians and gay men. Cultural perceptions of homosexuals during the 1950s and early 1960s as sick, perverted criminals were so deeply entrenched that public acknowledgment of one's homosexuality (often in news accounts of police raids on gay bars) almost always resulted in loss of employment, rejection by family, and/or commitment to an insane asylum. The American Psychiatric Association classified homosexuality as a mental illness until 1973.

In the 1960s, however, the emergence of the second wave of feminism, anti-Vietnam war protests, and a youth-based counter culture sparked challenges to prevailing gender and sexual norms (D'Emilio & Freedman, 1997). A shift toward a more liberationist/civil rights focus characterized new campus gay organizations and community activism, as the emerging lesbian and gay rights movement adopted some of the political strategies of the black civil rights and feminist movements of the 1960s. "Gay is Good" emerged as a slogan for the movement modeled after "Black is Beautiful," a slogan from the Black Liberation movement. The gay liberationist movement, in contrast to the homophile movement, challenged the status quo, celebrated difference, and encouraged pride in a distinct "gay" identity rather than assimilation into the mainstream and tolerance from heterosexuals (D'Emilio, 1983; Jagose, 1996).

In 1969, during a routine police raid on a gay bar in Greenwich Village, an angry crowd of primarily working class trans* people, lesbians, and gay men of color, including drag queens and butch lesbians, fought back. In an explosion of rage and frustration, bar patrons held police at bay for three days. The Stonewall rebellion is accepted as the event that triggered the birth of the modern lesbian and gay liberationist movement. However, it wasn't until the twentieth anniversary of Stonewall that the LGBT movement publicly celebrated the central role played by trans* working-class men and women and queers of color who sparked the rebellion in this pivotal historical moment in LGBTQ history.

The second wave of feminism, also emerging in the 1960s and 1970s, presented another challenge to traditional gender and sexual norms. The emergence of the feminist movement provided lesbians in the gay rights movement an alternative to male-dominated gay liberation organizations. Unfortunately, lesbians who participated in the early feminist movement were not welcomed with open arms by their heterosexual sisters (Abbott & Love, 1973). Lesbian feminists found their voices silenced and their needs subordinated to the needs of heterosexual cisgender feminists, who were afraid that an association with lesbianism would hurt the feminist cause and damage the reputation of feminist organizations.

By the early 1970s, fractures in the feminist movement and the gay rights movement developed as sub-groups within each movement demanded that their voices be heard. Many lesbians formed separatist communities in which both heterosexual women and all men were excluded, and members of the community worked to support and nurture each other in the face of homophobia from heterosexual feminists, sexism from gay men, and heterosexism in the larger culture (Faderman, 1991). Likewise, lesbians and gay men of color, working-class gay and lesbian people, trans* people, and bisexual people demanded recognition of their needs in lesbian and gay organizations, just as women of color and working-class women expressed their dissatisfaction with the middle-class white focus of mainstream feminist and lesbian organizations (Lorde, 1984; Moraga & Anzaldúa, 1983).

Some early gay, lesbian, and feminist writers understood the connections between gender and sexuality, and how rigid gender norms reinforced heterosexism and sexism (Jay & Young, 1992; Pharr, 1997). They called for challenging gender norms as well as sexuality norms in the service of liberation from sexism and heterosexism, and they called into question the categories of "heterosexual," "homosexual," "masculine," and "feminine" as constructions that enforce oppression.

Just as the needs of lesbians and women of color were not part of the agenda for the early feminist movement, the gay and lesbian rights movements of the 1970s did not address the needs of bisexual people. Many lesbians regarded bisexual women as "traitors" or "fence-sitters" who took advantage of heterosexual privilege. Other lesbians and gay men viewed bisexuality as a "phase" rather than an authentic identity (Hutchins & Kaahumanu, 1991). Lesbians who "changed teams" by being sexually involved with men were often regarded as traitors and shunned by lesbian friends. In response to this rejection and the failure of lesbian and gay organizations to meet their needs, a bisexual rights movement, related to but separate from the lesbian and gay rights movement, emerged in the 1980s. In reaction to this increasing bisexual visibility and voice, the names for many lesbian and gay organizations and pride marches were changed to incorporate bisexuals as recognized members of sexual minority communities.

The emergence of AIDS, which scientists called Gay Related Immune Disease (GRID), as a major health crisis among gay men in the early 1980s highlighted and intensified the stigmatization of homosexuality (Shilts, 1987). President Reagan did not mention AIDS publicly until 1987, despite the devastating effects of AIDS on an entire generation of gay men, intravenous drug users, women of color, and people who received contaminated blood transfusions. One positive outcome of addressing the AIDS crisis was a joining of lesbians and gay men, who worked together to care for their own community in the face of inaction from government and medical institutions. Political activism in the form of organizations like ACT UP, the AIDS Quilt Project, and the Lesbian Avengers demanded attention and action from silent legislators and health professionals.

TRANSGENDER RIGHTS MOVEMENT

Just as bisexuals created their own advocacy organizations in the early 1980s, the trans* rights movement gained visibility as separate from the lesbian, gay, and bisexual rights movement in the early 1990s (Feinberg, 1998). In the same ways that lesbians were often unacknowledged active participants in the early gay and feminist movements, trans* people were active in the early lesbian and gay rights movements, but they were often seen by lesbian, bisexual, and gay people as part of an unacceptable fringe group that made acceptance by the general public more difficult. Trans* people also raised uncomfortable questions about gender and sexual orientation that challenged long-held "truths" in not only the general population, but also in the feminist and lesbian, gay, and bisexual movements (Bornstein, 1994; Green, 2004). "Women Only" events, such as the annual Michigan Womyn's Music Festival, exclude trans* women since they are not "womyn born womyn." Women's organizations whose goals are to provide services to women or to challenge sexism also have struggled with how to include trans* women in their missions.

The existence and acknowledgment of trans* people challenges essentialist notions of bodies and identities, because trans* identities complicate the fixed binary notion of gender we are all socialized to believe as children and the "biology is destiny" mindset. One way this issue has played out is by forcing women's colleges to grapple with whether to admit trans* women and how to address the needs of students admitted as women who transition to a male identity after admission, all while maintaining a focus on their principles as an educational institution for women (Marine, 2011a; Troop, 2011). For example, in 2015, Mount Holyoke College publically announced a change in policy to admit transgender students and yet retain its commitment to its historic mission as a women's college. In their statement explaining their new policy, they recognize that the categorization of gender identity is not static nor independent on political and social ideologies:

> Just as early feminists argued that the reduction of women to their biological functions was a foundation for women's oppression, we must acknowledge that gender identity is

not reducible to the body. Instead, we must look at identity in terms of the external context in which the individual is situated. It is this positionality that biological and transwomen share, and it is this positionality that is relevant when women's colleges open their gates for those aspiring to live, learn, and thrive within a community of women.

(Mount Holyoke College website, https://www.mtholyoke.edu/policies/admission-transgender-students)

As an institution, Mount Holyoke utilizes positionality to make the connection between oppression and liberation.

As the trans* rights movement has matured, national organizations emerged to focus attention on trans* issues separate from lesbian, gay, and bisexual issues. Organizations like the Transgender Law Center and the National Center for Transgender Equality focus on education and advocacy for trans* civil rights for people of all gender identities and gender expressions. The emergence of a trans* rights movement separate from the lesbian, gay, and bisexual rights movements highlights the limitations of binary understandings of sex, gender, and sexuality, and challenges social justice educators to sharpen our awareness and understanding of these interrelated identity concepts and forms of oppression. The mainstream media has also increased public awareness of transgender people with the high-profile coverage of former Olympic gold medalist Caitlin Jenner's transition; and with the presence of LaVerne Cox, a trans* actor, in the public Netflix series, "Orange is the New Black."

Because the modern feminist movement, the lesbian and gay rights movement, the bisexual rights movement, and the trans* rights movement are all fairly recent developments (emerging over the last 50 years), each one continues to evolve in complexity and analytic sophistication as the dynamics of oppression that affect each group are clarified. In addition, each one is subjected to ongoing backlash from political, religious, and social groups, who contest every step toward social justice and equality taken by women, trans* people, and lesbian, gay, and bisexual people. Every advance in legal protection and change in social perspective is met with resistance from politicians and organizations whose interests are served by maintaining the status quo. Conservative religious and political groups have played an influential role in resisting such issues as abortion rights and equal pay for women, transgender rights and protection from violence, marriage equality for same-sex couples, and protection from discrimination based on sexual orientation in housing, immigration policy, and employment.

As in all social movements, language develops and changes along with a deepening understanding and analysis. Terms come into and go out of favor with different segments of each of the diverse communities that comprise the disadvantaged groups. Any attempt to hold fast to particular terms as "correct" or most "appropriate" is doomed to fail, as younger generations take on the struggles of older generations. Reclaiming such historically derogatory words as "queer," just as earlier generations of lesbians reclaimed "dyke," younger generations of LGBTQ people are claiming a future with a greater sense of empowerment to liberation and equality than their elders could have ever imagined. Younger generations of trans* people are not bound by sex and gender binaries that limited the experiences of their elders. Younger generations of LGBTQ people in the United States grow up in a changing social climate that has enabled many of them to identify themselves earlier, receive the support of their families and friends, become members of school Gay-Straight Alliance clubs, find support and information in a thriving online community, transition to live as the gender identity that is true for them, and envision a future in which they can legally marry the person they love.

As feminist and LGBTQ rights movements have evolved, it is apparent from their individual and collective histories that acknowledging interrelationships among them, and incorporating increasing complexity, strengthens each movement. Working in coalition to challenge the common dynamics of oppression that limit women and LGBTQ people increases the appeal and power each movement has when working on its own—or worse, fighting with each other for resources, public attention, and legal recognition. Despite differences in discrimination based on sexual orientation vs. discrimination based on gender identity or expression, lesbian, gay, bisexual, and trans* people often work in coalition based on an understanding of the interconnections among sexual orientation, gender identity, and gender expression, and how the struggle for social justice for each member of the LGBTQ community is enhanced by working in coalition. LGBTQ political organizations have changed their name in recognition of these interconnections. For example, the National Gay Task Force evolved into the National Gay and Lesbian Task Force, and is now the National LGBTQ Task Force. Feminist groups like the National Organization for Women include advocacy and programming to address the needs of trans*, lesbian, and bisexual women.

Sex, gender, gender identity, sexual orientation, and gender expression all interact in non-binary ways that both inform and "trouble" the categories upon which sexism, heterosexism, and transgender oppression depend. For example, health care professionals have had to adjust to lesbian patients who do not require birth control, which is a routine concern of most heterosexual women; or they have had to provide gynecological exams to trans* men or prostate exams to trans* women with penises. As Spade (2011) asserts, "A central endeavor of feminist, queer and trans* activists has been to dismantle the cultural ideologies, social practices, and legal norms that say that certain body parts determine gender identity and gendered social characteristics and roles" (p. 61).

CURRENT MANIFESTATIONS OF SEXISM, HETEROSEXISM, AND TRANS* OPPRESSION

As is characteristic of all forms of oppression, sexism, heterosexism, and trans* oppression operate at the individual, institutional, and cultural levels to confer normality and superiority on privileged social groups, and to assign abnormality and inferiority to disadvantaged groups. The brief historical overview of the activism and advocacy of the feminist, LGBTQ, and trans* liberation movements described in the previous section of this chapter illustrates how challenges to sexism, heterosexism and trans* oppression have resulted in changes at the individual, institutional, and cultural levels toward liberation for cisgender women, LGBTQ people, and trans* people. However, as is characteristic of all manifestations of oppression, challenges remain as systems of oppression, rather than completely disappear, often reshape into more subtle or nuanced forms. This section will describe some of these current manifestations of oppression and how sexism, heterosexism, and trans* oppression persist.

All three systems of oppression highlighted in this chapter share common elements of oppression (Young, 1990). Of these common elements of oppression, violence and discrimination are particularly salient social mechanisms that support and reinforce sexism, heterosexism, and trans* oppression.

VIOLENCE

Violence against women, lesbian, gay, bisexual people, and trans* people is well documented in United Nations and U.S. government statistics. According to the United Nations, 35% of women worldwide have experienced either physical or sexual violence (World

Health Organization, 2013). In the United States, 83% of girls aged 12–16 have experienced some form of sexual harassment in public schools (Hill & Kearl, 2011). Sexual violence against women exercised as an expression of male power and dominance, as well as the growth in a lucrative sex slavery industry that targets young girls and women, are worldwide problems reflecting the perspective that women are commodities to be controlled or sold for the pleasure of men. National statistics on the number of rapes on U.S. college campuses, and the often inadequate response to rape by school administrators and community leaders, illustrate how deeply sexual violence against women is embedded in U.S. culture (U.S. Department of Education, 2011).

The 2014 mass shooting at the University of California-Santa Barbara was carried out by a young man as an act of retribution against all women because he was denied what he believed was his right to sex from women, and his hatred of other men who he believed were receiving their rightful share of sexual attention from women (Jaschik, 2014). An otherwise "average" young man, the killer was fueled by a mix of patriarchal and misogynist beliefs that were reinforced on websites promoting "men's rights" as a response to feminism. Violence against women in relationships with men is also widespread, and the legal system response has failed to adequately protect women from the murderous rage of men who fear losing control over and sexual access to the women in their lives. Commonly used slurs like "slut," "bitch," "whore," and other derogatory terms dehumanize girls and women, and reduce them to sexual objects for boys and men to evaluate, ridicule, or conquer.

The pervasive portrayal of women as sex objects, and the extreme violence against women designed into video games, are intended to appeal to the young male-dominated "gamer" culture. When women, who are a marginalized part of video game culture, have protested or critiqued this portrayal, they have been subjected to terrifying and relentless anonymous online threats of rape and other violence that have caused them to leave their homes (Chu, 2014).

Viewed from a global perspective, cultural and religious beliefs often justify the murder, rape, and mutilation of women as a way to keep them under the control of fathers, husbands, and brothers. Many conservative religions are based in a strict patriarchal interpretation of the proper place and role of women as subordinate to men. Women who defy these cultural or religious norms are often subjected to state-sanctioned violence or death. The pervasiveness of these religious and cultural beliefs worldwide is a major obstacle to women seeking liberation, equality, and self-determination.

Violence plays a similar role in the oppression of lesbian, gay, bisexual, and trans* people. Though several (primarily North American and European) countries have enacted laws to protect LGBTQ people from discrimination, statistics demonstrate that violence targeting LGBTQ people is still commonplace, even in countries where nondiscrimination laws include protections based on sexual orientation or gender identity. According to the National Coalition of Anti-Violence Programs (NCAVP), overall reports of anti-LGBTQ violence in the United States remained steady in 2012 despite some progress in LGBTQ civil and marriage rights. Trans* women, LGBTQ people of color, and gay men face the most severe violence: 73% of anti-LGBTQ homicides victims in 2012 were people of color (NCAVP, 2013). The Gay Lesbian Straight Education Network (GLSEN)'s 2011 National School Climate Survey found that LGBTQ youth experience high levels of violence at the hands of their classmates, and that this violence is often ignored by adults in the school (Kosciw, Greytak, Bartkiewicz, Boesen, & Palmer, 2012). Over 60% of LGBTQ students felt unsafe in school because of their sexual orientation. For trans* youth, the figure was 44%. Over 80% of LGBTQ students reported being verbally harassed or threatened because of their sexual orientation, and 64% reported harassment due to their gender expression. Among LGBTQ students, 38% were pushed and 27% were physically harassed because of their sexual orientation or gender expression. Finally, the GLSEN report found that 18% and 12% of LGBTQ students were physically assaulted (kicked or injured with a weapon) because of their sexual orientation or gender expression.

Persistent bullying and harassment of young people who are, or who are perceived to be gay, lesbian, bisexual, or trans* by their peers (and sometimes their teachers) in schools, has prompted concerns that some of these young people may commit suicide rather than face daily violence and ridicule from classmates and the lack of response from teachers or other adults in the school. Though no single factor places young people at risk of being bullied, young people who are perceived to be lesbian, gay, bisexual, or trans* are frequently identified as targets (Kosciw, Greytak, Bartkiewicz, Boesen, & Palmer, 2012).

Many LGBTQ youth also face hostility and violence from their families. Often justified on the basis of religious beliefs about LGBTQ people, some parents commit children to discredited psychiatric treatment, "reparative therapy," or religious indoctrination in an attempt to make their sexual orientation or gender identity and expression conform to heterosexual and cisgender norms. When parents perpetuate this kind of violence on their own children's self-affirmed identities, the result is too often a legacy of self-hatred or suicide.

Fueled by extreme anti-LGBTQ prejudice coupled with legal sanctions against homosexuality, including imprisonment and death, violence against LGBTQ people in the Middle East, Eastern Europe, and several African nations, notably Zimbabwe, Uganda and Nigeria, is a constant threat—not only from the community and family members, but from the police as well. Russia's anti-gay culture was revealed in 2014 with the passage of a law prohibiting gay "propaganda" just prior to the Sochi Olympics. Though the law was promoted as a way to protect minors, the effect of the law was to unleash violent attacks on LGBTQ people by the police as well as other private citizens.

Violence toward those who challenge patriarchal beliefs about heterosexual cisgender male privilege and the subordination of women and LGBTQ people is dependent on misogyny and the vilification of LGBTQ people. Anti-LGBTQ and anti-woman epithets are employed as warnings to anyone who violates gender and sexuality norms, regardless of their actual identities. Gay men or men perceived to be gay based on their gender expression are often ridiculed as feminine, or demeaned as woman-like in a conflation of misogyny and homophobia. Similarly, women who challenge male privilege and power are often called lesbians as a way to marginalize and intimidate them. As an acknowledgment of this relationship, Suzanne Pharr (1997) called homophobia a weapon of sexism.

Among young people, being called a faggot, slut, or lezzy is deployed as a social control mechanism to let the targeted youth know she or he is violating gender or sexual expectations. As long as LGBTQ people are stigmatized as inferior, unnatural, or disturbed, homophobia, biphobia, and transphobia (the fear and hatred of lesbian, gay, bisexual, and trans* people, respectively) are effective tools to enforce traditional power relationships between men and women, heterosexuals, and LGBQ people, and between cisgender and trans* people. The message sent by this violence is that women must not challenge men's control over them; and lesbians, gay men, bisexual people, and trans* people must not challenge traditional sexual and gender binaries that privilege cisgender heterosexual men.

DISCRIMINATION

Women worldwide face marginalization (a manifestation of oppression) in almost every major social institution. Even in North America and Western Europe, where women enjoy more equal treatment than in many other parts of the world, issues of family and children are often marginalized as "women's issues" as if they are of no concern to men. Male legislators and jurists in the United States routinely pass and affirm laws restricting the rights of women to determine their own health care needs, particularly as they relate to reproductive rights. Legislated restrictions that are deemed unnecessary by most medical authorities on abortion clinics in Texas are expected to force the closure of 80% of the clinics performing abortions in the state (Deprez, 2015). Women's health concerns receive less attention in research, and male physicians often view women's health concerns as less serious than men's concerns (Risberg, Johansson, & Hamberg, 2009). National political leaders often reject legislation benefiting women and families, particularly poor and immigrant women, as unearned handouts that drain resources for more deserving women (Tolleson-Rinehart & Josephson, 2005).

LGBTQ people are marginalized by claims that they are seeking "special rights" or are undermining traditional (heterosexual) families. Anti-LGBTQ advocacy groups claim that being LGBTQ is comparable to being an alcoholic or drug abuser, whose addictive behaviors can be cured with prayer, a change of friends, or condemnation and shunning (Frank, 2015). Parents of LGBTQ children are taught to reject their sons' and daughters' self-definitions in order to save them or to make them "normal." Trans* women and men are routinely marginalized in the media as not real women or men, and who are acting against nature in asserting their trans* identities. Schools refuse to acknowledge trans* students' insistence that their gender identity or gender expression be accepted, often forcing them to use bathrooms according to their gender assigned at birth and refusing to respect their right to be addressed by their chosen name and pronouns. Several state government organizations refuse to change official identity documents, such as driver's licenses or birth certificates, to reflect a trans* person's gender identity.

Current statistics in the United States show that discrimination against cisgender heterosexual women and LGBTQ people is a persistent effect of sexism, heterosexism, and trans* oppression. Even a casual look at who occupies leadership positions in all major institutions reveals a consistent pattern of (white) heterosexual male dominance (Warner, 2014). Cisgender gender-conforming heterosexual men dominate leadership in government, religion, business, medicine, education, health care, and sports organizations, to name a few. According to the American Association of University Women (AAUW, 2014) the gender gap in wages earned by women and men has remained at a constant 77% for the last decade, with the gap being even wider for women of color. The gap holds steady across all occupations and in every state (AAUW, 2014.) Employment and income inequality also impact trans* people. In one study, trans* people were nearly four times more likely to have a household income of less than $10,000/year as compared to the general population (Grant, Mottet, Tanis, Harrison, Herman, & Keisling, 2011).

The ERA, a proposed amendment to the United State Constitution that would have mandated equal rights for women, failed to be ratified in the necessary 38 states by the 1982 deadline, and efforts to revive the ERA since then have been unsuccessful. As of 2015, 18 states and the District of Columbia outlaw discrimination in employment and/or public accommodations based on sexual orientation and gender identity/expression. Three more states ban discrimination based on sexual orientation. No federal non-discrimination law includes sexual orientation or gender identity/expression, though President Obama issued an executive order in 2014 banning discrimination based on sexual orientation and gender identity/expression in the federal government and with all federal contractors. This means it is permissible to discriminate on the basis of sexual orientation in 29 states and on the basis of gender identity/expression in 32 states.

A troubling trend surfaced in 2014 that highlights the role that religion plays in perpetuating sexism, heterosexism, and trans* oppression. Laws are being proposed that enable private businesses or educational institutions to obtain exemptions from LGBTQ non-discrimination laws, executive orders, or health care requirements to provide access to birth control or abortion services based on the religious beliefs of business owners or the faith-based tenets of the institution. An effort to pass a law exempting private businesses from laws requiring that they serve LGBT people failed in Arizona, but such a law passed in Mississippi. Similar laws have been introduced in several other states.

In 2014, the U.S. Supreme Court ruled that some private corporations were exempt from providing access to birth control or abortion services, as required in the Affordable Health Care Law, based on the religious beliefs of the owners (Liptak, 2014). These exemptions apply to individuals in the public and private sectors by giving them the right to opt out of providing services to LGBTQ people and women based on their religious beliefs.

In June 2015, the Supreme Court, in a landmark 5–4 decision, ruled that it is a constitutional violation of due process and the equal protection clause to deny same-sex couples the right to marry. This decision struck down the remaining marriage bans in twenty-three states, making same-sex marriage legal in all fifty states. There is no doubt that this victory for LGBT people will continue to be contested by opponents seeking exemption from abiding by the decision, just as they have continued to contest abortion rights by restricting access to abortion through state-by-state legislation, even though abortion is legal in all states. The hostility toward legal protections from discrimination for women and LGBTQ people reflects an enduring resistance to challenging deeply rooted prejudices and power imbalances. Violence and discrimination, as evidenced by the examples cited here, are used effectively to enforce sexism, heterosexism, and trans* oppression. Supported by patriarchy, misogyny, biological determinism, and genderism, these interrelated oppressions serve the interests of and privilege cisgender, gender-conforming heterosexual men, and subordinate all women, lesbian, gay, bisexual, and trans* people.

These common themes of subordination link heterosexism, sexism, and trans* oppression and illustrate why it is difficult to address them effectively as single issues. Violence and discrimination affect the ability of all members of disadvantaged groups to achieve self-determination, access to resources, and social power. A woman's right to choose when or whether to have children; a trans* person's access to affirmative medical services; and a lesbian, bisexual person, or gay man's ability to provide a spouse with medical coverage are all part of the challenge to the overarching dominance of male cisgender heterosexual privilege and power.

SEXISM, HETEROSEXISM, AND TRANS* OPPRESSION INTEGRATED DESIGN

The design presented in this chapter aims to provide participants with an introductory overview and understanding of the interrelationship of sexism, heterosexism, and trans* oppression. (Single-issue workshops on sexism, heterosexism, and trans* oppression are available on the associated website.) This presupposes familiarity with the SJE core concepts, including the conceptual frameworks about oppression described in Chapters 1 and 4 of this volume. We focus on helping participants develop an historical and conceptual understanding of sexism, heterosexism, and trans* oppression at the individual, institutional, and cultural levels. We also include possibilities for taking action and challenging sexism, heterosexism, and trans* oppression in our personal lives, institutions, and communities.

This design, like other designs in this volume, uses four quadrants as a way to sequence learning goals, key concepts, and activities. The quadrants generally follow the sequence "What? So what? Now what?" We use the four-quadrant design model because it helps us keep the learning sequence in focus. It can be easily adapted to other modalities, such as short workshops or semester-long courses. After the overview of the four quadrants of the design, there are learning objectives and core concepts specific to each of the four quadrants, as well as brief descriptors of the activities. Actual instructions, facilitation notes, and handouts for each of these activities can be found on the Integrated Approach to Sexism, Heterosexism, and Trans* Oppression website that accompanies this volume. The chapter closes with a general discussion of pedagogical, design, and facilitation issues that we have found to be specific to teaching about sexism, heterosexism, and trans* oppression from an integrated perspective.

Overview of the Sexism, Heterosexism, and Trans* Oppression Integrated Design

Quadrant 1: Connecting to Self and Shared Language
Total Time: 3.5 hours

1. Introductions (15 min)
2. Agenda & Goals (15 min)
3. Guiding Assumptions (15 min)
4. Developing Guidelines (15 min)
5. Icebreaker: Concentric Circles (15 min)
6. Exploring Language (75 min)
7. Gender Socialization (60 min)

Quadrant 2: Exploring Intersections & Privilege
Total Time: 3.5 hours

1. Identifying Personal Identities Matrix (60 min)
2. Identifying Experiences of Privilege and Disadvantage (80 min)
3. Noticing Assumptions about Gender and Sexual Orientation (60 min)
4. Closing Activity and Feedback (15 min)

Quadrant 3: Histories and Institutional Oppression
Total Time: 2.5 hours

1. Examining Historical Roots (60 min)
2. Identifying Institutional Oppression (75 min)
3. Free Write (10 min)
4. Closing

Quadrant 4: Possibilities for Creating Change
Total Time: 3.5 hours

1. Reflecting on Taking Action (30 min)
2. Developing Best Practices and Strategies for Creating Change (75 min)
3. Action Planning: Individual (40 min)
4. Action Planning: Broader Levels (50 min)
5. Closing Activity for an Integrated Design to Sexism, Heterosexism, and Trans* Oppression (20 min)

Overall Goals:

- To understand the distinctions and interlocking dynamics of sexism, heterosexism, and trans* oppression
- To reflect on learned behaviors and perspectives that contribute to our constructions of sex, gender, and sexuality identities
- To explore the multiplicity of identities and experiences that are negatively impacted by sexism, heterosexism, and trans* oppression
- To identify manifestations of heterosexism, sexism, and trans* oppressions
- To provide opportunities to explore how other social identities intersect and impact sexism, heterosexism, and trans* oppression
- To develop strategies and tactics individually, institutionally, and systemically that will interrupt heterosexism, sexism, and trans* oppression
- To envision a liberatory future free of sexism, heterosexism, and trans* oppression

QUADRANT 1: CONNECTING TO SELF AND SHARED LANGUAGE

Learning Outcomes:
- To help participants get to know each other
- To review the objectives of the course
- To create an environment for shared communication

- To reflect on gender and sexuality in broad and specific activities
- To develop a shared language to use throughout the course/workshop

1. Introductions (15 min)
   This activity allows facilitators and participants to share their name and pronoun to ensure each person is recognized for their name and gender.
2. Agenda and Goals (15 min)
   This activity provides time to review the design and the goals of the design, and to allow participants to reflect on their personal goals and group goals.
3. Guiding Assumptions (15 min)
   Take time to review the guiding assumptions located earlier in the chapter and on the website. Ask participants if they need any clarifications.
4. Developing Participation Guidelines (15 min)
   An integral part of creating an effective learning environment for individuals to reflect, share, and discuss their social identities requires mutually agreed-upon guidelines.
5. Icebreaker: Concentric Circles (15 min)
   This activity provides participants with a series of questions to explore with a partner for a short period of time, and to reflect on their own thoughts, ideas, and beliefs about their gender, sexual orientation, and allyship.
6. Exploring Language (75 min)
   This activity is designed to allow all participants to understand the complexities, nuances, and diversity in language about gender, sexual orientation, and trans* identities.
7. Gender Socialization (60 min)
   This activity guides participants through their gender and sexual orientation socialization processes to examine early memories, current influences, and identity groups.

QUADRANT 2: EXPLORING INTERSECTIONS AND PRIVILEGE

In this quadrant of the design, participants will continue the reflection process and identify privileges related to sexism, heterosexism, and trans* oppression.

1. Identifying Personal Identities Matrix (45 min)
   This activity allows participants to reflect on their social identities of sex, gender identity, gender expression, and sexual orientation, and encourages them to consider how they experience privilege and oppression based on those identities.
2. Identifying Experiences of Privilege and Disadvantage (60 min)
   This activity will give participants opportunities to identify how sexism, heterosexism, and trans* oppression manifest in privilege and disadvantage. The activity allows for participants to work from their own identities or to be assigned to identities to consider how privilege and disadvantage manifest.
3. Noticing Assumptions about Gender and Sexual Orientation (60 min)
   This activity allows participants to consider their own day-to-day assumptions of gender and sexual orientation, as well as their perception of peer opinions.
4. Closing Activity and Feedback (15 min)
   This activity provides participants with an opportunity to share their thoughts about their experience and to hear the thoughts of others.

QUADRANT 3: HISTORIES AND INSTITUTIONS

1. Examining Historical Roots of Sexism, Heterosexism, and Trans* Oppression (60 min)
   In this activity, participants will examine the historical roots of contemporary sexism, heterosexism, and trans* oppression.

2. Identifying Institutional Oppression (75 min)
   This activity will provide participants with an opportunity to consider the intersections of multiple social identities and the navigation of institutions.
3. Free Write (10 min)
   A free write allows participants to take time to write out their reflections, feelings, questions, and thoughts.
4. Closing

QUADRANT 4: POSSIBILITIES FOR CREATING CHANGE

1. Reflecting on Taking Action (30 min)
   This activity allows participants to consider a time when they took action to stop heterosexism, heterosexism, and/or trans* oppression, or a time when they wanted to take action but did not.
2. Developing Best Practices and Strategies for Creating Change (75 min)
   This activity will allow participant to use their prior and gained knowledge to develop a list of actions to create change that will end sexism, heterosexism, and trans* oppression.
3. Action Planning: Individual Level (40 min)
   In this activity, participants will engage in individual/personal action planning to consider ways to eliminate sexism, heterosexism, and trans* oppression.
4. Action Planning: Broader Levels (50 min)
   This activity invites participants to consider action within a specific context, and how to overcome barriers that make change difficult.
5. Closing Activity for an Integrated Design to Sexism, Heterosexism, and Trans* Oppression (20 min)
   This activity is an opportunity for participants to reflect on their experience in the workshop.

PEDAGOGICAL DESIGN AND FACILITATION ISSUES FOR TEACHING SEXISM, HETEROSEXISM, AND TRANS* OPPRESSION FROM AN INTEGRATED PERSPECTIVE

An integrated approach to teaching about sexism, heterosexism, and trans* oppression requires attention to several aspects of design and facilitation. First and most important is the need for facilitators to prepare themselves adequately on all three topics individually, as well as on intersecting oppressions that affect participants differently according to their individual identity profiles. Prior to leading an integrated educational session on sexism, heterosexism, and trans* oppression, facilitators need to read, discuss, and understand the nuances of how these related forms of oppression interact to affect lived experiences, not only for participants in classes or workshops, but for themselves.

Many social justice educators, particularly novices, are more knowledgeable about some forms of oppression than others, whether through their own personal experience and awareness or through intentional study and self-education. If a facilitator has more experience, comfort, and knowledge leading sexism classes, for example, they need to conduct some intensive research and think about heterosexism and trans* oppression, and how they intersect with each other and sexism, prior to designing an integrated educational experience. Because participants will also bring differences in awareness of and knowledge about these three forms of oppression to the class, facilitators need to design activities that build on what participants know about one or two of these topics to help them understand the other topics they are less aware of and knowledgeable about. This awareness builds a foundation for understanding how all three forms of oppression affect each other simultaneously—a much more complex task.

Other facilitation issues to attend to include the following:

1. The use of caucus groups: Forming "affinity" groups by gender or sexual orientation should avoid forcing participants to choose groups based on binary assumptions about gender identity and sexual orientation that will exclude people whose identities challenge these binaries. Participants who are genderqueer, bisexual, asexual, and other identities that challenge gender and sexual orientation binaries may feel excluded or discounted when asked to choose a group that does not represent their experience. An option to consider is to encourage the participants to identify the groups for which they feel an affinity to caucus. The first task in these groups might be to identify their unifying core, which in itself can be an interesting and illuminating conversation.

2. When creating caucus groups, avoid providing an "other" category for anyone who does not experience their identities on a binary from male to female, gay to straight, or cisgender to transgender, as this "other" category is equally marginalizing.

3. An integrated approach also challenges facilitators to create designs and monitor interactions so that the particular issues of privilege and disadvantage experienced by all participants are equally recognized and addressed. For example, it is equally important for trans* men to explore the privilege they may experience as men at the same time that they are targeted by trans* oppression.

4. Facilitators should also check their designs and monitor their facilitation to make sure that all three forms of oppression are given equal time in activities, processing questions, and discussions. This is particularly important when facilitators know that they feel more comfortable with and have more knowledge about one topic (sexism, for example) than another topic (trans* oppression, for example).

5. An integrated approach offers an opportunity to challenge binary thinking in relationship to sexual relationships. When participants' definitions of men and women are reorganized to include trans* people, and gender identity is disconnected from biology, then the typical labels we use to describe and understand sexual orientations are challenged. This can be disorienting to some participants, and it is prudent to make sure that enough time is planned so that they have time to make sense of these new concepts of identity.

6. Because an integrated approach challenges so many dominant conceptions of sex, gender, and sexual orientation at the same time, it is especially important to provide participants with the time to process and reflect on their confusion or resistance. Rather than leading several activities, plan to do fewer activities with more time for processing, reflecting, and asking questions.

7. With an integrated approach, it is more likely that most participants will have the opportunity to explore both privilege and disadvantage based on sex, gender, or sexual orientation. Take advantage of these opportunities to show how almost everyone can use these experiences to build a bridge to better understanding of other forms of oppression. For example, simultaneously holding one's privilege as a cisgender man and one's disadvantage as gay is an opportunity to better understand the complexities of oppression as a lived experience.

8. An integrated approach requires that facilitators be sensitive to the ways that we can fall into the binaries of privilege and disadvantage when using a single-issue approach. Asking participants to simultaneously think about their sex, gender, and sexual orientation in relationship to privilege and disadvantage invites a deeper exploration of

lived experiences, but it also calls for more complicated discussion questions that can lead participants to this realization. Take time to carefully plan processing questions to draw out these complexities.

9. Explore a variety of topics, such as relationship violence, employment discrimination, and civil rights laws, as anchor points for discussions about how sexism, heterosexism and trans* oppression are manifested in relationship to each of these topics, and as a way to highlight the varying degrees of privilege and disadvantage that participants experience depending on their identity profiles.

10. Welcome all self-affirmed descriptions of sex, gender, and sexual orientation that participants bring to the class. One of the important learning opportunities for facilitators and participants in an integrated approach is to recognize how the dominant discourse limits and legitimizes categories of identity in order to confer privilege on some and disadvantage others. This practice also encourages all participants to bring their authentic experience to the discussion.

Note

* We ask that those who cite this work always acknowledge by name all of the authors listed rather than either only citing the first author or using "et al." to indicate coauthors. All collaborated on the conceptualization, development, and writing of this chapter.

References

Abbott, S., & Love, B. (1973). *Sappho was a right-on woman: A liberated view of lesbianism*. New York: Stein & Day.

Altman, D. (1973). *Homosexual: Oppression and liberation*. New York: Avon.

American Association of University Women (AAUW). (2014). *The simple truth about the gender pay gap*. Washington, DC: AAUW. Retrieved from http://www.aauw.org/research/the-simple-truth-about-the-gender-pay-gap/

Aultman, B. (2014). Cisgender. *TSQ: Transgender Studies Quarterly*, *1*(1–2), 61–62.

Berger, P. L., & Luckmann, T. (1966). *The social construction of reality: A treatise in the sociology of knowledge*. Garden City, NY: Anchor.

Bilodeau, B. (2009). *Genderism: Transgender students, binary systems, and higher education*. Saarbrucken, Germany: VDM Verlag.

Blackwood, E. (1997). Native American genders and sexualities: Beyond anthropological models and misrepresentations. In S. E. Jacobs, W. Thomas and S. Lang (Eds.), *Two-spirit people: Native American gender identity, sexuality and spirituality* (pp. 284–294). Urbana-Champaign: University of Illinois Press.

Bornstein, K. (1994). *Gender outlaw: On men, women, and the rest of us*. New York: First Vintage Books.

Browne, K. (2004). Genderism and the bathroom problem: (Re) materializing sexed sites, (re) creating sexed bodies. *Gender, Place and Culture*, *11*(3), 331–346.

Chase, C. (2012). Hermaphrodites with attitude: Mapping the emergence of intersex political activism. In S. Stryker & S. Whittle (Eds.), *The transgender studies reader* (pp. 300–314). New York: Routledge.

Chu, A. (2014, May 27). Your princess is in another castle: Misogyny, entitlement, and nerds. *The Daily Beast*. Retrieved from http://www.thedailybeast.com/articles/2014/05/27/your-princess-is-in-another-castle-misogyny-entitlement-and-nerds.html

Clack, B. (1999). *Misogyny in the western philosophical tradition: A reader* (pp. 95–24). New York: Routledge.

DeCecco, J., & Parker, D. (1995). The biology of homosexuality: Sexual orientation or sexual preference? *Journal of Homosexuality*, *28*(1-2), 1–28.

D'Emilio, J. (1983). *Sexual politics, sexual communities: The making of a homosexual rights minority in the United States, 1940–1970*. Chicago: University of Chicago Press.

D'Emilio, J., & Freedman, E. (1997). *Intimate matters: A history of sexuality in America*. New York: Harper & Row.

Deprez, E. (2015). The vanishing U.S. abortion clinic. *Bloomberg Quick Take*. Retrieved from http://www.bloombergview.com/quicktake/abortion-and-the-decline-of-clinics

Ekins, R., & King, D. (2006). *The transgender phenomenon*. Thousand Oaks, CA: Sage.

Enke, A. F. (2012). The education of little cis: Cisgender and the discipline of opposing bodies. In A. F. Enke (Ed.), *Transfeminist perspectives in and beyond transgender and gender studies* (pp. 60–77). Philadelphia: Temple University Press.

Faderman, L. (1991). *Odd girls and twilight lovers: A history of lesbian life in twentieth century America*. New York: Columbia University Press.

Fausto-Sterling, A. (2000). *Sexing the body: Gender politics and the construction of sexuality*. New York: Basic.

Feinberg, L. (1996). *Transgender warriors: Making history from Joan of Arc to Dennis Rodman*. Boston: Beacon Press.

Feinberg, L. (1998). *Trans liberation: Beyond pink and blue*. Boston: Beacon Press.

Frank, N. (2015). Can gays turn straight? What the evidence says about "ex-gay" therapy. *Slate*. Retrieved from http://www.slate.com/blogs/outward/2015/04/20/can_gays_and_bis_turn_straight_what_the_evidence_says_about_ex_gay_therapy.html

Gilmore, D. (2007). *Misogyny: The male malady*. Philadelphia: University of Pennsylvania Press.

Grant, J. M., Mottet, L. A., Tanis, J., Harrison, J., Herman, J. L., & Keisling, M. (2011). *Injustice at every turn: A report of the National Transgender Discrimination Survey*. Washington, DC: National Center for Transgender Equality and National Gay and Lesbian Task Force.

Green, J. (2004). *Becoming a visible man*. Nashville: Vanderbilt University Press.

Harrison, J., Grant, J., & Herman, J. L. (2012). A gender not listed here: Genderqueers, gender rebels, and otherwise in the National Transgender Discrimination Survey. *LGBTQ Public Policy Journal at the Harvard Kennedy School, 2*(1).

Hill, C., & Kearl, H. (2011). *Crossing the line: Sexual harassment at school*. Washington, DC: American Association of University Women.

Hill, D. B., & Willoughby, B. L. B. (2005). The development and validation of the genderism and transphobia scale. *Sex Roles, 53*(7/8), 531–544.

Hird, M. J. (2000). Gender's nature: Intersexuality, transsexualism, and the "sex"/"gender" binary. *Feminist Theory, 1*(3), 347–364.

Holland, J. (2006). *Misogyny: The world's oldest prejudice*. New York: Avalon Publishing Group.

Hooks, B. (2000). *Feminist theory: From margin to center*. Boston: South End Press.

Hutchins, L., & Kaahumanu, L. (Eds.). (1991). *Bi any other name: Bisexual people speak out*. Boston: Alyson.

Jagose, A. (1996). *Queer theory: An introduction*. New York: New York University Press.

Jaschik, S. (2014, May 27). Deadly rampage. *Inside Higher Ed*. Retrieved from https://www.insidehighered.com/news/2014/05/27/uc-santa-barbara-students-killed-shooting-rampage

Jay, K., & Young, A. (Eds.). (1992). *Out of the closets: Voices of gay liberation*. London: Gay Men's Press.

Jeffries, S., & Gottschalk, L. (2014). *Gender hurts: A feminist analysis of the politics of transgenderism*. New York: Routledge.

Johnson, A. (1997). *The gender knot: Unraveling our patriarchal legacy*. Philadelphia: Temple University Press.

Johnson, A. (2006). *Privilege, power and difference*. New York: McGraw-Hill.

Johnson, J. R. (2013). Cisgender privilege, intersectionality, and the criminalization of CeCe McDonald: Why intercultural communication needs transgender studies. *Journal of International and Intercultural Communication, 6*(2), 135–144.

Katz, J. (1995). *The invention of heterosexuality*. New York: Dutton.

Kessler, S. (1998). *Lessons from the intersexed*. New Brunswick, NJ: Rutgers University Press.

Kessler, S. J., & McKenna, W. (1978). *Gender: An ethnomethodological approach*. Chicago: Chicago University Press.

Killermann, S. (2012). What does the asterisk in "trans*" stand for? [Weblog post]. *It's Pronounced Metrosexual*. Retrieved from http://itspronouncedmetrosexual.com/2012/05/what-does-the-asterisk-in-trans-stand-for/

Klein, M. (2011, May 20). To reclaim slut or not to reclaim slut: Is that the question? [Blog] *Ms. Magazine*. Retrieved from http://msmagazine.com/blog/2011/05/20/to-reclaim-slut-or-not-to-reclaim-slut-is-that-the-question/

Kosciw, J. G., Greytak, E. A., Bartkiewicz, M. J., Boesen, M. J., & Palmer, N. A. (2012). *The 2011 National School Climate Survey: The experiences of lesbian, gay, bisexual and transgender youth in our nation's schools*. New York: GLSEN. Retrieved from http://glsen.org/sites/default/files/2011%20National%20School%20Climate%20Survey%20Full%20Report.pdf

Lewontin, R., Rose, S., & Kamin, L. (1984). *Not in our genes: Biology, ideology and human nature.* New York: Pantheon Books.

Liptak, A. (2104, Jun. 14). Supreme Court rejects contraceptives mandate for some corporations. *The New York Times.* Retrieved from http://www.nytimes.com/2014/07/01/us/hobby-lobby-case-supreme-court-contraception.html?_r=0

Lorber, J. (1996). Beyond the binaries: Depolarizing the categories of sex, sexuality, and gender. *Sociological Inquiry, 66*(2), 143–159.

Lorde, A. (1984). *Sister outsider.* Trumansburg, NY: Crossing Press.

Marine, S. B. (2011a). Our college is changing: Women's college student affairs administrators and transgender students. *Journal of Homosexuality, 58*(9), 1165–1186.

Marine, S. B. (2011b). Stonewall's legacy: Bisexual, gay, lesbian, and transgender students in higher education. In K. Ward & L. E. Wolf-Wendel (Eds.), *ASHE Higher Education Report* (Vol. 37, No. 4). San Francisco: Wiley.

Messerschmidt, J. W. (2009). Goodbye to the sex-gender distinction, hello to embodied gender. In A. L. Ferber, K. Holcomb, & T. Wentling (Eds.), *Sex, gender and sexuality: The new basics, an anthology* (pp. 71–88). New York: Oxford University Press.

Meyer, W., III, Bockting, W. O., Cohen-Kettenis, P., Coleman, E., DiCeglie, D., Devor, H., Gooren, L., Hage, J. J., Kirk, S., Kuiper, B., Laub, D., Lawrence, A., Menard, Y., Monstrey, S., Patton, J., Schaefer, L., Webb, A., & Wheeler, C. C. (2001). The Harry Benjamin International Gender Dysphoria Association's Standards of Care for Gender Identity Disorders (6th ver.). Retrieved from http://www.wpath.org/documents2/socv6.pdf.http://www.wpath.org/documents2/socv6.pdf

Mogul, J. L., Ritchie, A. J., & Whitlock, K. (2011). *Queer (in)justice: The criminalization of LGBT people in the United States.* Boston: Beacon Press.

Moraga, C., & Anzaldúa, G. (Eds.). (1983). *This bridge called my back: Writings by radical women of color.* New York: Kitchen Table/Women of Color Press.

Morgan, R. (Ed.). (1970). *Sisterhood is powerful.* New York: Random House.

Mustanski, B., Chivers, M., & Bailey, M. (2002). A critical review of recent biological research on human sexual orientation. *Annual Review of Sex Research, 13*(1), 89–100.

Nanda, S. (2014). *Gender diversity: Crosscultural variations* (2nd ed.). Long Grove, IL: Waveland Press.

National Coalition of Anti-Violence Programs (NCAVP) (2013). *National report on hate violence against lesbian, gay, bisexual, transgender, queer and HIV-affected communities.* Retrieved from http://www.avp.org/resources/avp-resources/315

Nestle, J., Howell, C., & Wilchins, R. (Eds.). (2002). *Genderqueer: Voices from beyond the binary.* New York: Routledge.

Nicholson, L. (1995). Interpreting gender. In L. Nicholson & S. Seidman (Eds.), *Social postmodernism: Beyond identity politics* (pp. 39–67). Cambridge, UK: Cambridge University Press.

Nicolazzo, Z. (2014). Celluloid marginalization: Pedagogical strategies for increasing students' critical thought through the multiple (re) readings of trans* subjectivities in film. *Journal of LGBT Youth, 11*(1), 20–39.

Pharr, S. (1997). *Homophobia: A weapon of sexism.* Inverness, CA: Chardon Press.

Preves, S. E. (2003). *Intersex and identity: The contested self.* Piscataway, NJ: Rutgers University Press.

Risberg, G., Johansson, E., & Hamberg, K. (2009). A theoretical model for analyzing gender bias in medicine. *International Journal for Equity in Health, 8*(28). Retrieved from http://www.equity-healthj.com/content/pdf/1475-9276-8-28.pdf

Roughgarden, J. (2009). *Evolution's rainbow: Diversity, gender, and sexuality.* Berkeley, CA: University of California Press.

Serano, J. (2009). *Whipping girl: A transsexual woman on sexism and the scapegoating of femininity.* Berkeley, CA: Seal Press.

Shilts, R. (1987). *And the band played on: Politic, people and the AIDS epidemic.* New York: St. Martin's Press.

Smith, B. (2000). *The truth that never hurts: Writings on race, gender and freedom.* New York: Routledge.

Spade, D. (2011). Some very basic tips for making higher education more accessible to trans students and rethinking how we talk about gendered bodies. *The Radical Teacher, 92* (Winter), 57–62.

Spellman, E. (1988). *Inessential woman: Problems of exclusion in feminist thought.* Boston: Beacon Press.

Stryker, S. (2008). *Transgender history.* Berkeley, CA: Seal Press.

Tolleson-Rinehart, S., & Josephson, J. (Eds.). (2005). *Gender and American politics: Women, men and the political process.* New York: M. E. Sharpe.

Tompkins, A. (2014). Asterisk. *TSQ: Transgender Studies Quarterly*, *1*(1–2), 26–27.

Troop, D. (2011, Oct. 23). Women's university to reconsider hard line on transgender students. *The Chronicle of Higher Education*. Retrieved from chronicle.com/article/Womens-University-to/129490

U. S. Department of Education, Office of Civil Rights. (2011, Apr. 4). Dear colleague letter: Sexual violence. Retrieved from http://www2.ed.gov/about/offices/list/ocr/letters/colleague-201104.pdf

Warner, J. (2014, Mar. 7). *Fact Sheet: The women's leadership gap, women's leadership by the numbers*. Center for American Progress. Retrieved from http://www.americanprogress.org/issues/women/report/2014/03/07/85457/fact-sheet-the-womens-leadership-gap/

Weill, C. (Ed.). (2009). *What science reveals about the biological origins of sexual orientation*. New York: Routledge.

World Health Organization. (2013). *Global and regional estimates of violence against women*. Retrieved from http://www.who.int/reproductivehealth/publications/violence/9789241564625/en/ld

Young, I. M. (1990). *Justice and the politics of difference*. Princeton, NJ: Princeton University Press.

7

Classism

*Maurianne Adams, Larissa E. Hopkins, and Davey Shlasko**

The toll taken by the 2008 recession has focused public attention onto issues of class, economic status, and classism. People notice the glaring disparities between CEO and worker compensation, and between bank bailouts and personal bankruptcies or foreclosures, and wonder why executive bonus contracts are sacrosanct while union contracts and worker health benefits and pensions are stripped.

The authors of this chapter have noticed that in this climate, our students and workshop participants are more open to exploring economic injustice in the U.S. and globally, and to acknowledge the impacts of global and local economic forces on themselves and their families. Beliefs that are core to the U.S. class system—such as belief in universal upward mobility, meritocracy, and the reachable "American Dream"—are now being questioned.

In this chapter, we take a social justice approach to class and classism in the U.S., which pays serious attention to the historical legacies of economic injustice from the colonial period moving forward. We note some ways in which class-based oppression and race-based oppression have been entangled, and explore contemporary manifestations of class and classism that represent today's version of those legacies, reproduced throughout U.S. institutions and normalized in everyday life. Based on the historical legacies, the complex systemic manifestations, and the intersections with other social justice issues, we frame a social justice approach to teaching and facilitating about classism. Materials and activities that support our social justice approach can be found on the website for this chapter.

OUR APPROACH: CORE CONCEPTS IN A SOCIAL JUSTICE APPROACH TO CLASS AND CLASSISM

In this chapter, we describe our approach to class and classism and then examine the societal and cultural dynamics of class inequality, the reproduction of those dynamics at the institutional level, within groups and relationships, and as internalized through socialization. In order to make sense of the long-term economic inequities in our cultural, social, and political systems, a class analysis must address all three levels, and explore the sources as well as the indicators of economic difference.

Our approach to class and classism is shaped by the core concepts described in the introductory Chapter 1, such as power and powerlessness, privilege and disadvantage, the levels of oppression, the Five Faces of Oppression, and socialization. Our approach is additionally shaped by an analysis of the *myth of meritocracy* and by attention to *intersectionality*.

SOCIAL JUSTICE DEFINITIONS NEEDED FOR CLASS AND CLASSISM

Definitions of class are wide-ranging and contested, based on differences in theoretical orientation and in personal experiences. Some writers define class on the basis of occupational status (blue collar or white collar, professional or hourly, levels within a managerial hierarchy), while others define class based on relative levels of income and/or wealth. Some approaches (such as Marxist) emphasize the ownership of resources (such as land, factories, corporations, or financial instruments) while others (such as followers of Max Weber) note the impact of wealth and social position on an individual's life chances (Lareau & Conley, 2008).

To provide consistency and clarity in discussing the various dimensions of *class* and *classism*, we propose Leondar-Wright and Yeskel's (2007) definition of *class* as "a relative social ranking based on income, wealth, education, status, and power" and their definition of *classism* as "the institutional, cultural, and individual set of practices and beliefs that assign differential value to people according to their socioeconomic class," in a social system characterized by economic inequality (Leondar-Wright & Yeskel, 2007, p. 314; see also Fiske & Markus, 2012; Lareau & Conley, 2008).

Class as "a relative social ranking" is defined by a variety of indicators, many of which are relational rather than quantitative. There is no one number that definitively determines one's class location. Almost everyone is privileged relative to someone else, and at a disadvantage relative to others. Individuals internalize assumptions and stereotypes about different class positions, often based on misinformation about the economic system, and these simplified understandings define their relationships to others within a class hierarchy. Thus, classism implicates all participants in a social system in which the class categories are nuanced and opaque, and in which relative advantage and disadvantage are reproduced through a complex interaction of social, institutional, cultural, and interpersonal mechanisms.

In addition to examining a variety of class indicators, this approach allows us to consider the cultures and identities that form around shared *class location*. As a result, our understanding of class categories is not simply linear: A person may have higher relative ranking according to one indicator but lower ranking according to another. For example, a woman with greater wealth than another (because she's a professional athlete or she just won the lottery) may have lower class *status* (because she is less educated, or has less "sophisticated" language and dress). A nuanced view of class also allows us to examine the mechanisms of *class privilege*, by which we mean those advantages and resources accorded to some groups of people and not others (often at the expense of others), based on relative class ranking.

CAPITALISM

There are different understandings of the relationship between classism and capitalism, including the question (that we do not pursue here) of whether classism can be understood to exist independently from capitalism (as in pre- or non-capitalist agricultural, migratory, or socialist-industrial societies). Because we are focusing on the contemporary U.S., we limit ourselves to a discussion of the relationship between classism and capitalism as they manifest here and now.

Capitalism describes a type of economic system based on private ownership of the means of production (agriculture, industry, and technology) in which owners' profits derive from the labor of people who receive fixed wages (rather than a share of profits). Economic growth is driven by competition in the marketplace (thought of as a "free market") in which fairness is assumed to emerge from market forces in the absence of regulation (e.g., by government or unions). In fact, in our current U.S. capitalist system, there is significant interference in the "free" functioning of markets, primarily by corporate interests. Even when government regulations providing protections, like workplace safety and fair banking practices, a capitalist economic system by its nature creates and reproduces class inequality because of the different ways in which owners and workers can or cannot accumulate wealth. Economic inequality is a key part of classism, along with cultural- and interpersonal-level manifestations that we explore below.

CONFLATION OF CAPITALISM WITH DEMOCRACY

One challenge to understanding classism is the conflation of our U.S. *democratic political system*, which assumes political equality (one person, one vote), with the U.S. *capitalist economic system*, which assumes equality of economic opportunity. The democratic myth that every child can grow up to be President has been conflated with the capitalist myth that every child can become rich through hard work and talent.

Democracy is a political system, characterized by individual rights and responsibilities, and in the case of the U.S., a representative (as opposed to direct democracy) system of governance. The conflation of U.S. capitalism with U.S. democracy has often served as a tool for those with political and economic power to discredit poor and working people's movements (including organized labor and the civil rights movement, among others). When workers have organized to protest economic inequities, they have sometimes argued that some version of a socialist economic system would be fairer, because shared ownership of production would lead to people benefiting more equally from economic growth. People opposed to such a system of distribution have attacked socialism as if it were a political system opposed to democracy, rather than an economic system parallel to capitalism. This confusion of political with economic systems has stifled thoughtful and serious consideration of alternative economic policies and structures in the U.S.

Additionally, the capitalist assumption that markets are fair supports the psychological investment many Americans have in the American Dream—the idea that everyone can achieve prosperity, homeownership, and other markers of a middle-class life if they work hard. These assumptions make it difficult to challenge the problems of advanced capitalism, such as the extraordinary influence of large multinational corporations and wealthy donors on U.S. democratic institutions (Callahan & Cha, 2013; Collins & Yeskel, 2005; Hacker & Pierson, 2010).

WEALTH AND INCOME

It is important to understand two forms of *economic capital*: *Wealth* and *income*.

Wealth consists of what one owns (cars, stocks or securities, real estate) minus what one owes (credit card or school debt, home mortgages). It is obvious that wealth confers class privilege—there are advantages and resources available to people with higher wealth that are simply inaccessible to people with less or no wealth.

Wealth expresses the amount and type of assets one owns, whereas *income* refers to the periodic inflow of resources, whether from investments, salary, hourly wages, government benefits, or any other source. The type or source of income is relevant, as well as the overall amount. For example, families with inherited wealth often have significant income from long-term investments that do not require their ongoing labor to maintain, at a scale which is not possible for those who rely on salary or wages—even those whose salary or wages are very high. The privilege accorded to individuals who have steady high income without needing to work (even if they choose to do so) differs qualitatively and quantitatively from the privilege connected to a high income from working.

The complexities of class location, as well as the assumptions about class status or location that characterize classism, go well beyond wealth and income. These complexities grow out of the fact that indicators of class are not only material. There are non-material cultural and social indicators as well that include *class culture*, *status*, *cultural capital*, and *social capital*, and also political power (Fiske & Markus, 2012).

CLASS CULTURE

Class culture describes the norms, values, and ways of life shared by people with a similar class position. Class cultures develop in response to economic realities as well as other dimensions of experience, and can be thought of as those aspects of culture that help people to survive, thrive, and make sense of their roles in the economic system, whether or not people are consciously aware of that relationship (Shlasko & Kramer, 2011; Williams, 2012).

One's class culture is not shaped only by one's membership in a general class category, but also by a more specific location defined by context and by other social identities (Matos-Daigle, 2011; Yosso, 1996). For example, Lamont's (2000) research documents differences in culture among three groups: White factory workers, black factory workers, and white managers. Lamont found that some culture markers varied across class more than race (i.e., white and black workers shared a value, norm, or assumption that differed from that of white managers), and others varied across both class and race (i.e., each of the three groups was different from the others). Similarly, one could expect to find very different class cultures among new tech industry millionaires in Silicon Valley than among white Protestant families with multiple-generational wealth in New England.

Even as class culture is highly intersectional, recent research suggests that some aspects of class culture may hold true across a whole class category. Cultural patterns that seem to be highly correlated with class include parenting beliefs and practices, norms around conflict and politeness, beliefs about morality and values, and linguistic patterns, including abstract vs. concrete language and direct vs. indirect communication (Jensen, 2012; Lamont, 2000; Lareau, 2003; Leondar-Wright, 2014; Streib, 2013).

Like other kinds of cultures, the patterns of thought and behavior learned from one's class culture often remain unconscious. The fact that class cultures are rarely talked about makes it even more likely that people will fail to notice their own patterns of class culture, or will ascribe them to another aspect of their identity. Someone who does not "identify with" a class category, or who identifies generically as "middle class" without knowing what that means, may nevertheless be steeped in the internalized norms of a working- or middle-class culture that affects how they think, talk, act, and relate to other people and the world.

The normalization of the dominant class culture and the devaluation or disregard of others is a manifestation of classism. For example, the highly controversial idea of "the culture of poverty" links poor or working-class culture with cognitive deficits, educational failure, and criminal behavior in ways that appear causal, rather than analyzing the multiple dynamics of racial and class oppression (Moynihan, 1965; Patterson, 2010; Payne 1995; Wilson, 2009). The idea of a culture of poverty relies on stereotype and overgeneralization (Ng & Rury, 2006), and blames poor people for the disadvantages they experience while ignoring key systemic factors like power, status, and material resources (Gorski, 2005). As part of a social justice approach to classism, class culture needs to be understood within an analysis of the reproduction of power and wealth (Lavelle 1995; Smith 2010).

CLASS STATUS

Class *status* conveys the degree of prestige attributed to one's position (Leondar-Wright & Yeskel, 2007), or to a particular cultural marker, by people and institutions with power.

Because classism is often internalized, disadvantaged people may buy into the status hierarchy and agree with the power system's perspective on who or what is "highly regarded," and who or what may be looked down on or ignored, even at their own expense.

Cultural markers that are associated with wealth tend to have higher status than others. For example, Standard English pronunciation, or English spoken with a European accent, has higher status than rural regional accents, non-European immigrant accents, and African American vernacular English. However, the alignment between wealth and status is not perfect. Professors, clergy, and some artists are examples of occupational groups with relatively high status, but in many cases, relatively low income and wealth. Unexpected alignment between wealth and status also come up when someone gains or loses wealth. A family that lost some or all of their inherited wealth can sometimes retain the culture status that had been associated with their former wealth. Conversely, someone who grew up working class and has recently acquired wealth may continue to think and act from the norms of a working-class culture, and may not be highly regarded by other wealthy people.

CULTURAL CAPITAL AND SOCIAL CAPITAL

Cultural capital and *social capital* are concepts that help to explain the relationship among culture, status, and material resources. *Cultural capital* (Bourdieu, 1986) describes non-material resources, such as the knowledge, language, style, way of life, and self-presentation, that act as personal markers of class and that influence economic opportunity as well as quality of life (Lareau & Calarco, 2012; Swartz, 1997).

Class culture becomes *cultural capital* to the extent that someone's knowledge, familiarity and comfort with a given culture affords them material advantages. For example, students at elite private colleges whose class culture matches the dominant or normalized culture of the institution are likely to "fit in" and benefit from the range of campus resources, while students whose class cultures do not align with the dominant culture of the institution face barriers to accessing such resources (Hopkins, 2014).

People often use *cultural capital* to refer specifically to facility with the cultural markers of the more privileged classes, but in our view, *all* class cultures have their own forms of cultural capital, though these are valued and ranked differently by the broader society. For example, familiarity and comfort with the norms of interaction in a working-class community may help a person to navigate that social environment successfully and lead to work opportunities, access to aid from the community, and so on. At the same time, this does not mean that different groups' cultural capital are equivalent or interchangeable. In particular, attempting to leverage cultural capital from a lower-status class culture in a context characterized by a higher-status class culture is unlikely to be successful. Further, the cultural capital of high-status groups provides access to material resources on a much larger scale than that of lower-status groups.

Whereas *cultural capital* refers to "*what* one knows about," *social capital* refers to "*who* one knows"—that is, the social networks one is part of and to which one has ready access. Like cultural capital, *social capital* is sometimes used to describe connections to elite social networks that help people gain access to private schooling, professional advancement, and other forms of class advantage (Allan, Ozga, & Smith, 2009; Mohr & DiMaggio, 1995).

However, all communities' social networks can translate into material benefits, albeit at different scales. Working-class social networks can provide access to referrals for jobs, hand-me-downs from neighbors, and other forms of material aid shared within a class group. Being in close touch with one's family and extended family can be a form of social capital in itself, insofar as it provides access to direct and indirect material support that people with small families, or who are estranged from their families, cannot access. Although social capital can be quantified in terms of *how many* people are in one's network, it is often more useful to consider *who* is in one's network and how that network functions to provide access to resources in a particular context.

Cultural capital and social capital help to explain how class differences are reproduced and passed along from one generation to the next (Bourdieu, 1984; Mohr & DiMaggio, 1995). Those with higher wealth and status are likely to have the social connections and cultural capital that assure continued access to material resources, enabling them to replenish or grow their wealth, maintain their status, and pass on all forms of capital to their children (Kozol, 1991; Lareau, 1987, 2011). Their cultural and social capital also provide access to decision makers at organizational and political levels (and opportunities to become a decision maker) so that they can influence policy to their own advantage. Some individuals with significant class privilege may choose not to use it for their own advantage, such as members of United for a Fair Economy (UFE)'s Responsible Wealth network; yet the fact that it is a choice is in itself a privilege.

The cumulative advantages and disadvantages afforded by these class indicators—income, wealth, class culture, status, cultural capital, and social capital—largely determine the degree to which individuals and communities can leverage economic and political power, which may be used to maintain the status quo or to create change.

MYTH OF MERITOCRACY

One challenge to understanding *classism* in the U.S. is the pervasive belief in *meritocracy*—that is, the belief that hard work and talent will always be rewarded by upward economic and social mobility (McNamee & Miller, 2004). By this logic, people assume that those living in poverty have simply not worked hard enough or are less intelligent, in effect blaming the victim. The belief in meritocracy encourages U.S. citizens, especially those who already are middle or upper class, to believe that they and their children will have equal economic opportunities and that each generation will advance further than their parents.

Among many lower-income communities, it is more common to acknowledge that economic opportunities are persistently limited by a number of self-perpetuating cycles of race- and/or class-based disadvantage. Since the 2008 recession, the U.S. belief in *meritocracy* has been seriously undermined by the failure of the middle class to bounce back to its relative prosperity, despite great gains by the wealthy (Boushey, 2014).

Despite recent historical experience, some apologists for the status quo vehemently deny class inequality and shame or blame people in poverty, whose failure to thrive economically is mistakenly thought to be their own fault. Proponents of the economic status quo frame critiques of these economic inequities as efforts to inflame "class warfare" rather than efforts to create a fair and equitable economic system. For example, defenses of the status quo obscure the intergenerational economic disadvantages for Native American nations confined on reservations, African American descendants of slaves and debt peonage, and Mexican-American and Asian victims of wage inequity and unfair labor practices.

To explore evidence of economic disadvantage based upon cultural, political, linguistic, and race-based factors, we need to examine the intersections of classism with other systems of oppression: The economic, social, and cultural exclusion experienced by, for example, people with disabilities, youth, and elders marginalized on the two ends of the "ageism and adultism" spectrum, and women who, despite being integrated into almost all areas of the workforce, still receive less pay than men in comparable jobs. In this way, a social justice analysis of class and classism reverses the tendency to blame the victims—such as urban young men of color who are blamed for crime, immigrants who are blamed for lowering wages, and poor countries who are blamed for taking U.S. jobs. Instead, our approach recognizes the underlying forces of class inequality that create vast inequalities in wealth, the legacies of racism and gender oppression, as well as global factors such as imperialism, war, trade policies, global finance, and multinational corporations that unduly influence national tax and spending policies (Collins & Yeskel, 2005; Hacker & Pierson, 2010).

HISTORICAL LEGACIES OF U.S. CLASS AND CLASSISM

The historical legacies of U.S. class and classism offer a stark contrast to the narrative of "The American Dream." The American Dream paints a picture of equality of opportunity, meritocracy, upward mobility, and national prosperity enjoyed by all U.S. citizens as well as immigrants. But the historical record reveals harsh realities that undercut the dream's veracity. Some of the major themes include: 1) the reproduction in the colonies of class distinctions from Europe; 2) the racialization of a two-tier working class; 3) expansion, settlement, and immigration; 4) labor organizing and union movements; 5) ballot box and regulatory policies; and (6) the 20th century's "free market" and deregulation.

THE REPRODUCTION IN THE COLONIES OF CLASS DISTINCTIONS FROM EUROPE

The U.S.'s founding documents articulated egalitarian ideals as part of a rhetorical strategy to legitimize U.S. independence from England. However, the revolution mainly benefitted an emerging U.S. aristocracy, whose members were well placed to reproduce the class system they inherited from Europe. After independence, the revolutionary language of economic freedom, taxation based on representation, and opportunities for upward mobility became the rallying cry not of the colonial ruling class, but of tenant farmer and worker revolts against a newly entrenched system of class advantage and disadvantage.

Wealthy colonial settlers had benefited from English land-grants (available exclusively to white men) that situated them from the start as the economic and political elite, replicating the rank and class inequities of their homelands. Such disparities were maintained and enhanced by economic opportunities for those (primarily white men) who could control or speculate in land, trade, industry, or finance. Class and classism in the colonies and early Republic were characterized by disparities between a wealthy elite who could consolidate local and federal political power for economic benefit; a laboring class of tenant farmers who owned nothing and had little individual power; and unpaid, enslaved Africans whose labor was fundamental to the colonial economy and created a racialized lower tier of labor that is, in effect, still in place.

The 18th through 21st centuries have seen shifts in the specific characteristics of class difference (along lines of urban and rural, industrial and agricultural, small business and global finance). Yet history also demonstrates a continuity in class inequality, in which a self-perpetuating elite financed and benefited from building railroads, drilling oil and gas, mining copper and coal, and expanding banking and finance, all based on the exploitation of labor of people with less political power, including enslaved and free blacks, Latinos, white immigrants and immigrants of color, and others living in intergenerational poverty.

The political influence of the wealthy elite in the early U.S. resulted in federal policies that removed Native peoples from land that was desired for territorial expansion. Federal policies encouraged settlement of the West by an emergent "middle" class of farmers, skilled workers, and small- to medium-scale business owners. At the bottom remained the landless tenant farmers, hired-hands and service laborers, including African slave (and then freed) laborers and generations of exploited Irish, Italian, Jewish, Asian, and other immigrants.

The sheer size of the continental U.S. allowed for an optimistic belief that social mobility would be based on meritocracy. For example, the Homestead Act (1862) offered land that had been seized from Native peoples for sale as 160-acre homesteads for $1.50 per acre. Leaders talked about the act as providing nearly free land, equally available to anyone. In reality, homesteads were only available primarily to those settlers—almost all white—who could pay $200 up front (the equivalent of about $4700 today). Although 50 million acres were set aside for settler homesteads, much of the land went to well-financed speculators, and another 100 million acres went to railroads at no cost.

Meanwhile, working-class families in northern cities lived in overcrowded tenements, vulnerable to typhus and cholera and industrial accidents, with no garbage removal or clean water (Zinn, 2003). In the South, millions of southern whites were poor tenant farmers, or worked in cotton factories for 30 cents per day, while blacks earned 20 cents. The opportunities of settlement were not for them.

Working people have protested their lower wealth, income, and status throughout U.S. history. In the colonial period, they protested against excessive land rents. In the 19th century, they organized walkouts from textile mills and factories, despite accusations that their actions constituted "conspiracies to restrain trade" (Zinn, 2003, p. 223) and were therefore illegal.

On the other side of the class divide, a centralized banking system fostered symbiotic relationships among politics, business, and trade that enabled corporate monopolies to consolidate economic power in the hands of a wealthy corporate elite with formidable political influence. For example, railroad owners were bribed to ship Rockefeller oil, allowing the Standard Oil monopoly to consolidate iron, copper, coal, shipping, and banking, and building a fortune of two billion dollars (about 57 billion dollars today) (Zinn, 2003). The political corruption evident in such monopolies leads historians to conclude that "in industry after industry—shrewd, efficient businessmen building empires, choking out competition, maintaining high prices, keeping wages low, using government subsidies . . . were the first beneficiaries of the 'welfare state'" (Zinn, 2003, p. 257; see also pp. 253–295).

THE RACIALIZATION OF A TWO-TIER LABORING CLASS

The system of slave labor on Southern plantations was enforced through a legal system that segregated blacks from whites and hindered them from forming common cause. "Race laws" outlawed intermarriage and literacy among blacks, punished white workers who joined slaves in rebellion, and established "sundown towns" where black laborers were required to leave town at the end of each workday. Blacks, whether enslaved or free, ranked socially and economically below the "free" white men regardless of their skill or capacity. For white men, their presumed racial superiority obscured the fact of their economic exploitation.

Poor whites often lived in poor conditions similar to those of skilled slaves and free blacks, but work opportunities and salaries were racialized. Whites, no matter how poor, were still white and still free, would usually be hired before free blacks, and would earn more per hour for the same job. This two-tiered system provided the basis for a racialized union movement, which helped to create a white middle-class in the mid-20th century.

The system of de jure racism against blacks (vagrancy laws, laws against intermarriage, inferior schooling) and Native peoples (laws banning religious ceremonies and disbanding tribal authority), formalized in the 18th through the 20th centuries, is today perpetuated by racial disparities in policing, legal representation, and judicial verdicts. De facto economic racism, built into the plantation slave system and the forcing of Native peoples onto agriculturally unproductive reservations, continued as immigrants of color (including Sikhs, Chinese, and then Japanese) and Mexicans were shunted into menial labor—men in farms, factories, mines, and railroads, and women in domestic work. Factory and mine owners fueled interracial conflict, and discouraged union organizing, by exploiting blacks and Asians as strike-breakers at lower wages than whites.

The self-perpetuating legacy of this process was white elite ownership of industries that depended largely on a racialized labor force. Economic mobility belonged to the upper tier of skilled U.S.-born whites and European immigrants, while crushing poverty prevailed for the lower tier of blacks, immigrants of color, Native peoples, and Mexicans. The system was held in place by intersecting economic, legal, and social advantages for whites, and disadvantages for workers of color.

This racial divide also played out in late 19th-century U.S. overseas expansion and imperialism, in the plantations of Hawaii, Standard Oil's control of the global export market, United Fruit's control of the Cuban sugar industry, and the annexation of Puerto Rico and the Philippines (Zinn, 2003). Puerto Rican, Filipino, and South American immigrants soon joined the lower tier of the U.S. labor force.

Thus, the U.S. class system has always been racialized. The wealth of the owning class originated in the proceeds of racism: the plantation system based on slave labor, the government's redistribution of land stolen from Native peoples to wealthy investors, and the transatlantic slave trade. The owning class established racist and other policies that allowed them to maintain their wealth and power, giving them the primary control of and benefit from finance markets, land speculation, mining, and trade (Steinberg, 1989; Takaki, 1993; Zinn, 2003). A racially tiered labor market created and exacerbated racial tensions among the poor, hindering effective coalitions among poor people across race, and allowed owners to continue exploiting workers of all races. The historical legacy of this racialized class system appears today in the racially tiered workforce, in which darker peoples of color continue to be relegated to low-paid labor and service roles.

IMMIGRATION

Immigration has been central to the economic and class system of the U.S. since before its founding. The first immigrants, in the early-17th through late-18th centuries, included white, mainly Protestant landowners, financed by European investors, as well as skilled farmers and craftspeople and indentured workers. They settled the colonies by displacing and killing Native peoples and acquiring ownership of their lands, forming the basis for a landed elite. The second wave of migration (mid-17th through early-19th centuries) was entirely involuntary—millions of African people were kidnapped as part of the transatlantic slave trade and brought to the colonies for use as a racially marked workforce in the labor-intensive colonial export crops of sugar and cotton.

With each subsequent wave of migration, most new immigrants became part of the working class. Along with enslaved and indentured workers, and others who were kept from economic mobility, immigrants built the infrastructure and provided the domestic labor that allowed the owning class to make immense fortunes while the workers and their children largely remained poor.

A third wave of immigrants during the mid-19th through early-20th centuries came from diverse racial, ethnic, linguistic, class, and religious backgrounds. Irish fled famine and starvation, caused by British colonial policy, in the 1840s. Mexicans became absorbed into the southwest and western U.S. territories when the Treaty of Guadalupe Hildago (1848) shifted the U.S./Mexican border. Southern and Eastern Europeans (Italians, Jews, and Poles) immigrated in the millions, fleeing from poverty, war, and persecution. Arabs and Asians also fled poverty and war in Syria, Lebanon, India, China, and Japan.

The rate of immigration rose from 143,000 per decade in the 1820s, to 8,800,000 in the first decade of the 20th century (U.S. Department of Homeland Security, Office of Immigration Statistics, 2014). By 1860, the foreign-born American population was over four million (Jacobson, 1998). By 1920, 36 million Americans, more than a third of the population, were immigrants and their children, the majority from southern and eastern Europe with smaller numbers from China, Japan, and India (Daniels, 2002).

Irish immigrants were a significant part of the mid-19th century wave of immigration, with 1.5 million arriving between 1845–1855. They settled in East Coast and midwestern U.S. cities, where they faced anti-Irish (and anti-Catholic) resentment. Later, Italians, Poles, and Slovaks, fleeing from war and poverty, and European Jews fleeing from pogroms, settled mainly but not exclusively in urban centers. They interacted in factories but generally lived in ethnically segregated communities, often drawing upon social capital in networks of earlier arrivals for employment and housing.

The Mexican landowners who were absorbed into the new U.S. territories in the Southwest were vulnerable to extortion, discriminatory taxation, and fraudulent claims from whites who wanted their land. Many were forced off their land and pressed into a migratory labor force, along with Mexican tenant farmers, to compete with immigrant laborers for grueling and underpaid work building railroads and working copper mines (Takaki, 1993). Owners kept wages low by replacing Mexican workers with even lower-paid workers recruited directly from Mexico, despite workers' efforts to unionize in protest against the practice (Takaki, 1993).

Many Chinese immigrants became agricultural workers in California, and railroad owners hired them in the erroneous belief that they would not strike. But like the Irish and Eastern European railroad workers, Chinese workers organized against dangerous working conditions, long hours, and wages below those of white workers. Chinese workers made up half the labor force in San Francisco's low-wage industries; they built California's agricultural dykes and canals; Louisiana and Mississippi planters hired and pitted them against black laborers; and they created niche laundry businesses.

The white European immigrants were also an exploited, ethnically marked working class, whose poverty and desperation left them vulnerable to wage exploitation and to being pitted against even more vulnerable blacks, Mexicans, and immigrant Asians and Arabs (Steinberg, 1989; Takaki, 1993; Zinn, 2003). Economic competition was racialized, sometimes to the advantage of white ethnics who got priority and (slightly) higher wages, and sometimes to the temporary advantage of Chinese or blacks employed as strikebreakers against white workers who organized to protest unfair wages and working conditions. The white immigrants constituted the "upper" tier of the racialized two-tier working class at the bottom of the overall economic ladder (Brodkin, 1998; Guglielmo & Salerno, 2003; Ignatiev, 1995; Roediger, 1991). Irish women displaced black domestic labor, and worked alongside Italian and Jewish women in textile mills and sweatshops that didn't hire blacks. White ethnic generational upward mobility existed for Irish, Italians, Jews, and other white ethnic workers that was not available to blacks, Latinos/as, or other workers of color. The process by which white ethnics moved from the upper rung of the working class into a skilled factory worker or small-business owning "middle class" status, while most blacks, Mexicans, and Chinese remained in the lower tier, is part of this complex historical legacy (Foner, 1998; Roediger, 1991).

LABOR ORGANIZING AND UNION MOVEMENTS

Labor movements had a significant role in creating the kind of organized workforce that became the middle class. Railroad, mining, and factory jobs were particularly underpaid and exploitative. Workplace injuries and deaths were common, children labored along-side adults, and many workplaces lacked sanitation. When wages and work conditions improved, it was as a result of organized resistance to exploitative conditions. Union organizing required planning, skill, effort, and determination, as well as courage, solidarity, and self-sacrifice to face down the militias and armed security guards whose brutal government-sanctioned violence attempted to suppress organizing and protect owners' interests over workers' interests.

The United States has a tradition of homegrown class-based revolt, dating back to the colonies and early Republic. Throughout the 18th and 19th centuries, New England farmers, carpenters, and shoemakers revolted against conditions of work, while tenant farmers organized rent-revolts in New Jersey and upstate New York. Native peoples rebelled against broken treaties, and small-scale farmers against excessive land and agricultural taxes (Zinn, 2003). Bacon's Rebellion in Virginia (1676) exemplifies one such revolt that crossed lines of race and class. These rebellions were regularly and violently suppressed by local and state armed militias who maintained the economic status quo on behalf of the governing and owning class.

Labor unrest was accelerated by chronic instability of the U.S. economy (with major unemployment and economic depressions following financial crises in 1837, 1857, 1893, 1907, 1919, and 1929), and spread throughout many industries. In most cases, organizing was suppressed using police and military brutality. Workers meeting in Tompkins Square, New York (1874) were clubbed and beaten back by mounted police; Irish "Molly Maguires" on strike in the textile mills of Fall River, Massachusetts, were arrested and executed (Zinn, 2003).

Beginning in the mid-19th century, private mercenary forces were hired to supplement or substitute for government militias in the violent suppression of organized workers' rebellions. Owners of factories, mills, and mines hired private detectives (such as the Pinkertons) to use whatever force necessary to harass and disrupt union organizing. Notorious examples of such suppression include the Great Railroad Strike of 1877, the Homestead Strike of 1892, and the Battle of Blair Mountain in 1921 (Zinn, 2003).

In addition to economic hardship that accompanied financial crises, labor unrest and union organizing in the 19th century were motivated by the hardships of unregulated labor conditions: long hours and work weeks, unsafe work sites, powerlessness against wage theft, and wage cuts during periods of economic downturn. Rather than acknowledge these inequities, business interests and the media sought to blame "foreign influences" for the mass marches of unemployed, for periods of labor unrest, and for particular union organizing campaigns.

The stereotypic scapegoating of "foreign influences" succeeded in demonizing workers' rights movements that had been inspired, but only in part, by socialist movements in Europe. Although U.S. traditions of rebellion against unfair tax and labor practices had paralleled European labor movements, owners benefited from blaming immigrant activists, whose socialist critiques of unregulated capitalism could be labelled "un-American." Wealthy owners and popular media leveraged racist, ethnocentric, and antisemitic rhetoric to paint labor organizing as a threat to democracy itself, rather than as a threat to the owners' financial interests in maintaining unregulated conditions of labor. The ethnocentric and antisemitic legacy of early-19th century anti-socialism resurfaced during the anti-communist witch hunts of the 1950s.

Despite the formidable political, corporate, media, and military forces arrayed against them, a comparably moderate nationwide federation of labor unions—the American Federation of Labor (AFL)—emerged in 1886. It was initially organized as an umbrella organization for craft unions (Nicholson, 2004) and was composed mainly of skilled white ethnic workers. The success of the AFL was based in part on its opposition to more radical labor unions (still associated with "foreignness" and communism) and also on its exclusion of the many black workers seeking jobs in northern factories, who were forming their own labor unions, and of Chinese, Japanese, and Mexican workers (Nicholson, 2004; Takaki, 1993; Zinn, 2003).

The success of the AFL had enormous consequences for U.S. class and classism. First, their success in negotiating benefits, hours, and safety nets largely erased the ethnic or not-quite-white markers for an increasingly Americanized immigrant workforce. The unions enabled European immigrants to find productive employment with stable wages and benefits so that within two generations, the children and grandchildren of European immigrants had become assimilated as "white" middle-class Americans (Brodkin, 1998; Guglielmo and Salerno, 2003; Ignatiev, 1995).

Second, the termination of large-scale immigration after 1924 provided a 40-year breathing space, before immigration was reopened in 1964, during which the pre-1924 immigrant generations gained middle-class status by learning English, holding union jobs with reliable pay and good pensions, and graduating from public schools into an increasingly suburban middle class. Economic mobility was not universal for white ethnics—some remained in the working class and others (particularly Italians) emigrated back to Europe. But enough Italians became skilled construction workers, Jews became businessmen and professionals, and Irish moved into urban politics and policing to "create a middle-class cushion for class conflict" (Zinn, 2003, p. 349).

Many upwardly mobile white-ethnic immigrants supported the AFL and CIO and shared their vehement anti-communism. As a generation of new Americans, they were patriotic and suspicious of European radicalism. The children of former immigrants bonded in the trenches of World War I and battlefields of World War II, lost their ethnic markers, and benefitted from the military-industrial boom. The many who prospered came to believe the meritocratic narrative for their generation and to hold radical union organizing at arm's length.

As the moderate AFL/CIO membership became more upwardly mobile, they abandoned any hint of the egalitarianism of earlier labor unions. Instead, the AFL and CIO took the view "that workers must frankly accept their status as wage earners and seek higher wages" based on "the rigid segmentation of the job market along racial and ethnic lines" (Foner, 1998, p. 135). This created a skilled and union-protected majority white working class with limited demands for wages, hours, and working conditions. The U.S. economy became "more thoroughly racialized at the dawn of the twentieth century than at any other point in American history" (Foner, 1998, p. 135).

THE BALLOT BOX AND REGULATORY POLICIES: POPULISM, PROGRESSIVISM, AND THE NEW DEAL

The success of a relatively conservative union movement was aided in part by late-19th and early-20th century newspaper and muckraking exposés of the unregulated and abusive working conditions in many industries. Increased media attention and awareness generated public outrage and shored up working people's leverage at the ballot box. Organized labor's success at the ballot box had the ironic effect of diluting the movement's more radical and far-reaching demands for change.

Two threads characterize the story of this era: First, the continuity of labor unrest and the emergence of rural worker's alliances, and second, the absorption of moderate labor into the two-party political system.

At the same time that urban workers were organizing in protest against sweatshops and slums, farmers also were in crisis. In the aftermath of the Civil War, the U.S. army had forcibly removed Native peoples from the Great Plains, and railroads brought settlers westward. Many were farmers, intending to feed the rapidly growing U.S. population. But as the economy remained unstable, farmers went into debt, and many were driven into a crop-lien tenancy. In the South, 90% of farmers lived on credit (Zinn, 2003).

Farmers resisted by organizing Alliances throughout the South and West. They shared equipment, storage warehouses, and financing in "a drive based on the idea of coopera-tion, of farmers creating their own culture, their own political parties, gaining a respect not given them by the nation's powerful industrial and political leaders" (Zinn, 2003, p. 286). With 400,000 members by the 1880s, Alliances formed statewide cooperatives and met in 1890 to form a national Populist party. These agrarian resistance movements generated political clout for embattled white farmers in the cotton and wheat belts as well as white miners and industrial workers who the farmers supported politically (Foner, 1998).

A Colored Farmers National Alliance with around a million members organized in the South, and the populist Texas People's Party (1891) was interracial, but blacks and whites were in different social and economic positions. Blacks were field hands and hired laborers, whereas most white Alliance organizers were farm owners who opposed higher wages for the black cotton pickers (Zinn, 2003). The potential for interracial collaboration was over-whelmed by the prevailing racism as well as Jim Crow laws that sabotaged voting strength for blacks. As a result, it was primarily white populist alliances that became a political force within the Democratic party of the 1890s (Foner, 1998; Zinn, 2003). Southern blacks not only had no vote, but also were denied a place in farmers' Alliances, just as they were left unrepresented by nationally organized labor unions representing a skilled white working class. As unions and farmers' Alliances entered the political system, they lost vitality in a two-party system and were absorbed by political power brokers.

Rural populism was eventually drowned in a sea of Democratic party electoral poli-tics, while urban radical socialist labor organizing was deflected by the more conservative national unions (AFL and CIO), both of whom aligned politically with the Democratic Party. Those who remained outside the big tent had their strikes disrupted or violently bro-ken by the weapons of the system—local ordinances forbidding union gatherings, negative media coverage, and violent suppression by police, militias, and private mercenary forces. The "reluctant reforms" achieved through the combined efforts of muckraking journalism and (white) workers' political leverage proved sufficient to quiet the uprisings, but not to create fundamental change. Zinn uses the term "political capitalism" to describe a system "where the businessmen took firmer control of the political system because the private economy was not efficient enough to forestall protest from below" (Zinn, 2003, p. 350). Politics became the mechanism to stabilize and salvage capitalism, and in that spirit, the "Progressive" era established regulatory commissions to stem the worst excesses of inter-state commerce (the Interstate Commerce Commission, ICC), the financial and banking system (the Federal Trade Commission, FTC), and food safety (Meat Inspection Act, Pure Food and Drug Act) without the kind of fundamental change called for by radicals and socialists.

The term "Progressive Era" disguises the time's intense conflicts: Jim Crow, lynching, and race riots; a militant (white) women's suffrage movement, working against tremen-dous odds; the blacklisting, incarceration, and execution of union organizers; and mas-sacres of striking workers and their families.

The prosperity of the "Roaring Twenties" that followed WW I affected a limited seg-ment of U.S. citizens, mainly the wealthiest. Real wages in manufacturing went up 1.4% per year, while owning-class stockholders gained 16.4% (Zinn, 2003). Southern blacks remained sharecroppers, harassed by a burgeoning Ku Klux Klan (KKK) and cut out of unionized manufacturing jobs in urban centers. Workers continued to strike for fair wages and safer working conditions. But much of the wealth accumulated during the 1920s came from unsound financial speculation, and the economy collapsed after the stock market crash of 1929 that brought in the Great Depression. The election of Franklin Delano Roosevelt was taken as a mandate for change, and inaugurated an alphabet soup of regulatory experimentation and jobs programs, such as the National Recovery Act (NRA), the Agricultural Adjustment Administration (AAA), and the Tennessee Valley Authority (TVA). To address the explosion of strikes by the mid-1930s, the National Labor Relations Board (Wagner Act) gave unions legal status, created channels to address some grievances, and channeled union energy into meetings and contract negotiations rather than direct tactics like strikes (Zinn, 2003).

Although the New Deal (like the "deals" of the Progressive Era) provided benefits to poor and working poor people, it did not change systemic or structural inequalities of wealth and poverty, nor did it address the racialized distribution of wealth. The exclusion of people of color from economic advantages granted to whites is one of the persistent historical legacies of U.S. class and classism. African Americans were initially excluded from most New Deal programs. Similarly, in the aftermath of World War II, black, Mexican, and Asian veterans did not benefit from the G.I. Bill that enabled the children and grandchildren of 19th-century European immigrants to attend college, receive affordable home mortgages, and move into the rapidly growing (and racially segregated) middle-class suburban developments (Brodkin, 1998; Lipsitz, 1998).

Black veterans' disappointment and outrage upon returning from World War II to such a cold welcome from the government helped spur the civil rights movement. Black veterans would not allow Americans to forget that they had fought against fascism in Europe and also against racism in the U.S. The civil rights movement in turn inspired other poor people's movements, such as the United Farmworkers, the American Indian Movement, and the National Welfare Rights Organization, among others.

TWENTIETH CENTURY: THE FREE MARKET AND DEREGULATION

In the three decades between the entry of the U.S. into World War I (1917) and the end of World War II (1945), the U.S. emerged as a global power with a form of capitalism regulated by banking and workplace protections put in place following the 1929 depression. The industrialization in preparation for World War II marked the end of U.S. economic depression. A post-war "boom" based on wartime industrialization and post-war global supremacy supported a thriving middle class for several post-war decades.

But the post-war economic factors that had facilitated middle-class prosperity were soon undermined by changes in federal policy in the closing decades of the 20th century. These included changes in the tax code benefitting corporate interests, opportunities for corporations to go offshore and avoid U.S. taxes, the movement of factories and jobs to countries with lower pay scales and fewer protections for workers (supported by treaties such as the North American Free Trade Agreement, or NAFTA), the weakening of regulatory structures of banks and finances, and legal changes making it more difficult for unions to organize and negotiate on behalf of workers (Bartlett & Steele, 1994; Domhoff, 1983; Phillips, 1990). By and large, many of the union jobs whose paychecks, benefits, and pensions had supported a middle-class lifestyle disappeared, and with them the stability and prosperity of working families who depended on those jobs and networks (Henwood, 2003; Piketty, 2014; Reich, 2007).

Voters were encouraged to trust in "trickle down" economics, by which the accumulation of wealth by those already wealthy would somehow benefit everyone else. Political elections and longevity in public office came to depend increasingly on the deep pockets of corporate interests. Intricate tax codes provided loopholes for complex financial arrangements and stock options; unregulated financial interests found ways to garner enormous profits; and companies "too big to fail" were granted federal support not available to bankrupt individuals.

In this climate, labor regulations were relaxed and unions lost power. As industrial jobs became less secure and middle-class income levels decreased relative to booming stock markets, the middle-class lifestyle required the support of two or three jobs per family, supplemented by increased reliance on debt (in the forms of mortgages, car loans, and credit cards). At the same time, changes to welfare policy (such as welfare-to-work programs) meant that the poorest Americans were less and less able to meet their basic needs for food and shelter (Mishel, Bernstein, & Allegretto, 2007).

CURRENT MANIFESTATIONS OF U.S. CLASS AND CLASSISM

The historical legacies described above continue into the present time in the maintenance of an unequal and inequitable class structure, the many manifestations of classism, and organized movements of resistance. Major themes include: 1) the growing gap between rich and poor; 2) declining union membership; 3) immigration and employment; 4) racial disparities in wealth and income; 5) personal credit and debt, and 6) classism in education.

GROWING GAP BETWEEN RICH AND POOR

The uneven distribution of income and wealth has been growing since the early 1980s, at an ever-increasing pace. We can track growing inequality by comparing two periods of growth in the U.S. economy: 1947–1979 and 1979–2009. Between 1947 and 1979, the U.S. economy grew at a healthy pace, and the benefits were distributed more or less evenly across different income brackets. On average, families in every income category more than doubled their income in those 30 years.

By contrast, economic growth from 1979 to 2009 was less robust and the benefits were concentrated in the top fifth of income earners, whose average income grew 49%. In sharp contrast, the middle fifth saw only 8% growth, the second-to-lowest fifth's income was stagnant, and the poorest fifth had their income decrease by 12%. Even within the top fifth, inequality increased, with the top 1% gaining 185%, compared to 49% for the highest fifth overall (data from the U.S. Census and from Piketty & Saez, 2012, as compiled and summarized by UFE, www.faireconomy.org; see also Gordon, 2013).

Large tax cuts during the George W. Bush years (2001–2009) went disproportionately to the highest income brackets, creating a deficit in the federal budget. Earnings based on hourly income fell, and failure to enforce fair labor rights limited union and workforce leverage to counter declining wages.

Accelerating class inequities were disguised by the re-entrance of middle-class women into the workforce and by easy access to credit. Families that were previously supported by one income now needed two to maintain the same standard of living. With the collapse of global financial markets in 2008, the median net worth of U.S. families dropped by 39.4% from pre-recession levels (Fry & Kochhar, 2014). The U.S. Census Bureau reported that in 2011, 46.2 million Americans were below the poverty line (including 16.4 million children), and poor Americans became even poorer. Deep poverty rose 44.3%, the highest level in 36 years, with about one in eight Americans and one in four children dependent on government aid (Bishaw, 2013).

In the 2008 economic crash, many relatively wealthy people lost large sums of money when their investments lost value. However, the richest bounced back, while non-wealthy people continue to struggle for financial stability. In the short period from 2009–2012, the average growth in family income across all income categories was 6%, but the top 1% saw income growth of 31.4%, compared to only .4% for the remaining 99% (Pikkety & Saez, 2003, data updated through 2013).

The 2008 crash accelerated a process by which many people in the middle and working classes were already losing ground. Changes in tax policy during the Reagan years (1980s) provided windfalls to industrialists who moved manufacturing to low-wage countries, leading to the loss of whole categories of stable working-class jobs throughout the U.S. Financial investments followed industry overseas, where tax shelters meant less income was returned via taxes to potentially benefit people in the U.S. Global trade treaties, such as NAFTA, cost the United States hundreds of thousands of jobs that moved to South American and Asian countries in the 1990s.

As a result, public attention became focused on the destructive consequences of growing economic inequality (Stiglitz, 2013). The 2008 economic crisis called attention to the instability of global investments backed by pooled subprime mortgages rather than secure financial backing (Shiller, 2008). These revelations made clear that some of the wealthiest corporations and their stockholders were growing ever richer at the expense of working-class and middle-class homeowners, who had been lured by subprime mortgages and were now losing their homes to foreclosure as markets collapsed (Henwood, 2003; Reich, 2007). Since then, such mortgage-backed securities have been replaced by similarly unstable rental-backed securities and even car loan-backed securities. Although financial markets can seem impossibly complex, many people gained an increasingly clear understanding that both the causes and the consequences of the mortgage crisis represented a massive transfer of wealth from working- and middle-class people to wealthy corporations and their stockholders (Piketty, 2014; Shiller, 2008).

A global movement, largely led by youth and young adults, manifested in public protests that literally occupied public spaces in major cities around the world for months—in a continuation of the U.S. tradition of class-based activism (Leondar-Wright, 2014). The movement that started as Occupy Wall Street popularized the language of "the 1%" and sought to unify non-wealthy people with the slogan, "We are the 99%." By the time the most visible actions dwindled, the Occupy movement had succeeded in shifting the public discourse about class, making room for frank discussions of economic inequality in contexts where such discussions had previously been unthinkable. Many groups that began organizing around the Occupy encampments have continued their work around economic inequality in less visible ways (Collins, 2012, 2014; Korten, 2010; van Gelder, 2011).

DECLINING UNION MEMBERSHIP

Historically, unions had been an important way for working-class people to influence the terms and conditions of their labor through negotiation with employers. Union members earn an average of 10–30% higher wages than nonunion workers (Long, 2013; Mayer, 2004), and often provide better benefits (such as health insurance) and more favorable policies (such as grievance procedures for workers who experience harassment). The percentage of employed workers in the U.S. who are members of a union peaked in 1954 at 28%. The rate has declined more or less steadily since then, and between 1980 and 2013 it fell from around 20% to 11.3% (Bureau of Labor Statistics, 2014). The declining rate of union membership means that fewer workers are effectively protected from exploitation, low wages, and inadequate benefits.

Unions also serve as a vehicle for organizing workers' political voices, and they remain one of the primary mechanisms through which non-wealthy people's interests are represented in the U.S. political process. Unions mobilize and coordinate large numbers of workers to exercise their political rights through mechanisms like meeting with elected representatives and hiring lobbyists to advocate for workers' interests. Despite current efforts to unionize agricultural, domestic, and food service workers, the decline in rates of union membership has lessened unions' political pull and decreased the number of workers who are able to be politically involved as an organized group.

Government employees have a much higher rate of union membership than private sector employees (Bureau of Labor Statistics, 2014). In recent years, some politicians have blamed public employee unions, and public employees generally, for government deficits that are actually caused by macroeconomic policies and trends. Portrayals of unionized public workers as lazy or greedy illustrate classism playing out on a cultural level through stereotyped media representations. When such representations lead to policy changes that make it even more difficult to unionize, this becomes an example of institutional classism.

Workers and unions continue to organize to push back against the trend of declining union membership, including through new approaches to labor organizing (Mantsios, 1998). An example of recent organizing that highlights the intersectionality of class, race, gender, and immigration is the National Domestic Workers Alliance (NDWA), which supports state- and national-level organizing campaigns to improve working conditions for domestic workers (those who work in other people's homes). The National Labor Relations Act of 1935 (NLRA), which legitimized unions' role, established basic workplace protections, and helped the U.S. emerge from the Great Depression, specifically excluded both domestic and agricultural workers. Because of race and gender segregation in the workforce, most women (across races) and most people of color (across genders) did not benefit from the NLRA as much as white men. The NDWA works to correct this omission by creating new legislation protecting basic rights of domestic workers, such as the right to sleep uninterrupted, to get paid minimum wage, and to have paid sick days (Burnham & Theodore, 2012). As of January 2014, the NDWA has succeeded in winning these protections in New York, Hawaii, California, and Massachusetts, and for some home health care workers at the national level (see the NDWA website, http://www.domesticworkers.org/).

IMMIGRATION AND EMPLOYMENT

Agriculture is another sector of the workforce in which classism, racism, and immigration are deeply entangled. The Fair Labor Standards Act (FLSA, 1938, 1966) established basic employment protections, including the federal minimum wage and overtime system; however, it did not apply to farmworkers. The law was amended in 1966 to apply some provisions to farmworkers, including the minimum wage, but not overtime pay. There are about one million hired farmworkers employed in the U.S. at any given time of the year (Kandel, 2008). Compared to other workers, farmworkers are not protected from unfair practices such as substandard wages and housing, occupational safety hazards, and irregular work schedules—for example, being required to work 80 hours a week for several weeks (without overtime) and then having little or no work for several weeks after that (Kandel, 2008).

About half the farmworkers in the U.S. are not authorized to work in the U.S., which makes them especially vulnerable to exploitative labor practices, including wage theft and overwork. Additionally, about half of farmworkers move from place to place throughout the year to work on different crops as the seasons change (Kandel, 2008). Their mobility can make it difficult to receive benefits for which they may be eligible, such as food stamps or subsidized health care, and prevents their children from having regular schooling.

Some politicians and media outlets depict farmworkers, especially immigrants, as lazy people mooching off a generous public benefits system, despite the fact that farmworkers perform some of the most demanding labor and have less access to benefits than workers in other industries. These depictions are examples of classism (and racism) at the cultural level. The structural elements of the agricultural industry that keep farmworkers poor, such as different labor laws than other industries and a heavy reliance on seasonal and often unauthorized workers, are examples of institutional-level classism. At an individual level, one often-unconscious manifestation is the privilege many of us have to remain ignorant of the working conditions of the many people whose labor helps to bring food to our tables.

RACIAL DISPARITIES IN WEALTH AND INCOME AND THE RACIALLY TIERED LABOR MARKET

As a result of the historical and ongoing entanglement of racism and classism in the U.S., class position remains highly correlated to race. Black, Latino, and Native American people are about 2.5 times as likely as whites to have income below the poverty line (although whites still make up about 45% of those living in poverty) (Macartney, Bishaw, & Fontenot, 2013). Asian Americans have a similar poverty rate to white people overall, but within the category of Asian American, there are large disparities across different ethnic or national identities. For example, the poverty rates of East Asian and South Asian Americans are much lower than the rates among Southeast Asian Americans who arrived here as refugees. The same is true of different ethnic identities within the umbrella category of Latino.

The impact of the 2008 economic meltdown hit communities of color harder than white communities, reproducing and exacerbating the correlation of class and race (Sullivan, Meschede, Dietrich, Shapiro, Traub, Reutschlin, & Draut, 2015). The loss of credit and homeownership disproportionately affected black and Latino households, for whom home equity had been a source of wealth and upward mobility. Black and Latino families experienced 53% and 66% losses in wealth respectively, compared to the 16% loss for white families (Kochhar, Fry, & Taylor, 2011).

Educational inequities also reproduce racial disparities in income and wealth. Inequities in the quality of schooling, differential school funding, and disproportionate penalizing of students of color for breaking rules, lead to a higher dropout rate for youth of color (including the children of recent immigrants) (Cookson, 2013; Lui, Robles, Leondar-Wright, Brewer, & Adamson, 2006). Without a high school diploma, these young people are more likely to enter into a lower tier of the labor market, working in low-wage service jobs with no opportunities for economic advancement.

Combined with the disproportionate policing of communities of color, high dropout rates put poor youth of color at high risk of arrest and incarceration in what some have termed a "school to prison pipeline" (Heitzeg, 2009). Once saddled with a criminal record, released former inmates face severe obstacles in securing employment and remain at high risk of being arrested and incarcerated again. The school-to-prison pipeline, the pressures of poverty in the racially tiered labor market, and the "war on drugs" that disproportionately targets and punishes people of color, have together contributed to a mass incarceration of young black men (among other men of color) that Michelle Alexander (2010) has dubbed "the new Jim Crow." Alexander uses the term to highlight how current-day incarceration of black youth and other youth of color have negative impacts equivalent to the explicit legal segregation of the U.S. South before the civil rights movement (Alexander, 2010). In addition to damaging the social structure of families and communities, the New Jim Crow harms communities economically by removing potential wage earners, perpetuating a cycle of poverty and vulnerability to arrest.

PERSONAL CREDIT AND DEBT

Decades of weak and stagnant wage growth made it less feasible for many families to maintain a middle-class lifestyle (Emelech, 2008; Mishel, Bernstein, & Allegretto, 2007; Shierholz & Mishel, 2013). Families borrowed money through second mortgages and accrued increasing credit card debt in an attempt to meet their expectations of a middle-class life, including sending their children to college as well as paying for day-to-day necessities (Wolff, 2009). Weak or unenforced consumer protection laws allowed banks to prey on consumers by setting high, uncapped credit card interest rates, fees, and penalties (Garcia, Lardner, & Zeldin 2008), and lower-income workers were vulnerable to exploitative lending by paycheck cashing and loan outlets charging 20–35% interest (Williams, 2001).

As a result of these policies, the total revolving debt in the U.S. reached $890 billion in 2014 compared to $54 billion in 1980 (Federal Reserve, 2015; Soederberg, 2012). Banks continue to profit from targeting low-income communities, African Americans, Latinos, single women, undocumented workers, and the newly bankrupted, all of whom need cash to survive despite escalating debt obligations (Soederberg, 2012). The very communities with less financial security are subjected to higher fees and interest rates and home foreclosure.

CLASSISM IN EDUCATION

The widely held assumption that education leads to class mobility is contradicted by the disparities in K–12 education (Brantlinger, 1993; Kincheloe & Steinberg, 2007). These persistent disparities include unequal quality of instruction and resources, teacher-student ratios, local funding per student, and race- and class-based counseling for students to pursue vocational or academic paths (Allan, Ozga, & Smith, 2009; Ornstein, 2007). They are perpetuated by policies and practices that continue to funnel resources to wealthy communities at the expense of low-income communities (Biddle & Berliner, 2002; Kozol, 1991; St. John, 2003). Unquestioned class-based assumptions and stereotypes track low-income students into vocational programs and community colleges, and affluent students into elite colleges (Brantlinger, 2003; McDonough, 1997; Schmidt, 2007). These class-based assumptions and stereotypes play out in the dynamics of self-identity, relationships among peers, and doubts or hopes about one's future (Brantlinger, 1993; Fiske & Markus, 2012).

In higher education, escalating personal debt poses a major challenge to today's students and endangers investments in their future. Several factors converged over the past several decades to make higher education increasingly unaffordable and classed. Home foreclosures closed off one source of family collateral for student loans; states decreased their subsidies to public higher education; the cost of college tuition skyrocketed; federal Pell grants were cut; and many college scholarships became "merit" based rather than need based. Students have to resort to private loans with high interest rates to finance their education, unwittingly supporting a lucrative new income stream for private banks.

The soaring costs of higher education in the context of cuts to public-funded loans and grants have resulted in the accumulation of more than $1 trillion in student debt as of 2012, with about 70% of graduating students in debt, up from 45% in 1993; and individual debt loads average $23,300 per student but run as high as $100,000 (Fry, 2014). This debt burden needs to be coupled with the current youth unemployment figures (16.3%) noted earlier to grasp the human tragedy facing this current generation of college graduates and indebted dropouts, burdened by unprecedented levels of personal debt and aggressively pursued by student loan debt collectors.

Classism in higher education is perpetuated by admissions practices that reward applicants with enough class privilege to afford college tuition without aid (and/or with the cultural capital to receive "merit"-based scholarships), to participate in extracurricular and co-curricular activities, and to pay for SAT preparatory classes that boost their scores (Espenshade & Radford, 2009; Stevens, 2007). Once matriculated, lower-income students often encounter challenges to their academic and social success in college, including ongoing family responsibilities, differences between their cultural capital and that expected and valued by the institution, and having to catch up academically after receiving an average or below-average K–12 education (Hopkins, 2014). They may lack academic confidence, face barriers to harnessing campus resources, and experience classist microaggressions that can affect their psychological well-being (Hopkins, 2014; Smith & Redington, 2010).

Examples of classism in higher education also include inequities whereby students with more class privilege are able to focus on academic and extracurricular responsibilities, while students with less privilege have to work one or more jobs; relatively privileged students can take advantage of unpaid internships, which allow them to gain professional experience and build social capital for future career opportunities, while poorer students must work for income in jobs that do not contribute to a professional career path; and students have differential access to the many personal development opportunities offered by colleges (which are also means of building social and cultural capital), such as study abroad programs, student clubs, and fraternity or sorority membership.

INTERSECTIONS OF CLASS AND CLASSISM WITH OTHER FORMS OF INJUSTICE AND OPPRESSION

As mentioned above, we take a broad, intersectional social justice approach in order to address how other systems of oppression operate through classism and vice versa. For our approach to classism, an intersectional framework is key. Even as we focus on how oppression plays out along class lines, we also hold that classism operates both in parallel to other systems of oppression, and in mutual reinforcement with them.

For example, as noted above, the U.S. economy has depended upon occupational segregation by race, and many historical examples illustrate how class and classism are complicated by and entangled with race and racism. In the contemporary U.S., the school-to-prison pipeline, prison labor, and non-unionized migrant labor in agricultural and domestic work connect race intimately with economic exploitation. Race and class are so entangled that race continues to serve as a class indicator, as evidenced by the persistent racial disparities in wealth and income (Lipsitz, 1998; Sullivan, Meschede, Dietrich, Shapiro, Traub, Reutschlin, & Draut, 2015).

Historically, religion was used to justify economic exploitation. The presumed superiority of Christianity was used to justify the murder of Native peoples and appropriation of Native lands by European settlers, as well as the exploitation of black, Sikh, Muslim, Chinese, and Japanese talent and labor. In all these cases, resistance was met by violence from armed security forces, militias, and police.

Gender intersects with class and race for women in domestic service (mainly African American, Caribbean, and/or Latina), who have been vulnerable to wage uncertainty and sexual abuse, as it did historically for the women who rebelled against wage cuts, long hours, and unsafe working conditions in 19th-century New England mill towns and 20th-century sweatshops.

Occupational segregation and unequal pay mean that women have less of their own income and wealth than men (although they may access some class privileges through the income and wealth of family members). Women still perform endless hours of unpaid work caring for children and the elderly (Folbre, 2001), while men are socialized to equate their self-worth with their financial net worth.

The intersection of classism with heterosexism can be seen in part through the reproduction of class within families. It is still true that many lesbian, gay, bisexual (LGB), and queer people are estranged from their families of origin, which can lead to loss of economic and social capital. Those who have been ineligible to marry (and those who choose not to) are excluded from policies that reward marriage with economic benefits. Along with the risk of employment discrimination on the basis of sexual orientation, this means that LGB people are more likely to live in poverty than their heterosexual peers (Sears & Badget, 2012). Among youth, LGB, queer, and trans* youth are disproportionately likely to lose access to family support and become homeless, leading to increased risk of violence and criminalization (Quintana, Rosenthal, & Krehely, 2010).

Like LGB people, many trans* people suffer from downward mobility spawned by family rejection, in addition to potential loss of professional networks (social capital) due to transphobia. Discrimination in employment, health care, and safety net services; lack of access to an appropriate government-issued identification; and occupational segregation into criminalized work all conspire to make trans* people highly concentrated among those living in poverty (Shlasko, 2014).

Classism also intersects with ableism: People living in poverty are more likely than others to acquire disabilities (through factors like workplace injuries, poor nutrition, and limited access to health care), and people with disabilities are more likely than people without disabilities to experience downward mobility (due to factors like employment discrimination and lack of support for health- and accommodation-related expenses). A far higher percentage of people with disabilities live in households that are below the poverty level (29% as opposed to 10% overall), and a similarly disproportionate number report not having adequate access to health care or transportation (National Organization on Disability, 2000).

Youth and elder oppression intersect with class in multiple ways. Changes in the economy over the last few decades mean that younger people today face a much more challenging economic environment than their parents and grandparents did. Entire categories of stable working-class jobs that used to be available to people who did not attend college—such as manufacturing jobs—have moved overseas. Professionalization of some fields means that work that was previously performed by people with little formal education now often requires a bachelor's degree or more—such as in early childhood education—so that a college degree now in some cases has become equivalent to the high school diploma of the past. Meanwhile, the cost of college has escalated dramatically, and the availability of scholarships has decreased (St. John, 2003). As a result, today's college generation graduates with substantially greater debt than prior generations (Kamenetz, 2006), which often leads to postponing life milestones, like moving away from one's parents, purchasing or even renting a long-term home, and having children.

For elders, increasing health care costs and the economic collapse of 2008 have meant that many people were not able to retire when they expected to. People were forced to continue to work well into old age, while leaving fewer job openings for young adults entering the workforce. Elders who had depended on income from work often face poverty when they stop working. Elders who wish to work or need to work face discrimination in hiring, and may be forced out despite capability and experience.

In each of these examples, we've honed in on the intersection of classism with one or two other systems of oppression, but of course it's not that simple. An intersectional analysis acknowledges all of the interactions among all of the systems of oppression as well as the various levels at which they can be identified—a practically unimaginable complexity. We usually think about one, two, or perhaps three systems or levels at a time, in order to examine specifics at a scale that we can conceptualize. Yet we return to the broader framework to remind ourselves that no system of oppression can be isolated from the others; all of the systems or levels are relevant to each other all of the time. In the pedagogy and facilitation sections below, we present a design that attempts to strike a balance between zooming in on classism particularly, and maintaining a broad intersectional view.

CURRENT GLOBAL CLASS AND CLASSISM ISSUES

The collapse of financial markets and soaring private debt after 2008 shook up everyone from Main Streets to Wall Streets, in a global context where "Wall Street" referred to financial networks linking New York and Los Angeles to London, Paris, Frankfurt, Tokyo, and Shanghai. If we are to understand the international scope and local consequences of global financial interdependency, we need to trace the entanglements of global capital (finance, ownership, and trade) with global resources (cheap labor and raw materials) as well as with educational systems geared to produce a tiered workforce (Apple, 2010; Collins, 2012; Piketty, 2014).

Several specific examples will be obvious, such as the U.S. dependency on oil markets that have also affected our Middle East policy, the outsourcing of clothing manufacture to low-wage workers in South Korea and China to maintain a price-advantage within U.S. markets, and the outsourcing of technical jobs to college-trained workers in India and Pakistan. Another example is the geo-economics by which heroin from poppies grown in Peru and Afghanistan gets refined in local drug labs and transported by murderously competing drug cartels, who control trade routes across national borders to reach the drug markets in the U.S. and elsewhere.

Globalization has made an already complicated set of economic interdependencies all the more difficult to understand. Still, as social justice educators, we believe it is important to help participants not only to understand the broader context of our international economic interdependencies, but also to locate themselves in these systems and draw connections from broad economic contexts to smaller scale relationships and experiences. Only by coordinating these frames of reference and placing themselves in the shoes of people who have resisted class oppression in the past, and continue to resist in the present, does it seem possible for participants to understand the role of personal responsibility and agency (Taibbi, 2014; Young, 2011). This is our effort in the following design.

CLASSISM CURRICULUM DESIGN

The classism design presented in this chapter aims to provide participants with an overview of the core social justice education (SJE) concepts related to classism, together with a basic understanding of historical and current manifestations of classism at the individual, institutional, and cultural levels. We also focus on possibilities for taking action and making change to challenge classism in our personal lives, universities, workplaces, and communities.

This design, like other designs in this volume, uses four quadrants as a way to sequence learning goals, key concepts, and activities. The quadrants generally follow the sequence

"What? So what? Now what?" The design can easily be modified for other modalities, such as short workshops or semester-long courses.

This sample design presupposes familiarity with the core social justice concepts that we consider foundational to any social justice approach presented in Chapter 4. In the quadrants below, we incorporate these core concepts as organizers for an exploration of a social justice approach to classism. It is strongly recommended that instructors and facilitators will have read Chapter 4, and will have considered these core concepts fully, before applying them in a social justice approach to classism.

The sample design for classism is followed by learning objectives and key concepts specific to each quadrant, as well as brief descriptions of the activities needed to carry out the design. Detailed instructions necessary to carry out the activities, as well as any handouts needed for each activity, can be found on the Classism website, Part 1, that accompanies this volume.

Following the design with its learning outcomes, core concepts, and activities, the chapter closes with a general discussion of pedagogical, design, and facilitation issues that we have found likely to be needed in teaching and learning about classism. More focused facilitation considerations related to each activity can be found with each activity on the website.

Quadrant 1: Opening the Session and Introductory Material

1. Welcome and Logistics (10 min)
2. Icebreaker Option A: Common Ground (15–20 min)
3. Icebreaker Option B: Meet and Greet (10 min)
4. Assumptions, Goals, and Agenda (10 min)
5. Frameworks (10 min)

Group Norms and Guidelines

1. Option A: Creation of Group Norms and Guidelines (10 min)
2. Option B: Hopes and Concerns (30 min)

Self-Reflection and Sharing about Class Background

1. Class Background Inventory (20–50 min)
2. Defining Class Brainstorm (15 min)

Income and Wealth Distribution

1. Option A: Distribution of Wealth Activity: 10 Chairs (30–45 min)
2. Option B: Video & Discussion
3. Quintiles (UFE activity demonstrating changes in real income over two 30-year periods; highlights impact of government policy on individual class experiences) (20 min)

Quadrant 2: Class Culture Activity

1. Option A: Discussion of Class Culture Readings (assigned ahead of time or handed out during the session) (30–90 min)
2. Option B: Class Culture Guided Reflection (20–40 min)

Cultural Capital Activity

1. Option A: Cultural Capital Questionnaire (30–45 min)
2. Option B: Cultural Capital Brainstorm (60 min)

Social Capital Activity

1. Option A: Exploring Your Network (30–45 min)
2. Option B: Quantifying Your Social Network (30–45 min)

History

1. Option A: History Lecture Presentation (30–60 min)
2. Optional B: Participant Activity to Accompany Lecture Presentation (60–90 min)
3. Option C: Family History in Context (30–45 min)

Integrate Learning

1. Closure Activity (20–30 min)

Quadrant 3: Bring in Unrepresented Voices

1. Option A: Multimedia Activity (70–90 min)
2. Option B: Discuss Reading Assignments (70–90 min)

Bringing It All Together

1. Examples of Classism Using a Five Faces of Classism Activity (40–90 min)
2. Follow-up with Examples in Contexts:
   Option A: Web of Institutional Classism (20–40 min)
   Option B: Identifying Opportunities for Coalition (30–60 min)

Quadrant 4: Classism in Your [Insert Context]

1. Option A: Classism in Your . . . (60 min)
2. Option B: Organizational Classism Assessment (45–60 min)

Taking Action

1. Acting Accountably (4A's) (10 min)
2. Action Continuum (20–40 min)
3. Action Planning (60–90 min)

Closing Activity

1. Option A: Closure Using Sentence Stems Such as One Takeaway or One Next Step (15–30 min)
2. Option B: Asking and Offering (15–30 min)

QUADRANT 1: OPENING THE SESSION AND INTRODUCTORY MATERIAL

Learning Outcomes for Quadrant 1:
- Participants understand that this is an SJE approach to classism
- Participants understand principles of participating in an SJE learning community
- Participants can explain definitions of "class" and "classism" by drawing on multiple class indicators
- Participants can describe some key features of the distribution of income and wealth in the U.S., and how they have changed over two example periods in recent U.S. history
- Participants can define a set of class categories
- Participants begin to reflect on their own class backgrounds, and locate themselves in the macro- and meso- level discussions that follow

Key Concepts for Quadrant 1: Class, classism, class indicator, income, wealth, ruling class, owning class, professional middle class, buffer class, working class, poverty class.

Activities and Options for Quadrant 1
- **Opening the Session and Introductory Material**
  - The two icebreakers—Option A: Common Ground and Option B: Meet and Greet—are activities through which participants learn something about each other and get a sense of who is in the group.
  - "Assumptions, Goals, and Agenda" are brief presentations that establish some parameters for the classism workshop or course.
  - Frameworks: Instructors briefly explain the SJE approach and how it applies to classism, drawing on Chapters 1–4 as well as this chapter.
- **Group Norms and Guidelines**
  - Option A creates group norms and guidelines, and uses a brainstorm to generate the guidelines.
  - Option B begins with participants' hopes and concerns, and then uses a group discussion to create norms and guidelines that address those hopes and concerns.
- **Self Reflection and Sharing about Class Background**
  - "Class Background Inventory" is a reflection and discussion activity that helps participants begin thinking and talking about the multiple layers of their class background.
  - "Defining Class Brainstorm" is a brainstorm and guided discussion that draws out and formalizes participants' implicit definitions of class, and establishes a shared definition for the course/workshop.
- **Income and Wealth Distribution**
  - Distribution of Wealth Activity, Option A: 10 Chairs, is a participatory activity that uses a spatial metaphor to demonstrate the distribution of wealth in the U.S., and to introduce functional definitions of class categories.
  - Distribution of Wealth Activity, Option B, is a video and discussion.
  - Distribution of Income Activity: Quintiles is a participatory activity that uses a spatial metaphor to demonstrate changes in the income growth of different class groups as quintiles during two recent periods of U.S. history, and to begin to make connections with policies that impact income inequality.

QUADRANT 2: CLASS CULTURE ACTIVITY

Learning Outcomes for Quadrant 2:
- Participants can define and explain these class indicators: Class culture, cultural capital, and social capital, and they understand how each indicator is related to the reproduction of power
- Participants understand some historical context for the current class system
- Participants locate themselves and their families relative to each class indicator and the historical context they've learned
- Participants note intersectionality of other manifestations of oppression with classism

Key Concepts for Quadrant 2: Class culture, cultural capital, social capital, power, unionization.

Activities and Options for Quadrant 2
- **Class Culture Activity**
  - Option A: Discussion of Class Culture Readings. These readings are assigned ahead of time or distributed as handouts during the session.
  - Option B: Class Culture Guided Reflection. This activity uses guided reflection and discussion to explore participants' experiences of class culture mismatches and to discuss implications for cross-class relationships, cross-class situations, and the reproduction of class.
- **Cultural Capital Activity**
  - Option A: Cultural Capital Questionnaire. This activity helps participants understand how our personal/familial culture and cultural assets intersect with class, class privilege, and class inequality.
  - Option B: Cultural Capital Brainstorm. This activity helps participants think about the relationship between cultural capital and class cultures.
- **Social Capital Activity**
  - Option A: Exploring Your Social Network. This activity helps participants identify the people in their social network and who they can go to for certain kinds of connections, resources, and advice.
  - Option B: Quantifying Your Social Network. This activity helps participants identify recognize the relationship between cultural capital, material capital, and social capital, and how class inequality is perpetuated.
- **History**
  - Option A: History Lecture Presentation. The facilitator presents "historical legacies" described earlier in this chapter, supplemented by the U.S. Class and Classism History/Timeline Handout located on the website.
  - Option B: Participant Activity to Accompany a Lecture Presentation. The facilitator presents an overview (as above) and engages participants in an activity.
  - Option C: Family History in Context. This option is used as an in-class activity or as a homework assignment. This activity leads participants to either reflect upon (in-class activity) or interview (homework activity) their own extended family members and to place their extended family history in the historical context from the lecture (Options A or B) as well as their readings.
- **Integrate learning—Session Closure Activity:** This closing activity assists participants with bringing together the session's themes and integrating their learning, and provides an opportunity to air remaining questions and highlight additional themes to inform facilitators' planning for the next session.

QUADRANT 3: BRING IN UNREPRESENTED VOICES

Learning Outcomes for Quadrant 3:
- Participants incorporate unfamiliar examples from class positionalities that are un- or under-represented in the group
- Intersectionality
- Participants can identify manifestations of classism at different levels and in different forms

Key Concepts for Quadrant 3: Individual, institutional, and cultural levels; Five Faces of Oppression.

Activities and Options for Quadrant 3
- **Bringing in Unrepresented Voices**
  - Option A: Multimedia Activity. Video and Internet resources are set up in different rooms and stations so that participants can watch and respond to various depictions of class and classism.
  - Option B: Discuss Assigned Readings. If reading assignments have been completed, this provides a small-group opportunity for participants to either respond to guided questions about the readings, or generate their own questions, for whole-group discussion.
- **Bringing It All Together—Classism Examples**
  - Five Faces of Oppression Classism Activity: This interactive small-group activity draws out a variety of examples of manifestations of classism and explores some overlaps and interconnections with other systems of oppression.
  - Follow-up Option A: Web of Institutional Classism. This option is a visual and kinesthetic demonstration of how various manifestations of classism in institutions work together.
  - Follow-up Option B: Identifying Opportunities for Coalition. This structured problem-solving discussion in small groups highlights the overlaps and intersections between classism and other systems of oppression, and begins to transition participants toward thinking about steps for effective action.

QUADRANT 4: CLASSISM IN YOUR [INSERT CONTEXT]

Learning Outcomes for Quadrant 4:
- Participants apply concepts of class and classism to a specific organizational context of their school, workplace, etc.
- Participants apply concepts of class and classism to their own behavior as an "ally" to those with less class privilege than them
- Participants consider elements needed for an effective action plan

Key Concepts for Quadrant 4:

Acting as allies, advocates, in coalition, network building, spheres of influence

Activities and Options for Quadrant 4
- Classism in your [insert context]
  - Option A: Classism in Your . . . (school, workplace, etc.). This activity helps participants recognize manifestations of classism in their context, and to begin practicing effective ways to take action against classism in everyday situations.

    ◦   Option B: Organizational Classism Assessment. This activity helps participants apply concepts and information around classism to their specific organizational context.

- **Taking Action**
  - ◦ Acting Accountably (4A's). This activity helps introduce a framework for helping participants to think about accountable action for liberation.
  - ◦ Action Continuum. In this activity, participants go to stations around the room to discuss where individual participants are in relation to addressing classism, stand in groups and share examples, and share a few examples publicly. Participants then move to the station that describes where they would like to be and discuss ways of achieving that goal.
  - ◦ Action Planning. This activity helps participants identify ways to take action against classism in everyday life as well as in their organization; to reflect upon their spheres of influence and potential risks; to identify the skills, knowledge, and coalitions or networks needed; and to make commitments to carry through the change.
- **Closing Activity**
  - ◦ Option A: Sentence Stems. This closing activity is for groups that have come together only for this workshop/course.
  - ◦ Option B: Asking & Offering. This closing activity is for intact groups that brings closure to the learning experience and helps the group integrate new learnings into their ordinary work together.

NOTES FOR PEDAGOGY, DESIGN, AND FACILITATION

In classism workshops, as with any other social justice topic, there are challenges specific to the topic itself. Some are dilemmas related to overall pedagogical frameworks, others relate to design and sequencing decisions, and still others are facilitation challenges; many are a combination of two or more of these. In this concluding segment of the Classism chapter, we present specific issues of pedagogy, design, and facilitation that, in our experience, are important considerations for instructors and facilitators.

CLASS AS CATEGORY AND IDENTITY

As noted above, the public discourse on class tends to obscure economic realities, in part through encouraging nearly everyone to identify as "middle class." As a result, participants will have different relationships with their own social group memberships as members of class categories. Some may not "identify with" their class category; it may feel like a situation they are in and not part of who they are as a person. Others may identify with a class category that does not describe their current or previous class position. As a result, facilitators may find ourselves in the awkward position, when teaching about the realities of the class divide, of challenging participants' class-based self-identity. Although in general it is usually inappropriate (and, especially when in a position of power as an instructor/facilitator, unethical) to challenge someone's self-identity, in the case of classism, self-identity based on misunderstandings of the class-based categories may need further probing or clarification. Yet one of the ways classism is internalized is that people often misunderstand what their relative class ranking is.

For participants, being told or realizing during the workshop/course they have been mistaken about their class can come as a shock. As facilitators, we must balance respecting the ways in which participants have made sense of their experiences with supporting them to challenge those understandings with new frameworks and information. It is helpful to distinguish carefully between when we are speaking about class identity per se—meaning the class group with which someone identifies—and when we are speaking about class category—one's relative social ranking in more objective or at least describable terms.

The issue of class identification brings up a particularly acute facilitation dilemma around defining class categories. On one hand, participants may be anxious for definitive meanings with which to categorize themselves and others. Yet, since people's implicit definitions of these categories often include value judgments about the desirability of belonging to different class categories, participants may also be reluctant to categorize themselves honestly. Participants' processes of sorting themselves and their experiences into these categories—as ill-defined and emotionally laden as the categories are—can forestall open inquiry into class experiences. In addition, some participants may simply lack awareness about relevant class markers and/or analytic frameworks that would help them make sense of their experiences. For example, some participants may not have accurate information about the quantity, type, and origins of their family resources.

One way to address this challenge is to postpone defining class categories, and first encourage participants to discuss their own class backgrounds and situations with regard to specific class markers rather than general class categories. This approach creates space for important conversations about the range of experience (not just identity categories) in the group, and gives participants opportunities to discover and interrogate their own implicit definitions of the categories. However, it can be time-consuming. For shorter workshops, especially workshops with a specific goal that isn't served by such conversations, defining the categories at the beginning may be preferable.

Another way that class identification comes up is when participants have internalized beliefs about meritocracy. For example, a middle-class student may insist that their academic success is a result of their own hard work and cannot be attributed to class advantage. Or, a working-class student may insist that class barriers won't limit them and that their hard work is going to pay off in financial success, despite well-documented trends to the contrary.

Participants' beliefs about class expressed on a micro-level may seem like resistance to acknowledging the realities of classism, and may have the effect of distracting from macro-level discussions. At the same time, these beliefs are sometimes deeply ingrained parts of who participants understand themselves to be, and may serve important functions for them psychologically. The stories people tell themselves about meritocracy can help them to feel worthy and hopeful rather than guilty or hopeless. Rather than engaging with participants' beliefs about themselves as individuals, it is often most helpful for facilitators to distinguish between what may occur at a micro-level with any given individual, and the macro-systems that create trends, likelihoods, and overall inequity. As participants process their learning about macro-systems, their understanding of their own identities and roles will likely evolve as well.

WHO IS AND WHO IS NOT IN THE ROOM?

The class diversity among participants makes a significant difference in the overall experience of the course/workshop, along with diversity of other social identities, generation, family immigration history, and individual experiences. Since some activities have been designed to take advantage of the diversity of experiences and viewpoints in the group, it is important that facilitators be aware of the relative diversity or homogeneity of a group and plan accordingly.

In terms of generation, the economic moment in which people experience major life milestones, like finishing school, getting a first job, and retiring, have a large impact on their experience of class. Someone who grew up in a blue-collar family in the 1950s, when many blue-collar workers were unionized and well-paid, will have a markedly different experience of being "working class" than someone who grew up in a similar class situation in the 1990s. The difference is not only about their ages now, but also about their generations.

Families' immigration histories impact their experiences of class, both in terms of where they stand in the generational sequence since their family's entry to the U.S. as well as changes in the larger economic context that affect their class. For example, some immigrants who are highly trained professionals experience a drop in status and income upon immigrating because their credentials are not valid in the U.S.

Many class markers vary across region and urban/suburban/ruralness because of differences in the cost of living and the different resources needed to live comfortably in different contexts. For example, in some major cities, owning a car for each adult in the family is a luxury, while in most rural areas, it is a prerequisite for being able to work outside the home.

To account for these factors, facilitators should learn as much as possible about the group in advance of finalizing design decisions. In some cases, a pre-survey may be possible; in other cases, facilitators will have to make educated guesses based on the population of the school, organization, or community from which participants are drawn. If some class categories are likely to be very underrepresented or unrepresented, facilitators should explore ways to bring perspectives and issues relevant to those groups into the course/workshop. Additionally, facilitators should be cautious about assumptions or generalizations that may confuse or alienate participants based on differences in region, immigration, generation, and so on.

In some cases, a majority of participants may be within a relatively narrow range of class backgrounds, with a few outliers who have far more or far less class privilege. Facilitators should take care to address the needs of outliers, and avoid teaching only to the needs of the majority. It is especially important to consider those participants who are likely to experience themselves as "the only" representative of a particular class group (or other social group). Avoid appointing these participants as "experts" or examples for other participants' learning; yet do consider how the whole group might be served by discussions that seem at first to be mostly for/about the outliers. Often there are larger themes that might be elucidated by dedicating time to the perspectives and experiences of participants who are not in the majority.

In many college contexts (and some other groups as well), it is likely that a majority of participants will identify as middle class, whether or not they are middle class according to the "working definitions" of class indicators or class definitions that have been developed during Quadrant 1, either in the "Defining Class Brainstorm" activity or through the parameters of income in the "Distribution of Income Activity: Quintiles." It will be important that the group has agreed to stipulate "working definitions," however they are arrived at through the activities in Quadrant 1. If participants identify as "middle class" without nuance or qualification, the facilitator can remind participants that this assumption occurs partly because of the society-wide norm of describing practically everyone as middle class, and partly because of the class segregation that shapes student bodies and many workplaces to be relatively class-homogenous.

If a participant expressed the opinion that all or most of the participants are middle class, it may be difficult for participants who know they are not middle class to speak up and disrupt that normalized narrative. When someone says, "we are all middle class," facilitators can (1) remind participants that they do not know the experiences of others in the room,

(2) initiate discussion of why the group might not be as homogenous as it seems (that is, what institutional and societal forces lead to some groups not being represented), (3) initiate discussion of why people might believe that the group is more homogeneous than it is, and (4) remind the group of the multiple factors that shape class location and the difficulty of precision because of these factors. If this conversation occurs before more nuanced definitions of class categories are introduced, it can be useful to return to it later to ask participants to reassess their own class category in light of the new definitions, and to reflect on how that changes their understanding of the range of class experiences in the group.

One specific way the "we're all middle class" trope comes up is when participants assert that the fact of being a college student (or a student at a particular college) is such a privilege that it overrides any class differences. This statement often serves to silence discussion of the inequities within the student body and the micro- and meso-level classism that less-privileged students face on campus (see the Education section of this chapter). Facilitators can address such statements by briefly acknowledging the partial truth they contain, and then providing and/or asking for examples of how/why they are not true.

CLASS CULTURE AND CULTURAL CONGRUENCE

It is important to ensure that the course/workshop is culturally relevant for all participants. Instructors/facilitators should give particular attention to known class culture patterns, and should consider how they might unconsciously bring professional-middle-class assumptions to their pedagogy, design, and facilitation. Because of the normalizing and privileging of professional-middle-class culture in many organizations, this is a risk even if the facilitators/instructors did not grow up professional middle-class! Considerations of cultural congruence can come up in many ways, and they are addressed in the next several sections focusing on guidelines, risk and taboo, personal vs. academic understandings of class, and action.

GUIDELINES FOR PARTICIPATION

Establishing guidelines or group agreements will enable participants to feel more comfortable approaching challenging topics and give them a sense of ownership of the group process. For classism courses/workshops, it is especially important to set clear guidelines around confidentiality and participation, since participants may be invited to disclose sensitive information about their finances or family situations while participating in group activities. In order to address some participants' need for privacy while still encouraging reflection and participation, one guideline to consider is that when someone chooses not to participate in a particular activity, they should instead reflect, and if possible share their reflections, about the reasons for their choice.

The Case Against Guidelines

As valuable as guidelines can be, there are arguments against using guidelines in certain situations (Hunter, n.d.; Lakey, 2010). One of the potential pitfalls of group guidelines is that they tend to reflect the dominant culture of the group, the facilitators, and/or the organization (see Chapter 3). In a course/workshop about classism, it can be particularly counterproductive to establish guidelines that reflect professional-middle-class or owning-class cultural values as if these values are universal. Since most participants and many educators have little practice thinking about class culture, and since those cultural norms are reinforced in many organizations and in college and university settings, this is all too likely to occur, even when the facilitators do not come from middle-class or upper-class backgrounds.

Guidelines addressing how participants should manage conflict are one example. For many reasons, including cultural patterns and specific family experiences, participants may or may not view conflict as potentially positive or productive. In a classism course/workshop, it is important to acknowledge and value class culture differences about conflict. What we know about class culture patterns in general will not hold true for everyone, since personal experience and other identities also play a role; nevertheless, it is useful to be aware of the patterns.

Specifically, there is research that suggests that poor and working-class cultures value conflict and express it openly. For some people with those backgrounds, it may be productive for group members to explicitly express disagreement with another's perspective or actions (Lakey, 2010; Leondar-Wright, 2014). This contrasts with many professional-middle-class cultures, which tend to be conflict-avoidant. To many poor and working-class participants, professional-middle-class expectations of how to communicate disagreement may feel formulaic, or like "sugar coating." People from poor and working-class backgrounds who participate in majority-professional-middle-class settings (such as higher education) are already accustomed to having their communication styles stifled, especially around conflict, based on enforced professional-middle-class norms. To create a similarly stifling environment in a workshop/course about classism is an unfortunate and counterproductive contradiction. Instead, we encourage noting the variety of approaches to conflict (and other aspects of group communication) and supporting participants to communicate across differences as relevant, without norming or enforcing any particular communication style over another.

Knowing some of the pitfalls and complications of group guidelines, it is important that facilitators be thoughtful and deliberate in deciding whether to establish guidelines, and if so, how to use and revisit them. These choices have important implications for different expressions of class (and/or ethnic, racial, gender, and other) cultures. When guidelines are not used, the facilitators need another plan for how to keep the course/workshop productive for all participants. For example, they should build in more time for group process and/or for teaching communication and feedback skills that participants can use to help the course/workshop go well.

RISK AND TABOO

In considering sequencing, we generally encourage facilitators to start with those activities that present relatively low emotional risk for participants, and progress to higher-risk activities that ask participants to step farther out of their comfort zones. With regard to classism, participants will often have widely varying senses of how risky a particular activity feels, because of their class backgrounds and other factors.

To some participants, describing their class experiences at all may feel like a high-risk activity. Participants at the lower and higher ends of the income and wealth spectrum may be reluctant to disclose out of shame, embarrassment, or guilt, or out of fear that other participants will judge them. Many middle-class participants may believe that it is inappropriate to talk about family finance based on the widely held taboo against talking about class differences, especially in quantitative terms.

On the other hand, for some participants from poor and working-class backgrounds, it may feel normal and comfortable to discuss financial struggles in frank and specific terms. These participants may feel impatient with what feels to them like an unnecessarily cautious pace, especially if they see it as accommodating the discomfort expressed by participants with more privilege.

Disclosure about class tends to feel risky in different ways depending on whether participants are an intact group (who already know each other before the course/workshop) or a new group (who come together for the course/workshop). With intact groups, participants may feel nervous about disrupting existing assumptions and patterns in their relationships; on the other hand, they may have a base of trust that makes disclosure feel like less of a stretch. With new groups, the lack of established trust may make disclosure feel like a forced intimacy that participants may not immediately be ready for. In an ongoing course that focuses on classism for some sessions and other topics in other sessions, the group may be more like a new group or more like an intact group, depending on when in the course the classism section comes.

When considering activities and sequencing decisions, we urge facilitators to imagine the range of perspectives that participants may bring. Craft a sequence in which all participants are encouraged to push their comfort zones in different ways. Although different participants may feel challenged at different times, try to mix it up such that no group of participants spends a long time feeling far more or far less vulnerable than another group.

Additionally, consider initiating a discussion about the taboo itself. Questions to address include what is considered "private" information and why; what purposes shame and guilt play in maintaining the class system; for whom and in what contexts it is taboo to talk about money, and for whom and in what contexts it is not taboo; and in what ways the taboo serves and/or undermines justice.

TENSIONS BETWEEN ACADEMIC AND PERSONAL UNDERSTANDINGS OF CLASSISM

Most participants come into classes/workshops about classism from one of three different perspectives and positions about class and classism. First, some participants have thought very little about class or classism in any context prior to the course/workshop. Second, some participants may come with significant academic knowledge about class and classism (often gained from classes in Economics or Sociology), while having limited if any reflection on their own class background, classed experiences, or personal participation in the system of classism. This second group's understanding of class may be highly structured but impersonal, and they may exhibit unconsciously classist behaviors while articulating an anti-classist analysis. Finally, others may come motivated by their personal experiences of being *class straddlers* (i.e., people who grew up in one class category and later experienced class mobility putting them into another category) or of being outliers in relation to their peers. Their understandings start from the personal, may be emotional for them, and may or may not also include some systemic analysis stemming from learning in school or the community.

With participants coming from such different perspectives, the questions arise: Which kinds of knowledge are considered real and valid? Whose views and experiences are given credence? What is the value for the second sort of participant of adding personalized reflection to their understanding of classism, and what is the value for the third sort of participant in adding structured theoretical knowledge to their understanding?

As with all the curricula in this book, we believe a balance of personal and theoretical learning is most effective. Facilitators should acknowledge and appreciate the various kinds of knowledge participants may bring to the group, and participants should not be allowed to use any form of knowledge as a "trump" to discount or delegitimize other participants' perspectives. At the same time, it is important to highlight and interrogate the ways in which academic and impersonal knowledge is privileged over that drawn from personal experience—both in the sense that the former is taken more serious by the power structures, and in the sense that a level of class privilege is required to have access to it.

Participants with academic understandings about class may need to be reminded that their knowledge does not exempt them from learning about practical, everyday, micro-level impacts of classism; in fact, it may oblige them to approach the learning opportunity with particular openness. Participants with more personal understandings about class may need to be reassured that their lack of academic learning about it (for those for whom that's true) does not take away from their real lived knowledge; at the same time, they can be encouraged to explore what they might gain from also learning about classism on a more theoretical level.

FOCUSING ON THE SYSTEMIC/CULTURAL LEVELS TO AVOID THE INDIVIDUAL AND INTERPERSONAL LEVELS OF CLASSISM

A related but slightly different facilitation challenge comes up when some participants may tend to focus only on broad-scale structural analysis—the macro level—as a way of avoiding micro-level discussions that would feel too personal. This tendency may let some participants "off the hook" of examining their own experiences of privilege and/or oppression, and can silence other participants who could contribute insights based on their micro-level reflections.

Focusing on the macro level is important, but it should not be used to distract from or avoid other issues. If discussion seems to keep drifting back to the macro level while meso- and micro-level topics go unexplored, or if participants say or imply that macro-level issues should take precedence over other parts of the discussion, facilitators should steer the conversation toward a more balanced micro/meso/macro approach. It can be useful to remind participants that classism as a system relies on all three levels; the purpose of the course/workshop is not only to identify classism that happens "out there" in macro trends, but also to notice its manifestations "in here"—in our everyday lives, cultures, and institutions—and to seek ways to address it on all three levels.

Similarly, some participants may want to focus on a global context in a way that avoids or masks classism in the U.S. For example, someone may argue that, relative to people in many other countries, everyone in the U.S. is privileged economically. Such statements contain some truth, and can be an important part of the conversation. Yet too often they have the impact of obscuring the reality of classism and inequality within the U.S. Participants should be encouraged to consider the global context, and should also be urged to recognize and grapple with the reality of inequality and classism in the U.S., which is more extreme than they probably realize.

TAKING ACTION

As in any social justice course/workshop, it is important to address how participants can apply the new awareness and knowledge they have gained. In a successful course/workshop, participants' learning will generate a lot of energy and feelings. Reactions may include distress at the injustices they have become aware of, feelings of helplessness at the enormity of the systems they confront, relief at being able to articulate and explain something that they had previously noticed but not understood, and a desire to do something to make it better. A well-designed workshop gives participants options and tools with which to channel this energy into useful action.

Too often the question of how to act on new learning is relegated to a short segment at the very end of the course/workshop, but there are many ways to incorporate it throughout.

A benefit of starting to think about action earlier in the course/workshop is that participants' learning can be more solution-focused, and any helplessness they may feel upon confronting the scale of injustice in the world is less likely to be shorter-lived. On the other hand, if participants know very little about classism, starting to talk about action too soon can generate resistance from participants who are not convinced that classism is a problem. In group-action assignments, differences in understanding and analysis among participants can lead to difficulty agreeing on a project, especially in the beginning when participants may not yet have common vocabulary, knowledge, and skills to move their conversation forward. In these cases, introducing an action project in the second half or even toward the end of a longer course may be preferable.

In short one-time workshops, the action segment may be as simple as a closing reflection asking each participant to share one thing they will do next. Allotting even five minutes to reflection on next steps is far preferable to not addressing it at all. However, we urge facilitators to allocate as much time as is feasible to taking action. In the included design, we devote significant time to action, mostly in the fourth quadrant.

In some contexts, action will be built into every step of the design. For example, a training with an intact group may begin with acknowledgement of a specific problem the group is hoping to address through learning about classism. The problem can be revisited at different points throughout the training to make note of how participants' learning adds to their understanding of the problem and possible approaches to solving it, and the training can culminate with a more in-depth problem-solving and action-planning session. Similarly, in a course spanning multiple weeks, an action project may be assigned near the beginning or middle of the course, with periodic touch points and a culminating presentation or report due at the end of the course.

INTERSECTIONALITY

An intersectional framework should inform every aspect of a course/workshop, from planning to design to content to facilitation. Before planning a course/workshop on classism, facilitators should consider the possible impacts and implications of doing so in their particular context. Without a doubt, most groups need to learn about classism, but they also need to learn about and address many other systems of oppression. Which voices and conversations are amplified, and which might be talked over or silenced, by offering a course/workshop primarily focused on classism? Are there other topics that should be offered or at least announced simultaneously, in order to make the intersectional approach of the project transparent? Whose voices are centered and whose are marginalized in the planning process itself?

As the course/workshop begins, we encourage facilitators to introduce intersectionality from the very start. Doing so helps to set a tone of inviting complexity, and can reassure participants that a focus on classism does not preclude discussion of racism, sexism, or other systems of oppression; on the contrary, a robust exploration of classism *requires* that other systems be considered.

In terms of content and facilitation, many of the activities in our design include information and opportunities for discussion about classism's intersections with other systems of oppression. Even when intersectionality is not explicit in an activity, facilitators should be alert to opportunities for deepening discussion by giving examples and asking follow-up questions that highlight intersectionality.

For example, on an individual or interpersonal level, if participants are describing their class experiences in one-dimensional terms that only acknowledge class and not other identities/systems, saying things like "as a middle class person, I . . .," facilitators can follow up with questions like: "What other aspects of your identity might contribute to that experience? In what ways is that experience about class, and in what ways might it also be about your race, gender, age, religious background, . . .?" Similar responses are appropriate when participants make generalizations about class groups to which they may or may not belong. Intersectionality reminds us of the dangers of saying "*all* poor people experience such-and-such manifestation of classism." Rather, we should be holding as an ongoing question for participants to explore, "*Which* poor people experience such-and-such, how, and why?"

Similarly, on an institutional level, if participants describe examples of institutional classism in one-dimensional terms, a facilitator could ask, "How is racism (and/or another relevant system) also showing up in that example? How does the racism of that institution contribute to its classism, and vice versa? What could it look like to examine/address *both* the racism and the classism of that example at the same time?" On a macro level, if participants are discussing broad trends in culture or history in one-dimensional terms, a facilitator can add complexity with questions like, "What else would we learn about that story if we used an intersectional lens? In addition to class, what else is going on there?"

A common and unfortunate pitfall that many participants and facilitators fall into on the way to intersectional analysis is conflating race and class such that discussions hinge on combined categories, as in statements like, "Poor people and people of color are under-represented in the sciences." The phrase "poor people and people of color" often comes from a well-intentioned desire to acknowledge both racism and classism and to avoid leaving anyone out. Unfortunately, such statements fail to distinguish between the different mechanisms and impacts of racism and classism; used sloppily, they can imply that classism impacts poor white people identically to how racism impacts people of color (all of whom are assumed to be poor also). The conversations thus framed tend to focus primarily on those groups that come to mind easily because they represent large numbers of people or highly visible groups, or because they match our stereotypes—such as "poor black urban mothers" and "owning-class white men." Meanwhile, many other groups—"poor white rural elders," for example, or "professional-middle-class Latinas," are ignored.

Instead of conflating race and class, we should help participants to learn to specify *how* racism and classism each function, how they function together, and how they have similar and different impacts on different groups of people. In addition to offering a more robust analysis and leading to richer conversation, this framework helps to ensure that no participant's experience or identity will be invisible in the room because it doesn't match the stereotypical combinations of identities.

HISTORY

In a course/workshop that primarily focuses on the present day and on taking action, it can be difficult to justify spending time on history. Yet historical perspective is necessary for understanding the legacies that have led to current economic inequality, as well as traditions of resistance and change that activists draw on today. Since many, if not most, historical manifestations of classism are directly reflected in current manifestations, incorporating history does not mean having only a separate activity about it. Facilitators (and participants) should bring up relevant historical connections throughout the course/workshop. Additionally, the design we provide here includes a brief historical review to provide information that participants can then draw upon to make connections with their own experiences and contemporary manifestations of classism.

In addition to the societal-level history, it can be useful to bring in local or organization-specific history. For example, in a college course, facilitators might consider including historical material related to the college's financial aid system and/or the college's role in the economy of the community in which it is located. In a community-organizing context, a history of class in the specific city, profession, or demographic that unites that group can be compelling and instructive. It will sometimes be beyond the facilitators' capacity to research and provide such information; if so, consider incorporating an assignment in which participants research the issue and report back on both the information gleaned and the process of finding it.

SEQUENCING: INDIVIDUAL TO SOCIETAL/CULTURAL LEVELS

One of the key design decisions facilitators need to make is whether to start with an exploration of personal experiences (micro-level) before moving on to institutional (meso-level) and societal (macro-level) examples, or vice versa. There are strengths and liabilities of each approach, which vary depending on the nature of the group. Specifically, we've found that the micro- to macro-sequencing tends to work best for intact groups that already have a common base of knowledge (whether from reading assignments, from previous sessions in an ongoing course, or from the group's shared culture that has included talking about class outside of the course/workshop). Macro- to micro-sequencing tends to work best for shorter sessions with new groups in which participants don't know each other, have not completed pre-reading, and/or have little shared experience to draw on.

The four-quadrant design presented here adopts a hybrid model. We start by framing classism as a social justice and intersectional topic, which is itself a macro approach. The first few activities encourage micro-level reflection, before switching to meso- and macro-level activities to establish some shared understanding. Later we return to further, deeper, micro-level reflection incorporating the contextual factors participants will have learned about in the meanwhile.

BRINGING IT ALL TOGETHER

Whether the course/workshop starts with macro-level analysis or micro-level personal testimonials, there will come a point when the levels come together and participants are asked to generate examples at all levels and/or of various types, and to recognize the connections among the different manifestations. Facilitators face pedagogical decisions about how much to rely on the group's own knowledge, how much to insert new information, and how to integrate the two.

Because this social justice approach to classism may present a new framework for so many people, some participants may initially be unable to generate examples of classism. It is not that they are unfamiliar with the manifestations of classism, but rather that they may be unused to thinking of them *as* classism, or unused to thinking of class inequality or devaluation as being problematic. It can be helpful for the facilitator(s) to seed the discussion with a few examples to get started. The examples could be manifestations of classism and/or manifestations of other systems of oppression. In some cases, the latter may be even more generative: When participants see an example that they recognize immediately and obviously as racist, sexist, or heterosexist (for example), it may lead them to think of parallel or related manifestations of classism that would not otherwise have occurred to them.

The design we include here uses Iris Marion Young's "Five Faces of Oppression" to structure participants' brainstorm of examples during the second half of the course/workshop, after a series of activities that will provide many examples for participants to draw on and add to.

FACILITATOR PREPARATION

Even with the best design, there is some individual work that every facilitator will need to do in order to facilitate effectively about classism. In particular, it is important for facilitators to explore their own hot buttons on issues of classism and class as well as their assumptions about their own and participants' class positions. Ideally, facilitators should develop this self-awareness in conversation with one or more co-facilitators or colleagues.

CLASSISM IN THE CLASSROOM OR WORKSHOP

Similarly, all our preparation and design cannot keep classism out of the classroom. Even as we articulate and explore the many manifestations of classism, we can count on it manifesting right there and then in the course/workshop. At the very least, facilitators should be aware of such manifestations and seek to mitigate their impact on participants. In some contexts, facilitators may choose to draw attention to the classism in the room as a teachable moment, to enrich the discussion with real-life, real-time examples. Such discussions can be challenging to facilitate precisely because they are so "real" and present; for the same reason, they can be among the most powerful learning moments of a workshop/course.

Note

* We ask that those who cite this work always acknowledge by name all of the authors listed rather than either only citing the first author or using "et al." to indicate coauthors. All collaborated on the conceptualization, development, and writing of this chapter.

References

Alexander, M. (2010). *The new Jim Crow: Mass incarceration in the age of colorblindness*. New York: New Press.

Allan, J., Ozga, J., & Smith, G. (Eds.). (2009). *Social capital, professionalism and diversity*. Rotterdam, The Netherlands: Sense Publishers.

Apple, M. W. (Ed.). (2010). *Global crises, social justice, and education*. New York: Routledge.

Bartlett, D. L, & Steele, J. B. (1994). *America: Who really pays the taxes?* New York: Simon & Schuster.

Biddle, B., & Berliner, D. C. (2002, May). A research synthesis: Unequal school funding in the United States. *Beyond Instructional Leadership, 59*(8), 48–59.

Bishaw, A. (2013, Sept.). *Poverty 2000–2012: American community survey briefs*. (ACSBR/12–01). Washington, DC: U.S. Census Bureau. Retrieved from https://www.census.gov/prod/2013pubs/acsbr12-01.pdf

Bourdieu, P. (1984). *Distinction: A social critique of the judgement of taste*. London: Routledge.

Bourdieu, P. (1986). The forms of capital. In J. Richardson (Ed.), *Handbook of theory and research for the sociology of education* (pp. 241–258). New York: Greenwood Press.

Boushey, H. (2014, Oct. 15). *Understanding economic inequality and growth at the top of the income ladder*. The Washington Center for Equitable Growth. Retrieved from http://equitablegrowth.org/research/economic-inequality-growth-top-income-ladder/

Brantlinger, E.A. (1993). *The politics of social class in secondary school: Views of affluent and impoverished youth*. New York: Teachers College Press.

Brantlinger, E. A. (2003). *Dividing classes: How the middle class negotiates and rationalizes school advantage*. New York: Routledge Falmer.

Brodkin, K. (1998). *How Jews became white folks & what that says about race in America*. New Brunswick, NJ: Rutgers University Press.

Bureau of Labor Statistics (BLS). (2014 Jan. 24). *Union membership summary*. Retrieved January 11, 2015, from http://www.bls.gov/news.release/pdf/union2.pdf

Burnham, L., & Theodore, N. (2012). *Home economics: The invisible and unregulated world of domestic work*. New York: National Domestic Workers Alliance.

Callahan, D., & Cha, M. J. (2013). *Stacked deck: How the dominance of politics by the affluent & business undermines economic mobility in America*. Demos. Retrieved from http://www.demos.org/stacked-deck-how-dominance-politics-affluent-business-undermines-economic-mobility-america

Collins, C. (2012). *99 to 1: How wealth inequality is wrecking the world and what we can do about it*. San Francisco: Berrett-Koehler Publishers.

Collins, C. (2014, Dec. 15). Echoing in the streets: A growing racial wealth divide. *Huffington Post*. Retrieved January 17, 2015, from http://www.huffingtonpost.com/chuck-collins/echoing-in-the-streets-a-_b_6319740.html

Collins, C., & Yeskel, F. (2005). *Economic apartheid in America* (2nd ed.). New York: The New Press.

Cookson, P. W. (2013). *Class rules: Exposing inequality in American high schools*. New York: Teacher's College Press.

Daniels, R. (2002). *Coming to America: A history of immigration and ethnicity in American life*. New York: Perennial.

Domhoff, G. W. (1983). *Who rules America now? A view for the '80s*. New York: Simon & Schuster.

Emelech, Y. (2008). *Transmitting inequality: Wealth and the American family*. Lanham, MD: Rowman & Littlefield.

Espenshade, T., & Radford, A. W. (2009). *No longer separate, not yet equal: Race and class in elite college admission and campus life*. Princeton, NJ: Princeton University Press.

Fair Labor Standards Act of 1938 (FLSA, 1938). Chapter 676, 52 Stat. 1060 (29 U.S.C. 201 et seq.), passed June 25, 1938. Short title, see 29 U.S.C. 201. Ithaca, NY: Legal Information Institute, Cornell University. Retrieved from http://www.law.cornell.edu/topn/fair_labor_standards_act_of_1938

Fair Labor Standards Act Amendments of 1966 (FLSA, 1966). Pub. L. 89–601, 80 Stat. 830, passed Sept. 23, 1966. Short title, see 29 U.S.C. 201 note. Ithaca, NY: Legal Information Institute, Cornell University. Retrieved from http://www.law.cornell.edu/topn/fair_labor_standards_amendments_of_1966

Federal Reserve (2015, April). *Consumer credit—G.19* (Federal Reserve statistical release). Retrieved from http://www.federalreserve.gov/releases/g19/current/default.htm

Fiske, S. T., & Markus, H. R. (Eds.). (2012). *Facing social class. How societal rank influences interaction*. New York: Russell Sage Foundation.

Folbre, N. (2001). *The invisible heart: Economics and family values*. Philadelphia: Temple University Press.

Foner, E. (1998). *The story of American freedom*. New York: Norton & Co.

Fry, R. (2014, Oct. 7). *The changing profile of student borrowers: Cumulative student debt among recent college graduates*. Pew Research Center. Retrieved January 18, 2015, from http://www.pewsocialtrends.org/2014/10/07/cumulative-student-debt-among-recent-college-graduates/

Fry, R., & Kochhar, R. (2014, Dec. 12). *Wealth inequality has widened along racial, ethnic lines since end of Great Recession*. Pew Research Center. Retrieved January 17, 2015, from http://www.pewresearch.org/fact-tank/2014/12/12/racial-wealth-gaps-great-recession/

Garcia, J., Lardner, J., & Zeldin, C. (2008). *Up to our eyeballs: How shady lenders and failed economic policies are drowning Americans in debt*. New York: New Press.

Gordon, C. (2013). *Growing apart: A political history of American inequality*. Institute for Policy Studies. Retrieved from http://scalar.usc.edu/works/growing-apart-a-political-history-of-american-inequality/index

Gorski, P. C. (2005). *Savage unrealities: Uncovering classism in Ruby Payne's framework* (EdChange Working Paper). Retrieved from http://www.edchange.org/publications/Savage_Unrealities.pdf.

Guglielmo, J., & Salerno, S. (2003). *Are Italians white? How race is made in America*. New York: Routledge.

Hacker, J., & Pierson, P. (2010). *Winner-take-all politics: How Washington made the rich richer—and turned its back on the middle class*. New York: Simon & Schuster.

Heitzeg, N. (2009). Education or incarceration: Zero tolerance policies and the school to prison pipeline. *Forum on Public Policy Online: A Journal of the Oxford Round Table*, 5(2), 1–21.

Henwood, D. (2003). *After the new economy*. New York: New Press.

Hopkins, L. (2014). *Beyond the pearly gates: White, low-income student experiences at elite colleges* (Doctoral dissertation). Retrieved from Doctoral Dissertations 2014-current (Paper 96), http://scholarworks.umass.edu/dissertations_2/96

Hunter, D. (n.d.). *Break the rules: How ground rules can hurt us*. Philadelphia: Training for Change. Retrieved from http://www.trainingforchange.org/publications/break-rules-how-ground-rules-can-hurt-us

Ignatiev, N. (1995). *How the Irish became white*. New York: Routledge.

Jacobson, M. F. (1998). *Whiteness of a different color: European immigrants and the alchemy of race*. Cambridge, MA: Harvard University Press.

Jensen, B. (2012). *Reading classes: On culture and classism in America*. Ithaca, NY: Cornell University Press.

Kamenetz, A. (2006). *Generation debt: Why now is a terrible time to be young*. New York: Riverhead Books/Penguin.

Kandel, W. (2008). Profile of hired farmworkers: A 2008 update (Economic Research Report Number 60). Washington, DC: Economic Research Service, United States Department of Agriculture. Retrieved from http://digitalcommons.ilr.cornell.edu/key_workplace/559

Kincheloe, J. L., & Steinberg, S. R. (Eds.). (2007). *Cutting class: Socioeconomic status and education*. Lanham, MD: Rowman & Littlefield.

Kochhar, R., Fry, R., & Taylor, P. (2011, July 26). *Wealth gaps rise to record highs between whites, blacks, Hispanics*. Pew Research Center. Retrieved January 17, 2015, from http://www.pewsocialtrends.org/2011/07/26/wealth-gaps-rise-to-record-highs-between-whites-blacks-hispanics/

Korten, D. C. (2010). *Agenda for a new economy from phantom wealth to real wealth*. San Francisco: Berrett-Koehler Publishers.

Kozol, J. (1991). Savage inequalities: Children in America's schools. New York: Crown.

Lakey, G. (2010). *Facilitating group learning: Strategies for success with diverse adult learners*. San Francisco: Jossey-Bass.

Lamont, A. (2000). *The dignity of working men: Morality and the boundaries of race, class, and immigration*. New York: Russell Sage Foundation.

Lardner, J., & Smith, D. A. (Eds.). (2005). *Inequality matters: The growing economic divide in America and its poisonous consequences*. New York: New Press.

Lareau, A. (1987). Social class differences in family-school relationships: The importance of cultural capital. *Sociology of Education, 60*, 73–85.

Lareau, A. (2003). *Unequal childhoods: Class, race, and famly life*. Berkeley: University of California Press.

Lareau, A. (2011). *Unequal childhoods: Class, race and family life* (2nd ed.). Los Angeles: University of California Press.

Lareau, A., & Calarco, J. M. (2012). Class, cultural capital, and institutions: The case of families and schools. In S. T. Fiske & H. R. Markus (Eds.), *Facing social class: How societal rank influences interaction* (pp. 61–86). New York: Russell Sage Foundation.

Lareau, A., & Conley, D. (2008). *Social class: How does it work?* New York: Russell Sage Foundation.

Lavelle, R. (1995). *America's new war on poverty: A reader for action*. San Francisco: Blackside KQED Books & Tapes.

Leondar-Wright, B. (2005). *Class matters: Cross-class alliance building for middle class activists*. Gabriola Island, BC, Canada: New Society Publishers.

Leondar-Wright, B. (2014). *Missing class: Strengthening social movement groups by seeing class cultures*. Ithaca, NY: Cornell University Press.

Leondar-Wright, B., & Yeskel, F. (2007). Classism curriculum design. In M. Adams, L. A. Bell, & P. Griffin (Eds.), *Teaching for diversity and social justice* (2nd ed., pp. 309–333). New York: Routledge.

Lipsitz, G. (1998). *The possessive investment in whiteness: How white people profit from identity politics*. Philadelphia: Temple University Press.

Long, G. (2013). Differences between union and non-union compensation, 2001–2011. *Monthly Labor Review*, April 16–23. Washington, DC: Bureau of Labor Statistics. Retrieved from http://www.bls.gov/opub/mlr/2013/04/art2full.pdf

Lui, M., Robles, B., Leondar-Wright, B., Brewer, R., & Adamson, R. (2006). *The color of wealth: The story behind the U.S. racial wealth divide*. New York: New Press.

Macartney, S., Bishaw, A., & Fontenot, K. (2013, Feb.). *Poverty rates for selected detailed race and Hispanic groups by state and place: 2007–2011*. Washington, DC: U.S. Census Bureau. Retrieved from http://www.census.gov/prod/2013pubs/acsbr11–17.pdf

Mantsios, G. (Ed.). (1998). *A new labor movement for the new century*. New York: Monthly Review Press.

Martin, A., & Lehren, A. (2012, May 12). A generation hobbled by the soaring cost of college. *The New York Times*.

Matos-Daigle, J. (2011, Jan. 1). *Fulfilling their dreams: Latina/o college student narratives on the impact of parental involvement on their academic engagement* (Doctoral dissertation). Retrieved from Proquest (Paper AAI3465047).

Mayer, G. (2004). *Union membership trends in the United States*. Washington, DC: Congressional Research Service. Retrieved from http://digitalcommons.ilr.cornell.edu/key_workplace/174http://digitalcommons.ilr.cornell.edu/key_workplace/174

McDonough, P. M. (1997). *Choosing colleges: How social class and schools structure opportunity.* New York: State University of New York Press.

McNamee, S. J., & R. K. Miller, Jr. (2004). *The meritocracy myth.* New York: Rowman & Littlefield.

Mishel, L., Bernstein, J., & Allegretto, S. (2007). *The state of working America: 2006/2007.* Ithaca, NY: Cornell University Press.

Mohr, J., & DiMaggio, P. (1995). The intergenerational transmission of cultural capital. *Research in Social Stratification and Mobility, 14,* 169–200.

Moynihan, D. P. (1965). *The Negro family: The case for national action.* Washington, DC: Office of Policy Planning and Research, U.S. Department of Labor. Retrieved from http://www.domestic workers.org/

National Labor Relations Act (NLRA). 29 U.S.C. §§ 151–169. Passed July 5, 1935.

National Organization on Disability (2000). *Harris survey of Americans with disabilities.* Retrieved from www.nod.org/assets/downloads/2000—key—findings

Ng, J. C., & Rury, J. L. (2006). *Poverty and education: A critical analysis of the Ruby Payne phenomenon.* Teachers College Record. Retrieved from www.tcrecord.org

Nicholson, P. Y. (2004). *Labor's story in the United States.* Philadelphia: Temple University Press.

Ornstein, A. (2007). *Class counts: Education, inequality, and the shrinking middle class.* Lanham, MD: Rowman & Littlefield.

Patterson, J. T. (2010). *Freedom is not enough: The Moynihan Report and America's struggle over black family life from LBJ to Obama.* New York: Basic Books.

Payne, R. K. (1995). *A framework for understanding poverty.* Baytown, TX: RFT.

Phillips, K. (1990). *The politics of rich and poor: Wealth and the American electorate in the Reagan aftermath.* New York: HarperCollins.

Piketty, T. (2014). *Capital in the twenty-first century.* Cambridge, MA: Harvard University Press.

Piketty, T., & Saez, E. (2003). Income inequality in the United States, 1913–1998. *Quarterly Journal of Economics, 118*(1), 1–39. Data updated to 2013 in January, 2015; available at http://eml.berkeley.edu/~saez/

Piketty, T., & Saez, E. (2012, Nov.). *Top incomes and the Great Recession: Recent evolutions and policy implications.* Paper presented at the 13th Jacques Polak Annual Research Conference hosted by the International Monetary Fund, Washington, DC, Nov. 8–9, 2012. Retrieved from http://www.imf.org/external/np/res/seminars/2012/arc/pdf/PS.pdf

Quintana, N. S., Rosenthal, J., & Krehely, J. (2010). *On the streets: The federal response to gay and transgender homeless youth.* Center for American Progress. Retrieved from http://cdn.american progress.org/wp-content/uploads/issues/2010/06/pdf/lgbtyouthhomelessness.pdf

Reich, R. B. (2007). *Supercapitalism: The transformation of business, democracy, and everyday life.* New York: Random House.

Roediger, D. R. (1991). *The wages of whiteness* (revised ed.). London: Verso.

Schmidt, P. (2007). *Color and money: How rich white kids are winning the war over college affirmative action.* New York: Palgrave Macmillan.

Sears, B., & Badget, L. (2012, June). Beyond stereotypes: Poverty in the LGBT community. *TIDES/Momentum Issues 4.* Retrieved from http://williamsinstitute.law.ucla.edu/headlines/beyond-stereotypes-poverty-in-the-lgbt-community/

Shierholz, H., & Mishel, L. (2013, Aug. 21). *A decade of flat wages: The key barrier to shared prosperity and a rising middle class.* Economic Policy Institute. Retrieved January 17, 2015, from www.epi.org/publication/a-decade-of-flat-wages-the-key-barrier-to-shared-prosperity-and-a-rising-middle-class/

Shiller, R. J. (2008). *The subprime solution: How today's global financial crisis happened, and what to do about it.* Princeton, NJ: Princeton University Press.

Shlasko, D. (2014). Class inequality and transgender communities [Blog]. *Classism Exposed,* the blog of Class Action. Retrieved from http://www.classism.org/class-inequality-transgender-communities

Shlasko, D., & Kramer, T. (2011). *Class culture and classism in campus and community organizing.* Presented at the Pedagogies of Privilege Conference, University of Denver.

Smith, L. (2010). *Psychology, poverty, and the end of social exclusion: Putting our practice to work.* New York: Teachers College Press.

Smith, L., & Redington, R. (2010). Class dismissed: Making the case for the study of classist microaggressions. In D. W. Sue (Ed.), *Microaggressions and marginality: Manifestations, dynamics, and impact.* Hoboken, NJ: Wiley.

Soederberg, S. (2012). The U.S. debtfare state and the credit card industry: Forging spaces of dispossession. *Antipode, 45,* 493–512. doi: 10.1111/j.1467-8330.2012.01004.x

Steinberg, S. (1989). *The ethnic myth: race, ethnicity, and class in America.* Boston: Beacon Press.

Stevens, M. (2007). *Creating a class: College admissions and the education of elites.* Cambridge, MA: Harvard University Press.

Stiglitz, J. E. (2013). *The price of inequality: How today's divided society endangers our future.* New York: Norton.

St. John, E. P. (2003). *Refinancing the college dream: Access, equal opportunity & justice for taxpayers.* Baltimore: Johns Hopkins Press.

Streib, J. (2013). Class origin and college graduates' parenting beliefs. *The Sociological Quarterly, 54*, 670–693.

Sullivan, L., Meschede, T., Dietrich, L., Shapiro, T., Traub, A., Reutschlin, C., & Draut, T. (2015, Mar. 11). *The racial wealth gap: Why policy matters.* Demos. Retrieved from http://www.demos.org/sites/default/files/publications/RacialWealthGap_1.pdf

Swartz, D. (1997). *Culture and power: The sociology of Pierre Bourdieu.* Chicago: University of Chicago Press.

Taibbi, M. (2014). *The divide: American injustice in the age of the wealth gap.* New York: Spiegel & Gray.

Takaki, R. (1993). A different mirror: A history of multicultural America. Boston: Little Brown.

U.S. Department of Homeland Security, Office of Immigration Statistics (2014). *Yearbook of Immigration Statistics: 2013.* Washington, DC. Retrieved from http://www.dhs.gov/sites/default/files/publications/ois_yb_2013_0.pdf

van Gelder, S. (Ed.). (2011). *This changes everything: Occupy Wall Street and the 99% movement.* San Francisco, CA: Berrett-Koehler Publishers.

Williams, B. (2001). What's debt got to do with it? In J. Goode & J. Maskovsky (Eds.), *The new poverty studies: The ethnography of power, politics, and impoverished people in the United States* (pp. 79–101). New York: New York University Press.

Williams, J. C. (2012). The class culture gap. In S. T. Fiske & H.R. Markus (Eds.), *Facing social class: How societal rank influences interaction* (pp. 39–58). New York: Russell Sage Foundation.

Wilson, W. J. (2009, Jan.). The Moynihan Report and research on the black community. *Annals of the American Academy of Political and Social Science, 621*, 23–36.

Wolff, E. (2009). Finding the causes of educational debt. *Journal of the American Veterinary Medical Association, 235*, 3.

Yosso, T. (1996). Whose culture has capital? A critical race theory discussion of community cultural wealth. In A. Dixson & C. Rousseau (Eds.), *Critical race theory in education: All God's children gotta song.* New York: Routledge.

Young, I. M. (2011). *Responsibility for justice.* New York: Oxford University Press.

Zinn, H. (2003). *A people's history of the United States: 1492–present.* New York: Harper-Collins.

8

Religious Oppression

*Maurianne Adams and Khyati Y. Joshi**

Almost daily, we read or hear news about religious conflict and violence, globally as well as locally, including the murder of three Muslim students in North Carolina, the vandalism against two Hindu temples in Seattle and Virginia, and violence against Jews and Muslims in the U.S. and Europe. Attacks in the U.S. against non-Christian faith traditions lead us to ask these questions: How does U.S. religious difference impact who we are as a nation? Why do some Americans believe that Hindus, Muslims, and Sikhs pose a threat to the American way of life? Why are atheists and agnostics considered immoral or unpatriotic? Is this sense of threat a recent response to religious diversity or do these issues reach back into a long historical debate about U.S. national and religious identity, and about the meaning of our Constitutional "separation of church and state"?

Christianity was integral to U.S. national identity well before the colonial period and it remains important today. The significance of Christianity in U.S. life and the challenges it poses for minority religions is a social justice issue that requires the kind of historical knowledge and structural/cultural analysis we use to understand other forms of oppression that stand in the way of social justice.

In this chapter, we explore the role of religion in U.S. cultural, social, and political life. We consider how religion in the U.S. has served the needs of a dominant religious, ethnic, racialized majority by ensuring their access to institutional and cultural power. We explore the contradictions within U.S. traditions of religious freedom. We examine the historical legacies that survive in current manifestations of Christian hegemony, and their intersections with other forms of oppression in the U.S. We then raise some of the key concerns for religious pluralism as a form of social justice going into the future. The chapter concludes with a design for teaching about Christian hegemony and religious oppression with some discussion of pedagogical and facilitation issues. Materials and activities that support the design can be found on the website for this chapter.

DEFINITIONS OF KEY CONCEPTS

Religious oppression in the U.S. refers to the systematic subordination of minority religious groups, such as Buddhists, Hindus, Jews, Muslims, Sikhs, Native American spiritualities, and those who are atheists, agnostics, or freethinkers. The subordination of non-Christian religions occurs at all levels of society through the actions of individuals (religious prejudice), institutional policies and practices (religious discrimination), and cultural and societal norms and values associated with Christianity (Joshi, 2006).

The social structures, federal and local policies, and cultural practices that maintain and reproduce Christian norms in the U.S. through "the everyday practices of a well-intentioned liberal society" result in *Christian hegemony* (Young, 1990, p. 268). *Hegemony* generally refers to a society's unacknowledged and/or unconscious adherence to a dominant world view, without any need for external policing, through assumed cultural norms, policies, and practices whose maintenance depends not on any special effort but on "business as usual." *Christian hegemony* refers to the dominance of Christian observances, holy days, and places of worship without regard for those of non-Christians (Kivel, 2013, pp. 2–36). In the U.S., Christian hegemony refers to normalized Christian norms that are accepted as intrinsic to our national identity, even as a test of patriotism.

Christian privilege refers to the social advantages held by Christians in the U.S. who experience social and cultural advantages relative to non-Christians. Having *privilege* with respect to *normative* Christianity means participation in "the assumptions underlying institutional rules and the collective consequences of following those rules" (Young, 1990, p. 41). Christian *privilege* is generally unacknowledged by those who hold it, because it is maintained through the pervasive but largely invisible culture of *normative* religious practices (Blumenfeld, 2006; Joshi, 2006; Schlosser, 2003).

Whereas *Christian privilege* refers mainly to those who receive advantage, *Christian normativity* refers to the *norms, traditions, and belief systems* that characterize this advantage. Examples of the norms, traditions, and assumptions behind law and policy that benefit Christians but marginalize, harm, or disadvantage non-Christians, will be discussed later in this chapter.

OUR APPROACH

Our social justice approach examines religious oppression as one of the many ways that people are categorized in the larger society, resulting in advantage or disadvantage. A social justice approach to religious oppression emphasizes *structural and systemic patterns of inequality based upon religious group memberships, reproduced through interlocking social institutions and culture.*

This approach to religious oppression draws upon sociological, legal, and historical lenses. We analyze U.S. *history and current manifestations* of religious oppression to show the formative role of mainstream Protestant Christian culture in defining U.S. national identity and patriotism. We use a *sociological analysis* to describe pervasive religious values, beliefs, and institutions within U.S. culture, institutional policies, and social systems (Fox, 2000; Johnstone, 2004) rather than focusing on what specific religious beliefs might "mean" to individual believers or examining different rituals and theologies. We explore Constitutional protections of religion in light of the mixed history of legal interpretations. Our historical and sociological analyses lead us to explore the historical and current-day manifestations of religious privilege and religious oppression at the *individual, institutional, and cultural/societal* levels, in order to understand how these *manifestations of Christian hegemony* have historically reinforced and reproduced each other, and persist in the present day.

We also use an *intersectional* approach and focus on the interactions of religion with race, sexuality, ethnicity, national origin, and other categories of social difference that also have justified ongoing inequality. To these, we add the concept of *racialization or racial formation* (Omi & Winant, 2014), a term used to convey the processes by which northern European ethnicities (British, German, or Scandinavian) became "racialized" as white with access to white privilege, as distinct from the racial marginalization of the peoples of Asian, African, and Arab ethnicities. In this chapter, the *racialization of U.S. religions* applies to adherents of minority religions whose religious identities are considered in the U.S. to be race-based, while the white identity of U.S. European Christian or non-Christian Americans goes unnoticed racially. For example, many Americans believe that all Arabs are Muslim (although some are Christian or Jewish), that all Muslims are Arab (although many are Persian or Indonesian), that all Indians are Hindu (some are Muslim or Christian), and so on. By this process of dual religious and racial stigmatization, the racialization of religion reinforces the religious devaluation experienced doubly as religious and racial marginalization (Goldschmidt & McAlister, 2004).

HISTORICAL LEGACIES OF PROTESTANT HEGEMONY AND RELIGIOUS OPPRESSION IN THE U.S.

The focus for this chapter is religious oppression in the U.S. However, we highlight two global historical legacies that have been instrumental in the development and perpetuation of U.S. religious oppression. We will first discuss these two global legacies before turning to historical themes within the U.S. The first global historical legacy grows out of religious conflict rooted in the Old World of European Christianity, namely Protestant hostility and distrust toward Catholics and vice versa, and of all Christians toward Jews and Muslims. The second historical legacy involves the long-term negative consequences of both Orientalism and colonialism. Both of these global historical legacies have contributed to U.S. hegemonic Protestantism and to the oppression toward religiously "othered" peoples.

RELIGIOUS CONFLICT ROOTED IN EUROPEAN CHRISTIANITY

In Europe, Christianity emerged out of a small Messianic 1st century sect of Jews in Palestine to become the dominant European religious and political force by the end of the Roman Empire. European Christianity marked Jews and Muslims as enemies of the one true faith, asserting that Jews had rejected the deity of Jesus and were responsible for his Crucifixion, and that Muslims followed a false prophet. Anti-Judaism (later termed *antisemitism*) and antagonism toward Islam (now framed as *Islamophobia*) were therefore intrinsic to the core beliefs and self-definition of a militant European *Christian* culture that over many centuries shaped national identities for the Roman Catholic and Protestant nation states of Europe (Fredrickson, 2002; O'Shea, 2006; Reston, 2009).

The term *antisemitism* is a 19th century scientific-sounding euphemism for *Judenhass* (Jew-hatred) and reflects the European racializing of "semitic," which was a linguistic category that included Arabic and Aramaic as well as Hebrew. The term *antisemitism* is now used to convey the cumulative force of global and historic religious, economic, and racial oppression of Jews as a religion, an ethnicity, a race, and a people (Cohn-Sherbok, 2002).

Islamophobia is a term that uses "phobia" to convey dread, suspicion, and aversion toward "Islam," the religious group against whom those feelings are directed. The term emerged in part from early 20th-century French colonialism (Bravo López, 2011). Although Christian/Muslim religious conflict dates back into centuries of territorial military conflict between Christian and Muslim nation-states, the term *Islamophobia* is a relatively recent term that conveys Western prejudice, discrimination, and devaluation of peoples identified as Muslim. In this chapter we emphasize the stereotypical, prejudicial, and racist ingredients of Islamophobia (Frost, 2008; Rana, 2007) and see it as a complex brew of anti-Muslim religious animosity and distrust, combined with anti-African, Asian, and Arab racism.

In a single word, *Islamophobia* essentializes the diversity of Islamic nationalities, languages, religious sectarian affiliations, ethnicities, and cultures into a single undifferentiated and racialized religious group (Rana, 2007). Like antisemitism, Islamophobia conveys religious as well as racist fears and hostility, in this case largely against peoples of North African and Arab and Asian countries who are living in or migrating to Europe and North America. Also like antisemitism, Islamophobia is deeply rooted in Christian religious (and colonialist) assumptions of the superiority of the West over the East; this is described by Edward Said as "Orientalism" (1998) and by others as racism directed against Asians and Arabs, most specifically Muslims, through the racialization of religion (Joshi, 2006, 2009). Rana (2007) captures these complexities by describing how "[the] Muslim is constructed through a racial logic that crosses the cultural categories of nation, religion, ethnicity, and sexuality" (p. 148).

The religious cohesion of early Christian Europe was fueled in part by Papal-sanctioned military and religious Crusades against Muslims from 1095 to 1291, and legal restrictions or expulsion of Jews from the 4th to the 16th centuries (Fredrickson, 2002; Gilbert, 2003; Hilberg, 2003). Roman Catholicism was hegemonic throughout Europe until 17th century Protestantism challenged its dominance in what became a violent and brutal conflict between competing forms of Christianity, which affected the entirety of Europe and other continents colonized by Catholics or Protestants.

Antisemitism preached from both Catholic and Protestant pulpits blamed the Jews for the Crucifixion, accused them of poisoning wells, and demonized and dehumanized them as the anti-Christ. In Europe, it was widely believed that Jews murdered Christian boys (the "blood libel"), desecrated the Holy Sacrament, and caused bubonic plague (the "Black Death"). The hysteria about "blood libel" followed Jews to the New World, with documented accusations in upper New York State in the mid-20th century (Laqueur, 2006; Romero Castello & Macías Kapón, 1994; Weinberg, 1986).

In early Christian Europe, Jews were stigmatized for loaning money at interest, a practice ("usury") that was forbidden by Christian doctrine but was needed to fund Christian ventures, such as the Crusades, or to bankroll local authorities. The negative association of Jews with money comes from Christian attitudes toward "usury," and as Christian Europe developed a capitalist financial system based on the (now secularized) practice of usury, led to the scapegoating of Jews for the economic recessions built into European capitalism. Even more dangerous was the unquestioning acceptance of the belief that Jews were plotting global economic control, as capitalism became a global force. This view, propagated by the fictional *Protocols of the Elders of Zion* written by Russian anti-Semites, was trumpeted as historical truth in the European and U.S. press, and republished and distributed by Henry Ford in *The Dearborn Independent* in the 1920s (Bronner, 2000; Laqueur, 2006; Perry & Schweitzer, 2008).

Jews within Christian Europe were vilified on religious grounds as Christ-killers, and on economic grounds as money-lenders, tax-collectors, and landlords. They were also ostracized on racial grounds as an impure, "mongrel" people. This view of Jewish "racial impurity" grew out of the Jewish diaspora, as Jews looked like the people they settled among and had phenotypical differences that reflected 19th century "racial typologies"— Ashkenazy Jews (in Europe), Sephardic Jews (in Spain and the Americas), and Mizrachi Jews (in the Middle East and South Asia) (Fredrickson, 2002; Laqueur, 2006). Nonetheless, "the Jew" was stereotyped with dark hair, swarthy skin, and a big nose, features that had become racialized as "Semitic."

Jews were driven out of Christian communities and blamed for denying Jesus as the Messiah. They also were proselytized and at times absorbed into Christian society if they agreed to renounce Judaism. They were segregated in ghettos to prevent mixing the inferior racial group ("Semites") with the superior Aryan stock; they were expelled or murdered if they refused conversion, and tortured if suspected of maintaining secret Jewish observance. By the 18th and 19th centuries, these religious differences were becoming racialized based on the emerging pseudo-science of racial superiority that classified Aryans (whites) as superior peoples, and Jews (along with Africans, Arabs, and Asians) as inferior and impure (Laqueur, 2006; Perry & Schweitzer, 2008; Wistrich, 1991). Nineteenth-century eugenics movements in Europe as well as the U.S. were vigorously antisemitic (Michael, 2005). It is the recurrent "essentialism" of Jewish "differentness" that links the religious and economic antisemitism of the Middle Ages to the antisemitic racism behind the Holocaust of the 20th century.

The year 1492 is celebrated for European exploration and the discovery of the Americas. It is also the year in which Jews were expelled from the Iberian Peninsula, specifically those who did not hold "certificates of birth" to document their genealogical blood purity as Christian (Fredrickson, 2002). The requirement for documented "blood purity" as a test of religious and national identity in 15th century Spain suggests an early instance of the intersection of racial, genealogical, and religious identities that later came to characterize race-based antisemitism and other forms of racism (Fredrickson, 2002).

While antisemitism was taking root within Europe, the Crusades drove the Muslim "infidel" from the Holy Lands of Palestine and from Christian Spain into North Africa (O'Shea, 2006; Reston, 2009). In Spain, there had been a brief period of coexistence among Christians, Jews, and Muslims, until Christianity was forcibly established as an expression of national identity, and Muslim armies were driven out of Spain into North Africa.

It is important to note that Christian antagonism toward Islam was economic as well as religious, a function of intense competition for territory surrounding the periphery of Europe—in Spain, in Palestine, and in North Africa. But the relationships between Muslims and Jews, forged as trading partners across Europe, Asia, and Arabia, enabled Jews to live in Muslim countries across North Africa, central Asia, and the eastern Mediterranean for 1400 years as a subordinated, although legally protected, religious minority—not without violence, but also not with the unremitting patterns of forced conversion, expulsions, and genocide that characterized European antisemitism (Gilbert, 2003; Weinberg, 1986).

COLONIALISM AND ORIENTALISM

The colonial expansion of Europe by the 16th century came on the heels of the persecution of European Jewry and the Crusades waged against Muslims, positioning both as inferior to Christians. One long-term consequence of the situation in Europe was that Muslims and Jews were explicitly excluded from political roles in the English colonies, including colonial America. Indeed, the tactics and ideology that drove the expulsion of Jews from parts of Europe and the recurrent wars against Muslims at its fringes were precursors to the tactics Europeans later took against the indigenous peoples of the Americas (Winant, 2001).

The European powers' race to colonize Africa, Asia, and the Americas globalized the military and political basis for Christian hegemony and the marginalization and exclusion of non-Christians. This colonial legacy offers valuable insight into the racialization of religion in the United States as well.

Orientalism refers to the idea that European ways were superior to the cultures, people, and religions associated with Middle East, African, and Asian nations. "Orientalism was ultimately a political vision of reality whose structure promoted the difference between the familiar (Europe, West, "us") and the strange (the Orient, the East, "them")" (Said, 1978, p. 43). European encounters with the Orient (Africa, Arabia, Islam, India, Southeast Asia) were understood in Europe to be encounters with peoples inferior to and potentially antagonistic to European civilization (Said, 1978). Orientalism was combined with the developing pseudoscience of scientific racism—that is, the 18th and 19th century use of the term "race" to designate a genetic, intrinsic, and essentialized hierarchy based on bogus "racial" differences—to justify the European seizures and imperial management of South Asian civilizations, together with seizures of land, appropriation of mines, and enslavement of peoples from Africa, Arabia, Asia, and the Americas (Kapila, 2007).

Whereas for European travelers and adventurers, Orientalism was the term for race, color, civilization, and language linked to a supposed South Asian ("Orientalist") philosophy and world view, by the 1820s race intersected with religion as its co-accomplice (Kapila, 2007). Beliefs, ideologies, and theologies that were not Christian were distorted and essentalized. For example, religions that were not "revealed" in the way that Christianity was thought to be revealed—Hinduism, for example—were considered morally questionable. Other religions—Islam, for example—were considered morally questionable because the source of revelation was not Christian. As a colonizing legacy, Orientalism against peoples from "the Orient" (Arabia, Asia) intersected with U.S. racism (initially against indigenous peoples and enslaved African blacks), as well as a deeply rooted belief in Christian divine purpose. These beliefs and practices were used to justify the distrust and hatred expressed by generations of white U.S. Christians against those who were not white or Christian, and who, for those reasons, were considered incapable of the self-government required to become U.S. citizens.

Spanish, Portuguese, and English explorers on their voyages of discovery carried with them an ideology of Christian religious superiority which, also conceptualized as "blood-based," could be conflated with and mutually reinforce racial domination (Fredrickson, 2002; Smedley, 1999). Racism, Orientalism, and Christian entitlement reinforced the emerging racial hierarchies and provided a self-serving European colonial history—a history in which "the West" constructed "the East" as well as the South as different and inferior, and whose people would benefit from Western intervention and religious "rescue" (Rana, 2011).

The colonial mindset drew on multiple justifications—cultural, racist, religious—to rationalize the superiority of a Western civilization based on Christian faith over native and African indigenous religions, Buddhism, Hinduism, Islam, or Judaism. Thus, the colonial/orientalist encounters resulted in produced distortions, stereotypes, and patterns of misrepresentation about the multiple "others." Orientalism contributed to Christian hegemony and normativity by providing a way of looking at peoples, cultures, and religions as collectively superior (Christians) or inferior (all others). These religious/cultural attitudes fed into the arguments against naturalization of Asian and Arab immigrants, discussed later in this chapter.

European colonialism became a worldwide enterprise involving the taking of lands, minerals, and peoples in Africa, Asia, and the Arabian subcontinent as well as the Americas. Colonialism was justified by the presumed racial and religious superiority of the conquering peoples, a religious rationalization for their military conquest and economic exploitation. Because colonialism "in God's name" often went hand-in-hand with Catholic or Protestant missions to so-called heathen peoples, colonial exploitation could be explained away by the assumption that uncivilized, heathen peoples would benefit by the imposition of the presumed gifts of a superior white Christian culture and the "good news" of the one true gospel (Rana, 2011; Shohat, 2006).

Racism and religious oppression became mutually reinforcing, virtually indistinguishable tools of colonialism in the Americas as well as in Africa and Asia, where indigenous peoples of the Americas and Africa were classified both as heathen and as racially inferior. As European explorers and adventurers encountered different "others," race first reinforced, but ultimate gradually replaced religion as a way to distinguish among people, although in many contexts race and religion remained interchangeable.

Policies predicated on the inherent superiority of western Christianity impacted geographically dispersed areas at the same points in history. For example, the persecution, marginalization, and disenfranchisement of Jews in Europe (Middle Ages through 1940s) and Native peoples in the Americas (15th century into the 20th century) were concurrent, although geographically distinct. Although it is difficult to hold the two in mind as parallel processes of Christian oppression, both can be summarized by the historian Raul Hilberg's vivid summary of the long history of antisemitism (see Hilberg, 3 vols., 2003): "Since the fourth century after Christ there have been three anti-Jewish policies: conversion, expulsion, and annihilation" (Hilberg, 1961, p. 3). Hilberg understood that this was in itself a cyclical, historical trend:

> The missionaries of Christianity had said in effect: You have no right to live among us as Jews. The secular ruler who followed had proclaimed: You have no right to live among us. The German Nazis at last decreed: You have no right to live.
>
> (Hilberg, 1961, pp. 3–4)

The ethnic cleansing justified by Christian antisemitism in Europe parallels an ethnic cleansing that justified Christian massacres and relocations of Native peoples in the U.S. Both happened in the same historical timeframes, and both were rationalized by Christian entitlement. The deadly sequence from forced conversion, to expulsion and relocation, to genocide and extermination, is the same for Native peoples in the U.S. as for Jews in Europe: "You can't live among us as Indians" (forced conversions), "You can't live among us" (relocations), and "You can't live" (massacre).

United States anti-Muslim stereotypes are similarly rooted in Christian exceptionalism that assumed Christian capacity for democratic self-government but denied such capacity to Muslims (Feldman, 1996; Murray, 2008). Colonizing settlers had anti-Muslim as well as antisemitic stereotypes in their baggage from the Old World. Stereotypes against Muslims included the view that Muslims were intrinsically violent, that Sharia law was barbaric, and that Muslim loyalties undermined their capacity for democratic self-regulation or loyalty to a Christian nation—a view expressed in John Locke's highly influential 1689 "Treatise Concerning Toleration" that the "Mahometan . . . acknowledges himself bound to yield blind obedience to the Mufti . . . who himself is entirely obedient to the Ottoman Emperor" (quoted in Murray, 2008, p. 91). These views justified the denial of citizenship to Muslims in the 1920s. They have also motivated the current-day desecration of mosques, the burning of the Qur'an by self-righteous Evangelicals, and the attacks on U.S. citizens who appear to be Muslim by virtue of head-coverings, beards, or dark skin (Alvarez & Don, 2011; Hafiz & Raghunathan, 2014; Mamdani, 2004; Rana, 2011).

RELIGIOUS OPPRESSION AND CHRISTIAN HEGEMONY IN U.S. HISTORY

PROTESTANT HEGEMONY IN THE U.S.

The dominance of Protestantism in U.S. history reflects the English victory in the struggle between empires in which Protestant (English) and Catholic (Spanish and French) armies wrestled for control of the colonies. The English colonies established along the Eastern seaboard were Protestant, although they belonged to different sects and denominations.

Although U.S. history generally portrays the colonies as religious havens for peoples persecuted elsewhere, we now know that most early U.S. religious communities were themselves theocratic and exclusive, with their own church establishments that persecuted members of other faiths as well as dissenters viewed as "heretics" (Ahlstrom, 2004; Fraser, 1999). The legal foundation for the U.S., the world's first secular government, was based upon "an uneasy alliance between Enlightenment rationalists and evangelical Christians" (Jacoby, 2004, p. 31). The Salem witch trials in colonial Massachusetts offer an especially vicious example of religious cleansing, during which citizens accused of heresy and presumed Satanism were hanged, burned, or drowned, using religious justifications for accusations based on neighborhood feuds, class antagonism, and misogyny, and presided over by church-empowered magistrates (Adams, 2008; Boyer & Nissenbaum, 1972; Butler, Wacker, & Balmer, 2003).

United States history has numerous examples of religious persecution in the name of Protestant sectarianism: Against Quakers in Plymouth Colony, against Catholics and Jewish immigrants in the late 19th century, and against Mormons and Jehovah's Witnesses (Ahlstrom, 2004; Butler, Wacker, & Balmer, 2003; Wills, 2005). Missions to native peoples were federally supported by land grants to strengthen their role in "civilizing" and preparing the way for forced relocation, although these land grants and funds violated Constitutional prohibitions against political support for religious institutions (Echo-Hawk, 2010; Philbrick, 2004). Distrust of non-Protestants (including non-believers) showed up in state law: Massachusetts required that Catholics in public office renounce papal authority, and Pennsylvania allowed Jews but not atheists to hold office. Protestant domination lay behind the 19th century creation of a nationwide network of Protestant "common [public] schools" to maintain Protestant cultural homogeneity in the face of substantial Catholic and Jewish immigration (Fraser, 1999). For Protestants born in the U.S., these other faith traditions seemed incompatible with U.S. citizenship because of their presumed dual or split loyalties: Catholics to the Pope in Rome, Muslims to their Imams or an Islamic Caliphate, and Jews to Israel.

The religious freedom of the early U.S. Republic meant freedom for Protestants, which included Congregationalists, Episcopalians, Dutch Reformed, Presbyterians, French Huguenots, Baptists, and Moravian churches as well as Quakers, Amish, and Mennonites. The small Shearith Israel congregation (Sephardic Jews from Spain) was tolerated. The narrowly prescribed 18th century ecumenical toleration also left room for the free-thought and Enlightenment rationalism associated with the educated elite, and with their prized traditions of political freedom and free individual conscience—core U.S. values associated with this Protestant consensus.

Thomas Jefferson, a prominent Deist and freethinker, proposed a bill "Establishing Religious Freedom" (1779, passed in 1786) that granted complete legal equality "for citizens of all religions, and of no religion" in Virginia (Jacoby, 2004, p. 18). This bill became the prototype for the religious protection clauses added as a 1st Amendment to the new U.S. federal Constitution. The text of the Constitution itself was explicit about religion only in its assertion that *no religious test* be required for holding public office, a clear break from English precedent (Jacoby, 2004).

RACIALIZATION OF RELIGION

English, French, and Spanish colonizers became "white" in the same cultural and ideological process through which colonizers understood Native peoples to be racialized as "red," or African peoples as "black," although explicit and legalized racial segregation and inequality took a century or more to formalize (Lipsitz, 2006; Roediger, 1991). Thus, the foundational Protestant communities along the eastern seaboard were understood to be *white* communities, and their relocations of Native American Indians as well as their enslavement of Africans were justified by their presumed religious as well as racial superiority (Harvey, 2003; Loewen, 1995; Wills, 2005).

For native peoples whose ancestry predated white colonizing settlers, for African peoples brought involuntarily into the U.S., and for immigrants from Arab and Asian countries, the religious traditions of their ancestral communities established a foundational role in "making and preserving those very social boundaries that we call 'races' and ethnicities'" (Prentiss, 2003, p. 1). For the dominant Protestant federal and state power structures in the U.S., the presumed religious and racial inferiority of indigenous peoples became intersecting and mutually supportive justifications for their massacre throughout the Americas, and for expulsion from their ancestral lands and forcible removal of their children to vocational schools in preparation for menial work (Ballantine & Ballantine, 2001; Chavers, 2009; Grinde, 2004). Also, with the immigration of Arabs and Asians, religion and race became conflated and interchangeable markers of the religious and racial "Other."

United States Protestant churches were racially segregated, not only in the sociological sense of who worshiped with whom, but theologically, culturally, and politically as well (Jacobson & Wadsworth, 2012). Mainstream white Protestant congregations split over religious and ethical questions posed by slavery and racial segregation. Protestant denominations, both North and South, developed biblical interpretations and theological arguments that either rationalized or excoriated race-based bondage and segregation. Bitter denominational and sectarian disputes within white churches stimulated the growth of a separate Black Church. Black churches provided refuge, community, solidarity, and support for ex-slaves and black sharecroppers, and fostered black political leadership, economic development, and education. Black churches were centers for organized protest during the 19th and 20th centuries, including and beyond the civil rights movement (Fulop & Raboteau, 1997; Lincoln & Mamiya, 1990; Morris, 1986). Chinese, Korean, and Latino/a Evangelical and Catholic religious communities have also provided similar cultural/ethnic/linguistic solidarity (Carnes & Yang, 2004; Chen & Jeung, 2012 ; Espinosa, 2014; Garces-Foley & Jeung, 2013; Min & Kim, 2001).

The conflation of religious with racial difference justified slavery, even in cases in which slaves had become Christians (that is, black Christians); it was also evident in the anti-semitic policies and practices in private schools, colleges, and professional preparation, clubs, hotels, and employment (Diner, 2004; Takaki, 1991). The strength of Catholicism and its conflation with "Mexican" as a racial category helped to justify the 19th century appropriation of Spanish and Mexican lands into the new states of the "anglo" southwest and California (Menchaca, 2001; Takaki, 2008). The racialization of religion provided the basis for vehement U.S.-born white Protestant opposition to immigrants, such as the Chinese, Japanese, and South Asian Sikhs, Muslims, and Hindus; Irish, Italian, and Polish Catholics; and Eastern European Jews. The very notion of citizenship *itself* was racially and religiously charged (Eck, 2001; Jacobson, 1998).

RELIGION, RACE, AND IMMIGRATION

Prior to the Civil War, an estimated half of the U.S. population and 85% of Protestants were evangelical (Emerson & Smith, 2000), forging a white, Protestant evangelical national identity. This white and Protestant national identity remained largely unquestioned until the period from 1840 to the 1920s, when significant increases in immigration of non-Protestant peoples poked holes in a previously homogeneous, racialized, mainly Protestant American sense of nationhood. Total immigration rose from 143,000 during the 1820s, when most immigrants were northern Europeans, to 8,800,000 during the first decade of the 20th century, when most immigrants were from south or eastern Europe, or Arab and Asian countries (Office of Immigration Statistics, 2006). In 1860, the foreign-born American population was over 4 million, with more than 1.5 million from Catholic Ireland (Jacobson, 1998).

The Irish potato blight of 1844 devastated an already starving Irish and Catholic population, 90% of whose arable land had been enclosed for cattle by English (Protestant) landlords, leaving the rural poor to subsist mainly on backyard plots of potatoes. With the loss of their subsistence crop, a million Irish starved to death between 1845–1855, while English landlords converted even more Irish lands for grain and cattle export to British markets (Takaki, 1991). One-and-a-half million unskilled and pauperized Irish laborers fled starvation to migrate to U.S. east coast and Midwestern cities. Italian Catholics and Jews fled European revolution, poverty, and pogroms, settling mainly but not exclusively in urban centers. Wherever they settled, Irish, Italian, Polish, and Latino Catholics established separate parishes where they could worship in their languages of origin.

By 1920, more than a third of the total population of 105 million Americans included immigrants and their children (36 million), the majority of them Roman Catholic, Greek Orthodox, and Jewish, with significant numbers of Buddhists, Hindus, Muslims, and Sikhs from China and India (Daniels, 2002). Asian immigration (first Filipino and Chinese, followed by Japanese and South Asian) and Middle Eastern immigration (initially Syrian or Lebanese Maronite Christian) brought Buddhist, Confucian, Hindu, Muslim, and Sikh beliefs and practices, as well as Orthodox religious adherence, to the U.S. (Bald, 2013; GhaneaBassiri, 2010; Haddad, 2002; Jensen, 1988; Takaki, 1998).

There was often violent backlash against Irish, German, Italian, and Polish Catholics (Guglielmo, 2003; Ignatiev, 1995), who were perceived to challenge the white Anglo Saxon Protestant way of life. At the turn of the 20th century, intense anti-Catholicism, antisemitism, and opposition to Asians and Arabs, generically painted as "not like us," were enforced through intimidation by white nativist groups, who feared their brand of Protestant Americanism was under assault by foreign religions and ethnicities. This nativist activism resulted in the Immigration Act of 1917, which specifically eliminated Asian immigration—and thereby immigrant adherents of Buddhism, Confucianism, Hinduism, Islam, or Sikhism. This act was followed by the 1924 National Origins Act, which set the percentage for immigrants to the U.S. at a mere 2% of the total of any nation's residents as reported in the 1890 census. This law closed off southern and eastern European immigration, Jews, and Eastern Orthodox and Roman Catholics. These targeted and restrictive laws were part of a widespread xenophobia characterized at its extreme by the Ku Klux Klan and other Christian Identity groups, whose anti-Catholicism and antisemitism enlarged their earlier anti-black racist origins (Daniels, 2002; Lee, 2004).

Because of the immigration restrictions in place after 1924, Jewish Holocaust refugees were refused immigration status during the 1930s and 1940s, despite strenuous rescue efforts (Wyman, 2007). During the period 1924–1965, most assimilated and Americanized Jews and Catholics—whose ancestors had immigrated before 1924—became white or at least "almost" if "not always quite" white. At the same time, religious observance became increasingly private, with worship taking place in separate parochial, home schooling, or weekend Protestant, Catholic, or Jewish religious education (so-called "Sunday school").

In the decades following World War II, educational, residential, and professional barriers to upward mobility were slowly dismantled for white ethnic communities. The beneficiaries were mainly white Ashkenazy Jews and white Catholics (Italians and Irish), but not black or brown Catholics or Protestants (African Americans, Afro-Caribbeans, Puerto Ricans, Chicanos/as and Mexican Americans, and South or Central Americans) (Brodkin, 1998; Guglielmo & Salerno, 2003; Ignatiev, 1995; Roediger, 1991). European immigrants who had been seen as "ethnic" (as well as Catholic or Jewish) assimilated by giving up the languages and accents of their home communities, cooking and dressing "American," surgically altering telltale markers by having a "nose job," and in the aftermath of World

War II, moving to the "integrated" (interreligious, but not interracial) suburbs. All that remained of their communities of origin was their religion, but that was kept on the weekend "other" side of the "public face" of weekday life.

Not until 1965 did a new Immigration Act reopen the door to immigration that was religiously non-Christian and racially non-white, establishing a renewal of the earlier religious, racial, and ethnic national demographic. By 2010, immigrant and second-generation Americans numbered nearly 72 million, more than 40 million of them immigrants, many of them migrating as family units within strong religious community networks (Grieco, Trevelyan, Larsen, Acosta, Gambino, de la Cruz, Gryn, & Walters, 2012). A major outcome of the 1965 Immigration Act has been the growing number of Hindu, Muslim, and Sikh religious, cultural, and ethnic communities in the U.S. as well as major increases in Asian, African, and Latino/a Christian communities (Chen & Jeung, 2012; Ecklund & Park, 2005; Haddad, 2011; Joshi, 2006; Kurien, 2014; Min, 2010).

NATURALIZATION AND CITIZENSHIP

Religion played a role in who could enter the U.S., and it was also a factor that intersected with race for courts hearing appeals and making decisions about naturalization and citizenship for immigrants once they were here (Haney-López, 1996). The Naturalization Law of 1790 had restricted citizenship to "free white men," thereby excluding all women, blacks (until passage of the 14th Amendment in 1868), Native American Indians, and anyone else of non-white racial ancestry. Citizenship was not fully available to Native Americans until the 1968 Indian Civil Rights Act, which extended citizenship to native peoples living on reservations, thus providing them with legal standing and the ability to file claims for religious protection. These citizenship dates account for the relatively recent Native American litigation for religious protection of their sacred sites and their 1st Amendment rights to the free exercise of their traditional religious practices (Adams, 2012).

Chinese, Filipino, Hawaiian, Indian, Japanese, Mexican, Syrian, and Turkish immigrants turned to the courts for naturalization, using a range of arguments to buttress their claims for naturalization as white peoples, but with contradictory results that often involved the intersection of religious and racial identities. These applicants were considered racially ambiguous: Not black, but also not white, and marked by the perception that their religious cultures were unassimilable and "fundamentally at odds" with the American way of life (Ngai, 2004).

In cases involving Syrians, the intersection of religious identity (Muslim) and skin color became determinative, as in the 1909 case of the light-skinned Costa Najour, who was granted citizenship by a court that identified Syrians as members of the "white race" but also registered their concern that this "subject of the Muslim Ottoman Sultan, was incapable of understanding American Institutions and government" (Gualtieri, 2001, pp. 34, 37). By contrast, in 1942, the dark-skinned Yemeni Arab Ahmed Hassan was denied citizenship on the religious grounds that "a wide gulf separates [Mohammedan] culture from that of the predominantly Christian peoples of Europe" (Gualtieri, 2001, p. 81). Further, even Syrian Christian naturalization applicants who were deemed white and granted citizenship, faced discrimination, harassment, and violence from the Ku Klux Klan (Gualtieri, 2001).

Two pivotal Supreme Court decisions, *Takao Ozawa v. U.S.* and *U.S. v. Bhagat Singh Thind*, illustrate the crazy-quilt conflations of religion and race in Supreme Court naturalization cases. Takao Ozawa was a Japanese-born but California-educated and English-speaking church member who had lived in the U.S. for 20 years when he applied in 1914 for naturalization. To the courts, Ozawa was not "white" because the court accepted the pseudo-scientific classification of Japanese as "mongoloid" (Haney- López, 1996). Following this racial logic, Bhagat Singh Thind, an Indian Sikh, petitioned for citizenship as a white man, arguing that South Asian Indians were classified racially as Aryans/Caucasians and therefore white. The Supreme Court reversed its logic from the Ozawa case, arguing that while Singh might be classified as white, "the average man knows perfectly well that there are unmistakable and profound differences" between "the blond Scandinavian and the brown Hindu" despite their shared Caucasian ancestry. Further, the Court argued that "Hindus could not be assimilated into a 'civilization of white men,'" confusing Sikh with Hindu identity based on Thind's Indian roots (quoted in Snow, 2004, p. 268). The twisted and contradictory logics of Supreme Court naturalization litigation tied religious to race-based rationales against citizenship in order to have it both ways, but toward the same end point: Racialized religious minorities were not eligible for U.S. citizenship.

DISCRIMINATION AGAINST WHITE RELIGIOUS MINORITY GROUPS

The *racial* exclusion of Christian communities of color from white churches took place in tandem with the *religious* exclusion also of *minority white religious sects* from U.S. political life. For example, the violence directed against U.S.-born Christians who broke from denominational Protestantism to form the Church of Jesus Christ of Latter-day Saints (the Mormons), the Seventh-day Adventists, and the Jehovah's Witnesses, was triggered by outrage over their overt rejection of establishment Protestantism, and also by their repudiation of federal, state, or local political authority (Butler, Wacker, & Balmer, 2003; Mazur & McCarthy, 2001; Prentiss, 2003). The clashes of police and armed mobs against Mormons or Jehovah's Witnesses resulted in the withdrawal of these religious sects into relatively autonomous geographical spaces, or relinquishment of their sectarian claims to political autonomy (Mazur, 1999).

Although Mormons, Jehovah's Witnesses, and Seventh-day Adventists have been at times considered denominations within Christianity, their theological claims, political separatism, and aspirations toward autonomy alienated them from sectarian Protestant Christianity. Mormons, Jehovah's Witnesses, and Seventh-day Adventists experienced violence in the 19th century that was harshly similar to the colonial expulsions and executions of so-called heretics who threatened the earlier established religious/political status quo. The antagonism toward Mormons broke into the political and Constitutional arena when Congress prohibited polygamy in 1862, and the Supreme Court rejected Mormon claims to maintain multiple marriages under the free exercise case of the 1st Amendment (*U.S. v. Reynolds*, 1879). In this precedent-setting case, Reynolds, who was the defendant, argued that the anti-polygamy statute violated his free religious exercise as a Mormon. The Supreme Court reasoned that polygamy constituted an "action" not a "belief," and not only was not constitutionally protected, but should be restricted for the good of society (Feldman, 1996).

The *Reynolds* case is important because the Supreme Court narrowly defined "free exercise" to protect *belief* but not *action*, most notably when such actions seemed so far outside Christian norms as to pose a danger to Christian society. But from the *Reynolds* case on, one cannot find a clear, bright line between "belief" and "action" in keeping with the meaning of the Constitutionally guaranteed free "exercise" of religion. The line zigs and zags according to the faith traditions of petitioners for "free exercise" of their religion in relation to the Supreme Court's willingness to accept their claims that these practices were required by sincerely held religious beliefs. Two issues have been at stake here: (1) whether the religious practices oppose the public good, and (2) whether the religious practices are accepted as authentic by the Court.

DISCRIMINATION AGAINST AGNOSTICS AND ATHEISTS

Christian distrust of freethinkers, agnostics, and atheists became hardened once the evangelizing fervor of 19th century revivalist Protestantism overwhelmed the rationalist freethought traditions of an earlier period. Many of the framers of the Constitution, like Jefferson, had been freethinkers and Deists. The founding documents of the early Republic reflect their secular views. Until 1914, there was a vigorous freethought movement in the U.S. that linked secular beliefs to an "absolute separation of church and state, which translated into opposition to any tax support of religious institutions—especially parochial schools" (Green, 2012; Jacoby, 2004, p. 153).

These traditions of freethought and secularism, as well as atheism and agnosticism, came into collision with powerful religious organizations that emerged among immigrant Catholics as well as U.S.-born evangelical Protestants. Religious opposition to secularism and atheism became political, as the perceived threat of "foreign" socialism, anarchism, and radicalism among immigrant-identified activists gained visibility by the mid- to late-19th century. Irish union organizers, Italian radicals, and Jewish socialists were targeted by politicians and the media as serious dangers to U.S. business and commerce, threatening to drive a knife into the heart of U.S. capitalism. Immigrant European socialists were opposed on religious as well as political grounds, partly because some immigrant activists were Jewish, and partly because an atheist world view imagined that human progress could be achieved without divine intervention or sanction.

By the mid-20th century, the global threat of "godless Communism" to U.S. capitalism at home and abroad had discredited U.S. atheism or agnosticism and cemented the association of atheism with socialism. The Palmer raids on union organizers following the Red Scare of 1919 equated religious with political unorthodoxy, and atheism with socialism, so that earlier proud intellectual traditions of freethought, agnosticism, atheism, and secularism were tarred with the brush of bolshevism. All were positioned as potent political heresies that could undermine the powerful Christian-identified nation-state focused on capitalism and global finance that the U.S. considered itself to be (Kruse, 2015).

The McCarthyism of the 1950s, largely a repeat of the Red Scare of 1919, used theological grounds to purge the godless on behalf of the body politic. It was during the McCarthy era that the phrase "under God" was added to the Pledge of Allegiance (1954) as an ecumenical religious reference that would differentiate the god-fearing U.S. from the godless Soviets. A successful 2003 lawsuit brought by an atheist, who argued that the phrase "under God" violated the establishment clause of the 1st Amendment, led to hate mail against the plaintiff and furor in the media (Jacoby, 2004).

THE SEPARATION OF CHURCH AND STATE

Most U.S. citizens assume that freedom of religious expression has definitively been assured by the 1st Amendment to the U.S. Constitution, an assumption that is contradicted by more than a century of Supreme Court constitutional rulings that differentiate between "belief" and "expression" or "practice." In large measure, the findings are against plaintiffs whose religious *practices* do not accord with the Court's hegemonic understandings of Christian practices (Adams, 2012; Echo-Hawk, 2010; Feldman, 1996; Mazur & McCarthy, 2001).

The religious protection clauses of the 1st Amendment to the U.S. Constitution (1791) stipulate that "Congress shall make no law respecting an establishment of religion, or prohibiting the free exercise thereof." These clauses were added to provide a mutual assurance pact among the Protestant denominations of the 13 colonies that there would be no federally subsidized church supported by public taxes such as they had rebelled against in England (Fraser, 1999; Mazur, 1999).

The question whether religious freedom was extended only to Protestants across denominations, or to Catholics, Jews and all religions outside Protestantism, has haunted discussions of these religious protection clauses from the outset. On the one hand, the language of the Constitutional religion clauses declined to name the protected religions, reflecting the more inclusive language of Jefferson's 1779 *Act for Establishing Religious Freedom* for Virginia (1779), "that all men shall be free to profess, and by argument to maintain, their opinions in matters of religion, and that the same shall in nowise diminish, enlarge, or affect their civil capacities" (quoted in Feldman, 1996, p. 151). But the other side feared that the 1st Amendment became "a door opened for the Jews, Turks, and Heathens to enter in publick office" and an "invitation for Jews and pagans of every kind to come" to the U.S. (quoted in Feldman, 1996, pp. 162–163). Two centuries later, the Court ruled for the Jeffersonian perspective of religious inclusion:

> Perhaps in the early days of the republic these words were understood to protect only the diversity within Christianity, but today they are recognized as guaranteeing religious liberty and equality to the infidel, the atheist, or the adherent of non-Christian faith such as Islam or Judaism. . . . The anti-discrimination principle inherent in the Establishment Clause necessarily means that would-be discriminators on the basis of religion cannot prevail.
>
> (*County of Allegeny v. American Civil Liberties Union*, 1989)

The first of the "religious protection" clauses, the *Establishment Clause* ("Congress shall make no law respecting an establishment of religion") prohibits government from establishing or favoring any single religion, religious denomination, or sect. The second religious protection clause, *Free Exercise Clause* ("Congress shall make no law . . . prohibiting the free exercise thereof") has been interpreted to refer to religious belief and/or practice, although religious *practice* claims have been narrowly hedged and in many cases rejected in Supreme Court findings.

The well-known phrase "separation of church and state" comes not from the Constitution itself but from a letter from Jefferson (1802) to assure a Baptist congregation that the 1st Amendment had built "a wall of separation between Church and State" (Butler, Wacker, & Balmer, 2003, pp. 155–160; Fraser, 1999, pp. 18–21). This "wall of separation" between government and religion is still referred to as "the separation of *Church* and State," despite the proliferation of diverse religious places for worship such as Buddhist ashrams, Sikh gurdwaras, Muslim mosques, and Jewish synagogues or temples today.

In resolving legal questions brought under these two religious protection clauses, the Supreme Court has rarely used *strict separation* or a literal "wall of separation." Instead, most decisions have used *accommodation* or *non-preference* to avoid tilting any advantage to one religion over another. Accordingly, the Court found that students might be released from K–12 classes to receive religious instruction outside the school premises, but did not allow taxpayer (public) reimbursement to parochial schools for expenses incurred in teaching secular subjects inside the school premises (*Lemon v. Kurtzman*, 1971). In reaching these decisions, the Court asked questions such as: What is the secular purpose of any legislation in question? Is its primary effect to advance or inhibit religion? Will a legal decision avoid "'excessive government entanglement with religion'" (Maddigan, 1993, p. 299)?

The *free exercise clause* has generally been interpreted by the courts to affirm free religious belief, but not to affirm religious practices or behaviors that were in conflict with neutral-seeming legal restrictions. Freedom of religious *belief* has not been challenged because it is closely linked with freedom of speech (also a 1st Amendment right). But case law dealing with religious *worship*, *practice*, *behavior*, *expression*, or *action* have been balanced against the legal concept of *compelling state interests*. The Court generally has looked more favorably upon "free exercise" claims brought by Christian-identified groups, such as Seventh-day Adventists (*Sherbert v. Verner*, 1963) and Amish (*Wisconsin v. Yoder*, 1972).

Claiming their "free exercise" rights has proven more daunting for non-Christians. For example, in a free-exercise claim brought by an Orthodox Jew in the military who was required by religion to maintain head-covering at all times, the Court deferred to the military code. The Court argued that wearing the yarmulke was a personal preference, not a requirement of his religion; and that the standardized uniform needs of the military superseded his free exercise claims, and that military regulations were reasonable and did not violate the free exercise clause (*Goldman v. Weinberger*, 1986). By comparison, the Court had no difficulty affirming the "religious requirements" in cases brought by the Amish, Jehovah's Witnesses, and Seventh-day Adventists.

Similarly, Native American Indian free exercise claims from 1980 on were unsuccessful, and were evaluated by shifting, unfavorable criteria (Feldman, 1996; Long, 2000). The Court found that Cherokee and Navajo plaintiffs were not justified in claiming "free exercise" relief from federal land policies that prevented their religious practice in sacred sites that had been designated as federal parks or other public uses. In contrast to earlier findings (concerning the Amish or Seventh-day Adventists), the Court did not see that Native peoples, too, practiced ancient recognized religions; and that they, like the Amish, held their beliefs sincerely. The Court ignored the burden on free expression by federal land management policies or findings that the state interests in park policy were negligible and that the parks had not used the least-restrictive means (Beaman, 2003; Echo-Hawk, 2010).

If one were to apply a test of consistency to these and other Supreme Court 1st Amendment protection of free religious exercise cases, it would seem clear that these non-Christian cases met the criteria affirmed in the case of Amish or Seventh-day Adventist free exercise findings. The major difference appears to be that the cases rejected by the courts were cases in which the free exercise claims were not based upon traditional or (for them) recognizable norms of religious free exercise and worship. For example, it did not occur to the court that standardized uniforms "will almost always mirror the values and practices of the dominant majority—namely Christians. Put bluntly, the U.S. military is unlikely to require everyone to wear a yarmulke as part of the standard uniform" (Feldman, 1996, p. 247). The Court did not consider that in Orthodox Judaism (as in other orthodox religions), head-covering is required at all times. Nor, in the Native peoples' sacred sites cases, was the Court willing to protect Native peoples' capacity to conduct traditional religious ceremonies in ancient, well-established, and traditional sacred settings. In the numerous Native cases brought and lost, "free exercise" claims were subordinated to the federal government's authority in controlling what had become federal lands, with no regard for the ways in which such land had been acquired (Linge, 2000, p. 314).

At the same time, the Supreme Court upheld the use of politically sanctioned religious speech, ritual, and symbols that had been derived from Christian texts and traditions and used to describe the religious heritage of the U.S., and which they rationalized as a U.S. "civil religion" (Bellah, 1967; Jones & Richey, 1974). For example, the phrase "In God We Trust" was added to the U.S. currency in 1864, and Congress made Christmas a national holiday in 1865 during the crisis of Civil War. The phrase "In God We Trust" uses the Christian norm of naming the deity, an affront to orthodox Jews (who must not write or utter the divine name), to Muslims (who invoke Allah), or to the variously named deities in Hindu or other faith traditions. "In God We Trust" excludes freethinkers, agnostics, and atheists from the hegemonic Christian national identity ("we") assumed by this phrase.

Supreme Court decisions between 1890 and 1930 stated that the U.S. "is one of the 'Christian countries'," a "Christian nation," "a Christian people," although in 1952 the phrasing became more ecumenical: "We are a religious people whose institutions presuppose a Supreme Being" (Feldman, 1996).

RELIGION AND PUBLIC SCHOOLING

Religion has been central to U.S. education, from the colonial period when it was a family responsibility to educate one's young, into the 19th century when it became a priority for the state. The "common" (public) schools of the 19th century public education shared Protestant religious texts, prayers, and values as a nationalizing glue for a newly established system of primary schooling. The need for a "public" educational system had become evident following the Civil War, when immigrants as well as U.S.-born settlers migrated into western territories, all needing to ensure literacy and practical education for their children. There was also the perceived need to "Americanize" the children of Irish and German Catholic immigrants at mid-century, and the many other immigrants that followed. To meet these needs, Protestant leaders established a "nondenominational" network of "common schools," which were racially segregated and whose "common" curriculum forged the values for a shared national identity (Fraser, 1999).

The common schools formed the precursor for today's public school system. The common schools delivered a core curriculum upon which the major Protestant denominations could agree. They could be considered ecumenical or non-denominational only in the sense of bridging sectarian differences within a Protestant framework, although Amish, Mennonites, and Quakers more often maintained their own schools. Catholic immigrant communities established their own parish-based "parochial" school system, designed to maintain Catholic education by using the Douay Bible and Roman Catholic catechism, rather than the King James Bible and Protestant Book of Common Prayer used in the common schools.

The emergence of two major educational networks, each with explicit religious affiliations, led to political, financial, legal, and at times violent conflicts between a (largely Protestant) Christian population in the public schools and challenges from parochial schools. This conflict only intensified as the political leverage generated by Jewish, Catholic, and other non-Christian populations increased. Prayer and Bible readings in public schools came under scrutiny in "establishment" 1st Amendment cases of the 1950s and 1960s.

Two such cases went to the U.S. Supreme Court and continue to impact the dialogue about religion and public schools today. In *Engel v. Vitale* (1962), Jewish families in Long Island protested the daily prayer that had been mandated (by state legislation in 1951) to promote religious commitment and moral and spiritual values. The Supreme Court agreed with the plaintiffs that prayer in public schools violated the 1st Amendment's Establishment Clause. Then, in *Abington Township School District v. Schempp*, 1963, the U.S. Supreme Court ruled against Bible reading and recitation of the Lord's Prayer in public schools, but commented that *study about religions* (as distinct from *religious study*) in the nation's public schools is both legal and desirable. The justices stated that a student's education is not complete without instruction concerning religious influences on history, culture, and literature (Murray, 2008).

As the diversity of religions held by U.S. citizens increased, members of faith traditions challenging limits on their free expression turned to the courts to decide Constitutional issues of religion and public schools. These issues ranged from prayer in schools or school events, to the celebration of Christian holidays in public spaces, to curricular decisions concerning evolution or creationism in biology classes, to the appropriate garb (hijab, kippa) for public school students. School boards and religious communities across the country continue to debate whether public schools should be secular religion-free zones or whether *teaching about religion* (rather than *teaching of religion*) should be included in standard public school curricula. In this chapter, we take the position that to truly understand our own neighbors and to participate effectively in a diverse citizenry and global society, we will need to do a much better job of understanding each other's religions, beliefs and traditions of worship, as well as the salience of religion in our different cultures.

DEMOGRAPHICS OF CURRENT U.S. RELIGIOUS DIVERSITY

The national census does not provide the demographic information on religion that it offers for ethnic and racial self-identification. Non-governmental surveys that collect data on religion are often voluntary, based on self-reports from organized religious congregations or affiliations, and thus vary depending on whether religious identity is linked to organized, observant religious communities, or based on survey data and self-report. Since Buddhist, Hindu, Muslim, Sikh, and Native American religious practices are not necessarily congregational or documented by official listings, it becomes all the more difficult to gather demographic data on the numbers of adherents. The numbers in Table 8.1 are gathered from composite sources to provide an estimate of religious demographics.

The approximate numbers for *Buddhists* include converts of all races as well as immigrant first- and second-generation Americans. Buddhists come primarily from Japan, China, Tibet, Thailand, Cambodia, and other Asian nations. Approximately 75% to 80% of American Buddhists are of Asian ancestry.

Most *Sikhs* are of Indian origin, from Punjab. *Islam* is a pan-ethnic religion, with adherents in the U.S. from East, Southeast, Central, and South Asia, Africa, and the Middle East. There are also African American and European American (mainly Albanian) Muslims. African Americans, Arabs, and South Asians comprise more than three-quarters of all Muslims in the United States. South Asians make up the fastest growing Muslim immigrant population. Around 60% of native-born U.S. Muslims are African Americans (Pew Research Center, 2011a).

Table 8.1 U.S. Religious Demographics

Religion	Numbers	Source
Buddhist	2.2–3.6 million	Pew Research Center (Lipka, 2014) *Dharma World Magazine* (Tanaka, 2011)
Christian	240–262 million	Gallup Poll (Newport, 2012) Pew Research Center (Pew Research Center, 2011b)
Hindu	2.3–3 million	Association of Religion Data Archives (Melton & Jones, 2011) U.S. Census Bureau's American Community Survey (*Hinduism Today*, 2008)
Jewish	4.2–6.8 million	Pew Research Center (Lipka, 2013) Brandeis University's Steinhardt Social Research Institute (Tighe, Saxe, Magidin de Kramer, & Parmer, 2013)
Muslim	1.8–7 million	Pew Research Forum (Pew Research Center, 2011a) *The American Mosque* (Bagby, 2011)
Sikh	200,000–700,000	Sikh American Legal Defense & Education Fund (SALDEF, 2014)

The overall Christian share of the U.S. population dropped from 78% in 2007 to 70% in 2014, with the loss mainly to mainstream Protestants and Catholics, accompanied by increases in those who claimed to be "unaffiliated" or non-Christian (Pew Research Center, 2015, pp. 2–3). Pew also reported increased interreligious marriages, from 19% prior to 1960 to 39% in 2010 (2015, p. 5). Pew further reported that "By a wide margin, religious 'nones' have experienced larger gains through religious switching" in the sense that 18% of U.S. adults raised in a religious faith had come to identify with no religion in the Pew survey (2015, p. 11). There were gains in the populations of Catholics and evangelical Protestants of color. In broad brushstrokes, however, the U.S. has more Christians than other countries globally—70% people in the U.S. identify with some branch of Christianity.

CONTEMPORARY MANIFESTATIONS OF CHRISTIAN HEGEMONY

CHRISTIAN NORMATIVITY, HEGEMONY, AND PRIVILEGE

Many of the historical legacies noted above persist today in events and acts that, over time, became normalized within U.S. traditions while retaining their Christian associations. There are numerous examples of Christian normativity—contemporary rituals and practices that carry Christian culture into the public sphere yet are accepted as "normal," such as the lighting of the Christmas tree at the White House or in a local town, community Easter egg hunts, and the presumptively non-denominational prayer at the start of a city council meeting.

These public rituals have a basis in Christianity, and become repackaged as a U.S. "civil religion," meaning they are supposed to be seen as "American" traditions, widespread and propagated by the popular media (Steinberg & Kincheloe, 2009). This "civil religion" is maintained as a glue for U.S. national identity and an indicator of one's patriotism. Calling this marker of Christian hegemony a "civil religion" downplays the role of Christianity in the American way of life (Feldman, 1996; Murray, 2008).

Many people consider these events to be normal, appropriate, and joyous activities for all Americans. Few people think seriously about the ways in which U.S. Christianity has institutionalized its values and practices while marginalizing and subordinating those who do not adhere to Christian faith traditions. The above scenarios of "normalized" customs operate to privilege Christians while contributing to the marginalization and further invisibility of non-Christian faiths and atheists and agnostics. Christianity is a visible ingredient of U.S. patriotism in war-time or times of presumed conflict, as during the Cold War of the 1950s—when to be an atheist was to be un-American, and to be a Jew was suspect—or today with the suspicion of anyone thought to be Muslim. This issue emerged again in questions of President Obama's religious convictions (Protestant or Muslim), even to rumors whether he took the oath of office holding a Bible or the Qur'an.

Further, Christian norms shape assumptions about where and how to worship: In recognizable religious buildings (churches), but not in geographic sacred sites; and with hands clasped in prayer, but not stretched forward on the floor from a kneeling position. The respect shown to core Christian beliefs (the Virgin birth, the Resurrection, the Second Coming) is not accorded to the religious or spiritual beliefs of indigenous peoples. Mohammed's midnight flight to heaven (Islam) or Vishnu's periodic visitation of the Earth under different guises (Hinduism) are mocked and laughed at, reduced to the status of "myths" and "folkways." These views devalue them by removing their religious content through an implicit comparison with Christian beliefs or truths, and with Christian worship and religious observance (Joshi, 2006).

Because Christianity is culturally normative, non-Christians are asked, "What is 'your Bible'?" and "When is 'your Christmas'?" The normative force of these questions comes from the assumption that other religions have the same or equivalent versions of one sacred text or one or two major holidays. Hinduism, for example, has more than one sacred text, as does Judaism. Similarly, the respect accorded to U.S. depictions of God as a bearded (often fearsome) elderly man—or the Trinity that includes a white-bearded elder, a younger blue-eyed blondish Jesus, and a white dove—is not granted to Ganesh (half-elephant, half-human); or Krishna with his blue skin; or the four-armed Saraswati, goddess of knowledge, wisdom, and learning; or images of the seated Buddha.

Christian hegemony conveys the societal power inherent in these cumulative normative markers of Christianity (Kivel, 2013). The patriotism conveyed by "one nation under God" or the usual valedictory of U.S. Presidents, "God bless America," affirms identification with a Christian God. Beyond the cultural insult, hegemonic Christianity has real economic consequences for Jews who worship and rest from Friday sundown through Saturday; for Muslims who have weekly prayer obligations on Fridays; and for Hindus, Sikhs, and others whose major holidays may not coincide with the seven-day week at all. Across the U.S., historically and today, state laws and local ordinances, including strict regulations against work, shopping, and other activities, have been used to ensure that Sunday would be treated as the "Sabbath" (the day of rest). Even today, for example, retail businesses are closed on Sundays in Bergen County, New Jersey, and Georgia law forbids the Sunday sales of alcohol.

Christian hegemony at the institutional level and Christian norms at the cultural and societal level intertwine and result in Christian ideas and practices that are engrained and embedded in U.S. culture, law, and policy. The result is Christian privilege, a circumstance where Christians enjoy advantages that are denied to non-Christians.

At the interpersonal and individual level, there are many examples of Christian privilege in everyday life (Killermann, 2012; Schlosser, 2003). Americans who are Christian can:

- Easily find Christmas cards, Easter baskets, or other items and food for holiday observances;
- Have a religious symbol (a fish, for example) as a bumper sticker without worrying that their car will be vandalized, or they can wear a religious symbol without being afraid of being attacked;
- Travel to any part of the country and know their religion will be accepted and that they will have access to religious spaces to practice their faith;
- Fundraise to support congregations of their faith without being investigated as potentially threatening or terrorist behavior;
- Are likely to have politicians responsible for their governance who share their faith.

RELIGIOUS OPPRESSION: DISADVANTAGE, MARGINALIZATION, AND DISCRIMINATION

Religious oppression refers to the cultural marginalization and societal subordination of Buddhists, Hindus, Jews, Muslims, Native American spiritualties, Sikhs, and those who identify as atheists, agnostics, or freethinkers in the U.S. Religious oppression is present as individual biases and prejudices, in institutional policies and practices, and in the cultural norms and societal hegemony of Christianity in the U.S.

Many examples of bias, prejudice, and ignorance at the individual level have already been mentioned in the preceding section on Christian normativity, such as a personal sense of exclusion from team-based Christian prayer, or rude rather than respectful questions about one's practices, posed in language framed by the Christian norms ("What is your Bible?" "Where do you go to church?"). Other examples include being expected to speak as a representative of one's religious group, and dealing with stereotypes such as that Jews are cheap, or that Muslims are violent.

Non-Christians, whether adherents of other faith traditions or agnostics and atheists, are subject to the proselytizing encouraged in evangelical Christian practice. Christians who believe they are doing the "right thing" by carrying the "good news" to non-Christians would be shocked to know that such proselytizing can be experienced as bullying and harassment—and that when repeated, build up on a daily basis as microaggressions that cause anxiety and fear. The Butte, Montana, newspaper editor (1870) who wrote "the Chinaman's life is not our life, his religion is not our religion" (Eck, 2001, p. 166) sounds much the same normative note as the recent proselytizing claim "that all Hindus should open their eyes and find Jesus" (Hafiz & Raghunathan, 2014, p. x).

Finally, there is always the fear of personal violence. Many Hindus, Jews, Muslims, or Sikhs feel vulnerable on the basis of both dark-skinned physiognomy and religious attire that mark their outsider religious status, confounded with and multiplied by outsider racial, ethnic, and linguistic status. They and their families have bricks thrown through windows or vicious slurs from passersby. Sikhs who wear turbans are attacked and their turbans forcibly removed; Hindu women wearing a bindi or forehead dot are harassed and insulted. Hate crimes against Jews have increased at synagogues and Jewish day care centers. Individuals angry about Israel's actions toward Palestinians may target individual Jews who have no connection to and may not even support such policies. As numerous hate crimes studies have shown, such violence is regrettably neither rare nor a phenomenon of the past (Eck, 2001; Pew Research Center *passim*).

At the institutional level of the workplace, individuals whose religious identities are visible may not be considered appropriate for "front desk" or "client service" positions and have been denied employment. In these situations, grooming and dress policies reproduce mainstream cultural norms that clash with the kippa (yarmulke), turban, long hair, and beard that are required of observant Jewish, Sikh, or Muslim men. For example, a U.S. Supreme Court decision in 2015 revealed that clothier Abercrombie & Fitch had refused to hire a Muslim girl as one of its sales staff because she wore the traditional Muslim headscarf or *hijab*. When non-Christian religious groups have attempted to erect a house of worship in some towns and cities across the country, city councils and neighborhood groups have created legal roadblocks, and have in many cases prevented the construction or so poisoned the cultural atmosphere that religious minorities chose to go elsewhere (Eck, 2001; Esposito & Kalin, 2011; Singh, 2003).

The cultural devaluation by which religious beliefs of Hindus, Muslims and Native peoples have been represented as "myths" and "legends" is also expressed at the institutional level of the marketplace, where popular dress fads commodify and trivialize markers of marginalized or exoticized religion. Sales in gift shops of Native dream catchers, which is distinct from Native artists who reproduce Hopi spiritual items and whose proceeds support Native artists and communities, are one example of religious misappropriation. Another is the popularity of Hindu god and goddess images on candles, perfume, and clothing with secular purposes. On the mass-production market, these multi-armed gods and goddesses become cultish and fetishized, portrayed as cartoonish, despite their religious seriousness to believers as visible manifestations of the divine.

The overarching vision of social justice is one in which the current "privileges" held by Christians in the U.S. become considered "rights" that are protected for everyone, regardless of religion or non-religion. For this to take place, U.S. Christians will need to became far more aware of their privilege and of the cumulative and powerful normative influence of Christianity in everyday life, if they are to "level the living field" for their non-Christian colleagues, neighbors, and classmates.

CONTEMPORARY RACIALIZATION OF RELIGION

As noted in the earlier section on historical legacies, race had been "co-constitutive" with religion for the Jews, Arabs, and Asian immigrants from 1870–1924, and remains an important contemporary issue requiring special attention. Particularly since 9/11, brown-skinned, bearded Arab Americans and South Asian Americans, as well as Latinos and biracial, multiracial people, are assumed to be Muslim on the basis of their racial appearance, which is presumed to verify their religious identities. This is a period during which Muslims are among the most demonized members of U.S. society as a result of international events and domestic actions by those who commit violence abroad or in the U.S. in the name of Islam.

The notion of the "Muslim terrorist," powerfully etched in the minds of many Americans, is still in place. That this stereotype is the first assumption of the press and the police when violence occurs was demonstrated at the time of the bombing of the Oklahoma City Federal Building (carried out by a white right-wing extremist). We neglect the evidence on the other side—that threats and arson against medical clinics that provide abortion services, the murders of Jews, and the execution-style massacre of black worshippers at a South Carolina prayer service—all were conducted by white Christian ideological extremists who were not, however, described as "Christian terrorists" (Singh, 2013). Instead, the fanaticism and violence committed by these extremists were attributed to unique psychological or ideological factors. Indeed, "Muslim" or "Islamic" and "terrorists" seem a single, hyphenated term in media coverage, which emphasizes the threats posed by dark-skinned, bearded Muslims (Alsultany, 2008; Rana, 2011).

Islamophobia in the U.S. is not just a post 9/11 phenomenon, as noted in the earlier section on historical legacies. But there has been clear acceleration in the religious and racial stereotyping of Muslims—a "phobia" toward adherents of Islam (*Islamophobia*)—as if all were violent extremists. These assumptions have been reinforced in response to the oil crisis of 1973, the Gulf Wars of the 1980s and 1990s, the attacks of September 11, 2001, and the bombings in London and Madrid. Most recently, the stereotyping in the media builds on stories of Western-born young Muslims joining ISIS, and also accelerates fears of a geopolitical threat brought back to Europe and the U.S. by ISIS-trained jihadists.

Media representations designed to meet a 24/7 news cycle or focus on monitoring U.S. borders essentialize Muslims as if all were intrinsically violent, destructive, and incapable of self-regulation or democracy, whether on the basis of theology or genetics (Esposito & Kalin, 2011; Jamal & Naber, 2008). Remarks from political leaders and the news media reinforce caricatures that are filmmakers' or cartoonists' stock-in-trade (Alsultany, 2008; Shaheen, 2001). These negative images echo the antisemitic cartoons at the height of antisemitism in pre-World War II Europe and the U.S.

The widespread use of the term "Muslim terrorist" not only perpetuates fallacious and harmful stereotypes. It erases the complexity of religious traditions that are encapsulated within Islam, a religion as complex and multifaceted as Buddhism, Christianity, Hinduism, and Judaism. All (like Islam) contain a wide spectrum of beliefs that range from literal ultra-orthodoxy at one end (at times, marked by fanaticism) to progressive liberalism at the other (at times verging on secularism). In a variation of the ironic tag that refers to the racial profiling of African Americans, Singh (2103) notes the new racial designation "apparently Muslim" to capture the daily experience of Arab Americans when traveling, dealing with police, applying for jobs, and receiving poor service in restaurants.

GLOBAL RELIGIOUS AND POLITICAL VIOLENCE

While the focus of this chapter is on religious oppression in the U.S., the dynamics we describe occur globally. Most nation-states have one dominant religion that is hegemonic and that shapes national identity, thereby marginalizing or subordinating religious minorities in ways that intersect with class or caste, race, and ethnicity.

Some countries, such as Australia, Canada, France, India, South Africa, and the U.S., have religious protections built into their Constitutions. Others maintain formal religious establishments as part of the political framework, such as Great Britain's Anglican Church, or Islam as an official state religion in Pakistan and Saudi Arabia, or Judaism within Israel. These countries share with other democracies the dilemma of protecting the human rights of all peoples, in this case of religious minorities, despite political decisions driven by majoritarian electoral politics.

Many nation-states have experienced violent upheavals that reflect religious hegemony and marginalization, such as the Hindu/Muslim conflicts in India and Muslim/Christian violence in Pakistan. Religious claims are further complicated by ethnicity, class, or caste; historical and geographic competition for national identity; and resources (as in Bosnia, Croatia, and Serbia; or Israel and Palestine) (Armstrong, 2014; Fox, 2000, 2002). The conflicts in Northern Ireland and Israel reflect historical and contemporary inequities and grievances based on political and economic privileges/disadvantages that greatly complicate religious struggles for national identity. It is hard to grasp the complexity of global or local religious conflicts without accounting for decades, sometimes centuries, of religious, ethnic, and economic struggle, intensified and justified by competing historical narratives and claims for land, food, and water between dominating and subordinated peoples (Armstrong, 2014; Fox, 2000, 2002; Juergensmeyer, 2000, 2004; Said 1978, 1993).

The global and local have converged in the U.S., especially on college campuses, in ideological positions taken or assumed to have been taken by students on different sides of the seemingly intractable conflict between Israel and Palestine. This conflict is sometimes generalized as a conflict specifically between Jews and Muslims, a view that oversimplifies the complexities in the Middle East of competing nationalisms and territorial claims vindicated by conflicting histories, as well as different ideological disagreements within Islam and Judaism.

This conflict has come to U.S. college campuses by divestment efforts and the erroneous view that thoughtful critiques of Israeli policies and nationalism are necessarily antisemitic. This conflict seriously impacts the relations between Jews and Muslims in the U.S., whatever their convictions about the politics of the Middle East (Shavit, 2013; Tolan, 2006), and they play out in complex and challenging ways that negatively affect campus Jews (Kosmin & Keysar, 2015) and campus Muslims (Berlak, 2014). One dimension is the role of oversimplification, by which all Jews are faulted for Israeli settlement expansions and military policies, so that U.S. Jews (who largely are white) are also held responsible for the racism that is a component of the Israeli-Palestinian conflict. It is not often noted that many Israeli Jews are also peoples of color, refugees from North African and Arab countries. On the other end, Muslims are faulted and feared as if all were adherents of radical Islam.

These ideological conflicts leave no space for Jews who critique Israeli politics, but who also need to identify as Jewish (Karpf, Klug, Rose, & Rosenbaum, 2008; Kushner & Solomon, 2003)—or for Muslims who oppose radical Islam but who also (sometimes visibly) identify as Muslim. The Trinity College Anti-Semitism Report (February 2015) found alarmingly high reports by Jewish students of antisemitic incidents experienced or observed on their campuses, mainly one-on-one, sometimes in groups or classrooms, but generally ignored or downplayed by campus administrations (Kosmin & Keysar, 2015, pp. 10–12). The Political Research Associates report on antisemitism and Islamophobia on U.S. college campuses offers detailed analysis of the dilemmas facing observant as well as secular Jews and Muslims, with interviews and campus scenarios detailing the specifics of campus conflicts and controversies (Berlak, 2014). The essentializing inherent to antisemitism and Islamophobia disrupts efforts to build bridges and coalitions within educational settings, at a time when young people may be most open to cross-religious friendships, collaboration, and interfaith activism.

INTERSECTIONS OF RELIGIOUS HEGEMONY AND OPPRESSION WITH OTHER ISMS

While we particularly highlight the intersection of region and race, Christian hegemony and religious oppression intersect with other social identities and forms of oppression as well. Two Supreme Court split decisions in 2014 and 2015, reflecting the opposite sides of the Court, placed religious-freedom claims in direct opposition to women's rights to choose and gay couples' rights to marry. In *Burwell v. Hobby Lobby* (2014), a narrow conservative majority found that family-owned companies could be exempted from providing for insurance under the Affordable Care Act for contraception on the basis of their religious opposition to contraception. The Court's finding was based on a new interpretation of the Religious Freedom Restoration Act (RFRA, 1993), which had been originally crafted by Congress to protect marginalized religions, such as those of Native peoples. This new reasoning on RFRA would protect the religious exercise of individuals and for-profit companies whose religious convictions opposed the rights of marginalized groups—of women for contraception, and a year later, same-sex marriage.

In 2015, a liberal narrow majority in the Court found marriage equality to be a Constitutionally protected right. In nearly simultaneous protest, state legislatures passed local versions of RFRA protecting commercial enterprises (florists, bakeries) whose owners opposed marriage equality on religious grounds, and who denied services to gay couples. Civil rights groups immediately responded by stating that the denial of service by businesses to legally protected minorities is the very definition of discrimination. The resulting political firestorm over "religious protection" legislation in opposition to anti-discrimination laws protecting subordinated groups on the basis of gender and sexuality shows no sign of abating and is likely to be a hotly contested issue in the future (Cole, 2015; Eckholm, 2015).

Many global issues may wear a religious veneer, but below the surface one finds long-simmering conflicts among social classes, racial or ethnic groups, and the suppression of women's rights to their bodies and to education. Conflicts that have been framed as religious (in the Middle East, India, Pakistan, and Ireland) require closer analysis of economic inequality (land, jobs, education), sexual abuse and subordination, violence toward sexual and gender nonconformity, and competing nationalisms that have been subsumed by the religious dimensions that seem most visible (Little, 2007). Similarly, the sexual victimization of women in Africa, China, India, and Pakistan, or efforts to prevent their education (as in Afghanistan), may reflect ethnic authoritarian enforcement of religious patriarchy within families, reinforced by police or other authorities.

This intersectional approach to religious oppression explores the "co-constitutive relationships" (Goldschmidt & McAlister, 2004, p. 6) between religion and other social categories—race, ethnicity, economic class, gender, and sexuality—to which we must add nationalism. The intersection of religion with nationalism accounts for many of the most vicious attacks on members of "outsider" religious groups historically (such as pogroms against Jews in Russia) and currently (such as attacks on Sikhs in the U.S. and Christians in Pakistan). In such cases, it is extraordinarily difficult to try to hold in place one strand—religion—while also understanding that it is not truly a single strand but involves a "simultaneity of systems." Solo issues we call race and/or ethnicity and/or culture and/or class and caste and/or religion are interactive rather than unitary, "constructed in and through each other, and through other categories of difference" (Goldschmidt & McAlister, 2004, p. 7).

Adding religion as yet another category of analysis within systems of domination and oppression makes for a slippery slope if one attempts merely to isolate or freeze religious justifications from a complex web that includes cultural, ethnic, racial, class or gender-based rationales for oppression. The primary reason for attempting this disentanglement through a focus on specific isms—in this case, religion— is to better understand the previously under-examined religious justifications used in tandem with racism or classism to dehumanize the "Other," dismiss minority religions, relocate or restrict their living spaces, and eradicate their cultures. "Land acquisition and missionary work always went hand in hand in American history" (Deloria, 1969/1999, p. 22).

MOVING TOWARD JUSTICE

Although there have been Baha'is, Buddhists, Hindus, Muslims, Sikhs, Zoroastrians, and practitioners of Santería, Shinto, Native American spiritualties, and other world religions in the U.S. for decades, and in some cases for centuries, never have there been so many burgeoning religious-oriented communities and organized houses of worship as there are today. Just as the arrival of Catholic and Jewish immigrants spurred public debate on religion and schooling in the 19th and early 20th centuries, so today new waves of immigrants are creating new points of discussion and conflict in these areas. Along with the increase in faith traditions that are not Christian, we also see a rise in the number of people who think of themselves as non-affiliated, agnostic, atheist, or "nothing in particular" (Pew Research Center, 2015). Agnostics and atheists have become more outspoken and openly challenge the beliefs and traditions of formal religion (Andrews, 2013; Christina, 2012; Hitchens, 2007). Promoting religious pluralism needs to provide space for non-believers who may identify in various ways—as agnostic, atheist, non-believer, rationalist, secular humanist, or "nothing in particular."

One way for our society to be more inclusive is to not use religion as a rationale or excuse for discrimination against social identity groups that may seem outsider to one's own faith tradition. For example, individual religious beliefs have been used to perpetuate homophobia. The renewed attention on the free exercise of religion demonstrates the need for greater clarity and understanding about what can and cannot be done to express or suppress religion in the public arena, as in the case of Christmas nativity scenes on public property, sectarian prayer before public meetings, and denial of public services on the basis of religious objections to gays and lesbians. During the Christmas season, some public officials incorporate celebrations of Chanukah and Kwanzaa. In the case of Christian normative public celebrations, public officials need to consider how to be authentically inclusive and pluralistic as distinct from "additive." This includes questioning the hegemonic assumption that authorities should invoke a specific deity for guidance in public matters. While officials might look for guidance in their private moments, it can be argued that a public meeting should not presume agreement among participants as to the nature or the role of divine guidance.

The interfaith arena offers many opportunities for mutual understanding and respect, if not agreement, including but not limited to inter-religious dialogue (Forward, 2001; McCarthy, 2007; Patel, 2012; Smock, 2002). Interfaith councils have in recent decades included representatives of many religious traditions. Some interfaith groups focus on learning and understanding through dialogue; others address common social concerns; still others revolve around campus environments or public spaces, such as hospitals or prisons (McCarthy, 2007; Patel & Scorer, 2012). Despite their different approaches, interfaith groups share the unifying belief in intentional relationship-building to resolve intergroup conflict.

Interfaith groups have provided support to specific religious communities in times of crisis, as in the case of members of Jewish communities who were victims of white supremacist hate crimes in Billings, Montana (NIOT, 1995/1996). In the aftermath of 9/11, Church members reached out to local Muslim organizations and mosques to ensure their fellow neighbors could pray peacefully and without fear of violence. Protestant ministers came together in 2002 in New Jersey to advance dialogues among different religious communities (Niebuhr, 2008). After the massacre at the Oak Creek Gurdwara in Wisconsin, Sikhs and non-Sikhs alike made their way to *gurdwaras* in record numbers to show their support, while the Sikh community emphasized that their doors had been and would continue to be open. Interfaith efforts continue to focus on opportunities for members of each group to learn more about the others by meeting in different houses of worship and sharing meals to create bonds and communities.

Beyond interfaith coalitions, the vigorous theological as well as moral and pragmatic demands for economic justice by Pope Francis have reached a broad and enthusiastic public, with considerable media attention. Pope Francis's public apology for the participation of the Roman Catholic Church in colonial-era violence against indigenous peoples throughout the Americas offered a dramatic instance of the Church's willingness to acknowledge its share of responsibility for the horrors of Spanish colonialism. Pope Francis places responsibility on the inequities of capitalism for global poverty and economic injustice, with a critique that goes well beyond traditional Catholic social teachings and recalls the efforts of Liberation Theology, whose spirit this Pope now embraces.

As we hope for a future that includes religious justice, we must look not only to our religious and secular social movements, but also look for clarity about the role of religion in the public education curriculum. Educators have come to understand that modernization calls for pluralism, not secularization among its "diversity" concerns (Patel, 2015), although secularists or non-aligned non-believers must also be included in such religious pluralism.

Teaching about religion in public education has been hampered because of anxiety and misunderstanding about the applicability of the religion clauses of the 1st Amendment to public schooling. The Constitutional prohibition against devotional reading or sectarian prayer in schools has frightened policy-makers into choosing "non-religious" secularism over religious pluralism in efforts to maintain "total separation" between religion and public education. This approach misrepresents the Constitutional mandate, which does not require that public schools provide a "religion-free zone." The Supreme Court has encouraged that religion be made part of the school curriculum so long as the distinction between "teaching" and "preaching" is respected. The Court has made clear that schools may, and should, promote awareness of religion and expose students of all ages to the diversity of religious world views, but may not endorse or denigrate any particular religion or belief.

The Court on several occasions argued that the 1st Amendment calls for political neutrality, but not exclusion, with regard to religion, by describing the Constitutional requirement for "the state to be neutral in its relations with groups of religious believers and non-believers . . . State power is no more to be used so as to handicap religions than it is to favor them" (*Everson v. Board of Education*, 1947). In a subsequent decision (*Abington v. Schempp*, 1963), the Court suggested a path forward, namely, a renewed commitment to teaching *about* religion and religious traditions (not the teaching *of* any one specific religion) as part of the regular curriculum. Writing with the majority, Justice Tom Clark said:

> It might well be said that one's education is not complete without a study of comparative religion or the history of religion and its relationship to the advancement of civilization. It certainly may be said that the Bible is worthy of study for its literary and historical qualities. Nothing we have said here indicated that such study of the Bible or of religion, when presented objectively as part of a secular program of education, may not be effected consistently with the First Amendment.
>
> (*Abington v. Schempp*, 1963)

Understanding religious differences and the role of religion in the contemporary world—and in our students' lives—is important to personal growth and development, exposes religious prejudice, and helps build classroom communities where students develop the trust, knowledge, and skills to become thoughtful global citizens. Educators have prepared excellent guides to support these efforts in K–12 schooling as well as in higher education (Anderson, 2007; Haynes, Chaltain, Ferguson, Hudson, & Thomas, 2003; Haynes & Thomas, 2001; Jones & Sheffield, 2009; Moore, 2007; Murray, 2008; Nash, 2001).

There are many settings, classrooms, community groups, and religious organizations where members of different religious communities—and those who do not identify with any religion—can further explore the Christian hegemony and religious discrimination that characterizes our historical past and present, and consider how to foster religious pluralism and social justice in their future. We aim for something greater than merely to reduce religious discrimination against non-Christians, although that is surely an important intermediary step. Our aim is a genuinely pluralistic society that is socially just and in which religious communities, as well as non-believers, are visible, but without privileges accorded to some and disadvantages experienced by others. As we imagine ways of moving from "here" to "there," we focus upon how to challenge Christian hegemony in the public square and in educational settings, so that, in the words of an earlier Supreme Court, "The anti-discrimination principle inherent in the Establishment Clause necessarily means that would-be discriminators on the basis of religion cannot prevail" (*County of Allegeny v. American Civil Liberties Union*, 1989).

SAMPLE DESIGN FOR TEACHING ABOUT CHRISTIAN HEGEMONY AND RELIGIOUS OPPRESSION

The following design uses a social justice approach to Christian hegemony and religious oppression, drawing upon themes and information presented in this chapter. This is not an instructional design to teach "about" religion, nor does it focus on the differences among religions. It focuses on historical and contemporary manifestations of religious oppression as it plays out in the U.S. through pervasive Christian hegemony.

This design, like other designs in this volume, uses four quadrants to suggest ways to "sequence" the learning outcomes for students. These quadrants generally follow the sequence "What? So what? Now what?" by which we mean: "What is this issue all about?"(overview and personal awareness), "What do we need to know to understand this issue?" (conceptual frameworks, historical legacies, contemporary manifestations, intersections with other issues), and "Now that we know and care about this issue, what do we feel comfortable and have the knowledge and skills to do about it?" (advocacy, coalition building, action planning).

We use the four-quadrant design because it helps us keep this learning sequence in focus. It can easily be adapted to other modalities, such as short workshops or semester-long courses. Examples of other modalities appear on the chapter website.

The sample design for Religious Oppression offered below is immediately followed by learning objectives and core concepts specific to each of the four quadrants, as well as brief descriptors of the activities needed to carry out the design. Actual instructions and facilitation notes for each of these activities can be found on the Religious Oppression website that accompanies this volume (p. 281).

This design presupposes familiarity with the core social justice concepts that we consider foundational to any social justice approach (presented in Chapter 4). We incorporate these core concepts in ways that we believe "fit" an exploration of religious oppression. We assume that instructors and facilitators will have read Chapter 4 and will have considered these core concepts more fully prior to applying them to Religious Oppression.

Following the four-quadrant design, learning outcomes, core concepts, and activities, the chapter closes with general discussion of pedagogical, design, and facilitation issues that we have found to be specific to teaching about religious oppression. Specific considerations of pedagogy, design, and facilitation for each of the activities are explained more fully on the website, immediately following the description of each activity.

Quadrant 1: Personal Awareness of Religious Identity and Religious Difference in the U.S. (approx. 3.5 h)

1. Welcome and Overview, with Goals & Assumptions (30 min)
2. Community Building (30 min)
3. Group Norms and Guidelines (20 min)
4. Who's in the Room (20 min)
5. Personal Awareness and Reflection Activity Options (25–40 min)
6. Understanding Religious Oppression as a Social Justice Issue (20 min)
7. Social Justice Approaches to Religious Oppression (30–45 min)
8. Understanding Christian Privilege (30–45 min)
9. Closing Activity (5–10 min)

Quadrant 2: Historical and Conceptual Understanding of Religious Oppression in the U.S. (3 h 20 min)

1. Check-in (10 min)
2. Timeline: History of Religious Oppression and Christian Normativity in the U.S. (45–90 min)
3. Processing of Historical Legacies (activity segments as "breaks" in presentation) (15–45 min, 15 min each)
4. Intersections with Other Isms, New Insights, New Questions, and Takeaways (15–30 min)
5. Closing Activity (10 min)

Quadrant 3: Recognizing Examples of Christian Hegemony and Religious Oppression in the U.S. Today (3 h)

1. Opening Activity (15 min)
2. Examining Institutional Religious Oppression (30–90 min)
3. Examples of Everyday Christian Normativity and Religious Oppression (25–40 min)
4. Closure Activity: New Insights, New Questions, and Takeaways from the Quadrant (30 min)

Quadrant 4: Recognition of Manifestations of Religious Oppression, Steps Toward Change, and Action Plans (3–4 h)

1. Opening Activity (45 min)
2. Moving Forward (30–45 min)
3. Personal Considerations Prior to Action Planning (30–45 min)
4. Action Planning (45 min)
5. Next Steps (30 min)
6. Closing Ceremony

The Learning Objectives, Key Concepts, and Activities and Options for the Religious Oppression design are detailed below.

QUADRANT 1: PERSONAL AWARENESS OF RELIGIOUS IDENTITY AND RELIGIOUS DIFFERENCE IN THE U.S.

Learning Objectives for Quadrant 1:

- Understand social justice education (SJE) approach to Christian hegemony and religious oppression
- Understand the ingredients needed for an SJE learning community
- Recognize the impact of stereotypes and experiences of subordinated religious communities in U.S. history and contemporary life
- Explore personal implications of your own religious/non-religious experiences and perspectives in relation to those of your extended family and cultural context
- Understand the concept of privilege and disadvantage in relation to U.S. Christianity

Key Concepts for Quadrant 1: Religious oppression; social justice education; Christian hegemony, normativity, privilege; stereotypes; personal and institutional manifestations of religious oppression; personal bias, Christian advantage and non-Christian disadvantage

Activities and Options for Quadrant 1:

1. **Welcome and Overview** (30 min)
   a. **Goals and Assumptions:** This activity identifies goals/learning objectives in learning about religious oppression and overall assumptions for an SJE approach to religious oppression.
2. **Community Building** (30 min)
   a. **Option A: Introductions:** The instructor and participants introduce themselves by presenting the meanings of their own names in the context of their families' religious (or non-religious) history. This introduction establishes a context for names that is linked to the subject matter of religion and family religious identity.
   b. **Option B: Introductions:** The instructor and participants introduce themselves by presenting information relevant to the classroom or workshop context.
3. **Group Norms and Guidelines** (20 min)
   a. **Option A: Creation of Group Norms and Guidelines.**
   b. **Option B: Hopes and Concerns.** This activity helps to identify and name the hopes and concerns participants bring into the class on religious oppression through an active group process. These hopes and concerns become the basis for Norms and Guidelines.
4. **Who's in the Room** (20 min)
   a. **Option A: Common Ground** (20 min): The questions posed in this activity about religious identity, background, and modes of worship help participants see who is in the group and make personal connections while engaging with the different life experiences that participants bring to this subject.
   b. **Option B: Treasure Hunt** (20 min): The participants mix in the room to find the participants with religious experiences or identities described in the handout sheet.
5. **Personal Awareness and Reflection Activity** (25–40 min)
   a. **Religion and Stereotypes:** A short presentation on stereotypes is followed by an activity in which small groups generate stereotypes of marginalized religious groups, share their examples, and discuss the sources and common themes in the information generated.
6. **Understanding Religious Oppression as a Social Justice Issue** (20 min)
   a. **Presentation of the Social Justice Approach to Religious Oppression.** This activity places an emphasis on the structural and sociological analysis of institutional

manifestations and historical legacies of religious oppression, and not on personal religious beliefs or the content of different religions.

7. **Social Justice Approaches to Religious Oppression** (15–30 min)
   a. **Option A: Levels of Christian Advantage as an Organizer** (15 min): This activity offers examples of Christian advantage at the personal, institutional, and societal level.
   b. **Option B: Overview of "Five Faces of Oppression" as an Organizer** (30 min): This activity provides examples of religious advantage and disadvantage using Young's "Five Faces" framework.

8. **Understanding Christian Privilege** (30–45 min)
   a. **Knapsack of Christian Privilege.** This activity enables participants to identify and "unpack" the unconscious Christian privileges that enable Christians to navigate everyday life—a knapsack that non-Christians do not have.

9. **Closing Activity** (5–10 min)
   a. **Option A: Take the Temperature:** (10 min): This activity provides an opportunity for a brief check-in by asking participants to offer one word or a brief comment about how they are feeling at the end of this first segment.
   b. **Option B: Geometric Shape Check-in** (5 min): This activity provides an opportunity for participants to reflect individually and submit a handout with their new learnings and remaining questions.

QUADRANT 2: HISTORICAL AND CONCEPTUAL UNDERSTANDING OF RELIGIOUS OPPRESSION IN THE U.S.

Learning Objectives for Quadrant 2:

- Understand the historical legacies of Christian hegemony and the pervasive Christian norms, which result in advantages for U.S. Christians and disadvantages for U.S. marginalized religious groups such as agnostics/atheists, Buddhists, Hindus, indigenous and Native American Indian religions, Jehovah's Witnesses, Jews, Latter-day Saints/Mormons, Muslims, and Wiccans
- As time permits, understand the emergence of Christianity in early European history, and the patterns of antisemitism and anti-Islam built into early Christianity, which later parallels patterns in the U.S.
- As time permits, understand the Protestant policies and norms of U.S. Christianity until the mid-20th century
- Identify examples of the levels at which Christian hegemony results in unexamined norms, at the institutional, societal, and individual levels
- Understand the role of religion in national identity and nationalism
- Explore intersections of religion with other forms of identity at the individual, institutional, and societal/cultural levels

Key Concepts for Quadrant 2: Christianity normativity; religious hegemony; historical legacies and contemporary manifestations; social/cultural (macro), institutional (meso), and personal (micro) manifestations; antisemitism, Islamophobia or anti-Islam, Protestantism, Catholicism; national identity, nationalism; intersections

Activities and Options for Quadrant 2:

1. **Check-in** (10 min)
   Check-in at the start and close of a quadrant is an important ingredient of maintaining a learning community.

2. **Timeline: History of Religious Oppression and Christian Normativity in the U.S.** (45–90 min)
   This timeline activity allows participants to identify, explore, and discuss events that perpetuate Christian normativity and hegemony and the historical religious oppression against non-Protestant faiths and atheists in the U.S.

3. **Processing of Historical Legacies** (15–45 min)
   a. **Option A: Social/Cultural, Institutional, and Personal Manifestations of Christian (Protestant) Hegemony and Marginalization of the Religious Other** (30 min): Participants use worksheets for small-group discussions. They should include "intersections" or "reinforcers" from other forms of social advantage or disadvantage where they can.
   b. **Option B: "Five Faces" of Christian (Protestant) Hegemony and Marginalization of the Religious Other** (30 min): Participants use worksheets for small-group discussions. They should include "intersections" or "reinforcers" from other forms of social advantage or disadvantage where they can.

4. **Intersections with Other Isms, New Insights, New Questions, and Takeaways** (15–30 min)
   In this activity, a worksheet is provided for participants to complete while the information is being presented. The worksheet focuses on identifying intersections of religious oppression with other forms of advantage and disadvantage.

5. **Closing Activity**
   a. **Option A: Take the Temperature** (10 min): This activity provides an opportunity for a brief check-in by asking participants to offer one word or a brief comment about how they are feeling at the end of this first segment.
   b. **Option B: Geometric Shape Check-in** (5 min): This activity provides an opportunity for participants to reflect individually and submit a handout with their new learnings and remaining questions.

QUADRANT 3: RECOGNIZING EXAMPLES OF CHRISTIAN HEGEMONY AND RELIGIOUS OPPRESSION IN THE U.S. TODAY

Learning Objectives for Quadrant 3:

- Understand the historical context for adding the "protection of religion clauses" as part of the 1st Amendment to the U.S. Constitution
- Understand the issues raised by historical and contemporary cases brought under the "protection of religion clauses"
- Identify major topics in reading assignments
- Continue development and reflection within a learning community that respects different perspectives and personal experiences

Key Concepts for Quadrant 3: Historical context and legacies; "separation of church and state"; Constitutional "protection of religion" clauses; Christian hegemony in U.S. legal decisions; intersections among forms of religious oppression and other forms of oppression

Activities and Options in Quadrant 3:

1. **Opening Activity** (5–15 min)
   a. **Check-in** (15 min): Ask whether some of the questions participants brought into the session have now been addressed, and take note of those that have not yet been addressed.

2. **Examining Institutional Religious Oppression** (30–90 min)
   a. **Option A: U.S. Constitutional Protections Lecture and Activity** (90 min): Instructors can prepare a brief lecture covering material presented in this chapter. There is supplemental material for such a lecture on the chapter website. A brief lecture should include the historical context for the "separation of church and state" and the religion clauses of the 1st Amendment, if instructors use the activity "You be the Judge." The activity enables participants to use the Constitutional protection of religion clauses to guess at the outcome of real legal cases dealing with religious oppression.
   b. **Option B: Guided Discussion Groups** (30 min): Participants should choose one of three discussion groups: #1 and 2 are reading groups (readings from the Religious Oppression chapter of *Readings for Diversity and Social Justice*), and #3 is on Constitutional protections. Each group will provide newsprint to report their major insights to the whole group. Groups have an opportunity to report on their major insights, followed by whole-group discussion as time permits (15 min each group).
3. **Examples of Christian Normativity and Religious Oppression in the U.S. Today** (25–40 min)
   a. **Option A: Recognizing Everyday Christian Hegemony and Religious Oppression** (40 min): This three-part activity has participants identify current U.S. Christian hegemonic norms and the ways in which they become oppressive, exclusive, and discriminatory to non-Christians. The second part asks participants to generate a list of "intersections" or "reinforcers" for examples of Christian hegemony and religious oppression from other forms of advantage and disadvantage. The third part of the activity visualizes the ways in which these norms or exclusions operate as a societal and cultural "web" of religious oppression.
   b. **Option B: Everyday Scenarios** (25 min): Participants are provided the opportunity to analyze everyday situations to see how Christian normativity and religious oppression is present in schools and other workplaces.
4. **Closure Activity: New Insights, New Questions, and Takeaways from the Quadrant** (5–10 min)
   a. **Option A: Take the Temperature** (10 min): This activity provides an opportunity for a brief check-in by asking participants to offer one word or a brief comment about how they are feeling at the end of this first segment.
   b. **Option B: Geometric Shape Check-in:** (5 min): This activity provides an opportunity for participants to reflect individually and submit a handout with their new learnings and remaining questions.

QUADRANT 4: RECOGNITION OF MANIFESTATIONS OF RELIGIOUS OPPRESSION, STEPS TOWARD CHANGE, AND ACTION PLANS

Learning Objectives for Quadrant 4:

- Recognition of current examples of religious oppression at all three levels are necessary ingredients of action planning
- Considerations for planning
- Working in groups or coalitions to plan action

Key Concepts for Quadrant 4: Cycle of Liberation and openings for change; action plan considerations: Spheres of influence, risk levels, building coalitions, and networks; intersections among forms of religious oppression and other forms of oppression; building alliances and coalitions; advocacy and action planning

Activities and Options for Quadrant 4:

1. **Opening Activity** (45 min)
   a. **Option A: Interfaith Four Squares** (30 min). This activity provides an opportunity to see how much information participants have about religions in the U.S. This activity can be used to prepare for strategies for teaching about religion in U.S. public schools, as one kind of action. This activity also is helpful for interfaith groups.
   b. **Option B: Action Continuum—Room-Stations Activity** (30 min). In this activity, participants engage in small-group discussions based on the Action Continuum.
2. **Moving Forward** (30–45 min)
   a. **Option A: Walking the Line in Public Schools** (45 min). Legal and policy considerations concerning what can be done to teach about religion or change policy regarding religion in public schools are presented as a lecture followed by discussion, depending on the instructor's assessment of knowledge level of participants.
   b. **Option B: What's Possible in Professional, Organizational, or Community Settings** (45 min). Participants identify situations in which religion can be addressed in settings other than public schools.
3. **Personal Considerations Prior to Action Planning** (30–45 min)
   a. **Option A:** This option provides a structured approach to self-assessment on the personal factors that should be considered prior to identifying a situation for change and creating an action plan.
   b. **Option B:** In this option, participants tell personal stories about earlier experiences in which they were an advocate or change agent, and what those experiences taught them about becoming an advocate for action and change concerning Christian hegemony and religious oppression.
4. **Action Planning** (45 min)
   a. **Option A: Planning for Action in Schools: Calendar Activity.** This activity has the participants re-think a particular school district's calendar, observing who has their religious holidays off. Participants work toward creating a calendar that is more equitable by considering a number of factors.
   b. **Option B: Developing Your Own Plan for Workplace, Organizational, Professional, School, Community, or Other Settings.** This activity has the participants pick up where they left off in the "Personal Considerations" from Options 3A or 3B listed above to lay out the plan they need to take the action or change the policy or practices they identified in the earlier activity.
5. **Next Steps** (30 min)
   Depending on the number of participants, small groups or the whole group talk about their "takeaways" from the preceding two segments.
6. **Closing Ceremony**
   The closing ceremony can take place in a circle with participants using stems ("One thing I learned," "One thing I'm willing to do," "One thing I want you to know") or some other closing phrase that is appropriate to the group.

PEDAGOGICAL, DESIGN, AND FACILITATION ISSUES TO CONSIDER WHEN TEACHING ABOUT RELIGIOUS OPPRESSION

The classroom or workshop is one of many settings where the merest reference to religion elicits feelings of defensiveness, embarrassment, vulnerability, anxiety, appreciation, anger, and curiosity. These feelings may be heightened when the word "religion" is linked with the word "oppression." Because religion is often considered by many to be a private matter, it is not easy to talk about Christians having advantages in our society, or to identify intersections of religion with other forms of structural privilege and disadvantage. It can be easier to focus on the bias, prejudice, and discrimination experienced by marginalized religions, rather than the issues of cultural and systemic privilege that go along with Christianity in the U.S.

Often in these discussions, participants who are religiously observant and for whom religion has high salience as an identity may feel especially visible and uncomfortable. This is especially true of conservative Christians who may become defensive, even angry, when the terms *Christian hegemony* or *Christian normativity* become part of the workshop vocabulary.

If participants stray too far from the course or workshop design to discuss specific religious or theological beliefs, facilitators should acknowledge these remarks, but not get sidetracked by discussions about beliefs. Instructors need to remind the group that this class focuses on the ways in which the dominant religion has shaped the culture for all members of the society. It focuses upon the historical legacies that contribute to religious advantage and disadvantage in the U.S., and not religious or theological beliefs. It can be useful to have resources available to offer participants who want, in another setting, to explore their religious beliefs, or to learn more about other religions, but it is important not to allow the discussion of advantage and disadvantage to get sidetracked by ideological or theological issues.

It is also the case that some participants will self-identify as non-religious, non-affiliated, non-believers, agnostics, atheists, spiritual but not religious, secular or humanists, or "nothing in particular." It is important to keep space open for those positions, even if no one in the class explicitly owns such a position. The cultural bias in the U.S. against non-believers is very strong and needs to be acknowledged and addressed in the context of Christian hegemony. Religious or conservative Christians (and other religious groups) may also feel vulnerable in social justice spaces where being religious isn't always accepted. Instructors need to ensure that all participants are respected. Because feelings can arise unexpectedly in this (as in any other) course or workshop, we have some suggestions for instructor or facilitator preparation.

INSTRUCTOR/FACILITATOR SELF-AWARENESS AND KNOWLEDGE

Because religious identity is hardly ever thought of *as a social identity* or as a source of social advantage or disadvantage, it is important for instructors and facilitators to reflect upon their own religious upbringing, experiences, beliefs, assumptions, and values as they prepare for the course or workshop. If they are non-believers, this too is an important subject for self-reflection concerning the steps that have led to that identity and commitment. For facilitators to be effective in helping participants manage these conversations, they need to have thought in advance about their own religious position vis-à-vis specific religions as well as religion more generally, and to understand issues that might trigger them in such discussions.

They also need to have reflected in advance about how their own religious identities and experiences have shaped or intersected with their other identities, such as gender, sexual orientation, class, ethnicity, and race. They will need to have examples and anecdotes prepared in advance to illustrate various points and to encourage participant self-reflection. Finally, facilitators should consider their positionality as group leaders in relation to religious identity, and in relation to campus or professional or community religious norms.

This course/workshop does not call for expertise on U.S. or world religions, or religion and the law. But it does call for advance preparation on the topics in the design, and anticipating how to facilitate discussions where disagreement, withdrawal, silence, or avoidance can occur. Instructors and facilitators should use the information in this chapter and the website materials that support our sample design, and other materials on the website, as they prepare themselves to be knowledgeable on the following topics:

- A social justice approach to religious oppression that examines the ways in which historical legacies of Christian privilege have been reproduced culturally, institutionally, and in the socialization of generations of U.S. citizens;
- Some understanding of the major themes of U.S. history as they serve to illustrate Christian hegemony, the marginalization and disadvantage of non-Christian peoples, and the intersections between religious oppression, racism, ethnocentrism, classism, and other manifestations of oppression;
- Some understanding of current manifestations of Christian privilege and bias, prejudice, discrimination, and oppression of marginalized, excluded, and subordinated religious groups;
- The religious protection clauses of the 1st Amendment and some of the issues that complicate the separation of church and state;
- Some thoughts about the role of religion in complex global conflicts, as well as cautions about the issues that intersect with religion in such conflicts.

ESTABLISHING AN INCLUSIVE AND SUPPORTIVE LEARNING COMMUNITY FOR PARTICIPANTS

As with all social justice topics in this volume, the learning community is the context for support and challenge that encourage new learning. There will be varying degrees of comfort and knowledge in the classroom or workshop with this topic. Developing group norms and discussion guidelines is a crucial ingredient for establishing trust and commitment to the learning community from all group members. Here are some potential guidelines for the group that may be helpful:

- Respect what participants say about their religious identification and experiences.
- Be aware of your own ignorance and bias about various faith traditions and unbelievers.
- Name and acknowledge difficulties of discussing religion and religious oppression in a classroom setting with people from different religious backgrounds, legacies, and experiences.
- Do not expect members of marginalized faith communities to speak for other members of that community.

Freedom of religion in the U.S. is an important concept to explore. Participants may assume that the 1st Amendment assures the free exercise of religion (as distinct from freedom of religious belief), and it can be useful to consider what might be meant by "free exercise" and to illustrate some of the contradictions and the unexpected outcomes of Supreme Court cases dealing with the 1st Amendment cases. It can be illuminating to explore why courts might have such different interpretations of the religious protection clauses of the Constitution when they seem so clear cut. Like many issues, a legal mandate is not the same as a social mandate. There is a related Constitutional question that facilitators might want to anticipate, namely, the role of the 1st and 14th Amendments in protecting minority rights and the role of majority rule in a democracy. How do participants balance the protection of free religious exercise and the Constitutional protection of marginalized social groups, including, in this case, religious groups?

Because the topic of religious oppression seems so fundamentally to contradict a core U.S. belief in freedom, it is helpful to consider the difference between "beliefs" or conscience on the one hand, and "action" or practice on the other. This goes to the core of what is meant by "free exercise" of religion. Should belief and practice be separated, as they have been in Supreme Court decisions concerning "free exercise"

CONTEMPORARY U.S. AND GLOBAL EXAMPLES

We provide here a list of topics that instructors and facilitators should be aware of when teaching about religious oppression. Some of these issues may or may not always arise in the class/workshop as specific local or global religious conflicts appear in the media.

- When issues regarding global religious conflicts arise, remind the class that our main focus is to understand systems of advantage and disadvantage of religion in the U.S. At the same time, it is valuable to consider whether or how the core concepts apply to global religious conflicts. Conceptually, the social justice approach is applicable in every nation-state that has either a state religion or an "unofficial" state religion, like the U.S. However, unless the instructor/facilitator has planned to devote time to historical or geopolitical conflicts like those between Hindus and Muslims in India and Pakistan, or between Jews and Muslims in Israel and Palestine, it is wise to deflect such discussions—or to prepare oneself for the discussion by anticipating the likelihood it will come up, based on current events.
- It is possible to ask, "What questions would you need to answer?" or "Where would you find answers to these questions?" before bringing discussion back to the U.S.
- In a class or workshop that extends over many days, it is possible to set up assignments and plans for such discussions, or to ask a group of participants to use the social justice approach to frame such a topic.

ADDITIONAL FACILITATION CONCERNS AND TIPS

- It is helpful to know, in advance, the religious affiliation or non-affiliation of the students in the class, in order to specifically include activities that enable participants to see themselves reflected in the topic. In our curriculum design, we offer activities that will enable the instructor/facilitator and the participants to place each other in religious contexts—"Common Ground," the "name game" in introductions, and modifications of "meet and greet" introductions. Activities throughout the design can be modified to encourage further disclosure and information-sharing among participants.
- A question worth asking throughout the workshop or class is, "How can you get the information you might need, in the future, to understand the background and components of religious oppression in the U.S. or elsewhere?" Participants can help each other identify resources for continued exploration and learning on this topic.
- It is often difficult for participants who have Christian privilege to recognize and acknowledge that fact. Some may feel targeted and think of themselves as discriminated against because of being observant, and they are so focused on not feeling accepted that they are unable to recognize the ways in which they receive Christian privilege. Some may be in the midst of difficult journeys away from a Christian family background and find it hard to see their privilege. Some may be Christians of color for whom the intersections with racial, ethnic, linguistic, class, or gender identities (especially targeted and disadvantaged identities) undercut a sense of Christian privilege. Some may be currently questioning or confirmed disbelievers. Participants who

are non-believers from Christian backgrounds may not experience Christian privilege in their affirmed agnostic or atheist identity and may feel they have more in common with non-believers from Jewish or Muslim or other traditions.

- Although moving toward social justice means recognizing Christian privilege, it is important to hear what participants describe as their experiences and to question or explore the presence or absence of religious advantage or disadvantage. Often individuals are fearful about engaging in discussions about religion, because of the fear of making mistakes and offending other participants. It is important to stress that one cannot learn without making mistakes. This is an important guideline for the learning community, and if it does not initially emerge as part of the learning community's norms and guidelines, it should be added when it does emerge.

- Sometimes individuals are fearful about crossing the line that "separates" the public arena from religion, or saying something that could result in pushback or taking offense or even in litigation. This fear can become an excuse for silence and avoidance. There are many resources to help teachers and others in public service understand what the law prohibits, what it allows, and where the gray areas might be.

- The role of religion in public life, and the ways that communities experience religious homogeneity or diversity, plays out in different ways in various geographical regions of the U.S. For some communities, religion may be interfused with public life. In others, it may be considered private or taboo. It may be challenging for participants to separate their own regional and family experiences from the larger U.S. perspective, in order to talk about the role of religion in national culture, and to disentangle religion in the public sphere from religion in the private sphere.

- Participants may lack knowledge, or have misinformation, about their own religion as well as the religion of others. Knowledge about the strong and dramatic sectarian differences within religions (within Protestantism, within Catholicism, within Judaism, within Islam) may seem confusing. It is helpful to give examples that illustrate the broad continuum—from orthodox, fundamentalist, and observant, to liberal or reformist—within all religions. It helps also to understand that religions are "alive" and that they grow and change, that different religious communities emerge within a given religious belief—and may then break off to form a new religion—even if there are members of religious communities who believe their core documents (Bible, Qu'ran, Torah, Book of Mormon) were dictated by their deity or prophet in the distant past and should not be reinterpreted in the present. There is as much variability (theological, cultural, geographical) within religions as there is between them.

- Religious conflict is a painful subject, especially the indisputable evidence of violence in the name of a religion. The fact that all religions have, at some time, justified violence, provides an important perspective on this challenging issue from which no major religious group is immune.

- Participants may feel cynical or disillusioned by the contradictions between the high ideals of religions (peace, justice, love, caring for the stranger) and the behaviors of many peoples who claim those religions. Facilitators may need to point out other locations of contradiction—in politics, in organizational life, in families—to suggest that the contradictions may feel more dramatic in religion because the bar is often higher, and the ideals may be more visible.

- Participants may feel estranged and excluded by their religious communities because of gender or sexual identity or other forms of non-conformity with their religion's norms. They may express great anger and disillusionment with their religious community, whatever that community might be. This is an opportunity to note the intersections of forms of oppression and the ways in which advantaged as well as disadvantaged religious communities perpetuate those norms.

- Participants may feel daunted by the complexities of religious conflicts globally as well as domestically, and feel hopeless about achieving understanding of the issues or perspectives. It is worth the time to unpack the complexity of specific U.S. contemporary or historical examples of religious oppression. Here, again, the question, "Where can you go to find the information you will need to unpack this situation?" is a valuable question to ask, to make the point about participants' responsibilities for their lifelong learning.

- Sometimes greater respect seems to be shown to members of minority religious (Jews, Hindus, Muslims, non-believers) than to observant Christians. As a result, observant Christians may feel singled out, blamed, and defensive about the historical and systemic approach taken to their own faith. Some participants from Christian families or legacies may want the group to know that they themselves are personally not Christians, while other participants may want participants to know that they are deeply believing Christians. It is important to maintain space for both kinds of identity and affiliation, while emphasizing that the purpose of this class is not to share personal religious beliefs, but to understand the historical legacy and systemic power of hegemonic Christianity that is experienced by everyone in the U.S.

CLOSURE

It is not possible to "complete" an exploration of religious oppression generally or of Christian hegemony in the U.S. Nonetheless, classes and workshops need to come to closure, by openly naming their new insights or remaining questions, by sharing resources for further study, or by establishing networks, study groups, or informal connections to continue their conversations or action plans.

The common denomination in these tips is that the journey started within the course or workshop is a lifelong journey. The class or workshop should end with plans and attention to future action and continued learning, with support nets established among participants or plans to build support nets as part of participant action plans.

Note

* We ask that those who cite this work always acknowledge by name all of the authors listed rather than either only citing the first author or using "et al." to indicate coauthors. All collaborated on the conceptualization, development, and writing of this chapter.

References

Abington v. Schempp (1963). *School District of Abington Township, Pennsylvania, v. Schempp.* 374 U.S. 203, decided June 17, 1963.

Adams, G. A. (2008). *The specter of Salem: Remembering the witch trials in nineteenth-century America.* Chicago: University of Chicago Press.

Adams, M. (2012). Separation of church and state. In J. A. Banks (Ed.), *Encyclopedia of diversity in education.* New York: Sage.

Ahlstrom, S. E. (2004). *A religious history of the American people.* New Haven, CT: Yale University Press.

Alsultany, E. (2008). The prime time plight of the Arab Muslim American after 9/11. In A. Jamal & N. Naber (Eds.), *Race and Arab Americans before and after 9/11: From invisible citizens to visible subjects* (pp. 204–228). Syracuse, NY: Syracuse University Press.

Alvarez, L., & Don, V. N., Jr. (2011, Apr. 1). Pastor who burned Koran demands retribution. *The New York Times.* Retrieved from http://www.nytimes.com/2011/04/02/us/politics/02burn.html

Anderson, R. D. (2007). *Religion and teaching: Reflective teaching and the social conditions of schooling; A series for prospective and practicing teachers*. New York: Routledge.

Andrews, S. (2013). *Deconverted: A journey from religion to reason*. Denver: Outskirts Press.

Armstrong, K. (2014). *Fields of blood: Religion and the history of violence*. New York: Knopf.

Bagby, I. (2011). *The American mosque: Basic characteristics of the American mosque attitudes of mosque leaders*. Council on American-Islamic Relations (CAIR). Retrieved from http://www.cair.com/images/pdf/The-American-Mosque-2011-part-1.pdf

Bald, V. (2013). *Bengali Harlem and the lost histories of South Asian America*. Cambridge, MA: Harvard University Press.

Ballantine, B., & Ballantine, I. (Eds.). (2001). *The Native Americans: An illustrated history*. East Bridgewater, MA: JG Press.

Beaman, L. G. (2003). The myth of pluralism, diversity, and vigor: The Constitutional privilege of Protestantism in the United States and Canada. *Journal for the Scientific Study of Religion, 42*(3), 311–325.

Bellah, R. N. (1967). Civil religion in America. *Daedalus, Journal of the American Academy of Arts & Sciences, 96*(1), 1–21.

Berlak, C. (2014). *Constructing campus conflict: Antisemitism and Islamophobia on U.S. college campuses, 2007–2011*. Somerville, MA: Political Research Associates.

Blumenfeld, W. J. (2006). Christian privilege and the promotion of "secular" and not-so "secular" mainline Christianity in public schooling and in the larger society. *Equity & Excellence, 39*(3), 195–210.

Boyer, P. S. & Nissenbaum, S. (Eds.). (1972). *Salem-Village witchcraft: A documentary record of local conflict in Colonial New England*. Boston: Northeastern University Press.

Bravo López, F. (2011). Towards a definition of Islamophobia: Approximations of the early twentieth century. *Ethnic and Racial Studies, 34*(4), 556–573.

Brodkin, K. (1998). *How Jews became white folks and what that says about race in America*. New Brunswick, NJ: Rutgers University Press.

Bronner, S. E. (2000). *A rumor about the Jews: Reflections on antisemitism and "the protocols of the learned elders of Zion."* New York: St. Martin's Press.

Butler, J., Wacker, G., & Balmer, R. (2003). *Religion in American life: A short history*. Oxford, UK: Oxford University Press.

Carnes, T., & Yang, F. (2004). *Asian American religions: The making and remaking of borders and boundaries*. New York: New York University Press.

Chavers, D. (2009). *Racism in Indian country*. Bern, Switzerland: Peter Lang.

Chen, C., & Jeung, R. M. (Eds.). (2012). *Sustaining faith traditions: Race, ethnicity, and religion among the Latin and Asian American second generation*. New York: New York University Press.

Christina, G. (2012). *Why are you Atheists so angry? 99 things that piss off the godless*. Charlottesville, VA: Pitchstone.

Cohn-Sherbok, D. (2002). *Anti-Semitism: A history*. Gloucestershire, UK: Sutton.

Cole, D. (2015, May 7). The angry new frontier: Gay rights vs. religious liberty. *The New York Review of Books*. Retrieved from http://www.nybooks.com/articles/archives/2015/may/07/angry-new-frontier-gay-rights-vs-religious-liberty/

County of Allegeny v. American Civil Liberties Union (1989). 492 U.S. 573, decided July 3, 1989.

Daniels, R. (2002). *Coming to America: A history of immigration and ethnicity in American life* (2nd ed.). New York: Harper Perennial.

Deloria, V. (1969, 1999). Missionaries and the religious vacuum. In J. Treat (Ed.), *For this land: Writings on religion in America* (pp. 22–30). New York: Routledge.

Diner, H. R. (2004). *The Jews of the United States*. Berkeley, CA: University of California Press.

Echo-Hawk, W. R. (2010). *In the courts of the conqueror: The 10 worst Indian law cases ever decided*. Golden, CO: Fulcrum.

Eck, D. (2001). *A new religious America: How a "Christian country" has become the world's most religiously diverse nation*. San Francisco: Harper One.

Eckholm, E. (2015, March 31). Eroding in the name of freedom. *The New York Times*. Retrieved from http://www.nytimes.com/2015/03/31/us/politics/religious-protection-laws-once-called-shields-are-now-seen-as-cudgels.html

Ecklund, E. H., & Park, J. Z. (2005). Asian American community participation and religion: Civic model minorities? *Journal of Asian American Studies, 8*(1), 1–22.

Emerson, M. O., & Smith, C. (2000). *Divided by faith: Evangelical religion and the problem of race in America*. New York: Oxford University Press.

Espinosa, G. (2014). *Latino Pentecostals in America: Faith and politics in action.* Cambridge, MA: Harvard University Press.

Esposito, J. L., & Kalin, I. (2011). *Islamophobia: The challenge of pluralism in the 21st century.* Oxford, UK: Oxford University Press.

Everson v. Board of Education (1947). 330 U.S. 1, decided Feb. 10, 1947.

Feldman, S. M. (Ed.). (1996). *Please don't wish me a merry Christmas: A critical history of the separation of church and state.* New York: New York University Press.

Forward, M. (2001). *Inter-religious dialogue: A short introduction.* London, UK: Oneworld Publications.

Fox, J. (2000). Religious causes of discrimination against ethno-religious minorities. *International Studies Quarterly, 44*(3), 423–450.

Fox, J. (2002). *Ethnoreligious conflict in the late 20th century: A general theory.* Lanham, MD: Lexington Books.

Fraser, J. W. (1999). *Between church and state: Religion and public education in a multicultural America.* New York: St. Martin's Press.

Fredrickson, G. M. (2002). *Racism: A short history.* Princeton, NJ: Princeton University Press.

Frost, D. (2008). Islamophobia: Examining causal links between the media and "race hate" from "below." *International Journal of Sociology and Social Policy, 28*(11/12), 564–578.

Fulop, T. E., & Raboteau, A. J. (Eds.). (1997). *African-American religion: Interpretive essays in history and culture.* New York: Routledge.

Garces-Foley, K., & Jeung, R. (2013). Asian American Evangelicals in multicultural church ministry. *Religions, 4*(2), 190–208.

GhaneaBassiri, K. (2010). *A history of Islam in America: From the new world to the new world order.* Cambridge, UK: Cambridge University Press.

Gilbert, M. (2003). *The Routledge atlas of Jewish history* (6th ed.). New York: Routledge.

Goldschmidt, H., & McAlister, E. A. (Eds.). (2004). *Race, nation, and religion in the Americas.* Oxford, UK: Oxford University Press.

Green, S. K. (2012). *The Bible, the school, and the Constitution: The clash that shaped modern church-state doctrine.* Oxford, UK: Oxford University Press.

Grieco, E. M., Trevelyan, E., Larsen, L., Acosta, Y. D., Gambino, C., de la Cruz, P., Gryn, T., & Walters, N. (2012, Oct.). *The size, place of birth, and geographic distribution of the foreign-born population in the United States: 1960 to 2010* (Population Division Working Paper, 96). Population Division, U.S. Census Bureau. Retrieved from https://www.census.gov/population/foreign/files/WorkingPaper96.pdf

Grinde, D. A. (2004). Taking the Indian out of the Indian: U.S. policies of ethnocide through education. *Wicazo Sa Review, 19*(2), 25–32.

Gualtieri, S. (2001). Becoming "white": Race, religion and the foundations of Syrian/Lebanese ethnicity in the United States. *Journal of American Ethnic History, 20*(4), 29–58.

Guglielmo, T. A. (2003). *White on arrival: Italians, race, color, and power in Chicago, 1890–1945.* Oxford, UK: Oxford University Press.

Guglielmo, T. A., & Salerno, S. (2003). *Are Italians white? How race is made in America.* New York: Routledge.

Haddad, Y. Y. (2002). *Muslims in the West: From sojourners to citizens.* Oxford, UK: Oxford University Press.

Haddad, Y. Y. (2011). *Becoming American? The forging of Arab and Muslim identity in pluralist America.* Waco, TX: Baylor University Press.

Hafiz, S., & Raghunathan, S. (2014). *Under suspicion, under attack: Xenophobic political rhetoric and hate violence against South Asian, Muslim, Sikh, Hindu, Middle Eastern, and Arab communities in the United States.* South Asian Americans Leading Together (SAALT). Retrieved from http://saalt.org/wp-content/uploads/2014/09/SAALT_report_full_links.pdf

Haney-López, I. F. (1996). *White by law: The legal construction of race.* New York: New York University Press.

Harvey, P. (2003). "A servant of servants shall he be": The construction of race in American religious mythologies. In C. R. Prentiss (Ed.), *Religion and the creation of race and ethnicity* (pp. 13–27). New York: New York University Press.

Haynes, C. C., Chaltain, S., Ferguson, J., Hudson, D. L., Jr., & Thomas, O. (2003). *The First Amendment in schools: A guide from the First Amendment Center.* Alexandria, VA: Association for Supervision & Curriculum.

Haynes, C. C., & Thomas, O. (2001). *Finding common ground: A guide to religious liberty in public schools.* Nashville, TN: The First Amendment Center.

Hilberg, R. (1961). *The destruction of the European Jews*. New York: Harper & Row.

Hilberg, R. (2003). *The destruction of the European Jews* (3rd ed.), 3 volumes. New Haven: Yale University Press.

Hinduism Today (2008, Jan./Feb./Mar.). So, how many Hindus are there in the U.S.? U.S. Census Bureau's American community survey provides the best answer. *Hinduism Today*. Retrieved from http://www.hafsite.org/sites/default/files/HT_Census_USA_Jan08.pdf

Hitchens, C. (Ed.). (2007). *The portable Atheist: Essential readings for the nonbeliever*. Boston: Da Capo Press.

Ignatiev, N. (1995). *How the Irish became white*. New York: Routledge.

Jacobson, M. F. (1998). *Whiteness of a different color: European immigrants and the alchemy of race*. Cambridge, MA: Harvard University Press.

Jacobson, R. D., & Wadsworth, N. D. (2012). *Faith and race in American political life*. Charlottesville, VA: University of Virginia Press.

Jacoby, S. (2004). *Freethinkers: A history of American Secularism*. New York: Holt.

Jamal, A., & Naber, N. (Eds.). (2008). *Race and Arab Americans before and after 9/11: From invisible citizens to visible subjects*. Syracuse, NY: Syracuse University Press.

Jensen, J. M. (1988). *Passage from India: Asian Indian immigrants in North America*. New Haven, CT: Yale University Press.

Johnstone, R. L. (2004). *Religion in society: A sociology of religion*. Upper Saddle River, NJ: Pearson/Prentice Hall.

Jones, D. G., & Richey, R. E. (1974). The civil religion debate. In D. G. Jones & R. E. Richey (Eds.), *American civil religion* (pp. 3–18). New York: Harper & Row.

Jones, S. P., & Sheffield, E. C. (Eds.). (2009). *The role of religion in 21st century public schools*. Bern, Switzerland: Peter Lang.

Joshi, K. Y. (2006). *New roots in America's sacred ground: Religion, race, and ethnicity in Indian America*. New Brunswick, NJ: Rutgers University Press.

Joshi, K. Y. (2009). The racialization of religion in the United States. In W. J. Blumenfeld, K. Y. Joshi,, & E. K. Fairchild (Eds.), *Investigating Christian privilege and religious oppression in the United States* (pp. 37–56). Rotterdam/Taipei: Sense Publishers.

Juergensmeyer, M. (2000). *Terror in the mind of God: The global rise of religious* violence (3rd ed.). Berkeley, CA: University of California Press.

Juergensmeyer, M. (2004). Religious terror and the secular state. *Harvard International Review*. Retrieved from https://escholarship.org/uc/item/4w99n8tk

Kapila, S. (2007). Race matters: Orientalism and religion, India and beyond. *Modern Asian Studies*, 41(3), 471–513.

Karpf, A., Klug, B., Rose, J., & Rosenbaum, B. (Eds) (2008). *A time to speak out: Independent Jewish voices on Israel, Zionism and Jewish identity*. New York: Verso.

Killermann, S. (2012). *30+ examples of Christian privilege*. Project Humanities, Arizona State University. Retrieved from https://humanities.asu.edu/christian-privilege-checklist

Kivel, P. (2013). *Living in the shadow of the cross: Understanding and resisting the power and privilege of Christian hegemony*. Vancouver, BC, Canada: New Society Publishers.

Kosmin, B. A., & Keysar, A. (2015, Feb.). *National demographic survey of American Jewish college students 2014: Anti-semitism report*. The Louis D. Brandeis Center for Human Rights Under Law, Trinity College. Retrieved from http://www.trincoll.edu/NewsEvents/NewsArticles/Documents/Anti-SemitismReportFinal.pdf

Kruse, K. (2015). *One nation under God: How corporate America invented Christian America*. New York: Basic Books.

Kurien, P. (2014). Immigration, community formation, political incorporation, and why religion matters: Migration and settlement patterns of the Indian diaspora. *Sociology of Religion*, 75(4), 524–536.

Kushner, T., & Solomon, A. (Eds.). (2003). *Wrestling with Zion: Progressive Jewish-American responses to the Israeli-Palestinian conflict*. New York: Grove Press.

Laqueur, W. (2006). *The changing face of anti-Semitism: From ancient times to the present day*. Oxford, UK: Oxford University Press.

Lee, D. B. (2004). Religion and the construction of White America. In H. Goldschmidt & E. McAlister (Eds.), *Race, nation, and religion in the Americas* (pp. 85–110). Oxford, UK: Oxford University Press.

Lincoln, C. E., & Mamiya, L. H. (1990). *The Black church in the African American experience*. Durham, NC: Duke University Press.

Linge, G. (2000). Ensuring the full freedom of religion on public lands: Devils Tower and the protection of Indian sacred sites. *Boston College Environmental Affairs Law Review*, 27(2), 307–339.

Lipka, M. (2013, Oct. 2). *How many Jews are there in the United States?* Pew Research Center. Retrieved from http://www.pewresearch.org/fact-tank/2013/10/02/how-many-jews-are-there-in-the-united-states/

Lipka, M. (2014, July 17). *How many people of different faiths do you know?* Pew Research Center. Retrieved from http://www.pewresearch.org/fact-tank/2014/07/17/how-many-people-of-different-faiths-do-you-know/

Lipsitz, G. (2006). *The possessive investment in whiteness: How white people profit from identity politics* (rev. & expanded ed.). Philadelphia: Temple University Press.

Little, D. (2007). *Peacemakers in action: Profiles of religion in conflict resolution.* Cambridge, UK: Cambridge University Press.

Loewen, J. W. (1995). *Lies my teachers told me: Everything your American history textbook got wrong.* New York: The New Press.

Logiurato, B. (2014, July 3). Female justices issue scathing dissent in the first post-Hobby Lobby birth control exemption. *Business Insider.* Retrieved from http://www.businessinsider.com/sotomayor-ginsburg-kagan-dissent-wheaton-college-decision-supreme-court-2014-7

Long, C. N. (2000). *Religious freedom and Indian rights: The case of Oregon v. Smith.* Lawrence, KS: University Press of Kansas.

Maddigan, M. M. (1993). The Establishment Clause, civil religion, and the public church. *California Law Review, 81*(1), 293–349.

Mamdani, M. (2004). *Good Muslim, bad Muslim: America, the Cold War, and the roots of terror.* New York: Harmony Books.

Mariscal, G. (1998). The role of Spain in contemporary race theory. *Arizona Journal of Hispanic Cultural Studies, 2,* 7–22.

Mazur, E. M. (1999). *The Americanization of religious minorities: Confronting the Constitutional order.* Baltimore: Johns Hopkins University Press.

Mazur, E. M., & McCarthy, K. (Eds.). (2001). *God in the details: American religion in popular culture.* New York: Routledge.

McCarthy, K. (2007). *Interfaith encounters in America.* New Brunswick, NJ: Rutgers University Press.

Melton, J. G., & Jones, C. A. (2011). *Reflections on Hindu demographics in America: An initial report on the first American Hindu census.* Retrieved from http://www.thearda.com/asrec/archive/papers/Melton_Hindu_Demographics.pdf

Menchaca, M. (2001). *Recovering history, constructing race: The Indian, black, and white roots of Mexican Americans.* Austin, TX: University of Texas Press.

Michael, R. (2005). *A concise history of American antisemitism.* Lanham, MD: Rowman & Littlefield.

Min, P. G. (2010). *Preserving ethnicity through religion in America: Korean Protestants and Indian Hindus across generations.* New York: New York University Press.

Min, P. G., & Kim, J. H. (Eds.). (2001). *Religions in Asian America: Building faith communities.* Walnut Creek, CA: AltaMira Press.

Moore, D. L. (2007). *Overcoming religious illiteracy: A cultural studies approach to the study of religion in secondary education.* London, UK: Palgrave Macmillan.

Morris, A. D. (1986). *Origins of the civil rights movements.* New York: Free Press.

Murray, B. T. (2008). *Religious liberty in America: The First Amendment in historical and contemporary perspective.* Amherst, MA: University of Massachusetts Press.

Nash, R. J. (2001). *Religious pluralism in the academy: Opening the dialogue.* Bern, Switzerland: Peter Lang.

Newport, F. (2012). In U.S., 77% identify as Christian. *Gallup.* Retrieved from http://www.gallup.com/poll/159548/identify-christian.aspx

Ngai, M. M. (2004). *Impossible subjects: Illegal aliens and the making of modern America.* Princeton, NJ: Princeton University Press.

Niebuhr, G. (2008). *Beyond tolerance: Searching for interfaith understanding in America.* New York: Viking Press.

Not In Our Town (NIOT). (1995, 1996). Information retrieved from https://www.niot.org/

Office of Immigration Statistics (2006, Jan.). *2004 yearbook of immigration statistics.* U.S. Department of Homeland Security (DHS). Retrieved from http://www.dhs.gov/xlibrary/assets/statistics/yearbook/2004/Yearbook2004.pdf

Omi, M., & Winant, H. (2014). *Racial formation in the United States.* New York: Routledge.

O'Shea, S. (2006). *Sea of faith: Islam and Christianity in the medieval Mediterranean world.* London, UK: Walker & Company.

Patel, E. (2012). *Sacred ground: Pluralism, prejudice, and the promise of America.* Boston: Beacon Press.

Patel, E. (2015, Mar. 11). In promoting campus diversity, don't dismiss religion. *The Chronicle of Higher Education.* Retrieved from http://chronicle.com/article/In-Promoting-Campus-Diversity/228427/

Patel, E., & Scorer, T. (2012). *Embracing interfaith cooperation: Eboo Patel on coming together to change the world*. New York: Morehouse Education Resources.

Perry, M., & Schweitzer, F.M. (Eds.). (2008). *Antisemitic myths: A historical and contemporary anthology*. Bloomington, IN: Indiana University Press.

Pew Research Center (2011a, Jan. 27). *The future of the global Muslim population*. Retrieved from http://www.pewforum.org/2011/01/27/the-future-of-the-global-muslim-population/

Pew Research Center (2011b, Dec. 11). *Global Christianity: A report on the size and distribution of the world's Christian population*. Retrieved from http://www.pewforum.org/2011/12/19/global-christianity-exec/

Pew Research Center (2015, May 12). *America's changing religious landscape: Christians decline sharply as share of population; unaffiliated and other faiths continue to grow*. Retrieved from http://www.pewforum.org/2015/05/12/americas-changing-religious-landscape/

Philbrick, N. (2004). *Sea of glory: America's voyage of discovery, The U.S. exploring expedition, 1838–1842*. London, UK: Penguin Books.

Poole, E. (2003). Islamophobia. In E. Cashmore (Ed.), *Encyclopedia of race and ethnic studies* (pp. 215–219). New York: Routledge.

Prentiss, C.R. (Ed.). (2003). *Religion and the creation of race and ethnicity: An introduction*. New York: New York University Press.

Rana, J. (2007). The story of Islamophobia. *Souls: A Critical Journal of Black Politics, Culture, and Society*, 9(2), 148–161.

Rana, J. (2011). *Terrifying Muslims: Race and labor in the South Asian diaspora*. Durham, NC: Duke University Press.

Reston, J. (2009). *Defenders of the faith: Christianity and Islam battle for the soul of Europe, 1520–1536*. London, UK: Penguin Books.

Roediger, D.R. (1991). *The wages of whiteness: Race and the making of the American working class*. New York: Verso.

Romero Castello, E., & Macías Kapón, U. (1994). *The Jews and Europe: 2,000 years of history*. New York: Holt.

Said, E.W. (1978). *Orientalism*. New York: Vintage Books.

Said, E.W. (1986). Orientalism reconsidered. In F. Barker, P. Hulme, M. Iversen, & D. Loxley (Eds.), *Literature, politics, and theory* (pp. 210–229). London: Metheun & Co.

Said, E.W. (1993). *Culture and imperialism*. New York: Vintage Books.

Schlosser, L.Z. (2003). Christian privilege: Breaking a sacred taboo. *Journal of Multicultural Counseling & Development*, 31(1), 44–51.

Shaheen, J.G. (2001). *Reel bad Arabs: How Hollywood vilifies a people*. Northampton, MA: Olive Branch Press.

Shavit, A. (2013). *My promised land: The triumph and tragedy of Israel*. New York: Spiegel & Grau.

Shohat, E. (2006). *Taboo memories, diasporic voices*. Durham, NC: Duke University Press.

Sikh American Legal Defense & Education Fund (SALDEF). (2014). *Who are Sikh Americans*. Retrieved from http://saldef.org/who-are-sikh-americans/#.VfnQdnBVhBc

Singh, J. (2003). The racialization of minoritied religious identity: Constructing sacred sites at the intersection of white and Christian supremacy. In J.N. Iwamura & P. Spickard (Eds.), *Revealing the sacred in Asian and Pacific America* (pp. 87–106). New York: Routledge.

Singh, J. (2013). A new American apartheid: Racialized, religious minorities in the post-9/11 era. *Sikh Formations: Religion, Culture, Theory*, 9(2), 115–144.

Smedley, A. (1999). *Race in North America: Origin and evolution of a worldview*. Boulder, CO: Westview Press.

Smock, D.R. (Ed.). (2002). *Interfaith dialogue and peacebuilding*. Washington, DC: United States Institute of Peace.

Snow, J. (2004). The civilization of white men: The race of the Hindu in United States v. Bhagat Singh Thind. In H. Goldschmidt & E. McAlister (Eds.), *Race, nation, and religion in the Americas* (pp. 259–280). Oxford, UK: Oxford University Press.

Steinberg, S.R., & Kincheloe, J.L. (Eds.). (2009). *Christotainment: Selling Jesus through popular culture*. Boulder, CO: Westview Press.

Takaki, R. (1991). Between "two endless days": The continuous journey to the Promised Land. In *A different mirror: A history of multicultural America* (pp. 277–310). Boston: Little, Brown & Co.

Takaki, R. (1998). *Strangers from a different shore: A history of Asian Americans* (updated & rev. ed.). Boston: Little, Brown & Co.

Takaki, R. (2008). *A different mirror: A history of multicultural America* (rev. ed.). Little, Brown & Co.

Tanaka, K. (2011, July-Sept.). Dramatic growth of American Buddhism: An Overview. *Dharma World: For Living Buddhism & Interfaith Dialogue.* Retrieved from http://www.kosei-shuppan.co.jp/english/text/mag/2011/11_789_2.html

Tighe, E., Saxe, L., Magidin de Kramer, R., & Parmer, D. (2013, Sept.). *American Jewish population estimates: 2012.* Steinhardt Social Research Institute, Brandeis University. Retrieved from http://www.brandeis.edu/ssri/noteworthy/amjewishpop.html

Tolan, S. (2006). *The lemon tree: An Arab, a Jew, and the heart of the Middle East.* New York: Bloomsbury.

Weinberg, M. (1986). *Because they were Jews: A history of antisemitism.* New York: Greenwood Press.

Wills, D. W. (2005). *Christianity in the United States: A historical survey and interpretation.* Notre Dame, IN: University of Notre Dame Press.

Winant, H. (2001). *The world is a ghetto: Race and democracy since World War II.* New York: Basic Books.

Wistrich, R. S. (1991). *Antisemitism: The longest hatred.* New York: Pantheon Books.

Wyman, D. S. (2007). *The abandonment of the Jews: America and the Holocaust 1941–1945.* New York: The New Press.

Young, I. M. (1990). *Justice and the politics of difference.* Princeton, NJ: Princeton University Press.

9

Ableism

Benjamin J. Ostiguy, Madeline L. Peters, and Davey Shlasko[*]

INTRODUCTION

Ableism, or disability oppression, is the pervasive system that oppresses people with disabilities while privileging people who do not currently have disabilities. Like other systems of oppression, ableism operates on many levels, including institutional policy and practice, cultural norms and representations, and individual beliefs and behaviors. Our perspective on ableism is informed by critical disability studies, social justice education (SJE) scholarship, and our professional experience as disability access advocates. Rather than viewing disability as merely an individual trait, we take a social constructionist perspective that disability is a category constructed through social relationships. The purpose of this chapter is to introduce educators to major themes in disability history, current manifestations of ableism, and key concepts that support a systemic and personal understanding of ableism and disability justice.

In the first section we review key concepts in SJE as they apply to ableism, including social constructionism, the Cycle of Socialization, and levels of oppression, and we define important terms related to disability and ableism. Next, we address historical legacies of ableism and of disability movements, highlighting themes like stigma, institutionalization, the medical model, and the Independent Living Movement. The third section outlines current manifestations of ableism as well as current and recent disability activism, and explores the roles of people with and without disabilities as change agents toward disability justice. Finally, we introduce our four-quadrant workshop design for teaching about ableism, including the application of universal instructional design (UID) principles and discussion of some pedagogical, design, and facilitation issues that come up when teaching about ableism.

OUR APPROACH

SOCIAL CONSTRUCTION OF DISABILITY

Like other social identities, disability is often thought of as a trait of individuals, but it is actually a social categorization defined and reinforced by myriad institutional and cultural factors (Johnson, 2013). We understand disability not as a state of someone's body per se, but as a result of their interaction with the social environment. For example, being unable to walk is not necessarily a disability in itself, but being unable to walk in a society that assumes and normalizes the capacity to walk is a disability. Disability results when social designs and the built environment do not account for the presence and participation of people with non-typical physical, emotional, intellectual, or social abilities and needs.

Disability is "constructed" both in the sense that social forces cause injury and illness, and in the sense that society's failure to account for a wide range of bodies and minds creates barriers to full participation (Wendell, 2013). Some of the social forces that contribute to the construction of disability include poverty, technology, legal definitions of disability, and the expectation of economic productivity.

Poverty contributes to disability in both of the senses described above. First, it causes illness and injury that may become disabling: People living in relative poverty are more likely than those with adequate resources to experience workplace injuries (e.g., Occupational Safety & Health Administration, 2015), to enlist in the military (Lutz, 2008) and therefore be at risk of injury in the line of duty, and to be the victims of violent crimes (Harrell, Lanton, Berzofsky, Couzens, & Smiley-McDonald, 2014). Poor people are disproportionately incarcerated (Dolan & Carr, 2015), which has been shown to damage physical and mental health (Schnittker, Massoglia, & Uggen, 2012; Wildeman & Western, 2010). Poverty also increases the risk of chronic illnesses such as diabetes, cardiovascular disease, and many mental illnesses (National Center for Health Statistics, 2015).

In the second sense, people living in poverty are less likely to receive comprehensive medical treatment that could enable them to recover full functioning after an injury or to effectively manage a chronic illness (Agency for Healthcare Research and Quality, 2015). Poverty also limits access to accommodations and benefits that enable people to cope after a disabling event, such as paid time off work, help with daily tasks, and the latest assistive devices (World Health Organization, 2011).

Even as poverty can create disability, disability can also lead to poverty. Factors like job discrimination, lack of accessible to transportation and housing, inadequate government support, and expenses associated with health care and assistive devices lead to people with disabilities being poorer on average than people without disabilities (U.S. Senate Committee on Health, Education, Labor & Pensions, 2014; World Health Organization, 2011). Parents of children with disabilities often suffer financial stress and downward mobility due to the expense and time commitment related to advocating for their children (Cheatham & Elliott, 2013; Cheatham, Smith, Elliott, & Friedline, 2013). The U.S. Census Bureau finds that over 28.4% of people with disabilities live below the poverty line, compared to 12.4% of people who do not have disabilities (DeNavas-Walt & Proctor, 2014).

Technology contributes to the construction of disability in the sense that access to technology can make the difference between the same condition being disabling, or being a limitation that can be worked around. For example, before corrective lenses were widely available, having poor vision could be a disability that limited people's ability to participate in society. Now, many people use glasses or contact lenses to see, and poor vision is not a disability unless it is too severe to be corrected. Insofar as disability is created in the interaction between someone's body/mind and the social environment, technology alters that interaction. We often think of assistive technology in terms of special devices that most people don't need, such as an electric wheelchair or a voice synthesizer, but it also includes technology that is so ubiquitous we don't even notice, such as eyeglasses, spell-checking software, and computers with adjustable zoom and contrast. When a piece of technology becomes ubiquitous, the conditions it accommodates become less disabling and may eventually cease to be considered disabilities at all, as in the case of poor vision. Of course, technology interacts with poverty—the inability to afford needed technology is disabling.

Even more explicitly than many other social identities, disability is constructed in part by legal definitions. Laws that protect people with disabilities from discrimination, and in some cases provide funding and other resources for people with disabilities, require people to meet certain thresholds and definitions in order to qualify for those protections and resources. In the U.S., the Americans with Disabilities Act (ADA) establishes a legal definition of disability as an impairment (i.e., a physical or mental limitation) that "substantially limits one or more major life activities," such as caring for oneself, seeing, walking, speaking, learning, thinking, or communicating, or that limits the operation of a major bodily function. The ADA also prohibits discrimination against individuals with a documented history of disability, or who are regarded by others as having a disability, even if they do not presently experience a degree of limitation that would constitute a disability. (The "regarded as" part of the definition has been used to apply the ADA's protections to people living with HIV and AIDS who have no current limitations in functioning, insofar as other people's assumption about their capacities might lead to discrimination.) In 2008, the ADA was amended to expand the definition of disability to include conditions that are episodic or in remission, when the active impairment can substantially limit a major life activity (Americans with Disabilities Act, 2009).

While the ADA's definition is very broad, access to particular resources and services for people with disabilities is governed by more specific thresholds. For some programs, the qualifying factor is medical diagnosis; others utilize a quantitative scale (e.g., from mildly disabled to severely disabled), and still others rely on expert (medical) assessment of a person's capacity to perform certain tasks. In all cases, the definitions are necessarily less nuanced than would account for the variety of disability experiences people may have. As a result, some people who have a disability will not qualify for resources or services that might be useful to them. There are both benefits and disadvantages to being categorized as disabled, which we explore further in the section on current manifestations of ableism.

Expectations of economic productivity are central in the construction of disability, because they define what capacities people need to have in order to be considered functional "enough" to be non-disabled. For example, many jobs require someone to be able to operate at a quick pace, with high energy and consistent focus, for many hours in a row. Individuals who have to work more slowly, or who need to rest in the middle of a work day in order to keep performing effectively, may be considered disabled because they cannot work quickly for eight hours in a row. Yet the same people may be very capable of completing the job in other ways or with accommodations; it is not their capacity per se, but the interaction between their capacity and the expectations of most workplaces, that creates a condition of disability. Other people may not have the capacity to perform the kinds of work for which people are paid, but they may be able to offer caring, creativity, or other contributions to their communities that are not valued as "work." Equating a person's ability to contribute economically with their value as a person is part of ableism, and it is a significant factor in constructing disability.

An exploration of how disability is constructed helps to clarify the distinction between having physical or mental limitations and having a disability. Everyone has limitations simply by virtue of being human: There are limits to how fast we can think, how far we can run or walk, how much weight we can lift, and how much we can accomplish in an hour. We may not think of these as limitations except when one person's capacities are noticeably different from the assumed norm. Even then, not every noticeable limitation amounts to a disability. For example, at what point does being bad at math become a learning disability? Or, when does having a "bum knee" become a mobility impairment? With a social constructionist lens, the answer is that a limitation becomes a disability when the resources or accommodations are not available that a person would need in order to function adequately to meet society's expectations of them.

How we conceive of disability has implications for how we respond to the challenges faced by people with disabilities. When disability is regarded solely as a medical matter, defined by physical or mental traits of the individual, a common response is to try to change or "fix" people through medical or rehabilitative treatments. When we approach disability as a social construction, we begin to recognize stigma and marginalization as central factors impeding the life chances of people with disabilities (Shakespeare, 2006). Since disability is socially constructed rather than a "natural" or purely biological fact, the marginalization and stigmatization of people with disabilities is preventable. Through changes in ideology, behavior, norms, and policies, ableism can be mitigated and eventually ended.

DISABILITY AS IDENTITY

Even as we define disability as a socially constructed category to which people are assigned by legislatively and medically informed definitions, we must also recognize that individuals respond in different ways to being categorized as a person with a disability. On one hand, a person may experience an impairment that qualifies as a disability, yet not identify as a person with a disability. On the other hand, someone could experience an impairment that only ambiguously meets the legal standard for a disability, yet have a strong sense of disability in group identity. Our analysis of disability as socially constructed at cultural, institutional, and societal levels does not supersede the various and nuanced ways in which individuals and groups define themselves.

SOCIALIZATION

As with other systems of oppression, none of us asks to be born into an ableist system. The process of socialization teaches people with and without disabilities to fill particular roles in the system, and it is only through conscious resistance that we can break away from the status quo and enter a cycle of liberation and justice (Harro, 2013a). For most people, our first socialization occurs within our families. We may hear adults talking in ways that reflect the stereotypes of people with disabilities as incompetent, immature, dependent, or pitiable. As young children, when we innocently stare at or ask about a person with a disability, we are often shushed and told we are being rude, which can have the effect of associating disability with shame and secrecy. Media representations we see will tend not to include people with disabilities, or will re-inscribe dominant stereotypes. Our learning will be reinforced institutionally when we go to school and experience the ableism of tracking and testing, and when we interact with businesses, churches, and other institutions that are not accessible. We learn to accept the absence of people with disabilities in many community spaces as normal.

For people born with an apparent disability, the Cycle of Socialization begins inside a medical institution. Parents may learn about a disability when a doctor says, "We're so sorry," or "We have bad news." Because of stigma against disability, doctors and parents have probably learned to think of disability as an individual tragedy. They may feel the child is flawed or defective. Parents may grieve the loss of the healthy, non-disabled child they had imagined. Most children with disabilities are raised by parents who do not have disabilities, and some go through much of their childhoods without meeting anyone who has a disability like theirs. In school, they may be segregated into separate classrooms or programs, or they may be teased and bullied for looking or acting differently than other students. The cycle can lead to internalized ableism, in which people with disabilities unconsciously believe disempowering messages they have heard about people like them.

The Cycle of Socialization reminds us that our roles in systems of ableism are not our fault. We had no choice about being born into an ableist system, about being born with the minds and bodies we have, or about how society would interact with and judge our minds and bodies. Yet we have the ability to disrupt the cycle, and seek out other ways of thinking and acting about disability and ableism (Harro, 2013a, 2013b).

WIDE RANGE OF DISABILITIES

Approximately one billion people live with a disability globally—15% of the world's population (World Health Organization, 2014). This number includes people with a wide range of conditions. Without trying to be exhaustive, some types of disabilities include physical (such as quadriplegia, paraplegia, cerebral palsy, and any permanent mobility impairments), systemic (such as epilepsy, cancer, diabetes, multiple sclerosis, arthritis, and other chronic illnesses), sensory (such as visual impairment and hearing impairment), psychological (such as autism spectrum disorders, post-traumatic stress disorder, anxiety, depression, and schizophrenia), learning disabilities (such as attention deficit disorder, dyslexia, and auditory processing disorder), and intellectual disabilities.

Among people with the same diagnosis, the condition may manifest differently and lead to different types of disabilities. For example, a condition like cerebral palsy (CP) can affect someone's lower body, upper body, and/or speech and language abilities. Some individuals with CP use wheelchairs, others walk with crutches or canes, others have no mobility impairment but do have trouble speaking clearly, and still others have cognitive manifestations. Even two people with the same physical manifestation of a condition may experience different impacts on their lives: Someone who has had a leg amputated and uses a wheelchair will have different access needs than someone who uses a prosthetic leg and is able to climb stairs.

Anyone can become disabled through sickness, aging, accidents, or acts of violence, or even due to life stresses. We sometimes refer to people without disabilities as *temporarily able bodied* to acknowledge that our identities and roles as people with or without disabilities are not always permanent. However, the term is imperfect for at least two reasons. First, it implies that all disabilities are physical (in the body); in fact, someone can be able *bodied* and have a disability. Second, calling someone *temporarily able bodied* can have the effect of minimizing the privilege of their current position in a system of ableism. Whether or not someone may acquire a disability in the future (which is almost always unknown), it is important to have a way to name that the person does not have a disability now, and that they therefore benefit from living in an ableist system that is set up for people with minds and bodies like theirs. The work of disrupting ableism and moving toward disability justice includes grappling with our imperfect language to discuss the complexities and unknowns of disability in all our lives.

Some disabilities are apparent upon meeting someone, depending on context. For example, most mobility disabilities will be apparent in circumstances that require movement (e.g., a wheelchair user attending a dance); hearing impairment may be recognizable in settings that require verbal communication (e.g., a job interview); and learning disabilities may stand out in academic settings. Under different circumstances, those same conditions could be socially unrecognizable (e.g., the wheelchair user taking part in a phone interview, a person who is deaf corresponding via email, or a person with dyslexia going out to eat in a restaurant). Other disabilities are rarely apparent, including psychological disabilities, learning disabilities, and some systemic disabilities. A disability also might not be apparent if it is accommodated so smoothly that a casual observer would not notice, such as in the case of someone with hearing impairment who uses a hearing aide, or someone who uses a prosthetic leg.

Often when people hear the word "disability," they think of the most obvious or apparent disabilities. (The universal visual symbol for disability—a silhouette of a person in a wheelchair—contains and reinforces this assumption.) When considering less-apparent disabilities, people sometimes assume that anyone with an illness severe enough to be a disability must be confined to their home, or to a hospital or other facility. In fact, most people with disabilities live in the community, have jobs and families, and attend school alongside people without disabilities.

ABLEISM

Ableism is the system of oppression that disadvantages people with disabilities and advantages people who do not currently have disabilities. Like other forms of oppression, it functions on individual, institutional, and cultural levels (Griffin, Peters, & Smith, 2007). Ableism is not solely about the experiences of people with disabilities as targets of discrimination, but rather about the interaction of institutional structures, cultural norms, and individual beliefs and behaviors that together function to maintain the status quo and exclude people with disabilities from many areas of society.

Levels of Ableism

Subordination of people with disabilities occurs at the institutional level through laws, policies, and social conventions that discourage inclusion of people with disabilities in medical, educational, religious, economic, governmental, housing, and legal systems. For example, most homes are built with stairs, so that people who need ramps have many fewer housing options. In some regions, the only wheelchair-accessible apartments are in buildings designated for senior citizens, while in other places the accessible apartments are mostly found in newer developments, far from desirable downtown areas. Since there are so few options, people who need ramps cannot shop around, and often end up paying more for housing and/or for transportation to and from their home than people who can use stairs.

In education, teaching and testing practices are heavily weighted toward a particular learning style. Students who have learning disabilities that make that style difficult for them are often seen as less intelligent, may gain less from their school experience than their peers, and are required to get special documentation and oftentimes a stigmatizing diagnosis in order to prove their need to be taught in a way that works for them.

In the medical field, doctors are considered the experts on disabilities, rather than people who live with disabilities being the experts. Affected by the same cultural norms and biases as anyone, doctors sometimes urge families toward oppressive practices in caring for their children with disabilities, such as unnecessarily invasive treatments and institutionalization. Further examples of institutional ableism can be found in the sections on Historical Legacies and Current Manifestations below.

At a cultural level, ableism is about a dynamic between what is considered "normal" and what is considered deficient, limited, or abnormal. Expectations of what people "should" be able to do reinforce and justify institutional exclusion of people with disabilities. Our language, beauty standards, assumptions, and other social norms ignore or degrade people with disabilities. Images of people with disabilities tend to be absent from mainstream media, except when they are represented as violent (for people with psychiatric disabilities) or as objects of pity. The dominant (false) assumption that people with disabilities are rare means they are often not considered or included.

Language offers a window into some of cultural stereotypes of people with disabilities. Terms like *idiot*, *imbecile*, and *retarded*, all of which began as diagnostic categories for people with intellectual disabilities, are used as casual insults. People are called *stupid*, *slow*, or *lazy* if they don't learn easily in the same ways as their peers. Words like *crip*, *gimp*, *spaz*, *freak*, *dumb*, *mute*, or *sped* reduce people with disabilities to just their disabilities, rather than acknowledging them as whole people. *Disabled* and *handicapped* evoke images of people who are incapable overall, rather than people who have many qualities and capabilities no matter how severe their limitation in a particular area.

Crazy is another example of a commonly used term that reflects and perpetuates ableism. When used to describe someone with mental illness or psychiatric disability, *crazy* implies irrational, out of touch with reality, or violent, whereas actually, many people with psychiatric disabilities are none of these. *Crazy* is also used metaphorically to refer to practically any situation in which someone has feelings. We might say, "My neighbor's loud music is driving me crazy!," meaning that the music is irritating or distracting. This use of *crazy* implies that feeling irritated or distracted is tantamount to mental illness, which both minimizes the realities of mental illness and pathologizes ordinary, healthy feelings.

These trends in the language reflect and reinforce the conscious and unconscious attitudes many people have about people with disabilities. Because of the pervasive institutional and cultural-level ableism, many people believe stereotypes and misinformation about people with disabilities. Such beliefs are reflected in individual-level expressions of ableism such as these:

- Calling someone stupid, slow, or lazy for having a learning disability;
- Assuming or stating that there are no people with disabilities in one's school or workplace, based on the idea that people with disabilities wouldn't be smart enough or capable enough;
- Parking in the spot reserved for people with mobility impairments, if one doesn't need it;
- Staring at someone who has a visible disability, or on the other hand, avoiding looking at them at all;
- Talking to someone's aide or interpreter instead of directly to the person in question;
- Ignoring a person with a disability who needs help opening a door or getting their wheelchair unstuck from the mud, or on the other hand, insisting on helping someone who does not need or want help;
- Talking extra loudly to a person with a mobility impairment (or another disability irrelevant to hearing), or using baby talk to an adult with any disability.

Some of the behaviors listed above may be intended kindly, but because they rely on inaccurate and disparaging assumptions about people with disabilities, they contribute to ableism. Recalling the Cycle of Socialization, we recognize that it is no individual's "fault" that they have been socialized into the system of ableism. Someone who says or does something ableist can become aware of the impact and implications of their behavior and choose to change it.

Like all systems of oppression, ableism can be internalized. Many people with disabilities are socialized to believe harmful generalizations about themselves. People may feel abnormal, incapable, or undeserving, and assume that they cannot achieve their goals, enjoy entertainment or social activities, participate in the life of the community, or do certain kinds of work—even if these are within their capacities. Likewise, people who do not currently have a disability may internalize a sense of normalcy and deservingness, and may assume that everyone can or should be able to do everything.

Even when systems are designed inclusively and accommodations are made, people with disabilities may experience limitations that will prevent participation in particular elements of life. Shakespeare (2006) notes that "practicality and resource constraints make it unfeasible to overcome every barrier" (p. 201). Additionally, some disabilities, such as chronic pain conditions, will cause hardship no matter how well they are accommodated. Still, it is clear that society has not yet approached the limits of what is possible in terms of access and equity for people with disabilities. Despite all the pervasive manifestations of ableism, however, we believe that ableism is not inevitable and can be ended.

HISTORICAL LEGACIES OF ABLEISM

The historical legacies of ableism reflect shifting and overlapping frameworks. In this section, we trace major themes in the history of disability and ableism, including how different frameworks emerge and interact.

STIGMA AND MARGINALIZATION

In different societies throughout history, the role of people with disabilities has varied, but it has usually included some degree of stigma and marginalization. In pre-industrial societies, people with disabilities were construed as having a special relationship with the supernatural or divine, as sacred or evil, blessed or damned (Bryan, 2006; Pelka, 2012). People who experienced visions or heard voices (and might today be diagnosed with schizophrenia or a related illness) were sometimes honored as seers and other times persecuted as heretics. Infants with apparent disabilities were sometimes drowned or left outdoors to die of exposure (Bryan, 2006; Pelka, 2012).

In pre-industrial Europe, the dominant religious view of disability was as an unchangeable condition people brought on themselves by sinning (Covey, 1998). In particular, people with mental illness or intellectual disabilities (described at the time as *lunacy* and *idiocy*) were often thought to be possessed by the devil or evil spirits; as a result, many were whipped and tortured to make them repent (Pelka, 2012). Most people with disabilities were cared for at home by their families. The conditions in which people with disabilities lived probably varied widely, depending on their families' attitudes and abilities to care for them. Some people believed that people with disabilities were better off dead, including Martin Luther, the founder of Protestantism (Pelka, 2012). Infanticide was common, and children with disabilities were abandoned and left to beg for food and money to survive (Pelka, 2012).

Beginning in the 14th century, and escalating in the 17th century, laws against vagrancy were enforced against people with disabilities who had to beg. They were ejected from charity shelters because they were seen as dangerous and undeserving of the community's support. Instead, they were forced to beg in the streets for sustenance, and could be arrested for begging without a license and sent to pauper's prison (Pelka, 2012).

The social stigma continued through the early 18th century, although it began to take on a scientific framework in addition to the religious one. People with disabilities were seen as *freaks, monsters*, and less than human. Societal curiosity about people with severe disabilities made freak shows very popular. Paradoxically, *freak shows* became one of the few viable ways for people with disabilities to earn a living (Pelka, 2012). Ableism interacted with the particular racism and classism of the day: The diagnosis of *medical imbecility* applied to people with intellectual disabilities, along with homeless people, immigrants, and others unable to express themselves in English (Pelka, 2012).

INSTITUTIONALIZATION

The 18th century also saw the beginning of institutionalization of people with disabilities. From the 18th century through the 1960s, many families were convinced by physicians they could not care for their loved ones (Pelka, 2012). Children with intellectual disabilities or severe mobility disabilities were committed to residential hospitals and asylums by their physicians, who often had a financial interest in filling beds in those institutions (Hornick, 2012). There were hundreds of such institutions throughout the United States.

The policies that consigned people to institutions were focused more on protecting society from people with disabilities than on protecting the residents themselves (Pelka, 2012). Many residents had unpaid jobs, and some were subjected to experimental treatments that we would now call torture. The implicit belief that people with disabilities were less than fully human gave doctors permission to research cures or ways to control patients through techniques like dunking in cold water, electric shock, insulin shock, and lobotomy (removal of part of the brain) (Pelka, 2012; Russell, 1998).

Many institutions operated without external oversight, and overcrowding and understaffing were common. In some institutions, people with severe mobility impairments were rarely moved from their beds, while other residents went naked because attendants did not have time to change their clothes. Doctors performed otherwise unnecessary medical procedures in order make attendants' jobs easier, such as removing healthy teeth to make it easier for staff to feed patients who needed help eating. Staff members could abuse residents without repercussion. When discovered, the conditions were decried as horrific, medieval, and barbaric (Hornick, 2012; Pelka, 2012; Russell, 1998). Although the explicit framework of such institutions was scientific/medical, their operation was also informed by decidedly unscientific bias.

EUGENICS

In the early 19th century, an emerging eugenics movement, closely tied with scientific racism (see, e.g., Krisch, 2014), spurred policies to segregate and sterilize people considered to be "genetically defective." Eugenics describes a set of beliefs and practices ostensibly aimed at improving the quality of the human population, usually through limiting reproduction of people who are judged as inferior. At its most extreme, eugenics inspired state-sponsored murder and forced sterilization in Nazi Germany, the 20th century United States, and elsewhere.

During the 1920s–1930s, German proponents justified eugenics in part through a school of thought called Social Darwinism. Social Darwinism posited that the perceived degeneration of the German people was due to two factors: Medical care of the "weak" that interfered with natural selection, and people who were considered inferior (including poor people, people with disabilities, Jews and other ethnic minorities, people suspected of being homosexual, and people convicted of crimes) multiplying faster than those they considered superior. The Nazi sterilization program that began in 1933 required doctors to register anyone known to have an illness thought to be inheritable, including "feeble-mindedness" (intellectual disabilities or sometimes just lack of education), schizophrenia, "insanity" (any variety of mental illnesses), epilepsy, blindness, or deafness. Later, the program shifted from sterilization to murder. Despite protests against medical killings, a 1939 "euthanasia" program made it official: Doctors were ordered to let patients die through medical neglect, and later to actively kill them by lethal injection or gassing. In total, approximately 375,000 people with disabilities were killed or sterilized; by the end of the official phase, 200,000 people had been killed, including 5,000 children (Gallagher, 1995).

The horror of eugenics was not limited to the Nazi regime. During the 1920s–1930s, 30 U.S. states passed laws requiring the compulsory sterilization of the "criminally insane" (people with mental illness who had gotten in trouble, and people who had broken the law and were presumed to have mental illness) and others who were considered "genetically defective," including poor people, people with alcoholism, unmarried young women who became pregnant, and people with visual impairment (Singleton, 2014). By 1970, over 63,000 people had been sterilized, and many more institutionalized (Pelka, 2012; Singleton, 2014). Eugenicists in the U.S. advocated killing people with disabilities, and although it was never practiced officially, some institutionalized patients were killed through targeted medical neglect (Singleton, 2014).

Eugenics intersected with scientifically rationalized racism, and not only in the German concern for purity of the race. In the early 19th century United States, various forms of mental illness were thought to be more common among white people with "superior" minds than among black slaves. Psychologists with a eugenics agenda cited this phenomenon as proof of the superiority of the white mind, reasoning that black people's brains were less advanced, and therefore less sensitive to the stressors of modern life. Following the Civil War, when more free black people were counted in the national census, statistics showed them to have mental illness at similar rates to white people. Since the supposedly scientific basis for the racist and ableist belief was undermined, the medical industry concocted new theories to justify their bias, asserting that the forms of mental illness were distinct, with the mental illnesses of blacks being indicative of inferior minds, while the mental illnesses of whites remained signs of their superiority (Bryan, 2007).

MEDICAL MODEL

The medical model of disability also draws on a scientific framework, and emerges from the legacies of institutionalization and eugenics. But unlike eugenics, which uses science to justify killing and sterilizing people with disabilities, the medical model attempts to treat and cure them. The medical model is largely well-intentioned and has provided important improvements in the lives of many people with disabilities. At the same time, it has significant drawbacks.

The medical model understands disability as an individual condition, without attention to social factors. As a result, the medical model assumes that the proper response is to prevent, cure, or mask the manifestation of conditions. Of course, disability cannot be cured; when a condition can be cured by medical intervention, it ceases to be considered a disability, so disabilities are by definition not curable with current medical technology. In the meanwhile, the medicalization of disability draws on and reinforces the belief that people with disabilities need to be monitored and controlled by medical specialists. People with disabilities are referred to as "patients," who are assumed to be passive recipients of medical care. Doctors are considered the ultimate authority on treatments people with disabilities should undergo.

As with eugenics and institutionalization, the explicit scientific rationale for the medical model is overlaid with implicit cultural biases. Early medical textbooks included chapters on the benefits of eugenics programs, and prominent doctors were among the eugenics advocates who described people with disabilities as "genetically defective" (Singleton, 2014). The term conveys a value judgement of people with disabilities as broken, flawed, and "lesser than" people without disabilities, and also posits disability as inherent and inborn.

The medical model is also reflected in non-medical settings, including some charity organizations such as the March of Dimes and the Jerry Lewis Muscular Dystrophy Association. Such charities tend to focus on a single condition, and utilize images of children with disabilities to evoke sympathy and raise money, ostensibly to find a cure. Disability advocates have criticized such organizations for exploitative practices, such as encouraging pity rather than respect, implying that the money raised might cure the particular children depicted, and reinforcing the idea that only children with disabilities (and not adults) are deserving of support. Additionally, advocates point out that the unrealistic focus on prevention and cure, rather than on assistive technologies and accommodations, feeds into ableism and serves more to appease the guilt of donors than to improve the lives of people with disabilities. In the case of the Jerry Lewis telethons, the organization has admitted that most of the money raised has gone toward the cost of the telethon itself, as well as to research into genetic screening to prevent people with muscular dystrophy from being born (Fleischer & Zames, 2001; Shapiro, 1994).

REHABILITATION MODEL

The rehabilitation model emerged in the 1940s. Veterans returning from World War II with permanent disabilities spurred the medical field to focus on the development of treatments and devices to help soldiers return to work, even when a "full" recovery was not possible. The rehabilitation model combines a scientific/medical framework with an individual rights framework, asserting that people with disabilities have the right to medical assistance to become able to work alongside people without disabilities. In a rehabilitation system, people with disabilities are called clients rather than patients, and generally have some say over their treatment options.

Rehabilitation technology was still in its infancy in the 1940s, and there were many wounded veterans who could not return to their previous line of work even with rehabilitative services. Many people with disabilities continued to be segregated and treated as patients who needed supervision and care, rather than as autonomous people who could make their own decisions.

The rehabilitation model became more predominant in the 1970s with the passage of Section 504 of the Rehabilitation Act in 1973. The language of Section 504 mirrors that of the Civil Rights Act of 1964, and its passage was won through organized efforts of disability rights activists inspired by the civil rights movement. The act prohibits discrimination against people with disabilities in any program receiving federal funds, and opened up new opportunities for rehabilitation and employment for veterans returning from Vietnam as well as other people with disabilities.

It is no coincidence that the disability rights movement made significant gains in the aftermath of two major wars. Returning veterans were unlike many other people with disabilities in that they had acquired their disabilities in adulthood, in the line of duty. They were seen as respectable, contributing members of society, and many felt entitled to have their needs met by the society they had fought for. They were not subject to the same kind of internalized ableism as people who had experienced disability stigma their entire lives. Veterans' participation in the disability rights movement helped to win new laws, technologies, and acceptance that benefited non-veterans with disabilities as well (Fleischer & Zames, 2001).

Still, rehabilitation often fell short of meeting veterans' needs, especially when it came to the mental health impacts of war. Such impacts were acknowledged following World War I with the diagnosis of "shell shock," which was replaced after World War II with the term "combat stress reaction." It was only after many Vietnam veterans experienced severe impacts of war trauma that the term post-traumatic stress disorder (PTSD) came into use, and some psychological treatments became available. The rehabilitation someone might need to go to work with PTSD is different than in the case of a physical injury like a damaged leg, and there was no widespread effective treatment at that time. Additionally, mental health diagnoses carry a different quality of stigma than physical disabilities do, perhaps particularly among veterans, who may feel their masculinity or bravery is called into question by admitting to mental health difficulties, leading some to avoid diagnosis and treatment (Ben-Zeev, Corrigan, Britt, & Langford, 2012).

One shortcoming of the rehabilitation model is that rehabilitation tends to work best for the people who already have the most privilege. People who, if not for their disability, might have a relatively easy time finding employment because of privileges of race, gender, and class are more likely to gain employment through rehabilitation services than are people with disabilities who are also marginalized in other ways.

Another critique of the rehabilitation model is that its emphasis on getting people back to work prioritizes economic participation as central to someone's value as a person. The rehab model assumes that people with disabilities who *can* work *should* work, no matter how difficult it is or how much accommodation they need. The push for people with disabilities to work is further fueled by the inadequacy of financial assistance available to people with disabilities, and by cultural biases that lead people to feel strongly about not being a "burden" on their families or society. Some disability activists have challenged the assumption that people with disabilities should work if at all possible, and instead argue for the right *not* to work. Taylor (2004) argues that people's value should not be based on their economic contributions alone, and that the idea of "independence" should be broader than mere economic self-sufficiency.

INDEPENDENT LIVING MOVEMENT

In the 1960s and 1970s, a social movement among people with disabilities and allies began to emerge that became known as the Independent Living Movement. Inspired by other civil rights and justice movements of the era, disability activists drew on an individual rights framework to organize around a common social identity as people with disabilities and to advocate for needed changes. They began to refer to people with disabilities as "consumers" who make choices about accessing services. Slogans like "nothing about us without us" emphasized the importance of people with disabilities participating as a community in policy decisions, as well as participating as individuals in decisions that affect their lives.

Unlike the medical and rehabilitation models, the Independent Living Movement identified the "problem" of disability as primarily social rather than individual or biological, manifesting in the cultural and institutional patterns that forced people with disabilities to be dependent on medical professionals, family, and the community at large to meet their needs. Disability rights activists advocated for and created services by and for people with disabilities, emphasizing mutual support and self-help, and using collective political action to remove barriers to independent living and collective political action. The first independent living center (ILC) opened in Berkeley, California (Fleischer & Zames, 2001), and there are now hundreds of ILCs in the U.S. alone.

A key goal of the Independent Living Movement was to establish community-based services and support systems such that people with disabilities could live as independently as possible, integrated into communities rather than isolated in institutions. The Independent Living Movement contributed to a shift from institutionalization as the default for people with severe disabilities, to the majority of people with severe disabilities living in communities. Often referred to as deinstitutionalization (especially with regard to people with cognitive or psychiatric disabilities), this shift has had both positive and negative consequences, which we explore below under Current Manifestations.

The Independent Living Movement was instrumental in spurring the passage of Section 504 of the Rehabilitation Act and later the ADA in 1990—both significant federal policy victories that protect the rights of people with disabilities in areas including transportation, communication, and employment.

AMERICANS WITH DISABILITIES ACT

The Americans with Disabilities Act (ADA) was originally passed in 1990, and like Section 504, it was based partly on the Civil Rights Act. The ADA created people with disabilities as a protected class under the law, prohibiting discrimination against them. It also established a uniform basis for government definitions of disability.

The ADA is a powerful yet imperfect tool for advocating for disability rights. Unlike the medical model, the ADA's definition of disability is not purely individual or biological, but includes consideration of social relationships and expectations. For example, in terms of employment discrimination, the ADA defines a qualified person with a disability in terms of their ability to perform the essential functions of a job. Drawing on a social constructionist view, disability is defined not merely as a characteristic of an individual, but as an interaction between a person and the social and built environment of the workplace (Scotch, 2014). This gives the ADA potential to address a wide range of inequities for people with disabilities, yet also makes it confusing and difficult to implement uniformly. As with rehabilitative services, the protections offered by the ADA are likely to be most helpful to individuals who have the most privilege, and who are more likely to feel entitled to accommodations and to have access to support, including legal representation to enforce their rights. Furthermore, because of ongoing stigma, the ADA is underutilized: Many people who could qualify as having a disability under the law do not identify as disabled, and many more are unaware of their rights.

INTERDEPENDENCE AND DISABILITY JUSTICE

A framework for disability justice emerged in the mid-2000s from a group of disability activists who were primarily queer, poor, and/or people of color. A disability justice framework goes beyond a primary focus on independence to an acknowledgement of *inter* dependence. Disability justice recognizes that everybody, including those with and without disabilities, depends on each other. We are all interconnected in myriad ways, and all implicated in the system of ableism that excludes and devalues some kinds of minds and some kinds of bodies.

Disability justice encourages us to celebrate physical and mental differences, while also naming and addressing the ways in which people are categorized and oppressed according to disability and other social identities (Berne, 2015; Mingus, 2011). As an intersectional model and movement, disability justice has powerful potential to escape the shortcomings of previous models and create truly transformative justice and liberation practices.

CURRENT MANIFESTATIONS OF ABLEISM

The historical legacies of ableism, including competing frameworks for understanding disability, are still with us today. They play out in current manifestations of ableism on institutional, cultural, individual, and internalized levels.

STIGMA

Stigma remains a central element in ableism. Despite significant progress in institutional reforms, there remain widespread assumptions that people with disabilities are inferior to those without disabilities, and that people with disabilities are broadly incapable and a burden on their families and society. Accusations that particular illnesses and epidemics are "acts of God" or punishment for sin represent religiously justified stigma, and also often overlap with other systems of oppression (as in the case of heterosexist, racist, and classist rhetoric about HIV/AIDS). On an individual level, the irrational fear that a non-contagious disability may rub off, or that disability results from "bad luck," also demonstrates the ongoing influence of stigma.

Because of stigma, some people with disabilities are reluctant to seek diagnosis and assessment of their conditions, which can delay access to needed services and accommodations. The binary nature of many legal definitions and processes can contribute to this sense of stigma; although a person's particular diagnosis may be descriptive and value-neutral, the overall label of "disabled" may still feel stigmatizing. Beyond hindering an individual's ability to access services, stigma discourages people from organizing together as people with disabilities.

LEGACY OF EUGENICS

Although many official eugenics programs ended in the 20th century, the legacy remains strong. For example, arguments in favor of assisted suicide are complicated by culturally reinforced attitudes about the value of living with a disability. The assumption that living with a disability is worse than dying consigns people with disabilities to the same status as those who are terminally ill or living with extreme chronic pain. It is difficult to separate well-meaning arguments that terminally ill individuals should be able to choose when to die, from thinking that people with disabilities might be better off dead or that society might be better off without them.

Eugenics-type arguments also arise in discussions of reproductive technology, such as in sperm banks where sperm donors' desirable qualities, such as intelligence and beauty, are advertised as if they are genetic, reinforcing the (mistaken) idea that "good genes" guarantee a perfect, healthy, non-disabled child. Finally, public policy does not support people with disabilities being able to have and raise children; for example, tasks related to caring for children are not considered "activities of daily living" and so people with disabilities are not entitled to assistance with them even if they have care attendant services to help with other tasks.

INSTITUTIONALIZATION AND DEINSTITUTIONALIZATION

The theme of institutionalization shows up in current manifestations of ableism in two ways: The problems of deinstitutionalization, and the continuation of institutionalization in jails and prisons rather than psychiatric hospitals. Deinstitutionalization refers to the mass closures of long-stay psychiatric hospitals and transfer of people with mental illness or intellectual disabilities into community-based care. In the United States, deinstitutionalization began in the 1950s with the advent of antipsychotic medications and has continued in waves through the present. Motivations for policy shifts toward deinstitutionalization include awareness of the abusive conditions in many residential hospitals, the desire for people with disabilities to be less isolated and more integrated into communities, an increasing availability of effective medications to treat psychiatric conditions, and neoliberal pressures to shift funding of services from government agencies to private organizations. By 1994, the proportion of the U.S. population living in psychiatric hospitals had decreased by over 90% from 1950s levels (Torrey, 1997).

Although deinstitutionalization policies aimed to transition people into community-based care, the services available in communities often are inadequate. As residential hospitals closed, some residents were transferred to group homes or independent living, but many more became homeless. Some communities estimate that up to two-thirds of their homeless populations are people with mental illness (Treatment Advocacy Center, 2015). Homeless people with mental illness often rely on emergency rooms for acute psychiatric care, which is both ineffective and costly. In the absence of adequate care or housing, they may behave disruptively in public and end up getting arrested and incarcerated (Treatment Advocacy Center, 2015). As a result of these patterns, there are now approximately three times as many people with severe mental illness in prisons as there are in residential psychiatric care facilities (Torrey, Kennard, Eslinger, Lamb, & Pavle, 2010). Incarceration is the new institutionalization.

CONTINUING SHORTCOMINGS OF MEDICAL AND REHABILITATION MODELS

The medical model is the primary framework shaping public understanding of disability today. Advances in diagnostic and treatment technologies mean more people with disabilities are able to receive effective medical interventions than ever before; yet there remain downsides to medicalization. Some disabilities are over-medicalized, meaning that doctors are unreasonably seen as experts on everything about the disability, including what job duties someone is capable of or even what assistive devices they should be using. In many legal interactions (such as petitioning an employer for accommodations, or applying for disability-related financial assistance), a doctor's testimony is required to "prove" a disability, even though in most cases other professionals (such as occupational therapists, ergonomics experts, or educators), or people with disabilities themselves, could do a better job of describing someone's specific capacities and accommodation needs.

The medical model's imperative to "fix" people with disabilities sometimes comes into conflict with communities that understand disability through a different lens. For example, the development of cochlear implants (CIs) has made it possible for some deaf people to hear. But people who are culturally Deaf define themselves not only through the physical condition of not hearing, but also through a shared culture and language (American Sign Language, or ASL). Some Deaf individuals and communities consider the pressure from the medical community to get CIs as implying that Deaf culture and ASL are not as valuable as hearing culture and spoken languages. Deaf advocates argue that making CIs a default treatment is tantamount to cultural genocide.

A rehabilitation model also remains predominant, and is implemented in part through state Departments of Rehabilitation that provide services for people with disabilities who want to work. Both the medical and rehab models share a shortcoming in that their domain encompasses only one small aspect of the life of a person with a disability—in the case of the medical model, treatment or symptom management, and in the case of the rehabilitation model, getting accommodations and assistive technologies needed to work. Neither addresses a person with a disability as a whole person with many aspects to their life beyond a particular medical condition or accommodation need.

LACK OF RESOURCES FOR INDEPENDENT LIVING MODEL

Independent living centers serve as resource hubs for people with disabilities living in communities, and provide services that are peer-based (rather than centered around disability "professionals") and led by people with disabilities. Current issues that ILCs advocate for include people with disabilities being able to select and hire their own personal care attendants, maintaining state funding for in-home care rather than forcing people into residential facilities, and increasing the availability of accessible housing. Unfortunately, the resources available through ILCs are often inadequate to meet the needs of people with disabilities, especially those living in poverty.

ABLEISM IN K–12 EDUCATION

Ableism is apparent in many features of the U.S. education system, including implicit assumptions about the goals and nature of academic learning. The widespread assumption that the ability to succeed in school is of primary importance for young people can be seen as ableist, in that it values a particular way of knowing, learning, and interacting, and devalues other ways. Similarly, the idea of age appropriateness normalizes a single developmental path and pathologizes any students who have different needs or gain skills at different times than their average peers.

Tracking groups of students according to performance stigmatizes students in "lower" tracks, and allocates resources to higher tracks, all of which tend to exacerbate disparities in educational success. The origins of tracking trace to the late 1950s when, during the Cold War, U.S. leaders were concerned about preparing the "brightest" students to contribute in accelerating scientific and technological discoveries in order to stay ahead of the Soviet Union. It also came on the heels of *Brown v. Board of Education*, the Supreme Court decision that mandated the desegregation of public schools. From the very beginning, the biases inherent in testing and tracking assignments meant that tracking was not based on "intelligence" but on privilege.

In the early 1960s, children who were unable to keep up with the new standards and pace were categorized into five different groups: Slow learners, mentally retarded, emotionally disturbed, culturally deprived, and learning disabled (Sleeter, 1986). The "culturally deprived" category applied primarily to African American students, English language learners, and some white students from poor families, and represented an obviously racist value judgement about the relative worth of different cultures. The category of learning disabled (LD) was established in part to separate white, middle-class children from other low-achieving students so that resources could be directed to them. Students in the other low-performing categories were expected at best to catch up to minimum graduation requirements, whereas students categorized as LD were seen as capable of achieving highly alongside their average and above-average peers when given the appropriate accommodations (Sleeter, 1986). This is not to say that specific learning disabilities are not "real"— they are, but the disproportionate diagnosis into various "low-achieving" groups reflects racial bias in the education system rather than any actual differences in the prevalence of different learning needs across race.

Racist patterns in tracking and diagnosis continue today. African American students are more than twice as likely as white students to be labeled as "mentally retarded" (i.e., diagnosed with an intellectual disability) (Donovan & Cross, 2002). They are also often labeled by white, middle-class teachers as having behavioral problems based on high-energy behaviors that may be valued in the child's home and community, but not in school (Franklin, 1992; Rogers & Mancini, 2010). Similarly, English language learners may be inaccurately labeled as intellectually disabled, despite laws mandating culturally sensitive testing (Duhaney, 2000), and disproportionately assigned to special education programs (Harry & Klinger, 2006; Shepherd, Linn & Brown, 2005). The combination of stigmatizing diagnoses, tracking, and inadequate resources place many children of color in segregated special educational environments that are designed more to control than to teach or nurture, and which mostly do not prepare students for further education or for any but the most low-skilled work. Meanwhile, white students diagnosed with learning disabilities are more likely to be fully integrated into general education classrooms (Connor, 2006) where, with accommodations and high expectations, they can succeed academically and go on to higher education. The tracking system, including its relationship to diagnostic categories such as LD and mental retardation, still serves to sort and prepare students for a stratified labor market, such that those from advantaged social groups are educated toward more desirable jobs, while those from disadvantaged backgrounds tend to be channeled into low-pay, low-status work.

Alongside the tracking system, the school discipline system often disadvantages students with disabilities. Students with disabilities are more likely to receive disciplinary action, and about twice as likely to be referred to outside law enforcement, as the average student (U.S. Department of Education Office for Civil Rights, 2014). These rates are similar to those of black students with or without disabilities (U.S. Department of Education Office for Civil Rights, 2014). Inadequate educational services combine with disproportionate discipline to put students with disabilities (across race), black students (with and without disabilities), and sometimes other students of color in what some have termed a "school to prison pipeline" (Heitzeg, 2009). Even the relatively less-stigmatized diagnoses categorized as LD are associated with higher rates of poverty and of involvement with the criminal justice system (Cortiella & Horowitz, 2014).

Finally, ableism plays out on a cultural level in K–12 education in that the prevalence of a competitive framework leads some people to resist providing accommodations for people with disabilities on the grounds that it would be unfair to students without disabilities. For example, a common accommodation is extra time to take standardized tests—which demand a particular learning style and often pose significant barriers to people with learning disabilities. Opponents argue that all students could benefit from extra time, so giving it only to those diagnosed with a learning disability is not fair. If education were viewed as a cooperative or creative enterprise rather than a competitive one, this would not be an issue. An education system built on a disability justice model would start from the premise that every student deserves access to the different resources and supports they need to achieve their highest potential.

Several legislative interventions have been aimed at improving the situation for students with disabilities in K–12 schools. The Individuals with Disabilities Education Act (IDEA), originally enacted in 1975 under the name Education for all Handicapped Children Act (EHA), requires that students with disabilities receive free and appropriate public education along with their non-disabled peers, in the least restrictive environment that will allow each student to succeed academically. Previous to EHA, only about one in five students with disabilities were educated in public schools, while others were educated in special residential programs, in their homes, or not at all, and many states had laws excluding students with specific disabilities from public school (National Council on Disability, 2000).

As a result of EHA/IDEA, millions of U.S. students with disabilities now benefit from public education, many of them in their local schools, and are included part or all of the time in regular, non-special education classrooms (National Council on Disability, 2000). The positive impact of IDEA has been significant. For example, post-high school employment rates for people with disabilities are approximately double for those who benefited from IDEA compared to those who finished or left K–12 education before the law's enactment (National Council on Disability, 2000). However, there are many implementation shortcomings that limit the law's effectiveness, including resistance from some school districts and states, inadequate training for both regular and special education teachers, lax enforcement by state and federal governments, and the resulting burden on parents to advocate for the services to which their children are entitled (National Council on Disability, 2000).

Acknowledging the educational and social benefits of interaction between students with and without disabilities, IDEA regulations require schools to have a compelling rationale for removing students from a regular classroom for some or all of their school day (National Council on Disability, 2000). For most students with disabilities, appropriate accommodations and tailored instruction allow for full inclusion in a regular classroom, providing the best opportunity for academic and social success. However, the case of Deaf students who use ASL (American Sign Language) presents particular challenges to the idea of "least restrictive environment" (Cerney, 2007). Since deafness is relatively uncommon, most Deaf students who are included in regular classrooms will be the only non-hearing student and the only one using ASL to communicate. Students can be provided with an interpreter as an accommodation, but communicating through an interpreter is not the same as communicating directly with teachers or peers. Many Deaf educators have argued that inclusion in a regular classroom is actually *more* restrictive than the traditional residential Deaf schools, because it denies Deaf students the opportunity to have access to Deaf culture and to socialize with peers who share their language (Cerney, 2007). This example illustrates some of the complexity and potential shortcomings of a unified model for providing appropriate, empowering education for students with a very wide range of abilities, disabilities, and cultures.

ABLEISM IN HIGHER EDUCATION

Students with disabilities continue to encounter barriers, stereotypes, and stigma as they explore, transition to, and attend college. In addition to the questions all students considering college face (e.g., What do I want to study? What size campus is right for me?), students with disabilities must navigate questions of accessibility (e.g., How do I request and receive reasonable accommodations? Will the campus support all of my access needs? When should I disclose my disability and when not?). In the K–12 system, schools are responsible for assessing and accommodating students' disabilities, but in college, the onus is on students to disclose their disability status to the appropriate offices, provide supporting documentation, and advocate for the accommodations they require (Hamblet, 2009).

The processes establishing disability status differ from institution to institution, adding complication to students' process of choosing the right college—a process that is already known for rewarding students with relative privilege (Bergerson, 2009). Unfortunately, students with disabilities have often enjoyed fewer opportunities to acquire the knowledge and connections necessary for making skillful and informed post-secondary education decisions (Hitchings, Retish, & Horvath, 2005). Students with intellectual disabilities and some learning disabilities often encounter lower educational expectations than peers who do not have a disability (Grigal, Hart, & Migliore, 2011; Hitchings, Retish, & Horvath, 2005; Masino & Hodapp, 1996), and guidance counselors and college advisers may not bring up higher education because of false assumptions about students' learning potential. As a result, students may be less prepared to select a college that best suits their interests, to assemble a high-quality application, and to apply for financial aid. Furthermore, because students with disabilities disproportionately come from households with low socioeconomic status, many forego college due to concerns about the cost and about their ability to repay student loans (Cheatham & Elliott, 2013; Cheatham, Smith, Elliott, & Friedline, 2013). These are just a few of the ways in which students with disabilities are systematically disadvantaged even before they enter a college classroom.

Once students enroll in college, they can disclose their disability status in order to qualify for accommodations. The availability of accommodations and supports for students with disabilities is a key positive force against ableism in these settings. At the same time, stigma and inequities are built into the qualifying procedures at most institutions (Braba-zon, 2015; Loewen & Pollard, 2010). Students who seek accommodations must provide third-party verification of private medical information, and seek permission to do what they need to in order to participate fully and work to their true potential. Due to disability stigma and resulting desires to "fit in," as well as the difficulty of navigating an unfamiliar bureaucracy, many choose not to enroll with disability support services, thereby depriving themselves of resources that could be helpful or even critical for their academic success.

Underlying the qualifying procedures is an implicit assumption that students may seek to exploit the system to obtain "unfair advantage." Jung's (2011) research shows how many women with chronic health disabilities are met with suspicion and resistance to their accom-modation requests. Faculty members who support disability inclusion in general may dispute specific requests for accommodations based on their own judgements of which needs seem legitimate. Sometimes such resistance is rationalized as a concern for academic freedom, or for a limited conception of fairness. Such ableist dynamics frequently color the accommoda-tion experiences of students with disabilities, creating a *"backlash* discourse that seeks to pro-tect the privileged, usually male and white, academic status quo" (Jung, 2011, p. 270, italics in original). Along with other systems of oppression, ableism in higher education serves to enforce and perpetuate dominant, oppressive notions of what is "normal" and "abnormal," who is important and who can be ignored, who belongs in college and who does not.

Post-secondary opportunities for students with intellectual disabilities (ID) have been few, and typically involved "segregated life skills or community-based transition programs" (Hart, Grigal, Sax, Martinez, & Will, 2006, p. 2; Hart, Mele-McCarthy, Pasternack, Zim-brich, & Parker, 2004). Until recently, these marginalizing practices have largely gone unquestioned, supported by systematic enforcement of narrow definitions of cognitive "normalcy" and what counts as "intelligence" (Ball & Harry, 2010). Recently, a number of scholars, advocates, and policymakers have called attention to the inequitable social, economic, and "quality of life" experiences of people with ID (e.g., Grigal, Hart, & Weir, 2011; Hart, Mele-McCarthy, Pasternack, Zimbrich, & Parker, 2004; Ludlow, 2012; Scha-lock, Brown, Brown, Cummins, Felce, Matikka, Keith, & Parmenter, 2002), building sup-port for changes toward inclusion of some students with ID in higher education.

In 2012, the reauthorization of the Higher Education Opportunity Act established that stu-dents with ID who satisfy certain criteria can apply for and receive federal financial aid even if they have not earned a high school diploma (Think College, n.d.). This initiative appears to be a bellwether of significant changes in policies and attitudes toward people with ID in higher education, which increasingly recognize the expanding purpose of post-secondary education, the diverse academic and social interests of people with ID, the capacity and desire for greater autonomy among people with ID, and the *reciprocal* benefits of social rela-tionships between people with and without ID (Grigal, Hart, & Weir, 2011; Hendrickson, Therrien, Weeden, Pascarella, & Hosp, 2015; Ludlow, 2012; Martinez & Queener, 2010).

Early research into the effects of these inclusive post-secondary efforts reveal posi-tive outcomes. For example, Hendrickson, Therrien, Weeden, Pascarella, & Hosp (2015) found that participants in one inclusion program "experienced their first year at college/ university similarly to their peers without ID on a number of important dimensions asso-ciated with student engagement and good educational practices" (p. 215). While more research is needed to understand post-school outcomes (e.g., subsequent employment and quality-of-life effects), it is clear that interest in college among students with ID and their families is strong and growing (Hart, Grigal, Sax, Martinez, & Will, 2006). Unsurprisingly, these efforts have encountered resistance in the form of negative attitudes and low expec-tations (Hart, Grigal, Sax, Martinez, & Will, 2006), and future challenges will undoubt-edly emerge, but the momentum appears to be in favor of increased inclusion.

INTERSECTIONS WITH OTHER ISMS

On a systemic level, ableism intersects with all other forms of oppression and often functions as a means of justifying them (Pelka, 2012). Stigmatized diagnostic categories are used to further marginalize students of color. When formal racial segregation is no longer permitted, segregation by disability can serve the same function by justifying differential treatment and rationalizing schools' failure to help students achieve.

Another intersection of ableism and racism can be seen in mainstream media reactions to acts of violence. When a person of color commits a mass shooting or bombing, the person is often labeled a terrorist, especially if they are also Muslim. When a white person commits a similar crime, the person is often labeled mentally ill. In fact, none of these categories (race, religion, or mental illness) make someone more likely to do violence. Ascribing someone's violent act to a targeted identity—whether race, religion, or disability—can serve to obscure the actual power relationships at play, such as how sexism and racism implicitly condone white male violence. The media's excessive attention to notable acts of individual violence steals attention from the systemic violence that targets people of color, Muslims, and people with disabilities every day through disproportionate policing, military violence, and violence in prisons and other institutional settings.

Ableism is similarly mobilized to justify heterosexism and cissexism. Until recently, homosexuality was considered a psychiatric disorder, and in some circles, any non-heterosexual attraction is still regarded as a disorder that can be repaired (Arthur, McGill, & Essary, 2014). Proponents of this harmful attitude justify it in part through ableism by arguing that homosexuality is a mental illness that interferes with living a "normal" life and therefore needs to be cured. With regard to transgender people, the *Diagnostic and Statistical Manual of Mental Disorders* (DSM-V) continues to list gender dysphoria as a psychiatric disorder (American Psychiatric Association, 2013). The diagnosis is controversial, and its inclusion in the DSM has both pros and cons for trans* communities. The stigma attached to trans* identity as a pathologized category is in part due to the ableist assumption that anyone with a psychiatric diagnosis must be unhappy, unstable, and pitiable. These are just a few examples of how ableism intersects with other forms of oppression to justify the further marginalization of the targeted group.

Of course, people with disabilities are members of all social identities, and ableism can be compounded and complicated in myriad ways. For example, youth and elders with disabilities have even less power to make decisions about their own health care than young and middle-aged adults with disabilities. People with disabilities are often desexualized in the public imagination, which can harm women with disabilities in particular ways as women's value in society is often associated with sexuality and parenting. Women with disabilities also face particular employment discrimination; they are hired at lower rates and are paid less on average than men with disabilities (Seabrook, 2002). Class and disability intersect in many ways, as previously noted. People with less class privilege are more likely to acquire disabilities, and less able to afford needed treatment and accommodations, than people who have adequate resources.

Wounded warriors are veterans who have returned from military service with disabling injuries such as amputated limbs, traumatic brain injuries, and diagnoses of PTSD (Brown, 2008; Fischer, 2014; Stinner, Burns, Kirk, Scoville, Ficke, & Hsu, 2010), and they are primarily young adult men along with some women. Although veterans who sustain combat injuries are eligible for disability status and associated benefits, there is evidence that many are reluctant to avail themselves of these opportunities, and that they experience substantial challenges transitioning back to civilian life (Ben-Zeev, Corrigan, Britt, & Langford, 2012; Brown, 2008; Morin, 2011). Major reasons are disability stigma; a hyper-masculine norm of strength, stoicism, and endurance; and an associated identification of disability with weakness and lack of manhood (Ben-Zeev, Corrigan, Britt, & Langford, 2012).

GLOBAL ISSUES

In 2006, the United Nations adopted the Convention on the Rights of Persons with Disabilities (2006), which aims to protect the rights and dignity of persons with disabilities. The Convention describes specific obligations of signatory countries, including moving toward accessibility in all areas of public life (from voting to recreation), protecting people with disabilities from discrimination and abuse, facilitating access to effective and affordable assistance and technology, and ensuring that people with disabilities have the support and resources needed to live independently in communities. Richer countries are urged to provide financial aid to support the efforts of poorer countries to implement the Convention. The language of the Convention emphasizes the inherent worth and dignity of all people, including people with disabilities, and its framework is akin to an independent living model. Over 150 countries have ratified the treaty as of 2015.

In spite of the inspiring precedent set by the Convention, ableism continues to be a significant problem throughout the world, with discrimination, stigma, and inadequate resources remaining all too common. In so-called developing countries, where governments may be struggling to meet their populations' basic human needs for clean water, food, shelter, and safety, few resources are devoted to the protection and inclusion of people with disabilities (World Health Organization, 2011). The quality of care people receive, and the degree of independence they experience, may vary greatly depending on families' resources as well as the perspectives and frameworks they bring to understanding a family member's disability. When outside support is not available, the financial commitment of supporting a family member who is unable to work can have a detrimental impact on other family members, including children who may be required to leave school early in order to work to support the family (World Health Organization, 2011). Obstacles that are challenging to all, such as inadequate transportation and information infrastructure, can severely limit the lives of people with disabilities. Weak health care systems mean that more people are likely to become disabled by preventable illness, and that treatments and accommodations are too often unavailable or unaffordable (World Health Organization, 2011).

In more economically privileged countries, approaches to disability vary widely, and there remain significant unmet needs for accommodation and support services (World Health Organization, 2011) as well as differences in *how* different countries attempt to meet needs. For example, some European countries rely heavily on segregated special schools for children with disabilities, while others educate almost all students in mainstream classrooms with their same-age peers (World Health Organization, 2011).

A person's social and economic status within their country can have a great impact on their ability to access legal protections and services that are supposed to be available to them, so differences within countries can be nearly as large as those among countries.

MOVING TOWARD JUSTICE

DISABILITY JUSTICE, LIBERATION, AND ALLYSHIP

From an intersectional social justice and disability justice perspective, moving from ableism toward disability justice requires change at all levels. Disability justice includes changes to institutional policies and practices that limit the autonomy of people with disabilities, cultural shifts toward truly valuing and centering people with diverse minds and bodies, and individual and group transformation to liberate ourselves from internalized ableism, all as part of a broader intersectional social justice movement.

For individuals with disabilities, liberation from internalized ableism is a vital and ongoing process. The process often begins with a "waking up" moment (Harro, 2013b), which for many people with disabilities occurs when they are exposed to a model of disability different than the one they grew up with, such as through a peer support group, an online community, or the writings of disability justice organizers. Reflection and community support are key elements in helping people with disabilities disrupt the negative messages they have been taught about themselves. Rather than seeing themselves as dependent, incapable, or pitiable, they come to recognize and appreciate their own abilities and limitations, and understand themselves in the context of an interdependent world in which all people have limitations and depend on each other. Individuals can learn to take pride in their own successes in getting around the constructed barriers they encounter, both physical and symbolic. Communities of people with disabilities and their close allies can offer mutual support and work together, both to meet immediate needs and to push for cultural and institutional changes. The act of coming together as a disability community is itself an act of resistance, since it challenges the individualist lenses embedded in the medical and rehabilitation models, and to some extent even the independent living model.

Since disability communities are incredibly diverse, allyship around ableism is not only a matter of people without disabilities being allies to people with disabilities. People with different kinds of disabilities can also be allies to each other. The variety of stigma faced by people with disabilities, as well as practical problems related to different access needs, can make this challenging. In some cases, people whose disabilities are not always apparent to others may be reluctant to put themselves in the same boat with people whose disabilities are more obvious. People with physical disabilities may be reluctant to align themselves with those who have psychiatric or intellectual disabilities. Some people in the disability community require accommodations that others might experience as burdensome or expensive, and in rare cases the accommodations needed actually contradict each other. (For example, some people who have seizure disorders need to avoid fluorescent lights, while some people with visual impairment may need a room to be lighted as brightly as possible in order to participate. Depending on the lighting available in a building, there may be rooms or whole buildings where the two groups cannot meet together.) Yet all people share a common interest in dismantling ableism. With creativity, and acting from a disability justice analysis, disability communities can come together to make change.

People without disabilities also have a role in the movement. Since anyone can become disabled, and almost everyone has people in their families and communities who experience disability, it is not out of altruism but out of awareness of our mutual interdependence that people without disabilities should work for disability justice. Allies who do not have disabilities can challenge the patterns of oppression they observe, name privileges that would otherwise go unnoticed, and support the leadership of people with disabilities. As with all social justice movements, change can be slow and piecemeal, and people may not always see the results of their efforts, but that doesn't mean they are not having an impact. Sometimes people are reluctant to step up as allies around ableism because of fear of making a mistake. Rather than striving for perfection, an effective ally is someone who is consistently conscious of the needs of people with disabilities, and continues to reflect and take action in the direction of disability justice (Ayvazian, 1995).

CONSIDERATIONS FOR THE FUTURE

Over the past 25 years, remarkable advances have been made in the field of assistive technologies, particularly with the sophistication of computers and smart phones. People with disabilities who have access to these technologies have unprecedented opportunities for independent access communication, entertainment, education, and work. With built-in accessibility features and/or additional accessibility software, technology users are able to adjust their monitor options to suit their visual requirements (e.g., high contrast), dictate words into word processing and other text receiving applications, listen to digital text, navigate the screen by voice command or single keystrokes, and countless other tasks. Some touchscreen technologies have been designed with built-in accessibility features that cater to the access requirements of people who cannot see, so users can efficiently navigate the devices by listening to voice cues. As these technologies become ubiquitous, they will seem less like special accommodations and more like everyday tools that some people utilize more than others.

Proximity readers can identify a person in a wheelchair and open a locked door as the person approaches. Navigational software informs a visually impaired user of where they are in a building and instructs them how to get to their destination. Technologies can tell a person the ingredients in the food they are about to ingest in order to avoid allergens. There are even wheelchairs that can climb stairs. Aided by contemporary assistive technologies, people with disabilities experience greater independence than was once considered possible.

Emerging technology also presents some dilemmas. Increased availability of genetic testing during pregnancy raises the issue of selective abortion. Many disability rights activists who support access to abortion in general nevertheless have deep concerns about using a fetus's potential disabilities as justification for abortion, because that reasoning implies that it would be better not to be born than to be born with a disability, and ignores the meaning, value, and joy that one can derive from disability (see, e.g., Roberts & Jesudason, 2013). The apparent tension between the rights of pregnant people to make the reproductive decisions that are best for them, and the idea of disability as a form of diversity that should be respected and valued, has sometimes led to conflict between disability rights advocates and abortion access advocates.

Similarly, as new treatment techniques are developed (such as gene therapies and computer-assisted surgeries), a question sometimes arises: Just because we can "fix" something, does that mean we should? Our values around celebrating and respecting diverse minds and bodies can come into conflict with the medical and scientific imperative to strive for medical "perfection."

Another consideration is the impact of the aging baby boomer generation. As many people acquire disabilities in old age, the pressures on accessible housing stock, rehabilitation agencies, and the in-home health care infrastructure will be significant. As with the generations of veterans who pushed for new rights and resources that benefited all people with disabilities, this generation of elders may push society to find better solutions and establish better structures for meeting a wide range of needs.

UNIVERSAL DESIGN

Imagine a professor makes a last-minute decision to grab students' attention on the first day of class by starting off with a film clip. Among the students, there is one with low vision who is not able to see the film at such distance, another with hearing loss who is not able to hear the dialogue, and a veteran with PTSD who begins to panic upon seeing unexpected images of combat violence in the clip. Underlying this professor's decision was an assumption that all the students had similar capacities—that they could all see and hear the film and could tolerate violent images. Many instructors make similar assumptions all the time. The choices people make when designing physical spaces, products, programs, and services can have the effect of validating some people and marginalizing others. Universal design (UD) attempts to remedy this effect.

Universal design calls for designing buildings and other infrastructure to be accessible and functional for as many people as possible without the need for individual accommodations or retroactive modifications (Burgstahler, 2010; Hamraie, 2013). The seven core principles of UD are equitable use, flexibility in use, simple and intuitive use, perceptible information, tolerance for error, low physical effort, and size and space for approach and use (Burgstahler, 2010).

We experience UD when we visit a large grocery store that has motion sensitive, automatic doors and broad curb cuts marked with textured pavement leading to the entrance of the building. These design features were popularized in order to conform to ADA requirements for accessibility for people with disabilities, but people without disabilities also benefit. A person using a wheelchair will be able to enter and exit the store without assistance, as will a person with a visual impairment, but also a parent carrying a child or an elder pushing a grocery cart. Virtually anyone who approaches the door will find the grocery store accessible. Skillful adoption of UD principles can contribute to the destigmatization of disability. When accommodations are built in, people with disabilities can use the store like anyone else, and don't have to specially request unusual assistance or use different access routes. Although most educators will not have the power to affect the built environment of their classrooms, they can make sure to select spaces that will be accessible to the widest possible range of participants.

UNIVERSAL INSTRUCTIONAL DESIGN

The principles of UD can also be applied to curricula and teaching methods. *Universal instructional design* (UID) was first proposed in 1998 by Silver, Bourke, and Strehorn as a method of making college course content accessible to students with learning disabilities. Since then, the application of UD to teaching and learning has been championed by a number of scholars (Burgstahler & Cory, 2010; Scott, McGuire, & Shaw, 2003; Zeff, 2007) and is considered a best practice by many educational advocacy groups (e.g., Association on Higher Education And Disability [AHEAD]). The key goal of UID is to use practices, designs, and materials that are accessible to as many people as possible without the need for individual accommodations.

A practical example of the application of UID can be seen in the design of quizzes and exams. It is common for exams to include fill-in-the-blank questions as a way of measuring student learning. However, students with language-based learning disabilities may have challenges with word retrieval, difficulty discerning between homonyms, and/or spelling. For these students, fill-in-the-blank tests constitute barriers to access, not unlike manual doors for people with quadriplegia. The barrier is not necessarily physical (although a person who cannot hold a pen or write would find the exam inaccessible too), but the marginalization is no less real. To lessen this barrier, a course instructor who is informed by UID might offer all students a word bank to prompt word retrieval, avoid the inclusion of homonyms on the exam, and/or allow students to express their knowledge in another manner that best suits their expressive strengths (e.g., preparing a class presentation or answering the questions in short essays). Beyond exams, the principles of UID are applicable to all elements of teaching and learning, including in-class activities, homework assignments, field trips, modes of communicating expectations and feedback, and evaluation criteria.

As noted above, processes for requesting accommodations can be arduous, and are often marginalizing and stigmatizing in their own right (Loewen & Pollard, 2010). Universal instructional design lessens the burden on people with disabilities to assert their needs and expose themselves to stigma by accounting for the diverse access requirements of most students.

Universal instructional design benefits many people beyond individuals with disabilities, including people with different learning and communication styles, people with inadequate educational preparation, and people who experience learning challenges due to cultural and/or language mismatches. In some ways, UID is analogous to being a good host: When you invite people to your home for a meal, it is appropriate to consider how everyone can get to your home, whether you have enough space and chairs, whether any guests have dietary restrictions, and whether the activities you have planned will be appropriate for everyone. Too often, educators do not extend this level of courtesy to their students, and UID offers a useful model for rectifying this oversight. We encourage social justice educators to educate themselves about UID and incorporate its principles in their practice.

CRITIQUE OF UNIVERSAL DESIGN

Hamraie (2013) notes that UD is essentially a critique of the built environment as a reflection of dominant (white, masculine) subjectivity. Universal design is not only a set of principles from which one can construct inclusive environments, programs, and services; it is also a lens through which design can be analyzed and critiqued, and its power in this regard is far-reaching. For example, dominant biomedical and public health research methods have been examined through a UD lens and found to be exclusionary, stigmatizing, and methodologically invalid (Meyers & Andresen, 2000; Williams & Moore, 2011).

However, UD and UID are not beyond scrutiny, as they also rely on specific underlying values and assumptions. For instance, UID presupposes that instructors have the awareness, skills, and expertise to produce designs that will be appropriate for people with diverse access requirements. Hamraie (2013) challenges this assumptions and calls for UD that invites people with disabilities into the design process, shifting their role from that of consumers to that of co-creators. In this spirit, social justice educators should seek to establish a relationship of interdependence with people with disabilities, collaborating to understand and meet everyone's needs.

Further, Hamraie (2013) describes how UD should extend beyond matters of physical access and learning access to account for other forms of difference among people's minds, bodies, and experiences, including race, gender identity and expression, class, intellectual differences, and body sizes/shapes. For example, considering the correlation between disability and poverty, UD should address financial barriers to access, such as registration fees and transportation costs. Recognizing the intersectional relationship of ableism with other forms of oppression, we encourage educators to work toward Hamraie's broad concept of UD in all course/workshop designs, not only those focused on ableism.

Even the most broadly informed perspective on UD will not lead to completely universal access (Shakespeare, 2006). Sometimes individual, as-needed accommodations are the only way to provide access. Accommodations often result in a differential experience for people with disabilities who experience the content filtered through the accommodation and/or through the impairment itself (as with a participant distracted by chronic pain who misses some content while taking breaks for pain management, and tries to catch up later via a recording of a live lecture that they couldn't sit through). These dynamics illustrate the persistent challenges associated with UD and shed light on the complex nature of disability as both social construction and impairment (Shakespeare, 2006). In many ways, the concept of universal design remains aspirational.

INTRODUCTION TO THE ABLEISM DESIGN

The design presented in this chapter provides participants with an introductory overview and understanding of ableism, and draws on SJE core concepts, including the frameworks described in Chapters 1 and 4 of this volume. We focus on helping participants develop a conceptual and personal understanding of ableism at the individual, institutional, and cultural levels, and support them to move toward taking action toward disability justice. This design assumes participants may enter the course/workshop with a wide range of previous experience, but that a majority of participants will have limited if any experience talking about ableism as a system.

Like other designs in this volume, we organize learning goals, key concepts, and activities into four quadrants. The quadrants generally follow the sequence "What? So what? Now what?" Quadrant 1 focuses on defining key terms, beginning to explore the social construction of disability, and building a learning community in which participants can examine their own socialization about ableism. Quadrants 2 and 3 move to historical legacies and contemporary manifestations of ableism, and the application of legal and social movement frameworks to understanding ableism. Finally, Quadrant 4 turns to taking accountable action against ableism and developing action plans for change. Although this design uses four quadrants, the sequence and activities can easily be adapted to other modalities, such as short workshops or semester-long courses.

We assume that instructors and facilitators will read Chapter 4 for a "generic" design, and will have considered the SJE core concepts in that broad context, prior to applying them to ableism. Below is a sample design for ableism, followed by learning objectives and key concepts specific to each quadrant and brief descriptions of the activities needed to carry out the design. Instructions, facilitation notes, and handouts for each activity can be found on the Ableism website.

DESIGN FOR TEACHING ABOUT ABLEISM

Quadrant 1
Icebreaker (20 min)
- Option A: Scavenger Hunt
- Option B: Common Ground

Introductory Materials (35 min)
- Logistics, Goals, and Agenda
- Guidelines for Participation

Early Learnings (50 min)
- Option A: Storytelling Followed by Discussion of Themes and Stereotypes
- Option B: Cycle of Socialization

Social Construction of Disability (30–45 min)
- Option A: Brainstorm
- Option B: Reflection

ADA Definition and Spectrum of Dis/ability (30–60 min)

Quadrant 2
Opening Activity (20 min)
- Meditation on Stigma and Disclosure
- Check-in

History (40–60 min)
- Option A: Lecture
- Option B: Timeline Activity
- Option C: Video

Language, Identity, and Status (30 min)
- Option A: Interactive Activity
- Option B: Media Analysis

Experiences of Ableism
- Option A: Panel (90+ min)
- Option B: Videos (30–90 min)

Intersections of Identity (60 min)
- Option A: Gallery
- Option B: Scenarios

Quadrant 3
Opening Activity (20 min)
- Check-in
- Go Over Homework (if any)

Quadrant 4
Opening Activity (20 min)
- Check-in
- Go Over Homework (if any)

Dependence to Interdependence (20–60 min)

- Lecture
- Skits

Institutional-Level Ableism

- Option A: Broad Overview (30 min)
- Option B: Local Context (45–60 min)

Legal Context (20–40 min)

- Option A: General (lecture)
- Option B: Specific to Audience/Context (lecture + discussion)

Going Deeper (45–90 min)

- Discussion (on one or more topics related to current events or contemporary debates related to disability and ableism)

Imagining Disability Justice (60 min)

- Option A: Brainstorm and Discussion
- Option B: Group Drawing Activity

Frameworks for Allyship (5–20 min)

- Option A: Action Continuum
- Option B: 4 A's of Liberatory Consciousness

Taking Action (60 min)

- Option A: Discussion
- Option B: Scenarios

Closing (20 min)

- Option A: For Short-term Groups
- Option B: For Continuing Groups

QUADRANT 1

Learning Objectives for Quadrant 1:

- Define ableism and disability with a social justice lens
- Identify messages received from early childhood learning about disability
- Describe how disability is socially constructed
- Identify what qualifies as a disability under the ADA

Key Concepts for Quadrant 1:

- Disability
- Social construction of ability/disability
- Ableism
- Activity of daily living
- Reasonable accommodation

Activities and Options for Quadrant 1:

- **Icebreaker:** In both options, participants reflect on what they already know about disability and ableism, and have an opportunity to share information about disability and ableism with each other. The Scavenger Hunt is high-energy and social, whereas the Common Ground has a mellower tone of individual reflection and sharing.
- **Introductory Materials:** Review logistics, goals, and agenda; and establish guidelines for participation.
- **Early Learnings:** In both options, participants explore what they have learned from early and/or significant experiences with disability and ableism. **Option A** moves from low-risk individual reflection to storytelling in small groups, to a discussion of themes and stereotypes in the whole group. **Option B** uses the Cycle of Socialization (Harro, 2013a) to structure individual reflection and then small- and large-group discussion about how we are socialized into our roles as people, with and without disabilities, in an ableist society.
- **Social Construction of Disability:** In the brainstorm option, facilitators lead participants' through a group brainstorm about elements of their physical and social environment that make daily activities easier to perform. In the reflection option, participants reflect on the previous day/evening and identify elements of their environment that were enabling, then imagine what else they might need if they had a particular

disability. In both options, guided discussion builds on the reflections/brainstorm to illustrate concepts of accessibility and accommodation, and how an environment can be enabling or disabling, gradually building up to the idea that disability is constructed by social and cultural forces.

- **ADA Definition and Spectrum of Dis/ability:** Facilitators do a presentation and lead a discussion structured around the Impairments and Disabilities Handout, which shows a spectrum of impairment and disability. Participants consider the spectrum of human ability, and learn the ADA definition of what makes an impairment qualify as a disability.

QUADRANT 2

Learning Objectives for Quadrant 2:
- Develop empathy and understanding regarding disability stigma and experiences of disclosure
- Identify how ableist language reinforces disability stigma
- Explore intersections of disability and ableism with other identities and systems of oppression
- Understand historical legacies in understandings of disability and the treatment of people with disabilities
- Practice empathy (as distinct from pity) with the experiences of people with disabilities

Key Concepts for Quadrant 2:
- Levels of oppression
- Disability stigma
- Intersectionality
- Privilege

Activities and Options for Quadrant 2:
- **Opening Activity—Meditation on Disability Stigma and Disclosure:** This exercise serves to build empathy regarding the stigmatizing effects of ableism. Participants are asked to pair up and discuss their most recent medical interaction in great detail; the activity is halted before they actually do so, and facilitators elicit discussion about the thoughts and feelings that come up when confronted with the need to disclose a possibly stigmatizing experience.
- **Opening Activity—Check-in:** A flexible opener that can be used in any quadrant to bring the group back together, collect questions or comments left over from the previous session, and orient the group to upcoming activities.
- **History:** All three history activity options present information about the history of disability and ableism. The **Lecture** option provides the most flexibility for facilitators to focus content on issues of relevance to the particular group and context, as well as highlight themes in historical and ongoing frameworks of understanding disability. The **Timeline** option is most interactive, and requires participants to learn about a particular time period and teach the information back to their peers. The **Video** option can take less time than the others, and can be an engaging way to get some key themes and information into the room.
- **Language, Identity, and Status:** Both activity options help participants understand how language used to refer to people with disabilities supports the construction of

disability statuses and identities, and perpetuates disability stigma and marginalization. The **Interactive Activity** option elicits language examples from the group, while the **Media Analysis** option asks participants to collect examples from media.

- **Experiences of Ableism:** Both options provide an opportunity for participants to learn from personal experiences of people with disabilities and/or people who have expertise in ableism, disability access, and disability justice. In the **Panel** option, facilitators arrange for panelists to join the group (in person or by video conference) to discuss their experiences and expertise. In the **Video** option, publically available recordings are used in place of an in-person panel.

- **Intersections of Identity:** In both options, participants develop awareness of some ways ableism intersects with other forms of oppression to create specific experiences of identity, privilege, and marginalization. In the **Gallery** option, participants generate hypotheses of how intersectionality might look with regard to general categories of identity, e.g., race and disability, gender and disability, or age and disability. In the **Scenarios** option, participants analyze scenarios to identify the interaction of systems of oppression, including ableism.

QUADRANT 3

Learning Objectives for Quadrant 3:
- Become familiar with the interlocking institutional manifestations of ableism in, e.g., medicine, education, religion, law, housing, etc.
- Understand the spectrum of dependence to interdependence in different models of disability
- Understand the basics of relevant laws impacting people with disabilities
- Solidify understanding of intersectionality, social construction, and stigma through "going deeper" on one or more current issues in ableism

Key Concepts for Quadrant 3:
- Intersectionality
- Social construction
- Stigma
- Medical model of disability
- Institutional level oppression
- Dependence, independence, interdependence

Activities and Options for Quadrant 3:
- **Opening Activity—Check-in:** A flexible opener that can be used in any quadrant to bring the group back together, collect questions or comments left over from the previous session, and orient the group to upcoming activities.
- **Opening Activity—Review Homework:** If homework was assigned, debriefing participants' experiences with the homework can serve as an opening activity.
- **Dependence to Interdependence Model—Lecture:** A brief presentation followed by discussion that compares and contrasts prominent models of disability.
- **Dependence to Interdependence Model—Skits:** An interactive activity in which small groups present skits highlighting key components of prevalent frameworks of disability (e.g., medical model, rehabilitation model, independent living model, disability justice model). In discussion, the models are compared and contrasted.

- **Institutional-Level Ableism:** Both options are interactive activities in which participants identify examples of ableism at the institutional level. In the **Broad Overview** option, the focus is on macro-systems such as healthcare, education, housing, etc. In the **Local Context** option, the focus is on specific institutions, such as the local public hospital, the local school district, a specific housing complex, etc.
- **Legal Context:** The **General** option offers a brief overview of major legislation related to people with disabilities, and the **Specific** option focuses on law of particular relevance to participants' professional context.
- **Going Deeper:** Through discussion of current events and controversial issues related to ableism and disability justice, participants gain knowledge of one or more specific topics and practice applying concepts like intersectionality, stigma, and social construction.

QUADRANT 4

Learning Objectives for Quadrant 4:
- Imagine a world without ableism—practice thinking through the implications of full access and disability justice
- Apply frameworks for allyship to identify individual strengths and opportunities for growth in effective change-making toward disability justice
- Take lessons learned from Quadrants 1–3 and apply them to personal and professional roles

Key Concepts for Quadrant 4:
- Universal design
- Allyship
- Access
- Inclusion
- Disability justice

Activities and Options for Quadrant 4:
- **Opening Activity—Check-in**
- **Opening Activity—Review Homework** (see Q 3)
- **Imagining Disability Justice:** Both options are interactive activities that elicit ideas and encourage critical thinking about social change with respect to access, inclusion, universal design, and disability justice. The **Brainstorm and Discussion** option is primarily verbal, whereas the **Group Drawing Activity** option uses drawing to elicit nonverbal thoughts (and practice nonverbal communication and collaboration) before consolidating ideas in verbal discussion.
- **Frameworks for Allyship:** In both options, the facilitator begins with a brief presentation of a framework (the **Action Continuum** or the **4 A's of Liberatory Consciousness**) to help participants think through their own behavior as allies against ableism—with a definition of ally that can include people with and without disabilities. Participants then use the model to assess their current strengths and areas for growth as allies.
- **Taking Action:** Both options are interactive activities that help participants think through opportunities they may have to confront and transform ableism and work

toward disability justice. The **Discussion** option builds on the Imagining Disability Justice activity, with participants generating their own ideas in small groups. The **Scenarios** option works best for groups that share a professional context, and uses sample situations to engage in practical problem-solving.

- **Closing:** With both options, the goal is to bring a sense of closure to the experience and help participants transition back into their post-training lives. The option for short-term groups is a final debrief and closure, whereas the option for continuing groups emphasizes connecting their training experience into their ongoing work together.

PEDAGOGICAL DESIGN AND FACILITATION ISSUES WHEN TEACHING ABOUT ABLEISM

FOCUS ON ABLEISM AS A SYSTEM

As with all the designs in this book, we endeavor to strike a balance between attention to individual-level manifestations of oppression and systemic-level analysis. Ableism workshops should seek to build both awareness of the impacts of ableism on individuals with and without disabilities, and systemic analysis of how institutions and cultural construct disability and perpetuate marginalization of people with disabilities. Without attention to the systemic nature of ableism, education about disability issues can inadvertently reinforce existing stereotypes and beliefs, and since the dominant understanding of disability is individualist, the systemic aspect deserves emphasis. Facilitators may find they need to reinforce the systemic lens repeatedly in order to debunk some participants' strong and often unconscious assumption that disability is fundamentally an individual problem.

For example, many participants enter an ableism course/workshop with a tendency to focus on tasks people can't do rather than on what they would need to do those tasks. Facilitators may need to remind participants more than once to reframe in terms of access needs rather than inability. Such reframing enables participants to shift their perception of individual lacks to an exploration of the supports and accommodations that are or should be available through institutions, and it can be a powerful intervention to disrupt stereotypes and assumptions that are reinforced by the ableist dominant culture.

SEQUENCING

With ableism, it is frequently the case that participants have no previous understanding of ableism as a system, and many have very little previous knowledge of disability in any framework. The pervasive ignorance about ableism and disability presents both challenges and opportunities: On one hand, facilitators may find themselves spending more time on basic definitions and information, which can limit the time available for more in-depth systemic analysis and for action planning. On the other hand, participants tend to come into ableism courses with an awareness of their own ignorance, eager to learn with little of the defensiveness or privilege guilt often encountered when teaching other isms.

Because of the relative lack of privilege guilt with regard to ableism, activities that highlight some participants' privilege may be experienced as low- to medium-risk, even if a parallel activity would seem higher-risk when focused on a different ism. Yet that does not mean that activities focused on privilege should necessarily come early in an ableism sequence. If participants have not yet internalized an understanding of the systemic nature of ableism, discussions of privilege can lead them to focus on how hard it must be to have a disability (within an individual understanding), rather than on how ableism marginalizes people with disabilities, and on feelings of pity and impulses toward charity, rather than feelings of solidarity and impulses toward collective action. Later in the sequence, with a strong systemic lens, discussions of privilege can help participants understand disability as an issue that affects everyone, and ableism as a system they are part of and can help to dismantle.

We recommend setting clear expectations early on regarding the frameworks and goals that guide the course/workshop. Remind participants that the course/workshop is about ableism as a system. Although ableism does play out at an interpersonal level, the focus is not on a "how to" of interacting with or caring for people with disabilities, but rather on the need for systemic change and opportunities to contribute to it. It is also helpful to note that the course/workshop is an overview and cannot cover every example in the depth that participants may want. Some participants who have disabilities may want to make sure their particular disability is covered thoroughly so that they can feel understood; other participants may know someone with a particular disability that they are eager to learn more about. Facilitators can accommodate these desires to some extent, but not so much that it interferes with giving a broad overview and systemic lens on all types of disabilities.

PARTICIPANTS' EXPERIENCES WITH DISABILITY

Facilitators should be aware of and sensitive to the range of experience, awareness, and knowledge about disability that participants may bring so as to facilitate a meaningful experience for all participants/students. Some people with disabilities may come to a workshop with extensive knowledge and analysis about ableism. Many other people with disabilities may not be knowledgeable about or sensitive to the needs of people with disabilities different from theirs. Some participants who do not have disabilities may have experience with friends or family members who have disabilities; yet this does not guarantee that they will have awareness of ableism or their role in it. In most contexts, a majority of participants will not identify as having disabilities.

Participants who have disabilities or who have experience with disability in their families will vary in their willingness to discuss those experiences. People with non-apparent disabilities may or may not feel comfortable disclosing this information. Others may not think of themselves as having a disability when they begin an ableism course, but may come to identify as having a disability as a result of learning new frameworks and definitions. We recommend creating opportunities for participants to disclose disabilities or experiences with disability throughout the sequence of the course/workshop. Disclosure should always be optional, and the group should be reminded to keep such information confidential and to respect individuals' boundaries regarding whether/how they discuss their own disabilities.

Most people will know someone who has a disability at some point, but the dominant culture teaches people without disabilities not to think of disability as something relevant to our lives. All participants can benefit from an opportunity to explore their feelings about disability, including fears about their own fragility, loss of control, and death. In such discussions, participants may recognize patterns around privilege, including how fears cause them to avoid people with disabilities or feel anger toward people with disabilities for reminding them of these realities of life.

The characteristics of the group, as well as each participant's previous experience with disability, affect how specific activities or topics may be experienced as more or less "risky." For example, in our experience, participants without disabilities do not seem to be embarrassed or uncomfortable talking about disabilities in front of people with disabilities. However, they may avoid talking about the specific disability that someone in the room has disclosed (or that is apparent). Facilitators can address this simply by making sure to bring up that disability as an example among others, just as they would anyway. In some situations, it may also be useful to create an opportunity for participants to bring up topics or ask questions anonymously.

Another common dynamic is participants with disabilities falling into the role of expert with regard to their own disability or disability in general. Facilitators should remind participants that those with apparent or disclosed disabilities are not responsible for educating their classmates, and that participants with disabilities probably also have plenty to learn about ableism.

DISABILITY SIMULATIONS

Disability simulation activities are a popular educational intervention in many schools and workplaces, in which participants are assigned a disability to "live with" for a period of time. After the simulation, participants discuss the difficulty of performing daily activities with their disability. Such simulations tend to reinforce a view of disability as individual deficiency, and perpetuate negative assumptions about disability by focusing on what participants cannot do rather than what they can. The experience often reinforces participant fears of becoming disabled and enduring condescending attitudes toward people with disabilities. For example, people role-playing blindness may only remember their fear and incompetence, and they may leave the training still unaware of the tools and skills that blind people use to live independently. Rather than disability simulation exercises, we urge facilitators to use activities that highlight the interaction between individuals' needs and capacities, and the built and social environment. The social construction activities we include are examples of such activities.

INTERSECTIONALITY

In the design above, many activities address intersectionality at both an identity level and a systems level. In some activities, intersectionality is implicit, but it will sometimes fall on facilitators to nudge participants to fully engage with that aspect of the activity. Such concerns are noted in the facilitation notes for each activity. Beyond specific activities, an intersectional framework should inform every aspect of a course/workshop, from planning to design to content to facilitation. For example, in planning and pre-workshop assessment, facilitators should consider not only participants' likely experiences with disability, but also their other identities and experiences with other forms of oppression than may inform or mediate their experience of learning about ableism. What aspects of ableism might they find easy to identify with? What parallels with other systems of oppression might be useful to elucidate ableism for that group? If a group is likely to be particularly well-versed in the history of racism, an early mention of the use of ableism to justify racism, and the various ways in which eugenics has been used to target both people with disabilities and people of color, can help to spur participants' investment in the topic. Similarly, for participants who may have experience of having their bodies or identities being pathologized (based on gender, race, age, sexual orientation, or other identities), a critique of the medical model may be a useful point of entry into thinking through ableism.

Facilitators should be careful to avoid making parallels that seem to claim that ableism is "just like" another system of oppression. Even when the systems operate similarly, the differences matter. Highlighting both parallels and differences among systems of oppression, as well as the ways in which ableism may be deployed in support of another system of oppression, can lead to deeper and more complex understanding of oppression.

Throughout a course/workshop, facilitators should make room for intersectional analysis through the examples they give and the questions they ask. It is helpful to have many, varied examples about ableism and its intersections ready to use as appropriate. When providing examples of people with disabilities facing manifestations of ableism, facilitators should note how the person's other identities might impact their experiences. Likewise, when responding to participants' questions about hypothetical situations, facilitators should make sure to highlight how the answer might depend on the other identities of people in the situation. If participants are not bringing up social identities beyond ability and disability, facilitators can draw out participants' thoughts about intersectionality of identity and experience with questions like, "What might play out differently in that situation depending on the person's race [or class, gender, sexual orientation, age, etc.]?"

Sometimes the intersection of ableism and other systems of oppression can manifest during a workshop in ways that may be counterintuitive and challenging to facilitate. On an individual level, we sometimes notice intersectionality in terms of who feels entitled to accommodations. For example, in our professional practice working with people seeking accommodations, we have noticed that individuals who are privileged in terms of several salient identities and become disabled as adults often come across as very assertive and have a lot of relative success in getting their needs for accommodation met. Individuals who have had a disability their whole lives and/or who are members of other subordinated groups may tend to be more patient with delays in accommodation, or may assume that not all of their needs will be met and that there may be nothing to be done about it. If such a pattern emerges, facilitators should be careful not to "take a side" in terms of which approach is "better." Rather, the conversation should be used as an opportunity to draw out different ways in which we have all been socialized to get our needs met, to "make do" when our needs are not met, to persevere, and/or to accept disappointment.

On a systemic level, intersectionality of ableism and other systems can come up in the ableist rhetoric sometimes employed in social justice movements. Even though ableism so often operates as a tool for justifying or legitimizing other systems of oppression, people may also call on ableist assumptions when attempting to *de*legitimize or resist another system of oppression. For example, someone who is passionate about transgender liberation may argue against the categorization of gender dysphoria as a psychiatric diagnosis, using language like, "Trans people aren't sick or crazy. Gender diversity is healthy and normal." The speaker's intention is to support gender justice by disrupting the oppressive pathologization of gender diversity, and they may not realize that at the same time, their arguments implicitly support ableist tropes of people with mental illness as unpredictable, unreasonable, violent, and broadly unwell or incapable, and of illness generally as being outside the range of "normal" human experience.

If a participant makes such a statement, it is not enough to address the ableism in the statement; facilitators must engage with the intersectional complexities in all their messiness. In the above example, "calling out" the participant's use of ableist language without addressing the content of their statement about gender diversity could have the side effect of silencing an important discussion about the pathologization of trans* people—which is not unrelated to the pathologization of people with disabilities within the medical model. Instead of focusing on only one ism, or on trying to delineate which parts of a statement are "right" and "wrong," we encourage facilitators to dig into underlying issues, such as: How does pathologization work? How does it benefit and/or harm individuals and populations? What is the political impact when ableist language is used both in support of and/or in opposition to other systems of oppression? How could an intersectional lens help gender justice advocates and disability justice advocates work together to disrupt the harmful impacts of pathologizing discourses on everyone?

TAKING ACTION

In most cases, for short-term workshops on ableism, we address taking action in one or two specific activities toward the end of the workshop (as in the design provided here). This is because many people come into an ableism workshop with so little information, or so much misinformation, that the ideas for action they might come up with earlier in the workshop would tend to be misguided. Depending on the group of participants, it may be valuable to talk about visions for disability justice very broadly (e.g., in the whole community or in the whole world), or it may work better to contextualize the conversation in participants' specific professional or school environments.

With longer courses/workshops, or when participants can be expected to come in with a shared foundation of understanding, taking action can and should be incorporated early in the design. An action assignment can be broken down into steps that build on each other over the length of the course, and/or can include periodic check-ins so that participants can incorporate new information, frameworks, and analysis into their action projects. A benefit of starting to think about action earlier in the course/workshop is that participants' learning can be more solution-focused, which can help to disrupt problem-focused ableist thought patterns such as pity and paternalism.

INCORPORATING UID AND ACCOMMODATIONS

The activities in the four-quadrant design have been designed with a UID lens. Still, facilitators should be aware of students' potential needs and be ready to make adaptations. Some basic practices that can help make sessions accessible are provided in the "Universal Instructional Design for Social Justice Education" handout on the website, which provides a valuable checklist for planning.

FACILITATOR PREPARATION

As with all social justice education, facilitators must prepare themselves not only to teach content, but also to recognize and attend to the ways ableism has impacted their own thinking. Completing the activities that participants will go through is one way to raise one's awareness about ableism, and having in-depth discussions with a co-facilitator can also be helpful. In addition, facilitators should work to gather a variety of examples to use as appropriate during the workshop. Examples can come from published materials and/ or professional experience, but at least some should also be personal to the facilitator, and should acknowledge the facilitator's relationship to ableism as a person without disabilities or as a person with a particular disability or disabilities.

FACILITATORS' IDENTITIES

Facilitators who have disabilities should consider in advance whether and how to incorporate their personal experience into the workshop. For facilitators with non-apparent disabilities, the decision of whether, when, and how to disclose can be an important pedagogical one. In our experience, participants are usually eager to work with a facilitator who has a disability and to trust them as an "expert." On the other hand, participants may hesitate to ask questions that they fear may be offensive. Facilitators with an apparent disability, or who have disclosed a disability, should prepare themselves to field potentially offensive questions and reassure participants that well-intended questions are welcome.

Note

* We ask that those who cite this work always acknowledge by name all of the authors listed rather than either only citing the first author or using "et al." to indicate coauthors. All collaborated on the conceptualization, development, and writing of this chapter.

References

Agency for Healthcare Research and Quality. (2015, May 19). *2014 National Healthcare Quality & Disparities Report* (AHRQ Pub. No. 15–0007). Retrieved June 7, 2015, from http://www.ahrq.gov/research/findings/nhqrdr/nhqdr14/index.html

Americans with Disabilities Act of 1990, as Amended (ADA). (2009). Retrieved from http://www.ada.gov/pubs/adastatute08.htm

American Psychiatric Association. (2013). *The diagnostic and statistical manual of mental disorders: DSM 5*. Washington, DC: American Psychiatric Publishing.

Arthur, E., McGill, D., & Essary, E. H. (2014). Playing it straight: Framing strategies among reparative therapists. *Sociological Inquiry*, *84*(1), 16–41.

Ayvazian, A. (1995). Interrupting the cycle of oppression: The role of allies as agents of change. *Fellowship*, January–February 1995, pp. 7–10.

Ball, E. W., & Harry, B. (2010). Assessment and the policing of the norm. In C. Dudley-Marling & A. Gurn (Eds.), *The myth of the normal curve* (pp. 105–122). New York: Peter Lang.

Ben-Zeev, D., Corrigan, P. W., Britt, T. W., & Langford, L. (2012). Stigma of mental illness and service use in the military. *Journal of Mental Health*, *21*(3), 264–273. doi: 10.3109/09638237.2011.621468

Bergerson, A. A. (2009). College choice and access to college: Moving policy, research and practice to the 21st Century. *ASHE Higher Education Report*, *35*(4).

Berne, P. (2015, June 10). *Disability justice—a working draft by Patty Berne* [blog]. Sins Invalid: An unshamed claim to beauty in the face of invisibility). Retrieved from http://sinsinvalid.org/blog/disability-justice-a-working-draft-by-patty-berne

Brabazon, T. (2015). *Enabling university: Impairment, (dis)ability and social justice in higher education* (e-book). New York: Springer, 2015.

Brown, N. D. (2008). Transition from the Afghanistan and Iraqi battlefields to home: An overview of selected war wounds and the federal agencies assisting soldiers regain their health. *Workplace Health & Safety*, *56*(8), 343–346. Retrieved from http://whs.sagepub.com/content/56/8/343.full.pdf

Bryan, W. V. (2006). *In search of freedom: How persons with disabilities have been disenfranchised from the mainstream of American society and how the search for freedom continues*. Springfield, IL. Charles C. Thomas Publisher, LTD.

Bryan, W. V. (2007). *Multicultural aspects of disabilities: A guide to understanding and assisting minorities in the rehabilitation process*. Springfield, IL: Thomas Books.

Burgstahler, S. E. (2010). Universal design in higher education. In S. E. Burgstahler & R. C. Cory (Eds.), *Universal design in higher education: From principles to practice* (pp. 3–20). Cambridge, MA: Harvard Education Press.

Burgstahler, S. E., & Cory, R. C. (Eds.). (2010). *Universal design in higher education: From principles to practice*. Cambridge, MA: Harvard Education Press.

Cerney, Janet. (2007). *Deaf Education in America: Voices of Children from Inclusion Settings*. Washington, D.C.: Gallaudet University Press.

Cheatham, G. A., & Elliott, W. (2013). The effects of family college savings on postsecondary school enrollment rates of students with disabilities. *Economics of Education Review*, *33*, 95–111. Retrieved from http://doi.org/10.1016/j.econedurev.2012.09.011

Cheatham, G. A., Smith, S. J., Elliott, W., & Friedline, T. (2013). Family assets, postsecondary education, and students with disabilities: Building on progress and overcoming challenges. *Children and Youth Services Review*, *35*(7), 1078–1086. Retrieved from http://doi.org/10.1016/j.childyouth.2013.04.019

Connor, D. J. (2006). Michael's story: "I get into so much trouble just by walking": Narrative knowing and life at the intersections of learning disability, race, and class. *Equity and Excellence in Education*, *39*(2), 154–165.

Cortiella, C., & Horowitz, S. H. (2014). *The state of learning disabilities: Facts, trends and emerging issues*. New York: National Center for Learning Disabilities.

Covey, H. (1998). *Social perspectives of people with disabilities in history*. Springfield, IL: Charles Thomas.

DeNavas-Walt, C., & Proctor, B. D. (2014). *Current population reports, P60–249, Income and poverty in the United States: 2013*. Washington, DC: U.S. Census Bureau.

Dolan, K., & Carr, J. (2015). *The poor get prison: The alarming spread of the criminalization of poverty*. Washington, DC: Institute for Policy Studies. Retrieved May 12, 2015, from http://www.ips-dc.org/wp-content/uploads/2015/03/IPS-The-Poor-Get-Prison-Final.pdf

Donovan, M. S., & Cross, C. T. (Eds.). (2002). *Minority students in special and gifted education*. Washington, DC: National Academy Press.

Duhaney, L. G. (2000). Culturally sensitive strategies for violence prevention. *Multicultural Education*, 7(4), 9–17.

Fischer, H. (2014). *A guide to U.S. military casualty statistics: Operation Inherent Resolve, Operation New Dawn, Operation Iraqi Freedom, and Operation Enduring Freedom* (Congressional Research Services Report No. RS22452). Retrieved from the Federation of American Scientists website: http://fas.org/sgp/crs/natsec/RS22452.pdf

Fleischer, D., & Zames, F. (2001). *The disability rights movement: From charity to confrontation*. Philadelphia: Temple University Press.

Franklin, M. (1992). Culturally sensitive practices for African American learners with disabilities. *Exceptional Children*, 59(2), 115–122.

Gallagher, H. (1995). *By trust betrayed: Patients, physicians, and the license to kill in the Third Reich*. Arlington, VA: Vandamer.

Griffin, P., Peters, M., & Smith, R. (2007). Ableism curriculum design. In M. Adams, L, Bell, & P. Griffin, (Eds.), *Teaching for diversity and social justice* (2nd ed., pp. 336–358). New York: Routledge.

Grigal, M., Hart, D., & Migliore, A. (2011). Comparing transition planning, postsecondary education, and employment outcomes of students with intellectual and other disabilities. *Career Development and Transition for Exceptional Individuals*, 34(1), 4–17. doi: 10.1177/0885728811399091

Grigal, M., Hart, D., & Weir, C. (2011). Think College standards, quality indicators, and benchmarks for inclusive higher education. Boston: University of Massachusetts Boston, Institute for Community Inclusion. Retrieved from http://www.thinkcollege.net/images/stories/standards_F.pdf

Hamblet, E. C. (2009). Helping your students with disabilities during their college search. *Journal of College Admission*, 205, 6–15.

Hamraie, A. (2013). Designing collective access: A feminist disability theory of universal design. *Disability Studies Quarterly*, 33(4). Retrieved from http://dsq-sds.org/article/view/3871

Harrell, E., Lanton, L., Berzofsky, M., Couzens, L., & Smiley-McDonald, H. (2014). *Household poverty and nonfatal violent victimization, 2008–2012*. Bureau of Justice Statistics of the U.S. Department of Justice. Retrieved from http://www.bjs.gov/content/pub/pdf/hpnvv0812.pdf

Harro, B. (2013a). The cycle of socialization (updated). In M. Adams, W. Blumenfeld, C. Castañeda, H. Hackman, M. Peters, & X. Zúñiga (Eds.), *Readings for diversity and social justice* (3rd ed., pp. 45–52). New York: Routledge.

Harro, B. (2013b). The cycle of liberation (updated). In M. Adams, W. Blumenfeld, C. Castañeda, H. Hackman, M. Peters, & X. Zúñiga (Eds.), *Readings for diversity and social justice* (3rd ed., pp. 618–625). New York: Routledge.

Harry, B., & Klinger, J. (2006). *Why are so many minority students in special education? Understanding race and disability in schools*. New York: Teachers College Press.

Hart, D., Grigal, M., Sax, C., Martinez, D., & Will, M. (2006). Research to practice: Postsecondary education options for students with intellectual disabilities. *Research to Practice Series*, Paper 6. Boston: Institute for Community Inclusion.

Hart, D., Mele-McCarthy, J., Pasternack, R. H., Zimbrich, K., & Parker, D. R. (2004). Community college: A pathway to success for youth with learning, cognitive, and intellectual disabilities in secondary settings. *Education and Training in Developmental Disabilities*, 39(1), 54–66.

Heitzeg, N. (2009). Education or incarceration: Zero tolerance policies and the school to prison pipeline. *Forum on Public Policy Online: A Journal of the Oxford Round Table*, 5(2), 1–21.

Hendrickson, J. M., Therrien, W. J., Weeden, D. D., Pascarella, E., & Hosp, J. L. (2015). Engagement among students with intellectual disabilities and first year students: A comparison. *Journal of Student Affairs Research and Practice*, 52(2), 204–219. doi: 10.1080/19496591.2015.1041872

Hitchings, W. E., Retish, P., & Horvath, M. (2005). Academic preparation of adolescents with disabilities for postsecondary education. *Career Development for Exceptional Individuals*, 28(1), 26–35. doi: 10.1177/08857288050280010501

Hornick, R. (2012). *The girls and boys of Belchertown: A social history of the Belchertown State School for the Feeble-Minded*. Boston: UMASS Press.

Johnson, A. (2013). The social construction of difference. In M. Adams, W. Blumenfeld, C. Casta-ñeda, H. Hackman, M. Peters, & X. Zúñiga (Eds.), *Readings for diversity and social justice* (3rd ed., pp. 15–21). New York: Routledge.

Jung, K. E. (2011). Chronic illness and educational equity: The politics of visibility. In K. Q. Hall (Ed.), *Feminist disability studies* (pp. 263–286). Bloomington, IN: Indiana University Press.

Krisch, J. (2014, Oct. 13). When racism was a science: 'Haunted Files: The Eugenics Record Office' recreates a dark time in a laboratory's past. *The New York Times*. Retrieved from http://www.nytimes.com/2014/10/14/science/haunted-files-the-eugenics-record-office-recreates-a-dark-time-in-a-laboratorys-past.html?_r=0

Loewen, G., & Pollard, W. (2010). The social justice perspective. *Journal of Postsecondary Education and Disability, 23*(1), 5–18.

Longmore, P., & Umanski, L. (Eds.). (2001). *The new disability history: American perspectives*. New York: New York University Press.

Ludlow, B. (2012). College for all should really mean all. *Teaching Exceptional Children, 44*(5), 4.

Lutz, A. (2008). Who joins the military? A look at race, class, and immigration status. *Journal of Political and Military Sociology, 36*(2), 167–188.

Martinez, D. C., & Queener, J. (2010, Winter). *Postsecondary education for students with intellectual disabilities*. George Washington University HEATH Resource Center. Retrieved from https://heath.gwu.edu/files/downloads/pse_id_final_edition.pdf

Masino, L. L., & Hodapp, R. M. (1996). Parental educational expectations for adolescents with disabilities. *Exceptional Children, 62*, 515–524.

Meyers, A. R., & Andresen, E. M. (2000). Applying outcomes research to disability and health—Enabling our instruments: Accommodation, universal design, and access to participation in research. *Archives of Physical Medicine and Rehabilitation, 81*(2), S5.

Mingus, M. (2011, Feb. 12). Changing the framework: disability justice/How our communities can move beyond access to wholeness. *Leaving Evidence*. Retrieved from https://leavingevidence.wordpress.com/about-2/.

Morin, R. (2011). *The difficult transition from military to civilian life*. Pew Research Center—Social and Demographic Trends. Retrieved from http://www.pewsocialtrends.org/2011/12/08/the-difficult-transition-from-military-to-civilian-life/

National Center for Health Statistics. (2015). *Health, United States, 2014, with special feature on adults aged 55–64*. Retrieved from http://www.cdc.gov/nchs/data/hus/hus14.pdf

National Council on Disability. (2000). *Back to school on civil rights*. Retrieved from https://www.ncd.gov/publications/2000/Jan252000

Occupational Safety & Health Administration, United States Department of Labor. (2015). *Adding inequality to injury: The costs of failing to protect workers on the job*. Retrieved from http://www.dol.gov/osha/report/20150304-inequality.pdf

Pelka, F. (2012). *What we have done: An oral history of the disability rights movement*. Amherst, MA: University of Massachusetts Press.

Roberts, D., & Jesudason, S. (2013). Movement intersectionality: The case of race, gender, disability, and genetic technologies. *Du Bois Review, 10*(2), 313–328.

Rogers, R., and Mancini, M. (2010). "Requires medication to progress academically": The discursive pathways of ADHD. In C. Dudley-Marling & A. Gurn (Eds.), *The myth of the normal curve* (pp. 87–101). New York: Peter Lang.

Russell, M. (1998). *Beyond ramps: Disability at the end of the social contract—A warning from an uppity crip*. Monroe, ME: Common Courage Press.

Schalock, R. L., Brown, I., Brown, R., Cummins, R. A., Felce, D., Matikka, L., Keith, K. D., & Parmenter, T. (2002). Conceptualization, measurement, and application of quality of life for persons with intellectual disabilities: Report of an international panel of experts. *Mental Retardation, 40*(6), 457–470. doi: 10.1352/0047–6765(2002)040<0457:CMAAOQ>2.0.CO;2

Schnittker, J., Massoglia, M., & Uggen, C. (2012). Out and down: Incarceration and psychiatric disorders. *Journal of Health and Social Behavior, 53*(4), 448–464. Retrieved from https://www.soc.umn.edu/~uggen/Schnittker_Massoglia_Uggen_JHSB_12.pdf

Scotch, R. K. (2014, April). Models of disability and the Americans with Disabilities Act. *Berkeley Journal of Employment & Labor Law, 21*(1), Article 7. Retrieved from http://scholarship.law.berkeley.edu/cgi/viewcontent.cgi?article=1279&context=bjell

Scott, S. S., McGuire, J. M., & Shaw, S. F. (2003). Universal design for instruction. *Remedial and Special Education, 24*(6), 369–379.

Seabrook, K. (2002). *Class, caste and hierarchies*. London: Verso.

Shakespeare, T. (2006). The social model of disability. In L. J. Davis (Ed.), *The Disability Studies Reader* (pp. 214–221). New York: Routledge.

Shapiro, J. (1994). *No pity*. New York: Random House.

Shepherd, T. L., Linn, D., & Brown, R. D. (2005). The disproportionate representation of English language learners for special education services along the border. *Journal of Social and Ecological Boundaries, 1*(1), 104–116.

Silver, P., Bourke, A., & Strehorn, K. C. (1998). Universal instructional design in higher education: an approach for inclusion. *Equity & Excellence in Education, 31*(2), 47–51.

Singleton, M. (2014). The 'science' of eugenics: America's moral detour. *Journal of American Physicians and Surgeons, 19*(4), 122–125. Retrieved from http://www.jpands.org/vol19no4/singleton.pdf

Sleeter, C. (1986). Learning disabilities: The social construction of a special education category. *Exceptional Children, 53*(1), 46–54.

Stinner, D. J., Burns, T. C., Kirk, K. L., Scoville, C. R., Ficke, J. R., & Hsu, J. R. (2010). Prevalence of late amputations during the current conflicts in Afghanistan and Iraq. *Military Medicine, 175*(12), 1027–1029.

Taylor, S. (2004). The right not to work: Power and disability. *Monthly Review, 55*(10). Retrieved from http://monthlyreview.org/2004/03/01/the-right-not-to-work-power-and-disability/

Think College. (n.d.). *Higher Education Opportunity Act of 2008*. Retrieved February 10, 2015, from http://www.thinkcollege.net/topics/opportunity-act

Torrey, E. (1997). *Out of the shadows: Confronting America's mental illness crisis*. Hobokon, NJ: John Wiley & Sons. As cited by *Frontline*, May 10, 2005, on WGBH. Retrieved April 1, 2015, from http://www.pbs.org/wgbh/pages/frontline/shows/asylums/special/excerpt.html

Torrey, E., Kennard, A., Eslinger, D., Lamb, R., & Pavle, J. (2010). *More mentally ill persons are in jails and prisons than hospitals: A survey of the states*. Arlington, VA: Treatment Advocacy Center. Retrieved from http://www.treatmentadvocacycenter.org/storage/documents/final_jails_v_hospitals_study.pdf

Treatment Advocacy Center. (2015). *No room at the inn: Trends and consequences of closing public psychiatric hospitals*. Arlington, VA: Treatment Advocacy Center. Retrieved from http://www.tacreports.org/bedstudy

U.S. Census Bureau. (2013). *Income, poverty, and health insurance coverage in the United States: 2012* (Current Population Reports No. P60–245). Retrieved from http://www.census.gov/prod/2013pubs/p60–245.pdf

U.S. Department of Education Office for Civil Rights. (2014). *Civil rights data collection: Data snapshot (school discipline)*. Washington, DC: U.S. Department of Education.

U.S. Senate Committee on Health, Education, Labor & Pensions. (2014). *Fulfilling the promise: Overcoming persistent barriers to economic self-sufficiency for people with disabilities* (Majority committee staff report). Retrieved from http://www.help.senate.gov/imo/media/doc/HELP%20Committee%20Disability%20and%20Poverty%20Report.pdf

Wendell, S. (2013). The social construction of disability. In M. Adams, W. Blumenfeld, C. Castañeda, H. Hackman, M. Peters, & X. Zúñiga (Eds.), *Readings for diversity and social justice* (3rd ed., pp. 15–21). New York: Routledge.

Wildeman, C., & Western, B. (2010). Incarceration in fragile families. *The Future of Children, 20*(2). Retrieved from http://www.princeton.edu/futureofchildren/publications/docs/20_02_08.pdf

Williams, A. S., & Moore, S. M. (2011). Universal design of research: Inclusion of persons with disabilities in mainstream biomedical studies. *Science Translational Medicine, 3*(82), 82cm12.

World Health Organization (2011). *World report on disability*. Retrieved from http://www.who.int/disabilities/world_report/2011/report.pdf

World Health Organization (2014). *Disability and health* (fact sheet N 352). Retrieved from http://www.who.int/mediacentre/factsheet/fs352/en/

Zeff, R. (2007). Universal design across the curriculum. *New Directions for Higher Education, 137*, 27–44.

10

Youth Oppression and Elder Oppression

*Keri DeJong and Barbara Love**

INTRODUCTION

The mistreatment of young people and elders is so prevalent in the United States that laws in all 50 states have been enacted prohibiting child abuse and elder abuse. *Elder abuse* can take the form of violence, including physical restraint or assault; abuse, including emotional and mental neglect and economic mistreatment; bullying, including emotional, mental, and physical confinement; and the inappropriate prescription and administration of drugs (World Health Organization, 2002). Researchers interviewed 2,000 elders living in long-term care facilities and reported that 44% of those residents claimed they had experienced abuse and 95% claimed to have been neglected or to have seen another resident suffer neglect (Broyles, 2000). *Child abuse* can include "all types of physical and/or emotional ill-treatment, sexual mistreatment, neglect, negligence and commercial or other exploitation, which results in actual or potential harm to the child's health, survival, development or dignity" (World Health Organization, 2014, n.p.). The World Health Organization (2014, n.p.) reports that one-quarter of all adults report that they experienced child abuse as a young person. We characterize the widespread mistreatment of young people and elders as youth oppression or adultism and elder oppression or ageism.

In this chapter, we discuss our approach, our rationale, and how we conceptualize youth oppression and elder oppression as a social justice issue. We discuss some legacies that provide a historical context for our consideration of youth and elder oppression. Our discussion includes descriptions of manifestations of youth and elder oppression, both globally and in the United States, and provides a design for facilitating classes and workshops focused on understanding youth oppression and elder oppression in order to eliminate or transform these oppressions.

RATIONALE FOR ADDRESSING YOUTH AND ELDER OPPRESSION FROM A SOCIAL JUSTICE EDUCATION PERSPECTIVE

This discussion of youth oppression and elder oppression is based on assumptions that are embedded within and build upon key conceptual frameworks about oppression that are discussed in Chapter 4 of this text. These core concepts include an understanding of oppression as the manifestation of systemic inequalities organized around relationships of domination and subordination, the role of social identity categories as rationales for these relationships of inequality, and the hegemonic force of societal agreement and acceptance of relationships of domination and subordination based on advantages and disadvantages connected to social identities.

Based on these and other core concepts, we proceed from the assumption that ageism and adultism exist as cultural norms that inform and are reproduced by institutional policies and practices, and by individual relationships. We assume that youth oppression and elder oppression characterize U.S. society, similar to the ways in which racism, classism, sexism, or ableism also shape our social systems and play out at societal, institutional, and individual levels.

PREMISES THAT INFORM OUR APPROACH

In addition to assumptions about the institutional and cultural embeddedness of the marginalization and disadvantage experienced by youth and elders in the U.S., we also work from constructs about intersectionality, social constructionism, the normalization of mistreatment of young people and elders, and age as a social location through which other manifestations of oppression are experienced and internalized. Each of these constructs is defined below.

INTERSECTIONALITY

The experiences of both youth and elder oppression are mediated by other social identities, including race, gender, class, religion, ability, sexuality, and nationality. In addition to being devalued, excluded, or marginalized on the basis of young or old age, depending on other identities, young people and elders may be targeted by multiple combinations of racism, sexism, heterosexism, classism, ableism, transgender oppression, and religious oppression. Given their intersecting and multiple social identities, young people and elders will have different and unique standpoints through which they make meaning of and engage their life experiences as young people and as elders (Collins, 1990; D. E. Smith, 1987). For example, elders from upper-class backgrounds may be less likely to experience neglect in a nursing home. Owning-class white elders may be less likely to suffer the deprivations faced by poor elders targeted by racism, and may be more likely to receive life-saving and life-extending services than their poor counterparts.

The experiences of young people also differ based on intersecting social identities. Owning-class children, for instance, may be less likely to be followed in stores; middle-class white children may be less likely to face teacher assumptions about limitations of their intelligence. Young, white, middle- and upper-class students are more likely to attend schools with less security, more resources, and more flexibility when it comes to discipline. According to data released by the U.S. Department of Education, "nationally black girls were suspended *six times* more than white girls, while black boys were suspended three times as often as white boys" (Crenshaw, Ocen, & Nanda, 2015, p. 2). White boys are far less likely to be shot by police. Boys are not likely to be aborted on the basis of parental gender preference and are less likely to be sold into sexual slavery. All of these experiences are faced by some young people. Differing social identity group membership will determine which of these experiences a given young person is likely to face. Additional examples of specific intersections of oppressions will be discussed later in the chapter.

SOCIAL CONSTRUCTION, NOT BIOLOGY

We recognize and acknowledge the existence of different biological ages across the life cycle, from infancy to old age, along with "transformations in the organization of intellectual abilities and their underlying cognitive processes across the lifespan" (Li, Lindenberger, Hommel, Aschersleben, Prinz, & Baltes, 2004, p. 5). Learning to color inside the box, drive a car, or process higher-order questions occurs at different periods of development. While each age period has its own developmental tasks, according to developmental psychologists, "children show variations in intellectual abilities at different ages and some adults remain cognitively fit into old age while others show cognitive decline" (Baltes,1997, p. 27). Further, abilities shown by people at different ages across the lifespan may differ across societies. Rogoff (2007), for instance, describes tasks performed by children in different societies—such as four-year-old Kaware'ae children in Oceania skillfully cutting fruit with a machete, and three-year-old Efa children in Zaire taking care of younger siblings—that are considered inappropriate or prohibited to young people their age in western societies. Elders remain in charge of the extended household in some societies, but have a more marginalized role in others.

While humans experience developmental commonalities across the lifespan, conceptions of role, place, and appropriate behavior for people in different age groups, along with conceptions of what power they are to exercise and the nature of their participation in the social, political, and economic life of society, are socially constructed. These socially constructed roles and expectations for age-based groups vary in any given society across time, based, in part, on the needs of that society—for example, the needs of contemporary society to have children in school and not in a largely mechanized workplace. They also vary in the same time period across different societies.

Being young and growing old are realities that exist in our physical world. The mistreatment and denial of opportunities to young people and elders on the basis of age are primarily a product of our cultural, social, economic, and political world (Schieffelin & Ochs, 1986). Being young and growing old do not constitute a biological or developmental justification for exclusion, devaluation, powerlessness, and limitation of participation in society.

NORMALIZATION OF MISTREATMENT OF YOUNG PEOPLE AND ELDERS

The oppression of young people and elders is normalized and rendered invisible by the 'ordinary everydayness' of their mistreatment. Rather than focus on an individual person's knowledge, skills, or competence, many laws, policies, and procedures rely on age as the sole criterion to determine what rights a person can exercise, what resources one can have access to, and what relationships one can enter. For example, age is used to determine when a person can vote, drive, and get married, as well as when one is required to retire and when one is eligible to receive social security. These laws normalize allocating participation in society solely on the basis of age, rather than on some combination of individual circumstance.

The ethics of age-based rationing of medical care (Dey & Fraser, 2000), including life-saving services such as whether to resuscitate or not, whether to provide oxygen or transfusions, or extending medical care, such as organ transplants and dialysis, has been the focus of debate in the medical community (Debolt, 2010, Teutsch & Rechel, 2012). In their discussion of "Principles for allocation of scarce medical interventions," Persad, Wertheimer, and Emanuel (2009) recommend what they call the "complete lives system—which prioritizes younger people" (p. 2). Though such a system meets the authors' ethical framework, their discussion helps to normalize the idea of withholding medical care on the basis of age alone. Jokes, humor, and ridicule of young people and elders, commonly communicated by talk show hosts and greeting cards, not only normalize negative perceptions about and mistreatment of young people and elders, but make it a laughing matter.

AGE AS A SOCIAL LOCATION WHERE MANIFESTATIONS OF OTHER OPPRESSIONS ARE EXPERIENCED AND INTERNALIZED

Social justice education (SJE) and socialization theory contend that primary socialization of humans occurs when we are young. When we are born, "all the mechanics, assumptions, rules, roles, and structures of oppression are already in place and functioning" (Harro, 2013, p. 47). Though no human is born with attitudes and behavior patterns that reproduce and maintain systems of mistreatment on the basis of social identity, starting at birth, we learn those attitudes and behaviors through the socialization process (Harro, 2013, p. 47).

Few young people have the information, resources, or tools of analysis to contest, challenge, or resist the racism, religious oppression, sexism, classism, and other manifestations of oppression that are encountered, witnessed, or experienced when we are young. Since socialization into society is one of the primary life tasks of youth, and socialization includes learning the attitudes and behaviors that reproduce and maintain systems of mistreatment based on social identity, the experience of being a young person includes internalizing the attitudes and behaviors that are the defining features of all manifestations of oppression (Bell, 2010). In this way, young people both experience youth oppression while at the same time occupying the social location in which the defining features of all manifestations of oppression are internalized. Young people are both learning how to act out oppression, both dominant and subordinate roles, while occupying the social location of subordinate as young people.

KEY TERMS AND CORE CONCEPTS

We define youth oppression and elder oppression as the systematic subordination and mistreatment of young people and elders based on age through the restriction and denial of opportunities to exercise social, economic, and political power. Youth and elder oppressions both include restricted access to goods, services, and privileges of society, along with loss of voice and limited access to participation in society. The subordination of young people and elders is supported by institutional structures and practices of society, networks of laws, rules, policies, and procedures, along with the attitudes, values, and actions of individuals that combine to ensure the subordinated status of members of these socially constructed identity groups. Young people and elders are marginalized and excluded by practices that give middle-aged adults the power to act on and for them, often without their agreement or consent (Bell, 2010; Butler; 1969; Cannella, 1997; DeJong & Love, 2013; Jenks, 1996).

Conceptual frameworks for this discussion of youth and elder oppression are discussed extensively in Chapters 1 and 4 of this volume. Here, we relate the discussion of Memmi's (2000) criteria for oppression; Young's (1990) *Five Faces of Oppression*; and Hardiman, Jackson, and Griffin's (2007) discussion of levels and types of oppression, specifically to an examination of youth and elder oppression. In addition, we use Love's (2000) *Developing a Liberatory Consciousness* as a framework for considering strategies for ending oppression and the development of liberation movements.

MEMMI'S CRITERIA FOR OPPRESSION

Memmi (2000, p. xvii) describes four distinct criteria for oppression: (a) an "insistence on a difference, real or imaginary"; (b) imposing a "negative valuation" on those differences, (c) generalizing the negatively valued differences to the entire group; and (d) using the generalized negative valuations to justify and legitimize hostility and aggression against that group. Youth oppression and elder oppression share each of these four criteria.

Developmental theorists agree that humans differ, in physical as well as in mental and emotional development, across the lifespan (Li, Lindenberger, Hommel, Aschersleben, Prinz, & Baltes, 2004). These developmental differences are considered natural and normal. This discussion examines the "negative valuations" imposed by society as fixed social categories on the two ends of the age spectrum, youth and old age, the way those negative valuations are generalized to the entire group, and then used to rationalize and justify disadvantaged status for members of these two groups. Negative assumptions and valuations about the physical and mental capacities of young people (DeJong, 2014) and elders (Palmore, Branch, & Harris, 2005), assumptions about their inadequate knowledge or diminished intelligence (Calasanti & Slevin, 2001; Nelson, 2002), and assumptions about their capacity to make decisions regarding their own lives, arc generalized to the group as a whole and used to rationalize mistreatment and disadvantaged status.

For example, we noted earlier the variations in intellectual abilities demonstrated by children, adults, and elders (Baltes, 1997). Research has shown, for instance, that while some elders show cognitive decline, many elders remain "cognitively fit into old age" (Baltes, 1997, p. 370). When the cognitive decline of some elders is generalized to the entire group, this can become the basis for mandatory retirement laws that interrupt viable and gainful employment for all elders based on age, rather than on an individual elder's fitness to continue work. The massive increase in Equal Employment Opportunity Commission (EEOC) cases on age discrimination in the U.S. workplace reflects the growing impact of negative attitudes about elders' capacity for effective workplace participation (Winerip, 2013).

Similarly, "Must be 18" (MB18) policies restrict the entry and unsupervised participation of young people at shopping malls across the United States (Russell, 2005, p. A1). According to the mall manager at the Ingleside Mall in Holyoke, Massachusetts, "Just the fact that they're [young people], they are perceived by some people [adults] as intimidating. It might cause you [adults] to leave, or not shop in stores you [adults] want to shop in" (Russell, 2005, p. A1). Some young people have undoubtedly behaved inappropriately in a mall, as have some adults. Generalizing the inappropriate behavior of some young people to the entire group, and creating policies based on that generalization, is one example of the effect of negative assumptions and valuations on the lives of young people (Males, 2004).

YOUNG'S FIVE FACES OF OPPRESSION

Exploitation, Marginalization and Powerlessness

The Five Faces of Oppression discussed by Young (1990)—exploitation, powerlessness, marginalization, cultural imperialism, and violence—have also been discussed in greater detail in Chapters 1 and 4 of this volume, and applied in other chapters in this volume. Child labor and financial abuse of elders through misappropriation of their assets are examples of *exploitation* of young people and elders. Many young people and elders experience *marginalization* as well as *powerlessness* in their exclusion from participation in decision-making about policies and programs affecting their lives. Most young people, for instance, are marginalized from participating in decision-making about teacher and staff hiring, curricular standards, or their own daily schedule. Some states allow young people to state a parental custodial preference in divorce cases, and some do not. In some states, the law stipulates that "When a child is under the age of 14, the court must first determine whether or not it is in the child's best interest to listen to him or her" (Farzad, 2013). Many elders are excluded from participating in decisions about housing and day-to-day living arrangements, medical care, and their own financial affairs and undertakings.

Health care providers and others who direct questions about an elder's health and life to the elder's adult child, instead of to the elder, contribute to the *marginalization* of elders (Hart, 2012). Media addressed to "those who have an older loved one" reinforce this sense of marginalization. When the 'travel and dining out junk mail' is replaced by ads for 'hearing aids and funerals,' many elders experience the message that they are no longer sought after for active participation in mainstream society (Barnhart & Peñaloza, 2013).

Cultural Imperialism

Cultural imperialism centralizes the language, dress, music, and values of middle-age adults as the norm, and devalues these same aspects of young people's and elder's cultural practices. For example, cultural imperialism supported the dismissal and marginalization of rap music, b-boy dress, graffiti art, and other forms of hip hop culture (Dyson, 2007) until it became a financially lucrative phenomenon (Wyner, 2014). Many adults continue to express ignorance of and disdain for hip hop, the music and culture of young people.

Cultural imperialism is also manifested in the way "our society devalues old age" (Barnhart & Peñaloza, 2013, p. 1134). According to a study published by researchers at the University of Oregon, "Almost every stereotype we associate with being elderly is something negative" (Barnhart & Peñaloza, 2013, p. 1136). "When people in their 80's and 90's exhibited characteristics that society tends to associate with people who are not old, such as being aware, active, safe, or independent, they were viewed and treated as not old" (Barnhart & Peñaloza, 2013, p. 1136). Rather than being treated as an elder who is mentally alert, independent, active, and fully capable, they are treated as though they are not elders. This is similar to telling an effective, competent female leader that they 'don't act like a woman,' or an effective, competent African Heritage leader that they 'don't act black.'

Violence

Violence in the form of physical abuse is tolerated through the inferior health care experienced by many elders, often with life-threatening consequences (Acierno, Hernandez, Amstadter, Resnick, Steve, & Muzzy, 2010; National Center on Elder Abuse, 1998). Recent studies on elder abuse found that "7.6%–10% of study participants experienced abuse in the prior year" (Lifespan of Greater Rochester, Inc., Weill Cornell Medical Center of Cornell University, & New York City Department for the Aging, 2011, n.p.). Similarly, violence against young people in the form of corporal punishment in the home is lawful in all states in the United States (End Corporal Punishment, 2014). The use of corporal punishment in schools is approved in 36 states (End Corporal Punishment, 2014).

DEVELOPING A LIBERATORY CONSCIOUSNESS

A *liberatory consciousness* (Love, 2010) requires that people who are targeted by oppression be at the center of efforts to transform the oppression that imposes limits on their lives. Liberatory consciousness includes the idea that examining and understanding oppression is a first step in envisioning how to dismantle oppression. Four dimensions for developing a liberatory consciousness are identified by Love (2010): *Awareness, analysis, action, and allyship/accountability*. Developing *awareness* about the processes through which oppressions function supports *analysis* of norms, policies, behaviors, and practices that maintain youth and elder oppression. This analysis provides an informed basis for determining *action* that can be taken to challenge and transform these and other oppressions. Developing a liberatory consciousness can support thinking about how to build better and more *accountable allyship* with young people and elders. In the following section, we situate youth and elder oppression within their historical contexts in order to help readers to increase their awareness of these oppressions.

HISTORICAL CONTEXTS AND LEGACIES

The average age for a first marriage in Colonial America was 12–14 for a girl and 16–18 for a boy. A girl who reached her 20s unmarried was considered a social pariah (Taylor, 2002). In 2015, an online column about "The Childbearing Years" suggests that while teenagers are biologically capable of becoming pregnant, they are not "emotionally or mentally capable of caring for a baby" (Loop, 2015). These differing views of maturity reflect changing conceptions of childhood over time and across societies. Similarly, notions of old age have ranged from old at 25 during the Roman Empire (Rosenberg, 2014), to old at 30 at the turn of the last century (Taylor, 2002), to an average worldwide life expectancy of 78 in the 21st century (United Nations Department of Economic and Social Affairs, 2011). In addition to the biological realities of age across the lifespan, a range of factors helped to transform societal conceptions of youth and old age.

In this section, we explore four historical contexts and legacies that have influenced current conceptions of what constitutes 'young people' and 'old people,' and their role and place in contemporary society. Connections between the development of modern European colonialism and current constructions of childhood (Cannella & Viruru, 2004; DeJong, 2014), the industrial revolution (Hendricks, 2004), the printing press and the advent of modern and mandatory public schooling (Rogoff, 2003), and the growing elder population (Hendricks, 2004) are explored.

CONNECTIONS BETWEEN MODERN EUROPEAN COLONIALISM AND CURRENT CONSTRUCTIONS OF CHILDHOOD

In this chapter, we build on the work of scholars who have examined the parallels between concepts of modern European colonialism and contemporary constructions of childhood (Burman, 2007; Cannella & Viruru, 2004; Nandy, 1983). We explore evidence that principles of colonialism both borrowed from and influenced principles of human development, thereby contributing to current constructions of childhood.

The period of Western European colonial exploration and expansion—between the 16th and 19th centuries—was also a period during which childhood was conceptualized as "uncivilized" or "savage." Only adults were civilized, as the paradigm for "advanced" (Western) societies. The conceptual parallel between young people within families to peoples dependent upon colonizers was useful to colonizers and adults alike (Cannella & Viruru, 2004). The language of infantilization, using notions of biological development, rationalized the construction of hierarchical relationships of domination and subordination, evident in both colonialism as well as in contemporary constructions of childhood (Burman, 2007; Cannella & Viruru, 2004; Nandy, 1983). Some popular conceptions of childhood suggest that young people, in general, are biologically incapable of making decisions about their own bodies and lives because they are young people. These same notions hold that adults can think better and make better decisions because of their age, rather than because they have access to more information and experience on which to build a decision.

European colonial discourse in the 17th and 18th centuries that judged Africans and Native Americans as both childlike and savage was used to justify removing them from their land, taking their resources, and establishing European domination over them (Lakota People's Law Project, 2013; Swain, 2009). That they were cast as childlike justified colonial management and control; that they were cast as savage justified cultural and physical genocide. Native Americans have been subjected to genocide, and placed in the restricted environments of reserves controlled by the U.S. government. On the basis of their presumed 'child-likeness,' Africans were denied the right to self-government, governed through colonies, and sold into slavery. The infantilization of whole peoples, nations, and continents by imperial powers was used to justify the domination of those peoples, nations, and continents that were rendered as infants. Infantilization established and justified imperial powers as the mature, 'adult' power to dominate the economic, social, political, health, educational, and welfare policies and directions of the infantilized, subordinated nations and people.

Colonial discourse helped to firmly establish 'child' as a subordinated status in need of direction and control (Burman, 2007). Colonial discourse established 'childlike' as a pejorative term, indicating lack of sensibility, and the capacity for rational thinking. Fourteen-year-olds had been considered competent to marry and run a household until subsequent discourse held that young people are mentally and emotionally incompetent for such responsibilities.

This same judgment as 'child-like' is used to restrict self-determination and self-control for elders. For example:

> Researchers have documented the propensity . . . to use "baby-talk" (i.e., exaggerated tone, simplified speech, and high pitch) when speaking to [elders]. Physicians have been shown to condescend to and patronize older patients by providing oversimplified information or speaking to the family instead of the older patient.
>
> (Walker, 2010, n.p.)

This infantilization and rendering of elders as 'child-like' helps to justify their subordinated status.

INDUSTRIAL REVOLUTION

The European Industrial Revolution forced a transition from a rural, agrarian society to an urban, manufacturing society, and from skilled artisans and family commerce to machine production in factories. This had a profound effect on the role of and place for young people and elders in contemporary society. Work now took place in the factory instead of the home and community. Young people moved from work in the home and community to work in the new factories of the industrial revolution, where they were exploited (Thompson, 1968) and eventually excluded from wage-earning work (Freudenberger, Francis, & Clark, 1984; Hutchins & Harrison, 1911). Elders similarly moved from work as skilled artisans, who supervised the apprenticeship of others and passed on their knowledge and skills to apprentices and children, to marginalized participation in the workplace. This resulted in complete economic dependence of young people and elders on wage-earning adults for their livelihood. The child labor laws that resulted in the exclusion of young people from the factories did not focus on creating safe working conditions for everyone. Rather, these laws focused on the exclusion of children from the workplace and from wage-earning work. We also note that this exclusion of young people from the labor force was not universal. Young people were not excluded from farm work, and as recently as 2012, the U.S. Department of Labor withdrew proposed regulations that would have protected "child farmworkers from the most dangerous tasks" (Human Rights watch, 2014, n.p.). Many of those child farm workers are immigrants from Mexico and South America. This suggests that goals beyond child protection were served by these measures.

Elders experienced both restricted participation in the industrial workforce and diminution of their significance in society. The institutionalization and specialization of jobs requiring manual labor in factories replaced the role of skilled artisan once played by elders. This meant that elders were now excluded both from productive economic employment as well as from a valued social role in families and in the community.

IMPACT OF THE PRINTING PRESS AND MODERN MANDATORY PUBLIC SCHOOLING ON ROLE AND PLACE FOR YOUTH AND ELDERS

The invention of the printing press had profound effects on role and place for both young people and elders in contemporary society. With printed materials, the culture, tradition and history of a society could be learned in school, along with the basics required for future employment (Branco & Williamson, 1982). Most of what people needed to know could now be included in books.

Elders were no longer needed for the once treasured "knowledge they have acquired from their ancestors, through social learning" and the "key role [they played] in the evolution of [the] social species" (Coe & Palmer, 2009, p. 5). Literate societies were no longer dependent on the presence of an elder or their oral traditions for records of the culture and history of the group. The development of nuclear families and an accompanying rise in nursing homes, resulted in increased isolation of elders from active participation in society (Nelson, 1982; Stearns, 1986).

The printing press made modern public schooling possible (Rubinstein, 1999). According to Rogoff (2007), the exclusion of young people from factories made public schooling mandatory. Excluded from active participation in the workforce, modern society had the problem of finding a place for young people until they could enter the workplace from which they had been excluded. Schools serve a social and civic function. They are primary agencies of socialization, teaching young people what they need to know to participate effectively and appropriately in modern society. Schools also provide a societally approved placement for young people while adults earn wages at work (Rogoff, 2007, pp. 8–9).

GROWING ELDER POPULATIONS

Globally, there is a much larger population of elders than ever before. A decline in open warfare in certain parts of the world, combined with advances in modern medicine, have dramatically extended old age (Hendricks, 2004). Life expectancy has increased from "old" at 30 in 1900, to a current worldwide life expectancy of 78 nearly a century later (United Nations Department of Economic and Social Affairs, 2011). Elders are a dramatically larger percentage of the population in all parts of the world (National Research Council, 2012; Ortman, Velkoff, & Hogan, 2014). This shift in the age of the global population is, according to a report issued by the United Nations (UN) in 2014, " a process without parallel in the history of humanity" (Gacov, 2007, n.p.). By the middle of the 21st century, the global population under 15 will be outpaced by people over age 60 for the first time in human history (Gacov, 2007). The implications of this shift and the consequences for elders and for young people are only beginning to be understood.

In addition to the economic and social displacement of elders in family and community, other potential consequences for elders include rising costs of health care, more limited availability of people to provide care taking, more limited availability of trained health care workers, increasing percentages of national budgets required to pay for elder health-related costs, limited budgets to pay pensions and living costs, and generally fewer workers to do the work of society and pay taxes to fund our society's continually extending old age.

MANIFESTATIONS OF YOUTH OPPRESSION AND ELDER OPPRESSION

Oppression directed toward young people and elders can occur at individual, institutional, societal, and cultural levels; it can be conscious or unconscious, and intentional or unintentional (Hardiman, Jackson, & Griffin, 2007). Laws, policies, and individual behavior that make age the sole basis for determining how to treat an individual young person or elder reflects societal/cultural and individual beliefs about the capacities of young people and elders. Young people and elders experience individual-level oppression when they are excluded from making decisions about their own lives. The exclusion of young people from decision-making about teachers and staff hiring, curricular standards, or their own daily schedule is an example of exclusion at both individual and institutional levels. State laws stipulating that a court must determine whether a child will be "listened to" in determining the custodial parent in a divorce case (Farzad, 2013) is one example of exclusion of young people from participation in decisions affecting their lives at the institutional level. Excluding elders from participation in decision-making about their financial affairs has been accompanied by financial exploitation of elders reaching "epidemic proportions" in the U.S., according to a recent report issued by the U.S. Government Accounting Office (GAO, 2012). According to Bush (2013), financial exploitation of elders in the U.S. is estimated to cost nearly $3 billion per year.

MANIFESTATIONS OF YOUTH OPPRESSION

We note that even when young people make sound and informed decisions, they are described as adult-like, rather than as rational, capable young people. Similarly, when middle-age adults consistently fail to engage in rational, productive behavior, the prevailing societal attitude characterizes that behavior as childish, rather than as irrational, non-productive adult behavior.

John Bell points out that attitudes, beliefs, policies, and behaviors can be considered oppressive if they:

involve a pattern of consistent disrespect and mistreatment and have any of the following effects on young people:

- An undermining of self confidence and self esteem
- An increasing sense of worthlessness
- An increasing feeling of powerlessness
- A consistent experience of not being taken seriously
- A diminishing ability to function well in the world
- A growing negative self concept
- Increasing destructive acting out
- Increasing destructive acting in (getting sick frequently, developing health conditions, suicide, depression)
- Feeling unloved and unwanted

(Bell, 1995, n.p.)

Bell also identifies some common statements that reflect disrespect toward young people:

- You're so smart for 'your age'.
- Act your age.

- Children should be seen and not heard.
- What do you know, you're just a kid!
- Do as I say, not as I do.
- You'll understand it someday, just you wait.
- When are you going to grow up.
- Don't touch that, you'll break it.
- As long as you are in my house, you'll do it.
- You're being childish.
- Don't ever yell at your mother like that.
- You are too old for that.
- You're not old enough.
- What do you know; you haven't experienced anything.
- It's just a stage. You'll outgrow it.

(Bell, 1995, n.p.)

These negative attitudes and beliefs about young people, held by adults and which intersect youth oppression with other forms of oppression, can have harmful, sometimes devastating consequences for young people. Here are some examples resulting from the unchecked power of adults to act out and enforce their negative attitudes and behaviors toward young people:

- A Brooklyn school administrator demanded that a student "eat off the floor" ("Parents of Joel Robinson," 2014).
- A Dallas judge determined that a 14-year-old girl who was sexually assaulted was not a victim because she wasn't a virgin (Emily, 2014).
- Police arrested, handcuffed, and jailed a kindergartner who had a tantrum in school ("Ga. police arrest, handcuff kindergartner for tantrum," 2012).
- A 17-year-old rape victim committed suicide after officials at her Canadian high school ignored evidence that she had been raped ("Rehtaeh Parsons suicide," 2013).
- A teacher in China ordered a ten-year-old student to jump (to his death) from the 30th floor for failure to complete an assigned task (Thomas, 2013).

The school-to-prison pipeline is indicative of widespread negative societal attitudes toward young people as a group, especially young people of color (Rethinking Schools, 2011). This is demonstrated by the reality that since 2002, state budgets for prisons grew twice as fast as budgets for education (Mitchell & Leachman, 2014). It is demonstrated by the recent trend in schools to look more and more like prisons, particularly those schools attended by poor, working-class, and young people of the Global Majority (Hadi-Tabassum, 2015). It is demonstrated in the treatment of youth as criminals or potential criminals whose behavior must be watched, controlled, and regulated (in the name of protecting students) with zero-tolerance policies and procedures, school-based arrests, exclusions and expulsions, locker searches, and unregulated interrogation. At one Chicago high school, large numbers of students were arrested following massive locker searches. The substantial majority of those teens were arrested for possession of beepers or phones (Mitchell & Leachman, 2014). It is further reflected in the data about the widespread police killing of young black boys with apparent impunity (Gabrielson, Jones, & Sagara, 2014).

This *power-over* attitude is apparent in a few additional examples of institutional, societal, and cultural oppression toward young people:

- Discrimination in hiring people for being "too young" or "inexperienced";
- Programs designed by adults for young people without young people's input;

- Isolation of children and youth away from adults;
- Use of language that does not allow youth to easily understand what is being done to them;
- Adults evaluate young people, yet young people rarely get to evaluate adults in a similar way;
- Students are forced by law to attend schools that may not be effective;
- Classroom learning too often relies on adults as the sole holders of knowledge;
- Decisions about students, including learning topics, activities, punishments, budgeting, and teaching methods are routinely made without student input;
- Adults routinely grade students without giving equal weight to students' perspectives on their own academic achievement;
- Double standards in treatment, including the belief that when teachers yell at students, they are controlling classrooms; when students yell at teachers, they are creating an unsafe learning environment.

MANIFESTATIONS OF ELDER OPPRESSION

In *Ageism: Another Form of Bigotry*, Butler (1969) describes some negative societal attitudes and beliefs about old people:

> As a group, older people are categorized as rigid in thought and manner, old fashioned in morality and skills. They are boring, stingy, cranky, demanding, avaricious, bossy, ugly, dirty, and useless. . . . Old men become geezers, old goats, gaffers, fogies, coots, gerries, fossils, and codgers, and old women are gophers, and geese. A crone, hag or witch is a withered old woman.
>
> (Butler, 1969, p. 243)

These stereotypes and myths reflect societal attitudes of dislike, disdain, distaste, disrespect, and result in "scorn, subtle avoidance, and discriminatory practice in housing, employment, pension arrangements, health care, and other services" (Butler, 1969, p. 244).

The consistent experience of inferior health care (Acierno, Hernandez, Amstadter, Resnick, Steve, & Muzzy, 2010; National Center on Elder Abuse, 1998) is a major manifestation of elder oppression. Life-supporting and life-extending medical procedures, including transplants of organs, are sometimes withheld from elders on the basis of negative decisions about the usefulness and value of elder lives. Recent "guidelines from the International Society for Heart and Lung Transplantation caution against lung transplants for those over 65" (Span, 2013). Cervical disc disease is experienced by many elders. Spinal fusion is the traditional therapy for cervical disc disease, and results in loss of mobility of the neck and lower spine. The U.S. Food and Drug Administration has approved the use of lumbar artificial disc replacement (LADR) therapy as a treatment that both provides relief and retains mobility. Nevertheless, Medicare will only approve coverage for spinal fusion, the traditional, and less effective remedy. According to the Medicare website, "the Centers for Medicare and Medicaid Services (CMS) has found that LADR . . . is not reasonable and necessary for the Medicare population over 60 years of age; therefore, LADR . . . is non-covered for Medicare beneficiaries over 60 years of age" (Centers for Medicare and Medicaid Services, n.d., n.p.). The desire of elders, like other members of the population, to retain their flexibility and mobility, is deemed neither reasonable nor necessary by Medicare. This disproportionately impacts elders who can't afford private health insurance.

Elders, for example, experience persistent discrimination in the workplace (AARP, 2012). Elders experience a variety of financial targeting schemes, including predatory lending practices and disproportionate targeting of elders for reverse equity and other mortgage schemes designed to prey on elders' fears about financial viability in their final years. With the exception of a few wealthy white men who are regarded as more distinguished as they age, most elders are rendered invisible throughout society on all levels. When aging is referred to in advertising, it is to describe what everyone (especially women) is supposed to fear, to avoid at all costs, and to "reverse" if signs of aging appear. Advertisements urging us to fight back against aging are indicators of macro-level negative societal attitudes toward aging.

The invisibility of elders can have devastating consequences, especially in emergency situations. Evacuations of dogs and cats occurred within 24 hours after the September 11, 2001, attack on the World Trade Center in New York City (Butler, 2009). Elders and people with disabilities were abandoned in their apartments "for up to seven days before ad hoc medical teams arrived to rescue them" (Butler, 2009, p. 41). During the devastation of the Katrina disaster in New Orleans, elders suffered from delayed rescue efforts, and some elders were injected "with lethal doses of drugs" by their doctors to hasten their death (Fink, 2009).

On the societal and cultural level, elder oppression is constant and generally taken as a given. Talk show hosts and people in public life, who would never intentionally tell a racist or sexist joke, think nothing of telling disparaging jokes about elders. From greeting cards to cartoons to social media, elder oppression is taken for granted. A research team conducted a content analysis of "each publicly accessible Facebook group that concentrated on older individuals" to determine whether "ageism was found to exist in social networking sites" (Levy, Chung, Bedford, & Navrazhina, 2014, p. 172). Eighty-four groups with a total of 25,489 members were analyzed. The team examined six "age stereotype-based categories" including: (1) excoriating the old, (2) infantilizing the old, (3) banning the old from public activities, (4) nursing homes, (5) cognitive debilitation, and (6) physical debilitation. They found that "the majority of Facebook group descriptions about the old focused on negative age stereotypes" (p. 172). The research team found that "41% of the descriptions referred to physical debilitation, 27% to cognitive debilitation, and 13% to both forms of debilitation" (p. 173). Seventy-four percent of the descriptions excoriated the old, described their uselessness to society, and some suggested that when they "pass the age of 69 should immediately face a fire (sic) squad" (p. 173). Thirty-seven percent of the groups advocated banning the old from public activities, 26% included infantilization of the old, and 10% disparaged elders in general, including those in nursing homes (p. 173). It is interesting to note that the creators of these descriptors were found to live on "five continents; 51% from North America, 32% from Europe, 8% from Asia, 8% from Australia, and 1% from Africa. 65% of the creators were men" (p. 174). As the percentage of the population who are elders in societies around the world rapidly increases, so will the need for the development of policy and programs that are free of the negative attitudes, beliefs, and language of elder oppression.

INTERSECTIONALITY WITH OTHER FORMS OF OPPRESSION

Young people and elders, among the most vulnerable in any society, must also contend with the oppression by which they are targeted because of their other identities , as noted in many of the examples already presented. A poor, black, disabled, lesbian, Muslim girl/old woman, will have a life experience that differs from her owning-class, white, able, heterosexual, Christian, male counterpart. They will both experience the effects of society's targeting of young people and elders, but will experience that targeting with different cushioning and mediating circumstances. Young people and elders are targeted by racism, sexism, heterosexism, classism, ableism, transgender oppression, and religious oppression, along with the common experience of being targeted by youth oppression as young people and by elder oppression in old age. These multiple and intersecting social identities result in differential experiences for individual youth and elders (Collins, 1990; D. E. Smith, 1987).

Young people of color living in low-income neighborhoods are more likely to be targeted by zero-tolerance policies that increase the probability that they will interact with law enforcement, and that they will have a police record for minor incidents that have historically been dealt with by staff in schools. Young people with disabilities suffer an even great chance of being mistreated and ending up in prison (ACLU, n.d.).

Elders with accumulated wealth experience ageing very differently than poor and working-class elders. A report on ageism compiled by the Gray Panthers (n.d.) explains, "In 2004, the U.S. Equal Employment Opportunity Commission (EEOC) ruled that employers can deny health benefits to retirees at age 65 without violating age discrimination laws" (p. 11). While the Affordable Care Act in most states now makes health care accessible to most people, what is "affordable" is not the same for everyone. Life-saving operations, expensive cancer medicine, organ replacement operations, and other high-cost treatments are more affordable and therefore more likely for wealthy elders than for low-income elders. Some cancer treatment options are not available in hospitals that serve low-income elders and elders of color. Elders without wealth can be, and often are, turned down for life-saving medical procedures for lack of funds (Nash, 2012). The Gray Panthers (n.d.) reported that:

> . . . 60 percent of adults over 65 do not receive recommended preventive services, and 40 percent do not receive vaccines for flu and pneumonia. They receive even less preventive care for high blood pressure, hypertension and cholesterol, conditions chronically affecting Black and poor elders.
>
> (Gray Panthers, n.d., p. 8)

The experience of young people outside the western world varies widely based on class, caste, and gender. Young girls are still subject to forced marriages in many parts of the world. The Parliament of Afghanistan passed legislation in 2014 to *protect* abusers involved in domestic violence and those who arrange child marriages (Human Rights Watch, 2014). According to the International Labor Organization, "over 215 million children between the ages of 5–17 are involved in child labor" (Goodweave, 2010, n.p.). In India, where 12% of children are estimated to be involved in child labor, "Some children are forced to weave up to 18 hours a day, often never leaving the confines of the factory or loom shed" (Goodweave, 2010, n.p.). Child trafficking, a huge global problem, is compounded by the reality that:

> . . . children trafficked into one form of labor may be later sold into another, as with girls from rural Nepal who are recruited to work in carpet factories but are then trafficked into the sex industry over the border in India.
>
> (Goodweave, 2010, n.p.)

Infant mortality rates in many parts of the world remain startling, with rates of over 100 deaths per 1,000 live births in Somalia, Mali, and Afghanistan. Over 60 countries have an infant mortality rate exceeding 25 (Gendercide Watch, 2001). In its assessment of conditions for children in different regions of the world, The International Labour Office (2013) notes that in South America, "The persistent challenges of widespread and extreme poverty, high population growth, the AIDS pandemic, recurrent food crises, and political unrest and conflict clearly exacerbate the problem" for young people (p. 26). Severe malnutrition, homelessness, and extreme poverty plague the lives of young people. More than 6,000 teens and children crossed the U.S. border from Mexico in the first four months of 2014, seeking to escape dire economic conditions and escalating violence in their home countries, according to *Business Insider* ("More than 6,000 children were sent back," 2014).

Similar conditions prevail in sub-Saharan Africa. In addition to extreme poverty, disease, displacement, homelessness, and loss of community, many young people are forced to serve as child soldiers. Shirley Sirleaf Johnson, President of Liberia, describes the extreme brutalization that young people undergo when they are forced to become child soldiers (Johnson, 2009).

INTERNALIZED YOUTH AND ELDER OPPRESSION

Members of any group targeted by oppression internalize the messages that were developed by the dominant group to justify that oppression (Love, 2014). "Oppressive systems work most effectively when both advantaged and targeted group members internalize their roles and accept their positions in the hierarchical relationship between them" (Hardiman, Jackson, & Griffin, 2007, p. 44). Oppressive systems work because people are socialized to internalize the messages of domination and subordination that are necessary for them to play their part in the maintenance of the oppressive system. Freire (1970), Memmi (2000), Miller (1976), Love (2014), Rogoff (2007) and others have discussed the process by which members of subordinated groups internalize messages of domination and subordination, and the consequences of that internalization.

Young people and elders internalize the negative societal attitudes directed toward them and come to regard them as normal. Laws regulating age requirements for voting, holding office, receiving an education, and testifying in court; when and under what circumstances people can establish an independent domicile (unless they are poor, in which case they can live on the street with impunity); who can receive mortgage loans; and who can otherwise fully participate in the civil, social, economic, and political life of society are seen as normal and even necessary once youth and elder oppression is internalized. Both young people and elders internalize assumptions about the rightness of those who are mid-life adults to have more power and more resources, and to make decisions about their lives. Elders and young people act on the basis of these assumptions in their relationships with each other as well as in their relationships with members of the dominant group.

A key element of all internalized oppression is identification with the dominant group. Just as women often identify with men, and people of color often identify with white people, young people and elders will often identify with mid-life adults as the superior group. Encouraged and rewarded for enforcing youth oppression on other young people, young people act to keep each other in line:

> [Many young people] spend their entire childhood identifying with the perspective of adults . . . [and] feel that . . . other young people . . . actually deserve to be treated with disrespect . . . [Youth employ a variety of strategies] to dissociate themselves from other young people, trying to shed the negative status of childhood.
>
> (Bonnichsen, 2003, p. 2)

Similar to black people who may express greater respect and deference to black people who look, speak, and act more like white people, young people tend to accord respect on an age-based scale and act out the oppression on anyone weaker, with fewer resources, smaller, and especially anyone younger than themselves (DeJong & Love, 2013, p. 535). Older young people can give orders to younger people, who in turn can give orders to those younger, and so on down the age-based scale.

Identification with the dominant group is accompanied by collusion through behaviors that support the superiority of the dominant group. Elders, for example, are rewarded for their efforts to hold on to the appearance of middle age as long as they can. A multi-billion-dollar beautification/youth restoration industry supports them in this process. From hair dyes, which may be harmful to their health, to 'age defying serums,' to youth restoration spas and the age-old search for the fountain of youth, elders enact their internalization of society's contempt for aging and fear of getting old.

Young people learn from their own experience the conditions under which some groups of humans can be dominant over other groups of humans. They also internalize the attitudes and behaviors that accompany both subordinate and dominant status. Like members of any other targeted group, the quality of their survival depends on learning both sides of the oppression. Young people who learn to show appropriate deference and submission to parents, teachers, school administrators, police, and other authority figures, all of whom are adult, have a less troublesome experience than young people who don't 'mind their manners.' Internalizing the attitudes, beliefs, and behaviors of both roles of subordinate and dominant prepares young people for participation in those roles for the remainder of their lives. Childhood socialization helps people internalize the attitudes, beliefs, and behaviors required for effective participation in an oppressive society, whether called on to play the role of agent or target (Love, 2014).

Internalized oppression among elders often shows up as feelings of resignation and isolation. Elders may suffer depression stemming from internalized feelings of "loss of value, being a bother, worthlessness, feeling that they are unworthy of the caretaking of others, and the fear that they will one day be unable to take care of themselves" (DeJong & Love, 2013, p. 536). Both young people and elders internalize attitudes and behaviors of powerlessness, to not trust their own thinking, to give up their own voice and allow others to speak for them, and to allow others to make decisions on their behalf. Once the oppression is internalized, the perpetuation of the oppression is assured, for the subordinated groups will join with the dominant group to enforce and maintain the oppression.

MOVING TOWARD JUSTICE

Our goal for studying youth and elder oppression is the elimination of youth and elder oppression. The centrality of the voices and thinking of young people and elders from various social identity groups will broaden and enlarge our vision of a world without racism, sexism, classism, heterosexism, transgender oppression, ableism, and religious oppression. Intergenerational organizing and learning, where middle-aged people, elders, and young people share reflections and experiences about the impact of youth and elder oppression, can help shape the directions and scope of all liberation movements.

In many societies across the globe, many young people, elders, and their allies are actively challenging oppressive cultural attitudes and beliefs as well as individual and institutional policies and practices that maintain the oppression of young people and elders. They are developing policies, programs, and practices that enable young people and elders to contribute to their community and have real power in controlling their lives.

Youth oppression and elder oppression have likely always been challenged, and yet these movements have had different periods and levels of visibility. In the United States, elder oppression, or ageism, has been challenged by groups like the Gray Panthers, who began in 1970 by examining common experiences and problems faced by people in retirement (Gray Panthers, n.d.). The group members found that with their age also came an increased sense of freedom to speak openly about their experiences, and particularly about their opposition to the Vietnam War. The Gray Panthers focus their efforts on economic security, health care, civil rights/liberties, and political integrity for all people (Gray Panthers, n.d.). Though the American Association of Retired People (AARP) does not claim a liberation agenda, their efforts are focused on improving conditions in the lives of retired people who are most often elders.

Many young people, working with and supported by their adult allies, are working throughout the world to address young people's oppression. Indigenous youth in the United States are working to confront racism on reservations and in urban settings (Vena Ade Romero, Princeton University, at a panel at the conference "Beijing Plus 20 in NYC," March, 2015). Youthbuild-USA and Youth on Board are examples of youth-centered organizing to support young people's liberation. FIERCE is a membership-based organization committed to building the leadership and power of LGBTQ youth of color in New York City. Their mission states that they are an organization that works to develop:

> . . . politically conscious leaders who are invested in improving ourselves and our communities through youth-led campaigns, leadership development programs, and cultural expression through arts and media. FIERCE is dedicated to cultivating the next generation of social justice movement leaders who are dedicated to ending all forms of oppression.
>
> (FIERCE, n.d., n.p.).

In this organization, young people are at the center of addressing various forms of oppression that impact their lives, and they do so with the support and partnership of adults (and often young adults).

It is important to note some of the challenges faced by young people in organizing a liberation movement. A first challenge is that young people are taught to accept their mistreatment as a rite of passage, or something that is natural and normal. It is not easy to move from internalization of this perspective to organizing to challenge this perspective. Some adult researchers and activists work with young people in their local communities to address this challenge by creating space and organizing resources for young people to identify problems in their community, develop their own leadership, take action to transform problems, and reflect on this work to develop a vision for how their communities can thrive (Cammarota & Fine, 2008; Duncan-Andrade & Morrell, 2008; Tuck & Yang, 2013).

A second challenge is that young people often need the support of adult allies to organize resistance to adult mistreatment. Young people rarely have their own money or transportation, and they are forbidden to assume loans without an adult co-signer. They must say they are a certain age to have access to social media and electronic communication, which is a key organizing tool. Millions of people under ten years old have such accounts but do so illegally, or with the aid of an adult (Protalinski, 2011).

A third challenge of youth-based liberation movements is transiency in leadership. As young people grow older and are no longer members of this constituency group, they focus their attention on the challenges of being an adult. This sometimes precludes their continued involvement in youth liberation activities. Unlike other movements that can develop leadership over time, youth-based liberation movements often have a very short leadership trajectory.

Youth liberation work has been encouraged by the UN Declaration of the Rights of the Child (United Nations Cyber School Bus, 2014), and by the UN Conventions on the Rights of the Child. This treaty (1989) aims to protect "the civil, political, economic, social, health and cultural rights of children" (United Nations Human Rights, n.d., n.p.). Adopted by the UN because young people, globally, have not been adequately protected under the Universal Declaration of Human Rights, this treaty had been ratified by 194 countries as of 2009. The United States, Somalia, and a few other countries refuse to ratify the treaty because of the provision that "forbids the death penalty and life imprisonment for children." In addition, nations that ratify the treaty are subject to international law (Wikipedia, 2014, n.p.). Additional examples of groups working to address youth oppression and elder oppression can be found at http://www.routledge.com/cw/readingsfordiversity/s1/section9/.

Youth and elder liberation movements might benefit from analysis of the impact of the youth empowerment industry, and the elder protection industry, where middle-age adults receive a salary to tell young people how to be empowered, or how to protect and support elders. Youth liberation and elder liberation movements will be enhanced when young people and elders are paid for their intellectual labor in the same way that middle-aged adults are expected to receive compensation for their contributions. When middle-aged adults, elders, and young people work together to develop ways for young people and elders to be equal participants in every aspect of liberation movements, and when adults learn to follow the leadership of young people and elders, liberation movements for youth and elders will be enhanced. Globally, we can work together for a liberatory society.

SAMPLE DESIGN FOR TEACHING ABOUT YOUTH AND ELDER OPPRESSION

The design presented in this chapter aims to provide participants with an introductory overview and understanding of the oppression of youth and the oppression of elders. A number of the activities included in this design are based on an assumption that participants have already reviewed several SJE core concepts described in Chapters 1 and 4 of this volume, including the model of oppression, levels and types of oppression, social identities and social groups, the Five Faces of Oppression, definitions of oppression, and the Cycle of Socialization and Cycle of Liberation. We focus on helping participants develop an historical and conceptual understanding of youth and elder oppression at the individual, institutional, and cultural levels. We also include possibilities for taking action on youth and elder oppression in our personal lives, institutions, and communities.

This design, like other designs in this volume, uses four quadrants as a way to sequence learning goals, key concepts, and activities. The quadrants generally follow the sequence "What? So what? Now what?" We use the four-quadrant design model because it helps us keep the learning sequence in focus. It can easily be adapted to other modalities, such as short workshops or semester-long courses. After the overview of the four quadrants of the design, there are learning objectives and core concepts specific to each of the four quadrants, as well as brief descriptors of the activities. Actual instructions, facilitation notes, and handouts for each of these activities can be found on the Youth and Elder Oppression website that accompanies this volume. The chapter closes with a general discussion of pedagogical, design, and facilitation issues that we have found to be specific to teaching about youth and elder oppression.

Four-Quadrant Design for Youth and Elder Oppression

Quadrant 1: Conceptual Frameworks for Understanding Youth and Elder Oppression (3 hours)	**Quadrant 2: Individual Manifestations of Youth and Elder Oppression (4 hours)**
1. Envisioning a Liberatory Society (40 min) 2. Welcome, Introductions, & Course/Workshop Overview* (20 min) 3. Key Terms and Conceptual Frameworks for Understanding Youth Oppression and Elder Oppression* (1.5 hours) 4. Historical Context and Legacies: Colonialism & Capitalism (30 min)	1. Level and Types of Oppression: Examination of Individual-Level Manifestations (90 min) 2. Examination of Intersections of Individual-Level Youth and Elder Oppression with Other Forms of Oppression* (45 min) 3. Strategies for Change: Liberation at the Individual Level (75 min) 4. Developing a Liberatory Consciousness (30–45 min)
Quadrant 3: Institutional, Cultural, and Global Manifestations of Youth Oppression and Elder Oppression (4 hours)	**Quadrant 4: Liberation and Societal Transformation of Youth and Elder Oppression (4 hours)**
1. Examination of Institutional Youth and Elder Oppression (1.5 hours) 2. Societal, Cultural, and Ideological Manifestations of Youth and Elder Oppression* (30 min) 3. Examination of Intersections of Institutional-Level Youth and Elder Oppression and Global Connections* (2 hours)	1. Envisioning a Society Free of Youth Oppression and Elder Oppression (40 min) 2. Strategies for Change: Goal Progression Framework* (20 min) 3. Liberation Presentations and Closing the Workshop (3 hours)

* Optional activities and examples of how to flex activities for longer and shorter time frames are available on the website.

QUADRANT 1: CONCEPTUAL FRAMEWORKS FOR UNDERSTANDING YOUTH AND ELDER OPPRESSION

Learning Outcomes for Quadrant 1:
- Envision a society characterized by liberation and the elimination of ageism and adultism
- Define and describe youth oppression and elder oppression as manifestations of age-based oppression, and understand the common elements in the treatment of young people and elders as oppression
- Explore personal thoughts, beliefs, and feelings about ageism and adultism that contribute to the maintenance and perpetuation of ageism and adultism
- Identify and describe manifestations of individual, institutional, societal, and cultural manifestations of ageism and adultism, and ways in which they are internalized
- Examine the idea that our contemporary conceptions of young people and of elders are social constructions rooted in historical, social, and political forces rather than in biology

Key Concepts:
- Oppression
- Youth and elder social identities
- Socialization
- Liberation
- Colonialism
- Capitalism

Activities:
1. **Envisioning a Liberatory Society (40 min):** This opening activity allows participants to focus their attention on envisioning a society without youth oppression and/or elder oppression, before turning to historical and contemporary examples of youth and/or elder oppression.

2. **Welcome, Introductions, and Course/Workshop Overview (20 min):** This activity sets the tone; starts relationship-building, goal-setting, and developing community guidelines; and states the facilitators' assumptions about materials.
3. **Key Terms and Conceptual Frameworks for Understanding Youth Oppression and Elder Oppression (30 min):** This activity is a mini-lecture about oppression and age-related social identities using either the Five Faces of Oppression or the Common Elements of Oppression.
4. **Historical Context and Legacies: Colonialism and Capitalism (30 min):** This activity is an interactive lecture that introduces the following key points as they relate to youth oppression and elder oppression: Modern European colonialism, the European Industrial Revolution, the invention of the printing press, the development of public schooling, and the extension of old age.

QUADRANT 2—INDIVIDUAL MANIFESTATIONS OF YOUTH AND ELDER OPPRESSION

Learning Outcomes for Quadrant 2:
- Identify and describe manifestations of individual, institutional, societal, and cultural manifestations of ageism and adultism, and ways in which they are internalized
- Examine the notion that every human experiences adultism and faces the possibility of experiencing ageism
- Examine individual beliefs, attitudes, and assumptions about liberation and the creation of a society free of ageism and adultism
- Explore what young people and elders are doing to resist and transform youth oppression and elder oppression

Key Concepts:
- Individual manifestations and intersections of oppression
- Level and types of oppression, individual/interpersonal elder oppression, individual/interpersonal youth oppression
- Five Faces of Oppression (Young, 1990)
- Intersections with youth oppression and elder oppression: Sexism, racism, classism, ableism, heterosexism, religious oppression, transgender oppression, nationalism, linguicism, xenophobia
- Common Elements of Oppression (Pharr, 1988)

Activities:
1. **Level and Types of Oppression: Examination of Individual-Level Manifestations (90 min):** Review levels and types conceptual framework with a brief interactive lecture using examples of any type of oppression. Using a handout or the Powerpoint "Levels & Types" handout, have participants, in small groups, brainstorm, discuss, and plug in examples of youth oppression and/or elder oppression and then discuss in the large group.
2. **Examination of Intersections of Individual-Level Youth Oppression with Other Forms of Oppression (45 min):**
   a. **Option A: Young's Five Faces of Oppression:** Review Five Faces theory and have small groups complete a Five Faces handout focusing on youth oppression and/or elder oppression. This worksheet also focuses on intersections, including sexism, racism, classism, ableism, heterosexism, religious oppression, transgender oppression, nationalism, linguicism, and xenophobia.

b. **Option B: Pharr's Common Elements of Oppression:** In this activity, the option is to use Pharr's Common Elements of Oppression as a framework to examine intersections using one's own story, experiences, and social identities.

3. **Strategies for Change: Liberation at the Individual Level (75 min):** Using the Cycle of Liberation, have participants tell their own liberation stories from their own perspective across their own lifespan. Have them focus on individual-level transformation related to both youth oppression and elder oppression.

4. **Developing a Liberatory Consciousness (30–45 min):** Review the 4 A's of Developing a Liberatory Consciousness, including Awareness, Analysis, Action, and Accountability/Allyship. In pairs, have each person talk about where they see themselves in terms of developing a liberatory consciousness.

QUADRANT 3: INSTITUTIONAL, CULTURAL, AND GLOBAL MANIFESTATIONS OF YOUTH OPPRESSION AND ELDER OPPRESSION

Learning Outcomes for Quadrant 3:
- Identify, examine, and describe institutional, cultural, and global manifestations of youth oppression and elder oppression
- Identify and explore interconnections and linkages between youth and elder oppression and other manifestations of oppression
- Explore examples of youth oppression and elder oppression in a global context
- Apply one of two optional theoretical framework to generate examples of youth oppression and elder oppression
- Explore what young people and elders are doing to resist oppression of youth and elders

Key Concepts:
- Level and types of youth and elder oppression (institutional oppression, social oppression, cultural oppression)
- Violence
- Institutional power
- Norms
- Policies
- Stereotypes
- Intersections with youth oppression and elder oppression: Sexism, racism, classism, ableism, heterosexism, religious oppression, transgender oppression, nationalism, linguicism, xenophobia

1. **Examination of Institutional Youth and Elder Oppression (1.5 hours):** This is a group activity in which participants identify and analyze manifestations of youth and elder oppression in varied institutions of society.

2. **Societal, Cultural, and Ideological Manifestations of Youth and Elder Oppression (30 min):** In this brainstorm activity, participants identify and describe cultural forms in which oppression is manifested, such as media, humor, etc.
   a. **Option A: Oppression of Youth and Elders in Language and Communication Patterns:** Examine ways in which the oppression of youth and elders is expressed through language and communication patterns as examples of cultural oppression.
   b. **Option B: Youth Oppression and Elder Oppression in Humor (30 min):** Examine the range of attitudes and stereotypes that are communicated and perpetuated through humor.

3. **Examination of Intersections of Institutional-Level Youth and Elder Oppression and Global Connections (1–2 hours):** Examine intersections between youth and elder oppression and sexism, racism, classism, ableism, heterosexism, religious oppression, transgender oppression, nationalism, linguicism, and xenophobia on an institutional level.

   a. **Option A: Examination of Institutional Intersections through Media or Storytelling (1–2 hours):** Participants will watch selected clips from a film or will engage in a reading discussion and storytelling activity and will analyze the intersecting institutional, cultural, and global manifestations of youth and elder oppression.

   b. **Option B: Examination of Intersections and Global Connections (2 hours):** Participants work in groups to research examples of youth and elder oppression and intersecting oppressions in various countries and regions across the globe, and then share their findings with the class.

QUADRANT 4: LIBERATION AND SOCIETAL TRANSFORMATION OF YOUTH AND ELDER OPPRESSION

Learning Outcomes for Quadrant 4:
- Explore participants' conceptions of liberation, the characteristics of a liberatory society, and the strategies necessary to transform society toward liberation
- Identify and develop action strategies to eliminate youth oppression and elder oppression and contribute to the transformation of society
- Identify and analyze manifestations of internalized youth oppression and elder oppression
- Describe strategies for interrupting internalized ageism and internalized adultism
- Discuss the elements of a liberatory consciousness and how this might be applied to the elimination of youth oppression and elder oppression
- Develop a personal action plan aimed toward increasing participants' capacity and readiness to take action to eliminate youth oppression and elder oppression

Key Concepts:
- Internalized oppression
- Internalized youth oppression
- Internalized elder oppression
- Collusion
- Liberatory society
- Liberatory consciousness
- Transformation of society

Activities:
1. **Envisioning a Society Free of Youth Oppression and Elder Oppression (40 min):** This activity allows participants to extend and deepen their reflection on a society free of youth and elder oppression.
2. **Strategies for Change: Goal Progression Framework (20 min):** This activity looks at the importance of planning to start small and then go larger.
   a. **Option A: Spheres of Influence:** This activity supports a view of where one may be able to enact change in order to support planning action steps.
   b. **Option B: Personal Development Plan:** This activity is for moving forward with challenging/transforming youth oppression and elder oppression. It provides

participants the opportunity to examine "what I need to learn, heal, do" in order to move toward change goals.

3. **Liberation Presentations and Closing the Workshop (3 hours):** Conduct research in small groups and develop group presentations to share examples of movements and actions that challenge and transform youth and elder oppression on individual, cultural, and institutional levels. Participants will take into account global connection and intersections.

PEDAGOGICAL SEQUENCE AND FACILITATION ISSUES

The Youth and Elder Oppression design is organized into four quadrants. The activities presented in each of the four quadrants represent a sequence that begins by envisioning a non-oppression society, before introducing basic concepts and examining individual and institutional/social/cultural manifestations of the oppression. The fourth quadrant is focused on transformation and liberation. Considerations of liberation and transformation are presented at the beginning of the design and are included in each quadrant. The fourth quadrant brings together the visioning and reflections about transformation and liberation begun in Quadrant 1 with activities focused on individual personal development and action planning.

SEQUENCING AND LEVEL OF RISK

Depending on the characteristics of the participant group and the goals for the class or workshop, Quadrants 2 and 3 can be switched to focus first on institutional and cultural manifestations of oppression, and then transition to individual manifestations of youth and elder oppression. As noted in the level of risk discussion below, high-level risk activities should follow low-level risk activities. For risk-averse participants, beginning with individual manifestations of oppression, which often includes some degree of personal disclosure, might be experienced as high risk in the early phases of a class or workshop. In such cases, an analysis of institutional and cultural manifestations of oppression might be experienced as less personal, and therefore less risky.

The second sequencing of activities included in the design focuses on *level of risk*. Low-risk activities that require low-level participant disclosure or personal investment in learning outcomes are followed by activities that require higher levels of risk. The final quadrant returns to low-level risk activities. We recommend that this risk sequence be followed in all designs, whether a weekend workshop or a three-hour course. We do not generally recommend beginning or ending a workshop or class with high-level risk activities.

This design includes sequencing of activities that focus on *task and relationship along with a focus on content and climate*. Activities including introductions, goal setting, and guidelines; the early phenomenological listening exercises are designed to facilitate the development of a learning community characterized by safety, learner inclusion, and buy-in, and to help participants develop a sense of connection to other learners.

These activities help to *create a learning community* where participants feel comfortable acknowledging the edges of their current knowledge and awareness about youth oppression and the oppression of elders, and feel encouraged and supported to push against those limits. They are designed to interrupt the "culture of perfection" that grows out of typical schooling socialization, where the focus is on getting the right answer; the climate-setting and relationship-building activities are designed to support participant exploration and examination of new and unfamiliar ideas and concepts. While important for all learners, activities that are focused on creating connections between learners are especially important for the young people, young adults, and elders who participate in these classes and workshops. Such activities help to interrupt the internalized adultism and internalized ageism induced by schooling socialization, isolation, and the push to 'get the right answer.'

DESIGN AND SCHEDULE OF ACTIVITIES

The sequence of activities presented in this design can be the basis for a two-day workshop that includes 16 hours of instruction. A description of each activity is included on the website for this chapter that includes the goals for each activity. This allows for decisions about where each activity might fit in a weekend workshop or in a semester-long course. Instructors can select activities based on the specific goals and objectives for their course and the time frame to which they must adapt the activity.

However, for instructors who teach in a weekly class format, these sequences and activities can be adapted to a series of class meetings of two hours. A semester-long course that meets weekly or twice weekly will have different closure and summary needs than a weekend workshop format. The level of risk for most of the activities included in this design are assessed as low to moderate. We would not recommend including a high-risk activity in a weekly design due to the lack of time to adequately process and debrief such an activity.

DEFINITIONS AND KEY CONCEPTS

Key concepts and definitions are included in each module. Definitions for all core concepts are included on the website. We are quite specific in this design to use the terms *youth oppression* and *the oppression of elders*, avoiding the tendency to use these two terms interchangeably. We encourage distinguishing between these two specific manifestations of oppression, while acknowledging that they are both manifestations of oppression focused on age-based identity groups.

We use the term *charades of empowerment* (DeJong, 2014, p. 229) to describe practices used by adults to give the appearance of empowerment to young people, but which retain power and decision-making in the hands of adults. Such activities are often designed to make young people "feel" that they are included in decision-making. However, such inclusion typically falls short of actual sharing of power with young people. We use the term *liberation* to describe both an individual state as well as a condition of society. We use the term *transformation* to describe the process of engagement that leads to the creation of a society characterized by liberation.

We begin and end this design with a focus on liberation and transformation. Our thesis is that we study oppression not for the sake of knowing about oppression, but as a basis for learning what we can about liberation and transformation. Our goal is for participants to share the goal of liberation and transformation as a framework for entering the learning process, and to consider how the content and activities throughout the class or workshop can assist the overall goal of liberation and transformation.

FACILITATION ISSUES

Several dynamics commonly arise when facilitating workshops and classes on youth oppression and the oppression of elders. We discuss some commonly occurring dynamics and issues below.

Managing Resistance

We have encountered three key forms of resistance in facilitating on youth oppression and the oppression of elders. Often, this resistance is based on centrally held values and beliefs. The first is resistance to the idea that the oppression of youth and the oppression of elders constitute legitimate social justice issues. Some of this resistance is rooted in the idea that society's current treatment of youth is appropriate based on the developmental levels of young people. Many people believe that it is appropriate to deny young people the opportunity to participate in decision-making along with excluding young people from participation in the economic life of society. Many adults who are annoyed by the behavior of some young people feel that it is appropriate to ban all young people from certain spaces, such as malls or community centers. Some adults believe that as long as young people are 'under their roof, they must abide by their rules.' Some participants resist the notion that such a belief constitutes oppression.

Similar resistance is sometimes encountered about the oppression of elders. Some adults believe that being required to "take care" of older people gives them the right to make decisions for those older people. Some also believe that they should be able to decide when and under what circumstances they should be able to take over decision-making about the lives of those elders.

We have suggested that, where possible, the inclusion of young people in the design of the workshop or class constitutes a useful contradiction to the oppression. This is offered as both content as well as a pedagogical strategy. Including young people in the design and facilitation of the class or workshop provides a visual and experiential statement about the significance of young people. It elevates the story of youth liberation from a theoretical discussion to a practical reality, where young people are not simply discussed but are included in the discussion. Some adults may offer resistance to the idea of being taught by a young person.

Our strategy for managing such resistance is to remind participants that our goal is to offer ideas for their consideration, and that they retain the right and authority to determine the content of their belief system. At the same time, we remind them that the content of every manifestation of oppression was held as true, correct, and appropriate at some point in time by a majority of society. For instance, it was commonly believed by a majority of people, including many women, that women and children were the property of men, and that men had the right to do as they wish to and with those women and children, including punish and beat them. We remind participants that some people, including entire societies, still hold such beliefs. In the United States, some proponents of such beliefs would enact legislation preserving the right of men to regulate the lives and bodies of women. It is useful to remind participants that whether a majority of people approve of a specific attitude, belief, or practice is not a useful test of whether or not such idea, belief, or practice constitutes oppression. We apply philosophical and conceptual frameworks, such as Young's Five Faces of Oppression or Memmi's four criteria for oppression, to analyze any set of ideas, beliefs, or practices to determine whether they meet our criteria for oppression.

Managing power dynamics

When the participant group is mixed across ages, it is useful to pay particular attention to the power dynamics occurring in the group across ages. The types of power dynamics in speaking and use of airtime that occur across gender, class, and race/ethnic identity group will also occur across age. In a group of adults and young people, adults will often fail to notice that they use the majority of air time and that young people may feel reluctant to speak up and share their opinions. Similarly, older people may expect to be excluded, ignored, or belittled, and they may stay quiet. It will be useful for the facilitator to give attention to the use of airtime, how the group responds to participant input across age ranges, as well as seating patterns in the group. Just as men may often appropriate ideas shared by women and present them as their own, middle-age adults may appropriate the ideas shared by young people and by elders and put them forward as their own. Facilitators are reminded to interrupt the tendency of groups to respond to ideas that men have repeated from the sharing of a woman as though the idea originated with the man. Similarly, facilitators are reminded to interrupt this group tendency to respond to young people's ideas only after they have been claimed and repeated by an adult.

Note

* We ask that those who cite this work always acknowledge by name all of the authors listed rather than either only citing the first author or using "et al." to indicate coauthors. All collaborated on the conceptualization, development, and writing of this chapter.

References

Acierno, R., Hernandez, M. A., Amstadter, A. B., Resnick, H. S., Steve, K., & Muzzy, W. (2010). Prevalence and correlates of emotional, physical, sexual, and financial abuse and potential neglect in the United States: The national elder mistreatment study. *American Journal of Public*, *100*(2), 292–297.

Adams, M. (2010). Introduction. In M. Adams, W. J. Blumenfeld, R. Castañeda, H. Hackman, M. Peters, & X. Zúñiga (Eds.), *Readings for diversity and social justice* (2nd ed., pp. 1–5). New York: Routledge.

American Association of Retired People (AARP). (2012). *Age discrimination in the workplace*. Retrieved from http://www.aarp.org/work/employee-rights/info-06–2012/age-discrimination-ma1788.html

American Civil Liberties Union (ACLU). (n.d.). School-to-prison pipeline. Retrieved from https://www.aclu.org/school-prison-pipeline

Baltes, P. B. (1997). On the incomplete architecture of human ontogeny: Selection, optimization, and compensation as foundation of developmental theory. *American Psychologist*, *52*(3), 366–380.

Barnhart, M., & Peñaloza, L. (2013). Who are you calling old? Negotiating old age identity in the elderly consumption ensemble. *Journal of Consumer Research*, *39*(6), 1133–1153.

BBC. (2014). Cleopatra (c. 69 BC–30 BC). Retrieved from http://www.bbc.co.uk/history/historic_figures/cleopatra.shtml

Bell, J. (1995). *Understanding adultism: A key to developing positive youth-adult relationships*. Retrieved from http://freechild.org/bell.htm

Bell, L. A. (2010). Theoretical foundations. In M. Adams, W. J. Blumenfeld, R. Castañeda, H. Hackman, M. Peters, & X. Zúñiga (Eds.), *Readings for diversity and social justice* (2nd ed., pp. 20–25). New York: Routledge.

Bell, L. A., Castañeda, R., & Zúñiga, X. (2010). Introduction. In M. Adams, W. J. Blumenfeld, R. Castañeda, H. Hackman, M. Peters, & X. Zúñiga (Eds.), *Readings for diversity and social justice* (2nd ed., pp. 59–63). New York: Routledge.

Bonnichsen, S. (2003). *Objections to calling adultism an oppression* [blog]. Retrieved from http://www.youthlib.com/notepad/archives/2003/12/objections_to_c.html

Branco, K. J., & Williamson, J. B. (1982). Stereotyping and the life cycle: Views of aging and the aged. In A. G. Miller (Ed.), *In the eye of the beholder: Contemporary issues in stereotyping* (pp. 364–410). New York: Praeger.

Brooks, A. C. (2015, Jan. 6). An aging Europe in decline. *The New York Times*. Retrieved from http://www.nytimes.com/2015/01/07/opinion/an-aging-europes-decline.html?smid=tw-share

Brooks, S., & Conroy, T. (2010). Hip-hop culture in a global context: Interdisciplinary and cross-categorical investigation. *American Behavioral Scientist*, *55*(1), 3–8.

Broyles, K. (2000). *The silenced voice speaks out: A study of abuse and neglect of nursing home residents*. A report from the Atlanta Long Term Care Ombudsman Program and Atlanta Legal Aid Society to the National Citizens Coalition for Nursing Home Reform. Atlanta, GA: Author.

Burman, E. (2007). *Developments: Child, image, nation*. New York: Routledge.

Bush, M. (2013, May 8). *Financial exploitation of the elderly difficult to detect*. WAMU 89.5 American University Radio. Retrieved from http://wamu.org/news/13/05/08/financial_exploitation_of_elderly_difficult_to_detect

Butler, R. N. (1969). Ageism: Another form of bigotry. *Gerontologist, 9*, 243–246.

Butler, R. N. (2009). *The longevity revolution: The benefits and challenges of living a long life*. New York: PublicAffairs.

Calasanti, T. M., & Slevin, K. F. (2001). *Gender, social inequalities and aging*. Walnut Creek, CA: AltaMira Press.

Cammarota, J., & Fine, M. (2008). Youth participatory action research: a pedagogy for transformational resistance. In J. Cammarota & M. Fine (Eds.), *Revolutionizing education: Youth in participatory action research in motion* (pp. 1–12). New York: Routledge.

Cannella, G. S. (1997). *Deconstructing early childhood education: Social justice & revolution*. New York: Lang.

Cannella, G., & Viruru, R. (2004). *Childhood and postcolonization: Power, education, and contemporary practice*. New York: Routledge Falmer.

Centers for Medicare and Medicaid Services. (n.d.). *National coverage determination (NCD) for lumbar artificial disc replacement (LADR)* (Publication Number 100-3, Manual Section Number 150.10). Retrieved from http://www.cms.gov/medicare-coverage-database/details/ncd-details.aspx?NCDId=313&ncdver=2&bc=AAAAQAAAAAAA&

Central Intelligence Agency. (n.d.). *The world factbook. Country comparison: Infant mortality rate*. Retrieved from https://www.cia.gov/library/publications/the-world-factbook/rankorder/2091rank.html

Coe, K., & Palmer, C. T. (2009). How elders guided the evolution of the modern human brain, social behavior, and culture. *American Indian Culture and Research Journal, 33*(3), 5–21.

Cohen, T. (2013, Oct. 1). U.S. government shuts down as Congress can't agree on spending bill. *CNN*. Retrieved from http://www.cnn.com/2013/09/30/politics/shutdown-showdown/

Collier, F. (1964). *The family economy of the working classes in the cotton industry, 1784–1833*. Manchester, UK: Manchester University Press.

Collins, P. H. (1990). *Black feminist thought: Knowledge, consciousness and the politics of empowerment*. New York: Routledge.

Crenshaw, K. W., Ocen, P., & Nanda, J. (2015). *Black girls matter: Pushed out, overpoliced and underprotected*. African American Policy Forum and Columbia Law School's Center for Intersectionality and Social Policy Studies. Retrieved from http://portside.org/2015–02–04/black-girls-matter-pushed-out-overpoliced-and-underprotected

Dakss, B. (2005, Apr. 25). Handcuffed 5-year-old sparks suit. *CBS News*. Retrieved from http://www.cbsnews.com/news/handcuffed-5-year-old-sparks-suit/

DeBolt, K. (2010). What will happen to Granny? Ageism in America: Allocation of healthcare to the elderly & reform through alternative avenues. *California Western Law Review, 47*(1), 127–172.

DeJong, K. (2014). *On being and becoming: An exploration of young people's perspectives of status and power* (Dissertation). University of Massachusetts, Amherst.

DeJong, K., & Love, B. (2013). Ageism & adultism. In M. Adams, W. J. Blumenfeld, R. Castañeda, H. Hackman, M. Peters, & X. Zúñiga (Eds.), *Readings for diversity and social justice* (3rd ed., pp. 470–474). New York: Routledge.

Dey, I., & Fraser, N. (2000). Age-based rationing in allocation of health care. *Journal of Aging and Health, 12*(511), 511–537.

Duncan-Andrade, J. M. R., & Morrell, E. (2008). *Art of critical pedagogy possibilities for moving from theory to practice in urban school*. New York: Peter Lang.

Dyson, M. E. (2007). *Know what I mean? Reflections on hip-hop*. New York: Basic Civitas Books.

Dyson, M. E. (2014, Sept. 17). Punishment or child abuse? *The New York Times*. Retrieved from http://www.nytimes.com/2014/09/18/opinion/punishment-or-child-abuse.html?_r=0

Emily, J. (2014, May 2). Judge says sexually assaulted 14-year-old 'wasn't the victim she claimed to be'. *The Dallas Morning News*. Retrieved from http://www.dallasnews.com/news/crime/headlines/20140501-judge-say-14-year-old-who-was-sexually-assault-wasn-t-the-victim-she-claimed-to-be.ece

End Corporal Punishment. (2014). *Current legality of corporal punishment*. Retrieved from http://www.endcorporalpunishment.org/pages/progress/reports/usa.html

Facebook. (2015). *Community standards*. Retrieved from https://www.facebook.com/community standards

Farzad, B. R. (2013). How is a child's preference and choice in custody determined? *Farzad Family Law*. Retrieved from http://farzadlaw.com/california-child-custody/childs-preference-custody-how-when-choose/

FIERCE. (n.d.). *About FIERCE*. Retrieved from http://www.fiercenyc.org/about

Fink, S. (2009). The deadly choices at Memorial. *The New York Times*. Retrieved from http://www.nytimes.com/2009/08/30/magazine/30doctors.html?pagewanted=all&_r=0

Freire, P. (1970). *Pedagogy of the oppressed*. New York: Seabury.

Freudenberger, H., Francis, J. M., & Clark, N. (1984). A new look at the early factory labour force. *Journal of Economic History*, 44(4), 1085–1090.

Ga. police arrest, handcuff kindergartner for tantrum. (2012, April 17). *CBS News*. Retrieved from http://www.cbsnews.com/news/ga-police-handcuff-arrest-kindergartner-for-tantrum/

Gabrielson, R., Grochowski Jones, R., & Sagara, E. (2014, Oct. 10). Deadly force, in black and white. *ProPublica: Journalism in the Public*. Retrieved from http://www.propublica.org/article/deadly-force-in-black-and-white

Gacov, D. (2007, Oct. 1). Aging Europe: The demographic crisis is the defining issue for the continent's future. *The Vienna Review*. Retrieved from http://www.viennareview.net/news/special-report/aging-europe

Gendercide Watch. (2001). *Case study: Female infanticide*. Retrieved from http://www.gendercide.org/case_infanticide.html

Goodweave. (2010). *Child labor quick facts*. As reported by the International Labour Organization (ILO) in *Accelerating action against child labor*. Retrieved from http://www.goodweave.org/child_labor_campaign/facts

Government Accountability Office (GAO). (2012, Nov.). *Elder justice: Strengthening efforts to combat elder financial exploitation*. Retrieved from http://www.gao.gov/products/GAO-13–140T

Gray Panthers. (n.d.). *Gray Panthers priority issues*. Retrieved from http://www.graypanthers.org/index.php?option=com_content&task=blogcategory&id=33&Itemid=83

Hadi-Tabassum, S. (2015). Why do some schools feel like prisons? *Education Week*. Retrieved from http://www.edweek.org/ew/articles/2015/01/28/why-do-some-schools-feel-like-prisons.html

Hardiman, R., Jackson, B., & Griffin, P. (2007). Conceptual foundations for social justice. In M. Adams, L. Bell, & P. Griffin (Eds.), *Teaching for diversity and social justice* (2nd ed., pp. 35–66). New York: Routledge.

Harro, B. (2013). The cycle of socialization. In M. Adams, W. J. Blumenfeld, C. Castañeda, H. W. Hackman, M. L. Peters, & X. Zuñiga (Eds.), *Readings for diversity and social justice* (3rd ed., pp. 45–52). New York: Routledge.

Hart, A. (2012, Nov. 12). How elderly go from being perceived as capable consumer to 'old person'. *Examiner.com*. Retrieved from http://www.examiner.com/article/how-elderly-go-from-being-perceived-as-capable-consumer-to-old-person

Hendricks, J. (2004). Public policies and age old identities. *Journal of Aging Studies*, 18(3), 245–260.

Human Rights Watch. (2014, Feb. 4). *Afghanistan: Reject new law protecting abusers of women*. Retrieved from http://www.hrw.org/news/2014/02/04/afghanistan-reject-new-law-protecting-abusers-women

Hutchins, B. L., & Harrison, A. (1911). *A history of factory legislation*. London: P.S. King & Son.

International Labour Office. (2013). *The ILO in Latin America and the Caribbean: Advances and perspectives*. Retrieved from http://www.ilo.org/Americas

Jenks, C. (1996). *Childhood*. New York: Routledge.

Johnson, S. S. (2009). *This child will be great: Memoir of a remarkable life by Africa's first woman president*. New York: HarperCollins.

Lakota People's Law Project. (2013). *Lakota child rescue project*. Retrieved from http://lakotalaw.org/lakota-child-rescue-project

Levy, B. R., Chung, P. H., Bedford, T., & Navrazhina, K. (2014). Facebook as a site for negative age stereotypes. *Gerontologist*, 54(2), 172–176.

Li, S. C., Lindenberger, U., Hommel, B., Aschersleben, G., Prinz, W., & Baltes, P. (2004). Transformations in the couplings among intellectual abilities and constituent cognitive processes across the life span. *Psychological Science*, 15(3), 155–163.

Lifespan of Greater Rochester, Inc., Weill Cornell Medical Center of Cornell University & New York City Department for the Aging. (2011). *Under the radar: New York State elder abuse prevalence study*. New York: Authors.

Loop, E. (2015). *What are the childbearing years?* Retrieved from http://www.ehow.com/info_8105014_childbearing-years.html

Love, B. (2010). Developing a liberatory consciousness. In M. Adams, W. J. Blumenfeld, R. Castañeda, H. Hackman, M. Peters, & X. Zúñiga (Eds.), *Readings for diversity and social justice* (2nd ed., pp. 470–474). New York: Routledge.

Males, M. (2004, Feb.). Coming of age in America. *Youth Today*. Retrieved from http://home.earth link.net/~mmales/

Memmi, A. (2000). *Racism*. Minneapolis: University of Minnesota Press.

Miller, J. B. (1976). Domination and subordination. *Toward a New Psychology of Women*. Boston: Beacon Press.

Mitchell, M., & Leachman, M. (2014). *Changing priorities: State criminal justice reforms and investments in education*. Center on Budget and Policy Priorities. Retrieved from http://www.cbpp.org/cms/?fa=view&id=4220

More than 6,000 children were sent back to Mexico after illegally crossing the US border. (2014, June 14). *Business Insider*. Retrieved from http://www.businessinsider.com/immigrant-children-returned-mexico-us-2014-6#ixzz3B3sLrlFQ

Nandy, A. (1983). *The intimate enemy: Loss and recovery of self under colonialism*. Delhi, India: Oxford University Press India.

Nash, J. (2012). Sentenced to death for being old: The NHS denies life-saving treatment to the elderly, as one man's chilling story reveals. *Daily Mail.com*. Retrieved from http://www.dailymail.co.uk/health/article-2126379/Sentenced-death-old-The-NHS-denies-life-saving-treatment-elderly-mans-chilling-story-reveals.html

National Center on Elder Abuse in collaboration with Westat, Inc. (1998, Sept.). *The national elder abuse incidence study* (Final report). Washington, DC: The Administration for Children and Families and The Administration on Aging, U.S. Department of Health and Human Services.

National Research Council. (2012). *Aging in Asia: Findings from new and emerging data initiatives*. Washington, DC: The National Academies Press.

Nelson, G. (1982). Social class and public policy for the elderly. *Social Service Review, 56*(1), 85–107.

Nelson, T. E. (Ed.). (2002). *Ageism: Stereotyping and prejudice against older persons*. Cambridge, MA: The MIT Press.

Newcomb, A. (2012, Apr. 17). Kindergartener cuffed after tantrum in principal's office. *ABC News*. Retrieved from http://abcnews.go.com/blogs/headlines/2012/04/kindergartener-cuffed-after-tantrum-in-principals-office/

New York Civil Liberties Union (NYCLU). (n.d.). *Youth and student rights: School to prison pipeline*. Retrieved from http://www.nyclu.org/issues/youth-and-student-rights/school-prison-pipeline

Ortman, J. M., Velkoff, V. A., & Hogan, H. (2014, May). *Population estimates and projections: Current population reports*, P25–1140. Retrieved from https://www.census.gov/prod/2014pubs/p25-1140.pdf

Palmore, E. B., Branch, L., & Harris, D. K. (Eds.). (2005). *Encyclopedia of ageism*. New York: The Haworth Press.

Parents of Joel Robinson protest outside Brooklyn charter school after school administrator Amelia Clune allegedly demands students to eat food off floor. (2014, May 9). *News 12 Brooklyn*. Retrieved from http://brooklyn.news12.com/news/parents-of-joel-robinson-protest-outside-brooklyn-charter-school-after-administrator-amelia-clune-allegedly-demands-student-to-eat-food-off-floor-1.7970908

Persad, G., Wertheimer, A., & Emanuel, E. J. (2009). Principles for allocation of scarce medical interventions. *The Lancet, 373*(9661), 423–431. Retrieved from http://www.thelancet.com/journals/lancet/article/PIIS0140-6736%2809%2960137-9/

Pharr, S. (1988). *Homophobia, a weapon of sexism*. Inverness, CA: Chardon Press.

Pheterson, G. (1990). Alliances between women: Overcoming internalized oppression and internalized domination. In L. Albrecht & R. M. Brewer (Eds.), *Bridges of power: Women's multicultural alliances* (pp. 34–48). Philadelphia: New Society Publishers.

Protalinski, E. (2011, May 20). *Mark Zuckerberg: Facebook minimum age limit should be removed*. Retrieved from http://www.zdnet.com/blog/facebook/mark-zuckerberg-facebook-minimum-age-limit-should-be-removed/1506

Rehtaeh Parsons suicide: Two charged over photos in cyberbullying case. (2013, Aug. 8). *The Guardian*. Retrieved from http://www.theguardian.com/society/2013/aug/09/rehtaeh-parsons-suicide-charged-photos

Rethinking Schools. (2011). *Editorial: Stop the school-to-prison pipeline*. Retrieved from http://www.rethinkingschools.org/archive/26_02/edit262.shtml

Rogoff, B. (2003). *The cultural nature of human development*. Oxford, England: Oxford University Press.

Rogoff, B. (2007). The cultural nature of human development. *The General Psychologist, 42*(1), 4–7.

Rosenberg, M. (2014). *Overview of life expectancy*. Retrieved from http://geography.about.com/od/populationgeography/a/lifeexpectancy.htm

Rubinstein, G. (1999). *Printing: History and development*. Jones International and Jones Digital Century. Retrieved from http://karmak.org/archive/2002/08/history_of_print.html

Russell, J. (2005, Sept. 11). At regional malls, a teen test. *Boston Globe*, page A1.

Schieffelin, B. B., & Ochs, E. (Eds.). (1986). *Language socialization across cultures*. Cambridge, UK: Cambridge University Press.

Smith, D. E. (1987). *The everyday world as problematic: A feminist sociology*. Boston: Northeastern University Press.

Span, P. (2013, Jan. 8). *Who should receive organ transplants? The New York Times*. Retrieved from http://newoldage.blogs.nytimes.com/2013/01/08/who-should-receive-organ-transplants/?_r=0

Stearns, P. J. (1986). Old age family conflict: The perspective of the past. In K. A. Pillemer & R. S. Wolf (Eds.), *Elder abuse: Conflict in the family* (pp. 3–24). Dover, MA: Auburn House Publishing.

Steinhauser, P. (2013, Sept. 30). CNN poll: GOP would bear the brunt of shutdown blame. *CNN Politics*. Retrieved from http://www.cnn.com/2013/09/30/politics/cnn-poll-shutdown-blame/?hpt=hp_t1

Swain, S. (2009). Sweet childhood lost: Idealized images of childhood in the British child rescue literature. *The Journal of the History of Childhood and Youth*, 2(2), 198–214.

Taylor, D. (2002). *The writers guide to everyday life in colonial America, 1607–1783*. New York: F+W Media, Inc.

Teutsch S., & Rechel, B. (2012). Ethics of resource allocation and rationing medical care in a time of fiscal restraint - US and Europe. *Public Health Reviews*, 34(1), 1–10.

Thomas, E. (2013, Nov. 1). Ten-year-old Chinese pupil jumps to his death from 30th floor window 'on teacher's orders' because he had not written an apology for talking in class. *DailyMail.com*. Retrieved from http://www.dailymail.co.uk/news/article-2483313/Chinese-boy-commits-suicide-teachers-orders.html

Thompson, E. P. (1968). *The making of the English working class*. New York: Penguin.

Tuck, E., & Yang, K. W. (2013). Introduction to youth resistance research and theories of change. In E. Tuck & K. W. Yang (Eds.), *Youth resistance research and theories of change* (pp. 1–24). New York: Routledge.

United Nations Cyber School Bus. (1996–2014). *Declaration of the rights of the child*. Retrieved from http://www.un.org/cyberschoolbus/humanrights/resources/child.asp

United Nations Department of Economic and Social Affairs. (2011, May 3). *United Nations world population prospects: 2012 revision*. Retrieved from http://esa.un.org/wpp/

United Nations Human Rights. (n.d.). *Convention on the rights of the child*. Office of the High Commissioner for Human Rights (OHCHR). Retrieved from http://www.ohchr.org/en/profes sionalinterest/pages/crc.aspx

Walker, J. (2010). *Elder stereotypes in media and popular culture*. Aging Watch. Retrieved from http://www.agingwatch.com/?p=439

WFTV.com. (2007, Mar. 30). *Kindergarten girl handcuffed, arrested at Fla. school*. Retrieved from http://www.wftv.com/news/news/kindergarten-girl-handcuffed-arrested-at-fla-schoo/nFBR4/?__federated=1

Wikipedia. (2014). *Convention on the rights of the child*. Retrieved from http://en.wikipedia.org/wiki/Convention_on_the_Rights_of_the_Child

Winerip, M. (2013, July 22). Three men, three ages. Which do you like? *The New York Times*. Retrieved from http://www.nytimes.com/2013/07/23/booming/three-men-three-ages-who-do-you-like.html?_r=0

World Health Organization. (2002). *Facts: Abuse of the elderly*. Retrieved from http://www.inpea.net/images/Elder_Abuse_Fact_Sheet.pdf

World Health Organization. (2014). *World health statistics 2014: A wealth of information on global public health*. Geneva, Switzerland: WHO Press.

Wyner, A. (2014, Apr. 29). How hip-hop flourished in America. *The Harvard Crimson*. Retrieved from http://www.thecrimson.com/column/the-gospel-of-rap/article/2014/4/29/gospel-of-rap-how-hip-hop-flourished/

Young, I. M. (1990). *Five faces of oppression*. Princeton, NJ: Princeton University Press.

11

Online and Blended Pedagogy in Social Justice Education

*Andrea D. Domingue**

INTRODUCTION

Social justice education involves both a content and process that can be adapted to multiple formats or contexts. The other chapters in this book provide designs for face-to-face teaching in a semester or workshop format, typical of the way social justice education has been practiced for many years. Since the publication of the second edition of this text, considerable technological advances have changed the ways we as a society not only acquire and share information, but also communicate and build relationships (Allen & Seaman, 2014; Kim & Bonk, 2006). These societal shifts have also impacted the landscape of education, most notably through the increasing presence of online and blended learning (which includes both online and face-to-face formats), while also raising inquiry about how these changes influence the pedagogy, design, and facilitation of social justice education.

The purpose of this chapter is to show how and when social justice education pedagogical frameworks can successfully be used in online and blended learning formats. This chapter will first discuss the factors to consider when developing either an online or blended-format social justice education course. Second, the chapter identifies some of the opportunities and challenges of delivering social justice education through online and blended formats.

APPROACH, PREMISES, AND KEY DEFINITIONS

This chapter focuses on two kinds of formats that social justice educators increasingly are asked to design and facilitate: Blended and fully online.

- Blended facilitation of learning is both in-person within a classroom environment as well as through an online environment. The ratio of in-person to online facilitation can range from 30–79% of a course (Allen & Seaman, 2014).
- Fully online facilitation of learning is exclusively through online environments.

In this chapter, I follow the practice of other chapters in this volume by focusing on single isms/issues, although the material is typically presented in the context of a multiple-issue course that addresses several isms and draws attention to the core concepts (see Chapter 4) and to intersectionality. In doing so, I provide activity examples drawn from a multiple-topic, semester-long college-level course. Specifically, these examples illustrate single-issue or intersectional sessions within blended formats. While the examples provided are within the context of higher-education instruction, both the design and facilitation of these activities are adaptable across professional, disciplinary, or specialty contexts. Materials that support these activities can be found on the website for this chapter.

INFLUENCE OF TECHNOLOGY ON TEACHING AND LEARNING

Since the 1990s, there have been significant technological developments that continue to shift the ways in which individuals and groups communicate, learn, and engage in social activities (Watkins, 2009). Most of today's largely middle- and upper-class college students grow up in "technology rich" homes where they have access to personal computers, smart phones, and the Internet that allow them to continuously engage with peers and create virtual communities within and beyond their geographic location (Watkins, 2009). Higher-education institutions have responded to these trends by moving a significant amount of campus information to websites, establishing an online presence through social media, creating departments and professional positions to manage technological efforts, and offering academic programs through online and blended course formats (Hanna, 2000). Further, there is an increasing expectation that educators be knowledgeable of technology and incorporate these mediums into their practices (Kim & Bonk, 2006).

While technology and social media have become increasingly available over the last several decades, there has been little attention to how technology supports or hinders goals of educational diversity, inclusion, and social justice (Sull, 2013). Thus far, the research on technology accessibility provides data on differences of usage and structural barriers across race, social class, language, and ability (Boyd, 2012; Keeler, Richter, Anderson-Inman, Horney, & Ditson, 2007; Martin & Valenti, 2013). There is also a body of work on the "digital divide," which reflects the marginalization of people from lower socio-economic groups, including people of color, who face a variety of obstacles that prevent them from accessing the Internet and technology (Conner & Slattery, 2014; Watkins, 2009).

Further, social justice educators must navigate the challenges of using technology in ways that help rather than harm goals of social justice. For example, many colleges and universities are pursuing online course offerings as a cost-effective strategy to address student accessibility and institutional financial constraints. Online courses may allow campuses to use fewer resources (i.e., staffing, classroom space) and potentially reach a broader student population in terms of geographic location, age, academic interests, and social class. But, as higher-education institutions increasingly move toward online education and ask faculty to use technology more in their classes, social justice educators are faced with questions about equity so that we do not reinforce a digital divide or exacerbate inequities that currently exist. Online courses may provide access for some student populations while creating barriers for others. Cost-effectiveness may come at the expense of students who may most benefit from small classes with face-to-face instruction. Online learning is not a panacea for learning, nor is it the most effective way to deliver some course content, particularly for social justice education courses. Since social justice education values and pays great attention to group dynamics and interpersonal relationships (with the instructor as well as other students), online formats raise significant questions and concerns.

Given the aforementioned issues, these questions arise: When do online and blended formats work for social justice and when do they not? How can educators retain and incorporate essential principles of social justice education pedagogy through online and blended learning formats? This chapter addresses core principles of the social justice approach laid out in Chapters 2 and 3, keeping in mind the opportunities and challenges of an online and blended learning context.

SOCIAL JUSTICE PEDAGOGY IN ONLINE INSTRUCTION

My approach to social justice education pedagogy in online formats is informed by my experiences as an instructor in both face-to-face and online settings. I taught social justice education courses in face-to-face formats for eight, 13-week semesters to 30 undergraduate students per section. The curriculum for these courses included a unit on the conceptual frameworks, described in Chapter 4; and multiple-issue units that explored individual systems of oppression (racism, sexism, heterosexism, etc.) and the intersections among these systems. I also taught social justice education courses in online formats for one 3-week winter semester and two 5-week summer semesters.

The following are key elements for social justice education pedagogy for online courses. They incorporate my face-to-face experiences teaching social justice education topics with my experience using a social justice education approach for online teaching.

- Foster community and interpersonal relationships among students and the facilitator
- Create an inclusive learning environment that is adaptable to diverse learning styles and social identities
- Emphasize dialogue and solicit multiple voices and perspectives
- Facilitate the learning and model of dialogic, inclusive participation
- Provide course material that addresses contemporary social justice topics while also providing historical contexts for these legacies
- Promote experimental activities that provoke and involve question-posing, moving students beyond the "comfort zone" toward perspective-taking and new knowledge
- Provide for an exploration of social identities so that students can understand how these identities are situated within systems of power and privilege
- Provide opportunities for application of course material and experimentation of social action beyond the classroom context

Some of the assignments in the course include writing about personal experiences while situating these reflections in a larger structure of systematic oppression. It is important to reinforce to the students that grades are based on knowledge of content (specifically the conceptual frameworks), not on opinions or perspectives.

CONSIDERATIONS, OPPORTUNITIES, AND CHALLENGES

Despite some challenges, when done thoughtfully, the online format can provide a valuable arena for teaching social justice to participants who may be separated geographically. For online teaching, there are factors to consider when designing social justice education courses. There are several opportunities that this medium provides that make it favorable for delivering social justice education-based course content. Simultaneously, challenges arise in online courses that are similar and different from the challenges in face-to-face situations.

CONSIDERATIONS FOR DESIGNING ONLINE COURSES

There are several key considerations for designing online courses, as listed and described below:

- Student demographics
- Technological platform
- Learning formats
- Course structure and delivery
- Course activities
- Accommodations

STUDENT DEMOGRAPHICS

A major consideration in the design of social justice pedagogy in online formats is the demographic of students enrolled in the courses. While face-to-face courses largely attract traditional-aged undergraduate students, online courses have a considerable number of non-traditional students. Returning adult students have come to my courses wanting to change career paths toward education or to gain additional credentials for career advancement. In addition to creating intergenerational classroom environments, adult learners often enhance course topics by sharing their life experiences beyond the college campus, such as time spent in the workforce or on military duty, as well as discussing how the course resonates with what they observe in classrooms as teachers or as parents raising children.

It is important to consider the inclusion of students who are geographically located beyond the campus, such as in other parts of the state, other parts of the United States, or in other countries. Similar to the presence of non-traditional learners, students from diverse geographical backgrounds have resulted in richer conversations about course topics. For example, in one of my courses, there were rich conversations among students as they discussed manifestations of racism in education within the Unites States as one international student shared her experiences with racism living in Japan.

While there are advantages to having an intergenerational and geographically diverse class, these demographics also present some challenges. It is important to be mindful of addressing adultism (youth oppression) and ageism (elder oppression) while facilitating social justice courses in online formats. Non-traditional aged students will sometimes make comments that reflect their perceptions of traditional-aged students as having limited life experience and analyses of oppression. I have also observed ageism from traditional-aged students where their comments assume older students as less open-minded to diverse perspectives. In both instances, instructors need to be diligent about addressing these comments and using these moments as learning opportunities about prejudices, as well as remind students about the elements of sustaining an inclusive learning community.

Having students from diverse geographic locations also poses challenges. International students often face language and cultural barriers with online discussions. For example, slang words, idioms, and United States historical events and pop culture references are often confusing or new information for international students. Conversely, there are also moments when international students describe language, beliefs, or practices that are not readily familiar to U.S. students. To address these challenges, I utilize and model asking clarifying questions to make sure all students are clear on these references.

TECHNOLOGICAL PLATFORM

The technological platform is the medium in which course content is delivered. Many educational institutions host a learning management system (LMS) such as Blackboard or Moodle that is used campus-wide to deliver online courses. Some major benefits of using an institutionally supported LMS is that participants will likely have a familiarity with these formats. Instructors may or may not have information technology (IT) support services to help in the development and maintenance of these courses. As there is a greater push by institutions to offer online course offerings, it is important to note that some campuses face challenges supporting the development and facilitation of these courses. Examples of challenges include: Maintaining platform software updates, providing design resources for instructors, and supporting the demand of technical support for students. It is important for the instructor to know that any materials placed on the institutionally supported LMS become the intellectual property of the university.

Instructors may be limited to using instructionally supported systems; however, the continual evolution of public-access online tools such as Google applications, WordPress, or mobile applications offers facilitators additional options to teach online or blended courses. The decision of which technological platform to use for course delivery impacts the process in which social justice education pedagogy is facilitated, as the platform features largely influence how activities are adapted and communicated. While platforms such as Moodle and Blackboard share many similar features, each platform also has distinct features not available on the other. If an institution or instructor changes platforms, there might be challenges in not only what course activities are available, but also in the delivery (i.e., layout, instructions, etc.). Regardless whether one is using institutional platforms or publicly accessible platforms, it is suggested that facilitators should consider well in advance what design elements they want to incorporate in their courses and assess which platform best fits their needs.

LEARNING FORMATS

A second major consideration is the learning format to deliver the course. Typically there are two types of learning formats: Asynchronous and synchronous. *Asynchronous learning* is based on environments in which students participate in course activities within a given span of time, as compared to *synchronous learning*, which requires that students participate in course activities simultaneously at the same moment in real time. Courses that are set for asynchronous learning commonly use discussion posts and messaging tools, and students must respond to static content (Hrastinski, 2008). Asynchronous formats allow for flexibility in participants' schedules and time for reflection before responding to activities. In this format, students do not necessarily interact with each other or the facilitator at the same moment in time, which results in staggered learning moments. Synchronous learning formats use common media tools such as videoconferencing and chat features. An advantage of this format is that it allows for more social interaction, addresses student questions more efficiently, and gives instructors immediate feedback on student learning (Hrastinski, 2008). Challenges with synchronous learning include the more structured course time required of participants and facilitators, the requirement of Internet accessibility, and determining course times across diverse geographical locations.

Asynchronous learning is also a good approach to start with for a blended or online course, as it can use course activity features that instructors may already be familiar with from face-to-face formats (i.e., discussion threads, journals, and paper submissions from platforms such as Blackboard and Moodle). After delivering asynchronous courses for several semesters, I considered moving toward synchronous learning, as it simulates the dynamic nature of face-to-face course conversations.

While synchronous learning complements many pedagogical elements ideal for social justice pedagogy, there are several challenges when designing courses with this learning approach. First, synchronous learning requires that all participants be available for a common time to meet. This situation is exacerbated if students in the course are located in other time zones, both within the United States and abroad. Second, synchronous learning also requires students to have stable Internet access. Students may not always have access to the Internet at home, and even if they do, it may not be reliable. Students might only access the Internet and course materials at their employers or libraries to complete assignments. Also, unforeseeable events such as weather, course platform maintenance, or Internet provider outages can pose challenges to access course activities.

Based on my own experience having taught online courses using both asynchronous and synchronous activities—as well as having incorporated both formats into my face-to-face courses—I believe that elements of both formats support the key pedagogical elements of social justice education courses. However, it is important for facilitators to consider the advantages and disadvantages of each learning format when designing courses, and to make decisions on which format to use to best support the needs of the students, the topics being taught, as well as which format would complement the facilitation style of the instructor.

COURSE STRUCTURE AND DELIVERY

In addition to making decisions regarding the technological platform and learning format, facilitators will need to determine the structure and delivery of the course. The following are key questions facilitators must consider when designing and implementing an online course with social justice pedagogy:

- *How long will the course run? Will this course take place across a 14-week semester, intersession or summer session (3–5 weeks), or the span of several weekends?*
- *How many times per week will this class run, and what is the duration of time for each session?*
- *Will this course run fully online or will this course be blended? If blended, how many sessions will meet online? How many sessions will meet face-to-face?*
- *What will be the class size capacity of the course?*
- *What topics will the course cover? Will this be a single-issue or multiple-issues course?*
- *What course activities will be done during the online sessions? If the course is blended, what types of activities will be done during face-to-face sessions?*

These questions will help facilitators plan and design online social justice courses. It is important to note that some components of the course structure (i.e., length of course and class capacity) may not be at the discretion of facilitators and may be subject to institutional guidelines and practices. Upon addressing these questions, facilitators should draft a syllabus, including descriptions of learning objectives, course expectation, reading list, and explanation of course activities. Once this syllabus is complete, facilitators can begin to build a course site using the selected technological platform.

Many educational institutions require facilitators of online and blended courses to have their course sites fully or partially built several weeks before the course start date. The rationale behind this expectation is that students use this time period to browse the course site, using this information to make decisions about whether a course meets their needs and to get a sample of the course's facilitation. For this preview period, it is recommended to include the following components:

- A welcome letter or video to greet the students,
- Syllabus,
- Netiquette guide,
- Reading list, and
- At least the first two session modules with course activities (quizzes, discussion threads, etc.).

It is important to note that once a course site is built and available to students, changes should be minimal. The syllabus and course site provide an anchor for the course, and students find last-minute changes to be disruptive and confusing. While it is acceptable to make minor changes, such as adding or canceling a reading, changing an activity due date, or adjusting a discussion question, major alterations such as changing the topics covered or changing the structure of the course (platform, learning format, class meeting frequency, etc.) should not take place.

COURSE ACTIVITIES

The following are course activities for a blended social justice education course using asynchronous learning. The description below of the course activities is given based on using Blackboard as the platform for the blended course.

- **Course Units**—Using the Page or Module feature, class sessions are organized into units that include the objects of the unit, e-lectures, course discussion thread, listing of the required readings, assignments, and supplemental content, such as weblinks and resources.
- **Quizzes**—Using the Assessment feature, short quizzes assess understanding of course expectations (syllabus) and classroom participation guidelines (netiquette guide).
- **E-Lectures**—These are lectures on course content provided by either audio recordings of the instructor's voice as students navigate Powerpoint slides, or video recordings the instructor can create to discuss the course's concepts. The lectures can be uploaded to course unit pages or modules.
- **Discussion Threads**—Using the Discussions feature, class conversations can be facilitated on course units by posting a prompt of guiding questions. Students complete the assigned readings for the unit and submit an "Initial Post" by responding to the question prompts by a set deadline. After this deadline, students read and submit "Additional Posts," comments, or questions in response to their peers' Initial Posts.
- **Journals**—Using the Journal feature, students submit written reflections. These journal assignments strive to be dialogues between an individual student and the instructor to assess students' understanding of their social identities and insights students have on manifestations of oppression and social justice.
- **Papers and Exams**—Using the Assignment feature, students complete and submit formal paper assignments. I also use this feature to give midterm exams by posting a document students download, complete, and upload.
- **Final Projects**—Using the Assignment or Discussion feature, students work offline to complete individual or partnered project assignments where they apply course concepts

beyond the classroom. Students post projects in the form of PDFs, Powerpoint slides, or video links to the course site where other students (if using the Discussion feature) view and comment on projects.

ACCOMMODATIONS

The last major consideration for facilitating social justice pedagogy through online formats is thinking about accommodations for both English-language learners and students with disabilities.

For English-language learners, the online approach can serve as an accessible opportunity for students to participate in course discussions. Often in face-to-face courses, some English-language learners are hesitant to speak during class discussions out of concern of being misunderstood or difficulty translating words. English-language learners also express challenges with the fast pace of face-to-face course discussions and being able to process the information being presented and formulate timely thoughts. The asynchronous format of online courses allows English-language learners more time to respond to course discussions while also offering a space for students to practice articulating thoughts in English. Further, more opportunity to participate in course discussions supports long-term student engagement for English-language learners.

Despite online approaches to social justice pedagogy having benefits for students who are English-language learners, there are a few challenges for these students. First, while the asynchronous format requires students to write rather than speak within discussions, students may still struggle with articulating their thoughts. Students may face challenges with grammar, spelling, and word choice when writing responses. In addition, the large amounts of written text students will have to read, interpret, and respond to might be overwhelming for English-language learners. One way to address these issues is by checking in with students through private messages to assess how they are handling the volume of reading and writing, and by providing strategies or adjustments when necessary. These check-ins are a perfect opportunity to offer words of encouragement to validate that their posts are understood and valuable to the course discussions.

Another area of accommodation is consideration for students with disabilities. Based on a student's type of disability and the design of the course, online approaches can be spaces of opportunities and challenges for students with disabilities. For students who need additional time to complete assignments and readings, online approaches can offer that opportunity. Accommodations such as posting the materials in advance and designing an asynchronous course provide a helpful educational context for students with disabilities. For example, providing the course materials in advance, while perhaps challenging for instructors, is advantageous for students because they can browse the content and identify course expectations prior to the course start. Students with disabilities benefit from this approach, as they can be in communication with instructors and disability services prior to class to address accommodation needs, such as establishing adjusted assignment deadlines and gaining earlier access to assignment prompts.

Another benefit of online approaches and asynchronous learning techniques is the ongoing availability of course materials. In face-to-face courses, some students with disabilities struggle to balance being present in course discussions while also simultaneously taking notes. Within online courses, students are able to go back and watch lecture videos and re-read course discussion threads in the event information was missed or unclear. Further, online asynchronous formats also allow students to have some agency in how long and how often they engage with course materials, which is useful for students with attention-deficit disorders.

While online approaches can allow accessibility for some students with disabilities, online social justice education courses also create barriers for students with different disabilities. Perhaps the most difficult challenge for instructors and students might be receiving adequate accommodation support from disabilities services. First, students often have to register with disability services to receive documentation for accommodations, a particular challenge for students who do not have the time or are not geographically located near campus. Second, as students with disabilities begin to request accommodations for online courses, disability services may offer students resources that are typically compatible for face-to-face formats (e.g., notetakers, administering quizzes and exams, etc.) instead of accommodations for the blended learning environment. Realizing that disability services at colleges and universities may not have considered how to offer accommodations for students with disabilities in online courses, or that some institutions have assigned such duties to a staff or faculty member, instructors may have to address these issues independently on a case-by-case basis.

Despite offering additional time to complete assignments, students with learning disabilities struggle to keep up with the pace of online courses. Specifically, there are bound time frames for students to complete the course activities within a given unit (i.e., conceptual frameworks, etc.). Depending on the number of weeks of the semester, course units range from two days to two weeks. Even if students receive additional time to complete activities, such as discussion thread responses, this still proves to be challenging, because by the time students with disabilities post their initial thoughts in a course unit, their peers usually have read and responded to the posts. Thus, the posts that are posted late receive little to no attention, and students miss out on the discussion. One way to address this issue is to provide students with disabilities discussion thread prompts at the beginning of the semester so they may be able to align their posts in the same time frame as the class.

Another challenge for students with disabilities in regards to online courses is the substantial amount of writing and reading. In addition to the assigned readings and formal writing assignments, the primary way students engage in course discussions is through writing lengthy discussion thread posts and reading the responses from peers. Students with learning disabilities describe feeling overwhelmed by this format and struggle to synthesize information. One way to address this challenge is to allow students to upload video or audio clips of responses to decrease the amount of writing. I am also mindful to include video clips in lieu of some reading assignments and audio lectures to support students with disabilities and various learning styles.

It is critical that instructors of social justice pedagogy in online approaches identify course design strategies and institutional support options to include English-language learners and students with disabilities. It will be important to have conversations with students as early as possible so that instructors will be able to think through and offer options for students to not only complete assignments, but ensure their full inclusion in course discussions.

OPPORTUNITIES AND CHALLENGES IN ONLINE SJE COURSES

There are a number of opportunities as well as challenges in teaching SJE courses online. They are listed and discussed below.

- Online discussions
- Developing community
- Connecting with students (and students connecting with each other)
- Level of student engagement

POTENTIAL BENEFITS OF ONLINE DISCUSSIONS

Conversations on course topics largely take place through discussion threads, where students have to respond to prompts initiated by the instructor, such as questions based on readings and video lectures. While there are challenges for encouraging participation among students in face-to-face approaches, online courses can foster more student engagement. One reason for this increased participation is that in online courses, everyone is required to respond. For example, students in online courses can be required to submit an initial post introducing themselves to the class or course topic, followed by regular posts of their analyses of course topics. They can also be required to post comments on at least two of their peers' posts each session. Through this activity, each student has an opportunity to have their perspective recognized by their peers as well as the instructor. Further, since students have to write responses to posts rather than speaking, this activity requires students to think critically and craft intentional responses to best communicate their understanding of course materials.

In teaching these courses, I have found that online students often demonstrate an increased willingness to be vulnerable and candid when sharing personal experiences and opinions as compared to face-to-face courses. Students may feel less inhibited to share aspects of their identities (i.e., sexual orientation, religious beliefs, disabilities, etc.) and perspectives since they are "behind the computer screen." Unlike face-to-face settings, students can feel freer to share authentic feelings through written text rather than the potentially challenging conversational conflicts or closed body language reactions they may get from face-to-face peers.

POTENTIAL CHALLENGES FOR ONLINE DISCUSSIONS

While there are many benefits to online discussions, this approach also has several challenges. First, participants may not learn how to address challenging conversational conflicts and attend to cues of body language or facial expression that are evident in face-to-face encounters. Part of social justice education is learning how to deal with difficult discussions about racism, sexism, and other forms of oppression in a diverse group of people.

A second challenge is that discussion threads require students to have strong writing skills and construct well-organized responses that their peers and instructors can understand. I strive to model how to write and comment on posts by providing sample responses early in the semester. These examples remind students that this is an academic course where students must incorporate course readings and not just comment on personal experiences or opinions. I also stress that students need to proofread responses and avoid using abbreviated words or slang. There are instances when students in online discussions cite U.S. pop culture references, history, or idioms that are unfamiliar to non-native English speakers and international students. I am mindful to make sure to explain these references and encourage all students to ask clarifying questions of their peers.

In summary, it is critical that instructors are mindful of how social justice pedagogy through online context may foster different levels of participation among students. Facilitation in these spaces requires attention to different needs for validation and support of vulnerability, as well as strategies for recognizing and addressing potentially triggering discussion responses that occur differently in face-to-face encounters. Further, instructors must consider issues of accessibility both in terms of language barriers and writing skills. It will be important to have plenty of examples of how to meet written participation expectations and to make sure to provide explanations for cultural references.

DEVELOPING COMMUNITY AND INTERPERSONAL CONNECTIONS

A critical element of social justice pedagogy is fostering a sense of community while providing a challenging learning environment. Instructors in face-to-face settings use strategies such as icebreakers, name games, small-group activities, and large-group sharing to encourage students to develop interpersonal connections with their peers. In online formats, instructors use discussion posts to attempt to reach these same goals through requiring a "meet 'n' greet" thread and an identity collage assignment where students create a collage of words and images to represent how they view their personal and social identities.

While these strategies do contribute to community-building among participants in the class, these connections do not foster the same level of emotional connection as in face-to-face approaches. For the instructor, it can be difficult to assess and engage students on aspects such as empathy or perspective-taking. It is hard to assess the emotional engagement of students, because there are no verbal cues and few nonverbal cues. Both instructors and students must rely exclusively on what individuals post, and then pose follow-up questions to probe further about emotional engagement, or run the risk of misinterpretation.

LEVEL OF STUDENT ENGAGEMENT

Lastly, over the duration of the course, students' level of engagement with a discussion thread wanes. In face-to-face approaches, instructors use a variety of strategies to keep students interested in course topics, such as pair sharing, small-group work, and experiential activities. The continual reading and writing format of discussion threads grows tedious for both students and instructors after several course units. Despite the frequent reminders about posting requirements, students' posts gradually become shorter; responsiveness to readings may decrease, and some students stop responding to their peers' posts. Depending on the complexity of the discussion prompt, the length of the posts, and the number of students in the class, offering instructor feedback can also be quite time consuming.

A strategy for instructors to address student engagement and lengthy feedback processes is to combine selective and meta-commenting. Rather than trying to address every student's post, I selectively comment on students who demonstrate low engagement. I also pose questions to encourage such students to elaborate on their responses or more directly ask them to relate their response to a reading. Meta posting is a strategy where instead of responding to individual student posts, I make general comments and observations about what I noticed about the discussion. This strategy is also particularly useful to clarify any misunderstandings within discussions.

A common misunderstanding that arises involves word choice and language to describe social identity groups. For example, it is common in the racism unit that some white students use the word "colored" to describe black or African American identities, or assume the term is synonymous with the phrase "people of color." Similarly, students may use the term "homosexual" to describe gay and lesbian people or express discomfort viewing the word "queer" as a reclaimed or inclusive term, prompting conflict within discussions. In posting responses, it can be helpful to explain the historical legacy of language and also offer suggestions of more inclusive language to use when discussing social identity groups. Including links to articles or videos to supplement the explanations is a way to offer resources on these topics. It is helpful to post responses within the current discussion thread and also use the Announcement feature to make sure all students view and read these explanations on language.

Misunderstandings can also surface in discussions when students share their opinions on course topics such as affirmative action. While it can be difficult to assess emotions in these instances, it is important for the instructor to acknowledge potential misunderstandings and to remind students of the participatory guidelines. A specific strategy is to engage the students by posing clarifying questions in order to have students further explain their point of view. While this technique often helps to diffuse conflicts in discussions, facilitators may want to consider following up with students individually through messages or using synchronous tools, such as virtual chats, to create opportunities to further discuss areas of confusion or disagreement.

RATIONALE FOR SOCIAL JUSTICE BLENDED CURRICULUM DESIGN

As a social justice educator, it is important to take advantage of teachable moments. In my experience, some of this can be done online, and it has also been true in my experience that not enough of it can be done online. After some experimentation with online teaching, I came to prefer a blended approach. My own social justice practice requires me periodically to have a face-to-face opportunity to check-in with the students and have them also engage with each other, face-to-face and in real time, to clarify or expand upon their understandings of SJE and assumptions about each other as a learning community. Further, I find that the blended format is an effective strategy that highlights the opportunities discussed previously for online approaches while also mitigating its challenges. Facilitators who need to teach entirely online or have a preference must find ways of solving some of these challenges through online pedagogies and activities if they are to be inclusive and successful.

Within the context of blended teaching, intentional choices are required about the ratio of face-to-face and online sessions primarily based on the length of the course offering. The course design presented in the next section provides a quadrant design based on a 14-week semester course. Each quadrant has one face-to-face session. In addition to providing introductory information about the course topics, the face-to-face sessions continually create opportunities for community-building as well as assessing comprehension and application of course concepts. The sample course design in this chapter includes eight online sessions and six face-to-face sessions containing approximately 2.5 hours of course activities per session.

SAMPLE SOCIAL JUSTICE MULTIPLE-ISSUE, BLENDED CURRICULUM DESIGN

The curriculum design in this chapter offers one example of semester-long, continuous student participation in a blended format course. This design includes introductory quadrants presented in Chapter 4, which is multiple-issue focused. It also incorporates material from the quadrant designs from the single-issue ism chapters (Chapters 5–10). Attention is given to distinctions within, and intersections across, the manifestations of oppression presented in the ism chapters. It is important to note that this suggested design may differ based on course goals, student needs, duration of time allotted for the course, as well as technology available. At the conclusion of the course, participants will be able to achieve the following goals:

- Learn how to communicate and work with others
- Become aware of one's social identity through interactions with others and course material

- Exhibit an understanding of the dynamics and various manifestations of social oppression through examining racism, sexism, and ableism
- Incorporate strategies for interrupting oppression in daily life

Overview of Quadrants: Social Justice Education Blended Course

This design for a 14-week semester blended format course includes six sessions that meet online and seven sessions that meet face-to-face. In-person sessions are 2.5 hours long. Class size is 20 students.

Quadrant 1: Fostering an Inclusive Learning Community/Defining Social Justice Education

Session 1: Fostering an Inclusive Learning Community (Online)

1. Welcome and Introductions (two documents: Welcome Letter & Meet 'n' Greet)
2. Course Site Scavenger Hunt (or Syllabus Quiz)
3. Class Participation (or Netiquette Guidelines)

Session 2: Defining Social Justice Education (Online)

1. Defining Social Justice Education Gallery Walk and Discussion
2. Introductory Reflection Journals
3. Identity Collage Assignment

Quadrant 3: Historical and Contemporary Manifestations of Oppression

Session 6: Defining Race/Racism (Face-to-Face)

1. Bead Activity (20 minutes)
2. Defining Race and Racism Frameworks (30 minutes)
3. *Race: Power of an Illusion* (90 minutes)

Session 7: Contemporary Racism in Education (Online)

1. Separate and Unequal
2. Anti-Racism Task Force Activity

Session 8: Defining Sex/Sexism (Face-to-Face)

1. Gender Socialization (20 minutes)
2. Defining Sex, Gender, and Sexism Frameworks (20 minutes)
3. Miss Representation (110 minutes)

Session 9: Contemporary Manifestations of Sexism in Education (Online)

1. Messages about Gender Rules (15 minutes)
2. Testimonials and Caucus Groups

Quadrant 2: Conceptual Frameworks

Session 3: Social Identity, Social Construction, and Socialization (Face-to-Face)

1. Welcome, Course Overview, and Revisit Participation Guidelines (10 minutes)
2. What's In a Name (15 minutes)
3. Identity Collage Sharing (50 minutes)
4. Social Identity, Social Construction, and Saliency Frameworks (20 minutes)
5. Exploring Socialization through Storytelling (45 minutes)

Session 4: Prejudice, Discrimination, and Oppression (Face-to-Face)

1. Celebrity Taboo (10 minutes)
2. Discrimination and Prejudice; Oppression Frameworks (25 minutes)
3. Film Screening: Precious Knowledge (115 minutes)
4. Five Faces of Oppression Study Groups (30 minutes)

Session 5: Oppression, Privilege, and Liberation (Online)

1. Oppression, Privilege, and Social Action Frameworks
2. Social Change in Education Timeline
3. "What Would You Do" Action Scenarios
4. Action Projects

Quadrant 4: Envision Social Change and Taking Action

Sessions 14 and 15: Group Project Work (Online)

1. Action Projects Group Work (5 hours)

Session 16: Action Group Projects Presentations/Closing (Face-to-Face)

1. Action Project Presentations (120 minutes)
2. Closing (20 minutes)
3. Revisit Identity Collage (20 minutes)
4. Closing Reflection Journals

Quadrant 3 continued

Session 10: Defining Ability/Ableism (or Sexuality/Heterosexism) (Face-to-Face)

1. People Treasure Hunt (25 minutes)
2. Ability and Ableism Frameworks (25 minutes)
3. Best Kept Secret (85 minutes)

Session 11: Contemporary Ableism (or Heterosexism) in Education (Online)

1. Visioning an Accessible, Inclusive Society
2. Universal Design Gallery Walk

Session 12: Historical Manifestations of Heterosexism (Face-to-Face)

1. Human Bingo
2. History Timeline Activity
3. *Paragraph 175* Film and Debrief

Session 13: Contemporary Manifestations of Heterosexism (Online)

1. Heterosexism Across Institutions
2. Case Study and Debrief

QUADRANT 1: FOSTERING AN INCLUSIVE LEARNING COMMUNITY/DEFINING SOCIAL JUSTICE EDUCATION

Learning Objectives:

- Foster a welcoming learning environment through participant introductions and encouraging interpersonal group development
- Identify course expectations
- Discuss and begin to establish group participation guidelines
- Develop a shared understanding of key terms and ideas on social justice education, specifically the distinction between diversity and social justice and an inclusive learning community

Key Concepts: Social justice; diversity; (inclusive) learning community

SESSION 1: Fostering an Inclusive Learning Community (Online)

Time: 2.5 cumulative hours of online interaction

Activities:

1. Welcome and Introductions/Meet 'n' Greet Your Classmates (30 minutes)

The Welcome and Introductions activity uses a letter or video to introduce students to course learning objectives and topics. The Meet 'n' Greet Your Classmates activity allows students an opportunity to introduce themselves as well as meet the instructor and their peers.

2. Course Site Scavenger Hunt (or Syllabus Quiz) (30 minutes)

Using the Assessment feature in Blackboard, this activity helps students to gain familiarity with the course site, syllabus, readings, attendance policy, how to contact the instructor(s), assignment submissions, and resources. An alternative activity would be to have students complete a Syllabus Quiz.

3. Class Participation (or Netiquette Guidelines) (90 minutes)

Using the Discussion Thread feature and drawing from course readings on effective participation, students suggest participation guidelines that would contribute to fostering an inclusive learning community. For the online component of the course, Netiquette Guidelines provide an expectation for students of how they should participate in discussion. An alternative activity would be to have them complete a Netiquette Quiz.

SESSION 2: Defining Social Justice Education (Online)

Time: 2.5 cumulative hours of online interaction

1. Defining Social Justice Education Gallery Walk and Discussion (30 minutes)

Using multimedia sources, students explore elements of social justice and participate in an online discussion where they share themes they observed, how they would personally define social justice, and why social justice in education is critical.

2. Introductory Reflection Journals (30 minutes)

Using Blackboard's Individual Assignment feature on the course site, have students expand their introduction posts through questions on experience with social justice prior to the course. Students also identify their hopes and fears about participating in the course.

3. Identity Collage Assignment (90 minutes)

Drawing from course readings, students create a collage using words, pictures, symbols, etc., that represent their personal and social identities. An alternate assignment would be the Personal and Social Identity Wheel worksheets (see Chapter 4, Quadrant 2).

Pedagogical and Facilitation Notes for Quadrant 1

The first quadrant includes two online sessions with the goals of orienting students to the course expectations and beginning the community-building process. It is helpful to begin the blended class design with online sessions as they give students ample time to familiarize themselves with the course site and to begin to practicing participation within online discussions.

A significant benefit of beginning class with online sessions is that when students do come to face-to-face sessions, they come to class excited to meet their peers and the instructor in-person and have already learned about some aspects of their experiences from the discussion threads. Students are also more eager to participate in course topics and ask questions, which was a noticeable shift from teaching face-to-face classes, where it typically takes students several weeks and many group activities to reach a comparable level of engagement.

QUADRANT 2: CONCEPTUAL FRAMEWORKS

SESSION 3: Social Identity, Social Construction, and Socialization (Face-to-Face)

Time: 2.5 hours; face-to-face session

Learning Objectives:

- Practice group participation guidelines
- Describe the difference between personal and social identities

- Explore social group membership and experiences
- Develop an understanding of social construction and its role in the socialization process

Key Concepts: Personal identity; social identity; dominant identity group; subordinated identity group; social construction; saliency; socialization

Activities:

1. Welcome, Course Overview, and Revisit Participation Guidelines (10 minutes)

Welcome students to the first face-to-face session as well as review major course goals and expectations. Using the participation guidelines generated from Quadrant 1, post guidelines on newsprint or a Powerpoint slide. Ask students to revisit, clarify, and revise the items listed.

2. What's In a Name? (15 minutes)

For this activity, students tell the story of how they acquired their first name, surname, and/or nickname. Encourage students to share aspects of their name, such as the geographical origin, language, meaning, spelling, and people who influenced their name decision.

3. Identity Collage Sharing (50 minutes)

Students share collages that represent their personal and social identities in pairs or small groups. This activity concludes by having student identify thematic observations of similarities and differences of identities across participants.

Break (10 minutes)

4. Social Identity, Social Construction, and Saliency Frameworks (20 minutes)

This lecture offers definitions of the key concepts for this quadrant such as ability, disability, ableism, adaptive technology, and universal design, as well as how these terms are used in relationship with each other. Visual aids and observations noted from the Name Story and Identity Collage serve as examples to support understanding of these key concepts.

5. Exploring Socialization through Storytelling (45 minutes)

Students listen to the audio clip from the podcast *This American Life*, Episode 469: *Hiding in Plain Sight: Act 1, There's Something About Mary* (free audio clip available from http://www.thisamericanlife.org/radio-archives/episode/469/hiding-in-plain-sight; Chicago Public Media, 2012). In small groups, students identify examples from the clip that correspond with the Cycle of Socialization (Harro, 2013).

SESSION 4: Prejudice, Discrimination, and Oppression (Face-to-Face)

Time: 2.5 hours; face-to-face session

Learning Objectives:

- Identify the difference between stereotypes, prejudice, and discrimination
- Develop a common conceptual understanding of oppression dynamics
- Begin exploration of institutional and cultural forms of oppression

Key Concepts: Stereotypes; prejudice; discrimination; oppression

Activities:

1. Celebrity Taboo (10 minutes)

Based on the popular word guessing game *Taboo*, students take turns describing these celebrity individuals without using names, keywords listed on the cards, or physical descriptors. As a large group, students make connections to how this activity relates to assumptions, beliefs, and stereotypes that are associated with social identities.

2. Discrimination and Prejudice; Oppression Frameworks (25 minutes)

This lecture offers definitions of the key concepts for this quadrant as well as how these terms are used in relationship with each other. The model of oppression for this lecture draws from the Five Faces of Oppression (Young, 2013).

3. Film Screening: Precious Knowledge (75 minutes)

Show the film *Precious Knowledge* (available for purchase from www.preciousknowledge-film.com; Dos Vatos Films, 2011). This film provides an overview of an initiative to end the ethnic studies program in public schools at Tucson, Arizona. Ask participants to note examples of the Five Faces of Oppression observed in this film.

4. Five Faces of Oppression Study Groups (30 minutes)

Create groups with three students in each group to discuss reactions to the film *Precious Knowledge*. Assign each group one of the Five Faces of Oppression and have them compare examples of oppression they noted from watching the film. Have students as a large group offer highlights from their discussions and review the definitions of each of the Five Faces.

SESSION 5: Oppression, Privilege, and Liberation (Online)

Time: 2.5 hours cumulative of online interaction

Learning Objectives:

- Develop a common conceptual understanding of institutional, cultural, and individual levels of oppression
- Describe the relationship between internalized domination and internalized subordination, and their relationship to oppression
- Identity examples of privilege across different dominant social identity groups
- Begin exploration of strategies for allyship and social action on multiple levels of oppression

Key Concepts: Internalized domination; internalized subordination; privilege; liberatory consciousness; ally; social action

Activities:

1. Oppression, Privilege, and Social Action Frameworks (30 minutes)

This video lecture offers definitions of the key concepts for this quadrant as well as how these terms are in relationship with each other. The model of oppression used for this session is the levels, types, and intent of oppression (see Chapter 4). This lecture concludes with Barbara Love's model for liberatory consciousness and frameworks for social action (Chapter 10).

2. Social Change in Education Timeline (30 minutes)

Using video clips, quotes, pictures, songs, and articles that explore historical and contemporary elements of social change, students explore and share what themes they observed as well as what skills and resources are necessary to take social actions in educational settings.

3. "What Would You Do" Action Scenarios (45 minutes)

In virtual small break-out groups, have students review several scenarios depicting oppression and discuss how they would respond if they were personally in these situations. Ask students to develop and share a collective action plan to post to the full class.

4. Action Projects (45 minutes)

This semester-long activity asks students to work with 1–3 classmates where they will develop and implement a project to address oppression in educational settings. Students will select one of the isms explored in the course (i.e., racism, sexism, heterosexism, ableism) and will present the results of the project at the conclusion of the course.

Pedagogical and Facilitation Notes for Quadrant 2

For the second quadrant, there are three sessions: The first two meet face-to-face and the third meets online. The first session, focusing on social identity, social construction, and socialization, is the first face-to-face session of the course. Students create, bring, and share identity collages, a key activity where students make observations about their social identity groups, noting points of shared connection and differences among their peers. While this activity does work in the online format, it is more worthwhile to use it in face-to-face sessions as it promotes strong community-building and dialogue among students.

The goal of the second face-to-face session is to provide students with key understandings of prejudice, discrimination, and systems of oppression. After experiencing the conceptual frameworks unit in both formats, students will generate many questions and points of confusion in this unit. The face-to-face sessions provide students with detailed examples to better understand this concept as well as address their questions in the moment. This face-to-face session is also a space where students participate for the first time in small-group activities, offering a different learning style from the large-group discussion.

The final session in this quadrant takes place online. The rationale for this session being online is to have students extend the conversations they had in the first two sessions through online discussion threads. The first two sessions are filled with multiple frameworks that might be new learning for students, and the online session provides space to process this information. The discussion thread for the online session asks students to share memories of witnessing discrimination and consider past experiences with taking action. The journal activity encourages continued self-reflection on social identities while also assessing how a student is doing in the course so far.

QUADRANT 3: HISTORICAL AND CONTEMPORARY MANIFESTATIONS OF OPPRESSION

SESSION 6: *Historical Manifestations of Racism (Face-to-Face)*

Time: 2.5 hours face-to-face

Learning Objectives:

- Explore personal experiences about race and racism; explore the ways that racism is communicated and reinforced
- Develop an understanding of key terms, including racial prejudice, racism, colorblind ideology, and racial microaggression
- Begin identification of institutional and cultural forms of racism

Key Concepts: Race; ethnicity; racial prejudice; racism; colorblind ideology; racial microaggressions

Activities:

1. Bead Activity (20 minutes)

Through this activity, students will explore racial manifestations in their personal lives. Connections will be made to how these manifestations are influenced by institutional and cultural levels of racism. An alternate assignment would be the creation of a personal timeline using the Cycle of Socialization (see Chapter 5, Quadrant 1).

2. Defining Race and Racism Frameworks (30 minutes)

This lecture offers definitions of the key concepts for this quadrant as well as how these terms are used in relationship with each other. Attention will be on the distinction between racial prejudice and institutional racism, the limitations of a colorblind ideology, and how racial microaggressions contribute to cultural racism.

Break (10 minutes)

3. Race: Power of an Illusion (90 minutes)

Show episode 3 of *Race: Power of an Illusion: The House We Live In* (available from www.californianewsreel.com; California Newsreel, 2003). This film provides a historical overview of the social construction of race from the context of science, citizenship, and housing. Ask participants to note examples of the levels of oppression observed in the film as described in Chapters 1 and 4 (see also Chapter 5, Quadrant 3, Activity 2A).

SESSION 7: Contemporary Manifestations of Racism (Online)

Time: 2.5 cumulative hours of online interaction

Learning Objectives:

- Describe cultural and institutional privileges connected to "whiteness" within the U.S.
- Explore contemporary instances of racism in educational settings
- Identify ways to take action and interrupt racism on an institutional level

Key Concepts: White privilege; white supremacy; social action

1. Separate and Unequal (30 minutes)

Have students watch *Frontline: Separate and Unequal* (free video and streaming available from http://www.pbs.org/wgbh/pages/frontline/separate-and-unequal/; PBS, 2014). This episode explores the racial divide in K–12 school systems and features a proposed effort to create a new city within Baton Rogue, Louisiana, that would segregate students across race and social class. Using the Discussion Thread feature, ask participants to post their reactions to the episode and describe thematic similarities and distinctions with Episode 3 of *Race: Power of an Illusion: The House We Live In*.

2. Anti-Racism Task Force Activity (90 minutes)

In virtual small break-out groups, have students review several scenarios depicting racism and discuss how they would respond if they were a task force for a school system. Students will represent perspectives of a teacher, a parent, a student, and a superintendent where they will develop a collective list of recommendations to improve racial climates in schools.

SESSION 8: Historical Manifestations of Sexism (Face-to-Face)

Time: 2.5 hours face-to-face session

Learning Objectives:

- Explore the personal experiences about sex and gender; explore the ways that sexism is socialized
- Develop an understanding of key terms, including the distinction between sex and gender, patriarchy, and misogyny
- Begin identification of institutional and cultural forms sexism through media

Key Concepts: Biological sex; gender; gender identity; patriarchy; misogyny; objectification; femininity; masculinity

Activities:

1. Gender Socialization (20 minutes)

For this activity, have students free-write messages they received about feminine and masculine gender roles. Next, have students work in groups and apply these examples to the Cycle of Socialization (Harro, 2013). Move into a large-group discussion and have students identify where these messages were received.

2. Defining Sex, Gender, and Sexism Frameworks (20 minutes)

This lecture offers definitions of the key concepts for this quadrant as well as how these terms are used in relationship with each other. Attention will be on the distinction between sex and gender as well as how patriarchy and misogyny contribute to cultural sexism.

Break (10 minutes)

3. Miss Representation (110 minutes)

Show *Miss Representation* (available from http://therepresentationproject.org/films/miss-representation; 2011). This film provides a societal overview of the social construction of gender from the context of media, politics, and violence. Ask participants to note examples of the Five Faces of Oppression observed in the film.

SESSION 9: Contemporary Manifestations of Sexism (Online)

Time: 2.5 cumulative hours of online interaction

Learning Objectives:

- Describe cultural and institutional privileges connected to patriarchy within the U.S.
- Explore contemporary instances of sexism in educational settings
- Identify ways to take action and interrupt sexism on an individual and cultural level

Key Concepts: Patriarchy; feminization; male privilege

1. Messages about Gender Rules (15 minutes)

Have students listen to the podcast *This American Life*, Episode 530: *Mind Your Own Business: Act 1, Jill's House Rules* (free audio clip available from http://www.thisamericanlife.org/radio-archives/episode/530/mind-your-own-business; Chicago Public Media, 2012). This audio clip discusses a discrimination lawsuit filed by a professional cheerleader and how a gender-based rule book limits the lived experiences of women cheerleaders disproportionately to male athletes.

2. Testimonials and Caucus Groups (90 minutes)

Drawing from the film *Miss Representation* and the *Jill's House Rules* podcast clip, have students post a testimonial of how sexism has impacted their lives. Assign students to small break-out groups, and using the Discussion Thread or Blog feature, have students post testimonials as videos or text. Next, have students review the postings of each group's conversation and ask students to participate in a small-group discussion.

SESSION 10: Defining Ability/Ableism (or Sexuality/Heterosexism)(Face-to-Face)

Time: 2.5 hours face-to-face session

Learning Objectives:

- Use face-to-face discussions to allow participants to explore their own personal experiences with ability and ableism and to respond to what they hear from each other
- Explore the personal experiences about ability and ableism; explore the ways that normalcy of ability is socially constructed
- Develop a common conceptual understanding of ableism dynamics
- Use face-to-face setting to begin identification of institutional and cultural forms of ableism within educational settings

Key Concepts: Ability; disability; ableism

Activities:

1. People Treasure Hunt (25 minutes)

The goal of this activity is to have students consider what knowledge they and their classmates have on ability and ableism topics. Using a handout, students will ask their peers questions to assess if they know a particular concept on ableism and have them initial their handout if they have the correct answer. Facilitators will review each question as a large group and lead a discussion on observations and themes.

2. Ability and Ableism Frameworks (25 minutes)

This lecture offers definitions of the key concepts for this quadrant as well as how these terms are used in relationship with each other. Attention will be on types of disability, social construction of normalcy, and historical treatment of people with disabilities.

Break (10 minutes)

3. Best Kept Secret (85 minutes)

Show the film *Best Kept Secret* (available from https://www.academicvideostore.com/video/best-kept-secret-aging-out-autism; Filmakers Library, 2013). This film depicts the story of a teacher who works to support students of color with autism to live independently as they approach high school graduation and face decreased access to institutional resources.

SESSION 11: *Contemporary Ableism (or Heterosexism) in Education (Online)*

Time: 2.5 cumulative hours of online interaction

Learning Objectives:

- Describe cultural and institutional privileges connected to ableism within the U.S.
- Explore contemporary instances of ableism in educational settings
- Identify ways to take action and interrupt ableism on an individual and cultural level

Key Concept: Universal design

Activities:

1. Visioning an Accessible, Inclusive Society (75 minutes)

Using the Groups feature within the Assignment tool, arrange students into pairs and have them discuss an aspect of education such as the classroom, sports, residence halls, etc., and identify ways in which this area is accessible and inaccessible. Pairs will brainstorm ways to make these areas more inclusive by using principles of universal design. These visions will then be illustrated as pictures and diagrams.

2. Universal Design Gallery Walk (75 minutes)

On the course site, create a page of images from *Visioning an Accessible, Inclusive Society*. Have students browse these items, and using the Discussion Thread feature, post and ask students to share what themes they observed and identify tangible steps as students they could incorporate in their lives.

SESSION 12: Historical Manifestations of Heterosexism (Face-to-Face)

Time: 2.5 hours face-to-face

This alternate design can be used instead of or in any combination with racism, sexism, or ableism designs.

Learning Objectives:

- To investigate the historical and social foundations upon which heterosexism is built
- To explore examples of heterosexism throughout history
- To begin identifying institutional and sociocultural manifestations of heterosexism

Key Concepts: heterosexism; lesbian; gay; bisexual; queer; historical foundations

Activities:

1. Human Bingo (20 minutes) (Materials: Prepared Bingo Sheets)

Students will each receive a human bingo sheet related to historical and contemporary manifestations of heterosexism. The objective of the activity is to move around the room and find people to initial one of the boxes on the bingo sheet. The first student to get five initialed boxes in a row OR four corners will win. The activity can continue until there are several "winners." Once the activity is complete, review the correct responses and ask participants if they came across any terms or ideas that were new or surprising.

2. History Timeline Activity (30 minutes)

To understand the roots and maintenance of the forms of oppression, it is important to know history, for according to Santayana: "Those who do not learn from history are doomed to repeat it." This activity can be conducted one of two ways:

1. Distribute the individual segments of the timeline to students to read in sequence.
2. Randomly distribute the individual segments of the timeline but leaving off their respective dates. Ask students to line up chronologically, from earliest to most recent. After they have organized themselves, students will read their segments. Having the

complete timeline with the dates, notify students whether they are standing in the correct chronological position.

Break (10 minutes)

3. Paragraph 175 *Film and Debrief (90 minutes)*

The film, which can be shown in its entirety or in segments, presents first-hand accounts of LGBQ men and women survivors of the Nazi horrors and can be found on YouTube. Process or debrief the film by asking students to break into groups of three or four to discuss any emotions that came up for them during the film or information that was surprising or new for them, and to express any other thoughts they have related to the film. Students then come back as a large group to process what was expressed within their respective groups.

Facilitation Notes: Given the lack of emphasis on LGBQ peoples' experiences in history, students may have difficulty generating correct answers for the Bingo activity. If such is the case, ask students to think about the invisibility of LGBQ history in educational settings as it relates to contemporary manifestations of heterosexism. If time is running low, opt for the first option for Activity 2 and/or show segments of *Paragraph 175* instead of the entire film.

SESSION 13: Contemporary Manifestations of Heterosexism (Online)

Time: 2.5 cumulative hours of online interaction

Learning Objectives:

- Review levels of oppression as they relate to heterosexism within the United States
- Examine contemporary manifestations of heterosexism at the institutional level
- Identify ways to challenge institutional and sociocultural forms of heterosexism

Key Concepts: Heterosexual privilege; levels of oppression; taking action

Activities:

1. Heterosexism Across Institutions

Drawing on core concepts presented in Chapters 1, 4 and 6, this activity is meant to shed light on the pervasiveness of heterosexism across institutions and to generate ideas about how to take action against heterosexism. Students will be divided into five virtual small groups. Each group will be assigned one institution—either health care, education, religion, law/policy, or media—and asked to discuss ways in which heterosexism manifests in their assigned institution. Using the Discussion Thread feature, groups will generate a list of contemporary forms of heterosexism within their given institution. In a large-group discussion, other students will then have the opportunity to review and add to or comment on each group's list.

2. Case Study and Debrief

Students will research blogs, newspapers, television, social media, and other mediums to generate a specific example of contemporary heterosexism in one of the five institutions discussed during Activity 1. Using the Discussion Thread feature, students will post their example and express what steps they can take to take action against heterosexism within their chosen institution. To generate a larger dialogue, students will respond to two of their classmates' posts in addition to their initial post.

Facilitation Notes: To allow for the expression of diverse perspectives and encourage an inclusive learning community, facilitators should consider students' varying social identities when assigning groups.

Pedagogical and Facilitation Notes for Quadrant 3

The third quadrant consists of six separate course sessions that address historical and contemporary manifestations for three forms of oppression: Racism, sexism, and ableism. Alternatively, instead of ableism, an instructor could cover heterosexism. While the sample design in this chapter focuses on racism, sexism, and ableism, please refer to the companion website for a blended design for manifestations of heterosexism. This alternate design can be used instead of or in any combination with racism, sexism, or ableism designs. Each manifestation of oppression begins with one face-to-face session and ends with one online session for a total of six sessions. It is helpful to begin with face-to-face sessions, as it allows the instructor to make sure students understand key terms for these manifestations of oppression, and to make sure students are able to apply elements learned from the conceptual frameworks to these contexts. For example, within the Defining Race and Racism session, it is important to explain to students the difference between race and ethnicity as well as to clear up any misunderstandings on who is targeted by racism (see Chapter 5).

Face-to-face sessions often include the film screenings. Recognizing that there is a limited time in which I have students in-person, I find that film screenings develop a collective shared experience among the class and a rich follow-up discussion. For example, when the film *Race: Power of an Illusion* is shown, learning about government intervention of racialized housing practices is often new information for many students. Seeing the film together and recognizing that each person is not the only one unaware of these practices allows for more honest emotions and processing, which can be hard to emulate through online approaches. Also, it helps in informal assessment, allowing the instructor to assess what connections students are making between the movie and their learnings from conceptual frameworks. The instructor is also able to present an in-the-moment lecture based upon student-generated questions.

Online sessions in the third quadrant allow students to engage with manifestations of oppression on a deeper level by specifically examining racism, sexism, and ableism (or heterosexism) in contemporary educational systems. At this point in the semester, students tend to self-facilitate discussions, are less hesitant to voice disagreements and differing perspectives, and begin to apply course content beyond the classroom. What is valuable about these sessions is that students are able to practice dialogue skills such as empathy, perspective-taking, and inquiry because students have formed and continue to practice the principles of an inclusive learning community. Students also use the online discussions as opportunities to share resources and information (e.g., video clips, new articles, websites, etc.) relevant to the course to enhance their conversations.

QUADRANT 4: ENVISION SOCIAL CHANGE AND TAKING ACTION

This final quadrant contains two online sessions and one face-to-face session. The primary goal of the online sessions is to give students time to work on their projects with their group partners. This time also allows students to be in communication with me as an instructor to work through any challenges as well as to clarify what needs to be prepared for the final presentations. The single face-to-face session is largely for students to present the results of their action projects and their personal experiences experimenting with taking social action. This session also serves as a point of closure for students, as this is the last time the class has a group discussion. Students describe insights they have as a result of the course.

While this session can be online, I feel it is important that students have an opportunity to "teach" each other about their action processes across different topical areas and share strategies on how to overcome difficulties. I also want to allow space for students to raise any lingering questions about social justice and encourage students to make any acknowledgements of appreciation to individuals who impacted their learning.

SESSIONS 14 and 15

Time: 5 hours cumulative online interaction

Learning Objectives:

- Explore strategies to take action against oppression within educational settings
- Practice communication and collaboration skills when developing action strategies

1. Action Projects Group Work

Based upon the Action Project, students use this time to work in groups to complete projects and prepare presentations for the last session. Students do not meet as a class during these two sessions.

SESSION 16

Time: 2.5 hour face-to-face session

Learning Objectives:

- Explore strategies to take action against oppression within educational settings
- Practice communication and collaboration skills when developing action strategies
- Identify challenges confronted with implementing action strategies
- Encourage students to consider action for social change within their personal lives and social identity development

Key Concepts: Ally; privilege; action; collaboration; liberation

Activities:

1. Action Project Presentations (120 minutes)

Based upon the Action Project activity introduced in Quadrant 2, have students present the results and personal reflections from designing and implementing this assignment.

Break (10 minutes)

2. Closing (20 minutes)

Ask participants to make any observations from the Action Project presentations as well as how these projects will support their ability to take action in the future. To end the course, invite students to make any comments about new learnings, personal reflections, or appreciation to someone in the course.

3. Revisit Identity Collage (20 minutes)

If Identity Collages were introduced in Quadrant 2, an optional closing activity would be to return the collages to students. Give them 1–2 minutes for a free-write reflection, and have students share, in a round, what new learnings they have about their social identities or those different from their own.

4. Closing Reflection Journals

Using an Individual Assignment feature on the course site, have students revisit their Introduction posts. Have students describe what new learning they have gained as a result of the course as well as respond to how they addressed their initial hopes and fears about the course.

Pedagogical and Facilitation Notes for Quadrant 4

As noted above, this final quadrant contains two online sessions and one face-to-face session. The online sessions enable students time to work on their group projects and also to communicate online with me as an instructor to solve challenges and to clarify final presentations. By way of contrast, the face-to-face session provides the opportunity to present the results of their action projects and their personal experiences experimenting taking social action while practicing their verbal presentations skills in a real-life setting for participant feedback. This session also serves as a point of closure for students, as this is the last time the class has a group discussion. Students describe insights they have as a result of the course.

While this session can, if necessary, be online, I feel it is important that students have an opportunity to "teach" each other about their action processes across different topical areas and share strategies on how overcome difficulties. I also want to allow space for students to raise any lingering questions about social justice and encourage students to make any acknowledgements of appreciation to individuals that impacted their learning.

OVERALL PEDAGOGICAL AND FACILITATION NOTES

Creating an Inclusive Online Learning Environment. Critical to online social justice pedagogy is the facilitation of an inclusive learning environment. It is important to remember that students will have varying experiences not only with social justice learning spaces, but also may vary in experience with online settings. Facilitators should first make sure students have technological access to the course and clear instructions on how to navigate this space. Second, facilitators should focus on communication skills and interpersonal relationship-building among students. Create Netiquette Guidelines that not only highlight expectations of how to write responses (length, spelling, grammar, use of slang, etc.) but also help students explore how they should interact with peers during course discussions. It is vital that facilitators model this participation and provide individual and collective feedback regularly throughout the course.

Varied Course Activities and Student Engagement. In addition to creating an inclusive learning environment, facilitators should be mindful of student engagement with course topics, particularly for synchronous learning approaches. Given that synchronous discussions include a considerable amount of reading and writing, facilitators should consider how to keep students engaged with course discussions across different learning abilities and styles. A strategy to address both fatigue and accessibility includes varying course activity formats. Some suggestions include: Small-group work in lieu of large-group discussions, incorporation of audio and video responses over written text, and collaborative activities such as wikis and blogs.

CONCLUSION

The above course is one example of how instructors can design and facilitate social justice pedagogy through a blended context. Again, the goal of this chapter is to offer design ideas and facilitation considerations for instructors as they design their own online or blended courses using social justice pedagogy. Social justice pedagogy through online and blended settings is a relatively new focus where a rapid evolution of technology impacts discourses on this topic. It will be necessary to continually assess the applicability to pedagogical, design, and facilitation "process" goals of teaching issues using a social justice education approach, and we look forward to revisiting these topics in the future.

Note

* This this chapter grew out of conversations with social justice education instructors who worked with both face-to-face and online instruction learning environments. I would like to acknowledge the following individuals who participated in these conversations, some of whose work will be featured on the companion website: Keri DeJong, Maru Gonzalez, Taj Smith, and Warren Blumenfeld. I would also like to acknowledge Chase Catalano, who designed and facilitated our first online social justice education course that has served as a foundation for those of us who now teach social justice education in blended or online formats.

References

Allen, I. E., & Seaman, J. (2014). *Grade change: Tracking online education in the United States.* Retrieved from http://www.onlinelearningsurvey.com/reports/gradechange.pdf

Boyd, D. M. (2012). White flight in networked publics? How race and class shaped American teen engagement with MySpace and Facebook. In L. Nakamura & P. Chow-White (Eds.), *Race after the Internet* (pp. 203–222). New York: Routledge.

Conner, J., & Slattery, A. (2014). New media and the power of youth organizing: Minding the gaps. *Equity & Excellence in Education, 47*(1), 14–30.

Hanna, D. E. (2000). *Higher education in an era of digital competition: Choices and challenges.* Madison, WI: Atwood Publishing.

Harro, B. (2013). The cycle of socialization. In M. Adams, W. J. Blumenfeld, C. Castañeda, H. W. Hackman, M. L. Peters, & X. Zuñiga (Eds.), *Readings for diversity and social justice* (3rd ed., pp. 45–52). New York: Routledge.

Hrastinski, S. (2008). Asynchronous & synchronous e-learning. *EDUCAUSE Quarterly, 31*(4). Retrieved from http://www.educause.edu/ero/article/asynchronous-and-synchronous-e-learning

Keeler, C. G., Richter, J., Anderson-Inman, L., Horney, M. A., & Ditson, M. (2007). Exceptional learners: Differentiated instruction online. In C. Cavanaugh & R. L. Blomeyer (Eds.), *What works in K-12 online learning.* Eugene, OR: International Society for Technology in Education.

Kim, K.-J., & Bonk, C. J. (2006). The future of online teaching and learning in higher education: The survey says. *EDUCAUSE Quarterly, 29*(4). Retrieved from http://www.educause.edu/ero/article/future-online-teaching-and-learning-higher-education-survey-says

Martin, C. E., & Valenti, V. (2013). *#FemFuture: Online revolution* (Volume 8 in the New Feminist Solutions series, pp. 1–34). New York: Barnard Center for Research on Women. Retrieved from http://bcrw.barnard.edu/publications/femfuture-online-revolution/

Sull, E. C. (2013). Teaching online with Errol: Effectively teaching the multicultural online classroom. *Online Cl@ssroom, 13*(9). Retrieved from http://www.magnapubs.com/newsletter/online-classroom/story/6693/

Watkins, S. C. (2009). *The young and the digital: What the migration to social-network sites, games, and anytime, anywhere media means for our future.* Boston: Beacon Press.

Young, I. M. (2013). Five faces of oppression. In M. Adams, W. J. Blumenfeld, C. Castañeda, H. W. Hackman, M. L. Peters, & X. Zuñiga (Eds.), *Readings for diversity and social justice* (3rd ed., pp. 35–45). New York: Routledge.

12

Critical Self-Knowledge for Social Justice Educators

*Lee Anne Bell, Diane J. Goodman, and Rani Varghese*ᐟ

INTRODUCTION

What do we need to know about ourselves in order to teach about social justice issues and interact thoughtfully, sensitively, and effectively with students/participants and the broader communities and institutions in which we teach? In social justice education, instructors as well as participants are central to the learning process. All of us experience and respond to classrooms and organizations differently based on our various social identities. Thus, in this chapter, we turn the lens on ourselves as educators. We explore how our own social identities and dominant and subordinated statuses affect the way we engage with learners, and we discuss the critical self-knowledge we need to be effective social justice educators.

First, we discuss the significance of our social identities and positions in our role as educators within systems of inequality, such as schools, colleges/universities, organizations, and communities. We then explore how our social group memberships and positionality, along with our social identity development, affect various aspects of our teaching, such as our pedagogical approaches and curriculum design. For example, we examine our levels of awareness regarding content, our biases and assumptions, the experiences of different students, and our responses to participants as well as group dynamics in the classroom. Next, we look at issues of competency and authority and suggest how self-knowledge can help instructors navigate these issues in classrooms and in institutions. We end with considering how issues of social identity and positionality affect co-teaching or co-facilitating.

SITUATING OURSELVES

There are many factors that will affect our facilitation of social justice issues. Our particular and unique personalities, family backgrounds, life histories, and educational training, to name a few, all impact who we are and how we are in the classroom. In order to better understand what we need to know about ourselves to be more effective social justice educators, we consider how we are situated in the classroom and broader community, using the lenses of social identities, dominant and subordinated statuses, and related socialization. While our approaches as educators cannot be reduced to these factors, we consider their significant and complex role in shaping our senses of self, responses, and experiences as social justice educators.

Social Identities

Our various and intersecting social identities based on race, ethnicity, gender, sexuality, class, religion, age, nationality, (dis)ability), and primary language(s), along with socialization in our families and communities, position us in particular ways in relation to social justice content and pedagogical processes. Our social identities shape our cultural orientations, perspectives, and behaviors. "Social identity awareness includes analysis of one's multiple and interacting social identities as well as one's identity statuses and the impact of those identities and identity statuses on various dimensions of one's classroom practice" (Adams & Love, 2009, p. 11).

In conventional classrooms, where content or pedagogy may not take into account social justice principles, the particular social and cultural identities of instructors usually remain in the background. But in the social justice classroom or workshop, where social identity is central to the content, the significance of who we are often takes center stage. We may be more or less aware of different aspects of our identity and how they affect our capacity to be effective social justice educators. To explore their impact, we can reflect on questions like the following:

- What aspects of my social identities are most and least important to me?
- Which identities are most/least salient in different contexts?
- With which social identities am I most/least comfortable?
- How do my different social identities affect and interact with each other? Where are the alignments or tensions among my different identities in different contexts?

Self-knowledge about our social identities and how they shape us as social justice educators provides a critical foundation for this work.

OUR DOMINANT AND SUBORDINATED STATUSES AND POSITIONALITY

We are all located in societal hierarchies of power, mediated by our various social identities and our dominant and subordinated statuses. The constellation of our dominant and subordinated statuses affect how we perceive and respond to others, how they perceive and respond to us, and the content and pedagogies with which we are most comfortable. Thinking about these and other questions can help us examine and understand the potential impact of our social identities and dominant/subordinated statuses on our social justice teaching:

- How do I enact and experience my privilege or advantage due to my dominant identities?
- How do I experience disadvantage and oppression based on my subordinated identities?
- How do the intersections of my various dominant and subordinated identities affect my experiences of power and marginalization?
- How do my dominant and subordinated status affect my sense of competency and how I am perceived by others?

By asking ourselves such questions, we can recognize how our positions of advantage and disadvantage across different forms of oppression may enhance and impede our efforts as educators.

Our Intersecting Social Group Membership and Positionality

Our social identities and dominant and subordinated statuses do not operate in isolation from each other. Nor do we live as individuals removed from our social group memberships and how we are positioned within the social, historical, and political landscape in relation to other social groups. Although the three authors of this chapter identify similarly in terms of gender, we are positioned differently based on other aspects of our identities:

As a South Asian woman who gets "read" as younger than her actual age, I find myself at the beginning of the semester listing my degrees, the schools I've attended and my years of experience in order to get students to buy into the course and the topics that I am teaching (Rani).

As a white, middle-aged, full professor, I am more likely to be treated as an expert in my field, although when I initially asked my undergraduates to call me by my first name, instead of the title "Professor" typical at my new institution, only the white male under-graduates felt comfortable doing so (Lee).

Even though I am white, upper-middle-class, and got good academic preparation, it has only been as I've gotten older with many years of experience that I have felt more confident and more respected by others (Diane).

In these examples, our memberships in racial or ethnic groups, class status, gender identity, and categories of age are linked and impact how we show up in the classroom and how students see and interact with us. Scholars and activists engaged with intersectional issues raise awareness of how an intersectional lens changes the way we look at our social locations as well as how we experience specific isms and their intersections (Collins, 2008; Crenshaw, 1989, 1993). "We have still to recognize that being a woman is, in fact, not extractable from the context in which one is a woman—that is, race, class, time, and place. We have still to recognize that all women do not have the same gender" (Brown, 1997, p. 276).

Thus, it is important as social justice educators that we not only examine our own positionality in relation to others, but also consider how our different dominant and sub-ordinated statuses intersect to shape our experiences in distinctive ways. Our individual social group memberships in dominant and subordinated groups are also complicated by and embedded in larger historical, political, and social contexts with their own power dynamics:

As a faculty member teaching in the field of Social Work, I think it is important to share with students that we are situated within a profession that has historically had a complex relationship to subordinated racial and ethnic groups who have experienced social work as an imposition of white, middle-class values and beliefs. I want students to be aware of this history when they work in different communities so they are not surprised by a client's potential mistrust of them. In addition, I want them to reflect on the biases they may bring to their work (Rani).

This is also true in my field of Education and preparing teachers (still predominantly white, middle-class, females) to work respectfully and knowledgeably with young people from a range of social identities in diverse schools and communities. I've been in this field a long time and I am still learning about biases and assumptions in teacher education that prevent teachers from dominant groups from seeing the strengths, capacities, and perspec-tives of people from marginalized communities—the very information that would enable educators from outside of the communities where they teach to be more effective (Lee).

Our social identities, dominant and subordinated statuses, our positionality in larger systems and ways these interact affect many facets of our work as social justice educators. The more aware we are of how who we are affects our knowledge, awareness, approaches, and interactions, the more effective we can be.

OUR DEGREE OF KNOWLEDGE AND SELF-AWARENESS

Each of us has varying levels of self-awareness and critical consciousness about differ-ent forms of oppression and our identities related to them. There are some social justice topics that we have explored deeply, while there may be others that we understand more superficially. We may have a lot of relationships with and insight into the experiences of individuals from some social identity groups, but we may have had little exposure to the realities of other groups. We may have worked hard on rooting out our stereotypes and assumptions about people from certain social/cultural groups but still carry a lot of unconscious bias about others. Some questions to consider include:

- With individuals from which social groups do I feel most and least comfortable?
- Which students do I feel I educate most or least effectively?
- Which topics or isms do I feel most and least comfortable teaching?

Self-knowledge about our levels of awareness in relation to our own social identities and positionality, the experiences and lives of others, our knowledge of social justice issues and content are important considerations in our development as social justice educators.

Social Identity Development

As described in Chapter 2, social identity development theory describes a psychosocial process of phases of awareness and change in ways that people think about their own social group membership(s), other social groups, and social oppression. Where we are in our own journey of identity development influences how we intellectually understand and emotionally respond to particular social topics and interpersonal dynamics in the classroom.

Instructors who are early in their own process of social identity development may not be ready to teach about certain social justice issues where they lack a depth of knowledge in the subject, have not gained awareness of their own internalized assumptions, or have not developed knowledge to critique dominant narratives that support that particular form of oppression. At earlier stages of social identity development, it may be hard to clearly understand how we are affected by and participate in systems of inequality, or we may feel too self-conscious about our identity or knowledge of the oppression to be confident teaching the material. Consider these examples:

- A cisgender instructor, just learning about transgender issues, is tentative about addressing transgender issues and stumbles as he tries to find the right language.
- A white instructor's self-consciousness about her own racial identity and authority to speak on racial issues makes her reluctant to question an inaccurate statement about race made by a participant of color.
- A secular Jew, who has given little thought to his Jewish identity, is unprepared to address the questions and challenges Jewish students raise about the intersections of antisemitism, racism, and white privilege.

Some instructors at early points in their process may find it especially challenging to manage feelings such as anger, guilt, or frustration, or may be more likely to feel triggered by student comments or behaviors, and lack the patience or compassion to work with participants empathically and effectively. This dynamic can occur whether we are in the dominant or subordinated group working with people from our own or different social identity groups.

Early in my teaching about racism, when I was still grappling with guilt about being white, I sometimes found myself feeling disdainful and judgmental towards other white participants, in ways that interfered with my effectiveness. As I became clearer about my own white identity and my responsibility to educate other white people about racism, I was able to be more empathic about their struggles. I could then be more effective in helping them engage with the issues rather than resist or turn away from responsibly addressing racism (Lee).

When I first started teaching about sexism, I found myself being triggered by women in the class who were adamant that sexism was not an issue for "their generation." Over time, I was able to ask these women questions about why they didn't think sexism was relevant for them rather than bombard them with endless examples to try to get them to change their mind (Rani).

As instructors gain greater awareness and progress through their own social identity development around different issues, they can be more conscious and purposeful in dealing with students who are at various stages in their learning. Often the intensity of our reactions diminishes and we are better able to manage situations that arise.

Certain identities may also be more salient depending on where we are in our own development *across* forms of oppression. Sometimes when we are deeply involved with one identity or inequality, it can be more difficult to attend to other social identities or forms of oppression. As one instructor shared, *"I know it's really important that I'm white, but right now I'm dealing with coming out as a lesbian!"* Often we are not even aware that we are overlooking the significance of our other social identities.

While it can be helpful to focus on one social identity at a time when we are in the process of learning, ideally we want to become aware of our role in all forms of oppression. Undoubtedly, we will have varying degrees of awareness of different identities and will need to continually increase our self-awareness and critical consciousness across all forms of inequality. Moreover, instructors need to understand how our intersecting identities and positionalities affect our social identity development process.

I share with students that I didn't have to confront the ways in which I was privileged being Christian until later in college because most people assume that I am Hindu or Muslim. I use this example to illustrate my awareness about the complexity of identity, that I can simultaneously get "read" ethnically and religiously in a subordinate way but experience privilege because of my affinity to Christianity. Some of my students who don't feel "privileged" but are part of dominant social identity groups can relate to this example (Rani).

While I began to intentionally explore my white identity before my Jewish identity, understanding what it meant to be Jewish helped me deepen my understanding of the complexity and nuances of being white (Diane).

Reflecting on our process of social identity development can help us relate to the feelings and challenges our students may be facing as they move through their own social identity development with different issues of oppression. We can share with students how we have dealt with oppressive conditioning at different stages so as to continue to grow. When educators model self-awareness about their own identities, processes of identity development, and inevitable gaps in knowledge and consciousness, they are likely to garner more trust and respect from students. This is especially critical for educators from advantaged groups working with individuals from disadvantaged groups who may withhold trust until they see evidence from instructors that they are aware of their own social location(s) and what members of other groups experience. When we have worked on and are more comfortable with our own social identity development across the range of identities, we can be more authentic and competent in the classroom and teach with greater clarity, empathy, and effectiveness.

Awareness of Norms That Reinforce Privilege and Marginalization

Our social identities and relative privilege or marginality in different social groups will influence our perspectives on, and awareness of, particular social justice issues and dynamics. Dominant status generally makes us less conscious of our privileges and of the disadvantages and oppression experienced by members of marginalized groups, since dominant identities and experiences are normalized. The culture of higher education, for example, tends to assume and take for granted white, Western, middle- and upper-class norms that may or may not match the cultural styles and social experiences of our students/participants. This is common in other organizations as well. Our own familiarity and comfort with these norms may vary depending on the mix of social identities and dominant/subordinated statuses we bring to the institution.

As social justice educators, we need to acknowledge the norms that surround learning and be aware of the extent to which we accept or question those norms.

In a course with adult learners who were balancing the class with jobs and family responsibilities, students were upset with the cost of the textbook and the amount of out-of-class work. Even though I had experienced these same constraints as a student myself, it had not occurred to me to challenge institutional norms. I initiated a discussion with them about the challenges they were experiencing and connected this back to issues of classism and the unexamined assumptions that reinforce class privilege. The discussion led to more thoughtful decisions about having course texts and class assignments accessible to students who may not be able to afford them (i.e., develop a library of books to loan students, ensure multiple copies on reserve in the library, encouraging sharing of texts and collaborative assignments, etc. (Lee).

Other examples of how dominant status can lead to lack of awareness that can reinforce norms that marginalize students include:

- A cisgender instructor does not consider the location of gender-neutral bathrooms that may be needed by trans* students.
- An upper-middle-class instructor assigns students to attend a local theater performance or museum exhibit without considering the impact of transportation and ticket costs on students with limited means, or accessible transportation and access for students with disabilities.

As educators, it is hard to figure out what we don't know. Therefore, it is important that we regularly reflect on our identities and positionality in communities of other scholars or learners who are different and similar to us, knowing that a lack of awareness can lead us to have limited perspectives or leave out information and views that are central to a social justice curriculum. For example,

During a workshop, a Deaf participant objected to having deafness considered a disability because for her it is solely a culture. This was an important perspective for me and the class to learn about (Diane).

We may also treat marginalized group perspectives in tokenized ways and miss the nuances that can effectively challenge stereotypes and exclusions. Since educators from dominant groups are often less aware of and informed about the lives of people from subordinated groups, it is not surprising that it is more often people from marginalized groups who notice omissions and push to have their experiences and voices included in the curriculum. Consider these examples:

- Native American or indigenous people often feel their histories and realities are not included in discussions of racism that do not give adequate attention to colonization.
- People of color have fought for years to have their histories and realities included as important and accurately reflected in courses that are not exclusively about race.
- LGBTQ (lesbian, gay, bisexual, transgender, and queer) students have been the ones spearheading efforts to have their experiences and oppression included in diversity and social justice courses.

Sometimes, marginalized status can make us more aware of and sensitive to issues that others from our social group face.

As someone who grew up working class and a first-generation academic, I am intentional about discussing graduate school with the undergraduate students I teach, many of them first-generation college students, in order to dispel ideas that this is not a route for them and to explicitly encourage this route as a possibility they can consider for themselves (Rani).

While instructors from marginalized groups have some first-hand knowledge of oppression, they are not immune from lack of awareness and knowledge about social injustice and/or from internalized oppression (where they have internalized the stereotypes about their group). None of us knows everything there is to know about our own social group(s) since we are only expert on our own experience. Additionally, we are individually at different places in our process of social identity development. Even when well-informed about one form of oppression we experience, if we are not also knowledgeable about other forms of oppression, we cannot effectively see and address how these issues intersect.

For a long time I've been involved with feminism and women's issues, but I still need to stay conscious about the complex and varied experiences of women who have other social identities different than mine and face other forms of oppression that impact how they encounter sexism. Just because I'm a woman does not mean I understand their realities (Diane).

Clearly, developing greater insight into the complexity of our own and other social identity groups and experiences of privilege and marginalization is an essential and ongoing process.

ASSUMPTIONS AND BIASES

Everyone has biases, both recognized and unrecognized. Like our students, we have internalized assumptions and stereotypes about our own and other social groups through socialization and societal conditioning. We need to recognize that none of us stand outside of or above the systems we study, and that our perspectives are inevitably partial and shaped by our social locations.

Research reveals how insidious and harmful implicit or unconscious bias can be (Banaji & Greenwald, 2013; Staats, 2013, 2014). Scholarship about "microaggressions," the commonplace, persistent, and often unintentional, negative slights toward people from marginalized groups, shows how biases reveal themselves and affect others in profound ways (Huber & Solórzano, 2015; Solórzano, Ceja, & Yosso, 2000; Sue, 2010a, 2010b). Research in educational settings demonstrates how microaggressions negatively impact academic achievement, feelings of inclusion, and levels of stress (Sue, Lin, Torino, Capodilupo, & Rivera, 2009). To ensure we do not unwittingly perpetuate or allow microaggressions in our classes or workshops, it is critical that instructors examine our own assumptions and become conscious of how they may shape our interactions with participants in damaging ways we may not consciously intend.

During a fishbowl activity where different ethnic/racial groups talked about their specific experiences of race and racism, the Native American affinity group was listed to go last, resulting in the students having the least amount of time to talk and enacting structural racism, where indigenous voices and perspectives are silenced or made invisible. In my next class, it was critical that I named what my co-instructor and I had unconsciously done and the ways we, she as a white woman and I as a South Asian woman, could still engage in oppressive behaviors after having taught about race and racism for years (Rani).

As illustrated, there are innumerable ways prejudices, stereotypes, and assumptions can show up in the classroom. An instructor may treat students as "experts" or representative of their whole group rather than as individuals who may enact their experiences in the group in a range of ways. For example:

- Asking a Muslim person what Muslims think of the U.S. war on terror, as if all Muslims think alike
- Expecting a Latina student who is from Colombia to know about the history of the Mexican holiday Cinco de Mayo, not recognizing the variety of national, cultural, and historical experiences among people who are defined as Latina/o in the U.S.
- Requesting that a Jewish participant explain a particular Jewish holiday, assuming all Jews are knowledgeable about Judaism

Instructors may make presumptions that everyone shares the norms of the dominant culture, and/or may devalue subordinated group norms, styles, and experiences. For example:

- An instructor uses only hetero-normative examples or assumes all students are having heterosexual romantic relationships
- An educator complains that some students are "too quiet" or "too loud and emotional" or "not logical enough" and doesn't recognize their own limited knowledge about and inability to value different cultural orientations

Facilitators may also act out the ways they have internalized the pervasive societal messages about the superiority of dominant groups and inferiority of subordinated groups. This may be evidenced when:

- A facilitator pays more attention to male participants or gives more credence to their comments;
- An instructor takes a paternalistic stance that discourages independence and risk-taking by a student with a disability;
- A faculty member exhibits lower academic or intellectual expectations, such as being surprised or dubious when a working-class student hands in a particularly well-written paper.

While it can be unnerving to have our prejudices or unconscious biases revealed, we can learn to appreciate these missteps as important learning opportunities.

I mixed up the names of two black women in the class. One of them said she felt that it was a racist microaggression. I had to resist my urge to explain why I made that mistake, and instead, took a breath and apologized, said that I understood why she was offended, and would commit to not do that again (Diane).

We know that recognizing and rooting out deeply socialized prejudices and practices is a difficult and lifelong process. If we model willingness to acknowledge, get feedback, and reflect on our assumptions and biases (intentional or not) and demonstrate efforts to correct them, we show students that they, too, can be open to constructive feedback, will survive being challenged, and with practice and persistence, can develop more thoughtful and socially just ways to respond.

I have been fortunate to have the opportunity to spend a lot of time in Southeast Asia as part of the family I married into and have had many of my assumptions about my own and other ethnic groups or cultures challenged by these encounters. I try to share with students examples of some of the biases that have been uncovered and what I have learned through my experiences in another culture or with another ethnic group (Lee).

Only when we become aware of our biases and assumptions can we take active, conscious steps to overcome them and minimize their impact in our teaching. Research suggests that expanding our knowledge of and contact with different groups, monitoring our thoughts and biases, engaging in perspective-taking, and building empathy are ways to mitigate unconscious bias (Staat, 2013). This is important ongoing work for educators, since acting on our unconscious bias only undermines our educational effectiveness and efforts for social justice.

INTERPERSONAL AND GROUP DYNAMICS

Self-knowledge and self-awareness are also essential for understanding how we relate with participants and interpret and respond to the group dynamics in classes and workshops. In this section, we focus on the impact of our interpersonal styles and how we manage and develop skillful responses to the inevitably challenging situations that arise in social justice teaching. To be effective facilitators, we need to be aware of the complex mix of feelings, thoughts, behaviors, and experiences that make us who we are, as well as monitor how this affects our interactions with participants and handling of group processes.

INTERPERSONAL STYLES

Social identities shape communication styles, how we interact with others, and our comfort with self-disclosure. Families and communities have different norms around eye contact, touch, speaking patterns, expression of humor and emotion, and degree of directness and indirectness in conversation and gestures (DuPraw & Axner, 1997; Sue & Sue, 2013). Our socialization and cultural norms influence our teaching style as well. Some instructors (and students) are more familiar and comfortable with a formal and linear approach to teaching that focuses on facts and figures. Others may prefer a more personal, fluid, and experiential approach that draws on storytelling, sharing feelings and experiences, and using imagery and metaphors. In some social/cultural groups, it is viewed as improper and inappropriate to share or solicit personal information; while in other communities, such sharing is considered acceptable, appropriate, and valued.

These norms influence how an instructor teaches, interacts with, and is perceived by participants.

I have found that my sarcastic sense of humor and direct communication style, a product of my New York area Jewish upbringing, can be perceived as harsh to those unaccustomed to that style (Diane).

Additionally:

- A formal teaching and interpersonal style may be interpreted by some as distant and uncaring or as more proper and professional, while a more informal style may be viewed as warm and caring or as unserious and unprofessional, depending on the perceptions of different students.
- A fast-talking educator may make it difficult for a hearing-impaired participant who is reading lips or using an interpreter, or for people for whom English is a second language.
- An instructor who requests eye contact from students may be perceived as intrusive or insensitive by students raised in cultures where eye contact, especially with authority figures, is considered inappropriate or disrespectful.

The dominant and subordinated status of the facilitator may also affect how the same behavior gets read differently by participants. A soft-spoken man may be viewed positively as gentle and approachable, while a woman may be seen as unassertive and weak. A white woman who speaks strongly may be seen as confident and authoritative, while a black woman may be seen as angry and strident.

As we gain greater awareness of our social identities and related interpersonal styles and orientations, we can better appreciate how we may be perceived or misperceived by our students, adjust accordingly, and be prepared to deal with their reactions.

NOTICING AND RESPONDING TO GROUP DYNAMICS

Group dynamics in social justice education require attention to both content and process dimensions. The *content* of social justice education provides information about enduring historical injustice and inequitable patterns and practices that are normalized in mainstream society. It also includes information about struggles for justice and possibilities for change. The *process* of social justice education involves managing the individual, interpersonal, and group dynamics that arise as we and our students, with divergent levels of awareness, knowledge, and experience, grapple with social justice issues. Engagement with information that either confirms or questions what individuals have thought to be true typically generates feelings of anger, shock, guilt, disbelief, sadness, and powerlessness as they confront the enormity and pervasiveness of oppression.

While group dynamics are important in any learning situation, in the social justice classroom they take on added weight. Group members deal with emotional reactions, and negotiate asymmetric power relations and historically and culturally embedded patterns of interaction—whether tacit or explicit, acknowledged or not. What do we need to know about ourselves to create and maintain a learning environment that is respectful and inclusive for all? Facilitators who have spent time exploring how we typically respond to these process-level issues will be better prepared to address them rather than be taken off guard or unable to handle them when they arise.

For example, what do we do when a participant makes an offensive comment and all eyes turn to us to see how we will respond? The more we have reflected on our automatic feelings and reactions in such situations (fright, exposure, inadequacy, shutting down, or freezing), the more able we will be to respond in thoughtful and appropriate ways, rather than respond ineffectively by quickly avoiding and moving past the moment.

I was facilitating a fishbowl discussion on the film "Race: The Power of an Illusion" when an African American woman tearfully shared her deep sadness at realizing the structural barriers she had always taken as personal. When a white participant interrupted to say it was the same for her as a working-class white person and thus not about race, I could feel the air leave the room. By pausing the conversation to examine the dynamics of what had just happened, we were able to listen more carefully to both speakers and unpack relations of dominance and subordination reflected in the interaction. Had the conversation continued without fully discussing the dynamics involved, we would have reproduced the very dynamics of racism we were trying to challenge (Lee).

To a large extent, what we notice and how we respond to interpersonal dynamics are shaped by our families and communities of origin and the early injunctions we internalize about what is and is not appropriate. These messages affect how we respond to both verbal and nonverbal behavior. For example, those of us raised with familial or cultural norms that deem it inappropriate to comment on others' interactions or conduct may have a difficult time doing so in the classroom. For example:

- When a participant makes a rude face as another participant is speaking, a facilitator raised to "do as I say, not as I do" may ignore or fail to address nonverbal cues that impact relationships in the group in ways that interfere with learning.

- A trainer who was taught not to notice color or was "shushed" when noticing people with disabilities may be uncomfortable discussing differences and prefer to highlight similarities among people, thus avoiding important conversations about difference and discrimination.
- A female instructor raised to be "polite" and not interrupt may find it challenging to intervene when a participant is dominating or derailing the discussion.

Our ability to notice and respond to interpersonal dynamics is also affected by our various social group identities and relative positions of dominance and subordination. For example:

- White people are socialized to view the world from a white normative frame and thus may not notice the racial dynamics when a white participant interrupts or minimizes comments by classmates of color.
- Women are often socialized to harmonize and keep the peace, and may smooth over conflict rather than name and address it directly.
- Native English speakers may overlook participants for whom English is a second language, further marginalizing them in class discussions.

Facilitators who have not examined their own socialization may find it difficult to openly and effectively address racial, gender, sexuality, class, and other dynamics in ways that facilitate rather than block learning. Examining our own social identities and cultural conditioning can help us to be more conscious and willing to notice and name interactions we have been taught to ignore, even when we feel uncomfortable doing so. We can learn to address group dynamics directly, whether naming what is going on, asking clarifying questions, providing time for people to take a moment to reflect silently on the situation, or opening up a discussion about the impact of language and behavior and how people are feeling. Greater awareness of our own socialization will help us learn to facilitate group dynamics in ways that effectively interrupt oppressive interactions and promote learning.

UNDERSTANDING OUR RESPONSES TO EMOTIONAL INTENSITY

Exploring issues of social injustice in which we are all implicated and encountering information that challenges deeply held views and convictions, inevitably generates strong emotions. We have been shaped by the same damaging, misinformed view of the world as our students, and like them, we respond to learning about injustice emotionally as well as cognitively.

That social justice education is not only cognitive but also affective is a challenging awareness for those of us trained to show expertise in the subjects we teach, and to convey confidence and certainty in what we know. Many instructors have not been taught, nor do they feel prepared, to deal with emotionally laden content. Moreover, confronting the often fraught emotions raised by issues of injustice, and acknowledging that we don't have all the answers, places us as instructors in a very different position than how many of us have been groomed, especially in the academy. How we personally handle emotional intensity affects our ability to allow and handle emotion in the classroom in constructive ways. We can prepare ourselves by examining and reflecting on those emotions with which we feel most and least comfortable.

I grew up in a household with immigrant parents where I was taught to "keep to myself" and avoid conflict; and thus, in social justice classrooms where constructive conflict is encouraged and may be a part of dialogue, I've had to re-examine my comfort or discomfort with conflict (Rani).

I grew up in a family where I remember the elders yelling at each other, in good fun, as they discussed the issues of the day. I now realize that I am not unnerved by conflict or strong voices and emotions (Diane).

Being raised in a family or culture where feelings are not openly expressed, for example, further reinforces professional training to be "neutral" and suppress the display of emotions in the classroom—responses that are usually counterproductive to facilitating authentic discussion. On the other hand, being raised in a familial or cultural context where feelings are stated bluntly and directly may clash with student beliefs that such directness is rude or improper. Those socialized to read strong emotion as hostile or to be feared may withdraw or shut down in the face of such emotions. A facilitator who is uncomfortable with tears may refocus the discussion when a student starts crying while speaking passionately, rather than accept the tears and tune into what the student is saying. Even instructors who are comfortable with emotion may not know how to effectively work with it in a class or workshop. For example:

- An instructor who was conditioned to devalue emotions may find it hard to validate and support the expression of feelings.
- A faculty member who was raised in a family with a lot of emotional intensity may regard classes as ineffective unless they are highly emotionally intense.
- People from some African American and Latino communities may value emotional expressiveness and heated discussions of issues that matter to them and may be suspicious of those who are perceived as too restrained in a discussion.

Self-reflection becomes a critical tool for understanding our reactions to and ability to respond to emotions honestly and constructively rather than avoiding them.

Examining the emotional climate in our family and cultural background can make us more conscious of the feelings we find hardest to address, especially those we tend to avoid, distort, or fear. We can learn to moderate automatic first reactions or interpretations and consider how emotional expressiveness can be a reflection of cultural and familial styles of expression different than ours. For example, white people may read people of color as "angry" when they are simply expressing strong feelings. White facilitators who are aware of this pattern can be more conscious and open to participants who express themselves in this way. Men often read women as "irrational" when they are expressing emotion directly. Male facilitators who have examined their own response to emotional expressiveness can be more respectful and empathic of other styles of response.

Emotional reactions may also be affected by dominant/subordinated status. It is common for those in the dominant group to take a more distant stance in discussions of injustices we have been taught to ignore or accept as normal. In fact, one of the ways privilege works is through insulating people in dominant groups from the stress of dealing with the uncomfortable topics of oppression (DiAngelo, 2011). It is much harder for someone who is directly targeted by oppression to have a dispassionate view. Acknowledging one's own feelings of outrage at injustices perpetuated on our group can help an instructor be more empathic and understanding of participants from other groups who react intensely to examples of injustice. With such awareness, they can then can proactively help those from dominant groups understand and respect the intensity their classmates feel.

Learning to recognize different patterns of expression provides a frame for developing more comfort with emotional or "heated" discussions and respond in ways that support learning from such encounters. A group whose members are too guarded or mistrustful:

. . . may never move beyond the initial watchful stage as members fail to take the risks needed to move learning forward in the group. Or a group can become mired in conflict when there is not enough trust, skill or commitment to engage with and work through the challenges that inevitably arise.

(Bell, 2010, p. 93)

When a supportive climate has been established, "losing control" or facing strong emotions can become constructive and often transformative, enabling students and facilitators to connect on a deeper level. In fact, participants often make fundamental shifts in their perspectives after they have experienced someone "losing" control, revealing the deeper feelings, fears, and experiences surrounding oppression that are always operating but rarely expressed, especially in mixed groups. Our ability as facilitators to manage the group process thoughtfully, skillfully, and empathically is crucial for learning and relies on our own self-awareness. This self-knowledge is important preparation for managing emotions in the classroom and responding thoughtfully to participants, especially in moments of tension and uncertainty.

IDENTIFYING TRIGGERS THAT "PUSH OUR BUTTONS"

Dealing with comments and behaviors that "push our buttons" or "trigger" us is another common concern for social justice educators. Being triggered refers to getting "hooked" or having an unexpected, intense emotional reaction to a situation or person (Obear, 2013). Any number of things can trigger us for any number of reasons. When we are triggered, it makes it harder to pay attention to what is going on in the moment while we are caught up with our own internal thoughts, feelings, and physical sensations.

Given the social justice content and our personal relationship to it, it is especially likely that we may have strong emotional responses to the material or dynamics in the group. It is no surprise that certain content, behaviors, or words can trigger emotional reactions.

People from marginalized communities usually have a long history with and a heightened sensitivity to negative cues (language as well as verbal and nonverbal behaviors) that signal oppressive attitudes. They have been subjected to, suffered from, discussed, and thought about such cues throughout the course of their lives, and so they are often highly tuned to note them in the behavior and language used by members of the dominant group. Dominant group members, on the other hand, are more likely oblivious to the effects of their verbal and nonverbal communication on people from subordinated groups, and in fact are quite often shocked to realize their effect. Thus, the potential for breakdown in communication, hurt feelings, defensiveness, and recrimination is high.

I recall facilitating a discussion where a middle-class teacher commented on the "trashy" appearance of a child in her class. Two class members immediately reacted with outrage at the stereotyping and devaluation of people with few resources. As working-class mothers themselves, they were triggered by the classist assumptions in the statement of which the speaker was oblivious (Lee).

Since facilitators are not immune to being triggered, we need to recognize the comments and signals to which we are most susceptible. As noted previously, where instructors are in the process of their own social identity development around different forms of oppression can affect how likely they are to be triggered. Facilitators who are members of a marginalized group may understandably find it difficult to listen to hurtful stereotypes and attitudes they have been confronted with all their lives. Such expressions are painful and can re-stimulate past fears, anxieties, and intense feelings. We may feel angry and want to retaliate, even when we know that acting directly on these feelings would be inappropriate and counterproductive to the goals of the session. We may feel rejected and lose confidence, or become defensive and stuck while the "voices in our head" yammer on, reinforcing feelings of ineptitude or fear or anger.

I was doing a pre-planned role-play about addressing a homophobic comment. When we were done, my co-presenter, a lesbian, was supposed to lead the discussion. She sat there immobilized. She later explained that she was unexpectedly overwhelmed with emotion watching that interaction (Diane).

Other situations where triggers may arise include

- A facilitator who grew up in poverty may want to lash out when participants express disparaging stereotypes about poor people.
- A Native American instructor may be stunned into silence when seeing students jokingly do "tomahawk chops" and war cries while discussing conflicts between Indigenous people and settlers.
- A facilitator with a disability may bristle at listening to participants express pity and condescension toward people with disabilities.

Facilitators from dominant groups also can be triggered by situations in the classroom or workshop:

- A white facilitator may feel panic when challenged by a participant of color about a racial issue, feeling ignorant and exposed.
- A straight white male professor may react angrily when female students frame him as the "oppressor," feeling invalidated for all the work he has done on feminist issues.
- An instructor who grew up wealthy but has been committed to addressing income inequality may feel embarrassment and disdain when upper-class students express classist sentiments, reminding her of her own struggles.

We can notice and respond to triggers on several levels: We can look within at our own response and try to figure out what is going on for the participant who has been triggered, and we can consider the impact on the group. One level relates to reflecting on our own reactions to what is occurring in the moment: "Why am I so annoyed at this person or comment? What does it trigger for me?" On another level, we can consider how the individual who did or said the triggering behavior might be thinking or feeling and shift the frame to figure it out. Questions such as, "What prompted this behavior?" "What's really going on for this individual?" and "How can I help them try out a new perspective?" may help us respond more productively. Lastly, If we are feeling triggered, others may be as well, so we also need to consider the effect on the other members of the group. Not only do we need to try to gain clarity and composure about our own reaction and consider how to respond to the person who did the triggering behavior, but we need to assess what is happening for others in the class.

In a discussion about sexual assault where victim-blaming comments were made, I felt overwhelmed about how to engage those specific students as well as the whole class given my assumption that there were probably folks who identified as survivors of gender-based violence in the room (Rani).

In situations where we feel triggered, there are numerous options for what we can do. (Also see Chapter 3 for suggestions.) We can pause, take a deep breath, and try to refocus our attention to the situation at hand. We can utilize self-talk to help us regain composure and shift our reaction. We can acknowledge the tensions of the moment and take a short break, or have people sit, reflect, and free-write for a few minutes, and then come back and share their thoughts with a partner or with the group as a whole. We can pose questions to the group that help participants to process the situation in a reflective and thoughtful way.

Developing a support system of peers with whom we can discuss issues, share feelings, and get support can be extremely helpful. For example, meeting regularly with a colleague to debrief and talk, and/or keeping a journal to note and analyze our feelings and reactions to certain triggering statements or actions, provide outlets for ongoing self-reflection. Analyzing how we typically react, and thinking through other possible responses ahead of time, provides more options for responding in thoughtful ways in those loaded moments when our buttons are pushed.

I know that I am triggered by participants who dominate conversation and seem unable to accurately hear what others are saying. I think this comes from my own experiences as a child feeling unheard or misinterpreted by the adults around me and helpless to change the situation. The more I have thought about this issue, the better able I have been to acknowledge when I am feeling triggered and to respond in a way that is constructive rather than defensive and emotionally loaded (Lee).

The more we can stay open to our own internal process, the more insight we can gain into our own feelings and reactions. Knowledge of our triggers helps us anticipate and even plan for them. This awareness allows us to get less hooked by particular actions and gives us more options for how to address the situation. We likely can be more present to what may be going on for our students so that we can respond to them with compassion and understanding. An appreciation for the process we all go through in developing awareness about oppression can also help us acquire patience when dealing with our own frustrations and feelings toward participants.

NAVIGATING ISSUES OF COMPETENCE AND AUTHORITY WITHIN INSTITUTIONS AND COMMUNITIES

In this section, we look at issues of competence and authority we may face as social justice educators. *Competency* encompasses our knowledge of the content we teach and our ability to effectively convey relevant theories and concepts, as well as our ability to manage group dynamics and relationships with participants in ways that promote learning. *Authority* includes our ability to establish ourselves in the classroom or workshop as credible, and to use our position in strategic and effective ways to accomplish curricular goals. Our social identities and social locations affect both our felt and perceived competence and authority, and greater self-knowledge can help us deal with both internal and external challenges to our sense of efficacy as instructors. These dynamics can include navigating organizational cultures, norms, and rules as well as managing interactions with other members of the institution (colleagues, faculty, staff, administrators, students, or clients), and the larger community.

SELF AND OTHER PERCEPTIONS OF COMPETENCY AND AUTHORITY

Our social identities and social locations affect both how we experience ourselves as capable and authoritative, as well as how our competence and authority are viewed by others. "Despite decades of efforts to increase faculty, staff and student diversity, the culture of academia remains distinctly white, male, heterosexual, and middle- to upper-class"

(Gonzalez & Harris, 2014, p. 183). Faculty of color, women, LGBTQ faculty, and other faculty from subordinated groups are often perceived as less authoritative, may experience resistance to course content, and face questions about their competency and authority in ways that members of the dominant group(s), whose competence and authority are assumed, do not (Amos, 2014; Jean-Marie, Grant, & Irby, 2014; Messner, 2000; Gutierrez y Muhs, Niemann, González, & Harris, 2012; Tuitt, Hanna, Martinez, Salazar, & Griffin, 2009).

As a faculty member of color, I have had to ask students to call me "Dr." or "Professor," refer explicitly to my educational training, and dress in a more formal manner to project authority even though the culture of the institutions where I've worked is one where faculty are called by their first names and the style of dress is much less formal (Rani).

Questions about our competency and authority are heightened when the course includes social justice content and pedagogy. Moving away from hierarchical, banking models and facilitating an interactive process that invites engagement, exploration, and critical analysis represents a different definition of competence and authority than the traditional one of content mastery and expertise (Brookfield (2012); Brookfield & Preskill, 2005; Maher & Tetreault, 2001). Given these issues, it is important for us think through and be able to articulate and support with confidence the philosophies that undergird our pedagogical decisions.

Utilizing social justice education pedagogy may raise additional concerns for instructors from marginalized groups. For example, rather than use more interactive, learner-centered approaches that she believes are more effective for particular learning goals, a new young instructor may feel obligated to rely on PowerPoint in order to assert her authority in the class or workshop.

The privileged and marginalized statuses of instructors from different social identity groups influence how students are likely to perceive us. The interplay of race, class, gender, sexual orientation, age, ability, and other subordinated identities can impact how comfortable instructors feel acknowledging mistakes or gaps in knowledge, given they often already get constructed as less competent. For example:

- An older instructor may find it difficult to acknowledge when he says something inaccurate because of fears that displaying uncertainty will be attributed to his age.
- A gay or lesbian instructor who has to weigh the risks of self-disclosure may not invite the further scrutiny that personal sharing may bring.
- An immigrant instructor of color who speaks with an accent may not want to reveal lack of knowledge of an issue for fear of being further invalidated.

Issues of authority become especially complicated for those with multiple subordinated identities. For example:

- Given the typical black-white narrative about racism, an Asian American female instructor in a class on race and racism may not be seen as having legitimate knowledge about the material or authority to speak on the subject matter.
- A gay Latino may be perceived by students as politicizing class content when he teaches about heterosexism and linguicism.
- A working-class African American who teaches about race and racism in classrooms that are predominantly white may be perceived by students as teaching this content to deal with his "personal problem" or "agenda."
- A female instructor who uses a wheelchair may be patronized by students who fail to recognize her scholarly strengths and pedagogical skills.

Gender may influence issues of competency and authority in particular ways. Through the process of socialization, women are bombarded with messages about deferring to male authority, being "nice," and not seeing themselves as those with power and voice. Women who ultimately achieve positions of power may be pressured to embody a "male" style of leadership, distance themselves from other women, or struggle with feeling like imposters in these roles (Clance & Imes, 1978; Young, 2011). Students may evaluate and judge female faculty according to gender stereotypes.

I once co-taught with a female professor who used examples of her experiences raising her daughter to illustrate sexism. She received feedback in her end-of-semester evaluations that the course was based in personal narratives and not theoretically grounded (Rani).

Or students may expect a female faculty member to fulfill stereotypes, such as being more nurturing, and may push back when she does not fulfill these narratives.

A Latina faculty member at my institution was read by students as cold and distant because she resisted taking on a nurturing role and demanded hard work from her students (Lee).

Many times students are unaware of the stereotypes they project onto their instructors. As instructors, we need to anticipate and work with both conscious and unconscious projections that are at play in the classroom. In particular, we need to be aware of how participants' projections can trigger our vulnerabilities around competency and authority. Without consciously examining how we deal with the reactions from others, we may be susceptible to internalizing external constructions as who we are.

Given this pitfall, it is important to explore our own internalized oppression (i.e., internalized racism, sexism, classism, etc.). Instructors from subordinated groups may adopt the dominant group's ideology and accept their subordinated status as deserved, natural, or inevitable (Joseph & Williams, 2008; Niemann, 2012; Tappan, 2006); as a result, they may have too limited a view of themselves and their abilities, or second-guess what they have to offer or their pedagogy. For example, a faculty member who is a first-generation academic may struggle with the "imposter phenomenon" (Clance & Imes, 1978) and exhibit self-doubt and a lack of confidence, or unconsciously utilize their power in the classroom in overbearing and ineffective ways.

I have colleagues who earned an advanced degree, who are from low-income backgrounds and the first in their families to go to college. They are particularly vulnerable to self-doubts about being smart enough or belonging in academia when they get critical feedback on a manuscript or a class didn't go well (Diane).

Instructors from dominant groups may question their right and legitimacy to speak about social justice issues. Instructors need to continually try to distinguish between what is true about ourselves and what are participant assumptions and projections.

In addition, many courses that are identified as having social justice content are seen as less rigorous and often characterized as "soft science" (DiAngelo & Sensoy, 2014). Instructors who teach social justice-related courses often note that students come into the classroom expecting an "A" or have the misconception that the course will be "easy." Students who feel entitled to a particular grade may challenge the instructor's authority to assign grades, particularly a grade that the student does not want to accept. Faculty who hold privileged identities may be challenged less than other faculty members.

INSTITUTIONAL AND COMMUNITY CHALLENGES AND SUPPORT

One of the concerns about teaching from a social justice perspective is the response from the institution or organization when we depart from traditional formats and content. As we engage with social justice issues and change our classrooms accordingly, we often come into conflict with institutional norms of professed objectivity, authority, and professorial distance in ways that can undermine our confidence, and in some cases jeopardize our positions. Instructors who are female and instructors of color often receive lower evaluations in courses, and those who teach courses about social justice often receive lower ratings than those who teach traditional courses (Lazos, 2012; Messner, 2000; Pittman, 2010; Tusmith & Reddy, 2002). Faculty who most often choose to and/or who are asked to teach social justice courses are commonly from underrepresented groups and frequently untenured. Thus, the most vulnerable groups take on the most difficult and institutionally risky teaching. Instructors from marginalized groups often face heightened challenges and frequently receive less institutional support than colleagues from dominant groups.

- *A student's mother complained to the dean that her daughter's Latina professor (my colleague) was a bad teacher and that if she did not get the grade she "deserved" (wanted), the mother would take it up the chain of command. What was striking about this example was that while the dean was ultimately supportive, the faculty member felt interrogated and that she had to "prove" herself in ways not expected of her white colleagues (Lee).*
- *An African American instructor was accused of racial harassment and formally reprimanded for sharing with her Communication class her critique of the all-white college newspaper staff and pointing out a historical trend where the voices and stories of white men were centered.*

(Gibney, 2013)

These dynamics and risks are not limited to academe. In other contexts, such as human service and community or business organizations, leaders of social justice training can be invalidated as too "touchy feely" or "too political." Experiential approaches may be devalued as inappropriate or not serious, and the judgment and expertise of the facilitator may be questioned, especially when the facilitator is from a marginalized group. Facilitators who do not have traditional credentials or organizational status, or come from a lower socio-economic group than others in the organization, may be discounted as having "only personal experience" to offer.

Beyond the classroom or organization, instructors may have experiences within the community that further challenge their legitimacy. The following story exemplifies the difficulties instructors with multiple marginalized identities face. When relocating to a small town that was not racially diverse, a faculty member of color who was read as male because of her gender expression experienced difficulties from the day she arrived. The day before her first class, she was pulled over by a white police officer who refused to believe she was a faculty member and cited her for a minor driving violation. She had to consider who she could call on for support in a predominantly white institution and community where she did not know anyone, and had to cancel classes while she negotiated the possible legal and criminal justice consequences of this arrest (Patton, 2014).

How does this instructor manage the burden of knowing that she is perceived first by her race, skin color, and gender expression rather than her talents, credentials, and the valuable contributions she can make? What are the vulnerabilities she navigates if she decides to share her story with peers and students as an example of profiling? What are the costs of sharing such a narrative in class or publicly? How does not sharing what happened to cause her to cancel her first class create space for students to make assumptions or judgments about the instructor and judge her abilities to instruct them? Finding ways to name systemic inequities when they occur and discern what is true about ourselves are critical in order to cope and thrive. All faculty, but especially those from marginalized groups, need mentors who can help them navigate institutional challenges.

Being aware how we are constructed in the classroom, institution, and community can prepare us for some of the dynamics and challenges to our competency and authority. Self-knowledge about our own vulnerabilities and how we typically react to these challenges can enable us to develop ways to respond more skillfully and confidently and be more self-affirming. It is useful to recognize that we do not have to be all-knowing or perfect, that we do not operate independently of the contexts in which we work. Projections and judgments are inevitable, and we need and deserve a network of people who can help us sort through the feedback we receive, discern what is useful, and support our ongoing growth and development as facilitators.

CO-FACILITATION ISSUES

Issues related to our social identities and social location, perspectives and teaching styles, sense of authority and competency, and institutional and community context also affect how we co-facilitate with others. Not only is self-knowledge critical to what and how we teach, it impacts co-facilitation relationships as well. Our self-awareness affects how effectively we collaborate with another instructor, especially when we represent different identity groups and dominant/subordinated statuses. How we behave in a classroom or workshop is at least as important as what we say. Our self-awareness affects whether and how well we can model for participants equitable and respectful dynamics with our co-facilitator.

As we plan with our co-trainer, we can stay mindful of the impact of our personal and cultural styles, social locations, and preferred training approach to ensure that each person is having equitable input into developing the course or workshop. In the design process, we can watch for how we may be playing out power dynamics related to our social identities. We can assess if the design reflects and balances each other's styles, perspectives, and strengths and limitations (Maxwell, Nagda, & Thompson, 2011; Ouellett & Fraser, 2005; Zúñiga, Nagda, Chesler, & Cytron-Walker, 2007). When we are co-facilitating with people who have different dominant and subordinated identities, we can pay attention to how we may be enacting internalized dominance and internalized oppression (DiAngelo & Flynn, 2010). For example, people with dominant group identities may jump in unnecessarily, interrupt their co-facilitator, or take more time for their parts than was planned. Or they may overcompensate for their identities by "playing small."

I co-facilitated with a white man around the topic of sexism on campus where I felt like I was an impatient and overbearing facilitator. In checking in with my co-facilitator about what was going on, he realized that his fears of being seen as dominant was getting in his way of being authentic and speaking up (Rani).

People with marginalized identities may hold back due to a lack of confidence, or let the other facilitator routinely take the lead, or back off from handling more challenging moments. Given that facilitators have an intersectional mix of privileged and marginalized identities and may be addressing more than one form of oppression, these dynamics are not necessarily simple.

I have co-facilitated with men of color who were mindful of engaging in sexist behaviors while I was conscious of playing out my white privilege (Diane).

Instructors also need to be aware of when they may be colluding with participants' biases—for instance, by not addressing situations where students are talking to the man and ignoring the woman in a male/female team, or when participants accept information from the white person but challenge the information presented by the person of color in a mixed-race team. Moreover, when we know what gets us and our co-facilitator triggered, we can be prepared to support each other in handling a tension-filled moment.

Our internalized sense of competency and authority, and how we are seen by students/participants, colleagues, and the institution, affect the risks that different facilitators may be willing to take in terms of content shared, personal disclosure, and challenging of students.

For example, a colleague of mine, a younger, less experienced Latina, felt somewhat institutionally protected by regularly co-facilitating with a high-status, older white male faculty. The trust and knowledge built by their ongoing co-teaching relationship also allowed them to address and work through their interpersonal dynamics (Diane).

Knowing oneself and knowing one's co-facilitator allows for mutual support and the ability to model respectful and equitable dynamics.

CONCLUSION

Knowing ourselves as instructors and facilitators in social justice education is an ongoing process of exploration, challenge, new insights, and personal and professional growth. Self-examination about the effects of our socialization and experiences within systems of inequality ensures that we never take for granted the challenges of understanding systems of oppression and keeps us tuned into the struggles our students may be facing. We are continually reminded that we all have areas of limited awareness, particularly where we are members of the advantaged group(s) and where we have not yet explored how our intersecting identities position us vis-á-vis other groups and contexts. We need consistent vigilance and self-reflection to challenge internalized oppression and discern what is true about ourselves. Networks of support and mentoring relationships help guide and sustain us in this process. When we can stay open to ongoing learning, and accept the inevitable mistakes as we uncover new areas for growth, we show our students they can do this as well. Most crucially, self-reflection and self-awareness help us to take the long view needed to sustain our commitments and not retreat from this difficult but essential work.

Note

* We ask that those who cite this work always acknowledge by name all of the authors listed rather than either only citing the first author or using "et al." to indicate coauthors. All collaborated on the conceptualization, development, and writing of this chapter.

References

Adams, M. A., & Love, B. J. (2009). A social justice education framework for a post-Grutter era. In K. Skubikowski, C. Wright, & R. Graf (Eds.), *Social justice education: Inviting faculty to transform their institution* (pp. 3–25). Sterling, VA: Stylus.

Amos, Y. T. (2014). To lose is to win: The effects of student evaluations in a multicultural education class on a Japanese faculty with a non-native English Accent. *Understanding and Dismantling Privilege, 4*(2). Retrieved from http://www.wpcjournal.com/article/view/12220

Banaji, M., & Greenwald, A. (2013). *Blind spot: The hidden biases of good people.* New York: Random House Publishing.

Bell, L. A. (2010). *Storytelling for social justice: Connecting narrative and the arts in antiracist teaching.* New York: Routledge.

Brookfield, S. (2012). *Teaching for critical thinking: Tools and techniques to help students question their assumptions.* San Francisco: Jossey-Bass.

Brookfield, S., & Preskill, S. (2005). *Discussion as a way of teaching: Tools and techniques for democratic classrooms,* (2nd ed.). San Francisco: Jossey-Bass.

Brown, E. B. (1997). What has happened here: The politics of difference in women's history and feminist politics. In L. J. Nicholson (Ed.), *The second wave: A reader in feminist theory* (pp. 272–288). New York: Routledge.

Clance, P. R., & Imes, S. (1978). The imposter phenomenon in high achieving women: Dynamics and therapeutic intervention. *Psychotherapy theory, research and practice, 15*(3), 1–8.

Collins, P. (2008). *Black feminist thought: Knowledge, consciousness and the politics of empowerment.* New York: Routledge.

Crenshaw, K. (1989). Demarginalizing the intersection of race and sex: A black feminist critique of antidiscrimination doctrine, feminist theory and antiracist politics. In *University of Chicago Legal Forum 1989: Feminisms in the law, theory and practice* (pp. 139–167). Chicago: University of Chicago Legal Forum.

Crenshaw, K. (1993). Mapping the margins: Intersectionality, identity politics, and violence against women of color. *Stanford Law Review, 43*(6), 1241–1279.

DiAngelo, R. (2011). White fragility. *International Journal of Critical Pedagogy, 3*(3), 54–70.

DiAngelo, R., & Flynn, D. (2010, Aug.). Showing what we tell: Facilitating anti-racism education in cross-race teams. *Understanding and Dismantling Privilege, 1*(1).

DiAngelo, R., & Sensoy, O. (2014, Winter). Leaning in: A student's guide to engaging constructively with social justice content. *Radical Pedagogy, 11*(1). Retrieved from http://www.radicalpedagogy. org/radicalpedagogy.org/Leaning_In__A_Students_Guide_To_Engaging_Constructively_With_ Social_Justice_Content.html

DuPraw, M., & Axner, P. (1997). *Working on common cross-cultural communication challenges.* Retrieved from http://www.pbs.org/ampu/crosscult.html

Gibney, S. (2013, Nov. 30). Teaching while black and blue. *Gawker.* Retrieved from http://gawker. com/teaching-while-black-and-blue-1473659925

Gonzalez, C. G., & Harris, A. P. (2014). Continuing the conversation. *Berkeley Journal of Gender, Law & Justice, 29,* 183–194.

Gutierrez y Muhs, G., Niemann, Y. F., Gonzalez, C. G., & Harris, A. P. (Eds.). (2012). *Presumed incompetent: The intersections of race and class for women in academia.* Boulder, CO: University Press of Colorado and Utah State University Press.

Huber, L. P., & Solórzano, D. G. (2015). Racial microaggressions as a tool for critical race research. *Race, Ethnicity and Education, 18*(3), 297–320.

Jean-Marie, G., Grant, C. M., & Irby, B. (2014). *The duality of women scholars of color: Transforming and being transformed in the academy.* Charlotte, NC: Information Age Publishing.

Joseph, V., & Williams, T. O. (2008). "Good niggers": The struggle to find courage, strength, and confidence to fight internalized racism and internalized dominance. *Democracy and Education, 17*(2), 67–73.

Lazos, S. R. (2012). Are student teaching evaluations holding back women and minorities? The perils of "doing" gender and race in the classroom. In G. Gutierrez y Muhs, Y. F. Niemann, C. G. Gonzalez, & A. P. Harris (Eds.), *Presumed incompetent: The intersections of race and class for women in academia* (pp. 164–185). Boulder, CO: University Press of Colorado, Utah State University Press.

Maher, F. A., & Tetreault, M. K. (2001). *The feminist classroom: Dynamics of gender, race and privilege.* Lanham, MD: Rowman and Littlefield.

Maxwell, K. E., Nagda, B., & Thompson, M. C. (2011). *Facilitating intergroup dialogues: Bridging differences, catalyzing change.* Sterling, VA: Stylus Publishing.

Messner, M. A. (2000). White guy habitus in the classroom: Challenging the reproduction of privilege. *Men and Masculinities, 2*(4), 457–469.

Niemann, Y. F. (2012). The making of a token: A case study of stereotype threat, stigma, racism, and tokenism in academe. In G. Gutierrez y Muhs, Y. F. Niemann, C. G. Gonzalez, & A. P. Harris (Eds.), *Presumed incompetent: The intersections of race and class for women in academia* (pp. 336–355). Boulder, CO: University Press of Colorado and Utah State University Press.

Obear, K. (2013). Navigating triggering events: Critical competencies for social justice educators. In L. M. Landreman (Ed.), *The art of effective facilitation: Reflections from social justice educators.* Sterling, VA: Stylus Publishing.

Ouellett, M. L., & Fraser, E. C. (2005). Teaching together: Interracial teams. In M. L. Ouellett (Ed.), *Teaching inclusively: Resources for course, department and institutional change in higher education.* Stillwater, OK: New Forums Press.

Patton, S. (2014, Apr. 21). *When diversity doesn't come easy.* Vitae. Retrieved from https://chroniclevitae. com/news/455-when-diversity-doesn-t-come-easy

Pittman, C. T. (2010). Race and gender oppression in the classroom: The experiences of women faculty of color with white male students. *Teaching Sociology, 38*(3), 183–196.

Solórzano, D., Ceja, M., & Yosso, T. (2000). Critical race theory, racial microaggressions, and campus racial climate: The experiences of African American college students. *The Journal of Negro Education, 69,* 60–73.

Staats, C. (2013). *State of the Science: Implicit Bias Review 2013.* Kirwan Institute. Retrieved from http://kirwaninstitute.osu.edu/implicit-bias-review/

Staats, C. (2014). *State of the Science: Implicit Bias Review 2014.* Kirwan Institute. Retrieved from http://kirwaninstitute.osu.edu/implicit-bias-review/

Sue, D. W. (2010a). *Microaggressions and marginality: Manifestations, dynamics, and impact.* Hoboken, NJ: John Wiley & Sons.

Sue, D. W. (2010b). *Microaggressions in everyday life. Hoboken,* NJ: John Wiley & Sons.

Sue, D. W., Lin, A.I., Torino, G. C., Capodilupo, C. M., & Rivera, D. P. (2009). Racial microaggressions and difficult dialogues on race in the classroom. *Cultural Diversity and Ethnic Minority Psychology, 15*(2), 183–190.

Sue, D. W., & Sue, D. (2013). *Counseling the culturally diverse* (6th ed.). Hoboken, NJ: John Wiley & Sons.

Tappan, M.B. (2006). Reframing internalized oppression and internalized domination: From the psychological to the sociocultural. *Teachers College Record, 108*(10), 2115–2144.

Tuitt, F., Hanna, M., Martinez, L.M., Salazar, M., & Griffin, R. (2009). Teaching in the line of fire: Faculty of color in the academy. *The NEA Higher Education Journal: Thought & Action, 25,* 65–74. Retrieved from http://www.nea.org/assets/docs/HE/TA09LineofFire.pdf

Tusmith, B., & Reddy, M. T. (2002). *Race in the college classroom: Pedagogy and politics.* Rutgers, NJ: Rutgers University Press.

Young, V. (2011). *The secret thoughts of successful women: Why capable people suffer from the Imposter Syndrome and how to thrive in spite of it.* New York: Crown Publishing Group.

Zúñiga, X., Nagda, B.A., Chesler, M., & Cytron-Walker, A. (2007). *Intergroup dialogues in higher education: Meaningful learning about social justice.* ASHE-ERIC Report Series, Volume 32(4). San Francisco: Jossey-Bass.

About the Contributors

Maurianne Adams is Professor Emerita of Education at the University of Massachusetts Amherst and a founding member of the graduate faculty in Social Justice Education (SJE). She has written on SJE for *The Routledge International Handbook of Social Justice* (2014) and *The Praeger Handbook of Social Justice and Psychology* (2014).

Lee Anne Bell is Professor Emerita at Barnard College, Columbia University. Her publications include *Storytelling for Social Justice: Connecting Narrative and the Arts in Antiracist Teaching* (Routledge, 2010) and an award-winning film and teaching guide, *40 Years Later: Now Can We Talk?* (Teachers College Press, 2013).

Photo credit: Julianna Sohn

D. Chase J. Catalano is an Assistant Professor in the College Student Personnel (CSP) program at Western Illinois University. He previously served as Director of the LGBT Resource Center at Syracuse University. His research interests are trans* students in higher education, cultural centers in higher education, and social justice praxis.

Keri "Safire" DeJong, Ed.D. is a researcher, educator, and consultant focusing on social justice education, intergroup dialogue, technology, and digital citizenship. Her publications focus on centering young people in social justice education praxis, preparing intergroup dialogue facilitators, and developing theory and curricula about youth and elder oppression.

Andrea D. Domingue, Ed.D. is a scholar-practitioner who focuses on minoritized college student services, critical pedagogy, and college student leadership development. She is currently working as an administrator in student affairs and is the Chair for ACPA's Commission for Social Justice Educators.

Michael S. Funk is a Clinical Assistant Professor for the Steinhardt School of Culture, Education, and Human Development, Higher Education and Student Affairs program, at New York University. He earned his doctorate from the University of Massachusetts Amherst Social Justice Education program.

Diane J. Goodman, Ed.D. has been addressing issues of diversity and social justice issues as an educator, writer, and activist for over 30 years. She speaks, trains, and consults nationally and internationally with a wide range of organizations, community groups, and educational institutions. Her website is www.dianegoodman.com.

Pat Griffin is a Professor Emeritus in the Social Justice Education program at the University of Massachusetts Amherst. Dr. Griffin is co-editor of *Teaching for Diversity and Social Justice: A Sourcebook for Teachers and Trainers* (1997 and 2007) and author of *Strong Women, Deep Closets: Homophobia and Lesbians in Sport* (1998).

Larissa E. Hopkins is Assistant Dean for Undergraduate Students at Dartmouth College. She is co-editor of "Ableism" in *Readings for Diversity and Social Justice* (2015). Larissa received her B.A. in Women's Studies and Education from Hamilton College; and her M.Ed. and Ed.D. in Social Justice Education from the University of Massachusetts Amherst.

Khyati Y. Joshi is Professor in the School of Education at Fairleigh Dickinson University in Teaneck, New Jersey. She is the author of *New Roots in America's Sacred Ground: Religion, Race, and Ethnicity in Indian America* (Rutgers University Press, 2006). More information about her publications and presentations is available at www.khyatijoshi.com.

Barbara J. Love, Ed.D is Professor Emerita, Social Justice Education, College of Education, University of Massachusetts Amherst. Best known for her work on "Developing a Liberatory Consciousness," Dr. Love has written on self-awareness for social justice educators, internalized oppression, and teaching about social justice issues including racism, ageism, and adultism. Dr. Love can be reached for comment at info@drbjlove.com

Benjamin J. Ostiguy is a doctoral student in higher education and the associate director of operations for disability services at the University of Massachusetts Amherst. His inquiry focuses on institutional practices designed to support college students with disabilities. His work has appeared in *New Directions for Institutional Research*.

Mathew L. Ouellett is Associate Provost and Director of the Office for Teaching and Learning (OTL) and adjunct associate professor in the College of Education at Wayne State University (WSU), Detroit, Michigan. Ouellett's work promotes the implementation of multiculturally inclusive, evidence-based teaching methods for the academic success of all students.

Photo credit: Rick Bielaczyc, Wayne State University, Marketing and Communications/Photography Unit

Madeline L. Peters is the Director of Disability Services at the University of Massachusetts Amherst. She consults nationally on Accommodation Services. She co-wrote "Ableism" for *Teaching for Diversity and Social Justice* (3rd ed., 2016), co-edited *Readings for Diversity and Social Justice* (2000), and as a disability advocate, has won a national lawsuit for the disabled.

Davey Shlasko is an educator, consultant, and director of Think Again Training. Davey facilitates group learning about and in the context of social justice movements using creative expression, popular education, and practical skills-building to help communities and organizations deepen their understanding and practice of social justice principles.

Marjorie Valdivia is a doctoral student in the Social Justice Education program at the University of Massachusetts Amherst. Her doctoral research examines the reproduction of economic inequities, as well as pedagogical practices employed in college and university classrooms having to deal with issues of economic inequities.

Rani Varghese is Assistant Professor, School of Social Work, at Adelphi University. Her clinical training is from Smith College School for Social Work, and she received her Ed.D. in Social Justice Education from the University of Massachusetts Amherst. She brings an interdisciplinary approach to her teaching, consulting, practice, and research.

Ximena Zúñiga is Professor of Education and Coordinator of the Social Justice Education Concentration at the University of Massachusetts Amherst. She recently co-authored two books: *Dialogues Across Difference: Practice, Theory and Research* (Russell Sage Foundation, 2013), and *Intergroup Dialogue: Engaging Difference, Social Identity and Social Justice* (Routledge, 2014).

Index

Teaching for Diversity and Social Justice

For 20 years, *Teaching for Diversity and Social Justice* has been the definitive sourcebook of theoretical foundations, pedagogical and design frameworks, and curricular models for social justice teaching practice. Thoroughly revised and updated, this third edition continues in the tradition of its predecessors to cover the most relevant issues and controversies in social justice education (SJE) in a practical, hands-on format. Filled with ready-to-apply activities and discussion questions, this book provides teachers and facilitators with an accessible pedagogical approach to issues of oppression in classrooms. The revised edition also focuses on providing students with the tools needed to apply their learning about these issues.

Features new to this edition include:

- A new bridging chapter focusing on the core concepts that need to be included in *all* SJE practice and illustrating ways of "getting started" teaching foundational core concepts and processes.
- Expanded overview sections that highlight the social justice approach to each topic, the historical contexts and legacies of oppression, opportunities for action and change, and the intersections among forms of oppression.
- Added coverage of key topics for teaching social justice issues, such as establishing a positive classroom climate, institutional and social manifestations of oppression, the global implications of contemporary SJE work, and action steps for addressing injustice.
- A new chapter addressing the possibilities for adapting SJE to online and blended courses.
- New and revised material for each of the core chapters in the book complemented by fully developed online teaching designs, including over 150 downloadables, activities, and handouts on the book's companion website, www.routledgetextbooks.com/textbooks/_author/teachingfordiversity.

A classic for teachers across disciplines, *Teaching for Diversity and Social Justice* presents a thoughtful, well-constructed, and inclusive foundation for engaging students in the complex and often daunting problems of discrimination and inequality in American society.